Mad, Bad & Dangerous to Know

Also by Ranulph Fiennes

A Talent for Trouble

Ice Fall in Norway

The Headless Valley

Where Soldiers Fear to Tread

Hell on Ice

To the Ends of the Earth

Bothie the Polar Dog (with Virginia Fiennes)

Living Dangerously

The Feather Men

Atlantis of the Sands

Mind Over Matter

The Sett

Fit for Life

Beyond the Limits

The Secret Hunters

Captain Scott: The Biography
(*The Times* best biography of 2003)

RANULPH FIENNES

Mad, Bad & Dangerous to Know

HODDER &
STOUGHTON

Copyright © 1987, 2007 by Ranulph Fiennes

Parts of the text first published as LIVING DANGEROUSLY in Great Britain in 1987 by
Macmillan
This edition published in 2007 by Hodder & Stoughton
A division of Hodder Headline

The right of Ranulph Fiennes to be identified as the Author of the Work has been asserted by
him in accordance with the Copyright, Designs and Patents Act 1988.

A Hodder & Stoughton book

3

All rights reserved. No part of this publication may be reproduced, stored in a retrieval system,
or transmitted, in any form or by any means without the prior written permission of the
publisher, nor be otherwise circulated in any form of binding or cover other than that in which
it is published and without a similar condition being imposed on the subsequent purchaser.

A CIP catalogue record for this title is available from the British Library

Hardback ISBN 978 0 340 95168 2
Trade paperback ISBN 978 0 340 95183 5

Typeset in Sabon by M Rules

Printed and bound by Clays Ltd, St Ives plc

Hodder Headline's policy is to use papers that are natural, renewable and recyclable products
and made from wood grown in sustainable forests. The logging and manufacturing processes
are expected to conform to the environmental regulations of the country of origin.

Hodder & Stoughton Ltd
A division of Hodder Headline
338 Euston Road
London NW1 3BH

To my surviving sister
Gill
with love and many happy memories

Acknowledgments

My thanks to my late wife Ginny for a lifetime of love, friendship and inspiration. To my late mother and my late sisters, Sue and Celia, for being my loving family for sixty years. This book is dedicated to my surviving sister Gill. To our good friends for all the happiness and excitements we've shared.

To all fellow expedition co-travellers, sponsors and advisors, including those in Appendix 2 on page 356.

Also, for their help with this book, Gill Allen, Professor Gianni Angelini, Ian Bannister, Anton Bowring, Tom Briggs, Bob Brown, Tony Brown, Kenton Cool, John Costello, Dr Tim Cripps, Monty Don, Norman Dunroy, Simon Gault, Nick Holder, Gill Hoult, Morag Howell, Peter James, Mike Kobold, Andrey Kosenko, Arabella McIntyre Brown, Mac Mackenney, John Muir, Ian Parnell, Donald Sammut, Lord Saye & Sele, Steven Seaton, Ski Sharp, Neil Short, David Smith, Mike Stroud, Paul Sykes, Judy Tarring, Dr Gordon Thomas, Gary Tompsett, Yiannis Tridimus, Giles Whittell, Simon Wilde, Arabella Williams and John Yates.

Also, for the production of this book, my thanks to Ed Victor, Rupert Lancaster, Jill Firman, Maggie Body (my oft-times editor since 1968!), my wife Louise, stepson Alexander and daughter Elizabeth (for their patience), and to all those individuals mentioned in the text who went with me down the long years to 'the limits and beyond'.

Ranulph Fiennes
2007

Contents

Maps

1

At First

The *Guinness Book of Records* described me as 'the youngest posthumous baronet'. This unwanted claim to fame came about because my father, another Ranulph, was killed during the Italian Campaign in the Second World War four months before my birth. In June 1943 he came home on leave and I was conceived. When he left, my mother was never to see him again. He commanded the Royal Scots Greys at Salerno and, reconnoitring a bridge over the Pescara River unarmed and alone, he surprised three Germans in a cave and took them prisoner at the point of his briar pipe. Not far from Naples, checking out a possible route of advance, my father trod on a German S-type mine and died in a Naples hospital. My mother never remarried. From childhood I wanted to be as he was. Especially I wanted to command the Royal Scots Greys.

My grandmother, Florrie, had lost her elder son in the First World War, now she had lost her younger son, and her husband had also died. She had nothing left to keep her in Sunningdale, so as soon as the war was over she decided to return to her own family in South Africa and my mother, three elder sisters and I were wafted along in her wake. We arrived in Table Bay in January 1947. I was two and a half. A cousin came to meet us and welcome us to our new country. Turning to me, he asked Granny: 'And what is her name?' Granny exploded, for she was very proud of her only grandson. 'But,' protested the cousin, 'how can you blame anyone for mistaking his sex when you doll his curly hair up with these long blue ribbons?' My ribbons, the height of Sunningdale kiddies' fashion, were removed that very evening, never to be worn again.

There were thirty-three cousins in Granny's family, the Rathfelders, most of whom lived in happy harmony in Constantia, the Valley of the Vines, in the shadow of Table Mountain, which was an idyllic place for a small boy to grow up. There were no white children of my age in the valley except cousin Bella who cried all the time. Soon the coloured boys took me to their homes and showed me how to play their version of Pooh-sticks under the plank-bridge by their stream. Over the next four years our little gang often roamed the valley, avoiding the forest with its baboons and packs of wild dogs. Bamboo spears and short leather straps to whip the dirt were *de rigueur* and I became co-leader of the gang along with a one-armed lad named Archie. My mother, meanwhile, became fervently involved with a then relatively docile anti-apartheid movement known as Black Sash and drove about collecting signatures on behalf of coloured people's rights.

In October 1950 Granny Florrie suffered a stroke. She died quietly in the house she loved and was mourned by everyone in the valley. The funeral was held in the Anglican church in Constantia, although our normal place of worship was St Saviour's in Claremont, where Canon Wade had two skinny little daughters. The younger, Virginia, later became an English tennis star who won the Women's Singles at Wimbledon.

At prep school the severe-faced headmaster who beat me from time to time for good reason, awarded me the Divinity Prize. I decided briefly to become a priest, until Pathé News showed the first ascent of Everest. Somehow I was left with the muddled impression that Mr Hillary and a Chinese friend had been sent up this great mountain, higher even than Table Mountain, as a wedding present for the English Queen. I, too, would become a climber of mountains and stick the British flag into fierce features of far-flung landscapes; but only after being colonel of the Royal Scots Greys.

2

My mother had been brought up in another era and in different circumstances. She had married at nineteen and left her protected family environment without even knowing how to boil an egg or iron a shirt. When Granny Florrie died, she was on her own for the first time, with nobody to turn to for advice. Eventually, in 1954 she decided we should return to England. I promised, on saying goodbye, to write to Archie and the gang, but I don't think I ever did.

While Mother house-hunted, I was packed off to my new English prep school in purple blazer and cap and grey flannels. After sobbing into my pillow for the first week I came to enjoy Sandroyd School in Wiltshire as it transformed itself from a hostile planet into an exciting playground. My sisters and I had all developed the Afrikaaner way with English vowels, but English schooling soon eradicated this and in the dormitory I discovered my South African years were an unsuspected asset when it came to spinning 'tales of the jungle'. I only told my stories on Saturday nights, mainly because we were given our weekly chocolate bars on Saturday afternoon. I charged a square of chocolate from each listener.

About the time of my twelfth birthday my mother purchased St Peter's Well, a long, low house that had once been three cottages on the edge of the village of Lodsworth in Sussex. Right across the front garden wall, as far as the eye could see, stretched a paradise of fields, valleys and forest. The River Lod ran along the bottom of our valley and one day my sister Gill – then seventeen – and I canoed down past where it joined the Rother, paddling through the domain of dragonfly, swan and kingfisher, until we passed through a cleft in the South Downs and reached the Arun and, at length, the sea. Mother collected us and the canoe in her bull-nosed Morris Minor. She owned this car for twenty years and to the best of my knowledge never once exceeded thirty miles per hour, probably causing numerous crashes by frustrated speedsters.

A month before our own arrival, a family of five settled in the hamlet of River, a mile from Lodsworth. Mr Pepper ran a chalk pit at Amberley. There were two sons about my age and a daughter of nine, three years my junior. We were invited to tea.

'You must put shoes on, Ranulph,' my mother said sharply. 'People do not expect visitors with bare feet, especially on first acquaintance.'

'I don't want to go to tea with two boring boys and a silly girl. Can't I go down to the river this afternoon?'

Exasperated, my mother was firm. 'They are our neighbours. We can't be rude, and how do you know they are boring or silly since you've never met them?'

So we went to tea at the Peppers. There were excellent cakes which made up for lost time by the river, and the boys were not boring. In the attic they had an elaborate electric train set, the working of which they were happy to explain to me.

After a while a pin pricked my knee under the table and I knelt to spot the cause. I had quite forgotten the boys' sister, Virginia. Her brothers ignored her in a pointed fashion so I had done like-wise. Now I saw that she had been playing all along underneath the table and had fired a spring-loaded toy cannon at me.

'Stop it. That hurt,' I told her.

She screwed up her nose at me.

I went back to the trains, rather hoping that she might fire another pin. But she didn't. I had noticed that her eyes were very blue, almost violet, and that her eyelashes were long. Soon after-wards, I returned to school. Common entrance exams came and went. I passed with just sufficient marks to make it into Eton. My mother was proud and delighted and so was I, for luckily I could not foresee the immediate future.

My great misfortune was to be a pretty little boy. I can hardly blame Eton for that, yet my memories of the place are tarnished because of it.

My mother drove me to Mr Parr's House at Eton, the Morris Minor laden with suitcases, a colourful rug and two framed prints of spaniels. Accustomed to Sandroyd with its hundred pupils, I was awed by the thought of over 1,000 boys, many of them eighteen-year-olds and over six feet tall. Some, I was told, used razors.

At Sandroyd my baronetcy and my South African background had proved to be good for my street cred. Here there were numerous ex-colonials, and baronets were trashy nonentities eclipsed by a welter of earls, lords and viscounts. At first the customs, the colloquialisms and local geography left me bemused. Those first weeks were like an attempt to gain a set of daily changing objectives blindfolded in a swamp, with a host of hostile custodians shouting instructions in a weird language.

The fagging system was an ever-present bane of my existence. The six senior boys in each House had only to stand at their doors and scream '*Boyyyy!*' for every faggable boy within earshot to drop whatever he was doing and head at maximum speed to the source of the scream. He who arrived last was fagged. Trying to come to terms with this amazing new world, I had little time to be homesick and even less for leisure. But I did find myself attracted to the Drawing Schools where the senior master was a kindly soul named Wilfrid Blunt whose younger brother Anthony was in charge of the Queen's paintings and pursued other activities we knew nothing about at the time.

Quite when and how the horror started is now lost to me since the mind does its best to heal the deepest sores. But I believe I had been at Eton about a month when two older boys entered my room just before lunchtime.

'They say you're a tart, Fiennes. Did you know?'

'What,' I asked them, 'is a tart?' But they giggled together with much uplifting of eyebrows and wouldn't tell me. Eventually I discovered that in Eton slang a tart is a boy who sells himself for sexual activities in return for favours, be they in cash or kind. There could be no lower form of life. I must prove my innocence at once.

'I am not a tart,' I would protest. I did not realise that any pretty boy at Eton is going to be labelled a tart and that gossip is based not on what actually happens but on what the gossipers would like to think has happened.

Perhaps if some male relative had warned me of the impending problems adolescence at Eton would involve, I might somehow have forearmed myself. But I had no brothers, no uncles and no father. My tormentors were unremitting. I seriously contemplated throwing myself off the bridge over the Thames between Eton and Windsor, only restrained by the thought of making my mother suffer. Instead I decided to cultivate a perpetual scowl and join the school boxing team. I also enlisted my mother's support to allow me to switch early from the the bum-freezer, the short cutaway jackets worn by Etonians under five feet four, to the less provocative tailcoat of the bigger boys. But neither the new tailcoats that hung protectively over my backside, nor my well-practised scowl, nor even a gradually growing reputation as a pugilist could alter my girlish face. Boys had crushes on me and the verbal torment continued.

Fortunately, time was on my side. Each term brought a fresh crop of pretty faces to distract the gossips. Slowly, I began to enjoy one or two aspects of Eton life. History was my favourite subject, especially the study of British naval heroes and explorers. But one attempt to show off rebounded when I shot my hand up to the master's question: 'What did Stanley say at his famous jungle meeting?' My instant reply, 'Kiss me, Livingstone,' was greeted with the derision it deserved. At that time an attempt to complete the crossing of Antarctica was in progress, led by Sir Vivian Fuchs and my Everest hero Sir Edmund Hillary. Our history master traced the course of the expedition on an ancient chart of the frozen continent.

German, with a new master, David Cornwell, had taken on a new lease of life. He kept the language interesting and the lessons enjoyable. But he left Eton quite soon, sadly for us but profitably from his point of view, when his income rocketed thanks to the books which he wrote under the name of John le Carré.

I had always found making friends at Eton difficult and I only began to enjoy life at school after meeting Michael Denny who was 'in the Library' (i.e. a prefect) at Mr Crusoe's House, the House nearest to Eton's tallest and most imposing building, School Hall.

Since neither Denny nor I was an experienced climber it is difficult to conjure up quite why we began to climb together, but somehow the partnership was formed and, as a result, my last eighteen months at Eton included a good deal of nocturnal excitement.

There is nothing new about stegophily, the dictionary term for the practice of climbing buildings by night. It has nothing to do with the more normal sport of rock-climbing. Indeed, since I had no head for heights and easily succumbed to vertigo, daytime climbing was anathema to me. The beauty of night-climbing is that the thrill of danger is present without the full visual impact of the drop below. Denny and I hoisted assorted dustbins or lavatory seats onto various prized pinnacles and watched with secret pleasure while steeplejacks with ropes and long ladders brought them down again. In some of our activities we were were aided and abetted by Chris Cazenove, already an aspiring actor with the Eton Dramatic Society and adept at putting on an innocent face under questioning.

As my time at Eton drew to a close I had to decide on my future. But there had really only ever been one career choice. One day I would be commanding officer of the Royal Scots Greys, like my father. That was the summit of my ambitions and to that end I had joined the Eton College Corps and enjoyed every moment of the training. There were still officers and men in the Royal Scots Greys who had served with my father eighteen years before and remembered him by his nickname, 'Colonel Lugs', on account of his slightly prominent ears. But family connections were no longer a pass into the Army. Now, to enter the Royal Military Academy, Sandhurst, you needed at least two General Certificates of Education at Advanced Level, including mathematics or physics, and five certificates at Ordinary Level. This precluded any chance of my becoming a professional officer by the normal route. But there was a possible alternative: to obtain a short-service commission through Mons Officer Cadet School and, once in the Army on a two-year commission, to try to extend. Even for Mons, however, I would need a minimum of five Ordinary Level passes and nearly five years of Eton had only gained me four. After consultation with my house master, my mother told me the wonderful news that I could leave Eton at the end of the summer term and enrol in a specialist crammer abroad.

And so I became an Old Etonian. I wonder if I would be a different sort of person now if I had missed out on those early years of hell. In one sense it proved the perfect preparation for the trickier vicissitudes of life, since nothing would ever be so bad again. I arrived at Eton full of self-assurance, buoyant from happy days at Sandroyd. Public school and three long years of remorseless nastiness squeezed every last trace of confidence from me. It would take a long time to get back to a balanced state. I still find myself overly sensitive to the least criticism, a direct hangover from Eton days.

To summarise my old school: location hard to beat; facilities excellent; staff above average. My only complaint was the nature of some of my fellow inmates but all schools have their share of nasty little boys. The acid test must be: if I had a son, would I send him there? I cannot honestly say that I would not.

2

Young Love and the SAS

The Eton College Corps held an annual fourteen-day summer camp and, although I had left the school, I was eligible to attend. The Norwegian Army training base at Kvamskogen, north of Bergen, was deep in mountainous country. The captain of Parr's House, Neville Howard, led the enemy patrol and lived rough in the mountains throughout our fortnight at Kvamskogen. He was to become commanding officer of the SAS in later years. Sodden clothing and bruised bodies helped all 300 fledgling officers decide whether or not to plump for careers in khaki.

Rather than return to England with the rest, I hitchhiked back with another boy as far as Copenhagen. There we squandered dwindling funds at Tivoli, sat in sunny parks staring with longing at the abundance of leggy blondes, and wound up on the Tuborg lager factory guided tour. There were two types of tour ticket, one for German nationals and one for the rest of the world. Our non-Teuton group went first and polished off the bountiful supplies of free lager. These were not replenished for the Germans: war-time memories were still bitter.

Unable to cope with the lashings of alcohol, I misplaced my equally befuddled companion and did not see him again for several months. I continued alone through Denmark and Germany. That was my first expedition and, as I explained to my mother back in Lodsworth, its success proved I was quite ready to face

9

whatever challenges awaited me in the language cramming university I was to be sent to in Aix-en-Provence.

The challenge of the opposite sex still remained to be cracked. My first cousin, Greville 'Gubbie' Napier, lived in nearby Midhurst where he managed an antique shop called Keil's. Being five years my senior, he was worldly wise about those very beings my male-only public school had hidden from me but which now loomed enormous on my seventeen-year-old horizon – girls.

'France is *the* place,' he told me one day, sipping tea in the cluttered backroom of Keil's. 'French girls cannot say no or even *non*. They are unrivalled in both beauty and naughtiness.'

We determined to launch an invasion of Paris without delay.

'How do we get there?' I asked. 'I have £15 in the world.'

Gubbie waved his tin of Keil's Beeswax in the air. 'Absolutely no problem. You are the expert on hitchhiking and I am an expert on seventeenth- and eighteenth-century French furniture. We will have a wonderful time.'

The hitching went well as far as Dieppe. Thereafter, despite or because of the Union Jacks on our packs, our thumbs prodded the air in vain. Nobody stopped. We set down our packs in the steady French drizzle and applied ourselves to Plan B. We had been taught about the old Franco-Scottish *entente cordiale* at school, so we produced kilts from our packs and donned these. But the French truck drivers had not received the same history lessons and continued to roar past. This is where Gubbie's brilliance came into play. Another rummage in our packs produced scarves which we wound cunningly round our heads and necks so that from behind, if not examined too closely through windscreen wipers, we just might be taken for girls. It worked. A lorry stopped. The driver was from Yorkshire and before he had time to realise his mistake, we had swarmed aboard and were overwhelming him with gratitude.

And so, eventually, we got to Paris where we ogled the street ladies but declined their offers on the grounds that our exchequer was down to the bread-line. Gubbie, born and brought up in

Scotland, decided we would recoup funds by singing Scottish ditties in cafés, wearing our kilts of course. We made just enough to travel by bus back to Dieppe, where we called upon the British consul for a £10 loan to get us back to Sussex. He agreed, providing we told him a dirty joke. Amazing though it now seems, neither of us in our hour of need could remember a single joke, clean or dirty, but the consul relented and we were able to buy ferry tickets.

At home in Lodsworth I had long since made friends with Peter Tooth, son of the local chief woodsman. Together we roamed the countryside on our bicycles and also indulged in local roof-climbing between Lodsworth and Midhurst. We never read books or listened to music and we didn't have television. A favourite wet-weather wargame took place in the 'gallery' at home where my mother had hung Granny Florrie's portraits of Fiennes ancestors. One day my aim was poor and an arrow sped past Peter's ear, burying itself in the left cheek of Gregory Fiennes, the 14th Lord Saye and Sele. Today he hangs in our sitting room on Exmoor and I much regret his patched-up port jowl. Peter found instructions in some magazine for making explosives. I studied these for several days and experimented with growing quantities of granulated sugar and weedkiller until our activities were brought to a halt after I had blown up my mother's best brass flower vase and terrified the neighbours.

One Saturday, while still at Eton, I went to the Lodsworth Village Flower Show where my mother had great hopes for her marrow entries. The village hall was full, so I wandered off to see if Peter was about. He wasn't, but I noticed a slim girl of about thirteen wearing a blue and white skirt and a sports shirt with short sleeves. I was sure God had never designed any girl so perfectly. I sat on an onion display and watched her.

'Isn't it wonderful?' It was my mother.

'Oh, yes,' I said with enormous feeling. My mother looked at me surprised and pleased, for I did not normally enthuse over her vegetables. She had won a prize and so, both elated, we headed back to the Morris Minor. She stopped in the carpark to chat with the occupant of the next car, an Aston Martin. It was Mrs Pepper from River and beside her sat the vision.

'This is Virginia, remember her?' Mrs Pepper said. 'She's back from Eastbourne for half-term.' The girl smiled politely at my mother and looked briefly at me with total unconcern. That evening I told Peter about her.

'Does she like you?'

'I think she couldn't care less. I might have been a concrete gnome from the look she gave me.'

'Ah,' said Peter, knowingly. 'That is an excellent sign. They get taught at school nowadays that the best way to attract the man they want is to ignore him.'

The passport to success in adolescent society at that time was the ability to twist and knowing how to kiss. I achieved the former. The latter was a mystery. A life of kissing sisters and mother out of family love interfered with my zeal to kiss out of desire. Then some senior lady with little patience at a barbecue in Hook prised my teeth apart with her tongue and, after the initial shock, I learned what was required.

A fortnight after returning from France, Gubbie had involved himself with a fuzzy-haired beauty with long legs so I went alone to a Liss party on the Vespa scooter my mother had given me for Christmas. Two of the girls decided to raid their old school, a nearby mansion where Dame Margaret Rutherford had recently filmed *The Happiest Days of Your Life*. The entire party, armed with fireworks and smoke bombs, drove an assortment of motor-bikes, sports cars and old bangers to Bycylla School for young ladies. The raid was a noisy success but my girlfriend of the evening was a bad scooter passenger and, by the time we tailed the escaping cavalcade to the gates, the lodge-keeper had collected his wits and taken my number.

Two days later the police called at Lodsworth. The evidence, they said, was irrefutable and I was to be prosecuted for 'malicious damage resulting in costs of £8 3/6d'. None of the other raiders was caught and, at the Midhurst Court Sessions the proceedings were dropped after I had apologised to the headmistress and paid her £8 3/6d to replace an eiderdown burned by a smoke bomb. However the national newspapers were hard up for news and made tasty headlines out of the mixture of Bomber Baronet, Screaming Young Girls in Nightdresses and Margaret Rutherford.

My mother was at her wits' end, ashamed of her only son, and wondering where it would all lead. I was a liability and not to be trusted in England. What might I not get up to if let loose in France? She decided to find a language school rather nearer home than Aix and enrolled me, aged seventeen, at a crammer in Hove.

It was the time of the mini skirt or pussy pelmet and the place was full of sexy foreign girls. This impeded my concentration. I took a quiet English girl called Maggie to the cinema and afterwards down to the beach at nearby Climping Sands but I did not kiss her because she was too well mannered to look as though she expected to be kissed. So my sexual frustrations grew. To let off steam I introduced some of the crammer students to the delights of climbing buildings by night. I still hated heights but darkness meant that nasty drops were unseen. Over the next twelve months, the Sussex newspapers reported a rash of flagged spires. My finest climb was the lofty spire of Hove Town Hall which housed the police station.

Virginia Pepper kept two ponies at her father's chalk quarry at Amberley and one of my sisters got Mrs Pepper's permission for me to help exercise them. Ginny and I rode by way of woodland paths and long fallow fields which we both knew well. One day, before we rode back I gave Ginny a scarf I had bought especially for her in Paris. I watched as she opened the wrapping and, when I saw her smile, the whole world danced. She liked it. We left the ponies in the paddock and went in for tea. I learned that Ginny was going back to school in Eastbourne the following day so nonchalantly offered her a lift on the Vespa. To my surprise and delight her mother agreed. Her father would have been furious.

Ginny had a school suitcase which fitted on my rear seat when she kept well forward. I felt her pressed against my back and her hands lightly around me. I was definitely in heaven. In fact, if heaven is half as good as I felt that day, it will be worth the struggle to attain.

All went well as far as the school where we dropped off her case. She had agreed to have tea with me in town but on our way back I swerved to avoid a bicyclist. I do not remember the accident, nor the next fifteen hours. But when I woke up in hospital the nurse told me my passenger was in her bed at her school, my scooter was in good nick and the bicyclist, whose fault it had been, was unharmed. Apart from concussion and abrasions I, too, was undamaged. Ginny came to see me the following day with a bunch of flowers and I was fined £4 for riding a scooter without L-plates and carrying an unlicensed passenger. Ginny's father, who had never liked me, was volcanic and forbade her to see me again.

Thus encouraged, we agreed to meet by night in a bathroom at the school. For two hours I sat in the bath and Ginny, in her nightdress, sat on the loo. My cautious suggestion that we could perhaps make ourselves more comfortable were discouraged and I was determined not to risk alarming her. Towards the end of term, and daringly by day, I waited for Ginny with a bunch of other girls on their way back from lacrosse. She recognised me, despite the scooter helmet and goggles and dropped behind the others. We hid in a patch of rhododendrons.

'You are wicked,' she laughed. She was breathless. We kissed for the first time and I felt that I would love her for ever.

The following term I perfected a drainpipe approach to Ginny's new fourth-floor dormitory but was intercepted on the flat roof by a history mistress on night duty. I explained that I had been passing on my scooter and thought I had seen a fire on the roof, so had climbed up to extinguish it, only to find there was no fire . . .

The mistress nodded wisely. 'In that case, I might as well let you back down and out, don't you think?'

I never got my language A-levels (due to the mini skirts) but I did net a German O-level which brought my tally up to five and qualified me to attempt the Army's Regular Commissions Board, where I was put through a series of aptitude tests more taxing on the imagination and physique than the intellect. To my delight I passed. The next step was Mons Officer Cadet School at Aldershot. Day after day we learned drill movements with and without .303 rifle, submachine-gun or sword; how to attack machine-gun nests head-on under cover of smoke; and the enthusiastic application of brasso and blanco.

I discovered a fellow night-climber in the Honourable Richard Wrottesly, known to all as Rotters, who wore a monocle at all times and drove an E-type Jaguar. He proposed we scale the west wing of nearby Heathfield Girls' School which he said was a challenging climb. Three-quarters of the way up we were disturbed by a clamour from below. Rotters, above me on the same drainpipe, looked downwards and the beam of a powerful torch flashed off his monocle.

'We've been spotted,' Rotters hissed and, gaining the horizontal guttering, he swung himself across to a fire ladder that disappeared around the back of the building. But there was no escape. When we reached the ground a uniformed officer and the school bursar, a hefty man in his sixties, frogmarched us towards the main entrance. Without warning Rotters lashed backwards with the rope coil and shouted, 'Break.' I ran straight for the nearest rhododendrons, scaled the fence with wings of fear and sped to Rotters' car. I found it locked and decided to hitchhike back to Mons. First parade at 7.00 a.m. could not be missed.

The first car that stopped for me was a police van and I decided to play innocent. They took me to Ascot Police Station and there I found Rotters demanding his rights and complaining about police harassment of an innocent ornithologist. He showed no signs of recognising me so I responded likewise.

The police officer from the patrol van looked me up and down. 'Sir,' he said with heavy irony, 'you are wearing black Army gym shoes, red Army PT shirt and you have the haircut which can nowadays only be found on young Sandhurst cadets. Our bird-watching friend over there whom you have never seen before is wearing identical clothing with the sole exception of a monocle. He has a similar hairstyle . . . Do us a favour and tell us what you were both up to at the girls' school.'

An hour later the van dropped us off at Mons. Heathfield had agreed with our commandant that charges would not be pressed, providing we were suitably dealt with. Rotters, who had physically assaulted the bursar, was given the boot. I was awarded fifty-six days of Restrictions of Privileges, which was two days longer than I was meant to remain at Mons. I still don't know how I scraped through the exams. My platoon commander informed me unofficially that he suspected the authorities were not prepared to risk my presence for another five months while I redid the course.

Now there were four free months before I had to report to tank-training camp. A chance to see the world. An old school friend, Simon Gault, agreed to accompany me to Norway for a canoeing expedition. The only problem was the lack of a canoe. The cheapest suitable model cost £80, so I set to work to earn the money by doing three jobs in rotation, exercising polo ponies in the afternoon, washing dishes at a hotel in the evening and, after snatching a nap on cousin Gubbie's floor for a few hours, I would get up to hose down Southdown double-decker buses at 4.00 a.m. In three weeks I had the money and ordered the canoe. Maggie, whom I'd omitted to kiss on Climping Sands, came too. We arrived at Jotunheim with my double canoe and Simon's single kayak. For three miles we negotiated minor rapids with ease. Then the river dropped into a canyon, so I asked the other two to wait while I went ahead to film them in the rough stuff. The film, which I still possess, shows my hard-earned canoe hitting a rock and splitting in two. Maggie was caught underneath a spar but Simon rescued her further down the gorge. The canoe was not insured. We returned to England the same week. I had learned two lessons: the value of reconnaissance in unknown places and the futility of paying for expeditions from one's own pocket.

The tank gunnery school at Lulworth is carefully situated so that even the stupidest officers cannot knock off Dorset villages with

wrongly aimed high-explosive shells. I remember one gunnery sergeant explaining that a reasonably proficient Centurion tank crew
should be able to destroy three Soviet tanks 1,000 metres away
within ten seconds of sighting. My own range results indicated
that any number of Soviet tanks could safely picnic 600 yards
away. Despite this I passed the course eight weeks later: I suspect
no one is ever failed.

In February 1963 I made my way to Germany to join the Royal
Scots Greys. I was eighteen and had just bought my first car, an
elderly Peugeot 403, for £150. As in my father's day, the lion's share
of the officers were Scotsmen, as were over 90 per cent of the
troopers and NCOs. Only two Greys remained who remembered
Colonel Lugs, but the fact that he had been the CO and that
Fiennes, pronounced Feens by all the Jocks, was thought to be a
Scottish name, saved me from most of the mickey-taking suffered
by a number of the more obviously English. I grew to love the
Greys as much as I had loathed public school.

Immediately after the war tank-training in Germany was conducted in a cavalier fashion, with little respect for the vanquished
farmers whose crops were often crushed and barns destroyed. By
the 1950s 'Huns' were being referred to more often as 'German citizens' and, after the Berlin airlift, as 'our German allies'. Year by
year damage-causing training rights were curtailed until for
brigade or divisional exercises a complex scale of compensation
was laid down and upgraded each year. Slight damage to a twenty-
year-old pine tree could earn its owner £100 and a crushed
gate-post £50. Often smiling farmers would stand by open gates
waving invitingly to oncoming tank commanders. A poor crop
could be turned into a small fortune if a British tank could be persuaded to drive over it once or twice.

When no tank exercises were anticipated there was an Army
budget available for adventure training and on the strength of this I
received permission to train the regimental langlauf (cross-country)
ski team and form a canoe club, taking groups of Jocks down different European rivers. It all went wrong when I organised a

large-scale training exercise canoeing on the Kiel Canal, where officially we shouldn't have been in the first place, but it was night-time
so I thought our trespass would go unnoticed. Being crafty, some of
the canoeists waited for a merchant ship or tanker to pass, then,
braving the powerful backwash between hull and canal bank, they
would tuck in behind their chosen vessel which sucked them along,
making for less work and good camouflage from my watchers on the
bank. Unfortunately, a corporal on my staff accidentally landed a red
phosphorus flare on a ship's rear deck. He could not have chosen a
worse target, for it was a Soviet tanker with a liquid chemical cargo
so volatile that the crewmen wore rubber soles so as not to risk causing a single spark. A klaxon and red light system installed along the
canal began to honk and flash as though World War Three was
about to erupt. All canal traffic across Europe stopped for five hours
and I was later heavily fined by my brigade commander.

During my annual leaves Ginny and I contrived to meet, openly
when her father lifted his embargo, discreetly in the back of the
Peugeot when he did not. In 1965, my third year in Germany, we
spent four precious days together at a hotel in Dartmouth where I
signed in under a false name. But by then her father was growing
paranoid, made her a ward of court and hired a Securicor agent
whose enquiries among the chambermaids, a snoopy bunch, soon
established what had been going on. Mr Pepper telephoned my commanding officer in Germany to reveal the extent of my iniquity. Since
Ginny was by this time well over the age of consent, my colonel
clucked soothing noises at him and delivered me a mild scolding,
during which he was unable to keep the twinkle from his eye.

In the autumn I was sent to Berlin for a month with my troop to
man three tanks which, in the event of hostilities, were intended to
repel the Warsaw Pact from Hitler's Olympic Stadium. While my
tanks swivelled their guns about defiantly outside the giant arena,
I sneaked into the empty Olympic swimming hall and, attempting,
as I was periodically wont, to confront my horrible fear of heights,
jumped off the high competition board, scaring myself silly in the
process.

I was about to apply for a one-year extension to my short-service commission, when I spotted a three-line advertisement in regimental orders. 'Officers wishing to apply for secondment to the 22nd Special Air Service should obtain the relevant form from the Orderly Office.' Only a week before I had listened spellbound to a Mess story of SAS patrols in Borneo, the only war zone where the British Army was still in action. Here was an open invitation to a three-year secondment with this then little known but élite regiment. I consulted the only Scots Grey I knew who had served in the SAS, a sadistic corporal called Jones who had been to Bavaria on one of my ski courses. From him I discovered that map-reading and extreme fitness with a heavy backpack were important. He added, 'In Bavaria, you told me you hated heights. You're not going to be much use parachuting then, are you?'

By chance a two-week course in parachuting happened to be available in the south of France and the colonel let me go at short notice. The parachute school was at Pau, near Lourdes. A fellow student explained that this was no accident. 'You see, those men who are crippled here at Pau can seek speedy recovery in the holy waters just up the road.'

I was the only non-Frenchman in a class of eighty. The first jump, from a Nord Atlas transport plane, was by day. I tried to cure my terror of heights by the simple method of keeping my eyes firmly closed as I threw myself into space. A few seconds after exit, my parachute opened and tugged my body harness up sharply between my legs, jamming my family jewels in a painful position. But at least the canopy had opened. I looked up, expecting to see a neat array of rigging lines running away from my shoulders to the periphery of my chute. Instead there was a single knotted tangle which met in a bunch behind my neck. I experienced instant panic. The ground was already uncomfortably close.

In fact I was merely experiencing a common problem called 'twists', usually caused by a poor exit from the aircraft. The instructors had probably explained '*les twistes*', but I had failed to comprehend what they were saying. The normal process of elasticity slowly unwound the tangle, but I was spinning like a top on landing and hit the ground with a wallop.

I left the Royal Scots Greys in December, assuring my friends that I would be back in three years' time. After spending Christmas at home, I went to Dartmoor and the Brecon Beacons and trained alone with a forty-pound pack and Ordnance Survey map. Then, in February, I drove to Bradbury Lines in Hereford and through a security gate to the SAS barracks, a battered huddle of low huts or 'spiders'.

Altogether 124 would-be troopers and twelve other officers congregated in the barracks for the selection month. For the first week, officers were tested separately. The first night's activities included a naked swim across the River Wye in temperatures below freezing. There was a great deal of map-reading and fast cross-country movement and very little sleep. Our packs weighed only thirty pounds, but this was soon to be increased.

SAS staff with binoculars seemed to be everywhere. Any form of cheating led to dismissal from the course. Two officers twisted their ankles on the third day and one decided he was not cut out for the SAS. Then there were ten of us. On the fourth day another fell by the wayside. I was selfishly delighted with each new drop-out for we all knew that more than 90 per cent of applicants would be failed by the end of the month.

After a night in wet clothes tramping through woods without torches, we were ushered into a classroom and doled out question sheets involving complex military problems. I never discovered how I fared at this test – which is perhaps just as well. That evening we missed tea and went, feeling famished, on a fifteen-mile night march to reconnoitre an isolated reservoir. Back in the classroom, both hungry and tired, we were questioned one at a time by an intimidating group of veterans. Fortunately my short-term memory was good and I remembered every detail of the reservoir, down to water-height, construction materials and the nature of surrounding countryside.

At 10.00 a.m. on the sixth day, I returned from a twenty-mile trudge over the Black Mountains to find a brown envelope on my bed – instructions to carry out a theoretical but detailed raid on a specific bank in Hereford and to brief the SAS staff on its execution by 6.00 p.m. that evening. I gauged that there were two hours in hand to grab some precious sleep, set my alarm and crashed out.

The alarm failed to rouse me and the other candidates, each detailed to a different Hereford bank raid, naturally avoided waking me since their own chances of success would improve with my failure. I woke at 2.00 p.m. and rushed down to the relevant bank. Too late, for it had closed an hour before. I knocked on a side window and shouted at the young woman who appeared that I had an appointment with the manager. She must have decided my short haircut and tweed coat looked harmless, for she opened up and took me to the manager.

Thirty minutes later, after checking my passport, military ID, German bank account and SAS course papers, as well as phoning my London bank manager, he accepted that I genuinely wished to open an account. The only untrue frill that I added was the large amount of family silver I wished to store with him. He was quick to assure me how secure his bank was and thoughtfully explained the excellent alarm system. Thanking the manager for his help, I left to make detailed plans for the robbery, including a scale drawing of the offices and security devices I had been shown. The paper was ready on time and handed in to the staff.

That evening was the only free period of the week so three of us drove to a nearby town for a mammoth meal. I had kept a carbon copy of the bank raid plans and this somehow slipped from my coat pocket in the restaurant. Later the Italian restaurateur found it and called the police.

The first I knew of this turn of events was upon reading the headlines of the national newspapers the following day. These included 'Big Bank Raid Mystery' and 'Ministry Enquiry into Bank Raid Scare'. Two days later the headlines had changed to the

Daily Mail's 'Army Initiative Upsets Police' and comments in *The Times* that 'the Services are letting their zeal outrun their discretion'. A weekend-long security operation had stopped all police leave because every bank in Herefordshire had been surrounded, owing to the lack of a specific address on my plans.

I was summoned before the SAS adjutant. It was instantly clear to me that he thought I had planted the plans in the restaurant out of misplaced mischief. This appealed to the SAS sense of humour so I only received a warning. Had they known the plans had been genuinely mislaid, I would have been sent packing.

SAS selection courses no longer involve theoretical bank raids.

By the end of the first week, at which point candidates of all ranks came together, seventy men and six officers remained. Week two saw the departure of forty more men and two officers. I was still around, a lot thinner and craftier. The final test of the third week was known as Long Drag. This was a forty-five-mile cross-country bash carrying a fifty-pound pack, twelve-pound belt kit and eighteen-pound rifle without a sling. During most of the selection course I moved alone for greater speed but on Long Drag I set out with Captain Fleming, one of the three other officer survivors. We decided that the only way we could beat the clock on this last dreadful test was to hire the services of a local farmer with a black Ford Anglia.

At Pen-y-Fan we were lying sixth, about a mile behind a Scots Guards officer, the son of Britain's Chief Scout. We needed to maintain that position to avoid suspicion so, with adroit use of the Ford, binoculars and mist cover, we managed to arrive at isolated checkpoints, some of them several miles from the nearest feasible access point, almost a mile behind Lieutenant MacLean.

I felt guilty afterwards but not badly so, since subterfuge was very much an SAS tactic. I passed the selection but, sadly, Fleming, who finished Long Drag alongside me, was failed. In late February 1966 the SAS CO, Lieutenant-Colonel Mike Wingate Gray awarded three officers and twelve men their buff-coloured SAS berets and sea-blue stable-belts. Since all SAS

officers are ranked captain or above, I missed out the rank of first
lieutenant and became the youngest captain in the Army at that
time. But not for long. 'Pride came,' in the words of my CO,
'before a bloody great fall.'

'You are not in yet,' Staff Sergeant Brummy Burnett warned us, 'so
don't get cocky.' He was understating the facts. The selection
course proved merely a warm-up to the next four months of intensive training, during which we picked up eight personal skills basic
to any beginner sent out to join his first SAS unit: fast response
shooting-to-kill, static line parachuting in six-man sticks, demolition, signals using Morse, resistance to interrogation, CQB
(close-quarter battle), field medicine and survival techniques.

The CQB included self-defence against an assailant with knife,
pistol or blunt instrument and in each case we learned a two-step
response again and again until our movements were karate quick.
Field medicine was not my favourite subject as I become squeamish easily. Some of the lecturers were fresh back from Borneo and
taught us practical tips: 'When your mate's shot, treat him for
shock. Give him liquid if you have it, except when the bullet enters
between nipple and knee. Don't forget that, 'cos a bullet going in
above the knee might end up in the stomach and the poor feller
won't want liquid inside then, will he now?' Signals training began
in sound booths until we were Morse proficient to five words per
minute. Morse was no longer in use in most of the Army but with
the tiny but primitive SAS gear we could transmit quick bursts of
coded message thousands of miles with little likelihood of hostile
direction-finding equipment locating our position.

Brummy himself supervised shoot-to-kill and other sergeants
taught us demolition, from the mathematics of fuse-burning rates
to the tensile strengths of suspension bridge targets. We demolished old buildings, steel girders, railway tracks and pear trees, and
by the end of three weeks I possessed a boot-full of detonators,
fuse wire and plastic explosive, the result of demolishing my set
targets with less than the issued amounts. I should have returned

this volatile booty to the stores but I did not. My motives were acquisitive rather than criminal. I did not intend to blow up anything in particular but fancied the notion that I had the capacity to do so, given a suitable target.

Survival skills were taught by a tiny Welsh corporal who slit the throat of a sheep on our classroom table and watched over us as we skinned the animal, dug out its entrails and boiled the mutton. None of the meat was wasted and he stressed that no sign or scent of the butchery must remain. Theft from farms in winter, leaving no trace of our visit, or making it appear that our hen coop depredations were the work of foxes, were dealt with in minute detail. At the end of the Welshman's week, I felt confident of surviving anywhere short of the Gobi Desert.

At Abingdon airfield I discovered for the first time just how many things could go fatally wrong with a parachute jump, facts I had been protected from in Pau by the limitations of my O-level French. But I also found out I had glandular fever. I was despatched home to recover.

Ginny's father, an artist at blowing hot and cold, now decided Ginny could officially see me again and she appeared at my bedside in a light summer frock with a fashionably high hemline which can't have been good for my swollen glands.

'I picked these for you in the wood.' She gave me a bunch of late spring daffodils. Ginny was no longer just the little girl I had loved for so long. At nineteen she was tall, shapely and much sought after by a number of eligible West Sussex suitors. While in Hereford I had kept wary tabs on my competitors through Gubbie.

Later that summer I ran into an old Eton friend, William Knight, who wanted to register a protest at the way 20th Century Fox was desecrating a trout stream that ran through the picturesque village of Castle Combe in order to film Rex Harrison and Samantha Eggar in *The Adventures of Dr Dolittle*. William, then a wine salesman in the area, had learned about local anger whilst in the village pub. With my opportune supply of explosives, I was to mount the diversion which would draw away the security patrol and I was also to alert a friendly journalist to cover the story. The diversionary flares did their stuff but my tame journalist shopped us to the *Daily Mirror* who in turn informed the police who were lying in wait. The result was a pandemonium of excited cries and canine joy. Having but recently learned all there is to know about evading capture by various types of hound, I made good my escape by jumping into the stream which was the centre of all the fuss and submerging all but mouth and nostrils. But I was the only one of the conspirators to return to where we had parked our cars. It so happened that my fifth-hand Jaguar would not at that time start without a tow, so I changed into smart clothes, dried my hair and waited in the bushes for William to return for his Mini. He did not turn up but a police car did, sliding quietly and without lights into a corner of the park. After twenty minutes with no William and no movement from the police I decided I must make a move as I was due to fly out to Malaya for SAS jungle training the next morning and it would not do to miss the plane.

Retiring up the lane some distance, I reapproached the carpark whistling and, after surveying the dimly lit cars, spotted the police and went over to them. There were two officers and, when I hailed them, one put a finger to his lips. In a low voice I explained my car would not start and could they kindly give me a tow-start.

'Which car is yours, sir?' the driver asked. I pointed at my Jaguar.

'You must be Captain Fiennes, then.' It was a statement not a query. They must have been told my car's registration. 'I think you had better come with us.'

Considering I could have gone to gaol for seven years, the fine of £500, plus costs and legal fees at the subsequent court case, was an intense relief. But I was immediately expelled from the SAS and I realised that I would no longer achieve my dearest wish, for the Royal Scots Greys might not want a convicted arsonist for their commanding officer.

Ginny was another casualty of the Castle Combe affair, for her father, believing she had obtained my explosives from his Sussex chalk quarry, immediately packed her off to stay with cousins in Spain, which had no police extradition agreement with Britain. He warned her under no circumstances to contaminate herself further by even telephoning me. I was, he snorted, mad, bad and dangerous to know.

As for me, I was recalled to Germany and the tank troop. Here I was encouraged to channel my energies back into the canoe club, the langlauf ski team and boxing and in the summer I set up another Norwegian journey following an ancient cattle trail over Europe's largest glacier, the Jostedalsbre in Central Jotunheim, and then a canoe run down the glacial waste waters. These proved too rough for our canoes but on that journey I learned to lead by physical example rather than rhetoric and also to choose for challenging endeavours a selection of chiefs and Indians, not merely a gaggle of the former.

The langlauf Greys that year were better than ever. I was not to know it but the months of dedicated ski-training for the Greys were to serve me well for the future, just as the years of preparation in battle tanks subsequently proved about as useful as learning Latin, due to Gorbachev, Reagan and Thatcher interfering with and eventually closing down the whole Cold War set-up. During our final week of ski-training in Bavaria Ginny came over from England. We skied together and drank hot chocolate by log fires. We laughed and talked, threw snowballs, and Ginny learned to langlauf.

By now I realised that my Whitehall file was marked in indelible red for caution. I might wriggle my way up to major over the years but I would go no further. I had no wish to mark time in khaki mediocrity and so made up my mind to call it a day as soon as my three years' contracted service were up. Such was my state of mind when my Greys friend Major Richard John suggested I volunteer to serve in Oman in the Sultan's Armed Forces. Postings lasted two years for seconded officers and the pay was marginally better than in Germany. More important, there was sun, sand and excitement aplenty. My CO approved my application without delay, in fact with indecent haste.

My old world was breaking up. I felt no urgency to marry and settle down. Far from it. I had a powerful urge to do and see things and to be free as I had never truly been before. I thought not at all of married life, but a great deal about Ginny. I knew I could have easily lost her after Castle Combe and, soldiering in remote Oman, might risk her again. Sitting in Ginny's battered Mini van in a Midhurst side street, the tarmac shining from a summer shower, I asked her to marry me. By then I had loved her for twelve years.

At the end of June I left England for Arabia.

3

Fighting for the Arabs

In the late 1960s few people had heard of Oman or knew of its links with Britain. So long as Britain had held neighbouring Aden, the Omani Sultans were able to keep their country together, but the British withdrew from Aden in 1967. Marxism then had a firm base in Arabia, and Dhofar, the impoverished southern sector of Oman, was a natural Soviet target. Oman was also all that blocked the way between Aden, now the People's Republic of Southern Yemen, and the Straits of Hormuz, gateway to the Persian Gulf, through which two-thirds of the free world's oil needs were daily tankered. The aged Sultan of Oman did nothing to prepare for the impending storm. At the time I joined the Sultan's Army there were but 200 fighting men in Dhofar under a dozen British officers and their standard weapons were bolt-action rifles dating back to the Second World War.

With seven other officers I flew out to Muscat via Bahrain where we were marooned for eight days by a BOAC strike back home. It was here I learned that a British officer had just been flown out from Muscat with one shoulder and a portion of his chest shot away by the Communists, and I was told, 'They say he was on a stretcher in the mountains for ten hours before they evacuated him. Your Sultan uses mules instead of helicopters. What a place to volunteer for!'

I asked the officer's name. It was Richard John, my only friend in Oman.

The vintage Fokker to Muscat staged via Sharjah where we took on our first real-life mercenary. The Sultan hired freelance officers as well as seconded Brits as insurance against the British government getting cold feet. The new arrival, Captain David Bayley, was from Hove, so we had common ground.

More to the point he had recently spent three interesting years fighting for royalist guerrillas in the mountains of North Yemen. Nerve gas attacks by Egyptian aircraft on his cave headquarters, he explained, were the most dreaded events.

I was destined to command a reconnaissance platoon in Dhofar. The men were a mix of Omanis and Baluchis who cordially hated each other, so I had to be doubly careful to appear even-handed at all times. The enemy were the *adoo*, and a large part of our task was to ambush them before they could target us. The *adoo*, well trained and armed in the Soviet Union, knew all the tricks of night warfare without benefit of Hereford.

My immediate priority before we went south was to nurse our meagre equipment up to combat condition. Weapons were cleaned and oiled. Some were in a filthy state and the two-inch mortar had gone missing altogether, a fact which in the British Army would have involved a major enquiry and heads would have rolled. I set out to find a replacement mortar. Richard John was still away recovering from his wounds and there was no other British officer in his company at the time, so I 'borrowed' a mortar and, for good measure, a machine-gun from his armoury. Over the next two years neither was missed by its previous owner and both weapons saved our lives more than once.

On our patrols we were sometimes offered coffee, even in remote cave dwellings. This was always poured to guests in order of importance. Sometimes I came after all the others for, being a Nasrani or Christian, I rated lower than the poorest Muslim.

Sick people would come to our vehicles. We had first-aid satchels but no medical orderly. The population was riddled with eye trouble and our aspirin and Optrex dispensing seemed starkly inadequate.

'Hundreds of our people go blind each year,' said my staff sergeant, Abdullah. 'There is nothing to be done about it. To God be the praise.'

There were three hospitals in all Oman and eight out of every ten babies born died within a year. The Sultan would not allow foreign units such as Save the Children Fund into his country. He seemed determined, as far as I could make out, to perpetuate his country's backwardness and poverty. When I cross-questioned Abdullah about the lack of medical care he was not impressed. 'The government has little money. We are not a wealthy country. There are more pressing matters. Anyway this southern region is a poor area with miserable people. Illness comes to those who sin.'

My conscience was increasingly ill at ease: I was clearly a part of the military machine that upheld the Sultan in denying 800,000 Omanis their rightful inheritance. Away from the large towns of the north the people did not know what they were missing but ownership of cheap transistor radios was spreading and discontent increased alongside awareness.

All around us the Arab world was in ferment – from Egypt to Jordan, from the Sudan to the Yemen. Oil revenue was changing lifestyles radically for our nearest neighbours along the Persian Gulf, known to the Omanis as the Arabian Gulf. I listened in to Aden Radio because it was good for my Arabic and heard the People's Republic of Yemen urging the Omanis: 'Throw off the harness of British imperialism. Take back the wealth that is yours but is stolen by the Sultan.'

Before heading the 500 miles south to the Dhofar war zone with my own men, I was sent there without them for a familiarisation month's secondment to the Northern Frontier Regiment. At B Company headquarters in Umm al Ghawarif David Bayley and I were issued camouflaged clothing and headcloth, three blankets, 100 bullets and a bolt-action Mark 5 .303 rifle. Also a set of maps of the mountains on a weird scale I had never seen before, 0.36 inches to the mile. There were few place-names and many of the existing ones had the words 'position approximate' in brackets beside them. We were each given command of a platoon.

Our work at first was simple and unpleasant. We were to scour the wadis and cave-riddled cliffs and arrest every able-bodied male who might conceivably be an *adoo*. The policy was to subdue the people of the plain and the foothills into refusing food supplies to the guerrillas. Arrests, harassment and interrogations would in theory cow the locals. In practice our patrols served only to increase their hatred of Army, government and Sultan. It was only fear of being branded a coward that prevented me from resigning from the Sultan's forces as the *adoo* regrouped in force and threatened the major towns of Salalah and Marbat.

Back in the north again after my first taste of Dhofar, I confided my doubts about the efficacy of what we were doing to Staff-sergeant Abdullah. But he was adamant that the British were better than the Communist alternative.

'You must not feel the British do wrong here, sahib. They do not meddle with our way of life or our religion. Listen to me.' He lowered his voice. 'It is said in the sooq that Qaboos, the son of the Sultan, will rule before long. With oil money, he will give us those very things the Communists are promising, but without taking away our religion, as they will do. If you British leave before that can happen, then the Communists will take over without a doubt. They will force us to denounce Islam or they will kill us.'

I was impressed by Abdullah's sincerity but unconvinced. It was several days later that I finally came to justify my own role without misgivings.

Captain Tim Landon, from whom I had taken over the Recce Platoon, had returned briefly from an intelligence course to see old friends before going to a different part of Oman. He had, I knew, a special relationship with Qaboos bin Said, the Sultan's son. They had been at Sandhurst together but then had gone to separate regiments in the British Army, Tim with a cavalry regiment and Qaboos to a Scottish infantry unit. In due course Qaboos was ordered back to Salalah by his father. Because their family history included an unhealthy number of inter-familial coups and even murders, Qaboos was kept by his father under a sort of loving paternal house-arrest for seven years in the Salalah palace. To keep him happy, the Sultan allowed him a weekly visit from his old Sandhurst friend Tim Landon. This seemed harmless enough to the old Sultan who was unaware that they were plotting a coup to oust him. I knew nothing of this, of course, but recognised Tim's extensive knowledge of Oman and the current crisis. After talking to him I felt reassured with our role in fighting Marxism.

Change was inevitable in Oman. Either the Sultan must use his new oil revenue for progress or a more enlightened ruler must take over. The critical period was now. Unless the British ensured the status quo during this dangerous time, the Communists would, via Dhofar, take over all of south-eastern Arabia. Once Dhofar fell, the rest of Oman would follow. If Dhofaris were not soon given at least basic proof of support by their existing government, they would continue to swell the ranks of the *adoo*, or to use their official title, the People's Front for the Liberation of the Occupied Arabian Gulf (PFLOAG).

From Tim Landon's summary it was clear to me that I must stay and do all in my power to help keep PFLOAG at bay, at least for as long as it took Tim and others to remove the Sultan and replace him with Qaboos.

Weekly reports signalled from Dhofar indicated that newly trained *adoo* bands with modern weapons had arrived in many regions of the Jebel. Their tactics were imaginative, their firepower impressive and their shooting accurate. I was given eight weeks to prepare Recce Platoon for operations there.

My five years with Centurion tanks had done little to prepare me for an infantry Recce Platoon, but I did find my SAS training useful. One of the few hard and fast Hereford rules was movement by night whenever feasible and my previous brief visit to Dhofar led me to apply this maxim. In the SAS four men form a basic operational group, not two dozen, so I had to work on my own system of control by night. The resulting drills were not to be found in any textbook but they emphasised speed, simplicity, silence and common sense. All our training involved live ammunition and advances over broken ground by night, with frequent switches from single file to line abreast and back to file, practised time after time, along with twenty simple hand signals.

I took my six weeks annual leave while my platoon transferred to Dhofar's safer northern zone, and when I caught up with them again they were operating from the desert base of Thamarit. As the plane taxied in the men rushed out from the shade of the huts to grab my bags and gun and pump my right hand in greeting. I felt moved by this unexpected welcome. I knew all thirty men by name now and they called me Bachait bin Shemtot bin Samra, for reasons which I never discovered. The nearest English equivalent is John, Son of Rags, Son of the Thorntree.

For weeks I trained with the men in the gravel wastes outside our Thamarit base. Searing hot winds from the Empty Quarter blew sand through the air day after day. The camp, a long-deserted oil prospectors' base, was beside a well where bedu of the Bait Kathiri called with their thirsty camels. I went to greet each new arrival and we gave out flour or aspirins in exchange for information about the *adoo*. It was a one-way trade: all aspirins and no information.

From Thamarit the CO ordered me to the Yemen frontier to verify a suspected *adoo* infiltration route by locating camel tracks. This was at the time approaching Ramadan, the month of fasting, when the men were excited about a proper sighting of the new moon which would signal Ramadan's beginning. In Muscat it was already in force.

'In Pakistan,' muttered one of the Baluchis, 'three chief *qadis* fly up in an aeroplane to see the moon arrive. Once they report by radio, it is Ramadan for all.'

When our 'local' moon arrived a sigh came from the men and all of them knelt to pray. I remained standing but I also prayed since it felt appropriate. I prayed for my mother and sisters and Ginny.

For two days we pushed south, shedding broken-down vehicles

and their men to fix their own repairs since we had too little water to wait for them. Huge boulders blocked our way and the wadi narrowed to a winding corridor as dark as a Manhattan alleyway. The men began to complain. The Army had never been in these parts before. It was Ramadan, no time to be pushing heavy vehicles through soft sand until the forehead veins bulged. The Baluchi mullah was especially vociferous but I told him we must obey orders. I too had scrupulously drunk and eaten only during the sunless hours so my argument did not seem unfair.

We came to the high, bald escarpment of Deefa, not far from the Yemen border, the farthest west that we could travel without risking certain cut-off in enemy-held territory. The *adoo* grip on Dhofar was tightening and we returned to Salalah to be briefed on further ambushes.

Once we were scaling a hillside when we encountered a herd of cows. In the dark we listened to the sharp tac-tac of the herdsman's stick. Then someone halted above us and there came the falsetto cry much used by Dhofari herders. One of my men whispered, 'They heard the Land Rovers and sent the cowman to find us. Those men move their cows only by day. We must be more careful. He smelled us, sahib. We must cover ourselves.' We smeared the liquid green spattering of the cows on our shirts and trousers and smelled satisfactorily unpleasant, but it took another day holed up in a cave before we could make good our retreat undetected. We became skilled at the game of cat and mouse in the mountains. Ambush or be ambushed.

To stop the flow of heavy weapons from the Yemen into central Dhofar, our colonel devised the Leopard Line – a loose blockade running north from the coast to the sands of the Empty Quarter. Our company manned the line on the plain and in the foothills. To cover such a vast region with only five Land Rovers meant non-stop patrolling and recognising *adoo* signs when we chanced upon them. For this our bedu guide was invaluable. Water points dictated the route of camel travel and he knew the location of most of the springs in the Nejd, a narrow band of steppe country between the monsoon belt and the true desert. By kneeling beside the prints of a lone camel he could glean a mine of information. Sometimes he knew the name of the camel's owner by the shape of the hoof, where and when it had last drunk by the amount and frequency of its droppings and, by their texture, in which wadi it had last eaten.

Early in 1969 I was referred to patrol the ancient Dehedoba camel trails in the rugged country immediately north of the Qara mountains and up to the Yemeni border. For months we lived on the move in the scorching, gravel deserts, dodging enemy traps, suffering ulcerating desert sores, straying many miles over the Yemeni border and never developing a routine. The key was always to respect the enemy, but never to allow that respect to overawe and blunt the scope of our own strategy.

In the Sands we were more at ease. The men talked into the small hours, squatting with fingers sieving the pure sand or simply watching the stars. They never spoke derisively of one another or tried to score over a neighbour as British soldiers are wont to do. Each man had his say and the Baluchis sat at peace among the Arabs. The months of shared dangers had dissolved previous hostility. They were happy to talk for the pleasure of communicating, and needed no alcoholic stimulus nor swearwords to help express themselves. I thought of other nights by other fires: of the Jocks in Germany, the clatter of beer cans, the filthy language with every sentence and the crude laughter as someone rose to urinate into the fire. I felt happy and at one with these Muslim soldiers in a way I had never felt in Germany or with the SAS.

We did one night mission for Tim Landon deep into enemy-held territory to intercept some important *adoo* we had been told about by an informer. We had to scale steep cliffs and the men were jittery as we jogged from cover to cover, racing the dawn. Then we waited through the heat of the day, burrowed into a thorn bush and observing, a few hundred metres below our tiny hide, the movements of our enemy building stone sangars in defensive positions. A narrow goat trail ran between our thicket and the top of a steep grassy slope. Two tall men were approaching along it. I saw their dark clothes and the glint of weapons in their hands. The second *adoo* wore a shiny red badge in his cap, not the Mao button badge worn by many of the militia, but the hexagonal red star of a political commissar. These were our men. I was sure of it. There was no time to think. They were fifteen yards away. The first man stopped abruptly, appearing to sniff the air. His face was scarred, his hair closely shaven. I watched his fully automatic Kalashnikov, its round magazine cradled in his elbow, swing round as he turned to face us. Inch by inch I lifted my rifle. The sun outlined the man. He peered directly at me now. I remember thinking, he has seen us. He is weighing his chances.

My voice seemed to come of its own volition. 'Drop your weapons or we kill you.'

The big man moved with speed, twisting at the knee and bringing his Kalashnikov to bear in a single movement. I squeezed my trigger. He was slammed back as though caught in the chest by a sledgehammer. His limbs spread out like those of a puppet and he cartwheeled out of sight. Behind him the commissar paused for an instant, unsure what to do. I noticed his face beneath the jungle cap. He looked sad and faintly surprised. His rifle was already pointing at my stomach when a flurry of shots rang out from either side of me. The man's face crumpled into red horror, the nose and eyes smashed back into the brain. Further bullets tore through his ribs and a pretty flowering shrub caught his body at the top of the grassy slope.

One of my men cautiously retrieved from the commissar's body a leather satchel stuffed with documents. He handed it to me and crawled back to place a grenade with the pin removed under the commissar. I hissed at him, 'Forget it, Said. Come back.' I knew we were deep inside enemy territory, many miles from our own scattered troops and with no helicopter support in all Oman. We would be surrounded and cut off in minutes. I whispered the retreat. '*Rooch feesa. Guldi. Guldi.*' Mixed Omani Baluchi slang for instant withdrawal north to the desert and our Land Rovers.

36

Later in camp I found sleep elusive. I had often shot at people hundreds of yards away, vague shapes behind rocks who were busy shooting back. But never before had I seen a man's soul in his eyes, sensed his vitality as a fellow human being, and then watched his body torn apart at the pressure of my finger. A part of me that was still young and uncynical died with him and his comrade the commissar, spreadeagled on a thorn bush with his red badge glinting in the hot Dhofar sun.

In 1970 a palace coup, orchestrated largely by my friend Tim Landon, replaced the elderly and ineffectual Sultan with his son Qaboos who was himself half Dhofari and the amnesty he immediately declared triggered a trickle of *adoo* deserters that soon became a flood. By 1975, with ongoing help from Britain, as well as Egypt, Jordan and Iran, the tide was turned and the Marxist threat removed from Dhofar. The old Sultan, exiled to the Dorchester Hotel in London with a group of retainers, died there in 1972, a sad but charming old man. In three short years, Qaboos heaved Oman from the Middle Ages into the twentieth century. He used his blossoming oil revenues to the benefit of his country and in doing so whipped the propaganda carpet from under the feet of the revolutionaries.

By the year 2007 Qaboos still reigned supreme in twenty-first-century Oman, popular with his people who, being Ibadhi Mulims, were uninvolved in Shia and Sunni strife and were not infected by the innate hatred of most Arabs for their biblical brethren, the Israelites.

On 2 March 1970, the day that Ian Smith proclaimed Rhodesia a republic ruled by whites, I flew back to England. I was twenty-six and my chosen career was ended. I must find a new civilian life that suited my startling lack of qualifications.

4

The Fastest River

In my absence Ginny had been busy on my behalf and signed me up with George Greenfield, the best literary agent in the adventure business who, seeing something interesting in her if not yet in me, procured an advance of £400 from Hodder & Stoughton for me to write a book about an expedition I had made up the Nile during my six weeks annual leave the previous year. Five of us had travelled by Land Rover and hovercraft, the latter then being a novel means of transport in Egypt so it removed barriers that might otherwise have cut our travels short in that volatile part of the world.

I was thankful to both Ginny and George and set to work on my first book. I also joined Foyles lecture agency and started to go round the lunch club circuit earning £25 a talk and selling my own book at the same time. *A Talent For Trouble* earned under £600 but it did seem I might be able to make a basic living if I could plan and execute an expedition every year between June and October and then write and lecture about it from November until May.

From a sofa in Ginny's London flat, shared with three other girls (the flat, not the sofa), I set about organising my next project, an unambitious summer journey in central Norway. My only firm business rules were to spend no money on mounting an expedition. Everything must be sponsored. And, should any income result from an expedition through lecturing, writing or photography, this must be mine and mine alone. To this end I would take on no one who did not fully and happily accept this principle before signing on. After a lifetime of school and army, I was now on my own for the first time, with no capital, no income and no academic qualifications.

I had no itch to become wealthy – which was just as well – and absolutely no desire to marry and settle down. It never occurred to me to ask myself why on earth I had proposed to Ginny two years before if I never intended marrying anyone, not even her whom I adored. I can only assume that, dog-in-the-manger-wise, I had selfishly staked my claim on her with a diamond ring to warn off the competition. But Ginny was not someone to be misused. If I was not prepared to set a date for our wedding, even a distant date, now that I had left the Army, what was the point of remaining engaged? Did I really love her? Did I want children by her? As I listened to her, I felt like the worm that I was. I was truly ashamed but could not bring myself to accept the dreaded state of wedlock. Ginny made up her mind. If I would not promise her marriage, she would return her engagement ring and go away. She left for Scotland the following week and I returned to my mother's home in Lodsworth.

My mother had grown attached to Ginny and was sorry to hear of our break-up. As usual she was comfortingly fatalistic: 'Life must go on. You won't find another Ginny but it's not the end of the world.' I immersed myself in organising the Norwegian expedition and tried to forget that Ginny was no longer a part of my life.

The general purpose of the expedition was to tackle a physically difficult task and to succeed, so that subsequent more ambitious schemes would more readily gain sponsorship. The specific purpose was to survey the Fabergstolsbre Glacier on behalf of the Norwegian Hydrological Department to see whether or not it was receding. Today global warming has made this kind of research a top priority but in 1970 we were merely considered an economical way of picking up a dropped thread. In 1966 the Hydrological Department had made a comprehensive survey of the twenty-eight glaciers flowing off the 10,000-foot Jostedal Ice-cap to compare with their 1955 survey. But the Fabergstolsbre had eluded them due to an error with the aerial dye-bomb markers. A land-based survey party like us would mop up the omission at no cost to the Norwegian tax payer.

We planned to be parachuted on to the ice-cap, but once the survey work was done we would have to descend on foot with the expensive and delicate loaned survey gear. The simplest route appeared to be straight down a glacial tongue and from there to the nearest roadhead via a glacial river in light boats. This would mean that all the team members must know or learn how to parachute, ski, river-boat and climb. Assembling such assorted talents took some time.

At weekends I jogged in the Welsh mountains with a sixty-pound backpack and a compass. For four years I had brooded about my time with the SAS, not my sacking which I had deserved, but the fact that I had only passed the final hurdle of the 1965 selection course with the help of a taxi. On applying to join the Territorial Army soon after returning from Dhofar, I discovered there was a curious anomaly known as Reserve Squadron, 22nd SAS Regiment, which was neither regular nor Territorial, but whose role was to provide reinforcements for the regular SAS in time of war. Applicants to join R Squadron had to pass the regular SAS selection course. Here was my chance to banish a ghost. Thanks to my Welsh jogging stints, I found no difficulty in keeping ahead of the hundred or so regular Army applicants. I passed into R Squadron, but only as a trooper. No matter. I had completed Long Drag without motorised help.

The sergeant-major in charge of my new unit turned out to be my old SAS training sergeant, Brummy Burnett. After six months with R Squadron, desirous of more pay, I asked Brummy if I might get a commission to captain. He looked down at me. 'If you're very lucky, Fiennes, you might make corporal in five years. But no promises. Pigs might fly.'

Many of the older SAS sergeants, though not I think Brummy

himself, still held a grudge against me for my indiscretions of 1966 because I had caused a shaft of public scrutiny to fall on a unit with an obsession for secrecy and obscurity. In years to come the SAS was to be used as a public relations tool in the struggle against IRA terrorism, but my own peccadillos occurred when, to most people, SAS still merely meant Scandinavian Airlines System.

Norwegian preparations were all in order and I was living off my earnings from SAS weekends when I learned via the grapevine that Ginny, at work with the Scottish National Trust, had become good friends with the son of the Lord Lieutenant of Ross-shire. With no precise plan in mind, but aware that I must not let Ginny get too involved with this most eligible Scotsman, I decided to go to visit her on her birthday.

I owned a Triumph Tiger motorbike at the time and decided to ride all the way to Ginny on it. Proof surely of my devotion. By the time I reached London I was soaked through, so the Tiger and I used British Rail to Inverness before riding the last two hours to Ginny.

The Trust caravan where Ginny lived was parked close to Loch Torridon. Not stopping to think what I would say, I knocked on the door. When Ginny's little face peered, startled, through the misted window, I saw quite clearly that I must marry her: if necessary that very week in Torridon kirk.

I revved the Tiger's throttle. 'Hello,' I said. I did not mention British Rail.

'Why have you come?'

'I brought you a birthday card for next week.'

'Couldn't you have posted it?'

Gradually, over the next two days she thawed out a bit. On her birthday she drove me in her Mini to Applecross and we walked along the deserted coast which looks west to Skye. She let me hold her hand as we walked along the white beaches to the cry of gulls. But when I tried to kiss her and tell her I could not exist without her, there were bitter tears and she said I must leave and stay away for ever.

I promised to go the next day and that night, when it rained, Ginny let me into the caravan where I slept on the floor beside her narrow bunk. Before leaving for Inverness I asked if she would drive down to Newcastle in early August to see me off on the ship to Norway.

'Maybe,' she said.

A month later she was there. I told Ginny that if she would only agree to marry me, we would hold the wedding within ten days of my return from Norway. She looked happy but shook her head and refused to give me an answer. I confided in one of the team, Patrick Brook, an Army friend of many years, that she had turned me down and later saw him speaking to her urgently with much gesticulation. As I kissed her goodbye at the gangplank she whispered 'Yes', the most precious single word in my life.

'What did you say to Ginny in Newcastle?' I asked Patrick later.

'Oh, only that if you were to fall down a crevasse in Norway – which is quite likely – she would never forgive herself for having said no.'

The likelihood of intimacy with a crevasse arrived soon enough when, in Bergen, we boarded a Cessna sea-plane after we had been taught, in theory, how to jump off its floats. As the engines roared, I licked my lips. My stomach felt furry-lined as squadrons of butterflies free-fell within it. I would be first to jump and did not relish the idea. *The Sunday Times* described the occasion as 'The World's Toughest Jump', but they had paid £1,000 for coverage rights and wanted their money's worth. I looked down 6,000 feet at the slits of crevasses big enough to swallow a regiment of parachutists without leaving a trace. I fought back the rising panic of vertigo.

Awkwardly, we levered ourselves into kneeling positions facing the door. The rough hand of our instructor, ex-SAS Don Hughes, shook my shoulder as he prodded meaningfully at the exit. But something was wrong. I had been waiting for the sound of the engines cutting back, the necessary preliminary to any free-fall jump. The Cessna was still at maximum speed. I pointed at the pilot, but Don's 'shove off' gesture was repeated. I forced one arm through the slipstream and grasped the wing strut as we had been instructed. Then I lunged my legs outwards, aiming for the float. As my boots scrabbled for a foothold my hands lost their grip on the strut and I was sucked bodily into space. Out of control, I passed close by the fuselage and struck the side of the float with the back of my hand.

'One thousand and one. One thousand and two . . .' I heard my voice inside my helmet churning out the seconds and I opened my eyes. I will freeze solid in this ridiculous position, I thought, for coldness was the first sensation. Then came fear as I recognised the early signs of body-spin. Without warning I began to keel forward into a nose-dive. My arms snapped inwards to locate my ripcord but a camera had come loose inside my anorak and lodged itself against the ripcord bar. Grovelling in the folds I found the red handle and ripped it outwards. Then I snapped both arms back to the star position to arrest a rapidly materialising somersault. A second or two later, with a whipcrack sound and a breathtaking jerk, my orange canopy deployed fully. Two crevasse fields passed beneath my boots. The ice surface provided no perspective. I braced my legs, knees bent for impact. When it came I hardly knew it, as my landing was cushioned by the softness of a snow-bridge spanning an old crevasse. Four of the others landed close by, followed by our gear.

After some initial confusion as to which glacier we had actually landed on, and after a torrential storm, the survey work began in earnest as we liaised by radio with our ground party below. The work was cold and boring but allowed no lapses in concentration since even the slightest mathematical slip could render the whole project a failure. Geoff Holder, a Royal Engineers captain and our surveyor in chief, finally announced that the survey was complete. The paperwork was evacuated and we were free to look forward to the next stage of our enterprise, the descent of the Briksdalsbre Glacier. For this we had hired two of the Norwegian Tourist

Board's top guides. But we were in for a shock. The guides were unwilling to take us in dangerously thick mist on the forty-kilometre ice-cap journey to the top of the Briksdalsbre. On skis with light packs they could do the trip in eight hours. Pulling over-loaded sledges, they reckoned we would take two days, if indeed we could get that far.

At length we reached a compromise. They would ski along the ridge for thirty kilometres, at which point they would leave one of our ice-axes pointing in the direction of the Briksdalsbre. They would then veer north to descend a different route. It took us eleven hours of non-stop hauling to reach the ice-axe marker. As it grew dark we entered our first crevasse field and gingerly threaded a maze-like route through wicked-looking fissures. We knew we should be roped up but were too tired and cold. Each new chasm forced us off our chosen bearing. From every side came the booming echoes of avalanches. With numb fingers we erected two tents and pegged their guy-ropes to ski sticks.

Next morning the mist cleared at dawn and we saw the first ice-fall of the Briksdalsbre Glacier directly below us. The descent was sudden and, in minutes, one of our laden sledges slid out of con-trol and cartwheeled down into a crevasse. Alarmed, we donned helmets and roped up. About a hundred yards further down the yawning incline our second sledge turned turtle, dragging Roger Chapman and Patrick Brook behind it. Using a sawtooth sheath-knife, Roger slashed through the harnesses and saved both their lives. The pulk disappeared down a crevasse. All our skis were lost and our only remaining gear was in our backpacks, including one two-man tent between the five of us.

I winced at the thought of thousands of pounds' worth of lost gear, of angry sponsors and the effect on my future expeditions. But there were more immediate worries to hand: 3,000 feet of near sheer ice, and none of us were climbers. At noon we were con-templating an unstable causeway of ice-blocks which we would have to cross to reach the main descent line. It looked lethally inse-cure. We sought radio advice from the boss of our Land Rover mobile base in the valley below, and were not comforted to learn that of the twenty-eight glacier tongues that pour off the Jostedalsbre, this was the only one still unclimbed by Norway's ace glacier specialists. I edged warily over the causeway. In places only thin wedges spanned the gap and twice I froze as lumps of ice, disturbed by my passing, fell away like rotten planks from a footbridge. Once across, I made the rope firm and one by one the others joined me. I noticed blood on the ice and discovered that my fingers were bleeding. There was no pain, for my hands were numb. The others found the blood-trail a help when we passed through labyrinthine piles of loose ice boulders.

A twelve-foot crack that stretched across the entire glacier finally foxed us, forcing us back on to the rockface deep inside the bergschrund. Streams of icy water ran down our backs and a knife-like wind whistled down the dark cranny. Subterranean torrents roared below us in the nether regions and I prayed I would not slip from my fragile holds on the wet rock. When we emerged from the cavern we had bypassed the crack but evening stars were already visible and we were forced to camp for the night, all five of us in our two-man tent. Next day we survived the perils of avalanche rubble and two 400-foot abseils to the glacial lake where our base team awaited us in an inflatable boat.

Ten days after returning to England, and with Gubbie as best man, I married Ginny in Tillington church, a mile to the east of Lodsworth and her River home where we had met as children.

I did not marry Ginny because I had decided she was more important than my freedom, but because I considered it should be possible to have both. The early days of our marriage were to test this bland assumption sorely, starting from day one. I did not consult Ginny about our honeymoon programme since my understanding of tradition was that bridegrooms do not interfere with wedding arrangements nor brides with honeymoon details. Unfortunately, she did not find the prospect of a tour through Eastern Europe only two years after Soviet tanks had crushed

Dubcek's Czechoslovakia as intriguing as I did. She also complained at not getting a turn to drive my MG and nearly abandoned me in Munich. Things did not improve. In eastern Yugoslavia the exhaust pipe fell off. The officials at both ends of Czechoslovakia were painstakingly unpleasant, the Bulgarian and Hungarian police hounded us, due to our noisy exhaust, and the East Germans screwed every pfennig from us at the obligatory campsites. As a last straw, when we reached Vienna, I went off to find us a couple of ice creams, leaving Ginny in the queue for the Opera House, but I didn't manage to find my way back to where she was waiting before the last on-the-day ticket had been sold. To make amends I told Ginny we would visit Vienna's famous Lipizzaner Riding School. Only to discover that the wonderful white horses were all away in Spain on holiday.

After this inauspicious start, we settled temporarily in a rented cottage in Wester Ross where I buckled down to meet my deadline on a book about Norway and Ginny went for long walks in between dishing up Irish stew or scrambled eggs, the extent of her cookery repertoire. I never complained, since I liked both. We were both strong characters in our late twenties who had long practised doing our own thing. We were in love and had yearned for each other, despite powerful paternal opposition, for over a decade. But the institution of marriage closed about us like a cage and we began to fight like chained tigers. Having no money and no job did not help.

One day out of the blue I received a telegram from the William Morris Agency asking me to go to London to audition for the part of James Bond. Sean Connery had retired, his successor George Lazenby had been pensioned off, and the prime mover of the Bond films, Mr Cubby Broccoli, was on the lookout for a new 007. Mr Broccoli, I was told over the phone, was looking for 'an English gentleman who really does these things'.

'What things?' I asked.

'Shoot rapids, climb drainpipes, parachute, kill people, you know . . .'

The fact that I couldn't act seemed irrelevant, and it was an expenses-paid trip to London so I went down. The final interview after all the screen tests lasted all of ten minutes, sufficient for Mr Broccoli to decide I was too young, most un-Bond-like and facially more like a farmhand than an English gentleman. He settled on Roger Moore instead, so the cinema-going world had to wait for my cousins Ralph and Joseph to come along before the Fiennes name made it on to the silver screen.

In the new year we moved back south to Sussex, which didn't make Ginny any happier, and I got taken on as a captain by the 21st SAS Regiment (Territorial) in London and spent most weekends with my new unit, very grateful for the pay packet. Then in February, a letter arrived from the Royal Scots Greys, on whose list of reserve officers I still figured. They had an expedition for me to lead.

In 1971 British Columbia was celebrating the centenary of its joining the Canadian Confederation and wished to commemorate the early pioneers, most of whom had been Scots who had explored their impenetrable territory by river. The centenary committee in Vancouver had suggested a river journey by Scotsmen from their northern border with the Yukon to the United States border on the 49th parallel would be a feat to match those of their forebears. If successful, it would also be the first recorded north-south transnavigation of British Columbia. The route, along nine interconnecting water systems, ran deep through the Rocky Mountains and included some of the roughest rivers in the world. The Canadians approached the Ministry of Defence and they passed the suggestion on to the Greys, who liked the idea, especially since in June they were due to lose their identity and their famous grey berets through regimental amalgamation. The expedition would be a fine last fling but, as they had no regular officers available to lead it, my name came up. I was told the regiment would provide 'two or three soldiers and some supplies'.

Ginny agreed to join as road party leader and radio operator,

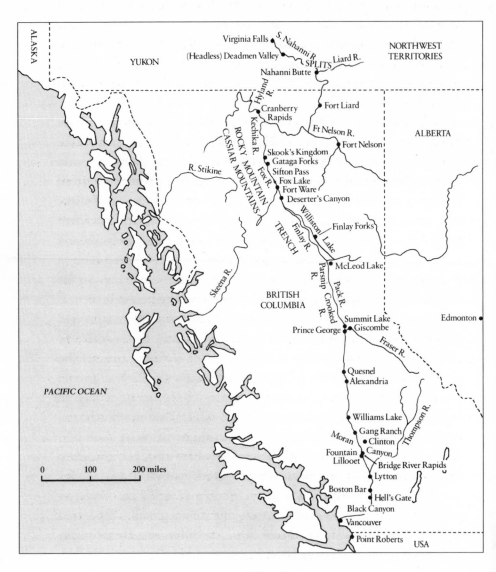

British Columbia

and when two of my old langlauf team volunteered I accepted both at once. One was an ex-butcher's apprentice from Edinburgh called Joseph Skibinski (we used to call him an Oatmeal Pole); the other, Jack McConnell, was a skilled radio operator. My last acquisition was a tank mechanic called Stanley Cribbett who, though short in size, could, according to Skibinski, repair anything from a clock to a sputnik. *The Observer* sent their top photographer, Bryn Campbell, and the BBC *World About Us* supplied a two-man film team and a Yorkshire policeman, Ben Usher, with lifeboat experience was recruited to steer for them.

An RAF Hercules flew us to Edmonton from where we drove our sponsored Land Rover and a four-ton lorry lent by the Canadian Army north-west to Fort Nelson. Here the plan was for the three boats to undertake a 400-mile trial journey before committing ourselves to the main expedition and attendant publicity. This seemed sensible since our UK training had only been on the Thames and none of us had wild water boating know-how. The trial goal was to reach the little known Virginia Falls, twice the height of Niagara, and 110 miles up the South Nahanni River. American river-runner and author Colonel Snyder, not given to understatement, described the South Nahanni as 'the fastest river in North America and the most dangerous in five continents'. To reach the Nahanni itself involved a further 290 miles of river travel. It would be a fair test.

We Royal Scots Greys wore our grey berets with their silver eagle badges as we left Fort Nelson. This was out of respect for our famous regiment which four days previously had ceased to exist after 300 years as Scotland's own cavalry regiment. My father during World War Two had seen the last of the grey horses in the 1940s; I wore the last grey beret in the seventies.

The three boats slid away, edging into the current as we gathered speed. A Mountie, two Indians and a group of press from Vancouver waved us off. Ginny stood alone on the bank, small and forlorn in her dusty jeans, soon a fading blur in the willows.

The river was 300 yards wide, both banks were thickly wooded and the world passed by quite silently but for the rush of water, the soft plunk of paddles and the sudden boil of converging eddies. An hour from Fort Nelson things changed with a vengeance.

'The current's racing along,' Bryn mused, 'as though there's a waterfall ahead.'

'There's no rapid on this river,' I assured him.

From up ahead I heard a sound as of breakers lashing a shingle beach; the same dull double boom and the rushing hiss of under-tow. The channel ahead curved right but the local current sucked us left. The other boats were out of sight.

Along the left-hand bank fallen trees rose and fell in the water. Torn down by the force of the floods upon the elbow of the river's curve, their gnarled roots clung to the bank and their trapped trunks threshed to the pulse of the rushing water. If a boat was sucked into this chaos of tangled roots, the tubing would be torn and punctured. We stabbed deep with our paddles, straining to move into mid-river. Before Stan could reach the outboard, a branch lashed across and cut his face. A splintered root dug into the hull behind Bryn and ripped it open. The port air tube wrin-kled and subsided and the boat shuddered as we struck a grounded log. We bounced off. If the boat had been of wood, we would probably have foundered and been sucked beneath the mass of heaving vegetation.

For a moment we were free, spun away from the bank by an eddy. This was merely a brief respite, for the shock of our narrow escape was soon eclipsed by the horror of the scene ahead. Now we could see the source of the earlier wind-borne roar, an island in mid-river on which, it seemed, every log borne downriver by recent floods was impaled. The whole force of the current, channelled by the acute bend, ran full tilt against the upstream apex of the island, and every piece of flotsam, from floating stumps of juniper to eighty-foot logs, was ensnared where the current split in two against the island.

We could not go left because that channel was a moving mass of tangled debris. So we swung right, sweating over the paddles.

Stanley wrestled with our outboard, swung its drive-shaft down until it locked vertically and tugged hard on the ignition cord. Again and again he pulled and twice the engine spluttered hopefully. Bryn stopped paddling to look over his shoulder, distracted by the shocking sound of log crashing onto log.

The water about us was disturbed now by back eddies surging around the jam. We were sucked inexorably backwards to where the river rushed under the sieve of logs. I thought to myself: 2,000 miles to go and here we are drowning on the first day. Then we smashed into the logs, sharp branches whipped at us and the boat up-ended. Someone screamed and a heavy object rammed my chest. I felt a branch rip down my back and the shock of cold water.

For a moment the boat was held by a branch and I scrabbled up from the floor to the mid-tubing. The branch broke and our bows disappeared, sucked inch by inch under the churning debris. Water poured over the bagged gear and the lashed fuel drums.

A branch flailed at Bryn and tore him away. He disappeared underwater, his hands clawing the air as he went.

The boat was about to go under. We must get on to the logs while there was a chance or we would all drown. I shouted to warn Stan and tried to scramble on to the nearest log above us. But it was too large and too slimy to grip. Then the boat shuddered and I fell back among the fuel drums. Stan shouted with excitement. He had started the engine. All this time he had single-mindedly tugged at the cord, not noticing the disappearance of Bryn. Now he engaged gear and the forty-horsepower engine roared in reverse cavitation.

There was hope. We both jumped up and down on the half-submerged craft to vibrate the trapped bows loose. A lashing line snapped, a ten-gallon drum broke loose and the bows shot free. Stanley grabbed the tiller and, with painful slowness, we edged away from the log jam.

Then I saw Bryn, or rather his mop of black hair. An underwater surge had spewed him up further down the log jam and his smart denim 'ranger' jacket was caught up on a branch. As we watched, his head sank a few inches. The full force of the undertow was dragging at him from the waist down.

We donned life-jackets and Stanley nosed the boat as near as possible to the downstream end of the log. I jumped on to it and edged along its bucking length towards Bryn. Sometimes the tree spun through half a turn. Reaching Bryn, I held his jacket scruff firmly and, with our combined strength, he came clear of the water. He was white, cold and shaken, but managed a rueful grin. His frail stature and normally immaculate garb belied a tough and resilient spirit.

The other crews both managed to keep clear of the great jam. We learned our lesson about the danger of snags and thereafter warmed our engine for a while each morning and started it at the first sign of any likely threat.

At Fort Liard we stopped to visit the Hudson's Bay Company store with the sign outside which proclaimed 'HBC 1886'. The Scotsman who ran it told us the locals said this stood for 'Here Before Christ'. He warned us the mosquitoes would be far worse in Nahanni country. 'The upriver Indians say the air is so thick with them, you canna starve. Simply keep breathing with your mouth open and you will get your daily meat ration.'

More practical was the advice of the local French priest who indulged in a fit of Gallic shrugs on inspecting our three inflatables and urged us, as he doled out moose stew and carrots, to get a flat-bottom river boat like his.

I followed his advice as soon as we reached Nahanni Butte, the point where the South Nahanni River joined the Liard. Here I hired from a local Indian a thirty-two-foot river boat for $50 and a bottle of our sponsored Black & White whisky. It would make a more solid platform for the BBC crew and would also enable us to carry extra fuel for the two inflatables.

Next day we entered the first canyon of the Nahanni. The towering walls acted as an echo chamber to every gush and twirl of the current, the sky above narrowed to a faraway strip of blue and we shivered in deep shadow, three waterbeetles struggling against the flow in a sheer-sided drain. The wiles of the river had to be watched at all times. There was no time to relax and enjoy the incredible scenery. To do so would be as suicidal as studying the Arc de Triomphe while driving round it.

High above us soared sheer red walls with successive pine-clad tiers of rock teetering atop the lower cliffs. The sun seldom touched us as we inched along the gloomy corridors of the canyon. Elsewhere, fighting for every inch of progress, we had to tug the river boat upstream on tow-lines with the eight of us hauling knee-deep in icy shallows. Policeman Ben, the strongest of us, was built like an Aberdeen Angus bull and, when he slipped, we all went under. The rope ripped away, tearing free of my numbed grip. On our next attempt we lined her, the jockey-light Stanley stayed aboard and cleverly nosed the boat upstream as we took in slack on the ropes.

Eventually we entered a region much favoured by the Canadian press due to its macabre associations. In Deadmen Valley, tucked between the Headless Mountains and the Funeral Range, three headless skeletons were found in the early 1900s. Canadian newspapers had been clocking up the unexplained deaths score in the area ever since and put the toll as high as thirty-two, but Ginny's research at the Royal Geographical Society and the Royal Canadian Mounted Police records confirmed only seventeen unexplained deaths or disappearances. Which might be considered enough. We did not add to those statistics and left Deadmen Valley with our heads intact.

In less than a hundred miles we had climbed over 1,000 feet. The final canyon was an impressive display of water force. A pocket of converging currents very nearly defeated us. We inched up the wall of water in the eddy-trap and water poured out of the butterfly valves in our boat bilges. Stanley zigged the tiller of our boat, shouting with relief as we crested the last rapid in an explosion of spray. Then the roar of pounding water intensified to an overall boom and from the heavens, or so it seemed from river-level, there appeared a waterfall of Olympian grandeur beneath a halo of high-flung spray. We had reached the Virginia Falls. Even the dour features of Constable Ben softened with pleasure at the majesty of the place.

The current whisked us back to Nahanni Butte where Bryn and the film team caught a bush plane to Fort Nelson to film firefighting in British Columbia. The trial journey was over. We drove north-west to the Yukon border ready to launch the boats on our 1,500-mile attempt to transnavigate British Columbia.

No sooner had we been rejoined by the BBC film crew than I sensed an overtly hostile atmosphere. Earlier they had fretted about not having a more definite timetable and again about not having enough time to sort out their gear at the end of the day. But I had been able to ignore that. Now I could tell I was in for trouble.

The Hyland River took us gently over the Yukon border into the Liard River and all went well as far as the Cranberry Rapids, where the Jocks overturned and Stanley ripped our own boat open on a snag. Jack's morale was dented by the experience, for he was sucked below by undercurrents, despite his life-jacket, and battered against submerged rocks.

Not far beyond the Cranberry Rapids and above the Rapids of the Drowned, we entered the mouth of the Kechika (or Big Muddy) River. This tributary of the Liard was sourced from a high swamp in the Rocky Mountain Trench known as the Sifton Pass and every authority I had consulted assured me our inflatables would not penetrate very far upriver. When we could get no farther I planned to canoe or to walk with rucksacks and had brought from England two portable canoes which, when dismantled, would be divided between our four backpacks. The point at which we would have to give up on our inflatables was probably going to be a spot known as Skook's ranch. This was the kingdom of Skook Davidson, *skookum* being the local Indian for The Tough One.

Skook ran a camp for big-game hunters, all his clients, guides and stores being flown in by float-plane. When the film crew learned that Skook had pack-horses for hire they approached me with the, to them, reasonable-sounding proposal that they hire these for their heavy camera gear. They could not see my view that the ethics of the expedition precluded outside support. Either we travelled the river or, where we ran out of waterways, we walked. Ever since my use of a taxi on the SAS Long Drag I had developed a fixation about cheating. But as far as the BBC crew were concerned I was being wilfully obstructive for no good reason. From that moment my fate was sealed. I would be the villain in their documentary film.

Skook was over eighty. Leaving Scotland as a teenager with £10 to his name, he became the finest rodeo rider in British Columbia and settled in his valley in 1939. Now he looked after twenty big-game hunters a year, specialising in grizzlies, bighorn sheep, cougars and mountain rams. The great man welcomed us from his bed, an old gnarled pioneer crippled by arthritis. He fumbled to light a candle. 'Sit down, darn you,' he barked. 'You folk from the old country never seem to know what the Lord gave you asses for.' Candlelight revealed a row of medals nailed to a log. Skook had done a stint as a sniper in the 29th Vancouver Battalion during the First World War.

From Skook's the boats went back downstream with Ginny, and the film team flew south to meet up with us at Fort Ware.

I asked Skook about the country to the south.

'When you can canoe no further,' he advised, 'you'll find my old trail beside the river, all the way to Sifton Pass.'

The Rocky Mountain Trench and the Kechika both lie north-south and, on the far side of the Sifton Pass, a new river, the Tochika or Fox, flows south all the way to Fort Ware. Skook's memories of his trail from thirty years ago were difficult to check and I found it ominous that a surveyor whose book I had studied described the trail, only six months after Skook had made it, as 'requiring much work every season if it is to be kept open, due to washouts, rapid growth and windfalls'. I consulted a local Indian guide. 'You'll be all right,' he said, 'so long as you don't follow a game trail by mistake. They're all over the place.' When asked how we were to recognise the real trail from the game trail, he replied:

'Why, you just do.' Then as an afterthought he warned us to watch out for bears. 'You surprise a grizzly on the trail with her kids and she can get real mean.'

We ran out of waterway at Gataga Forks where the river became too narrow and too powerful, so we collapsed the canoes we were then using, lashed them to our 110-pound packs and started following a trail blazed with old tree slashes. Jack fell off a tree-bridge into a thorn thicket and lay pinioned by the weight of his rucksack until rescued. Little Stanley Cribbett, not much larger than his pack, stumbled along, his face pale as he winced from a spasm of coughing and spat blood. Joe fell off a log and wrenched his back. Unable to carry his load, he had tried hauling it on a two-pole 'sled' but fallen trees made this impractical. Reluctantly, but unanimously, we agreed that Stanley and Joe should return to Skook's ranch, our last point of contact with civilisation, and radio for a plane to take them south to Fort Ware to rest and recover.

This left Jack and me. Things only got worse. Jack sprained his ankle and we lost all signs of any trail to the south. Rations were running out and eventually the only course was to return to Skook's and start again. Skook could not understand how we had missed the trail, but it was a long time since he had been on it. We set out again, but Jack's ankle was worse than before. Crying with frustration, he agreed he too had to give up. He gave me his pistol and we shook hands.

Route-finding continued to be a nightmare. I was ready to throw in the towel myself until the possibility occurred to me that the local Sikanee Indians might have moved Skook's trail across the river. I waded across and six hours later picked up the clearly marked triple slash which indicated their traplines. Forgetting sores, hunger and blisters, I covered the next twenty miles in two days to the headwaters of the Kechika, high on the flats of the Sifton Pass, a cheerful place of flowering plants and berry bushes. This was good trapping country, flush with beaver, marten, mink and otter. Now the Indian trail became easy to see, no longer a will-o'-the-wisp passage through undergrowth but a trodden path with blaze marks every few yards.

Late in the afternoon after crossing the pass I rounded a bend to find Jack and Joe hunting squirrels and they led me down to their camp at Fox Lake where the film crew were also installed.

Everyone seemed rather subdued. There was no welcome for me. Jack brought me tea and a pot of stew and, when the others were out of hearing, told me what was going on. 'The Beeb are out to get yoo's, Ran,' summed up the situation. He explained how the film team had been passing the waiting time prompting Stanley and Joe to complain about their treatment on tape. They had pictures of the diminutive Stanley staggering about under the weight of his pack. They had film of Joe declaring that 'Ran couldna' organise a piss-up in a brewery', and by way of proof that I was an egomaniac glory-seeker, the suggestion that I had encouraged the others to drop out so I could cross the Rocky Mountain Trench all by myself. On top of everything else I was plainly a lousy navigator. All that was now needed was for the journey to fail somewhere along the miles of violent rivers to our south. Then the BBC could make a fascinating in-depth study of leadership failure.

To select the perfect expeditionary team, in my opinion, is nearly impossible. There is no foolproof selection process and the longer, the more ambitious the endeavour, the more time there is for each person's failings to rise to the surface. The most I hope for is to find at least one true companion on each journey. In Canada I was lucky. Jack became a loyal lifelong friend, a man I would ask again on any expedition and trust whatever the stresses.

We launched ourselves back on the river at Fort Ware then followed the boisterous Finlay, the log-jammed, storm-tossed Williston lake, the mosquito and black-fly-infested Parsnip, Pack and Crookford Rivers until at last we reached Summit Lake. One night Ginny, waiting to contact us in a thickly forested swamp beside the river, was surprised by a black bear. She lost her nerve and screamed. The bear came closer and she pulled her .38 Smith and Wesson out of her anorak pocket. Somehow she pressed the trigger before the gun was clear and a bullet passed through the outside welt of her rubber boot, within a couple of millimetres of her foot. The bear departed and so did a terrified Ginny. Next time I met her she was furious. Why had I not made the rendezvous? Why did she have to wander through stinking woods and portage heavy gear? Nobody ever thanked or acknowledged her. I did, I pointed out.

'No, you don't. You just use me. You couldn't care less what happens to me so long as I'm in the right place at the right time.'

I did not try to argue as, by that time in our marriage, I knew that would be useless. Instead I thought of my favourite quote from Albert Einstein: 'Some men spend a lifetime in an attempt to comprehend the complexities of women. Others preoccupy themselves with simpler tasks such as understanding the theory of relativity.'

All the rivers we had travelled prior to reaching Summit Lake had flowed to an Arctic destination. Summit Lake was a dead-end, a high-altitude source of this Arctic watershed. To continue south we carried our boats nine miles along the ancient Giscombe Portage trail, over the Intercontinental Divide and down to the Pacific watershed and the biggest river of British Columbia, named after the great Scots explorer Simon Fraser.

We launched the boats on to the Fraser River late on 20 September and within minutes swept over the Giscombe Rapids wearing black frogsuits and life-jackets. From Giscombe, the river, the lifeline but also grave of so many pioneers, flowed for 850 tempestuous miles to Vancouver and the sea. Between Prince George, British Columbia's most northerly city, and the Fraser-side town of Lytton the river drops 1,200 feet, four times the height of Niagara Falls. Seventy miles south of Prince George it penetrates a deep trough many hundreds of feet below the surrounding land mass. The uncertainty of not knowing the state of the river in the boiling canyons ahead wore at all our nerves. When we attempted to glean local knowledge along the way we were met by the universal response that nobody knew what 'the river does down there'.

We entered the Moran Canyon, a rushing, roiling cauldron squeezed between black walls 1,000 feet high. The underplay of currents was impressive. Huge surface boils, bubbling like hot water in a saucepan, twice turned us about completely and thrust us chaff-like against the granite walls. By nightfall we stopped a mile above the great killer rapid of the Bridge River confluence. The press were waiting in Lillooet below the Bridge River Falls, licking their lips.

When the time came to run the falls, Stanley climbed on to our boat as though it were a tumbrel. The film team waved from a high boulder. I pushed the boat off and sprang aboard. Plucked from the bank like a feather we plunged into the white water. A roar like the thunder of doom rushed at us as we shot downwards. For a while I could see nothing. We were awash within a cartwheeling tunnel. The craft keeled over, forced to the side of a monster wave by centrifugal force. It was a wall of death on the horizontal plane and our hull clung to the inner side of the spinning liquid tube. At the lower end the boat was gripped by an undertow, dragged around and around, then spat out into a whirlpool. Our outboard roared frantically as we swung around the sinkhole and the cliffs of the river disappeared as we sank deep within the river's bowels. Then the sinkhole closed and regurgitated us towards the left-hand cliff. Stanley, water gushing from his helmet, tried to steer away from the rocks. He failed and we dashed against a boulder. The hull screamed in rubbery protest and crumpled along one side as the tube split open. But we were through. We shook hands and felt on top of the world. Our second boat also managed to defy the Bridge River Rapids.

After repairing the boats we continued south as the river flowed fast and furious through the Coastal Range and the Fraser's final monster rapid, Hell's Gate. Four days later we passed through the suburbs of Vancouver and navigated with care into a Pacific sea fog until a police launch met us with a bullhorn. 'This is it, folks. You're in Yank territory now.'

The two BBC films that were made from this expedition led their sixteen million-strong British audience to believe I was a cruel and incompetent publicity-seeker. The innuendoes which helped paint this picture certainly added spice and colour to the films, but did surprisingly little to discourage my sponsors in the future and helped me in a small way to develop a tougher skin when later expeditions were laid open to public scrutiny and criticism in the future.

Jack and Stanley left the Army a year after the expedition and emigrated to Western Canada where they both married. Jack called one of his sons Ranulph.

5

Ginny's Idea

Early in 1972, Ginny was stirring the stew when she came up with a weird suggestion. 'Why don't we go around the world?' She had mooted the idea once before in Scotland, and I had ignored it as impractical because what she envisaged was a longitudinal route – through the Poles – which was, I knew, neither physically nor administratively possible. A year passed and with no other projects on hand, we visited the Royal Geographical Society's map vaults and, grudgingly, I began to accept that her idea might after all be feasible. We could follow the Greenwich Meridian around the world's axis. We could start at Greenwich and head south to Antarctica, then up the other side of the planet, over the North Pole and back to Greenwich. A simple plan on the face of it.

For the next seven years we worked non-stop and unpaid to launch the endeavour, during which we often despaired of eventual success. Luck and hard work saw us through. At the weekends and on free evenings we lectured in civic centres, borstals, ladies' luncheon clubs and men's associations. We attacked the problem with total dedication and a determination that every item of equipment, every last shoelace and drawing pin, must be sponsored. We opened no bank account and possessed no chequebook, so there was no danger of the expedition overspending.

In the beginning I approached my 21st SAS Regiment CO to see whether the SAS group of regiments would sponsor the expedition.

But the Director of the SAS, a brigadier, at first refused to consider the idea because of my involvement with the Castle Combe raid. 'This expedition,' the brigadier expostulated to our CO, 'is unbelievably complex and ambitious. That Fiennes is not a responsible person. I can tell you straightaway that the SAS will not attach their good name to a plan such as this under a fellow like Fiennes.'

We were disappointed to hear the CO's account of his meeting. But a week later he summoned us to his office. They had evolved a workable solution. Brigadier Mike Wingate Gray, who, as CO of the regular SAS seven years before, had sent me packing after the Castle Combe incident, was appointed overall boss of the Transglobe expedition. If I accepted his loose supervision, then the SAS group would nominally sponsor the whole venture and provide us with office space in the Duke of York's Barracks just off the King's Road, Chelsea. We were in business.

Over the next two years our new office, a high attic which had earlier served as the 21 SAS rifle range, filled with sponsored equipment and its walls became papered with maps showing the more remote stretches of our proposed 52,000-mile journey. There was no telephone in the attic, but a friend who was a telephone engineer and Territorial trooper fixed up a phone one night which he clipped into the rooftop Ministry of Defence line. This was critical, since no phone meant no contact with sponsors. The expedition aim was that a core group of our team must travel over the entire surface of the world via both Poles without flying one yard of the way.

Early in 1975 Ginny, who was to be chief radio operator and mobile base leader, joined the Women's Royal Army Corps to learn about radios, antenna theory and speedy Morse operation. Oliver Shepard, a 21 SAS lieutenant, applied to join us. He looked overweight. I remembered him vaguely from Eton and had decided he was definitely not Transglobe material. By then we had a system of testing all volunteers in North Wales. Each weekend that winter and over the next two years, the Territorial SAS provided army trucks and rations for me to train a mountain racing team in

Snowdonia and, from the team hopefuls, about sixty SAS men in all, I would pick the three best ones for the expedition. Oliver Shepard joined the Welsh training weekends and proved to be more determined than he looked. He resigned his job and slept on a floor in the barracks, breakfasting on expedition rations and working evenings in a nearby pub, the Admiral Codrington. Oliver introduced me to an out-of-work friend named Charlie Burton, who had spent four years as a private soldier in an infantry regiment. His rugged face bore a pattern of rugby and boxing scars. Charlie passed the Territorial SAS selection course and joined our Welsh mountain training sessions. So too did Geoff Newman, who gave up his career with a printing firm. Finally, a part-time secretary, Mary Gibbs, joined us as nurse and generator mechanic. The six of us seemed to work well together, despite the strain of the tiny office and single telephone. By the autumn of 1975 we were sponsored by over 800 companies.

Andrew Croft, an Arctic explorer of note, advised me: 'Three men is a good number if you all get on. Two men is relatively suicidal. Four men can create cliques of two. In extremis, with three men, two can gang up against the leader. My advice is that you should decide whether to have two or three companions only after you have seen your potential colleagues in action during trials in the Arctic.'

From the moment Ginny and I started our joint struggle to launch Transglobe, we began to grow together. Our continued dedication to the venture survived even our total lack of know-how in all polar matters, the assurance of experts that our plans were impossibly ambitious and the long morale-sapping years of negative responses. For four or five years the British Antarctic Survey and the Royal Geographical Society (without whose blessing it would have been impossible, short of being a millionaire, to enter Antarctica) genuinely believed the projected journey to be hopelessly ambitious and probably impossible. Our prospects were summed up by one of Britain's polar godfathers, Sir Miles Clifford, an ex-director of the Falkland Islands Dependencies

Survey. 'You are saying, Fiennes, that your group will, in the course of a single journey, complete the greatest journeys of Scott, Amundsen, Nansen, Peary, Franklin and many others. You must understand that this sounds a touch presumptuous, if not indeed far-fetched.'

Sir Vivian Fuchs advised me that we could not hope to achieve Transglobe without polar training, so I began to plan two separate trial journeys. The first, to the Greenland Ice-cap in 1976, would train us for similar terrain in Antarctica. Next, in 1977, as there was nowhere suitable merely to simulate the Arctic, we would try to reach the North Pole itself.

Ginny's painstaking lobbying with the Ministry of Defence gained us permission for our first polar training and after four years in our barracks office, the RAF flew us to Greenland in July 1976 with 30,000 pounds of equipment. We landed at a US forces airbase in the north-west of the great ice-bound island. Along with two similar sites, one at Fylingdales in Yorkshire and the other at Clear in Alaska, this base formed part of a Soviet missile-spotting radar screen across the top of the world. Hills of grey gravel enfolded the base and eight miles inland we could see the rim of the ice-cap which covers all of Greenland save for the rock-girt fringes.

The redoubtable polar traveller Wally Herbert had advised me that fur parkas are unbeatable for Arctic winter travel. He also recommended that the ice-covered parts of our journey would best be attempted by some sort of machine rather than by dog teams, since we did not have time for the couple of years he considered essential for intensive dog-handling training. The snowcats we were going to use, which we called Groundhogs, were fitted with home-made buoyancy bags, and would float, swim and steer reasonably well between the cruising islands of pack-ice. Each towed two 1,000-pound sledge-loads separated by long safety lines.

During our first week on the Greenland Ice-cap a two-day blizzard kept us tent-bound and we learned simple lessons which would have been second nature to seasoned polar travellers: which way not to position the tent's entrance; how not to leave anything anywhere except on a Groundhog or inside the tent; how to string the radio's antenna wires to ski sticks rather than laying them along the snow surface where, after a blow, they became hard to dig out without damage. We quickly determined that snow for melting for drinks would come from one side of the tent foyer and the 'loo' would be on the other.

The Groundhogs, which started easily at temperatures down to −10°C, thereafter revolted and, on our first −20°C day they failed to respond to the electric circuit or the manual crank until Oliver poured the two Thermos flasks of hot chocolate, prepared for the day's travel, over the starter motors, whereupon the engines roared into life. Over the next months these machines caused non-stop trouble. The vehicle manuals were all in German which did not help, being beyond the scope of my hard-won O-level in that language.

I learned that neither my jungle nor my desert experience helped me much as ice-cap navigator, for the cold made my hand compass frustratingly slow to settle, while all manner of new problems cropped up to confuse and hinder accurate use of the theodolite. My first computed theodolite position in Greenland, following altitude shots of the sun at noon, was wrong by some sixty-two nautical miles. As our Groundhogs twisted their way through narrow snow valleys beneath the coastal mountains I used obvious features for compass backbearings. Later we climbed on to the inner ice-fields of the Hayes Peninsula, passing between heavily crevassed slopes. Blizzards pinned us down, inclines overturned the heavy sledges, throttles jammed, carburettors blocked, fuel lines leaked, a gearbox gasket blew and sprocket tyres shot off, landing up to sixty feet away. Finally we ran into serious trouble when both Groundhogs plunged into crevasses at the same time. We spent three precarious days tunnelling down to and under the stricken machines to retrieve them with pulleys and aluminium ramps.

But by the end of our ordeal we were working well together. Oliver's mechanical procedures were slick and we could strike or break camp in under an hour, compared with six hours a month before. Although no polar veterans, we had mastered deep snow ice-cap travel in temperatures of −20°C. The next step, a different game in every sense, was apprenticeship to Arctic Ocean ice-floe travel in temperatures of −40°C.

I arrived back in London from Greenland weighing thirteen stone. Over the next three 'office-bound' months I lost sixteen pounds and grew my first grey hairs as every possible political hurdle that might hinder our Arctic Ocean training plans was raised by the authorities. With limitless funds, we could have bought our way around most obstacles but we were, in Oliver's words, 'skint as squirrels'. In desperation I explained our immediate requirement − £60,000 to charter a ski-plane − to my old Dhofar contact, Tim Landon, and he introduced me to a wealthy Omani businessman, Dr Omar Zawawi, whose company agreed to sponsor the cost. In February 1977 a chartered DC6 flew the six of us into the polar darkness to try for the Pole.

Alert Camp, the world's most northerly settlement, is supplied only by air since there are no roads for hundreds of miles and all sea access is permanently frozen over. Sixty Canadian soldiers and scientists known as the Chosen Frozen manned the base in six-month stints. On the day of our arrival the temperature was −48°C and the night was pitch black. There would be no sign of the sun for a month. Our own camp, a deserted huddle of four wooden shacks, was perched along the very shore of the frozen sea a mile or so north of the Army camp. Between our huts and the North Pole lay nothing but 425 nautical miles of jumbled ice and black sea-smoke emanating from seams of open sea.

Oliver and Charlie prepared our new snow machines called skidoos. Much lighter than the Groundhogs, they were powered by 640cc two-stroke engines and steered by way of handlebars controlling a single short front ski. Skidoos are the snow traveller's motorbike: they provide scant protection from the elements.

I practised with my theodolite in a twenty-eight-knot wind at temperatures of −45°C, fairly average conditions for the time of year. One night the shooting of a single star took an hour and fifty minutes. In England I would have shot a dozen in twenty-five minutes. My eyelashes stuck to the metal of the scope and my nose cracked with the first symptoms of frosting. If I carelessly directed my breath on to the scope, even for a second, it froze; if I then wiped its lens with my bare finger, ungloved for even just a few seconds, this brought on circulation problems. Each time I tried to turn my head my beard hairs were tugged by the ice that meshed them, my eyes watered and more ice formed on my lashes which then froze together. But I persevered, for my ability to keep track of our position on the moving ice of the Arctic Ocean, whether by the sun or stars, would be key to our survival. An error of four seconds would put my position wrong by a mile.

We set out on 1 March, a few days before there is any glimpse of the sun at that latitude, and travelled five miles along the shoreline west of our camp before driving on to the sea-ice. A mile later we camped at −51°C, two men to a tent. Geoff tried to send a message back to Ginny, but his Morse key froze up and his breath simply froze on the inside of the fine wire mesh of his microphone. Then the main co-axial power line cable cracked when he tried to straighten it out. Next morning, after an unforgettably evil night, none of the skidoos would start.

During the two months of our North Pole attempt our chartered Twin Otter ski-plane visited us eight times. But there were other days when the pilot did not manage to spot us and returned to Ginny with a glum face and a negative report. Ginny sat at her radios for ten hours a day, often longer, knowing we were passing through areas of unstable breaking ice. She never missed a schedule and at times of major ionospheric disturbance, when even the major Canadian radio stations were blacked out, Ginny would tirelessly change antennae on her high masts, hop from frequency to frequency and tap out or yell out her identification sign hour after hour in the hope we might pick up her call. Out on the ice we were dependent on her ability. In the the tent, hearing her faint Morse signal or, in good conditions, her voice was the happiest moment of any day.

We never tried to drive skidoos and sledges north until we had first prepared a lane with our axes, work we dreaded because of the body sweat it caused which turned to ice particles inside our clothing. A typical stint of axe-work would last nine to eleven hours and clear a skidoo lane of between 500 and 3,000 yards. At first, aware of the dangers of polar bears, we each carried a rifle, but soon dropped the practice through sheer exhaustion. Slipping, sliding and falling into drifts made it difficult enough to manage a shovel and axe without worrying about a rifle as well.

Geoff and Oliver in particular suffered from frost-nipped finger ends. For long minutes in the dark I thought of nothing but my eyes. The eye-pain was a living thing. With a wind chill factor of −120°C the natural liquid in our eyes kept congealing. It was difficult to avoid outbursts of temper and hours of silent hostility in such conditions. For three years in London and four months in comparatively temperate Greenland, relations between us had been idyllic. But the Arctic put an end to the harmony. Any outside observer would have thought we were a close-knit group, but the new level of strain was beginning to get to us. Apsley Cherry-Garrard, describing Scott's winter party, wrote: 'The loss of a biscuit crumb left a sense of injury which lasted for a week. The greatest friends were so much on one another's nerves that they did not speak for days for fear of quarrelling.'

Over the weeks we inched north until the pressure ridges were no longer an unbroken mass. We began to find flat icefloe pancakes where travel was easy and quick flashes of hope, even elation, would then upset my determined cocoon of caution. I experienced exhilaration as the ice flashed by, my sledge leaping like a live thing but settling back on its runners instead of overturning.

During the second week of April the pack-ice showed the first symptoms of break-up. The temperature soared to −36°C and nights of creaking, rumbling thunder gave way to mornings of black or brown steam-mist, a sure sign of newly opened water-leads. For days we crossed open canals and lakes of *nilas*, which is newly formed dark grey sludge-ice. Winds picked up surface snow and filled the air with the glint of freezing ice particles. White-out conditions resulted when clouds blocked the sun and then we travelled slowly, for navigation was awkward without shadow or perspective. No hole in the ice was visible until you fell into it; no hummock or thirty-foot wall evident until you collided with it. One of us would walk ahead with a prod before the skidoos slowly followed.

Open water, being black, was clearly visible but new ice, mere centimetres thick, was quickly covered by spindrift and formed traps for the unsuspecting. Conventional wisdom has it that white ice is thick and grey thin. I discovered that this was not always true while gingerly exploring a recently fractured ice-pan. The ice felt spongy underfoot at first, then more like rubber. Suddenly the surface began to move beneath my boots, a crack opened up and black water gushed rapidly over the floe, rushing over my boots and weighing down on the fragile new ice. As the water rose to my knees, the crust under my feet cracked apart. I sank quickly but my head could not have been submerged for more than a second since the air trapped under my wolfskin acted as a life-jacket.

The nearest solid floe was thirty yards away. I shouted for the others, but there was no one in earshot. Each time I tried to heave myself up on to a section of the submerged crust, I broke it again. I crawled and clawed and shouted. Under my threshing feet was a drop of 17,000 watery feet down to the canyons of the Lomonosov Ridge. Sailors in the world wars, I recalled, survived one minute on average in the North Sea. I began to tire. My toes felt numb and there was no sensation inside my mitts. My chin, inside the parka, sank lower as my clothes became heavier. I began to panic.

After four, perhaps five minutes, my escape efforts had weakened to a feeble pawing movement when, ecstatic moment, one arm slapped down on to a solid ice chunk and I levered my chest on to a skein of old ice. Then on my thighs and knees. I lay gasping for a few seconds, thanking God, but once out of the water, the cold and the wind bit into me. My trousers crackled as they froze. I tried to exercise my limbs but they were concrete-heavy in the sodden, freezing parka. I trudged robot-like via a solid route back to my skidoo which I could not start. For fifteen minutes I plodded round and round. My mitts were frozen and the individual fingers would not move.

Oliver came along my tracks. He reacted quickly, erecting a tent, starting a cooker, and cutting off my parka, mitts and boots with his knife. Twenty-four hours later, with me in spare clothes and a man-made duvet, we were on our way again. I was lucky to be alive. Few go for a long swim in the Arctic Ocean and survive.

During the latter half of April we pushed hard to squeeze northerly mileage out of each hour's travel. Only three teams in history had indisputably succeeded in reaching farther north towards the Pole – Plaisted, Herbert and Monzino. By 20 April we had exceeded the records of all previous travellers but these three. On 5 May we passed 87° North, a mere 180 miles from the Pole. The transpolar drift was what stopped us. The two major currents of the Arctic, the Beaufort Gyral and the Trans-Siberian Drift, meet and diverge somewhere between 87°and 88° of latitude, causing surface chaos, tearing floes apart in places and jumbling others up to heights of thirty feet. On 7 May there were wide canals and slush pools every few hundred yards. The entire region was in motion.

At this point the engine of my skidoo blew a head gasket and we could not progress without a re-supply drop. By the time Ginny had cajoled a ski-plane into dropping a new part we had drifted sixty miles to the south and east and a six-mile belt of sludge surrounded us. We waited for a further week, hoping for a freak temperature drop, but on 15 May, with temperatures rising to 0°C, I decided to call it a day.

Our funds ran out with the flight that extricated us from the floe and took us back to Alert. There Ginny gave me a radio message from London: Prince Charles had agreed to become patron of the main Transglobe Expedition.

The Arctic journey confirmed that the main expedition would have to have its own dedicated Twin Otter ski-plane and crew for re-supply purposes. I spent three years and numerous interviews with big company bosses before finally persuading Lord Hayter of Chubb Fire to sponsor us with the three-year loan of a Twin Otter with skis.

Back in the London office we carried on much as before. But the Arctic journey had humbled me, my first expedition failure. Soon afterwards Mary and Geoff were married and left the expedition. Mary's place as Ginny's base camp companion was taken by a young Cumbrian named Simon Grimes. A scruffy-looking man with a black beard, Anton Bowring, applied to join up as a ship's deck-hand. He was quiet and unflappable. He listened impassively when I explained there was no ship as yet for him to be a deck-hand on. But his first job, to keep him busy, could be to find one. It must be an ice-breaker and free of charge. A year later he located a thirty-year-old ice-strengthened vessel and persuaded the insurance brokers, C.T. Bowring, once owned by his family, to buy her on our behalf. This they did, with an eye to the fact that they had sponsored Captain Scott seventy years previously with his ship, the *Terra Nova*. Anton recruited sixteen unsalaried but qualified crewmen for his ship which he christened the *Benjamin Bowring*, after an adventurous ancestor. I was meanwhile lucky enough to obtain the services of Britain's most skilled Twin Otter polar pilot, Captain Giles Kershaw. The British Army loaned the expedition the services of Gerry Nicholson, an electrical and mechanical engineer specialising in Twin Otter maintenance who had spent time in Antarctica with the British Antarctic Survey.

By the end of 1978, after six years of unpaid full-time work, we had 1,900 sponsors from eighteen countries, £29 million worth of goods and services support and a team of fifty-two unpaid individuals giving their time and expertise towards Ginny's dream of the first circumpolar journey round earth.

One summer weekend Ginny's pet terrier drowned in a slurry pit. For weeks she was inconsolable until a friend turned up with a Jack Russell puppy with which she instantly fell in love. We called him Bothie in honour of his donor whose surname was Booth, and Ginny informed me she was not coming on Transglobe without him.

At Farnborough, in the spring of 1979, Prince Charles opened the Transglobe's press launch, arriving at the controls of our Twin Otter. He announced that he was supporting the expedition 'because it is a mad and suitably British enterprise'. Late in the afternoon of 2 September 1979 the *Benjamin Bowring* left Greenwich with Prince Charles at the helm. He wore a black tie because his uncle, Lord Mountbatten, had been killed three days before by the IRA. There were many people lining the pier. I spotted Geoff who was shouting rude messages at Oliver, and Mary, smiling through her tears. At the end of the jetty Gubbie held up one of his daughters who, with misplaced priorities, was busily waving her arm at the nearby *Cutty Sark*.

6

The Bottom of the World

On the day we set out from England, Prince Charles commented, 'Transglobe is one of the most ambitious undertakings of its kind ever attempted, the scope of its requirements monumental.' *The New York Times* editorial column, under the heading 'Glory', stated, 'the British aren't so weary as they're sometimes said to be. The Transglobe Expedition, seven years in the planning, leaves England on a journey of such daring that it makes one wonder how the sun ever set on the Empire.'

Our initial plans were mundane enough. With three Land Rovers we would cross Europe, the Sahara and West Africa. The ship would take us from Spain to Algeria and again from the Ivory Coast to Cape Town. Departure from Cape Town had to be timed precisely in order to enter Antarctic waters in mid-summer, when the ice-pack should be at its loosest. This was the reason we left England in early September and why we had to leave South Africa by late December.

Anton Bowring's crew of volunteers were a wonderful bunch, professional at their posts but fairly wild when off duty. They included Quaker, Buddhist, Jew, Christian and atheist, black, white and Asian. They came from Austria, America, both ends of Ireland, South Africa, India, Denmark, Britain, Canada, Fiji and New Zealand. Most of the crew were Merchant Navy men who gave up promising careers, at a time of growing unemployment, to join a three-year voyage with no wage packet. Paul Anderson from Denmark, who had signed on as a deck-hand, had worked with us for a year in the office and on the ship but died of a heart problem just before we left England.

Ginny was not the only female aboard, for Anton had selected an attractive redhead, Jill McNicol, as ship's cook. She soon gained a number of ardent admirers from among the crew.

In Algiers the port officials showed ominous interest in our three-year supply of sponsored spirits and cigarettes. When the first wave of officers departed, promising a second visit in an hour, our skipper decided to make a run for it and quickly unloaded our vehicles and gear. As the crew waved us goodbye, the *Benjamin Bowring*'s thirty-year-old variable pitch control jammed itself in reverse. So the vessel retreated out of the harbour and out of sight steaming backwards.

In our three sponsored Land Rovers we drove through Algeria to the sand-dunes of El Golea, a sticky-hot hell-hole dubbed 'El Gonorrhoea' by Oliver. We were pleased to leave the sweltering sands and head south to the Hoggar Mountains. At 8,000 feet we reached the Pass of Asekrem, the haunt of French monks. We savoured views of vast mountain ranges disappearing to Chad and the centre of Africa. From Tamanrasset we rattled down ever-worsening trails to lonely Tit and thence over trackless miles of sand and scrub to Tim-Missao and the Touareg lands of the Adrar des Iforas. Wide starry nights and wind-blown dunes brought back memories of the Dhofari Nejd and desert days long past.

From the Forest of Tombouctou to Goundam on the Niger we roared and skidded over dunes of thirty-foot-high sand in low gear to the cheer of barefoot donkeymen in sampan hats driving cavalcades of pint-size mules along the same trail.

At Niafounke we learned that extensive flooding barred our planned route to the Ivory Coast, but a 700-kilometre westerly detour took us at length to Loulouni and the Ivorian border at Ouangolodougou. For a week we camped in thick jungle beside the Bandama Rouge River, an excellent collection point for bilharzia-bearing water-snails, one of Oliver's tasks for the Natural History Museum, then south to the lush and hilly coastline. In Abidjan harbour, we were met by the *Benjamin Bowring*. Simon and two members of the crew were weak from malarial fever but we pressed on and sailed across the Equator close by the Greenwich Meridian.

Somewhere off the Namib coast, the Benguela Current coincided with a Force Seven storm. The electrical system of the stern refrigerator room broke down and a ton of sponsored mackerel turned putrescent. Brave hands volunteered to go below and clean up the mess, slipping about, as the ship rolled and heaved, in a soup of bloody fish bits. They fought their way up the ladders and tossed the sloppy bundles of rotten fish overboard. Then a forklift truck burst its lashings, crushed valuable gear and spattered battery acid about the cargo hold. Nowhere on the bucking ship, from cabins to fo'c'sle, could we escape the fumes of acid and mackerel. We were in the tropics and there was no air-conditioning system. This was, after all, a ship designed for work at polar temperatures. With each roll to port our cabin porthole spat jets of sea-water on to our bunks. All night the clash of steel on steel and the groan of hemp under stress sounded from the cargo holds.

The old ship struggled on at a stately eight knots and delivered us, slightly dazed, to Saldanha Bay, near Cape Town, on 3 December. Jackass penguins squawked from the rocky shoreline, hundreds of thousands of them, as we anchored to take on fresh water.

We stayed two weeks in Cape Town to mount an export sales-orientated exhibition of our equipment, one of eight such events to be held during the course of the voyage. On a free evening I drove to Constantia with Ginny and visited our old house, built by Granny Florrie thirty-four years before. Nothing was as I remembered it. The valley was no longer the wild and wonderful place of my dreams. Residential expansion had tamed and suburbanised the woods and vineyards. The vlei where I had roamed with Archie and the gang was now a row of neat bungalows for foreign embassy staff. Our own house, Broughton, was a transitory post for US Marines on leave and nobody had tended the garden in years. There was no longer a view of the valley, for Granny Florrie's

The Transglobe Expedition, 1979–82

shrubs had flourished unchecked and the four little palm trees named after my sisters and me were now roof-high.

We wandered in silence through the old vegetable patch. No trace remained of the summerhouse, a place of bewitching memories. My mother's rockery, tended with so much care and love, had run amok. Up the valley, beside a building lot where caterpillar trucks were at work, we called on my cousin Googi Marais, whose rifle bullets passing over the roof at night had once caused our English nanny to pack her bags and flee. Googi was now crippled with arthritis, but he and his wife gave us tea and filled

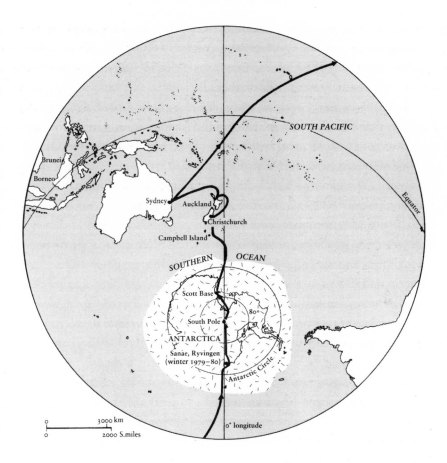

me in on the past quarter century of happenings in our valley.

Over the next ten days I was reunited with twenty-two other cousins, one of whom, an alderman of Cape Town, showed me a family tree which proved he and I shared a close relationship with Karl Marx. I regret not having taken away a copy to shock the family back in England.

We left South Africa three days before Christmas, passing by Cape Agulhas, the last land for 2,400 miles, and set a course south to Antarctica.

Bothie, our Jack Russell, appointed himself ship's mascot and, respecting no privacy, left calling-cards in all cabins. Ginny tried hard to remove all his indiscretions before they were discovered by the crew but it was an uphill struggle.

The Observer, covering the expedition, sent Bryn Campbell to Antarctica with us to record the ship's arrival. A four-man film team was also on board – provided by millionaire octogenarian Dr Armand Hammer, a friend of Prince Charles – intending to film the entire three-year journey by joining the team in the more accessible areas. The actor Richard Burton was to provide a background commentary.

Swelling the ship's complement still further were a number of oceanographers. At certain stages of the voyage there were eight scientists on board and at all times our own resident boffins, an Irishman and a Cape Town University researcher, worked with their bathythermographs and nets to study current patterns and the interaction of water bodies at sub-tropical and Antarctic convergences.

Christmas spirits were dampened by a Force Eight storm which tore away the Christmas tree lashed to our mast and made eating rich festive fare a risky business. Giant Southern Ocean rollers forced the ship to list 47° both ways and, fearing the worst, I asked Anton if the ship could cope. His eyes glinted evilly and he proceeded to tell me a number of Antarctic shipwreck horror stories.

As the old year slid away, we entered pack-ice and the sea slowly settled. Anton reflected that Scott and Shackleton had been active in these waters less than seventy years before. The skipper sent a lookout up to the crow's nest to shout directions to the fo'c'sle through the antiquated intercom. The loose pack-ice yielded to our steel-clad bows and only once did we need to halt and slowly ram a new path through the floes.

On 4 January 1980, we sighted the ice-cliffs of Antarctica and the same day gouged ourselves out a nest at Sanae, in the thin bay-ice of Polarbjorn Bite, where we could climb straight down a ladder on to the ice. The unloading of over 100 tons of mixed cargo, including 2,000 numbered boxes and 1,600 fuel drums, began at once.

To ensure that the ship could leave before the pack solidified and cut off her escape, we raced to carry every item two miles inland to more solid ice. Everyone helped, even the film team. Our sole tow-machine apart from skidoos was a Groundhog rescued from Greenland but, in only eleven days, the complex operation was complete.

Halfway through the unloading a storm broke up the ice and I watched from the bridge as eight drums of precious aircraft fuel sailed north on a floe. It was as if the bay-ice all about the ship were pieces of a jigsaw all coming apart at the same moment.

Our steward Dan Hicks, a permanently merry character, drank too much whisky and fell off the gangplank, floating belly-up between the hull and the ice-edge, in imminent danger of being crushed, until someone hauled him out on a boathook. One of the engineers slipped and broke three ribs and Bothie lost a fight with an angry chinstrap penguin. The chief engineer, who had hoisted his Honda motorbike on to the ice for a quick ride, lost the machine for ever during a storm. Otherwise the unloading went well and those of us who were to stay behind waved goodbye to the ship and crew on 15 January. All being well, they would pick us up again in a year or so, 2,000 miles away on the far side of the frozen continent.

Ten days later, in conditions of nil visibility, Ollie, Charlie and I took our skidoos and laden sledges on a 370-kilometre journey inland to set up a base on the high polar plateau in which to spend the next eight months of polar winter and the long disappearance of the sun. The base-site beneath Ryvingen Mountain was chosen because of its height above sea-level and its distance inland, the furthest which the Twin Otter could be expected to reach carrying a 2,000-pound cargo load. We hoped, by wintering at 6,000 feet, to become acclimatised to the bitter conditions before the main crossing journey the following summer, when the average height would be 10,000 feet above sea-level. Until we reached our winter site we would be simple travellers. But once south of our camp, we would become true explorers of one of earth's last untrodden regions. For 900 miles we would pass through terrain neither seen nor touched by mankind. Oliver would be mapping this whole unexplored area using an aneroid barometer, as he had been trained to do by the British Antarctic Survey.

The Twin Otter flew in Ginny, Bothie and four cardboard huts Ginny had designed, and the race began to prepare our camp for the long winter. The Twin Otter crew completed their seventy-eighth ferry flight from Sanae to Ryvingen and we wished them a safe flight back to Britain via the Falkland Islands and Argentina.

The weather clamped down on the ice-fields, travel for any distance became impossible and we were soon cut off from the outside world. We were 400 miles from and unreachable by the nearest humans, the twelve South African scientists in their snow-buried seaside hut at Sanae. For eight months we must survive through our own common sense. Should anyone be hurt or sick there could be no evacuation and no medical assistance. We must daily handle heavy batteries, generator power lines and heavy steel drums, but avoid the hazards of acid in the eye, serious tooth trouble, appendicitis, cold burns, fuel burns or deep electrical burns. Temperatures would plunge to −50°C and below. Winds would exceed ninety knots and the chill factor would reach −84°C. For 240 days and nights we must live cautiously and mostly without sunlight.

After a few days the huts disappeared under snow drifts, and all exits were blocked. So I dug tunnels under the snow and stored all our equipment inside them. In two months I completed a 200-yard network of spacious tunnels with side corridors, a loo alcove, a thirty-foot-deep slop-pit and a garage with pillars and archways of ice.

Since our huts were made of cardboard with wooden struts and bunks and our heaters burned kerosene we were apprehensive of fire. A Russian base, 500 miles away, had been burnt out the previous winter and all eight occupants were found asphyxiated in an escape tunnel with blocked hatches.

Katabatic winds blasted our camp and snuffed out our fires through chimney back-blow. We experimented with valves, flaps and crooked chimneys, but the stronger gusts confounded all our efforts. The drip-feed pipe of a heater would continue to deliver fuel after a blow-out and this could cause a flash-fire unless great care was taken on re-lighting the heater.

Generator exhaust pipes tended to melt out sub-snow caverns which spread sideways and downwards. One day Oliver discovered a fifteen-foot-deep cave underneath the floor of his generator hut. He moved his exhaust system time and again but nearly died of carbon monoxide poisoning three times despite being alert for the symptoms.

Without power from the generators, Ginny's radios would not work, so our weather reports, which Oliver must send out every six hours, could not be fed into the World Meteorological System, nor could Ginny's complex, very low frequency (VLF) recording experiments for Sheffield University and the British Antarctic Survey be undertaken. So we fought hard against snow accumulation in certain key areas of the camp.

At night in the main living hut we turned the heater low to save fuel. We slept on wooden slats in the apex of the hut roof and in the mornings there was a difference of 14° between bed level and floor temperature, the latter averaging −15°C.

Ginny and I slept together on a single slat at one end of the hut, Oliver and Charlie occupied bachelor slats down the other end and Bothie slept in a cavity behind the heater. The long black nights with the roar of the wind so close and the linger of tallow in the dark are now a memory which I treasure.

There was of course friction between us. Forced togetherness breeds dissension and even hatred between individuals and groups. After four years at work together our person-to-person chemistry was still undergoing constant change. Some days, without a word being spoken, I knew that I disliked one or both of the other men and that the feeling was mutual. At other times, without actually going so far as to admit affection, I felt distinctly warm towards them. When I felt positive antagonism towards the others I could let off steam with Ginny, who would listen patiently. Or else I could spit out vituperative prose in my diary. Diaries on expeditions are often minefields of over-reaction.

Each of us nursed apprehensions about the future. The thought of leaving the security of our cardboard huts for the huge unknown that stretched away behind Ryvingen Mountain was not something on which I allowed my thoughts to dwell.

On 2 May the wind chill factor dropped to −79°C. Windstorms from the polar plateau blasted through the camp with no warning. Visiting Ginny's VLF recording hut one morning, I was knocked flat by a gust, although a second earlier there had not been a zephyr of wind. A minute later, picking myself up, I was struck on the back by the plastic windshield ripped off my parked skidoo.

Even in thirty-knot wind conditions we found it dangerous to move outside our huts and tunnels except by way of the staked safety lines which we had positioned all around the camp and from hut to hut. Charlie and I both lost the safety lines one day when an eighty-knot wind hurled ice-needles horizontally through the white-out. We groped separately and blindly in circles until we blundered into a safety line and so found our way to the nearest hut's hatchway. That same day the parachute canopy covering the sunken area of Ginny's antennae-tuning units was ripped off, and by nightfall two tons of snow had filled in her entire work area.

Before the sun disappeared I taught Oliver and Charlie the rudiments of langlauf skiing, for I knew, if we succeeded in crossing Antarctica, that we would meet many regions in the Arctic where only skis would be practical.

On a fine autumn day we left camp with laden sledges for a quick sixteen-kilometre manhaul trip to a nearby *nunatak*, a lonely rock outcrop. A storm caught us on the return journey and, within minutes, the wind had burned every patch of exposed skin and frostnipped our fingers inside their light ski mitts. At the time we were each moving at our separate speeds with a mile or so between us. This was not acceptable by current mountain safety practices but it was a system encouraged on all SAS training courses. The fewer individuals in a group, the faster the majority will reach their goal. This presupposes that the weakest link can look after himself. Oliver was last to arrive back at camp, his face and neck bloated with frostnip. For a week he took antibiotics until his sores stopped weeping.

Ginny's problems were mostly connected with her radio work. Conducting low-frequency experiments with faraway Cove Radio Station in Hampshire, she worked a 1.5 kva generator in the foyer to her hut. A freak wind once blew carbon monoxide fumes under her door. By chance I called her on a walkie-talkie and, receiving no reply, rushed along the tunnels and down to her shack. I found her puce-faced and staggering about dazed. I dragged her out into the fresh −49°C air and told the Cove Radio operator what had happened. Next day we received a worried message from their controller, Squadron Leader Jack Willes.

Even in a comfortable environment the operation of electrical radio components is a hazardous operation. In your location the dangers are considerably increased . . . Remember that as little as thirty mA can kill. Never wear rings or watches when apparatus is live. Beware of snow from boots melting on the floor . . . Your one kilowatt transmitter can produce very serious radio frequency burns . . . Static charges will build up to several thousand volts in an aerial. Toxic berillium is employed in some of the components . . .

Only four days later, with all her sets switched off and no mains power, Ginny touched the co-ax cable leading to her forty-watt set and was stunned by a violent shock that travelled up her right arm and 'felt like an explosion in my lungs'. The cause was static, built up by wind-blown snow.

Not being a technical expert, Ginny used common sense to repair her sets, replace tiny diodes and solder cold-damaged flex.

When a one-kilowatt resistor blew and she had no spares, she thought of cutting a boiling ring out of our Baby Belling cooker. She then wired the cannibalised coil to the innards of her stricken radio and soon had everything working again, the home-made resistor glowing red-hot on an asbestos mat on the floor. The chief back at Cove Radio described her as 'an amazing communicator'.

To keep our little community happy, Ginny listened to the BBC World Service and produced *The Ryvingen Observer*. On 6 May we learned that the bodies of US airmen were being flown out of Iran following an abortive attempt to rescue American hostages, that Tito's funeral was imminent, that SAS soldiers had killed some terrorists at the Iranian Embassy in London and that food in British motorway cafés had been summed up in a government report as greasy and tasteless.

Bothie spent his days following Ginny from hut to hut. She kept old bones for him in each shack and dressed him in a modified pullover when the winds were high. I fought a non-stop battle with the terrier for eight months, trying to teach him that 'outside' meant right outside the tunnels as well as the hut. I lost the struggle.

Charlie, in charge of our food, rationed all goodies with iron discipline. Nobody could steal from the food tunnels without his say-so, a law that was obeyed by all but Bothie. Our eggs, originally sponsored in London, were some eight or nine months old by mid-winter and, although frozen much of that time, they had passed through the tropics en route. To an outsider they tasted bad – indeed evil – but we had grown used to them over the months and Bothie was addicted. However hard Charlie tried to conceal his egg store, Bothie invariably outwitted him and stole a frozen egg a day, sometimes more.

The months of June, July and August saw an increasing workload in the camp, due both to the scientific programme and our preparations for departure in October. The sun first came back to Ryvingen, for four minutes only, on 5 August, a miserably cold day. Down at our coastal Sanae base hut, Simon, overwintering with one other Transglober, Anto Birkbeck, recorded a windspeed in excess of 100 miles per hour. July 30 was our coldest day. With the wind steady at forty-two knots and a temperature of −42°C, our prevailing chill factor was −131°C, at which temperature any exposed flesh freezes in under fifteen seconds.

In August Ginny had to complete a complex research task which involved working with two other remote Antarctic bases, Sanae and Halley Bay, to pick up Very Low Frequency signals emanating from the Arctic. All pick-up times (once every four minutes) had to be exactly synchronised between the three bases. But Ginny discovered the oscillation unit in her VLF time-code generator had failed due to the cold. To complete the VLF experiment without the instrument meant manually pressing a recording button every four minutes for unbroken twenty-four-hour periods. Wrapped in blankets in the isolated VLF hut she kept awake night after night with flasks of black coffee. By October she was dog-tired and hallucinating but determined to complete the three-month experiment.

As the sunlit hours grew longer, the ice-fields reacted. Explosions sounded in the valleys, rebounding as echoes from the peaks all about us. Avalanches or imploding snow-bridges? There was no way of knowing.

With departure imminent, I realised how much I had grown to love the simplicity of our life at Ryvingen, a crude but peaceful existence during which, imperceptibly, Ginny and I had grown closer together than during the bustle of our normal London lives. Now I felt pangs of regret that it was ending. Also tremors of apprehension. As the days slipped by my stomach tightened with that long-dormant feeling of dread − once so familiar during school holidays as the next term-time approached.

'I wish you weren't leaving,' Ginny said.

In the last week of October it should be warm in the −40s°C and light enough to travel at 10,000 feet above sea-level. Then we would attempt the longest crossing of the Antarctic continent, the first crossing attempt to use vehicles with no protective cabs for the drivers and the first to travel from side to side, rather than split-teams approaching the Pole from both sides. The frozen land mass we must cross was bigger than Europe, the USA and Mexico combined, than India and China together, and far larger than Australia. The ice-sheet was five kilometres thick in places and covered 99 per cent of the entire continent. Four days before we set out, a news release through Reuters quoted the New Zealand Antarctic Division boss as criticising our intended journey as under-equipped and our skidoos as under-powered. The official view was that we would fail: it was 'too far, too high and too cold'.

On 29 October we left Ginny and Bothie in a drifted-over camp and headed south. The wind blew into our masked faces at twenty knots and the thermometer held steady at −50°C.

Clinging to a straight bearing of 187°, we crossed the sixty-four kilometres to the Penck Escarpment, a steep rise of several hundred feet of sheet ice. Spotting the curve of a slight re-entrant, I tugged my throttle to full bore and began the climb, trying to will the skidoo on with its 1,200-pound load − a heavy burden for a 640cc two-stroke engine operating at 7,000 feet above sea-level. The rubber tracks often failed to grip on smooth ice, but always reached rough patches again before too much momentum was lost. Renewed grip and more power then carried me on − just − to the next too-smooth section. The ascent seemed interminable. Then came an easing of the gradient, two final rises, and at last the ridgeline. Fifteen hundred feet above our winter camp and forty miles from it I stopped and looked back. The peaks of the Borga Massif seemed like mere pimples in the snow, Ryvingen itself just a shadow.

We pressed south and by dusk there was no single rock feature in any direction. Only endless fields of snow. Nothing to navigate by but clouds and soon − once we left the weather-making features of sea and mountain behind us − there would not even be clouds.

On the second day, at −53°C, we climbed slowly into the teeth of high winds and a white-out, the true plateau still 4,000 feet above us. After four hours Oliver staggered off his skidoo and lurched

My father, Palestine 1940.

With my mother, 1944.

Me at 11; Ginny (left) and family. Her father (right) was the man who described me as 'Mad, bad and dangerous to know' – perhaps with some justification, given the newspaper coverage below.

Not even her father could stop us getting engaged –
even though I nearly missed my opportunity.

On patrol in the Omani southern deserts, 1969.

Training with the SAS (Territorials): this was a good way of keeping fit when I was no longer part of the regular army.

Parachute training prior to the glacier drop, 1970.

The first recorded descent of the highest glacier in Norway, 1970, the author third from left.

Even in those days my hands caused me problems.

The majesty and beauty of ice has always captivated me –
the Jostedals Glacier, 1970.

The Headless Valley Exedition, 1971: the Virginia Falls,
twice the height of Niagara.

Ginny sometimes had to resupply our boats in thick forest and
once had a seriously close encounter with a black bear.

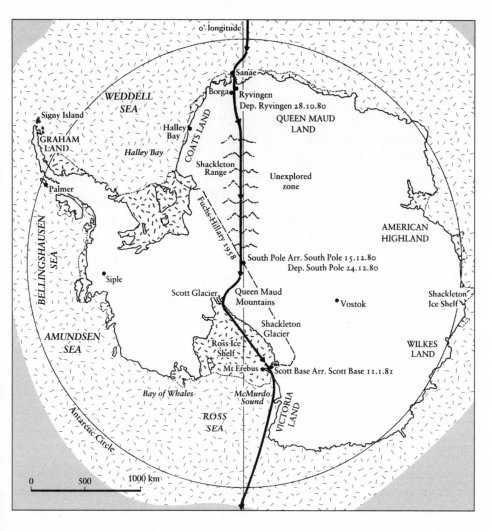

The Transglobe Expedition's route across Antarctica

over to me, his speech slurred. 'Must stop. I'm getting exposure.' We boiled water and gave him tea. He was physically the toughest of us and wore five layers of polar clothing. But the cold was cruel and wore us down hour after hour. We travelled for between ten and twelve hours a day.

That night Oliver wrote: 'Very bad weather. I think we should have stayed in the tent.' I saw his point but Greenland five years earlier had taught me that we could travel in high wind and white-out and every hour of progress, however slow, helped our slim chances of success. We had 2,200 miles to go, 900 of them unexplored.

I took a bearing check every ten minutes against the clouds: as these moved slowly and maintained their silhouettes for quite a while, they served me well. At times when partial white-outs hid sun and clouds, all I could do was aim my compass at imperfections in the snow ahead. When the sun shone I navigated by means of the shadows of a series of penknife-scratched lines on the plastic windshield of my skidoo. To check on the accuracy of this crude system and to put some life back into our frozen limbs, I stopped for five minutes in every hour. We always maintained a space of a mile between each of us so, as soon as I stopped, a backbearing on the two specks back along my trail provided a good check on the angle of travel.

For four days and nights the temperature hovered around −50°C, creating weird effects such as haloes, sun pillars, mock suns and parhelia.

In the mornings the skidoos were difficult to start. Any wrong move or out-of-sequence action caused long delays. Try to engage gear too soon and the drive belt shattered into rubber fragments. Turn the ignition key a touch too hard and it snapped off in the lock. Set the choke wrong and the plugs fouled up. Changing plugs at −50°C in a strong wind was a bitter chore which no one fancied.

Often the whole day would pass without a word spoken between us. Our routine was slick and included, after camping, the drill of ice-core samples at every degree of latitude, a full coded weather report by radio to the World Meteorological Organisation, and the taking of urine samples as part of our calorific intake programme.

Back at Sanae, our coastal base, Giles and Gerry had returned from England with the Twin Otter and took Simon up to help Ginny at Ryvingen. Every 300 or 400 miles we would run out of fuel and Giles would have to locate us from my theodolite position. In ten days' travel we were 404 nautical miles from Ryvingen with a suspected major crevasse field just to our south. Since no man had been there before us, we had only satellite photographs from which to try to detect such obstacles.

On 9 November we ran into our first bad field of sastrugi, ridges of ice cut by the wind and resembling parallel lines of concrete tanktraps. Due to the prevalence of east-west winds, these furrows were diagonal to our southerly direction of travel. The sastrugi were from eighteen inches to four feet high and, being perpendicular, they often impeded any advance until we axed out a through-lane. They buckled our springs, bogey wheels and skis. Oliver struggled to improvise repairs.

At 80° South we camped in one spot for seventeen days to allow Giles to set up a fuel dump halfway between the coast and the Pole.

For weeks our progress was painfully slow. Sledges with smashed oak spars were abandoned, frequent overturns caused minor injuries, axe-work through sastrugi fields progressed sometimes at a mere 800 yards in five hours, and the ever-present fear of crevasses gnawed at our morale. One morning, stopping on an apparently harmless slope, Charlie stepped off his skidoo to stretch his legs and promptly disappeared up to his thighs. He was parked right over an unseen cavern, with less than two inches of snow cover between him and oblivion.

Close to 85° South, in a high sastrugi field, we had stopped for repairs when we heard from Ginny that a team of South African scientists, operating at the rim of the coastal mountains near Sanae, were in trouble. One of their heavy snow tractors had plunged sixty feet down a crevasse together with its one-ton fuel sledge. One man then fell ninety feet down another crevasse and broke his neck and their rescue party, returning to their coastal base, became lost in the ice-fields. They had, by the time Ginny contacted us, already been missing with minimal gear for five days. Already short of fuel and with a recurring engine start-up problem, highly hazardous in Antarctica, Giles nonetheless flew over 1,000 miles to search for, and eventually locate, the missing South African scientists. This saved their lives.

From 85° South we struggled on, detouring east to avoid a mammoth crevasse field and running into total white-out conditions. Navigation became critical and on 14 December, after nine hours of travel in thick mist, I stopped where I estimated the Pole should be. There was no sign of life, although a sixteen-man crew of US scientists worked in a domed base beside the Pole. We camped and I radioed the Pole's duty signaller.

'You are three miles away,' replied a Texan twang. 'We have you on radar . . . Come on in.'

He gave us a bearing and, an hour later, the dome loomed up a few yards to my front. At 4.35 a.m. on 15 December, 900 miles south of Ryvingen and seven weeks ahead of our schedule, we had reached the bottom of the world.

Giles flew Ginny, Bothie and Simon to the Pole, complete with the radio station stripped from Ryvingen. The temptation to spend Christmas Day with Ginny at the Pole was powerful, but we had to press on. With each passing day the crevasse systems between the polar plateau and the coast were growing more rotten, snow-bridges accumulated from drifts the previous winter were daily sagging and collapsing.

For five years I had tried to discover a straight-line descent route from the polar plateau to the coastal ice-shelf. The Scott Glacier appeared to be the straightest, but no one knew anything about it and I only had an aerial map to go by. This showed extensive crevassing at the glacier's crest some 9,000 feet up, fractures in belts down its course and massed around its mouth where the ice debouched on to the ice-shelf 500 feet above sea-level.

We left the Pole on 23 December. I thought of Captain Scott, whose team had reached the Pole sixty-nine years earlier. 'All day-dreams must go,' he had written, for his Norwegian rivals had arrived there first. 'It will be a wearisome return.' They never made it back.

From the Pole we steered north. Every direction was of course northerly but my compass setting was 261° for 180 miles. There were no sastrugi all the way and no crevasses, so we reached the plateau edge in only two days. At 5.00 p.m. on Christmas Day I stopped on a small rise and saw far ahead the summit of Mount Howe, guardian of the Scott Glacier Valley and the first natural feature we had seen in well over 1,000 miles. It made an excellent Christmas present. That night there was an air of apprehension in the tent, not in anticipation of Christmas stockings but through fear of the impending descent.

My map dotted Scott Glacier with vaguely delineated rashes of crevasse belts, an artist's impression rather than an exact record from which an optimum compass course could be set. I decided to play Scott Glacier by ear rather than compass. Oliver changed all our carburettor jet settings for the lower altitudes and we swapped our one-metre sledge tow-lines for six-metre safety lines.

A series of east-west pressure swellings heralded the first obsta-cle. We breathed in as we passed over huge crevasses but all were bridged well enough to take the minimal ground pressure of our skidoos. The narrower fissures, from four to twenty feet wide, were the greater danger, for many were spanned by sagging snow-bridges that collapsed under the slightest weight.

Each time I crossed a relatively weak bridge, my sledge, heavier by far than my skidoo in terms of ground pressure, broke through, partially, plunging a cascade of snow down into the fissure below. Only forward momentum saved the day at such times. Charlie, behind me, would have to find himself another crossing-point. So too, later, would Oliver.

The La Gorse range for which I was headed was soon obscured by mist, as were all other features, so we camped in the centre of a wide crevasse field. Next morning the white-out was still clamped about us and, impatient, I decided we should move on. This was perhaps a rash decision.

From about this period of the expedition Charlie underwent a subtle change that I cannot, to this day, explain. He radiated a muted hostility which never broke out into rage. Instead it simmered away month after month, nursing itself quietly.

After six years of working together with two men for whom I had no prior affection or common ground – save for the single desire to achieve Transglobe – the vicissitudes of our common experiences had slowly led me to grow fond of Oliver and to dislike Charlie. I disliked being disliked. Hostility bred hostility. I was fully aware that the major part of the expedition, and by far the more hazardous sector, lay ahead and that one of my two companions and I were silently at loggerheads. Since this situation was only known to the two of us and it was never openly acknowledged, I saw no reason why it should impair our chance of success, which was, after all, all that mattered. The fact remained that we worked well together and there were no arguments.

Our nightmare trail down the glacier led us into a cul-de-sac, surrounded by open crevasses. We retraced our tracks and tried again via another narrow corridor between blue ice-walls. A maze of sunken lanes beset with hidden falls finally released us, shaken but unhurt, close by the Gardner Ridge and 6,000 feet above our ice-shelf goal. In forty-knot winds and thick mist, we followed the Klein Glacier for twelve miles until forced along a narrow ice-spit between two giant pressure fields, a chaos of gleaming ice-blocks.

I knelt to study the map to find a way through, but the wind tore it away. I carried one spare chart with my navigation gear and, using it, plotted a course to the eastern side of the valley. Halfway through the smaller pressure field, a sudden drop revealed the lower reaches of Scott Glacier, a breathtaking show of mountain and ice-flow, rock and sky, dropping 600 metres to the far horizon and the pinnacles of the Organ Pipe Peaks. A crevasse field five miles deep crossed the entire valley from cliff to cliff and halted us short of Mount Russell, so we detoured east over a 1,000-foot-high pass and, three hours later, re-entered Scott Glacier – beyond the crevasse field – by way of a wicked ravine. We had travelled for fourteen hours and covered five days' worth of scheduled progress. The next day our mad journey continued. More ice-walls and skidding, out-of-control sledges. At the foot of Mount Ruth we cat-footed along the ceiling of an active pressure lane as rotten as worm-eaten wood.

The last concentrated nightmare, south-west of Mount Zanuck, was a series of swollen icy waves pocked by broken seams.

Beyond the powerful in-flow of the Albanus Glacier the dangers lessened hour by hour until, at the final rock outcrop of Durham Point, there was nothing ahead but flat ice and the Pacific. We had reached the Ross Ice-shelf. Dog-tired, we camped after fifteen hours of travel and awoke next day to Oliver shouting, 'Welcome to the tropics! It's *plus* 1° on the thermometer.'

For nine further days I held to a bearing of 183°, which took us well north of the disturbed zone known as the Stagshead Crevasses. On the seventh day we crossed the 180° meridian which, at that point, is also the International Date Line. I experienced a zany temptation to zigzag north along it singing, 'Monday, Tuesday, Monday, Tuesday.'

On the ninth day, passing the region where Oates groped his frostbitten way to a lonely but honourable death, we first saw the mushroom steam-cloud of Mount Erebus, a hundred miles distant but marker to our destination. Beneath the 13,000-foot volcano lies Scott Base where, on 11 January, we arrived at 6.00 p.m. We had crossed Antarctica in sixty-seven days.

Much of our strength, despite our lack of polar experience, lay in our collective ability – remove any one of us and the other three became a far less capable entity. Unfortunately, that is precisely what happened. Oliver's wife Rebecca, from whom he had been separated – then re-united for the past few years – had grown sick with worry during the Antarctic crossing. Oliver was faced with the cruel choice of wife or Transglobe. He took the long-term option because he loved Rebecca more than his six-year-long ambition to achieve Transglobe's goals.

Oliver's loss caused wider problems than the mere mechanics of food supplies and weights to be carried in the Arctic. Back in London the committee who represented the expedition, including ex-SAS Brigadier Mike Wingate Gray, decided it would be irresponsible for us to attempt the northern hemisphere with a team of only two. They were solidly in favour of a third man, probably from the Royal Marines or SAS, being recruited to replace Oliver. A committee deputation to decide the issue of the third man was to be sent to meet us in New Zealand after the *Benjamin Bowring* penetrated the pack-ice again and removed us from Antarctica.

7

Full Circle

On arrival at Christchurch, New Zealand, I received a warning message from Anthony Preston, the ex-RAF man in charge of our London office. He had discovered that an American, Walt Pedersen – one of the 1968 team that reached the North Pole under Ralph Plaisted – was all set to sledge to the South Pole early next year. Determined to become the first man in the world to reach both Poles overland, he had spent twelve years getting his act together. It looked as though he would beat us to the double by four months, since the earliest we could hope to reach the North Pole would be April 1982. I reflected that virtually none of our Antarctic experience was applicable to our coming Arctic struggle. The two places were as alike as chalk and cheese.

Mike Wingate Gray, our chairman, Sir Vivian Fuchs and other key members of our London committee, held long meetings with Ginny, Charlie and me, but we could not agree to the recruiting of a third man. I resolved to put the final decision to our patron, Prince Charles, and at Sydney, where he opened our trade fair, I explained the whole problem to him in the skipper's cabin. I was as firmly against taking on a replacement for Oliver as the committee were in favour of the idea. I quoted Wally Herbert who during his pioneering Arctic crossing stated: 'As a two-man party we would travel harder, faster and more efficiently than as a three-man unit.' I stressed to Prince Charles that Charlie and I had already spent six years together, including travel in Greenland, the

Arctic Ocean and Antarctica. We knew each other's limitations and strong points. We had worked out a mutually acceptable *modus vivendi*. Should a third man be forced on us, his very presence, no matter how we interacted with him, might undermine our own mutual compatibility for the Arctic crossing which we knew would be far more testing than Antarctica. The upshot of the various discussions was that Charlie and I should carry on alone, but Sir Vivian Fuchs warned me that if things should go wrong, the blame would be entirely mine.

On the *Benjamin Bowring*'s boat deck we gave Prince Charles three cheers and a miniature silver globe, marked with our route, to congratulate him on his engagement to Lady Diana Spencer. Bothie joined the cheering, yapping aggressively until Prince Charles patted and spoke to him.

While we were in Sydney, Charlie married the girl that he loved and Anton married Jill, our ship's cook. The *Benjamin Bowring* was becoming quite a family ship. All in all the expedition was to witness seventeen marriages of its members to each other or to outsiders. One *Daily Mail* headline talked of 'The Love Boat'.

From Sydney we steamed north over the Equator to Los Angeles, where President Reagan had kindly agreed to open our trade exhibition. Sadly, someone took a shot at him just beforehand so he sent us a message instead, acclaiming our 'can-do' spirit.

Our final exhibition, in Vancouver, was completed on schedule and we followed the coastline north to the mouth of the Yukon River in Alaska.

If the ship had been able to continue north through the Bering Strait – between Russia's eastern tip and Alaska – she would have sailed on to the North Pole, over the top and back to England via Spitsbergen. But because the Arctic Ocean is full of moving ice the best the *Benjamin Bowring* could do was to drop Charlie and me overboard with two 12-foot long rubber boats in the Bering Strait, as close as she could get to the mouth of the Yukon.

Eight years earlier we had scheduled our arrival off the Yukon for the first week of June because, in a bad year, that is the latest time when the northern rivers shed their load of ice and become navigable. All being well we would now ascend the Yukon for 1,000 miles, then descend the Mackenzie River to its mouth in the Arctic Ocean at the Inuit settlement of Tuktoyaktuk. From there we would make a 3,000-mile dash east through the fabled North-West Passage and north up the Canadian archipelago to Ellesmere Island and Alert, our old stamping-ground. It was imperative to complete the entire boat journey from the Bering Strait to Alert within the three short summer months when the Arctic Ocean ice-pack should be at its loosest. We had to reach Alert by the end of September or risk being cut off by freezing seas and twenty-four-hour darkness.

Fewer than a dozen expeditions had ever successfully navigated this passage in either direction. Those few all used boats with protection from the elements and took an average of three years to get through, due to blockage by pack-ice en route.

The *Benjamin Bowring*'s skipper tried hard to close with the Yukon mouth but, when still fourteen miles away in heavy seas, the echo sounder showed only six to eight feet clearance below the hull, with a ten-knot offshore wind making the ship's position highly risky.

Our two twelve-foot dinghies slammed up and down in the lee of the ship as we loaded them. Bryn Campbell of *The Observer* was to accompany Charlie and me as far as Tuktoyaktuk and he clambered atop the fuel drums on Charlie's madly tossing boat. I experienced a sudden flashback to the very first day of that other Canadian boat journey, ten years before, when Bryn had come within an ace of drowning. Bryn's diary on leaving the *Benjamin Bowring*:

We waved until the ship was out of sight. Soon the waves were breaking over us, hitting us hard from behind. Often we were completely awash . . . As we watched Ran's boat pounded by the sea and disappearing in the ten-foot troughs, we had all too vivid an image of how vulnerable we were. I turned to talk to Charlie and saw him lifted bodily by a surge of water and thrown clean over my head. As the boat capsized, I tugged my feet free of the fuel lines and jumped as far away from the propeller as I could. Then the hull crashed down on me.

I was attempting to keep to a compass bearing despite the silt-laden water smashing on to my boat, stinging my eyes and covering the compass glass. At the top of a breaker I risked a quick glance backwards and to my horror saw Charlie's boat upside-down with no sign of either passenger.

It was a while before I could try to turn round. The secret of survival in such shallow riotous waters was to remain totally alert and keep the bow at all times into the next breaker. In just such rubber boats we had come safely through far worse conditions on the rivers of British Columbia. It was a matter of aim and balance. After a big wave, I whipped the tiller round and the boat sped through 180° in time to face the next attack. In a while I saw Charlie crawl on to his boat's bottom and then haul Bryn up by his hood. I breathed out with relief. They began to try to right their inflatable using the hull hand-grips, but they were too exhausted. I flung a rope across to Charlie but a wave ripped the line's fixture point away from my hull. With my propeller blades threshing only inches from their prancing rubber tubing, I flung the rope over again. Timing the arrival of the next big wave, we succeeded in flipping the boat back over. I slowly towed the stricken boat with its waterlogged outboard back towards the distant silhouette of our ship.

Charlie had lost only his rifle, but Bryn's cameras had sunk and he was decidedly unhappy. Overnight, back on the *Benjamin Bowring*, a Force Seven gale blew up and the hull began to strike the sea floor in the heavy swell. The skipper weighed anchor at once and we headed 200 miles north to another mouth of the Yukon, known as the Apoon Pass. With 120 miles to go and off a dangerous lee shore, one of the main tie-bolts – which hold the ship's engine in place – sheared. This had happened before and the engineers had only one set of replacement bolts. After eight hours of toil below decks and anxiety above, the engines restarted and we reached Apoon.

Seventy cold, wet miles in the inflatable boats followed before we came to the river village of Kotlik where we bedded down in the local gaol. The Kotlik sheriff warned us that the summer winds could turn certain stretches of the Yukon into no-go areas.

At Kravaksavak we joined the brown and powerful Kwikpak River, which is the main arm of the Yukon. The banks were thickly forested but we saw fox, bear and river birds. Continuing through half the moonlit night we covered 150 miles to the village of Marshall. The river then narrowed and for days we fought an eight-knot current.

Fifteen miles short of the village of Holy Cross we noticed duststorms raging on both banks. With little warning the river erupted into a cauldron which caught us in mid-stream. Pine trees crashed down into the river and whole sections of the banks collapsed. The forest swayed towards the river, its upper canopy pressed flat by the force of the wind. There was no question of trying to land in such conditions. In mid-stream we battled through five-foot-high waves which followed one upon the other with hardly a breathing space for recovery. Once or twice my bows failed to rise from a plunge and the next wave swamped the boat. I thanked the Lord for positive buoyancy chambers. Then the river twisted to the east and the storm subsided. My long-nurtured idea of the Yukon as a gentle Thames-like river had been shattered. At Holy Cross, the keeper of the travel-lodge told us we were lucky to be alive. We had been travelling north, he said, in the first big southerly blow of the year, with winds exceeding seventy knots. Local river men stayed land-side on such days.

For long days of glare and heat we moved on across the face of Alaska towards Yukon Territory and the Canadian border. On 15 July we reached the only river-bridge anywhere from the sea to Dawson City, having boated over 1,000 river miles. Ginny and

Bothie met us in their Land Rover, on to which we lashed our deflated boats and gear. She drove us 500 kilometres up the recently opened Dempster Highway. Floods held us up for four days where this dirt highway was washed out but, a hundred miles from the sea, we reached the end of the road at Inuvik on the Mackenzie River.

Simon awaited us at Inuvik airstrip with a sixteen-foot open fibreglass whaler boat. Ex-Scots Greys Jack McConnell of the 1970 Headless Valley expedition, now a Canadian citizen, joined us for the journey to Tuktoyaktuk. He took the helm of Bryn's boat while the rest of us squeezed aboard the whaler and set out for the mouth of the Mackenzie.

The little whaler was a last-minute idea which had come to me back at Kotlik. I had used the sheriff's radio phone to ask Ginny to obtain one from a sponsor. Somehow she had, after phone calls to Hong Kong, London and New York, obtained the boat, outboards and a cargo plane flight from Vancouver to Inuvik, all free of charge. While we boated upriver she had worked at a motel out-side Dawson as a waitress – in return for free telephone calls and a bedroom. Ginny was not just a pretty face and lovely legs.

On the afternoon of 24 July, back on our tight schedule, we entered the harbour of Tuktoyaktuk in the North-West Passage. Jack and Bryn flew south. Ginny and Simon set up a radio base and Charlie and I loaded the whaler for our 3,000-mile journey through the passage.

Worried about navigation, I visited a local barge skipper with sixteen years of experience. I was planning to navigate the passage by magnetic hand compass plus my watch and the sun. The skip-per said simply, 'You are mad.'

'But I have good charts and a hand-made balanced prismatic compass,' I assured him.

'Throw it away,' he muttered.

'What do you use?' I asked him.

He pointed at his sturdy barge-towing tug. 'She has everything. She goes in the dark, out in the deep channels. Radar beacon responders, MF and DF, the works.' He shook his head dismissively. 'You must hug the coastline to escape storms so you will hit shoals, thousands of shoals. Also you cannot go across deep bays for fear of wind and big waves so you must hug the coastline which is like crazy pavement. You have to use more gas and take extra days. Most of the time there will be thick fog. No sun means you use your compass. Yes?'

I nodded.

He flung his hands up. 'Ah, but you cannot use a compass. Look . . .' He prodded his desk chart of the passage and I saw the heavily printed warning 'MAGNETIC COMPASS USELESS IN THIS AREA'.

'Too near the magnetic Pole, you see. You stay here in Tuk. Have a holiday.'

On 26 July we headed out into the choppy bay of Tuktoyaktuk. In thirty-five days we must not only complete the 3,000 miles of the passage, which traditionally takes three years, but also cover an additional 500 miles further north, attaining some point within skiing distance of our intended winter quarters at Alert before the sea froze, forcing us to abandon the whaler.

Four or five isolated Inuit settlements and eight Defence Early Warning camps were the sole inhabited points along our route. Five years previously I had set up a complex arrangement with the air company which supplied the bases, to take our ration boxes and fuel cans to these outlying sites. To cover the intermediate distances was just possible (given the maximum fuel load capacity of our whaler), providing I made no navigating errors en route.

The coastline, on leaving Tuktoyaktuk, was flat as a board and quite invisible whenever shallow water forced us out to sea. The treeless tundra of the Tuk Peninsula might just as well not have been there. Fortunately the sun was out to give us direction, so we headed due east until the glint of breakers off Cape Dalhousie showed like silver froth on the horizon. A conical hill, or pingo, stood proud from the otherwise unseen coastline, giving me a rough indicator of our position.

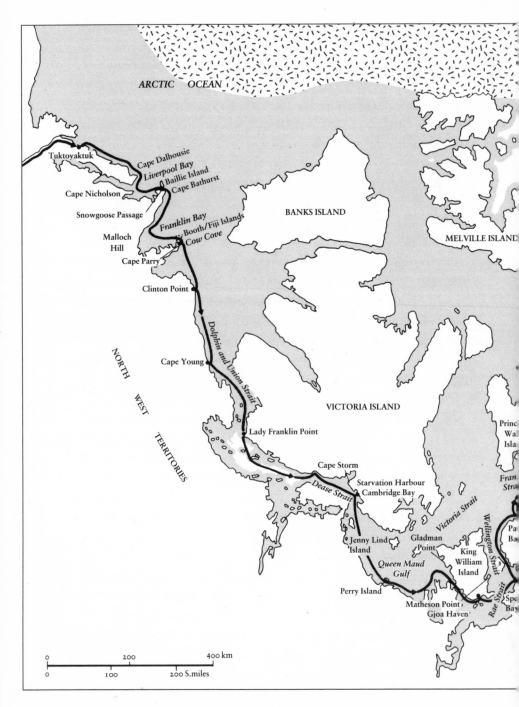

The North-West Passage

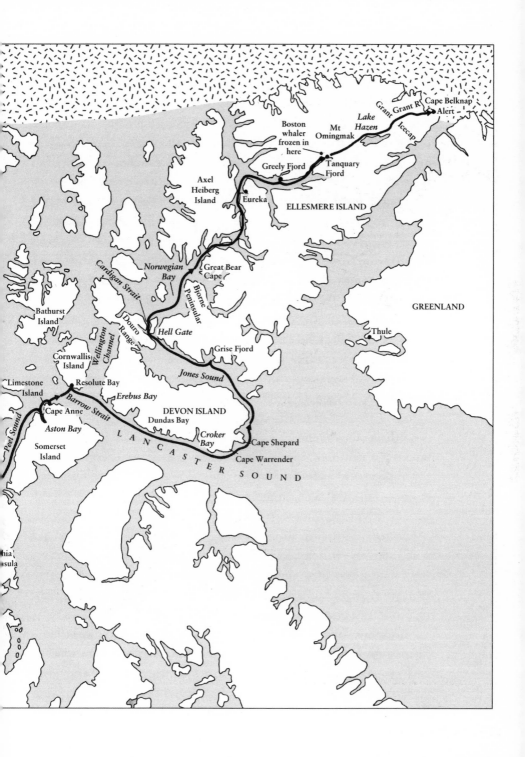

Cape Belknap
Alert
Grant R
Grant R
Icecap
Boston whaler frozen in here
Mt Omingmak
Lake Hazen
Greely Fjord
Tanquary Fjord
ELLESMERE ISLAND
Axel Heiberg Island
Eureka
GREENLAND
Norwegian Bay
Great Bear Cape
Cardigan Strait
Bjorne Peninsular
Thule
Douro Range
Hell Gate
Grise Fjord
Wellington Channel
Cornwallis Island
Jones Sound
Bathurst Island
Limestone Island
Resolute Bay
Erebus Bay
DEVON ISLAND
Dundas Bay
Cape Anne
Barrow Strait
Croker Bay
Cape Shepard
Aston Bay
Peel Sound
Somerset Island
Cape Warrender
LANCASTER SOUND
hia sula

East of the cape we bucked forty miles through a rising sea which soaked us anew at every crest. A flat tongue of shingle south of Baillie Island was the cache-point agreed a year previously with a government helicopter pilot, then in the area, for two drums of fuel.

The sea was too rough on both sides of the spit to allow a beaching. So Charlie dropped our light anchor overboard and I waded through the surf, back and forth with twelve jerry cans. Three hours later, re-fuelled, we entered Snowgoose Passage via a vicious tide-rip toothed by shoals. Once in Franklin Bay the full force of wind and wave struck us and for fifty miles we ran the gauntlet between fourteen-foot breakers and the wave-pounded cliffs to our west. We were soaked and our teeth chattered in unison. Each wave that broke over the whaler showered us. Salt-water poured down the neck-holes of our survival suits, running down back and chest and legs to collect in slowly rising pools inside our waterproof boots. Our underclothes were salty and sodden. Time and again we were forced to swing off our course to face into rolling waves which raced at us from the flank. Once the boat hung almost on its side as a green wall of water surged by in a rush of power.

As dusk approached I saw fires ahead and, an hour later, we passed a section of low cliffs wherein the mineral components smouldered and gave off an acrid chemical odour. Dante's Inferno. Sulphur deposits glowing red and yellow, for ever burning. Yellow smoke curled up from deep rock crevices.

The storm grew in intensity but, by a piece of good luck, we penetrated the beach breakers via a ten-foot-wide channel into a tiny lagoon beneath Malloch Hill. Next morning, shaking with cold, we marched up and down the beach in our wet clothes until the blood ran again. Then we set out east into thick mist.

'Surely we should head further to the right?' Charlie shouted.

Knowing how easy it is to be tempted to distrust the compass at the best of times, I closed my mind to his suggestion: 'The compass says this way,' I shouted back, 'so just keep aiming for that darker patch of sky.'

I had a local error of 43° set on the compass, with five more degrees added to cope with the effect of the boat's engine and metal fittings. How great the magnetic Pole's influence was I could not tell but I had, over twenty years of navigating, developed a certain faith in the compass.

To our great relief, after two hours of nothingness and our first chunks of floating ice, Rabbit Island loomed close ahead and, an hour later, we stopped in Cow Cove, a leeward beach. A flat stretch a hundred metres from the beach-anchored boat provided our camp spot. The next morning we returned with our camp-kit to the boat to find the wind had boxed through 180° and the whaler, now on an unprotected shore, was full of water and being pounded by breakers.

For two days we drained the fuel system and dried our gear; then, in a twenty-knot wind and the usual fog, we entered the narrows of Dolphin and Union Strait. For thirty-six hours without a break we ploughed east. We grew very tired and had to shout and sing to force our brains to stay alert. We determined not to stop, for there was no beach with a stitch of cover from the surf. The evenings, when the mists rolled back, were full of wild beauty which faded from red dusk to purple dawn with no darkness between. But winter menaced us unseen like some Damoclean sword. Already the sun at midnight caressed the silent surface of the sea.

For 340 miles we stood in the narrow bucking space between helm and fuel cans until at last, dodging a rash of inlets, we crossed a narrow channel to Victoria Island and left the mainland coast for the first time. We spent the night at Lady Franklin where I set up the radio. Ginny came through clearly from Tuktoyaktuk. She and Simon were watching live coverage of Prince Charles's wedding. The previous night a storm had sunk many of the local Inuit boats, complete with outboard engines and fishing gear, so she had been worried about us.

Over the next four days we were delayed by outboard troubles 130 miles east of Lady Franklin but limped on through rain and high winds. Wild storms lashed our passage across the mouths of bays, one wider than the English Channel, and past forlorn capes of twisted red lava domes. There was no shelter, no landing beach until we reached Cambridge Bay Inuit settlement.

Because Ginny was losing radio contact with us, she and Simon moved their base to Resolute Bay on Cornwallis Island. On their way north they had stopped in at Cambridge Bay and I noticed a black dog, smaller than Bothie, in Ginny's kit-bag.

'What,' I asked, 'is this?'

'Ah,' she said. 'This is Tugaluk. Two months old and a good dog.'

'Whose is she?' I pressed. Ginny blustered and I knew she was feeling maternal. If she had left the dog in Tuktoyaktuk, she said, it would have been shot as a stray. Bothie had fallen in love, she added, but he would doubtless get over it in Resolute and then Ginny would give the puppy to a new owner. The matter was closed, Ginny was clearly intimating, but the very fact that she had given the dog a name struck me as sinister.

Ginny and the others flew on and, a day later, we too left Cambridge Bay.

Originally I had planned to strike east across Queen Maud Gulf by way of Jenny Lind Island, but a tongue of pack-ice had recently slid down in a northerly wind and blocked off this entire route, so we detoured south an extra 200 miles to creep around the pack. The navigation was complex and only possible with total concentration. All day a mist obscured the coastline. We passed through corridors between nameless islands filled with shoals where the sea boiled between gaunt stacks of dripping rock. Hour after hour I strained my eyes through the misty glare to recognise some feature but there were islands of all shapes and sizes and the coastline was so heavily indented with fjords, bays and islets that the fog made it easy to mistake a through-channel for a dangerous cul-de-sac.

After 130 miles of nerve-racking progress between these shoals, a storm came at us from the west and threw great rolling waves over the reefs. I deemed it too risky to continue and we camped on

Perry Island in a sheltered cove. After twenty-four hours the storm showed signs of abating so, impatient, we ploughed on east for ten hours, often out of sight of land.

Since the compass was useless and the sun made no appearance all day I kept my nose glued to the charts. At dusk the storm renewed its attack and we plunged through cresting breakers. I prayed we would not strike a reef in the dark.

Close to midnight, a break in the cloudbanks revealed a low gap along the dim silhouette of the cliff-line. Nosing inland, we were rewarded with a sheltered islet where we spent the remaining four hours until dawn. We shivered uncontrollably in the tent and agreed to broach a bottle of whisky. By dawn the bottle was empty and we were shivering less.

With the first streaks of eastern light we squelched back into the survival suits, our thighs red-raw from the long days of salty chafing. For nineteen hours we weaved our way through innumerable gravel islands, a task made easier when the sun decided to show itself weakly through the post-storm haze.

At Gjoa Haven settlement, the Inuit warned us that pack-ice blocked the Humboldt Channel and the Wellington Strait to the north, my planned route, and we would be crazy to attempt to travel to Resolute Bay without first calling at the last Inuit settlement in the region, Spence Bay, to hire boat guides. I eagerly concurred and, after crossing Rae Strait in fine weather, we entered Spence Bay – the halfway point on our voyage to Alert.

Here we obtained the services of an Inuit hunter with an unrivalled knowledge of the area. He was accompanied by the local Mountie and three Inuit boatmen. We followed our guides whose boats, like ours, were some sixteen feet long and outboard-powered. An hour or two north of Spence Bay the Inuit turned inland and shelved their craft on a beach. We hovered offshore. 'What's wrong?' I shouted.

'There's a storm coming,' the Mountie shouted, 'a bad one. Our friends will go no further and advise you to stop here or head back to the village.'

The sky looked clear and my overall fear of winter catching us in the passage overrode any suspicion that the Inuit might be right. I was also suffering from the delusion that I knew better than the Inuit. There was no apparent danger, so why waste precious time?

For a hundred miles we moved north until the storm caught us. The coastline was not blessed with a single nook or cove where we could seek shelter. Committed, and caught between heavy pack-ice and a hostile lee shore, we had no choice but to struggle on. After six hours of drenching with ice-cold water our eyes were inflamed and our fingers ached with cold. Thankfully, we reached a keyhole-cove named Parsley Bay and turned east – directly away from the wind – to gain shelter.

But the next two miles proved the wisdom of the Inuit and only luck saved us from a watery end. The bay was a boat-trap. Waves followed one another, steep and close, so that our bows plunged off one six-foot wall, down its front and into, not over, the next. The whaler was awash. Waves smashed on to the prow and filled the cockpit. Visibility was difficult. As soon as we opened our salt-filled eyes, more water would cascade over our heads. Surf pounded against the beach when we finally made the crossing, but we located the mouth of a small river and the boat was flung into the safety of its estuary on a surge of flying foam. Next day the sea was down to an angry but manageable swell outside the bay and we clung to the coastline to avoid the ever-increasing presence of ice.

A day later, some miles past the vertiginous cliffs of Limestone Island, a strong northerly wind sprang up and set the entire ice-pack of Barrow Strait on the move. It became painfully obvious that, inching along a north-facing coastline with no likely place of shelter, we stood in grave danger of being crushed. Much to Charlie's annoyance I decided to retreat until conditions were safer. This involved back-tracking twenty miles to a shallow bay for protection.

On the morning of our third day in this cove a skein of new ice sheened the surface of the bay, a nasty reminder of the approaching freeze-up. Next day the wind changed and we threaded our way out of the cove, now all but beset by crowding bergs. Later we crossed Barrow Strait, forty miles wide, and nudged past pack-ice into the cove of Resolute Bay, capital city of the archipelago.

Resolute is home to over 200 Inuit and a number of transient Canadians, mostly technicians and scientists. Ginny was housed in a tiny shack with her radio beside her bunk, Simon lived in the main scientists' accommodation. The black dog from Tuktoyaktuk had grown to almost twice Bothie's size and Ginny was plainly infatuated. Our boating outlook from Resolute to Alert, Ginny warned us, looked bleak. In a week or so the sea would almost certainly undergo a general freeze-up, stranding us *in situ*.

The Resolute meteorological station commander proved to me by way of his ice-charts that we were all but blocked into Resolute for the year. The strait east of Bathurst Island was frozen, as was the northern end of Lancaster Sound. All routes to the west and north-west were already solidly iced. We could still attempt a 600-mile detour round Devon Island but its eastern coast was storm-bound and a maze of icebergs. I thanked him and opted for the last course through lack of a positive alternative.

For four days our whaler, very nearly crushed in one overnight ice-surge, was blocked inside Resolute Bay. Then, on 25 August, a southerly wind allowed us to escape east along the coastline of Cornwallis Island. The seas were rough and high for hundreds of miles and the coast to our north was either teetering cliff or glacier, pounding surf or disintegrating icebergs. With over 1,000 miles to Alert and under a week before freeze-up, we slept little.

With high waves breaking violently upon icebergs all about us, we were caught ten miles short of any shelter at nightfall. Two propeller blades broke against chunks of growler ice. Straining my eyes up at the mountain tops silhouetted against the moonless night sky was not easy, for the boat bucked and danced in the waves. Charlie fought the tiller to avoid icebergs visible only at the last moment. By weak torch battery and wet chart I guessed at the location of Dundas Bay and we nosed cautiously past cliffs against which waves smashed twenty feet high, luminous in the darkness. The mouth of the bay was crammed with grinding bergs and only lack of choice made us risk pressing on. Once past the outer ring of clashing icebergs a huge swell took over from the breakers. Soaked to the skin and numb-handed, we secured the boat between two grounded bergs and camped in a long-deserted Inuit hut. For an hour before sleeping we let the tension unwind as we lay on the floor propped up by our elbows, sipping tea by candlelight and chatting of Army days long ago in Arabia. Charlie's not such a bad old sod after all, I thought to myself.

The next five days are etched on my memory. I remember a blur of danger, a race against the dropping thermometer and constant cold. The nastier the elements, the further the natural barrier of restraint between Charlie and me dissipated. Our latent antagonism disappeared altogether once the predicament of the moment entered the danger level and became positively unpleasant.

Glacial valleys draining enormous ice-fields created bergs larger than cathedrals, which sailed seaborne from their dark spawning valleys to collect off the coast. Battered ceaselessly by waves containing broken ice-chunks, these bergs disintegrated bit by bit. A course running parallel to the cliffs and mere yards offshore seemed the least dangerous.

Waves smashed against cliffs and icebergs in a welter of thundering surf. Our port propeller's shearpin split against a growler, a half-submerged chunk of ice, entailing a repair job only possible at anchor. We prayed the second engine would keep going or we would soon be fibreglass matchwood, ground to pieces by rock or ice.

Eventually we found a deep inlet between cliffs. At the only possible landing point a large polar bear sat watching us, so we stopped in rocky shallows and fought to steady the craft among basking beluga whales. I stood in the sea holding the stern as still as I could while Charlie worked as fast as he could on the propeller. The bear dived into the sea and swam around us. We kept the rifle to hand but only the animal's nose and eyes remained above water as it swam.

After 300 miles we rounded the north-eastern tip of Devon Island and aimed across Jones Sound for Ellesmere Island. At Grise Fjord, the most northerly Inuit village in Canada, we beached the boat in a safe cove and rested for twenty-four hours. Our skin was the texture of etiolated bacon, our faces burned dark by the wind and the glare. We had lost a good deal of weight and various parts of our bodies, especially our crutches, thighs and armpits, were suffering from open sores and boils. The sea was due to freeze over in two or three days, should the winds drop and flatten the water.

Back in Resolute, Ginny, fully aware of the dangers of Devon Island's east coast, had awaited my radio call for twenty-eight hours. At Grise Fjord I fixed up an antenna between Inuit drying frames and, although her voice sounded faint and faraway, I could detect Ginny's happiness that we had reached Ellesmere Island.

With forty-eight hours to go and 500 sea miles to cover to the most northerly point we could hope to reach, Tanquary Fjord, we slid into our damp survival suits after emptying the last of our foot powder down the leggings.

The journey to Hell's Gate Channel was a blur of black cliff, freezing spray and increasing pack-ice. The channel was blocked with bergy bits but, through good fortune, the only alternative corridor, Cardigan Strait, was partially open and we edged into it beneath the great mountains which guard the western gateway of Jones Sound.

The long detour had paid off, but that same evening the surface of the sea began to freeze, congealing silently and quickly. Twenty miles south of Great Bear Cape we were caught between pack-ice and newly forming frazil ice, a paper-thin crystalline cover.

Forcing our way back south through the new crust, we spent an anxious night camped at the edge of Norwegian Bay and Ginny promised to obtain aerial guidance if she could. At noon on 29 August, Russ Bomberry, a Mohawk chief and one of the best bush pilots in the Arctic, flew his Twin Otter overhead for two hours to guide us, by a labyrinthine route, through sixty miles of loose pack to Great Bear Cape. When Russ flew away back to Resolute, we broached our last bottle of whisky. We slept five hours over the next two days and prayed for once that the wind would continue to blow. It did and the surface grease ice did not settle thickly enough to prevent us ascending Greely Fjord, Canon Fjord and finally the dark narrows of Tanquary Fjord, a cul-de-sac deep within glacier-cut mountains.

Tiers of snow-capped peaks rimmed the winter sky as we snaked into a twilit world of silence. Wolves stared from shadowed lava beaches but nothing moved except ourselves to sunder in our wash the mirror images of the darkened valley walls. Twelve minutes before midnight on 30 August we came to the end of the fjord. The sea journey was over. Within a week the seas behind and all about us were frozen.

Alert camp lay 150 miles to the north-east of Tanquary Fjord. With the temperature dropping daily and sunlight hours fleeing over the polar horizon, we needed to reach Alert within three weeks. The eastern heights of the main United States Range and the Grant Ice-cap block a straightforward overland route. We planned to use skis and snowshoes, rucksacks and light fibreglass sledges to cross the ice barrier, carrying fourteen days' food and cooking fuel from Tanquary Fjord where we abandoned the boat.

Charlie carried his bear-gun and I packed a .44 Ruger revolver into my eighty-pound rucksack. We followed a series of riverain valleys, trudging slowly, for we were weak from the months of boat travel and many salt-chafed sores that rubbed as we walked. In one narrow valley a huge ice-tongue, an offshoot from the ice-cap, tumbled into the canyon blocking our advance. Summer floods had cut a long tunnel through this icy barrier so, with heads bent and rucksacks dragged, we crept underneath the glacier and through the dripping culvert.

Charlie slipped on ice and his forehead struck a rock. Hearing him shout, I dropped my pack and ran back, thinking a bear had attacked him. Blood filled one of his eyes and covered one side of his face and neck. He felt sick and faint. An hour later, bandaged and dizzy, he carried on. That night we checked his feet and found broken, weeping blisters covering both his soles and most of his toes. He said he ached all over.

Charlie and I seldom walked together. Sometimes we were separated by an hour or more. In a film made later of the expedition, Charlie said: 'Ran is always pushing himself. He can't do it the easy way. I don't know what drives him but he always pushes himself. I'm not that way inclined. I'm a slow plodder. If I tried to keep up with him, I wasn't going to make it.'

Each time I stopped to wait for Charlie, I became cold and impatient and swore at him. If I had moved at his pace I could have avoided this, and I did try once or twice to do so. But I just could not maintain such a desultory amble.

On the third morning ice crystals lined our tent, although we were merely 1,000 feet above sea-level. Snow covered the land and walking was difficult. Skis were not practical due to long stretches of ice and rock. Charlie's left eye was quite closed and puffed up like a yellow fungus. His back and his knees and his blistered feet all hurt him. The blister wounds had gone septic and walking must have been purgatory for him.

In mid-September we passed Omingmak Mountain and Charlie could go no further without a rest. His groin glands were swollen with poison and his knees with fluid. But winter was coming and I urged him to keep going, for we had to complete the journey over the high ice-caps before polar sundown. There seemed little point anyway in waiting for new skin to replace the open sores on Charlie's feet since the first few miles on snowshoes would soon re-open them.

We emptied the contents of our rucksacks on to our light portable sledges and, strapping on snowshoes, set out in a cuttingly cold wind. The temperature fell to −18°C as we passed Lake Hazen. North of the lake I tried to follow a bearing of 130° but the compass was sluggish. Musk-oxen snorted and stampeded as we loomed through the freezing fog.

There were no distinguishing landmarks. At 2,200 feet above

sea-level we camped in a frozen gulley at –20°C, a temperature which remained steady for three days' hauling through deep snow-fields where the stillness was immense. No musk-oxen now. Nothing and nobody.

Over the rim of the Grant Ice-cap, spurred on by increasing cold, we limped at last to the edge of the high plateau beneath the twin glaciers of Mount Wood, dwarfed by the blue ice-falls which rose to the sky. A wary hush presided below these 2,000-foot ice-formations. A cataclysmic event seemed imminent. Craning my neck back to ease my knotted shoulder muscles, I glanced up and felt momentary unease as the sky-high ice-falls above seemed to teeter on the verge of collapse.

Towards dusk we found the narrow entry-point to the upper canyon of Grant River, a winding ravine that falls thirty miles to the sea. The canyon kinked, snaked and was blocked by black boulders, so that often we manhandled the sledges over solid rock for hundreds of yards.

On 26 September, towards noon, the river-bed plunged thirty feet down a frozen waterfall. From the top of this cleft we could see the Arctic Ocean, a jagged vista of contorted pack-ice stretch-ing away to the polar horizon. Nine hours' travel along the edge of the frozen sea, dreaming of warmth and comfort, brought us to Cape Belknap and, by dusk, to the four little huts that we knew so well, the most northern habitation on earth.

We had travelled around the polar axis of the world for 314° of latitude in 750 days. Only 46° to go but, looking north at the chaotic ice-rubble and remembering our failure in 1978, we knew that the journey to date had been easy compared with what lay ahead.

Five days before our arrival at Alert, Ginny had flown in with winter equipment, our old Antarctic skidoos and the two dogs. The three of us spent the next four months of permanent darkness in the Alert huts preparing equipment, completing a new series of scientific research tasks and training on the local pack-ice.

In mid-January the Alert met-man warned me that his sea-ice recordings showed a thickness of 87cm, thinner than that of any previous January on record, the average being 105cm. The true cold, which crackles the nose and ears like parchment, congeals the blood in fingers and toes like rapidly setting glue and fixes the sea-ice slowly into a precarious platform to the Pole, finally came in late January. Better late than never. The camp thermometer hovered around −51°C with a fresh ten-knot breeze. One night a fox outside the hut awoke me and I noticed Ginny's hot-water bottle lying in between her bed-sock'd feet – frozen solid.

We received a radio message from a Californian friend. Walt Pedersen, the American aiming to reach both Poles, had given up his impending attempt on the South Pole due to stonewalling by the US National Science Foundation. We could still become the first people in history to reach both Poles. Prince Charles radioed through to Ginny and mentioned that he had heard rumours of a Norwegian team racing us to cross the Arctic. 'No racing,' he said to me with a stern edge to his voice.

By the last day of January I must decide when to set out to cross the Arctic. To start prior to the first appearance of the sun would be to lay myself open to accusations of irresponsibility. On the other hand it was imperative that we reach the North Pole before the annual summer break-up. Once at the Pole we would at least be in the zone of currents which float their ice-cover in the general direction of Spitsbergen or Russia. If we delayed our departure from Alert until after sun-up in March, as in 1977, we would again risk falling short of our target. Whenever we set out we could not be certain that success was attainable, for the simple reason that no man had ever crossed the Arctic Ocean in a single season.

On 13 February 1982 I said a quick goodbye to Ginny. We had spent the previous night in our hut closing our minds bit by bit to reality. Over the years we had found it better that way. The wrench of departure was worse than in Antarctica for we both knew the southern crossing was a mere nursery slope compared with the Arctic.

The weather was clear, although the day was as dark as night, when we pulled away from the huts. I glanced back and saw Ginny clutching her two dogs closely and looking up at the passage of darkness by which we had left.

Charlie and I sat astride the open, heavily laden skidoos, each towing 600 pounds of fuel and gear. Our beards and eyelashes were ice-laden within minutes, for the chill factor was −90°C when stationary, increasing with the speed of our advance. We followed a wild zigzag way along the dark and ice-girt coast. I remembered the 1977 travels which helped me not to get lost, although that year we had of course travelled in daylight. Crossing a high pass somewhere on the Fielden Peninsula, Charlie turned his sledge over on a steep slope above sheer cliffs. He managed to extricate himself some yards from a long drop into the dark.

On 17 February we came in twilight to a canal of newly open water from which emanated dark clouds of frost-smoke. In the depths of winter, long before sunrise and at a point of maximum coastal pressure, this was an ominous sign. We had not expected open water so early. With extra care we skirted the canal and entered a narrow corridor of blue ice, emerging a short distance east of Cape Columbia, that coastal point off which the southerly sea currents split west and east. This makes the cape a sensible jumping-off point from land-ice to sea-ice. After axing ourselves a ramp of ice-blocks we took the skidoos for a twenty-foot slide over the tide-crack. We were now 'afloat' at sea.

We camped 300 yards out from the coast in a field of broken ice. In a way I was glad of the darkness for it prevented a wider and therefore more depressing view of our route north. I pressed a mitt to the raw end of my nose and was silent as a host of vignettes flooded my mind, memories of what had passed last time we tried to pit our wits against the power of the Arctic pack. We had learned a lot of lessons then about what not to do.

During the first day of twilit labour with our axes we cleared 800 yards of highway through the pressure rubble. Our axed lane was precisely the width of a skidoo and it followed the line of least

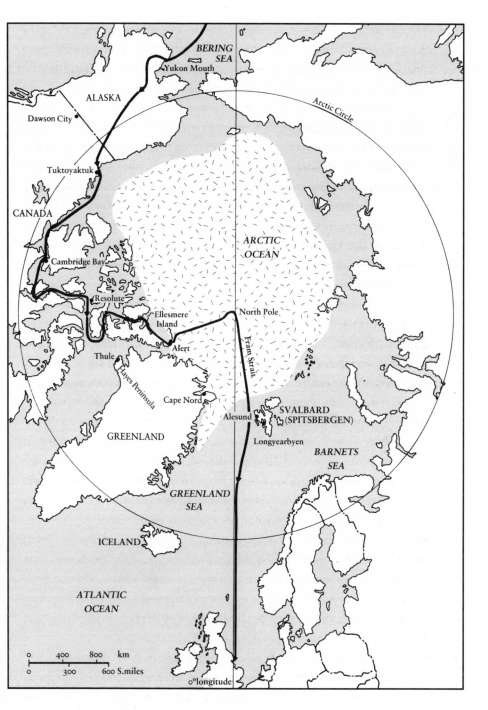

The Transglobe Expedition's route across the Arctic

resistance, which unfortunately added 75 per cent of extra distance to the straight course we would have taken were it not for obstacles. To gain the Pole we must cover 825 miles – then much further again on its far side to reach a potential rendezvous point with the ship.

There were two dangers: failure to reach the Pole – and therefore the Spitsbergen current – by summer floe break-up time, and the subsequent worry of failing to reach the *Benjamin Bowring* before the end of summer when the ship must retreat to more southerly waters. We could not hope to achieve either goal without air re-supply with food and cooker fuel from the Twin Otter which was to fly out from England with Gerry Nicholson and a skilled Arctic pilot called Karl Z'berg, a Swiss Canadian who had flown our chartered Otter in 1977.

We axed our skidoo lane through 200 yards of twelve-foot-high ice-blocks. Damage to equipment was inevitable as the only way to negotiate the switchback lane was at full tilt, bouncing off walls and over iron-hard slabs. On 19 February my drive axle snapped. That did it: I determined to switch to manpower and abandon the skidoos – at least for the first hundred miles where the pressure rubble would be at its worst.

The previous winter at Alert, preparing for this eventuality, I had tested two lightweight eight-foot-long manhaul pulks and it was with these fibreglass sledges, carrying 190 pounds each, that we pushed north on 22 February. After eight hours of haulage, our underwear, socks, facemasks and jackets were soaking wet or frozen, depending on which part of the body they covered and on whether we were resting or pulling at the time. But, by the end of four dark days, we had logged eleven northerly miles. This would not sound very impressive except to someone who has also pulled a load in excess of his own bodyweight over pressure rubble in the dark and at a temperature of −40°C.

Charlie plodded on at his own pace and, unable to slow down, I stopped every hour for twenty minutes or more for him to catch up. I attempted to avoid freezing solid during these long waits by cursing the Arctic in general and Charlie in particular. Sheer exhaustion overcame any fear of bears or indeed of falling into the sea.

Charlie and I saved time daily by never cooking breakfast. We merely drank a mug of coffee from our vacuum flask, heated the night before. This gave us the courage to unzip our bags and climb into our frosted clothes and boots. For seven months we were to remain in precisely the same clothing without washing.

We dragged behind us, man for man, the same weight as Scott and his team. Their aim was to be first to reach the South Pole, ours was to be first to reach both Poles. Like them, we were racing the clock. On 3 March, at –49°C, the blood-red ball of the sun slid briefly along the rim of the sea. Sunlight, although welcome to improve visibility, was our number-one enemy. Ultraviolet rays would now begin to eat at the structure of the pack-ice and, by mid-April, so weaken the ice that the least pressure from the wind would crack up the floes and halt our progress.

At 4.00 a.m. on 4 March, at –40°C, a fire broke out in our stores hut back at Alert. Ginny rushed out with an extinguisher but, 'It was just one big fireball inside with smoke issuing from the seams in the walls and flames filling the windows . . . There were forty-five gallon drums of fuel stacked by the wall. They had been there for years and were frozen into the ice.' While they watched, eight drums of gasoline exploded, as did fusillades of rocket flares and 7.62 FN rifle bullets.

Until that point the world's press had ignored the expedition. Now newspapers and television screens all over the world carried headlines such as 'Conflagration at Polar Base' and 'Polar Expedition in Flames'. After the night of the fire every action we took – and one or two that we didn't – became news from London to Sydney, from Cape Town to Vancouver.

Seven years beforehand Ginny had argued that I should lay an equipment cache at Tanquary Fjord as well as at Alert – just in case. With the generous help of the Canadian Coastguard's icebreaker two years before, we had done so. This meant that the expedition need not now be abandoned. Spare, radios, generators, ice rations and skidoo gear were available for our Twin Otter to collect from Tanquary as soon as the weather allowed. I made a mental note to tell Ginny once again she was not just a pretty face.

With enough food for eight days we digested the news of the fire – about which we could do nothing – and concentrated on northerly progress, yard by painful yard. Our shoulders and hips were raw from the rub of the pulk harnesses. My nose, weeping blood and fluid for the last two weeks, was now frost-nipped as well. The rough and frozen material of my facemask chafed the wound and I could no longer wipe away nose-dribble with the back of my mitts, so a sheen of ice, constantly growing in size, covered the bottom half of my facemask, punctured only by the small hole over my mouth.

At night the act of breathing caused the worst discomfort. Generally speaking, polar travel would be quite pleasant if it was not necessary to breathe. When we tried to snuggle down inside our sleeping bags, our breath formed a thick rime of frost where it met cold air. The resulting frost layers cascaded down our necks whenever we moved. To avoid this I blocked both nostrils up with plugs of Kleenex and tried to position my mouth to breathe out of the bag's hood-hole. This worked well except that my frostbitten nose remained outside the bag's warmth and, unprotected from the tent's average temperature of −40°C, was far colder than a deep-freeze.

A storm blew up and shattered the ice-pack. All about us were vast areas of open sea where, for at least the next two months, the ice should have remained largely solid. On the coast behind us, the five-man expedition of our Norwegian rival Ragnar Thorsketh, which had announced its intention to beat us across the Arctic, were astonished to find open sea and no ice at all in sight. They made camp on the land and waited.

Simon and Karl Z'berg located the two skidoos we had abandoned along the coastline and managed to land the Twin Otter beside them. Later they delivered the skidoos and steel sledges to us on a flat floe. Overjoyed at shrugging off the harnesses, we continued by skidoo and were blessed by a patch of good going.

Still travelling at dusk, I swerved to avoid a sudden canal and drove straight into a trench full of *shuga* porridge-ice. I was flung clear and watched my skidoo sink out of sight within a minute. The steel sledge slowly up-ended but I caught hold of its lashing strap. Charlie ran over in response to my yelling. He attempted to save our tent by removing his mitts in order to undo a lashing buckle. In seconds his fingers began to freeze and, before we could loosen the tent, the sledge disappeared underwater. We saved only our radio and theodolite.

Charlie's hands were in immediate danger. I erected a makeshift shelter from the tarpaulin with which Charlie used to cover the vehicles and started up the cooker. He spent an hour forcing blood slowly back into his hand and so saved his fingers from anything worse than painfully nipped ends. We passed an extremely uncomfortable night at −40°C under the tarpaulin with one sleeping bag between us.

Two days later Karl found a landing floe half a mile from our location and brought in a skidoo, sledge and gear from Tanquary Fjord. 'Don't sink any more skidoos,' he advised. 'That's your last.'

Forty-knot winds battered the pack and we headed north in a semi-white-out. With no visible sun, I followed my compass needle.

On 16 March, with millions of tons of ice on the move all about us, we camped and lay listening to the awe-inspiring boom and crackle of invading floes. The anemometer rose to fifty-five knots and weaker pans fractured all about us, nipped and flaked by their larger jostling neighbours. One crack opened up twenty yards from our tent and cut us off on an island for a day.

Ginny warned me that the press were turning critical. In England the *Daily Mail* stated that the Transglobe sponsors were considering finding a new leader since our chances of success were looking bad. One reporter interviewed the cameraman on our 1970 Canadian expedition, who said the soldiers on that journey had mutinied and threatened me with knives. In Vancouver, a reporter pointed out that SAS members Fiennes and Burton had cleverly cut themselves off in the Arctic beyond all possible recall by their regiment for service in the Falkland Islands war which was raging at the time.

When the storm died away we packed up in conditions of total white-out and moved off into a curtain of brown gloom, a certain sign of open water. Within minutes I narrowly missed driving into the edge of a river of moving sludge. Charlie and I took a deep breath and spent two perilous days pussy-footing through a sludge swamp, often crossing lakes of half-inch-thick ice which writhed under our skidoos and broke under the sharp runners of the sledges. God was good to us on both days. The next two days passed by in a haze. We pushed on our bruised bodies and mutinous minds and craved more sleep.

My chin was numb one evening when I came into the tent. I must have pulled my frozen facemask off too hard. When thawing the garment out over the cooker and picking ice-bits from around the mouthpiece, I found a one-inch swatch of my beard complete with skin implanted in a bloody patch of iced wool. It took a while to detach this from the mask. Where the skin had torn away from my chin, there was an open patch of raw flesh the size of a penny. In a while my chin warmed up and bled. Then it wept liquid matter which froze once the cooker was turned off.

On 22 March I shot the sun with my theodolite and found the loose pack had drifted us many miles too far east. I applied a 15° westerly correction and we moved on at a good rate. My chin throbbed like a tom-tom by nightfall and, running out of antibiotic cream, I applied some pile cream.

'He's got piles on his chin,' Charlie shrieked with mirth. It was lucky we shared a weird sense of humour. Unlike during the latter part of our Antarctic crossing, there was now no tension between us. I hugely respected and admired his ability to suffer and keep going.

For a week we averaged fifteen miles a day, sometimes travelling for sixteen hours at a time in what we called a double-shuffle.

Charlie was frostnipped along the length of his nose and one of my eyelids puffed up with wind-burn. Navigation was becoming more or less instinctive, with or without the sun.

A memorably evil day was 29 March, during which we pushed to the limits of skidoo travel. Streamers of brown vapour wafted through the overall fog and soft squeaking, grinding sounds emanated from the moving sludge banks we passed. To check each apparently weak section, before charging it on my skidoo, I went ahead gingerly on foot with my ice-prod. Charlie advanced halfway between me and the sledges, calling from time to time when I lost sight of him in the gloom.

When we made it at last to solid ice I felt elated. If we can cross that, I thought, we can go anywhere. We stopped at 87°02′, within nine miles of our most northerly camp in 1977 but forty days earlier in the season. If our aim had been solely to reach the Pole we could have felt reasonably confident.

As we crept north in early April the movement and noise of the floes increased. It seemed as though we were rushing pell-mell, caught in an unseen tidal race, towards the maw of the world, Poe's maelstrom. For three days the troubled fissure zone of the convergence, the area where the Beaufort Gyral current ends, slowed us to a crawl. For some time we crossed a no-man's-land where floes spun around in limbo, uncertain which way to go. Then the fringe of the transpolar drift began to take hold of all surface matter and we entered a new gyral with a strong north-easterly pull. A great deal of rubble was piled up in pyramidal heaps within this convergence and at 87°48′ North we were stopped by the bulkiest wall I had ever seen in the Arctic. Rising to thirty feet high, the barrier was well over 100 yards wide. It took us four hours to axe and four to cross.

After the convergence we entered a sixty-mile region of fissures and high barriers. On 8 April we crossed sixty-two sludge cracks, often by shovelling snow into the water and then ramming the resulting weak bridge before it sank.

Twenty miles short of the Pole the going improved dramatically. At mid-day on 10 April I carefully checked our noon latitude and each subsequent mile until we were at 90° North. I had no wish to overshoot the top of the world. We arrived there at 11.30 p.m. GMT and passed the news to Ginny early on Easter Day 1982. We had become the first men in the world to have travelled the earth's surface to both Poles.

Apprehension about what lay ahead overshadowed any sense of achievement that we may otherwise have felt, for the *Benjamin Bowring* was still many cold months beyond our horizon.

I aimed south along a line some 15° east of the Greenwich Meridian. We changed to a routine of travel by night and sleep by day so that the sun would project my body's shadow ahead and prove a natural sundial.

As we left the Pole, the Transglobe crew steamed from Southampton harbour en route for Spitsbergen.

Over 1,000 miles still separated us from the latitude to which the *Benjamin Bowring* might, with luck, be expected to smash her way when, in August, the pack was at its most penetrable. The *Benjamin Bowring* would not be able to penetrate heavy Arctic pack, being merely an ice-strengthened vessel, but, if we could reach as far down as 81° North, she might – through the skill of her skipper and the eyes of Karl in the Twin Otter – be able to thread her way into the pack's edge.

From the Pole all went well for four days – in reality, nights – during one of which we achieved a distance of thirty-one miles in twelve hours over a freakishly unbroken pan of floes. From 88° down to 86° the conditions deteriorated slowly with an increasing number of open leads. I had grown accustomed to keeping an eye ever open for potential Twin Otter landing strips. But for the last forty miles there had been neither a single floe flat enough for a landing nor a pan solid enough to camp on safely during a storm.

The temperature rose to –20°C and stayed there. New ice no longer congealed over open leads within twenty-four hours, so wide canals with no crossing-points became permanent stoppers, not mere hold-ups. Tedious foot patrols to find crossing-points became increasingly necessary. Following a brief storm on 23 April we axed for two hours through a forest of twelve-foot-high green rafted blocks and reached a series of winding couloirs of new ice packed with black pools of sludge. Alongside this marsh I tripped and fell. My hands shot out to ward off a heavy fall. My axe disappeared and sank. My arms pierced the surface up to the elbows and one leg up to the knee, but the snow-covered sludge held my body weight. Seven miles later seawater cut us off in all directions except back north, so we camped. The wind blew at thirty knots and chunks of ice, floating across pools and along canals, all headed east.

That night I told Charlie I would begin to search for a floe on which to float south. He was horrified, feeling we would never reach the ship if we did not make much more southerly progress before beginning to float. Stop now, he feared, and the expedition would fail. I argued with him that wind and current should take us to 81° before winter, providing we could only locate a solid enough floe to protect us during storm-crush conditions. If we waited one day too long before locating such a floe we could easily be cut off on a rotten pan and then there would be no answer to our predicament. Better safe than sorry. Charlie agreed to disagree. But, he reminded me, in the future – whatever happened – I should remember the decision to risk a float from so far north was mine alone.

Two days later we escaped from the weak pan and managed to progress another five miles south on increasingly thin ice before having to camp. Four days later I thought the river-ice had congealed and attempted to cross by skidoo. To my surprise my sledge runners broke through the sludge at a point where I had safely walked an hour earlier. Thereafter this sludge-river remained at the same tacky consistency, insufficient for sledge weight. The temperature rose towards 0° and we ground to a halt.

Charlie searched for cracks and weak points on the floe we were on and eventually decided upon a line of hummocks along the impact point of an old pressure ridge. We flattened out the top of this high ground with axes and made a camp there.

During the first week of May I asked Ginny to send us two light canoes and rations for a long float. She flew with Karl and Simon from Alert to the north-east corner of Greenland and at remote Cape Nord set up her last radio base. She told me that the remnants of the Norwegian expedition racing us to cross the Arctic had reached the Pole too late to continue and had been evacuated.

On 11 May, without a sound, our floe split apart 500 yards east of our tent and we lost a third of our original real-estate. Bending over the edge of the newly opened canal, I saw that our two-thirds was some five or six feet thick. I had hoped for a minimum of eight feet but – too bad – we were committed to this place.

Our tent floor of axed ice was uneven and daily became more sodden with water as the surface of the floe melted down. Soon, all about our slightly raised platform, the floe became a floating pool of vivid blue salt-water, five feet deep in places.

Late in May two members of our London committee travelled to Spitsbergen to visit the ship. Karl flew them over the pack and, horrified at our overall predicament, they returned to London and warned the committee that our chances of success this summer were minimal. We must be airlifted out at once while such a course was still possible or any subsequent disaster would be on their hands. Ginny queried the committee's follow-up message, a direct evacuation order, and rallied those in London who were against such a course. Only when the order had been softened to a recommendation that we abort the float but that the final decision should be mine, did Ginny inform me.

I felt, and Charlie agreed, that there was still a strong chance of success without risking an international search-and-rescue operation, so we continued to float at the mercy of wind and current. For five days a southerly storm blew us back towards the Pole and for several days our southerly heading veered sharply towards Siberia, but overall we continued south at a steady rate towards Fram Strait, between Greenland and Spitsbergen. Karl managed to land on a rare mist-free day. He dropped us off two tents, two canoes and a two-month supply of rations. He warned us that in another week

126

he would no longer be able to take off from our increasingly soggy floe. We were on our own. On 6 June in thick fog our floe was blown against its northerly neighbour and, where the ice fronts clashed, a fifteen-foot-high wall of broken blocks reared up.

The sense of smell of the polar bear is phenomenal: they can detect a seal from ten miles away. Large males weigh half a ton, reach eight feet tall and tower to twelve feet when standing. They glide over ice quietly, yet can charge at thirty-five miles per hour.

One night in my sleeping bag I was woken by loud snuffling sounds beside my head on the other side of the tent cloth.

'Ran?' Charlie called.

Since his voice came from his own tent I knew with a sinking feeling that he was not snuffling about outside my tent. It must be a bear. Grabbing camera and loaded revolver, I peered outside. So did Charlie, whose eyeballs grew huge as he spotted – behind my tent – a very big bear. I craned my neck and three yards away saw the face of the bear which was licking its lips with a large black tongue. We photographed the fine animal and after a few minutes it shuffled away.

A week later another bear would not leave and showed signs of evil intent. We fired bullets and even a parachute flare over its head but the bear only grew irritable. We agreed to shoot if it approached closer than thirty yards. It did, so I fired a bullet at its leg. The bear hesitated in mid-stride then broke sideways and loped away. There were blood splashes but no sign of a limp. Over the next few weeks many bears crossed our floe and eighteen visited our camp, tripping over our guy-ropes. This kept us from getting bored by our inactive existence.

The uncertainty of our situation, especially at times when communications blacked out, was a great strain on Ginny. She had a long history of migraines and spastic colon attacks and her life at Nord was full of pain and stress. She had no shoulder to cry on and no one from whom to seek advice. She hated this part of the expedition but kept steadily on at her job. Late in June she made contact with the *Benjamin Bowring*. The sooner she could remove us from our floe the better, for the remnant of our floe was fast approaching a danger area known as the Marginal Ice Zone, the ice pulverisation factory of Fram Strait. Two million square miles of the Arctic Ocean are covered by pack-ice and one-third of this load is disgorged every year through Fram Strait. Very soon now our own floe would enter this bottleneck, where currents accelerate by 100 per cent and rush their fragmenting ice burden south at an incredible thirty kilometres a day. Keenly aware of our danger, the skipper and crew agreed to take a risk. Arctic pack-ice is far more hazardous than the Antarctic equivalent.

On 2 July, after a game attempt, the ship was forced back some 150 miles south of our floe. On 10 July the mist cleared at noon long enough for a sun shot. After seventy days on the floe we were at 82° North. That night a chunk of two acres split off our floe. The next-door floe rode up over a forty-yard front and 80 per cent of our pan was covered in slush or water up to seven feet deep. New ridgewalls rose up daily and noisily where we struck our neighbours. Off our seaside edges humpback whales sang at night and huge regattas of ice sailed by before the wind. There was seldom any sign of the sun and the low-hung sky reflected the dark blotches of great expanses of open sea to the south and north of our floating raft.

As we approached nearer to Fram Strait we began to gyrate like scum heading for a drain. To remind us that summer here was short, the surface of our melt-pools began to freeze over.

The *Benjamin Bowring* tried a second time to reach us in mid-July and again they failed, this time putting themselves in considerable danger. Anton recorded: 'hurling the ship at six- to seven-feet thick floes which are breaking without too much difficulty. But the ice is more solid and further to the south than before . . . Evening: We are stuck solid at 82°07′ north, 01°20′ east, 82 miles south of Ran . . . Jimmy has spotted a cracked weld.'

Cleverly the skipper rammed a low floe and managed to lift the damaged bows clear of the sea. Two engineers worked, squatting on the ice, to effect temporary repairs with welding gear.

During the last week of July our floe was daily buffeted and diminished in size. Charlie had chosen our camp spot with great skill, as it was about the only part of the floe still uncracked. But on 29 July he showed me a widening seam close beside his tent. We had been on the floe ninety-five days and our entry into the crushing zone was imminent.

I told Ginny and she spoke to the skipper. They decided to make a final dedicated push northwards. Karl flew Ginny from Greenland to Longyearbyen where she boarded the *Benjamin Bowring*. They set out on the first day of August, our seventh month out on the pack ice, and – within twelve hours of smashing a straight route through medium pack – they reached a point forty-nine miles to our south.

Late on 2 August after a twenty-four-hour fight north-west through heavy ice and thick fog, the skipper reported sinister signs of a wind change. The pack would close about the ship if the wind rose. Throughout the long night the skipper and crew willed the ship north yard by yard in a potentially suicidal bid to reach us.

At 9.00 a.m. on 3 August Ginny spoke on my radio. She sounded tired but excited. 'We are seventeen miles south of your last reported position and jammed solid.'

Charlie and I packed basic survival gear into our two canoes. We had hoped the *Benjamin Bowring* would smash her way to our floe, but this was clearly impossible. For us to attempt to travel from our floe might easily prove disastrous, for everything was in motion about us: great floating blocks colliding in the open channels and wide skeins of porridge-ice marauding the sea lanes. At noon I took a sun shot which put us only twelve miles from the ship. A southerly wind or current could easily widen this gap. We left our bedraggled tents and I took a bearing south-east to the probable current position of the *Benjamin Bowring*. The wind blew at twelve knots as we paddled nervously through the first open lead.

Having lain in our bags with scant exercise for so long, we were unfit. Charlie was nearly sick with the sudden effort. Every so often I filled my water bottle from a melt pool and we both drank deep.

Makeshift skids attached to the canoes snapped off on rough

ice and then we dragged the boats along on their thin metal hulls.

Trying to negotiate a spinning mass of ice-islands in a wide lake, I glanced back and saw two high bergs crunch together with an impact that sent a surge of water towards my canoe. Luckily Charlie had not yet entered the moving corridor and so avoided being crushed.

At 7.00 p.m., climbing a low ridge to scout ahead, I saw an imperfection on the horizon along the line of my bearing. I blinked and it was gone. Then I saw it again – the distant masts of the *Benjamin Bowring*.

I cannot describe the feeling of that moment, the most wonderful of my life. I jumped high in the air, yelling at Charlie. He was out of earshot but I waved like a madman and he must have guessed.

For three years I had always known our chances of overall success were heavily loaded against us. I had never dared allow myself to hope. But now I knew and I felt the strength of ten men. I knelt down on the ice and thanked God.

For three hours we heaved and paddled. Sometimes we lost sight of the masts, but when they re-appeared they were always a little bigger.

At fourteen minutes past midnight on 4 August at 80°31′ North, 00°59′ West, all but astride the Greenwich Meridian, we climbed on board the *Benjamin Bowring*.

Ginny was standing alone by a cargo hatch. We hugged each other as though we would never let go. Her eyes were full of tears, but she was smiling. Between us we had spent twenty years of our lives to reach this point, the fulfilment of her dream.

Revelry lasted well into the night. There was no hurry now, which was just as well because the ship remained stuck fast for twelve days, until the wind changed.

From the lonely islands of Spitsbergen we steamed south through the Greenland Sea and the North Sea. On 29 August Prince Charles joined us on the Thames and brought the ship back to our starting-point at Greenwich, almost three years to the day since we had set out. Ten thousand cheering people lined the banks. Our polar circle around the world was complete.

That night, when all the crew and our friends had gone, Ginny and I slept in our old cabin. I watched as she fell asleep and the lines of stress fell away from her face. I felt as happy as I had ever been.

8

Hammer and Sickle

Three days after returning home I learned that Transglobe had accumulated debts totalling £106,000. We had no funds to pay them off. This was where Anton Bowring appeared in our hour of need to announce that he considered the expedition complete only when all debts were paid. For the next eighteen months he and Ginny worked full-time to that end, a thankless task, but they eventually even turned a modest profit through sales of T-shirts and old Transglobe gear at Camden Lock street market. Anton and his wife Jill, the *Benjamin Bowring*'s cook for three years, became our best friends. Ginny was godmother to their eldest daughter, Mini Ginny, who was conceived during Transglobe. They were to have three daughters, all red-haired like Jill, and collectively known as the Carrots. I meanwhile was writing the expedition book, *To the Ends of the Earth*, which made the *Sunday Times* bestseller list. Bothie achieved fame by nipping TV host Russell Harty and I was decoyed into *This Is Your Life*. Family and friends assembled from all periods of my past, included Chris Cazenove and Jack McConnell, as well as the history mistress who caught me on Ginny's school roof in Eastbourne and the entire Transglobe team. Eamonn Andrews' researchers were put off the military aspects of my life when one asked my former CO in Oman whether he could regurgitate any heart-warming tale of my 'bravely saving someone's life'. The colonel replied with vehemence. 'Saving lives?! Fiennes wasn't out there to save lives. He was there to kill Communists.' Not what we would today describe as PC.

I turned forty in March 1983 and one of my presents was a sweatshirt emblazoned with the words 'I'm over the hill'. But I was discovering what happens to so many polar travellers, the urge to return. As the less comfortable memories of the Transglobe years receded, I increasingly felt the lure of the North. I determined to ignore this mesmeric polar attaction with the same vehemence as a smoker must shun thoughts of tobacco. For a while I was helped by a phone call from Los Angeles at 2.00 a.m.

'Is that Ran Fiennes?' The voice was gravelly and brusque. 'This is Armand Hammer.'

Assured that it was me, the good Dr Hammer continued, 'I want you to work for me in London. You will be my Vice-President of Public Relations in Europe.'

This was my very first offer of a civilian job. The octogenarian head of Occidental Petroleum knew me because, at Prince Charles's behest, he had financed the film-making on the Transglobe expedition and approved of our success. So, aged forty, I experienced the joys of commuting for the first time. I discovered that 'nine to five' actually meant 'seven to seven'. I made after-dinner speeches in French and German on behalf of Dr Hammer at glittering European functions. I tried hard to sell an unwanted oil terminal for him on Canvey Island and saw that his visits to Europe ran without a hitch, despite his penchant for changing his mind and schedule with little warning and requiring a meeting at two days' notice with Prince Charles or Robert Maxwell or Mrs Thatcher. In the same week he had me rushing to Rome with secret papers for the ex-King of Afghanistan (who Dr Hammer was hoping to reinstate) and making a speech to Raisa Gorbachev in Moscow. I learned to chat up airport officials to allow me to meet the doctor's private Boeing 727 with a bevy of rented Rolls-Royces on the airstrip to avoid the tiresome business of customs and immigration. This worked everywhere in the world, including Moscow, Peking and Cardiff, but not Heathrow, where the rules were inflexible and, when I finally gave up trying to buck their system, I felt quite proud to be British!

Amid all this Hammer-inspired rushing about, Oliver Shepard called me one day in 1985 with a proposal for the ultimate polar journey, the grail of the international polar fraternity: to reach the North Pole with no outside support and no air contact. No one had yet achieved it. I found myself reacting with unexpected enthusiasm and realised that, ever since the end of the Transglobe travels, I had without knowing it been yearning to return to the cold white unknown. There is a Danish word, *polarhullar,* an ache for the polar regions, that grips the soul of a traveller so that nowhere else will ever again satisfy his or her appetite for the essence of 'over there and beyond'. A victim of *polarhullar* will forever be drawn back to the very extremities of earth.

Part of my annually renewed contract with Dr Hammer allowed me to go off on expeditions for three months in any year. After the success of Transglobe, sponsorship had become much easier to obtain. Equipment, food, travel and insurance could all be quickly lined up free of charge in return for promises of publicity. To obtain the interest of a major newspaper or television film producer was, however, still no easy business.

I failed to find a documentary film-maker but, since such films are statistically watched only by a maximum of two million TV viewers, I concentrated on the main TV News channels which were watched twice daily by over sixteen million. I had once worked as a TV News reporter for ITN in Oman and so approached them first. This began a great working relationship with their reporter Terry Lloyd who ITN agreed to send north with us that year to the base we would make on Ward Hunt Island in the Canadian Arctic.

In the winter of 1985 Ginny was due to lecture about her Very Low Frequency work in Antarctica to a conference in Chicago. At little extra cost she flew on to Resolute Bay in the North West Territories and hitched a lift on to Ward Hunt Island, a remote former scientific summer camp, in a Twin Otter ski-plane that was positioning sonar buoys in the Arctic pack. Ginny measured the skeletal ribs of one of the long abandoned Ward Hunt huts and a sponsor back home constructed a tough new custom-made hut cover. But after reconnoitring the place for us, Ginny would sadly no longer be our base leader.

Back in England, and thanks to my salary from Dr Hammer, we had found our dream home, a near derelict farm in the wilds of Exmoor. There was no electricity but Ginny had started to build up an organic beef herd around an initial six Aberdeen Angus cows. She was also breeding from Bothie's girlfriend Blackdog, the stray Inuit puppy who had come back with us from Tuktoyaktuk and who Ginny had mated to a Crufts champion black labrador. In 1985 Ginny recommended one of our Transglobe team, Laurence Howell, known as Flo, to take her place in the Arctic as our base leader and radio operator.

Ollie and I completed our winter sledge trial runs and in March 1986 were established at our Ward Hunt base with Flo, preparing to set off. A few days later a Twin Otter brought in the French manhauler, Dr Jean-Louis Etienne. He was aiming to be the first solo traveller to the North Pole. We agreed to show him the best route we had discovered through the chaotic pack-ice that formed a high wall just north of the Ward Hunt ice-shelf. Then we shook hands with the diminutive doctor and watched him disappear into the moonlit icescape.

'I wish we had sledges like his,' Ollie commented. The French sledge weighed a mere four pounds and its load eight. Our own 450-pound loads included seventy pounds of bare sledge. Jean-Louis would be resupplied by air every eighth day and his sledge replaced whenever it was damaged so he could afford to travel light. But if we were to be unassisted this could never be for us. We were finding that even the superior design of our new sledges did little to improve our snail-like performance. We kept paring down equipment to a bare minimum, even shaving the Teflon runners with Stanley knives.

At this moment Ollie had the rug pulled out from under him. He received an ultimatum by radio. Either he returned to London within four weeks or he lost his job, then with Beefeater Gin. He had no alternative but to cry off. This left Ginny back home in England with the task of finding a last-minute replacement from the very small field of fully fit polar sledgers. Polar expert Roger Mear suggested that Ginny call Dr Mike Stroud from Guy's Hospital who had been first reserve for Mear's own and very recent Antarctic journey. He would still be manhaul-fit.

When, a week later, Mike climbed off the Twin Otter at Ward Hunt Island I was shocked at how short he was. Small people, in my book, were not built to drag over 300-pound sledges for hours on end. You needed carthorses. Mike's head came to a level with my shoulder. But, on closer inspection, it became clear that Mike was built like an ox, with the biceps, chest and thighs of a body-builder. He pulled like a husky, digging his boots in and leaning so far forward that his nose seemed to scrape the ice. I was soon to discover he could drag his sledge, more than twice his bodyweight, alongside mine and trudge on relentlessly for hour after hour. So we waved goodbye to Flo Howell and set out north three days after Mike's arrival. I reflected that if a committee had been running this expedition, after the fashion of our Transglobe committee, we would never have resolved things so quickly. I remembered reading that 'a committee is a group of people who individually can do nothing, but as a group decide nothing can be done.'

At the time Mike Stroud arrived on Ward Hunt Island the world record for human travel without support towards the North Pole stood at ninety-eight nautical miles following the near fatal journey of the Simpsons and Roger Tufft in 1968. Subsequent attempts, such as those of David Hempleman-Adams and Clive Johnson in the 1980s, had ended in failure and frostbite less than fifty miles from the Arctic coast. The terrain included some 2,000 walls of ice rubble up to twenty-five feet high, regions of rotten ice that break up and overturn as you try to negotiate them and zones of open waters, sometimes as far as the eye can see, which are often skimmed with a treacherous *shuga* ice layer of porridge-like consistency. Add to these obstacles a temperature that is often lower than a deep-freeze and a northerly wind that cuts into exposed skin like a bayonet and it is no wonder that, despite intense international competition, the challenge had yet to be met.

Some seventy miles from the coastline we were struggling in a field of broken ice-blocks and thin floes. My sledge cannoned off a twelve-foot chunk and knocked me from my hauling position. I broke through the ice and was instantly immersed. Mike was luckily close at hand and dragged me out, but the damage was done, for we could not stop in such a fractured zone. So it was four unpleasant hours later before Mike could erect the tent. By that time my hands were lumps without feeling and I could not help him. More seriously, I had no feeling in my feet. Inside the tent I struggled to remove my sledge jacket, but since both it and my clumsy mitts were encased in a thick film of frozen sea-ice, I had no success. All the while I battered my two boots together in an attempt to force blood to flow.

Mike at last appeared through the tent's tunnel entrance with some four inches of frozen nose mucous stuck to the chin of his balaclava like a gnome's beard. Unlashing the sledge had quickly made him cold. Any pause from the exhausting action of man-hauling soon results in a lowered heart rate, so that the blood flow rapidly retreats from the extremities and shivering begins. Sweat caught between layers of clothing turns to ice and there is an urgent need to do one of two things: you can either return to the treadmill of manhauling or, if too tired, erect the tent and eat into the sternly rationed daily quota of fuel to provide life-giving heat.

To cut down cargo weight, our fuel ration allowed only for cooking, not for tent heating or clothes drying, so an immersion like mine caused major problems with the vital fuel supply. This sort of setback could lead to bitterness between team members, since to fall in could be considered the result of stupidity. On all previous expeditions I had gone to considerable lengths to vet every team member but circumstance had obliged me to accept Mike sight unseen. That we proved to be totally compatible was remarkably lucky. There was no strained atmosphere, no recrimination, not even the occasional heated exchange.

Mike managed to remove my mitts and I shoved my hands inside the ski jacket and under my armpits. There was a chance they might return to life, according to Mike's practised eye. More seriously, my boots would not come off, however hard Mike struggled with them. The obvious answer, since it was vital we extricated my toes with minimal delay, would have been to cut through the frozen bootlaces with our pin-nosed pliers. Since the laces were completely encrusted, the actual boot canvas would need cutting too.

'If we cut up the boots,' Mike said, looking at me from beneath a fringe of iced-up eyebrow, 'it will mean the end of the expedition: failure.'

I nodded. We carried no spares. To save weight every item not vital to progress had been jettisoned: and that meant none of those spares normally considered indispensable, such as extra mitts, goggles or bootlaces. We had a choice between dangerously delaying the resuscitation of my feet while thawing the laces out and cutting through the obstacles at once to give my feet a better chance but the expedition none. Ruefully I remembered a day eight years before when I had fallen through Arctic ice and Ollie Shepard had saved my feet by cutting my boots off with the help of an axe.

Reluctantly, I asked Mike, by now shivering with cold himself, to thaw the boots out as quickly as possible. I could feel no sensation at all in either foot. The thawing process seemed to take for ever. Once the boots were off, Mike declared my left foot 'redeemable' since it had remained miraculously dry, except for the toes and the sole.

'Not so good,' he said, shaking his head as he examined my other foot. Three of the toes and an adjoining area of skin were parchment-white and devoid of any feeling. Slowly he warmed up both my feet, expending valuable fuel, before applying dry dressings. Breaking the normal rule against using the cooker merely for damp clothes, he dried out my socks and slipped them over the bandages.

Next day we set out on time. I felt no pain throughout the day and was surprised when, back in the tent, Mike swore aloud on removing the dressing. What appeared to be the outer half of my little toe and a segment of flesh had come away with the bandage. A large area of raw flesh and bone was left exposed which felt, as soon as my foot warmed up and blood returned to the nerve ends, as though it were on fire. For the rest of the journey I dreaded the mornings until, after an hour or so of travel, the foot grew cold enough to deaden the nerves. Likewise the evenings, when the reverse process took place. Nevertheless, despite our heavy loads and my early morning limp, our progress continued to outpace that of the two fully air-supported expeditions to our north. After fifteen days we passed the ninety-eight nautical miles point, the existing unsupported world record, and celebrated with an extra cup of tea.

In bad conditions we craved each tea break, yet at the same time feared the intense cold that accompanied a halt. One evening Mike announced that he had broken one of our two vacuum flasks. Since this cut us down to a single intake of hot liquid a day, I felt distinctly hostile towards him, although I made no comment.

'We have a choice from now on,' Mike said. 'We can use the remaining flask either for tea or for Pre-stress.'

Pre-stress was a specially prepared quick-energy drink that helped to stave off hypothermia and which we normally alternated with tea.

'As a doctor, what do you advise?' I asked Mike.

'We'd better stick to Pre-stress, despite the taste,' he said, giving the reply I had expected.

Two days later Mike was unusually quiet in the tent and after a while broke the news that he had somehow managed to break the second and last vacuum flask. Mike's solution to the problem was that we should use our communal plastic pee-bottle.

'You must be joking,' I replied. 'Are you suggesting peeing into it each night and drinking Pre-stress out of it each day?'

'Why not? We can call it Pee-stress. Urine will do you no harm, after all.'

'*Mine* won't,' I retorted. 'But I can't say I fancy the idea of drinking from a container with your frozen pee stuck to the outside.'

'I never thought of you as fastidious. But I'm happy if you don't wish to share the contents.'

'It's one short step from cannibalism,' I muttered. But the following day I noticed no change in the taste of the Pre-stress.

Some days later the tent was filled with a foul smell when Mike changed my foot bandages. Gangrene. It spelt the end of our attempt for 1986. We found 400 yards of comparative flat surface on a well-weathered floe and marked out an airstrip with coloured ration bags. Then I radioed Flo Howell at Ward Hunt Island. We had passed the record of the previous best unsupported northing by nine miles but we were still over 300 miles from the Pole.

Back home I learned I was to be installed in the *Guinness Book of Records*' World Hall of Fame as the 'World's Greatest Living Explorer' (alongside Paul McCartney for music and Billie Jean King for sport). I hobbled on to the BBC stage to receive my award from David Frost and Norris McWhirter wearing a black sock over the bandages and no shoes. Ginny and I gained more quiet satisfaction from receiving the Polar Medal from the Queen, with unique bars for Antarctica and the Arctic. Ginny was the first woman to receive the medal, and soon afterwards the first woman to become a member of the prestigious Antarctic Club.

Ollie, Mike and I had another try for the Pole in early 1988. Flo Howell was again base leader, this time with his wife Morag manning the radio with her colourful Orcadian accent. This attempt foundered after sixty miles in the face of appalling terrain and weather. The following spring Mike Stroud and I set off yet again from Ward Hunt Island. The conditions were average but we fell well short of the record we had set in 1986 and I opened up a skin graft on my right foot which had been applied after the gangrene episode. As we left Ward Hunt Island for the last time I asked Mike if he would like to try once more, next time from the Siberian side of the Pole.

'Glasnost permitting,' he replied with a grin.

The thawing of relations with Russia had indeed opened the field and in 1990 there were, as well as ourselves, Russians, Canadians and Norwegians all preparing to be the first to make it unaided to the Pole. Although the North Pole is some 100 miles further from Russia than from Canada, the sea currents carry the ice floes towards not away from the Pole which should, we all thought, prove a great help. In Moscow I was delighted that Arctic hero, Dr Dmitry Shparo, was prepared to organise my bid. He warned me of stiff competition from Colonel Vladimir Chukov of the Soviet Special Forces. On the other side of the world the Canadians were led by none other than my old friend Jack McConnell.

From Moscow in the spring of 1990 Mike, Flo, Morag and I were flown to the depths of Siberia and stayed one night in a scientific camp where only a year earlier we would never have been allowed, for the station was the Soviet equivalent of Canada's Defence Early Warning line which Charlie and I had encountered on our 1981 push to Alert. Our Soviet hosts entertained us to dinner at the even remoter station of Golomiany where we were told proudly that we were the first foreigners to visit since the days of the Tsar. One of the six-person station's occupants had been killed the previous month by a polar bear outside their cookhouse. Once the sun arrived along the Siberian coast, Dmitry organised an ex-Afghan gun-ship to fly us north to Cape Arktikiski, the most northern point of land in Severnaya Zemlya. As on our previous Arctic journeys, Terry Lloyd of ITN was on hand to see us off.

On the other side of the world three Norwegian ski champions had declared their intention to reach the Pole first and two separate teams of Soviet skiers were somewhere behind us. Flo and Morag Howell manned our radio base, together with two Russian operators, and through the electronic clutter of our HF radio Morag's voice came and went from a Soviet Army shack on the island of Sredniy, keeping us up to date with the competition as we made our own careful progress north.

'Kagge and his Norwegians are out of the race,' she told us some weeks later. 'One of them has been airlifted to safety with a frostbitten foot. The other two are carrying on but their challenge has obviously been compromised by their air contact.'

Now we had only the Russians to worry about, for Jack McConnell's Canadian team had also withdrawn with frostbite.

'Chukov's men are doing well. We estimate they are less than one hundred miles to the south of you.'

'What about Fyodor Konyukhov?' I asked Morag.

'Also compromised,' Morag replied. 'A Soviet helicopter picked him up. He was in trouble with breaking ice in a bear-infested zone.'

I knew that Vladimir Chukov was ranked high in the lists of Russian polar explorers. He had led two unsupported journeys to the Pole in previous years. Both times he had reached the Pole but death and injury to team members on each occasion had necessitated air contact. Chukov played by the unwritten rules of unsupported polar travel. These stipulated that any contact at all en route to the Pole compromised the attempt. So Chukov was trying again. He had learned many lessons. He knew the hazardous nature of the drifting Russian pack-ice, far looser and more volatile than the corresponding sea-ice on the Canadian side. Here, a single error could quickly lead to death. I knew his team's progress would be slow and methodical.

After about 400 miles Mike and I abandoned our heavy carbon-fibre sledge-boats and continued with basic food, fuel and camp gear carried in rucksacks. These weighed nigh on 100 pounds each and it was all but impossible to stand up unaided after struggling into the harness. Our chances of making the last two degrees of latitude, 120 miles, to the Pole rested on luck and avoidance of hypothermia. Sometimes I skied, sometimes I strapped my skis to the pack and walked. Mike had no option but to walk as one of his ski bindings had broken irreparably only seven days out. This slowed us to the speed of a walking expedition but that we kept going at all was a tribute to Mike's tenacity.

One day on a drifting hummock I spotted the fresh prints of an adult polar bear. I knew I must warn Mike, for bears will usually attack the rear member of any group and we had heard that the Norwegians had had to shoot a large male bear close by their tent. I regretted the fact that only a few days previously we had abandoned our radio and our revolver as being too heavy to keep carrying. I tried to bury negative thoughts but the total concentration necessary for successful navigation in broken pack-ice was absent that morning which was perhaps why I misjudged the width of a canal through the porridge-like slush and fell in. Fettered by my skis and rolled face-down by my heavy rucksack, I struggled in panic until Mike arrived and, lying on his stomach, reached down into the canal. He managed to grasp a loose strap from my sack and, with no means of leverage and with fingers already lacerated from broken blisters, he hauled me to safety through sheer force of willpower.

Over the following weeks we each fell in six or seven times, mercifully not both at the same time. Around 88° North, with 447 miles behind us and within a tantalising eighty-nine miles of the Pole, our strength quite suddenly disappeared as the extreme loss of bodyweight reached the point where we became debilitated. Cold pervaded our bodies and sleep, always difficult on ice that shrieks and shudders, grew impossible lying on thinly padded bones. In addition my eyesight became too poor to navigate. To pull a heavy sledge you must lean forward. Your heavy breathing if wearing a balaclava and goggles will mist up the goggles when below −40°C. So, as navigator, needing constantly to scrutinise the ice ahead, you travel with no goggles, squinting into the glare. Not good for your long-term sight. Though we were only ten days from the Pole we recognised it was time to give up and activated a miniature radio beacon to request our evacuation.

A Soviet helicopter extricated us and took us to their nearest scientific base on an ice-floe. This unfortunately split up in a storm, cutting their landing zone in half, so the Aeroflot plane which commuted scientists weekly to and from the Soviet Union was delayed by ten days awaiting the bulldozing of a new runway. While we waited I experienced a severe kidney stone attack, my third in twenty years, and Mike dosed me with his remaining store of pain-killers. When we eventually returned to Moscow we learned that Chukov's group had also failed to reach the Pole and had been evacuated further south than us. We were given medals and assured by the Russians that we had made the longest and fastest unsupported journey towards the Pole to date. Polar records are seldom without controversy. The Norwegians, Erling Kagge and Borge Ousland, did reach the Pole that season but only after the third member of their party had been airlifted out, so their claim to be wholly unsupported was not recognised by the Russians, the Canadians or the British. To us it was as blatant a piece of assistance as an Olympic athlete taking drugs. I said so in the press. The Norwegians called me a bad sportsman and we left it at that. In 1994 Ousland was at last to achieve a proper record when he made it solo and unsupported to the Pole in fifty-two days.

After the last of these Arctic journeys I went to London's top eye surgeon, Eric Arnott, worried about double vision. He diagnosed that the long weeks of travel with no horizon and no real focus point had made my eyes focus at a distance of one metre ahead of my boots and it took weeks for this 'convergence of the visual axes' to relax.

'You failed again, then?' Dr Hammer growled when I first met him after the Siberian journey.

'Not exactly, Doctor,' I bridled. 'We broke the existing world record by over 300 miles.'

A few months after our group finally abandoned our North Pole attempts, Charlie Burton and Ollie Shepard began to come down with South Pole fever. How about us making an unassisted crossing of Antarctica, they suggested, manhauling sledges just like Scott. It sounded good, but I already had other expedition plans under way at the time, so I listened to them cajoling me persuasively but in vain in the map room of the Royal Geographical Society. *Polarhullar* notwithstanding, I had had enough of frozen climes for a while.

9

The Frankincense Trail

Back in 1968, when I was serving in Dhofar, a bedu guide had told me about a fabulously wealthy city of antiquity which was reputed to be lost in the sands. Over the years, on occasional return visits for other purposes, I had investigated possible sites of this lost city but never with enough time to take things to a conclusion. Now Ginny and I had taken on the planning and mounting of a fully fledged expedition. Some historical sources called the city Ubar, others Irem. My hunch was that the site must be somewhere astride the trade route which carried the precious high-quality Dhofari frankincense to the markets of the north.

On the first maps of the Arabian Peninsula, drawn up by Ptolemy in AD 150, there was a major market town which he located on the southern rim of the region now known as the Empty Quarter, the greatest sand desert of the world. Lawrence of Arabia records being told of ruined castles seen by wandering tribes. Bertram Sidney Thomas, an administrator of Palestine, and financial advisor to the then Sultan of Muscat, received permission in 1925 to attempt a crossing of the Empty Quarter from south to north. The journey took him fifty-eight days. He received the personal congratulations of King George V and the Founder's Medal of the Royal Geographical Society, but the mystery of Ubar remained unsolved.

Our own interest evolved into a joint venture with an old friend, Nick Clapp from Los Angeles, who had edited Dr Hammer's film of the Transglobe expedition. I would liaise with Sultan Qaboos of Oman, organise sponsors and lead the expedition in the field, Nick would do the archaeological research and the filming. His researches led him to NASA in quest of space photographs, hoping these would give us a head start, but all the eventual NASA shuttle photos produced was an L-shaped site way out in the dunes. All the same, the connection between buried biblical cities and space-age technology remained a good talking point for raising sponsorship.

We began with a short reconnaissance trip in July 1990, taking along with us an eminent archaeologist from Missouri called Juris Zarins who had a vaguely reassuring resemblance to Indiana Jones, complete with battered brown trilby. Juris didn't think we had a cat in hell's chance of finding Ubar, if indeed it existed, but he was keen to have a chance to conduct archaeological work in southern Oman and if searching for Ubar provided a pretext, fair enough. Our timing coincided with Saddam Hussein's invasion of Kuwait, but as nobody was expecting the trouble to spread to Dhofar, our visas were duly stamped. Our main guide on the ground would be Major Trevor Henry, my instructor on an SAS jungle course back in the 1970s. He told me bluntly that if there had been any surface ruins in Dhofar they would have been spotted by oil prospectors, talkative bedu or land and air patrols from the Sultan's Armed Forces. But he was happy to help.

First of all we flew by helicopter to inspect the mysterious NASA-provided L-site. On the ground it was as clear as it had been from 160 miles in space, but Juris was quick to dismiss it as merely an ancient lake bed, though he did find the stone patterns of some ancient dwellings and hearths nearby. We then flew to other possible locations that might have a bearing on the frankincense trade. I revisited caves from which I had once spent many days and nights ambushing Marxist soldiers.

Trevor pointed out the spoor of leopards and some aloe trees – 'very good for curing wounds' – and castor-oil trees – 'you know what that's good for'. He led us to Jebel Kasbah, a lofty crag above a spring. Hidden by thorn and mimosa, a tangle of ruined walls puzzled Juris. A large rectangular room, well plastered and hardly damaged over the centuries, had perhaps served as a reservoir for monsoon water. It was reasonable to deduce this was a mountain garrison from which the incense trade was once policed, an interesting fragment in our jigsaw puzzle, but not a clue to Ubar's whereabouts.

After a whirlwind tour of the plain, the mountains and the Nejd, we drove from Thamrait to my earlier Ubar hunting grounds of Shis'r and Fasad on the edge of the Sands. Both places had undergone considerable change. Where in 1968 there was only barren desert at Shis'r and a crumbling *Beau Geste* mud fort, there now flourished cultivated plots of palm, fruit and vegetables. At Shis'r there was also a modern Arab-style housing development not far from the rock cleft waterhole.

Shis'r's very location, so close to the Sands and astride the best aquifer in the region, indicated that ancient camel trains may have watered here en route for Yemen and previous visitors had recorded tracks running west from here to the Sands which our satellite photographs had confirmed. We spent three hours wandering about a heap of rubble and Juris was delighted to find fragments of pottery and various ambiguous mounds, evidence of former springs. He was sure people had lived here longer ago than the 300 years theorised by the only previous archaeologist to have visited Shis'r. There was plenty for Juris to explore, but as to locating Ubar, we were really no further forward. The interim report I eventually submitted to the Sultan and our sponsors made the best of a bad job.

We postponed our main expedition until the autumn of 1991, because of ongoing troubles caused by Saddam Hussein. On the day we set out I discovered that in my rush I had collected the wrong travel bag from our London gear store. Instead of tropical shirts, sun-cream and malaria tablets, I had a duffle bag with snow goggles, balaclava and mitts. I decided not to mention this to the larger party we had now assembled in case it alarmed them as to my administrative efficiency.

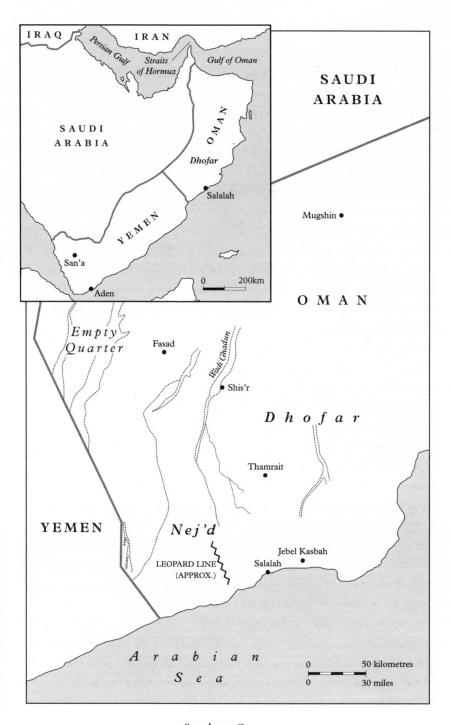

Southern Oman

We based ourselves at Shis'r, where Ginny set up our HF radio base, because it seemed a good place to branch out from. I linked up with desert bedu and mountain folk I had known from the late 1960s who were useful as scouts or advisers, and there were many long and inconclusive debates as to Ubar's likely location between the film director, the explorer, the archaeologist and the Imam of Fasad, through whose home terrain we were hesitantly creeping and who agreed to take us out into the Sands. At least we felt confident that wherever we ended up, he would know the most direct way back.

Terry Lloyd and his ITN cameraman Rob Bowles joined and recorded many of our desert wanderings. I savoured the beauty of the stars at night and read the Qur'an to Ginny: 'It is Allah who makes men laugh and weep, it is He who kills and makes alive . . . He is the Lord of the Dog Star, He who destroyed Ad of yore, and Thamud, and left none of them, and the people of Noah before them. Their cities, he threw them down and there covered them what did cover them.' The Dog Star, I mused, could tell me every secret of the Sands and where to find Ubar, which the Qur'an called Ad.

I knew well from my Arab Army days that there were three main aquifers running north into Dhofar's southern fringe of the Empty Quarter. The existing water sources at Fasad, Shis'r and Mugshin all lay at a latitude through which an incense road hypothesised by Bertram Sidney Thomas might have passed. The water at Fasad is very sulphurous, and at Mugshin highly salty, but Shis'r's water, that of the Wadi Ghadun aquifer, is famous for its sweetness. Though historians had written Shis'r off as a mere 300 years old, we decided to start digging here, for reasons quite unconnected with archaeology.

Three days before Christmas 1991 I overheard the two Omani students, who worked with us on loan from the Ministry of National Heritage and Culture, commenting on the fact that we had been in Shis'r for ten days, that our dig-teams were sitting around doing nothing and that all we seemed to do was film each

Geoff, Charlie and Ollie, 1977: our first experience of travel at minus 50°C. Even wearing Inuit wolfskin parkas, our learning curve out on the Arctic Ocean sea-ice was steep - and nearly cost Geoff his fingers.

Antarctica 1980: Ollie is halted by a bank of iron-hard sastrugi ridges.

Easter Day 1982: the first men in history to reach both Poles. But over 1,000 miles of broken ice lay ahead.

The mouth of the Yukon – rough seas and no land in sight.
This photo was taken just before the near fatal capsize.

Arctic man-hauling in early march. Not an activity
to be generally recommended.

Self-taught radio operator Ginny survived near poisoning by carbon monoxide and two hours sleep a night to keep the expedition in touch. She became the first woman to receive Britain's elite Polar Medal.

The crew of the Benjy B forcing a way for our old ship between Arctic ice-floes.

One of my favourite photos: Bothie the dog is fearless in approaching
the strange frozen jeans monster. Rygvingen Montain, the last
known feature for 900 unexplored miles, is in the background.

1989: an unusual sight, the author in suit and tie,
working for Dr Armand Hammer . . .

. . . but not for long: searching for the lost city of Ubar,
deep in Arabia's Empty Quarter, 1991.

As epic a natural force as I've seen anywhere in the world:
a sandstorm about to engulf my old base at Thamrait.

The longest track – the first unsupported crossing
of the Antarctic continent, 1992.

other. This seemed a fair summary, but it would not sound good at all in the wrong quarters. On Christmas Eve I had a quiet but urgent word with Juris and suggested he start digging *anywhere* so that the Ministry students could see the action. So he took his dig-team some 200 yards from our camp to the rubble around the old Shis'r well. Desultory work began. Two days later Juris looked smug. He had found a piece of red pottery identical to the style of the Jemdet Nassir period in Uruq, Mesopotamia. If carbon dating proved this to be so it would pre-date previous thinking as to the start of trade between Mesopotamia and south Arabia from 4000 to 5000 BC. He was not yet ready to go out on a limb and say we had discovered Ubar, but he was clear that our Shis'r dig was already proving to be a very important Roman-period site and probably went back at least 4,000 years.

Two months later Juris summed up what we had by then unearthed: 'So far we have walls and towers that are square and round and horseshoe-shaped. There was clearly a central tower, an inner sanctum and an outer wall which had a minimum height of between ten and fifteen feet and a consistent thickness of eighty centimetres. Some of the original rooms, complete with hearths, did not collapse as others did and these have already yielded rich finds for the key periods between the second millennium BC and around AD 300.'

When free time was available, I took a shovel and pickaxe to the site and attacked any area that did not require more delicate attention using trowel and handbrush. But the archaeologists in our team, who were allergic to shovels, would scream and chase me away, so Ginny and I spent more time plodding about in the desert searching for subsidiary camps, rich in axe-heads and Fasad points, arrowheads from between the sixth and fourth millennia BC, places where travellers would have camped within sight of the many-towered citadel that Shis'r had clearly once been.

As we dug down, we found the original building work of our city was excellent, consisting of semi-dressed stone cemented with a white plaster similar to that used in the north of the peninsula by contemporary peoples such as the Nabataeans of Petra. Our archaeologists came across the only ancient chess set ever to be found in south Arabia, six soapstone pieces, each two or three inches high and well polished by the fingers of the players. After a month the diggers were three feet down in places and pottery from Rome, Greece and Syria joined Celadon and Ming pieces from China, glass bracelets of bright clear colours from Aden and Neolithic flint weapons from 5000 BC. But was this Ubar? Was it Irem?

Each new artifact helped to fill in the puzzle which Juris needed to reconstruct about Shis'r's unknown past. Between 8000 and 6000 BC the region was too arid for humans. In 5000 BC, with wetter weather, Neolithic folk from Syria and further east arrived and built hearths. Even then, Juris believed, they traded in incense and travelled the then less arid interior, now the Sands, on foot and, after 4000 BC, by donkey. By the seventh century AD, when the Qur'an and later Islamic writers described the fabled city, the site itself was gone, a place only of fanciful legend. The decline would partly have been due to natural catastrophe, the decline of Rome, the spread of Christianity and the dwindling demand for frankincense.

When I was summoned to report on our finds to Sultan Qaboos in person, and he asked me if our Shis'r excavation was definitely Ubar, I felt able to reply, 'I believe so, Your Majesty. It is difficult to know what else it could be.' There is after all only one Dhofar 'place of trade' marked on Ptolomy's map of Arabia.

The carbon dating tests confirmed Juris's hunch and the worldwide attention aroused by the expedition brought tourists and television teams aplenty to Shis'r. Sultan Qaboos recognised that oil revenues would diminish in time and tourism could offer a lucrative alternative source of income. I like to think that the eventual success of my long search for Ubar has in a small way repaid the people of Oman, the country that has given me some of the best times of my life.

10

The Longest Track

While Ginny and I had been in Oman, I had done nothing about the Antarctic crossing journey originally mooted by Ollie and Charlie, but back in London I heard that Norwegian plans for an Antarctic record-breaking journey were afoot by Erling Kagge, our earlier rival in the north and an exceptionally fine cross-country skier. Without delay I started to raise sponsorship for Antarctica. With Kagge as a rival, speed and endurance would now be a high priority for our team and I was concerned about our collective stamina. I had recently noticed what looked like a paunch on Charlie.

In mid-May 1991 I went to a trade fair at Olympia where Oliver had organised a sales stand for his employers. By chance, Charlie Burton was in charge of security there, so I was able to explain my worries to them both, and suggested that I ask Mike Stroud to join our team.

'He is like a bull terrier,' I stressed, 'small in stature but incredibly powerful.'

'That's great,' Charlie remonstrated, 'but where does that leave us oldies? Surely a team moves at the pace of its slowest member?'

It was agreed that some thought would be given to the idea of inviting Mike along and, not long afterwards, Ollie called me to say that he and Charlie had both decided to change their role in the project. 'We would want to enjoy the experience,' Charlie told me later, 'and I know that, once you get competitive, you take any

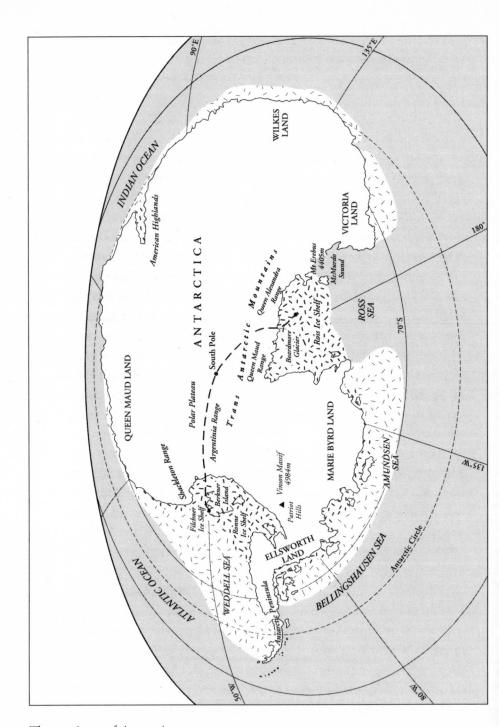

The continent of Antarctica

signs of enjoyment on my part as being tantamount to mutiny and a clear sign that we should be travelling faster.'

So he and Ollie took on the role of organisers from London, and I approached Mike Stroud by telephone.

Usually, the only position that I can tolerate on an expedition is that of team leader. Ollie, Charlie and Mike were totally aware of my peculiarity in this respect, but all three were strong personalities and not yes-men. My policy with everyone on any journey is to follow the democratic route (*when* there is time), of talking about options rather than pronouncing dictatorial and unilateral decisions. If others, whether or not they form a majority, favour an opinion which I believe to be stupid, dangerous or unlikely to help attain the goal of the expedition, then I overrule them, no matter how disaffected this may make them feel. In fact, because most fellow polar travellers know how to progress over snow and ice, we normally all agree on the best way forward, so contretemps are quite rare.

I knew very little in depth about Mike. This may seem strange as he had, by 1990, already come on four of my Arctic expeditions and we had been through a great deal together. To take *friends* on stressful expeditions has always seemed to me to be foolish, since I can think of no easier way of marring a friendship for ever. An expedition's aim is best achieved by individuals who can look after themselves, need little or no directing or nursing and are tough in body and mind. I look for professional or dogged people and treat any friendship resulting from an expedition as an unexpected bonus.

Polar expeditions are well known for causing stress and enmity between participants and quite why Ollie, Charlie, Mike and I had never come to blows, literally or even verbally, during our Arctic journeys remains a mystery to me.

'I know you. You like to lead from the front,' Mike observed. I conceded we would take hourly turns in navigation before he finally agreed to join. He also wrung out of me the agreement that he could conduct an extensive physiological research programme throughout the journey. This was bad news since I hate the sight of blood, especially my own, but it seemed a reasonable penalty in order to secure Mike's participation.

Prince Charles was once more our patron and he asked us to use the expedition to raise funds for multiple sclerosis research. We partly based this on members of the public pledging a penny a mile covered. Since Antarctica is over fifty times the size of Great Britain, a lot of pennies were involved.

Timing, as ever, is crucial when contemplating the Antarctic. Because the Antarctic plateau is so high and so cold, the period when humans can travel over it is severely limited. So is the availability of transport to and from Antarctica. We would be flown in on the Atlantic side and taken off by cruise ship on the Pacific side, which meant walking 1,700 miles between 1 November 1992, the very earliest flight date, and 16 February, the cruise ship's departure date. We would be pulling sledges at least sixteen miles a day for 108 days with loads likely to exceed 350 pounds, well in excess of any manhauling achievements to date.

In 1903 Scott, Shackleton and Wilson hauled loads of 175 pounds. Eight years later, on 'the worst journey in the world', Wilson, Bowers and Cherry-Garrard started out with 253 pounds. Especially unnerving for us were the much more recent observations of Reinhold Messner, the world's greatest mountaineer, and Arved Fuchs, Germany's top polar explorer, during their own crossing attempt. I had serious doubts that Mike and I could outperform such a team. Of his Antarctic journey Messner wrote: 'With sledge-loads of 264lbs, the longest stretch would be murderously strenuous. Perhaps even impossible . . . 264lbs is a load for a horse not a human being.'

By early October the projected weight of our sledge-loads had gone up to 400 pounds. We were entering the realms of the theoretically impossible but it was too late to back out now. To mention 400 pounds per load to anyone with the slightest knowledge of manhauling was to invite ridicule . . . so we didn't. The starting loads finally climbed to 485 pounds each. And that despite paring our gear down to minimal necessities.

On a gusty morning in late October Ginny drove me to Heathrow. We said goodbye in the carpark for there would be many people in the terminal. I waved as she drove off and thanked God for her. I had told myself after many previous journeys that I would never again leave her at our bleak Exmoor home for the long and lonely winter. As she left I felt wretchedly guilty. It occurred to me that *I* had never spent a single night alone at our house on the moor.

As Mike and Morag Howell, again in charge of our communications, chatted on the plane, I idly considered their motives in coming along. I knew Mike's. He had spent two years of his life, seven years earlier, hoping to walk to the South Pole with Swan and Mear but, to his dismay, another man was eventually selected, leaving him merely first reserve. Now, whether or not we managed to cross the whole continent, he knew that he stood a chance of at least making it to the Pole.

When I am asked for my own life motives I openly admit that expedition leadership is quite simply my chosen way of making a living: and under 'occupation' in my passport the entry has always stated 'travel writer'. Mike found my financial motivation upsetting and 'commercial'. His own rationale was more romantic. He talked of stunning landscapes and equated his adventures with a more intense version of the pleasures he had found as a boy from mountaineering, hill-walking and rock-climbing. I am not introspective and find it awkward having to dig within myself to produce replies to journalistic questions about motivation. I liked the response of Jean-Louis Etienne when asked why he went on polar expeditions. He replied: 'Because I like it. You never ask a basketball player why he plays: it is because he enjoys it. It is like asking someone why he likes chocolate.'

The KLM Boeing stopped at Sao Paulo, Montevideo, Santiago, Puerto Montt and finally Punta Arenas on the southern tip of Chile. We were met here by Annie Kershaw of Adventure Network (ANI). Annie was the widow of Giles Kershaw, our Transglobe Twin Otter pilot in Antarctica, who had later died in a gyrocopter accident. Annie had taken over running ANI, his polar air charter business on his death. Her first DC6 passenger flight of the year to her tented camp and ice runway at Patriot Hills in Antarctica was scheduled to depart two days after our arrival in Punta Arenas, South America's most southerly city. Until the Panama Canal replaced the Cape Horn route, Punta Arenas flourished with 138 brothels to cope with visiting sailors. Now it is a strategic Chilean naval base. The 200,000-strong population are mostly descended from nineteenth-century immigrants: Spaniards and Germans just outnumber the descendants of Scottish shepherds and Croatian goldminers. Chilean grannies in fur coats could still be heard speaking English in Scots accents almost as thick as Morag's. Unfortunately, engine problems delayed take off for six days, the first dent in our tight schedule.

We flew south over the South Atlantic and then Antarctica for nine hours. At last, in the endless white sheet below we glimpsed a flash of tiny figures, tents and two Twin Otters. The notorious blue ice airstrip of Patriot Hills flashed beneath us. Twice our Canadian pilot rehearsed his landing to test the cross-wind. Then, with a shattering impact that could not have done any part of the DC6 much good, we struck the ice and bounced, rattling over the rippled blue surface. I do not remember any other landing even half as impressive in thirty years of arriving at remote spots in small aircraft.

Three hours later, Mike and I had transferred to one of the Twin Otters bound for Antarctica's Atlantic coastline. With us were Terry Lloyd, Rob Bowles and our radio base leader, Morag Howell. The Twin Otter ski-plane roared over the ice-front of the Weddell Sea, a vertical cliff forming the seaward face of the Filchner Ice-shelf. Antarctica is composed of two vast ice-sheets divided by a mountan chain. The sheets contain ten million square kilometres of ice which, in places, is four and a half kilometres thick and moves slowly but surely seawards. This huge wilderness provides scientists with a unique playground of volcanoes, fast-flowing glaciers, mobile ice-sheets, katabatic winds of frightening power and a perfectly pure and sterile interior where temperatures in winter can reach −100°C. After several cautious rehearsals, our pilot found a relatively smooth stretch of snow at the point where Berkner Island meets both the ice-shelf and the sea. We were set down at 78°19.8′ South and 43°47′ West on Antarctica's Atlantic seaboard.

Morag helped us unload and wished us well. For the next few months she would attempt to keep radio contact with us from a tent at Patriot Hills and with our UK base which was manned by her husband Flo at their home in Aberdeen. We watched the little aircraft depart until the engine noise was a distant drone and the great silence of Antarctica closed about us.

Months of unspoken apprehension were coming to a head. The key question was whether or not full loads of 485 pounds each, including the hundred days' fuel taken on at Patriot Hills, could be moved by the two of us. The main bulk was rations. These were equally important both to our chances of success and to Mike's physiological research. Each bag was packed to provide two men with twenty-four hours of food at a daily intake of 5,200 calories. This packing system had evolved over a period of sixteen years of polar journeys, beginning with my first North Pole attempt in 1976.

The average daily intake of both Scott's and Amundsen's teams was 4,500 calories per man. This proved enough for the Norwegians who skied unencumbered and with husky power. But to support the hard labour of the British manhaulers, the amount was insufficient and they slowly starved. The first man to weaken and die was Taff Evans, the biggest and heaviest on Scott's team, the man they 'least expected to fail'.

I considered our team's vital statistics. I was eleven years older than Mike and approaching my fiftieth birthday. I was taller by five inches and heavier by three stone. But in terms of sheer strength, especially of the vital lower limb powerbase, Mike was clinically tested as considerably stronger.

At home on our Exmoor farm, Ginny would give me twice her

own food portions, although she worked harder than I did. Over the months ahead I would be consuming exactly the same calorific intake as Mike. I feared that, like the heavily built Evans on Scott's team, my performance would deteriorate first and more markedly than Mike's. I determined from the outset, therefore, to avoid my normal course of forging ahead at maximum output.

As each piece of equipment was loaded we ticked it off in our notebooks, alongside its weight, down to the nearest ounce. The total was, as we had feared, 485 pounds each, constituting far heavier loads than those of any previous polar manhaul journey on record.

We finished loading the sledges and looked at their bulk. Then at each other, and shrugged. The moment of truth had arrived. We adjusted the manhaul harnesses about our stomachs and shoulders. I leaned against the traces with my full bodyweight. The near half-ton sledge paid no attention. I looked back and spotted an eight-inch ice rut across the front of the runners. I tugged again with my left shoulder only, and the sledge, avoiding the rut, moved forward. I will never forget that instant. I *could* pull a 485-pound sledge. Mike was also on the move. The expedition was under way.

After a hundred yards I stopped, out of breath. I was pleased to see, looking back, that Mike was also labouring hard. The thought of pulling my sledge for an entire mile, never mind to the South Pole and beyond, was appalling. The map, or strictly speaking chart (since the sea was beneath us), showed a rash of blue lines, the crevasse symbol, running south along the foot of Berkner Island for some eighty miles.

Should we fix a safety line between us before reaching the first crevasse? I knew this was our agreed drill but the sheer weight of the sledge had already biased me against any action beyond the sheer task of progress. Even though we were descending a gentle incline, the sledge was totally inert. The very instant I stopped pulling, it stopped moving. There was not the least glissade. I conjured up a parallel. If I were to lash together three average-sized adults, each weighing 160 pounds, dump them in a fibreglass

160

bathtub with no legs and then drag them through sand-dunes for 1,700 miles, the difficulties involved would be similar.

My sledge-load soon grew to represent something animate and hostile. I knew the pattern well. First my inner anger would be directed at the weather, the equipment and the ice. Later at my companion. The same would hold good for Mike. I determined never to allow myself to think unnecessarily far ahead. Sufficient unto each day is the mileage thereof . . . providing daily progress tallies with the schedule.

After two hours I felt certain we had reached the ice-shelf. About a mile behind us and to our immediate north was the ice-front, a chaotic jumble of giant ice fragments where shelf met true sea-ice. In every other direction there was nothing but mirage shimmer and the great white glare of Antarctica.

After five and a half hours it was time to halt for we had been awake for twenty-four hours since leaving Punta Arenas. For navigation purposes, we must keep to a carefully timed daily schedule. I intended to use my watch and body shadow to establish direction all the way to the Pole and that meant keeping the sun due north at local midday. There were, I reasoned, only another 1,696 miles to cover and, since we had rations for a hundred days, there was yet time to find a way of increasing the daily average to sixteen miles. There must be absolutely no rest days or we would fail.

Remembering the promise I had made to Mike, I alternated the navigation with him at hourly intervals. I found this increasingly annoying since I had spent well over twenty years leading expeditions from the front and mistrusted anyone else's navigating abilities. Another thing that annoyed me, I reflected as my legs dangled inside my first mini-crevasse of the trip, was the ignorant complacency of journalists who said that of course it was 'different nowadays' with all our technological gadgetry. Crevasses are today, just as in the time of Scott and Mawson, the chief threat to Antarctic travellers and the danger has not lessened one iota over the intervening years.

Up to my armpits in deep soft snow, with my lower torso

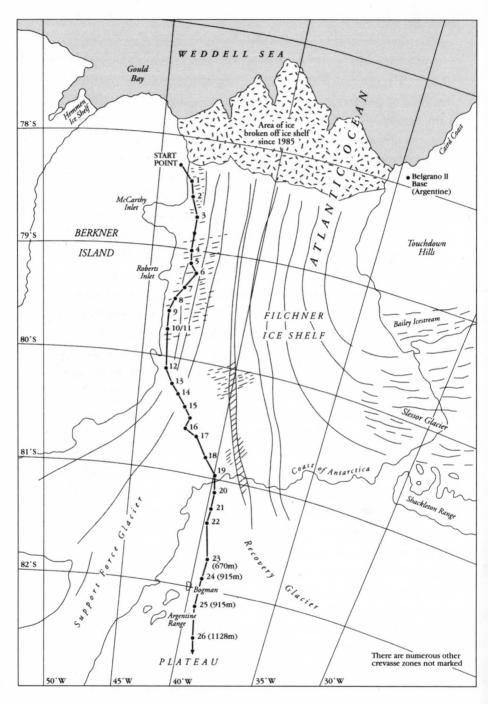

Ascent from the Atlantic Ocean to the Antarctic Plateau

treading air over nothingness, I only wished the gadgetry fallacy had some basis in reality. Too much movement on trying to extricate my body could in an instant collapse the whole snow-bridge. My attempts to look back at my sledge failed, for the hood of my parka and my cotton balaclava prevented sufficient lateral movement of my neck. Furthermore I had breathed into the balaclava as I fell, which had the immediate effect of misting up my goggles and the mist had frozen across the insides of the lens. To all intents and purposes I was blind since I had no hand free to tear off the goggles.

The alloy poles leading back from my body harness to the sledge had snapped close behind me, which actually helped me by allowing sufficient movement for me to wriggle up, inch by inch, until my hips were out of the hole. The rest was easy. I replaced the broken poles with rope traces.

Many of the crevasses we were to negotiate were over a hundred feet wide with sagging bridges. The weakest point was not, as might be expected, in the centre but along the fault-line, where the bridge was joined to the crevasse wall's lip. In the most dangerous cases the whole bridge had already descended a few feet down into the maw before catching on some unseen temporary stopper. New snow had then partially filled the resulting trough.

Hauling the sledges down on to such teetering bridges presented no great physical task since gravity was on our side. If the bridge held under our initial weight, we pulled onwards over the centre span. At this point the going became singularly off-putting because, in order to manhaul our monster loads up the far side of the disintegrating bridge, maximum downward pressure with skis and sticks must be applied to its weakest point. There were moments of sickening apprehension as our straining ski sticks plunged through the crust, or part of a sledge lurched backwards, its prow or stern having broken through. I never grew inured to the crevasse hazard and continued to sweat and silently curse as each new death trap passed beneath us.

Fifteen miles above us was a feature first discovered by the British Antarctic Survey nine years before, the hole in the ozone layer, which is also the nest where man-made pollutants called chlorofluorocarbons come to roost. Stratospheric winds carry these compounds, long used in aerosols and coolants, south, where they mix with high-altitude clouds in the cold and dark of the Antarctic winter. As the sun returns in spring, these frozen chemical clouds react with its rays, releasing chlorine molecules that temporarily dissolve the thin layer of ozone that protects earthbound life from harmful solar radiation. Since we were travelling directly below this hazard, it made sense to cover our skin. But, hauling huge loads in our tight dog harnesses, we needed to breathe deeply, gasping for air without fogging our goggles, so the sun shone day after day on our uncovered lips and noses. Mine deteriorated rapidly. The lip scabs always stuck together overnight and, when I woke, the act of tearing my lips apart in order to speak and drink invariably opened up all the raw places. Breakfast from a communal bowl consisted of porridge oats in a gravy of blood.

Soon our minds churned over the fact that we were not averaging ten miles a day. We had to cut the loads.

'Mike, I'm chucking my duvet jacket. I have hardly worn it all week. We work so hard we will keep warm even when winter comes.'

He nodded. We both knew it was a big decision. The weather was now warm, in polar terms. Maybe we would have second thoughts later. But there would be no later if we could not get a move on now. Next morning we buried the two down-filled jackets along with the empty ration packs. I was later bitterly to regret the decision but it is easy to be wise with hindsight.

At the end of the first week we entered a zone of great instability. Thunderous roars warned us that the whole ice-shelf had entered a hyperactive phase, causing hitherto safe snow-bridges to collapse all around us into their crevasses. No amount of ice lore could keep us out of trouble here. A gaping hole opened up with an explosion of snow spray as we watched. Some ten paces ahead of Mike, and 45 feet wide by 120 feet in length, it lay directly across his intended path. Had it occurred but a few seconds later he and his sledge would have disappeared, along with several tons of plunging snow-bridge. All around us renewed implosions announced further cratering. The sensation was memorably frightening. We must escape at once to a safer area. But where was safer? Only the looming bulk of Berkner Island offered certain stability. We roped up with nervous fingers, fearing that at any moment the snow beneath us would open up and dump us hundreds of feet. The surface of the ice shelf all about us rumbled and reverberated again and again. Geysers of snow dust rose into the air. The feeling was similar to closing on enemy troops when under mortar fire. As each new crump exploded at random, the fear increased that the next catastrophe would have our name on it.

The nylon rope between us was sixty feet in length. We moved as fast as the sledges and the wings of fear allowed. Time stood still. I came to an abrupt halt as a wave of cold air rushed past, accompanied by the loudest and closest of the explosions. I ducked, for the all-engulfing sound seemed to pass both overhead and underfoot.

Immediately between Mike and me an immense crater appeared. One moment the ice-shelf ahead was solid and white. The next a maw like the mouth of the Underworld, steaming with snow vapour, lay across our intended route, wide enough to swallow a double-decker bus. The roaring echoes of imploding snow cascading into the bowels of the ice-shelf returned in successive waves, like shore ripples from an undersea volcano. Although a cold wind scoured the ice-sheet, I sweated with fear. The next hour was a nightmare of apprehension; nowhere was safe. Only pure luck enabled us to escape from this volatile zone.

On the ninth day the ice-shelf showed signs of climbing towards the interior. There were no spot heights on my local chart and my small-scale map of Antarctica showed only that we were about to enter the largest crevasse field on the Filchner Ice-shelf. Mike agreed that we seemed to be climbing but maintained that the undulating series of rising steppes, which I could see through the wafting mists, was in reality only an illusion in our minds caused by the heavy loads and mirage effects. We could not actually see any gradient.

Fortunately the deep drifts of the ice-shelf did not extend to these wind-scoured flanks so the going was easier than at any time since the firm coastal strip. Temperatures of around −15°C were not low enough to coarsen the surface and Mike, when navigating, set a pace that seemed to me as the day went by increasingly and unnecessarily fast.

I resolved to make no comment and at first found no difficulty in keeping hard on his heels. My shoulder blades and lower back screamed at me but the old competitive urge came back. Why let this guy steam ahead? For almost twenty years now I had pulled sledges, in all conditions, faster than any colleague of any age, and on the northern expeditions over the past six years I had out-pulled Mike, day after day, in even the worst of Arctic conditions.

I talked persuasively to myself in this vein but all the time Mike's small but powerful legs pulled on piston-like and I began to realise it was self-defeating for me to keep up such a pace. At thirty-nine Mike was in his prime. In Siberia, when he was thirty-six and I was forty-seven, I had no difficulty keeping well ahead. So, at that stage, his eleven-year advantage made no difference. Something must have happened since.

Like Shackleton, the first man to plan a crossing of Antarctica, I found myself preoccupied with the ageing process. Each new ache of muscle or tendon soon achieved obsession rating and blisters and chafing sores screamed their presence through every long and toilsome day. I swore silently when Mike was leading and moving faster than suited my pace for then I was forced by pride to abandon the rhythm of my polar plod. Self-pity is not an attractive trait and I do not remember indulging in it on previous occasions. As the days struggled by and the stress mounted, we faced increasing tensions between us. We could not ease the pain, the fear, above all the sheer burden of the sledge-loads by kicking our sledges, so we took it out on each other, at first silently, as had been our wont in the Arctic, but then with controlled outbursts.

After only five miles on the seventeenth day Mike's foot blisters became painful and he told me he thought it would be sensible to stop. I said nothing in the interests of diplomacy and we camped four hours early, to my mind a dangerous precedent.

We reached the Antarctic coastline some time during the twentieth morning. We could not actually see where the floating ice-shelf stopped and the continental ice began since the joining point was covered in seamless snow, but once we crossed over we began the true continental crossing journey. At first any uphill gradient was imperceptible but by the afternoon each and every heave on the traces required concentrated mental and physical effort. And then we reached the start of the first sastrugi field, a great rash of iron-hard furrows lying directly across our route. I know no other way to advance when the ice gets nasty than to attack it head-on with every ounce of gristle at your disposal. Tightening my harness and stick-straps, I focused on each successive wall of ice and threw energy conservation to the winds. Towards the end of the day, after eleven hours of uphill hauling, we came to an especially rugged zone of serrated ice and Mike lagged well behind, despite my pauses for him to catch up. At the end of the final hour I had the tent up in time for his arrival and knew at once that he was livid. Mike let rip. I had surged irresponsibly ahead despite the evil terrain and, worse, I had gone straight at the sastrugi instead of taking a sensible indirect route through the worst of it. Fortunately, the hostility we nurtured towards each other on the route almost invariably evaporated once we were in the tent, which saved the journey for both of us from becoming a non-stop nightmare.

That is not to say that our irritations with each other eased. He would surge far ahead and complain at my steady plod, when not attacking sastrugi. I was infuriated when his watch stopped because he had not put in a new battery before leaving England, despite several reminders. This meant I had to let him have mine and shout when it was my turn in front. His blister and diarrhoea stops also outraged me. I was all set to have the whole thing out with him when he announced that the abscess on his heel was so swollen that he had decided to operate. I watched with intense admiration as he gave himself two deep injections of anaesthetic and then plunged a scalpel deep into the swelling with diagonal incisions. Pus poured out and the swelling visibly decreased. Mike then bandaged up his heel and packed away his medical kit. I am not sure whether or not he felt faint but I certainly did. I said nothing more about the early halts or the stricken Rolex.

Over the next three days we climbed to 5,000 feet above sea-level with constant Force Eight winds in our faces. Arriving some distance ahead of Mike one evening, I began to erect the tent by fixing a safety line to my sledge before trying to slot the ten-foot alloy poles into the sleeving. The fourth and last pole was almost positioned when an especially violent blast tore the tent from my mitts and buckled one of the poles. Since I only carried a single eighteen-inch spare pole section for the entire journey, I left the bent pole in place and prayed we would be spared a big katabatic event in the days ahead.

I thought of Ginny back on Exmoor. She had lit an outsize church candle in our kitchen and intended to keep it burning day and night until I returned. It was four feet long but so many hundreds of miles stretched ahead of us I could not help but think the candle would run out long before I came home.

One morning I noticed a black item behind Mike's sledge. It turned out to be a spare battery. Mike looked grim, as well he might, for he had packed the battery deep inside his load and there was no way it could have escaped but through a hole in the hull. We rolled the sledge on to one side and then the other, revealing a ragged split across its entire width. This had been caused by Mike falling twenty feet into a crevasse days earlier. We had done our best to repair it at the time, but not, it now seemed, well enough. We erected the tent as a new gale blew up, unloaded, repaired and reloaded his sledge, then set off again to make mileage over the last four hours of the day.

The following day brought our first true white-out as well as sastrugi. When we camped, after a memorably nasty ten hours lurching over unseen obstacles and crashing into invisible trenches, I found both my cheeks burning and inflamed by UV rays. I had exposed my cheeks to help demist my goggles but it had been a mistake. Mike's eyes, even though he wore goggles for all but two hours, were also affected. Soon after we camped he developed snow blindness symptoms. Only the mildest of attacks, but enough to have him lying back in considerable pain.

Since our overall speed and rate of progress for the first forty days were slightly better than for any previous Antarctic manhauling journey on record, our pace should not theoretically have caused dissension. But we were both under increasing strain and our bodies, under the stress of slow starvation combined with enormous energy expenditure, were altering chemically. Subsequent analysis of our blood samples was to show that our whole enzyme systems, everything that controlled our absorption of fat, were changing and we were recording levels of gut hormones twice as high as were previously known to science. We were adapting to our high-fat rations in a way hitherto unrecognised. Furthermore, with zero remaining body fat, we were losing muscle and weight from our hearts as well as our body mass.

By the fifth week Mike's intermittent surges of speedy sledging were telling on him. He confided to his diary that he was feeling hypoglycaemic. He told me that he could 'feel the weight falling off'. On Christmas Eve we were able to take full advantage for the first time of a wind driving us south and use the sails we had optimistically brought along to attach to our sledges. But on Christmas Day the wind veered again. I was now suffering from haemorrhoids, which at least allowed me to forget the pain in my feet due to the new aggravation. Cherry-Garrard wrote: 'Sometimes it was difficult not to howl.' I understood how he felt.

One day Mike produced from his science pack two small bottles of very expensive water for us to drink in the interest of his urine sample analysis. He told me not to spill any because each bottleful cost hundreds of pounds, and it was like atomic heavy water, but non-radioactive. I never ceased to admire Mike's dedication to his research work. One of his science projects measured our calorific experience. The results were startling: 'When we made the ascent to the plateau, the isotopes gave daily energy expenditure of 10,670 calories in Ran and 11,650 in me. They confirmed the highest maintained energy expenditures ever documented – values that must lie close to the physiological limit.'

On our sixtieth day Mike had a very bad time and told me he must be wrong about the effects of altitude. He was worried within himself about his ability to continue fending off negative thoughts. He wrote: 'Last night I did express to Ran my fears of not being able to hack it if things go badly. Needless to say I got a sort of "we will be tough" type talk rather than true understanding. He gets his strength from "God and family and the whole clan here inside me". All very useful but I know it won't help me if I can see the whole chance of success slipping away and us just slogging on.'

That night I gave Mike two chocolate squares and he seemed to appreciate the gesture. I am not good at being sympathetic. I knew that Mike was agnostic and did not expect him to gain any mental help in that direction. I had hoped, however, that he might be able to invoke his family and the knowledge that they were all gunning for him but he seemed to scoff at this as too contrived a mental aid.

My practice was to hype up my mind during the first hour of every day, when the pain from my feet was at its worst, by simply remembering that I was not alone in facing the dreaded hours ahead. I pictured my grandfather who had trapped in northern Canada and fought for his country all over the world. I thought of my father and uncle who were killed in the two world wars. I pictured my wife, my mother and my sisters and I knew that all of them were right behind me, helping to suppress the ever-lurking urge to put a stop to the pain and the cold by giving up.

The last 200 miles before the Pole involved us in climbing above 10,000 feet. The altitude effects added to our debilitation and the loads were beginning to change us in many subtle ways. Mike reached the end of his tether, grinding to a halt in his tracks, head lolling, as if he were about to succumb to hypothermia. I set up the tent, got the cooker going and he accepted a mug of tepid soup in a trance. My mind was in a turmoil. I had little doubt but that he was pushing himself far too hard. I was doing likewise. We had no alternative. We had to earn our daily ration with the mileage are put behind us.

On our sixty-eighth day the wind dropped and the mists cleared. Towards evening there was a *thing* ahead. For the first time in over 700 miles a man-made object was visible in the snow. Could it be the Pole? The item turned out to be a half-buried meteorological balloon. After seven hours' hauling on 16 January, on the eighty-first anniversary of Scott's sad arrival at the same point, we topped the final rise and came to the South Pole. The journey was far from over but we had dragged to the Pole just enough stores to allow us to cross the continent and survive. If our luck held. It was a moment of sheer elation. Especially so for Mike, who had not been selected back in 1985 when Roger Mear was finalising his Pole team.

All the isolation of the past months fell away. The polar site had vastly altered, even in the twelve short years since my last visit. Strangely shaped installations on jacked-up steel legs reared monstrously in every direction from the main black-roofed dome in which over-wintering scientists lived and worked. A small huddle of nine figures had come out to greet us, but we put aside thoughts of the food available in the dome canteen as we forced ourselves to continue north. In all, we paused at the Pole for only eighty minutes.

Only then, beyond the Pole, did we discover the true meaning of *cold*. Our condition in terms of body deterioration, slow starvation, inadequate clothing, wind chill temperature, altitude, and even the day of the year, exactly matched those of Scott and his four companions as they came away from the Pole in 1912.

We learned from Morag that Erling Kagge had reached the Pole before us and had been airlifted out the previous week. The Norwegian press talked of his winning the race, but our sledges were twice as heavy and our journey twice as long so our morale was not too badly dented by this misleading piece of media spin.

I could sense that Mike was in a bad way, despite his continued power surges. I knew that even now he would never recognise

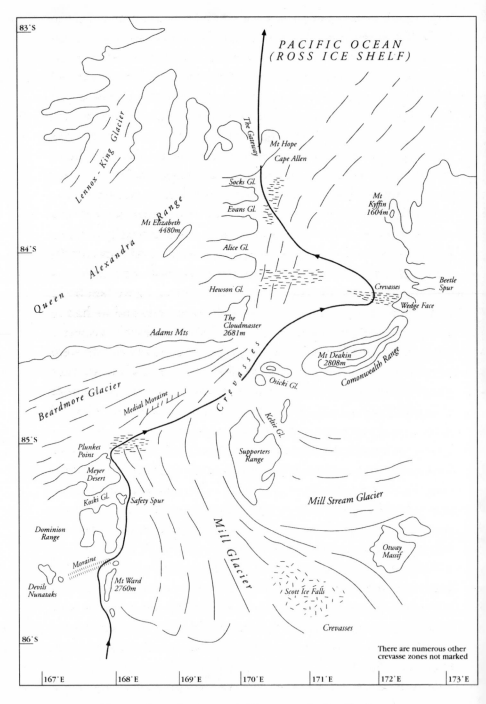

Descent from the Antarctic Plateau to the Pacific Ocean

that his pace was his own worst enemy. I would never be able to 'bully' him into copying my polar plod. I could only try to compromise with him over matters of pace wherever necessary. I had my own mounting problems with harness sores, diarrhoea and haemorrhoids, and the most agonising throbbing pain in my feet. Mike diagnosed possible bone infection and put me on antibiotics. I realised how lucky I had been for fifty years in experiencing little pain. Broken bones and teeth, torn-off digits, frostbite and chronic kidney stones had seemed unpleasant at the time. But now I knew real pain and I feared lest it overwhelm me.

On 30 January we recorded our first barometric descent of a few hundred feet, but this welcome news was balanced by a potentially disastrous discovery. Mike had lost both his ski sticks off his sledge. Trying to share mine and progress with one each was unbalancing, and when Mike again fell behind, I gave him both, but he was once more on the edge of hypothermia and we had to camp early. Our bodily condition was becoming highly suspect. I was not in the business of leading suicide expeditions. We were approaching the edge of our ability to cope safely with very extreme conditions and this was, we both knew, because we were starving, losing ten ounces every day through a deficiency of 3,000 calories each and every day for three months.

The next day Mike began to work out a satisfactory way of forcing his sledge to move with just one stick and I constantly checked the compass for I knew we would need great accuracy to enter the Mill Glacier, the start of the long descent from the plateau to the Pacific coast. Mike and I needed to make no mistakes from now on. We were committed to the 9,000-foot descent as if in a rubber boat at the moment of yielding to the first pull of a great rapid. The horizons which now opened to us were awesome, a sprawling mass of rock and ice in motion. These were the headwaters of a slow-moving ice-river. Huge open chasms leered ahead and standing ice-waves reared up at the base of black truncated cliffs.

I scanned the skies north and saw no clouds. So long as the

good visibility conditions remained, I could find the best route. I felt a God-given confidence and, for the first time on this journey, the warm pleasure of challenge. I knew the rules. Never waste a minute. Pause for nothing. Here there could be no place for my polar plod. So long as the weather held we must go like the wind. This was the region of monster holes described by Cherry-Garrard as 'vast crevasses into which we could have dropped the *Terra Nova* with ease'.

We came at last to where the Mill joins the Beardmore Glacier and another breathtaking vista opened up. Messner and Fuchs, the only others to have attempted our route, had lost their way at this point. We had to cope with more crevasses, interrupted for a while by a field of sharp sastrugi. Unable to cross these with my skis on, I made the fatal error of unclipping and strapping them to my sledge. The very first crevasse bridge I attempted to cross without skis was a minor affair, no more than four feet wide and similar to hundreds we had safely traversed. Because my harness waistband was unfastened the sledge ropes did not restrain me as they should have done and my abrupt plunge into the dark shaft was halted only by the thin webbing strap of my ski stick looped over my right wrist.

I dangled for a moment more surprised than frightened. The fear came as soon as I realised that only my ski stick, wedged above me and still fastened to my wrist, was postponing my imminent demise. Any movement that dislodged the stick was liable to send me downwards. Throwing caution to the winds, I lunged upwards with my free hand, my feet scrabbling against each smooth ice-wall. With my arm strength sapping, I lifted my body high enough to reach the crevasse lip with my mitted hand and then to heave my chest over to safety. For a minute I lay shaking with relief until, with dismay, I realised that my stick and the other mitt in its wrist loop were loose down the hole. I inched to one side until I could squint down, my breath rushing out in a sigh of relief as I spotted the ski stick now loosely lodged some four feet down. Using my boots as grabs, I managed to retrieve both stick and vital mitt.

A few days later we strayed into a treacherous crevasse field, as lethal as any Marxist minefield, but our guardian angels saw us through successive obstacles of a hairy nature. At last we reached a steep slope some 500 feet above the edge of the Ross Ice-shelf and pitched our ninetieth camp. We were within half a mile of having walked over the highest, coldest, most inhospitable continent on earth from Atlantic to Pacific. How much longer did we stand a chance of surviving? Since all our main aims were now achieved, the only practical rationale for continuing must be to reach the ship before its departure in eight days' time.

On our ninety-second travel day, clear of crevasses at last, we hauled for ten and a half hours over the floating Ross Ice-shelf. On 12 February, our ninety-fifth day of travel, the last US aeroplane left Antarctica. In five days our ship would steam out of the Ross Sea. We were still 289 nautical miles from Ross Island. The time for procrastination was over. I radioed the Twin Otter which picked us up from the ice forty miles 'out to sea' on the Pacific Ocean.

Mike wrote in his diary that evening:

While Ran made the radio call for our pick-up, I went and stood outside. Our tent was pitched in the middle of a huge white plain and the sun was shining. To the south, a thin line ran back from where I stood to disappear beyond the horizon, towards mountains and wind-sluiced valleys. There it ran back up the glacier and then due south to the Pole. It continued on – straight for the rest of the plateau, and dropped tortuously through valleys, dune and sastrugi to the ice-shelf on the far side and so to the Atlantic coast. It was the longest unbroken track that any man had ever made.

We will never know how much farther we could have continued over the ice-shelf because there are too many ifs and buts. As it was, our achievement took us into the *Guinness Book of Records* and Mike and I were awarded OBEs. If, like Scott, we had had no option but to battle on, it is my opinion that we would have died short of Ross Island.

Scott's modern detractors make much of his stupidity in championing manhaul travel over the use of dogs. Amundsen's colleague Hanssen is often quoted as concluding: 'What shall one say of Scott and his companions who were their own sledge dogs? Anyone with any experience will take his hat off to Scott's achievement. I do not believe men ever have shown such endurance at any time, nor do I believe there ever will be men to equal it.' All attempts for a century, whether by Norwegians, Russians or Americans, to cross the continent unaided and using snow-machines or dog teams had failed miserably. In hauling our own loads across this area, greater in mass by far than the United States, we have shown that manpower can indeed be superior to dog-power and, in doing so, have partly exonerated Scott's much-abused theories on the matter.

Our record in the *Guinness Book* simply states: 'The longest totally self-supporting polar sledge journey ever made and the first totally unsupported crossing of the Antarctic landmass was achieved by R. Fiennes and M. Stroud. They covered a distance of 2,170 km (1,350 miles).'

A year later various types of kites and para-wings emerged that enabled Antarctica to be crossed with far less effort in a mere fifty days. Now it is possible to traverse both Antarctica and the Arctic Ocean with no outside support by harnessing the wind with light-weight sails. A sledger, using modern kites, can pick up and harness winds from over 180°. Until 1994 the great journeys of Shackleton and his successors, including Mike and me, made use of crude sails which could only run before a directly following wind. Should Mike and I have described our 1993 expedition, or Shackleton's for that matter, as 'unsupported' when we harness the wind, albeit in a minimal way? It is a question of definition, for there is, after all, no polar version of the International Olympic Committee.

11

How Not to Get Old?

The media in Britain reacted to our Antarctic journey in a mostly positive vein, but there are always some who will rattle on about the point of it all. Few people bother to write to counter-attack columnists unless they feel very strongly. Several letters bounced back this time, including one from John Hunt, the leader of the first ascent of Mount Everest, who reprimanded *The Independent*'s Margaret Maxwell: 'It ill becomes Ms Maxwell to question the motives underlying this astonishing feat of human endurance and courage . . . Surely at a time when, as never before, we need to develop these qualities in the young generation, this story should be accepted at its face value, as a shining example to Britain's youth.'

Various letters also flurried between the polar pundits as to precisely what had been the previous record. Dr Geoffrey Hattersley-Smith, a great polar traveller of the 1950s, wrote: 'Shackleton's party, without support, covered a distance of 1,215 statute miles. They picked up depots laid by themselves on the outward leg of the same march. It is this record that they have broken. All honour belongs to both Sir Ernest's and Sir Ranulph's parties, men of different eras whose achievements approached the limits of endurance. Comparisons are superfluous if not impossible to make.'

Another aspect which exercised the media was a supposed falling out between Mike and myself. It is as if the press cannot believe two people can survive great dangers together without being at each other's throats with recriminations immediately afterwards. Sometimes it is the newspapers that help bring this state of affairs about. Reinhold Messner and Arved Fuchs completed their supported crossing of Antarctica in a reasonably friendly fashion but *Stern* magazine contrived to portray Fuchs as the quiet hero and Messner the villain which drove a fatal wedge between them. Roger Mear and Robert Swan managed things better. After their 1985 South Pole journey they maintained what Mear called 'an outward pretence of cohesion', but in their joint book they were open and honest about one another's failings and their relationship did not degenerate into a mud-slinging match that would ruin whatever mutual feelings of respect had withstood the journey itself.

For eighteen years of polar expeditions Charlie Burton, Oliver Shepard and I managed to survive these post-expedition strains. Ollie and Charlie were loyal and honourable men. They nursed the odd grudge, as did I, but they kept these to themselves and we remained the most solid of friends as a result and despite constant rumours to the contrary. I can say the same for my good friend of twenty years, Mike Stroud.

The Director of the Scott Polar Research Institute at the time, Dr John Heap, told me that he considered that Mike and I were 'a marriage made in heaven, with your initiative and drive and Mike's scientific ability'. After our return, Mike's sister, Debbie, told a reporter: 'When I heard that Mike nearly died through hypothermia, I didn't know whether to run up to Ran and hug him for saving my brother or whether to shout at him for putting him in that danger in the first place.' Mike told the press that we had got on 'extraordinarily well' together and, when asked if he would consider another expedition with me, replied: 'I can think of nobody I would rather do these things with.' My own responses had been on similar lines.

Five peaceful months after our return from Antarctica, a tabloid reporter produced a full-page article which claimed to be based on

Mike's writings, which began: 'The smiles and mutual backslapping that marked the return of Fiennes and Stroud from their record-breaking Antarctic expedition was a sham and their ninety-five day trek was peppered with bitter arguments.'

Mike phoned me the day that the article appeared, apologised profusely and explained that he was furious with the newspaper which had completely misquoted him. He wrote back to the paper to say they had published 'unadulterated rubbish' and that he hoped to be able to go on another expedition with me before too long. For my part I had no intention of switching from Mike, should another expedition plan crop up.

At this point however I had had enough of polar travels for the time being and found I could be happy and fulfilled just living at home with Ginny and her ever-increasing Aberdeen Angus herd, by that time over a hundred head of cattle. Each animal had a name and Ginny would often ask me to go and check on Gravity or Umberto or Bakhaita or whoever in one of the fields. The farm was situated at 1,300 feet above sea-level in the heart of the Exmoor National Park and attracted fog off the surrounding moors a good deal of the time. Locating a particular cow or bull was never easy, since to me they were all black, furry and identical. Only by their yellow ear tags could I initially identify any individual, although by 1995, after two whole expedition-free and domesticated years on the farm, I had become personally acquainted with the looks and foibles of at least two dozen of the Angus and a good handful of Ginny's Black Welsh Mountain sheep.

There were also her birds, about 200 at the time, ranging free in a fenced-off field with two ponds. Quail, guinea fowl, ornamental ducks, geese and egg-laying bantams rootled, swam and squawked alongside coots, pheasants, mallards and Canada geese. Iridescent Kayuga ducks were Ginny's favourites. In the summer of 1994 Ginny entered her best looking cows at a number of West Country shows and won a great many awards. My job was to lead her bulls around the rings, wearing an NHS doctor's white coat, tweed cap and Aberdeen Angus Society tie. Ollie Shepard was often at the same shows manning the mobile stall of the country clothing out-fitters for whom he was working. That year Ginny and I also went to the Chelsea Flower Show, not to check out the exhibits, but to take the mickey out of Charlie Burton who was the head security officer controlling traffic and entry gates in a peaked cap and lapelled police-type jacket. The four of us met up on Exmoor or in London from time to time to yarn or to plan new projects that never left the drawing board.

Ginny's farm activities were profitable, though not hugely so. She did much of the work herself, including calf-delivery, basic husbandry, mucking out, feeding and field maintenance. She was self-taught as she had been in the fields of polar base leading and radio communications. To augment our income I worked for a number of lecture agencies who hired me as speaker for business conferences, dinners and awards ceremonies all over the world.

I had started to lecture about travel back in the early seventies for £18 per talk, mostly in London town halls to audiences of ladies with hats and hearing aids. As many as two or three dozen would turn up but as Ginny, who handled the slide show projector at the back, noted, 'They don't listen to you, Ran. I think they only turn up for the company and the free council cuppas.' By 1994 audiences at some of the events exceeded a thousand and, even after paying the lecture agency's 20 per cent plus 40 per cent to the Inland Revenue, we were able to live well enough and go skiing for a fortnight every December when the lecture season was over.

Ginny made many friends among the people who bought the Black Dog puppies that she bred from the original Arctic Black Dog – one was Monty Don, who later became a famous gardener. We spent a weekend with his family helping to clear some scrub on his property. Taking a rest, I observed, as though in slow motion, Ginny cutting down a fairly large tree. I watched as it fell and saw Monty, right in its path, bending over to start a chainsaw. I tried to scream a last-second warning but it was too late; the tree hit

Monty right across the back of his neck and knocked him flat. Both Ginny and I were sure he was dead. But somehow he wasn't, and he survived to become the Percy Thrower of the 21st century.

We had a good circle of friends, mostly from previous expeditions, my old regiments, or our school days, and we kept in close touch with our families. Ginny's father had died finally approving of our being married, her mother Janet and my own mother still lived in West Sussex and were good friends. My three sisters were all married, respectively to an Army colonel, an American surgeon and a Yorkshire-based farmer, so I had plenty of nephews and nieces who often stayed with us on Exmoor. Ginny's brother Charles had for years exported British-made goods to Asia and the Middle East, so we formed an export company together. I located suitable UK manufacturers, many of which had at some point sponsored our expeditions, and Charles found foreign buyers. We took a small percentage of the resulting sales contracts. Ginny's only sister, Abby, who had helped us with the Transglobe Expedition, moved to Liverpool and started her own publishing business there.

In March 1994 Ginny booked a surprise holiday for my fiftieth birthday. I was still ignorant of our destination when we followed the transit signs at Amsterdam's Schiphol Airport. The Scandinavian Airlines loudspeaker finally gave the game away – Iceland. We hired a Land Rover and spent a second honeymoon touring that weird and wonderful island of sagas, geysers and moonscapes. We had known and loved each other for four decades, we had no children and I knew that, without Ginny, there would be no point to my life.

Back home I had suffered financially due to the Lloyds insurance crash and, more ominously, I had noted an alarming drop in the number of contracts for conference presentations booked for 1995. Since this business had become 90 per cent of our income, I consulted Jeremy Lee, the acknowledged doyen of conference speakers. His advice was simple. You are, as in the movie business, only as good as your *next* project. At the time Maggie Thatcher had just dropped her speaker's fee to £20,000 but was still in great demand, as was ex-England Rugby captain Will Carling at £8,000. Conference agencies want celebrities, and if you have done nothing for a while, your chances of being chosen decrease with alarming speed. There was only one answer: another expedition, and in order to get the necessary sponsorship, it must have attendant media coverage, which in turn meant that its aim must be to complete a 'first'.

I had less than happy memories of the most recent Antarctic trip, so I would have favoured the Arctic for any future polar project. But in the autumn of 1995 I heard from Morag and Flo Howell in Aberdeen that the gossip grapevine in Norway was buzzing again. Not Erling Kagge this time, but his colleague Børge Ousland was planning an attempt to cross Antarctica solo and unsupported in the 1996–97 travel season. Ousland's rationale was clear. All the great polar challenges, north and south, had already been achieved by groups of two or more. All that was left was for an individual to try unaided.

Solo travel had never appealed to me. Half the fun of an expedition is the planning of it and, as with old soldiers, the shared memories afterwards. Also, since I make a living through books and talks about the expeditions, I need good photographs and film, which are difficult to get when by myself. On the plus side, however, a lone traveller can experience fewer frustrations caused by rivalry, discontent and, as with Mike and me, differences of pace.

The Howells warned me that Børge Ousland was an even better skier than Erling Kagge. This was the equivalent of a footballer even more skilled than Pele. Proof of this was not long in coming when, in the spring of 1996, Ousland reached the South Pole unsupported in a staggeringly quick forty-four days. Mike and I had taken sixty-eight days to reach the Pole during our 1993 crossing.

I discussed with Ginny the idea of competing with Ousland for the solo Antarctica crossing laurels. She shrugged and observed, 'You're not very fit.'

This was true. If I was to enter such a race, I had eleven months in which to train hard, for Ousland would start his solo crossing attempt in October 1996. At thirty-four years of age he was at the peak of his ability. At fifty-two I was getting rusty round the edges, but Mike Stroud had the answer – the Eco-Challenge race.

'It lasts for seven days and nights,' he told me, 'and I am entering a team. You need to be super-fit to stand any chance of even finishing the 500-mile course. Join my team.'

Mike explained that Eco-Challenge races occurred only once a year and involved athletes from all over the world. Teams from elite special forces units, physical training instructors from American universities, marathon-runners and orienteering clubs enter every year. Some are sponsored by Nike, Reebok and the like, who pay team members $10,000 each if they win, so the competition is fierce. Participants are usually selected for their supreme fitness and capacity for great endurance. The average age of the contestants is twenty-five. I agreed to sign on.

Mike had decided that his five-person team's make-up would buck the age trend. His idea was to have an age range stretching over five decades, in order to prove that endurance is not the prerogative of the young. Rebecca Stevens, Britain's first woman up Everest, was in her thirties. Mike was himself forty-one, I was fifty-two, Chris Brasher – the man who with Chris Chataway had paced Roger Bannister's first four-minute mile – was in his sixties, and Mike's father, Vic Stroud, a retired businessman and keen fell-walker, was seventy-one. In the end Chris Brasher had to withdraw, to be replaced by David Smith, a forty-four-year-old cardiologist from Exeter.

On day one at 5.00 a.m. in a high mountain pasture near Whistler Mountain in Jasper, British Columbia, seventy-four five-person teams charged away to the echo of the starting gun's signal reverberating through the forests all about us. On every side the broken silhouette of the Rockies reared above us until it was obscured by the dust cloud generated by 370 competitors.

Each team had two mountain ponies for the first twenty-six miles. Vic and Rebecca rode our stocky steeds and the rest of us ran. Then at a checkpoint, we wrapped up our gear in polythene bags and leaped into a raging river, the only way forward. Vic was swept away, and for several agonising moments we feared he would drown, until Mike rescued him. For four days we slogged up and down high mountains, through tangled undergrowth in forests, along streambeds, over crevassed glaciers and down cliffsides. Mike's face was so swollen from hornet bites that he could hardly see; Vic's backside remained badly blistered from the initial pony ride.

By day three we had moved from fifty-sixth position to forty-ninth. People from younger, tougher teams were dropping out. Next came the river section. The five of us crammed into two canoes and paddled hard day and night without pausing to rest, through some of the most beautiful scenery in North America. At the next checkpoint we exchanged the canoes for mountain bikes and, still unrested, pushed on all night and for most of the next day, suffering several falls in the process. Our final position was twenty-ninth.

The event and the previous months of training for it had successfully dragged me back to a reasonable level of fitness, but the solo Antarctic crossing attempt would need a lot more than physical abilities. I needed a support team, nutritional and medical advice, a communications network and the sort of media coverage that would persuade somebody to sponsor the whole project with at least a quarter of a million pounds.

As always before those journeys which Ginny could not join, she was a tower of strength and sound advice, based on her own wide polar experience. She would check my preparations with meticulous care and home in on key items I might have forgotten. She was never keen on my leaving her for an expedition, but she never tried to dissuade me from going. This time she was more worried than usual because I was going solo. I felt guilty and selfish and tried to salve my conscience by repeating to myself that when we married Ginny had been fully aware of how I intended to make a living.

Flo Howell was by 1995 a senior employee of Philips Petroleum in the North Sea oil fields and so was not able to take time off for this Antarctic trip. But he agreed instead to man his own radio station in the garden of his Aberdeen home and keep in contact with Morag who would base herself again at Patriot Hills and attempt to keep in daily contact with me as I crept across the Antarctic icecap. Morag had meanwhile been finding out more about Børge Ousland. The secret of his phenomenal speed, Morag said, was his adept use of the very latest hi-tech wind-chute.

'You mean a kite?' I asked.

'You'd better get one yourself,' Morag nodded, 'and learn how to use it fast.'

I found a kite-maker in South Wales and practised flying it at home on windy Exmoor. At first the string lines became frequently and hopelessly tangled with bushes and heather but I persevered until I had mastered the rudiments of keeping the kite aloft whenever the wind was reasonably strong. Even mild gusts pulled me off my feet and, had I been on skis manhauling a heavy sledge, would surely have pulled me over ice or compact snow at a goodly speed. I was impressed. But my arms were quickly sore, as were muscles in my shoulders and back whose existence I had not previously suspected. I called Brian Welsby of Be-Well Foods in Lincoln who had provided my expeditions with high-nutrition rations for sixteen years. He agreed to devise a complex carbohydrate diet for me to eat for the eleven months prior to the journey. He would also put together, with Mike's advice, special rations for the trip itself, very similar to those Mike and I had eaten in 1993.

As for my sore muscles, which in reality indicated an actual lack of muscles, Brian introduced me to my first ever fitness trainer, Jonathan Beevers, a member of the British Olympic sailing squad's training team at the recent Olympic Games in Atlanta which won more sailing medals than any other nation. I called Jonathan Adolf, for he was a hard taskmaster. In the month before the expedition a single day's programme included a brisk walk with seven-pound weights in each hand carried for two and a half hours, repeated weight exercises in a gym for one hour, pulling lorry tyres cross-country for two hours and a run for one hour and ten minutes.

I sorted out an ongoing, and sometimes incapacitating, back problem by seeing a Harley Street specialist, Bernard Watkin, for deep injections of dextrose, glycerine and phenol solution into the ligaments of my lower back on either side of the spine. This was followed up with a dire exercise regime laid down by Mary Bromiley, our next-door neighbour and famous horse physio, who advised the New Zealand Olympic equine team. She had helped Bernard Watkin keep my back from crippling me over the previous two decades. For manhauling mega-sledgeloads a working spine is fairly critical.

So is a financial sponsor to underwrite an expedition, but past experience had taught me never to waste time seeking one out until I could promise maximum media coverage of the event as a whole and said sponsor's corporate logo in particular. Astute PR reps will often turn their noses up and advise their directors accordingly if I merely promise 'a documentary film and general news reports'. Adventure documentaries, they observe, are statistically watched by a mere 1.5 million viewers at best, and general news reports can never be assumed in advance since they will be easily eclipsed by any 'heavier' news such as ministerial scandal or murder. In 1996 both ITN and *The Times* signed up to cover my solo Antarctica crossing bid, and I came across our sponsor quite by chance.

Ginny's Japanese vacuum cleaner broke down after years of sucking up the considerable output of long black hairs shed by her many Black Dogs and the fallout from her own boots and overalls on her daily return from the cattle shed. She bade me get her a new machine from the retailer in Porlock, our nearest shopping town.

'The Panasonics are still okay,' I was advised by the salesman, 'but would you like to try this new marque, the Dyson, which is bagless? It's been getting rave reviews.' Ever a sucker for clever sales angles, I paid the extra amount for the ultra-modern-looking, bagless model and, unpacking it at home, glanced at the brochure which was stuck to the box. Details of the bagless idea's inventor, James Dyson, were given, stressing that he was British. I phoned him and he agreed to meet up on Exmoor. We went for a run together to Dunkery Beacon and, a fortnight later, he wrote, 'I did enjoy our run and enclose some good running socks. I can also confirm I would be delighted and excited to sponsor your crossing attempt to the tune of £275,000.' He later stipulated that the charity we should work with should be Breakthrough, which concentrated on funding research into finding a cure for breast cancer. Both his parents had died young of cancer, and Breakthrough needed £3 million to start a special clinic at the Royal Marsden Hospital in London, the first such in Europe.

Unlike my previous sponsors, James Dyson took a personal interest in the project. As the *Telegraph* noted, he was clearly 'not a man to throw his money away on a whim'. His research engineers helped with various sledge-haulage gear designs and his graphics boss, a keen parachutist, helped my kite training on the Dyson factory's football ground. This was less than a success. A gust of wind lifted my instructor in the air, he let go, the kite took off for the main road and got run over by a Volvo. Stupidly, I failed to follow up kite-work beyond the basic principles. This was to prove a costly omission. By the time I was ready to go, I had spent eleven months becoming what one newspaper described as 'the fittest 52-year-old in Britain, albeit with defective vision, arthritic hips, lower back pain and chronic piles', but I had only spent a few days attempting to master the complex art of kiting.

Mike Stroud gave me a well thought out container of medicaments, tailor-made for the crossing attempt. He also advised me on exactly what rations I should ask Brian Welsby to provide, aiming at 5,600 calories per day as a result of his analysis of our previous expedition work. Mike was now the senior lecturer on nutrition at Southampton University and the most experienced specialist in survival nutrition in Britain. He also agreed to be spokesman for the expedition, fielding all polar queries from the media.

In the course of my two years at home I had been busy writing books and one of my last obligations before setting off for Antarctica was to complete a nationwide promotion tour for my latest title. *The Sett* was the biography of a Welsh accountant whose wife had been murdered. Unfortunately, the man partly responsible for her murder had himself been shot and killed by a man, then in gaol, who had become my friend in the course of my researching the book. I started to receive threats by telephone and the police advised twenty-four-hour security for Ginny. It could not have happened at a worse moment. James Dyson kindly lent us two ex-Paras whose job was normally to spot and apprehend industrial spies at the Dyson factory. They took turns to patrol our farm and slept there in my absence. As for the book which had landed us in this trouble, *The Times* compared it to Hemingway and it reached number four in their bestseller list. But I was grateful for the brace of ex-Paras all the same.

At the Dyson press conference at Heathrow I was told Børge Ousland was not the only man after the crossing record. The top polar Pole, Marek Kaminski, at six foot five even taller than Ousland, had been on many a fine expedition, including solo to the South Pole the previous year. Of the two, I feared Ousland more, probably due to my long-fought rivalry with the Norwegians. Like football team managers before a match, I thought it diplomatic to play down my own chances, so, when asked what I thought of Ousland, I replied, 'He's very impressive. Tall and well built. When I stand near him I feel small, like a worm.'

Ousland's pre-race tactics, however, were those of a boxer psyching his opponent. He told the press, 'Fiennes's competitors are much, much stronger.'

12

Solo South

A n American once wrote that 'nothing is more responsible for
the good old days than a bad memory', and on my way back
to Antarctica, as long latent memories of gangrene and crutch-rot
wormed their way back into my mind, I had to agree with him.
Horrid times and subsequent self-promises never to do it again
had so often been eclipsed by rose-coloured recollections of journeys past. Now I was at it again. And yet, had I stayed home and
watched the news, I would surely have forever regretted letting
somebody else grab one of the last remaining polar records without even giving it a go myself.

The trouble with the narrowness of the polar windows of
opportunity is that competing expeditionaries do not have much
choice but to turn up at the same time in the same place. There's
no sidling unnoticed in to Antarctica when you all have to collect
in Punta Arenas and await the vagaries of the weather for a flight
south to Patriot Hills. I had hoped to set out as early as possible,
ideally by 1 November. But blizzards kept me and my rivals
champing at the bit throughout October 1996 and well into
November. At least it gave Morag and me a chance to eye up the
opposition. Incongruously, we did this at a drinks party given by
Annie Kershaw who would be responsible for flying all expeditions
to their various Antarctic starting-points.

Børge Ousland was tall and well built, with a stern and
guarded manner. I was impressed by his professionalism and

focused dedication, as well as his youth – he was eighteen years my junior – and obvious physical power. I sensed that our competitive status, or maybe the memory of our row in the Norwegian press in 1990, made him reserved and that, in other circumstances, he would have been friendly enough. Marek Kaminski was thirty-three years old and, in 1995, had travelled by ski to both the South and North Poles, the first person ever to do so in a single year. He was a friendly giant of whom both Morag and I grew quickly fond.

We had all succumbed to Antarctica's magnetic pull. We each wanted to implant at least a part of it in our memories, whatever other personal quests we sought. For a while I had been the only person to cross the continent twice and, on both journeys, had met not a single other human being (apart from at the Pole Station) in a country bigger than China and India joined together. But now there were regular tourist flights in to Antarctica, as well as visiting cruise ships, with around 15,000 people a year visiting the continent. These included groups of the wonderfully named sphenisciphiles or penguin lovers.

A third party, going for the same end goal as us, was Heo Young-ho from South Korea. In fact there were six Heos, each with an identical sledge. All were wreathed in smiles and all professed earnestly to be 'going solo but as a group'. Collectively Morag dubbed them the So-Hos. Small, stocky and bright-eyed like so many Jack Russells, they were in some ways even more impressive than Ousland and Kaminski.

Three members of a team led by Lloyd Scott, an Englishman with leukaemia raising funds by walking to the Pole, arrived when the weather had held us in Punta for two frustrating weeks. One of them, Clive Johnson, was using a para-wing similar to that used by Ousland and Kaminski the previous year, and he showed me how it worked in the nearest flat field, but it was too late for me to beg or borrow one of these state-of-the art models. We left at last on the seven-hour flight by Hercules to Antarctica, three weeks behind our intended start date.

The Hercules landed gently this time and Chilean skidoo drivers ferried our cargo to a nearby Twin Otter ski-plane. Within three hours we were climbing above the Ellsworth Mountains and heading north towards the seaward edge of Berkner Island. I had wanted to reconnoitre the ice-shelf five miles out from Berkner's eastern coast, but the pilot said this would be highly expensive in both fuel and extra dollars. I had to abandon my favoured route and go for a more westerly approach from the edge of the Antarctic ice for the 250-mile haul to the true edge of the continent. Both Ousland and Kaminski had used this western route when, with far lighter loads, they had hauled to the Pole the previous year.

Group by group the rival teams were dropped off at appointed spots along the Antarctic coastline in high winds and thick fog. I waved goodbye to Morag and Terry Lloyd, hitched the sledge's dog harness around my chest, shoulders and waist, set my compass for due south and took the strain of my 495-pound load, enough fuel and food to last me for 110 days.

A fifty-knot wind from the east slammed at me, blasting my goggles. I could see nothing about me and marvelled at the skill of the recently departed ski-plane pilot. Somewhere to my right lay the western flank of Berkner Island, perhaps half a mile away. I must keep clear of its crevasse fields which had caused Mike and I so much trouble. So I allowed myself to veer left in the white-out. After eight hours' stumbling progress the wind speed shown on my hand anemometer was gusting to eighty knots in the howling polar 'night' and I was falling asleep on the move. Erecting my tiny tent took thirty minutes. Later, on the high polar plateau, I knew this job would have to be done in just three or four minutes, with a wind chill factor of −90°C, to avoid hypothermia.

The next day the wind lessened and blew miraculously from the north-north-west, a rare event in that area. So I unfurled my kite and, to my great delight, felt my skis surge forward, hauling me and my 495-pound sledge-load in the approximate direction of the South Pole. Several times gusts slammed the sledge into my legs and I collapsed in a welter of skis, sticks and tangled ropes. One high-speed crash gave me a painful ankle and smashed ski-tip – I bandaged both with industrial tape. This was the learning process. Necessity is the mother of invention and for the first time I began to develop the knack. To my enormous delight, I learned to catch the wind and hold it. But only in the direction which the wind dictated. A GPS check showed that all my wonderful sailing had taken me east of my destination. So I was forced to return to the grind of manhauling: the difference between Formula One racing and carthorse riding. Everything in my tent was wet that night. Both lips wept pus from burns like cold sores which cracked and bled when I ate chocolate.

On 18 November I made weak contact with Morag in her tent at Patriot Hills, more than 300 miles away. She told me that over two days I had gained nearly thirty miles to Ousland's twenty-one. The following day, however, saw the arrival of a steady east wind, enabling Børge to use his para-wing and cover a staggering ninety-nine miles in two days.

Throughout 21–22 November there was no wind, only white-out, and both Ousland and I manhauled due south along our separate routes. He managed nineteen miles; I completed 19.3, despite my 100-pound extra load. Not exactly catching him up, but a good sign for the 500-mile plateau ahead, where manhauling would come into its own. The So-Hos, Morag said, were progressing extremely slowly and were having sledge problems. And Marek Kaminski had been lucky to escape with his life after an accident soon after starting out.

In a high wind and thick fog he had been trying to adjust his sledge harness when a sudden gust knocked him over and concussed him. He came to some time later to find that he had been dragged by his para-wing for an unknown distance but unattached to his sledge and its life-supporting contents. He would die within hours if unable to find his tent and stove. Noticing a small bloodstain, he took a compass bearing on it, since he must have arrived from that direction. After many minutes of desperately retracing his route, with no help from tracks due to blowing snow, he felt overwhelming relief when a dark shape materialised up ahead. His head ached but he was alive! He shrugged and carried on, the Polish flag affixed to his jacket.

My heels developed blisters, so I strapped on foam snippets cut from my bedmat and tried to ignore them. My chin, windburned, became poisoned and swollen, so I lanced it with a scalpel until the swelling subsided. My eyes lost their long-distance focus after a week staring at the glare through goggles. As usual, the lids puffed up with liquid. My eyes became mere slits. I resembled a rabbit with advanced myxomatosis. Every evening I attended to my developing crutch-rot with Canestan powder and applied lengths of industrial sticky tape to raw areas. My back and hips were sore, but not as painful as on previous journeys because my Dyson harness-designers had developed an effective new padding system. For the first time, life was truly bearable, almost enjoyable, on a heavy polar manhaul journey.

The sun provided no relief. It burst through the white-out one day and almost instantly I was hot. I went on dressed just in my underwear. Any bare strip of skin quickly burned purple; the ozone hole was at its worst at that time of year. I fashioned a head cover from a rationbag which covered my neck and shoulders like the flap of a kepi. A day later the white-out returned but I still managed eleven hours of non-stop manhauling. This despite long tiring stretches of pie-crust snow, known to glaciologists as firn or névé, which is fallen snow that is granular but still has aerated cells. Its effect is to hold your footfall for a second prior to collapsing and allowing your foot to sink. This can cause the alarming sensation of a crevasse fall and can sound like a snowquake or mini explosion.

One improvement to my manhaul gear of previous years was in the ski skins department and the superior adhesive mix which glued them to my skis. No longer did they come adrift on uneven ice, so I avoided the frozen fingers caused by repeatedly having to reattach them.

A rare north wind and conditions of good visibility allowed me to try my luck at kiting again. Without stopping for chocolate and taking quick gulps of energy orange from my Thermos, I kited 117 miles in one day. I now thought I was almost certain to succeed in the entire crossing. That evening I was only able to eat my day's 5,600 calorie ration by stuffing myself. I did not *need* more than half the ration for I had not exerted myself, merely steered the kite, braced my legs against occasional rough bumps and slid at speed along Berkner Island's rim. So easy. The exact opposite to manhauling which would use up 8,000 calories in a typical ten-hour day. That night I unloaded and buried eight full days of rations weighing twenty pounds, due to the extra mileage covered.

Before leaving Punta Arenas, Marek Kaminski and I had discussed possible routes from Berkner Island up to the inland plateau. Glaciers often serve as the most sensible corridors to inner Antarctica, but only if you know the nature of the glacier in question. Not all of them move gently. Galloping glaciers, those that advance more than five centimetres a day, can surge with huge power, ice streams shatter, a wave of ice bulges to the front or snout, the surface buckles noisily and becomes no place to travel over. The Columbia Glacier in Alaska was measured advancing at thirty-five metres a day, and the Kutiah Glacier in the Himalaya surged twelve kilometres in just three months, burying forests and villages.

I did not favour the idea of trying to climb on to the plateau south of Berkner Island by way of any unknown glacier, for I remembered the troubles we had had during the Transglobe Expedition on the Scott Glacier. So I had been happy when Marek had shown me a photograph of the mountains with an arrow marking the whereabouts of the Frost Spur, the best route, he reckoned, to climb from Berkner Island's surrounding ice-shelf up to the high polar plateau. I had a mental picture of a hard climb. I was not to be proved wrong. About six hours away from the escarpment three days of poor visibility ended and brilliant sunshine revealed the Frost Spur dead ahead.

I came to an abrupt halt, overcome by disbelief and apprehension. Then I remembered a chance remark by Børge Ousland about Erling Kagge, his fellow Norwegian who had manhauled to the South Pole in 1993. 'I can't understand how Kagge took his gear up the spur without crampons.'

I had no crampons and I had never travelled alone before over a known crevassed zone. My ice-axe had fallen off my sledge during the wild kiting ride, leaving me with only a twelve-inch hammer screw. Ahead lay a crevassed and seemingly impassable barrier, a dark ice-sheathed blue wall rising to an abrupt horizon of blue sky, the rim of the polar plateau. I carried two ice-screws with foot loops and a small ice-hammer in a waistbag. In theory I might be able to rescue myself and perhaps even my sledge after falling into a reasonably shallow crevasse, but crevasses have been measured as deep as forty-five metres.

I am no climber and would not have relished the ascent with a day rucksack on my back, let alone a sledge-load still weighing about 470 pounds. Black clouds promised further bad weather. I began to haul myself up the icy incline, but repeatedly slid backwards. Exhausted, I pitched the tent and decided to split my sledge-load into four. If I could make my first ascent while sunlight still bathed the wall of the spur, showing me the best route, I could descend again, eat and sleep, and complete three more climbs the next day.

My hands were cold, and the ice-wall was about to switch from brilliant sunlight to deep shadow when I was seized by vertigo. Shaking my head to break its mesmeric spell, I gingerly retrieved my ice-hammer from its sledge bag and, using its pick end, started to grope my way up the frozen face of the spur. It was four hours before I could find an even vaguely prominent place to leave my first load. Here, in a wide expanse of nothing, I cached the rations and marked the pile of bags with a single ski.

The journey back down to the tent took just forty minutes and, with relief, I cooked my rehydrated spaghetti bolognese and drank two pints of tea. Ten minutes after I had fallen asleep, a series of katabatic wind-blasts struck the tent. Katabatic winds in Antarctica, the highest, driest, coldest continent on earth, can blow at 190 mph and arrive with just a few minutes warning. I was alarmed, but I waited for an hour before I realised I must move or the tent would be damaged. In a quarter of a century of travel, I had not encountered winds of such ferocious aggression. Sleep was out of the question. Timing the brief lulls between each fresh blast, I dismantled the tent in seconds and tied all my gear together, lashed to a fixed ice-screw. I climbed the spur again, though the wind blew me several times from my fragile holds. Once I slipped thirty feet or more, desperately trying to dig the hammer's pick into the face. Gulping air, I rested, shivering against the ice until I could resume my snail-like ascent.

The third ascent was the worst because I took a wrong route in poor visibility, heading too far to the right. That meant I had to climb twice as high to reach the rock-lined upper rim of the spur. With the clouds to the east now obscuring the escarpment, I immediately made a fourth ascent, but was too tired to manage the last two twenty-five-pound ration bags. That meant I had to descend a fifth time to retrieve them. The final climb, with the fifty-pound load over my shoulders, was easier. However, the storm clouds from the east reached the top of the spur before I did. Light snow began to fall and I could find no trace of my equipment cache. I grew cold as the day's sweat cooled my skin. I knew that twenty days of bagged rations over my shoulders would do me little good if I had lost all the rest of my gear.

I prayed hard and an hour later I stumbled on the dump. Such moments of relief and joy almost make these journeys worthwhile. Hearing the news of winning a lottery jackpot could not even approach the sheer happiness of the instant I found my tent above the Frost Spur.

I could not actually see the Antarctic plateau – in fact, I could see no feature at all in any direction – but I knew I had reached the true gateway to the Pole. The dangers of the ice-shelf and the escarpment were behind me. For the next seventy miles there would be crevasses and wicked moraines, the masses of ice debris that formed difficult barriers. But after that there was nothing but the vast open plain of the polar plateau. Somewhere in this great white land, perhaps halfway between the Pole of Inaccessibility and the isolated Russian base of Vostock, lay the Pole of Cold where winter temperatures can drop to −100°C. I ate an extra bar of chocolate and thought again of Børge Ousland's comment to the Chilean film crew: 'Fiennes's competitors are much, much stronger than him.' I might yet prove him wrong. I had caught up more than seventy of the miles he had gained by sailing the east winds. Both Marek Kaminski and the tough little Korean manhaulers were well over a hundred miles behind me after only seventeen days of travel.

I felt elated. To hell with being too old. It's all in the mind. At this stage of our 1993 Antarctic crossing, Mike Stroud and I had already been in a state of semi-starvation and severe physical decline. Yet this time I was still feeling on top form, no more hungry than after a day's training on Exmoor. I was accustomed to the raw skin, poisoned blisters and screaming ligaments which returned on every manhaul trip. The pain in my ankle from the sailing crash was better now, as were the ulcerating blisters on my heels. Life was good and my competitive urge bubbled up as I set out the next morning, the sledge dragging through the soft new snow.

If only the east winds stay absent all the way to the Pole, I would beat Børge, I thought. The harder the manhauling the quicker I will catch him. Then, on the far side of the Pole, the winds will be behind us and my newfound kite skills will cope with his para-wing expertise. After all, in a single day on Berkner Island, my 117 miles were greater even than Ousland's best day's sail. Such were my thoughts.

Only twelve hours later I made radio contact with Morag and my optimism was dashed. Ousland had used his wonderful skill at para-wing control to travel 134 miles in only four days. Ahead of me stretched the Jaberg Glacier and the heavily crevassed snowfields. This was one of the most wild and beautiful places in Antarctica and, in parts, one of the most dangerous.

On 2 December Morag told me through whining static that our charity, Breakthrough's Expedition Appeal, had already raised over £1 million towards the £3 million needed to fund a London breast cancer research centre. The further I progressed, the more money we would raise. I found this a big help when the going was especially hard. The new snow continued to grip my sledge runners, making every step a battle. For long periods my skis disappeared and often snagged one another, tripping me up. My speed dropped to a mile an hour, sometimes even less. The constant rub and strain reblistered my heels and snapped one of the steel ski bindings. The leather upper halves of my ski boots came away from the plastic foot shells and needed four hours of restitching.

On the twentieth day of my journey, I was already ten days ahead of my previous Antarctic crossing. Not because of faster manhauling, but entirely due to the single day of southerly kiting. I had no major health troubles but various sores. Crutch-rot was an old problem I knew well, caused by trouser-rub. I had treated it as usual with Canestan powder and strips of industrial sticky tape over the raw areas. Sometimes the tape would come unstuck and tear at the sores with each step. Now my morale dipped as the bandages on my privates came unstuck and the new skin on my inner thighs tore with each step. When the sun was out, sweat poured down my face. My forehead and the back of my neck were sun-seared. The ultraviolet light pouring through the ozone hole was far more noticeable than on my 1993 journey with Mike. On previous occasions in Antarctica I had seen mirages of mountains and many strange tricks that rays of light play with ice and vapour, such as moondogs, parahelia and fogbows. But this time the light was mostly too intense, too dazzling, despite my ski goggles, to gaze about at all.

Panic can arise from fear of failure, leading to the sudden collapse of the reservoir of willpower needed to sustain enormous effort and discomfort for long periods. Mike and I had already discovered the best way to keep panic at bay is to have a bank of prepared positive thoughts you can produce on demand. For example, when approaching a crevasse field, it is a great help to conduct a mental rehearsal of exactly what you will do, step by step, should you plunge into the maw of a 100-foot fissure. Thoughts can also be stretched out to help the long hours and slow miles pass by without constantly dwelling on the sheer size of the task ahead and the slow and painful breakdown of your body. Mike's term for getting lost in his thoughts was 'mind-travelling'.

Sometimes I would check my watch only to find to my disgust that a really excellent run of absorbing thoughts had after all only eliminated a few minutes of reality. I often wished to howl like a dog, anything to master my thoughts and banish the insistent desire to halt because the whole task was simply too hard and hurt too much. I would imagine that my grandfather, a pioneer in Canada and Africa, my father and my uncle, both killed in the world wars, and I knew my living family were all right behind me, willing me on. As the last mountain peaks passed by with infinite slowness, I imagined that I was hauling a heavy sledge at a gulag in Siberia, that I was undernourished and poorly clothed, and I would chant, in time to the creak of my sticks, 'Gulag, gulag, gulag.' The extra responsibility of solo travel weighs heavily.

On the night of my twenty-third day, Morag sent me a message from Børge Ousland's base leader at Patriot Hills. Børge had passed the moraine zone in conditions of good visibility and had kindly radioed to warn me of an uncharted crevasse field. By the time I received the information, I had already passed that particular area of danger. But I was grateful for his thoughtfulness. Falling into a crevasse is a bad idea at any time, but doing so alone in Antarctica can lead to a slow and lonely death, for many are mere narrow slits that can trap a human body in a slowly tightening embrace. I was fairly adept at spotting the tell-tale shadowy hollowing of crevasse lids, but many blind crevasses are so well lidded as to be invisible.

On my twenty-fifth day I was sick a few minutes after eating breakfast gruel. I felt faint and started out four hours behind schedule on a fine sunny day, neither too hot nor too cold. In six hours I manhauled six miles, despite a long, steep climb. The improved surface continued but I felt queasy and took two Imodium tablets.

A muffled explosion sounded, vibrating through the snow under my skis. Then two further rumbles in quick succession. Either avalanches or imploding snow-bridges in the great, largely uncharted, crevasse fields to my immediate west. Behind me the deep tracks of my runners disappeared to the north, where countless mountain peaks shimmered as though floating on waves of air. Ahead lay only a blue sky and the gently sloping snowfields leading without further obstruction to the South Pole. I was halfway to the Pole and 125 miles ahead of the point Mike and I had reached in the same time in 1993. I tried not to feel over-optimistic. Things could still go wrong.

To my surprise, I was violently sick again after eating my evening meal, a delicious mixture of ghee milk fat with rehydrated shepherd's pie and Smash mashed potato. I stared at the results on the tent floor and wondered how I could recycle the mess, since I had towed that ration for 400 miles and it represented energy for ten miles of further manhauling. I informed Morag that night that I had been sick, but was uncertain why, since I did not have diarrhoea. She told me to call her at any time if the symptoms persisted so she could relay advice from the camp doctor at Patriot Hill.

Two hours later the first cramps attacked my gut and I recognised at once the symptoms of a kidney stone blockage. The pains of a kidney stone, doctors say, are very similar to those of birth contractions – except that they don't produce such a wonderful result. I knew the pain only too well. In 1990 I had had a similar attack on a floating Soviet scientific sea-ice base 200 miles from the North Pole. Another time I had been working in an office, and the stone had been removed surgically within two days. I lit my cooker and heated water. I would flush the bloody thing out of my system. Drown it with water. Groaning and talking aloud, I wrenched open the medical pack that Mike had meticulously prepared in the knowledge of my 1990 attack which he had treated.

I gulped down morphine substitute tablets, two Buscopan

anti-pain pills and inserted a Voltarol suppository for quick pain relief. Within half an hour the initial pains, which I think I can safely describe as excruciating, had dulled to a background throb. But the relief didn't last.

No living cell can withstand much change to its environment. Even slight changes in acidity will kill a highly developed structure such as a human nerve cell. That's why we have kidneys: to prevent such changes in our bodies. Fifteen gallons of blood flow through the kidneys every hour and a minimum of one pint of water per day is needed to wash away all the harmful waste products that collect there. My doctor had recommended six pints a day. But I had been saving fuel instead of melting snow on my stove for drinking water, and now a chip of calcium in my urinary tract had me writhing on the ground. Had the Gestapo been involved I would have told them anything just to lessen the pain.

For six hours, every hour on the hour, I tried to call Morag. My home-made radio set was the brainchild of her husband, Flo, who had put it together in their Aberdeenshire kitchen. Once I briefly heard Morag calling 'Victor Lima, Victor Lima', my call sign. Then her voice faded into the electronic disturbances that cluttered the ionosphere. Flo had warned us, via the powerful transmitter in his garden, that severe geomagnetic disturbances were likely to cut communication for several days. I feared that, by the time I eventually made contact, bad weather would leave me stranded for further days, without relief.

At the moment the weather was excellent. I yearned to be on my way. Since I was eating nothing and using fuel only to heat snow for water rather than to heat the tent, I was not technically reducing my overall chances of success. True, Ousland was ahead of me and widening the distance, while Kaminski and the Koreans were creeping up from behind. But there was no way I could carry on until I had shifted the stone from my urinary tract. When I finally made brief contact with Morag, the doctor at her camp – a former flying medic from north-west Australia – advised me to take pain-killers every six hours and drink lots of water. For twenty-four hours, possibly the least enjoyable period I can remember ever having spent, I took more pain-killers than the doctor had advised and drank a great deal of water, but the stone failed to shift and the pains from my lower stomach, back and sides stayed with me. For an hour or so after each intake of MST, Voltarol and Buscopan the pain was muted and my desire to continue the journey mounted. Then the dreaded spasms returned with ever-increasing intensity, and I writhed about on the cold floor of the tent clasping my flanks and rolling into a foetal ball incapable of constructive thought processes.

At 11.00 a.m. on 27 December, with two days of tablets left, I decided that the danger of irreparable damage to my kidneys, as well as the risk of running out of pain-killers, was too great a price to pay for the chance of being first to cross the Antarctic solo. I pulled the pin of my emergency beacon which, a few hours later, informed a satellite signal watcher in England, who called Morag, who in turn alerted the Twin Otter ski-plane crew at Patriot Hills as to my exact position.

Nine hours later, with the fine weather beginning to change, the Twin Otter landed by my tent. Throughout the flight back to Patriot Hills, the Australian doctor fed morphine into my blood system through a drip. I was soon completely stoned and in wonderful, painless bliss. Morag recorded: 'I was quite shocked when I saw you, as you were in huge distress. We took you down to the camp after securing you on a stretcher.' My journey had ended almost exactly halfway to the South Pole and a quarter of the way to my destination on the far side of the continent.

Even if I had not been zapped by a kidney stone, Ousland with his superior para-wing skills would have beaten me. He made the crossing in fifty-five days, having sailed for over three-quarters of them. My congratulatory signal was at Scott Base to greet him when he arrived. Kaminski and the SoHos reached the Pole too late to continue.

Morag called my medical insurers, who advised immediate evacuation to a clinic in Punta Arenas. The weather, miraculously, held just long enough for me to fly on a stretcher on a scheduled Hercules flight from Patriot Hills to Punta. After an exhaustive series of x-rays, an enema and fluid injections, the Punta surgeon sent a report to my insurers, who advised that, should I then, or at any time in the future, try such a journey again, they could no longer cover any further stone-related costs. Although the stone had shifted once the morphine had relaxed my nervous system, the condition could return at any time. Any future Antarctic evacuation flight could cost over £100,000 with no insurance cover. I would have to make do with the 1980 and 1993 Antarctic crossings.

Assessing the whole enterprise afterwards, my big mistake, I realised, had been concentrating during training on manhaul fitness rather than on becoming a wind-assistance expert. Using wind assistance with kites or para-wings is very different from using following-wind devices such as parachutes or dinghy sails, employed by Amundsen, Shackleton and Scott. The toil and the suffering is cut to a minimum and that, after all, is what leads to success.

Back at home a month later James Dyson called to say the Breakthrough fundraisers had already raised £1.7 million and that he would personally add £700,000 to that total. He had produced a new 'polar-blue' Dyson model that month, and £10 from the sale of each unit was added to our fund. Many housewives bought his vacuum cleaners and, at the time, one in every twelve British women was being hit by breast cancer. The money raised by the expedition, even though it failed to achieve its physical goal, allowed Breakthrough to help set up Europe's first dedicated breast cancer research centre.

13

Sorry Straits

Trying to plan and organise two expeditions at the same time is something I have usually avoided, but whilst I was training for the solo Antarctic crossing in 1995 I was approached by a Canadian professor in his sixties with an unusual plan which he had named Transglobal. This would involve the first overland crossing of the world on a set of wheels. I met and immediately liked Gordon Thomas, who went by the nickname of Sockeye, and agreed to co-lead Transglobal. I would organise the West European sector of the journey, Dmitry Shparo, who had helped organise our 1990 North Pole bid, would handle the Soviet Union, and Sockeye would deal with North America.

Earth's widest west-east landmass stretches 21,000 miles from Clogher Head in south-west Ireland to St John's in Newfoundland. Various bits of water get in the way en route, including the Irish Sea, the English Channel, the Bering Strait and the Gulf of St Lawrence between the Canadian mainland and Newfoundland. So our vehicles would need to be amphibious. Ford had recently failed in a well-publicised quest to motor across the semi-frozen Bering Strait, but I had a longstanding love for Land Rovers and approached their then owners, BMW, who agreed to sponsor us with three vehicles and a budget of £300,000 to include the cost of rendering them amphibious.

Whilst preparing for the Antarctic expedition, I had also spent time on the Transglobal plans and had visited many vehicle components suppliers, winch manufacturers and design engineers. Eventually a method of making Land Rovers swim emerged, so I asked the Prince of Wales to be patron once again. He agreed and nominated the charity we would work with as the Macmillan Cancer Relief Fund. I called Terry Lloyd and the senior Foreign News Editor at ITN, who agreed to send a team on the expedition. Because I needed to concentrate on Antarctic preparations, I asked Anton Bowring to take over organising the European and the ocean-crossing sections of Transglobal. Flo and Morag Howell agreed to handle all the communications, whilst Charlie Burton and Oliver Shepard dealt with many of the sponsors. They also agreed to run a selection course in Wales to choose suitable individuals for the Land Rover team.

Steve Holland, an old friend from British Aerospace who had helped design my manhaul sledges for many years, joined our team, and we approached a famous yachtsman from Cornwall, Pete Goss, to help design a catamaran-shaped float which could be pulled over sea-ice by a Land Rover. On reaching open sea the vehicle could then push the float into the water, drive up ramps on to the float and provide the motor to power the float.

I went to Antarctica and left the rest of the team to progress with the Transglobal plans. Dmitry in Russia and Sockeye in Canada did various reconnaissance journeys up north to check likely routes through the most difficult regions. Dmitry was by far the most active of Russian explorers and his fame right across Siberia ensured that regional bosses would cause us minimal bureaucratic delays, even in those chaotic post-glasnost and perestroika times.

Dmitry, born in 1941, was a teacher in Moscow who, in the seventies, had risked the wrath of the Politburo by leading a North Pole expedition which they had expressly forbidden. When it proved a success the authorities changed their attitude, Dmitry became a Hero of the Soviet Union with the Order of Lenin and never looked back. Nobody could be better suited to handling the mammoth task of organising our trans-Russia drive.

On hearing that a rival Fiat expedition was making claims that confused the exact goal of what we were attempting, we clarified our precise aim as 'attempting to achieve the first self-propelled journey around earth's horizontal landmass'.

Charlie and Oliver's selection course produced a tough, bossy, highly self-confident and much given to complaining New Zealander who had a superlative record in vehicle maintenance and recovery in extreme regions of the world. Looking at his CV and comparing it with Oliver's second choice, an ex-RAF officer with comparatively little vehicle experience but really good character references, I was surprised and a touch apprehensive. However, Charlie and the other selectors were all in agreement, so I accepted their judgment.

That summer we all assembled at the Royal Marines amphibious testing area at Barnstaple in Devon. There was no public access to Instow Bay so, if our prototype amphibious Land Rover were to sink, the press could not take embarrassing photos. But all went well and our subsequent debrief sent the nine engineers involved in the amphibian's design scurrying off to complete various modifications in readiness for the Alaskan trials we planned for the spring of 1997.

Sockeye had selected the Inuit village of Prince of Wales as our trials site since we would land there after crossing the Bering Strait from Russia on the main journey. It made sense to try the vehicles out in the exact sea-ice conditions that we would encounter and, on the landward side of Prince of Wales, high snowbound mountains would also have to be crossed, using prototype track and winch methods. These too must be tried out.

Even Sockeye knew little about Prince of Wales and its inhabitants. Captain James Cook charted the Bering Strait for the Royal Navy in the 1770s and named it after an efficient but timid Danish navigator, Vitus Bering, who worked for Tsar Peter the Great and, fifty years before Cook, had sailed a Russian ship into the strait but failed to reach the American coast or even to spot it through thick fog. Russia did, however, possess colonies in Alaska with some 600 Russian settlers in the 1860s and, had the Soviet Union still owned the region during the Cold War, President Kennedy might have found things even more troublesome than the Cuban missile crisis. Luckily American dollars in the nineteenth century did good acquisitive work, which would normally have been the task of the military. In 1803 they bought Louisiana from the French, Florida from Spain (for $5 million) and Alaska from the Russians (for $700,000).

Inuit had hunted around Prince of Wales since pre-historic times – the Yupik tribe in the south and the Inupiat in the north. A Royal Navy officer who worked for the Hudson's Bay Company was sent to find copper in 1770 and commented approvingly: 'the women were made for labour; one of them can carry or haul as much as two men do. They also pitch our tents and keep us warm at night . . . Though they can do everything, they are maintained at a trifling expense for, as they always cook, the very licking of their fingers in scarce times is sufficient for their subsistence.' A US government school was set up at Prince of Wales, but the first teacher was murdered there in 1893. In 1900 up to half the community died in a measles and flu epidemic, and an American visitor in 1901, describing Prince of Wales, wrote: 'There is probably no place in the world where the weather is so persistently vile as on this cheerless portion of the earth's surface.'

On arrival at Wales I could see the writer's point, although by 1998 there was the landing strip, a public laundry house, a post office, a grocery store, a schoolhouse and the reasonably neat houses of the 150 Inuit inhabitants. I had flown out with the ex-RAF officer, Andrew 'Mac' Mackenney whose place on the team had gone to the New Zealander. As first reserve, I had asked Mac to become our base camp leader, stores supervisor and, as I grew to trust and like him, chief administrator for Transglobal's Europe sector.

Our rented quarters at Prince of Wales consisted of a large garage with work benches and space enough for both vehicles but not the float. Close by in the same ramshackle building were tiny bedrooms and a cosy kitchen which we shared with Big Dan Richards, the building's owner, a bearded ex-USAF technician with the air of a genial giant hippie. Dan had married a local Inuit lady, left the Air Force and settled down in the village to raise a family. His hobbies included solving complex computer video puzzles and hunting game on a skidoo in the wilderness that stretched east from the village and over a coastal arm of the Rockies to the nearest town of Teller. Dan operated a radio telephone, so I was able to speak daily to Ginny.

Sockeye taught us how to lassoo bucking steers. All his life he had entered steer-roping contests, despite losing a testicle when gored by a bull, and won whatever team event he and his eldest son entered, including at the 'big one', the Calgary Stampede. I went on an outing with Sockeye, towing a couple of days' food and safety gear, to scout out the coastline to the north for a suitable vehicle training area and a bay that was at least partly ice-free. After eight hours Sockeye dropped behind and when at length I lost sight of him, I turned back. He was lying in the snow amidst blood stains from some cut to his leg and not looking at all well. He had lost a glove and the temperature was well below freezing. He spoke with a slurred edge to his consonants and I sensed hypothermia was not far off. We drank tea from a Thermos before turning about and trudging slowly back along our trail. Normally I was the old man on expeditions. It felt good to have a yet more senior citizen along too. I started calling him 'Old Sockeye'.

But watching Sockeye floundering in the Alaskan snow set me thinking. I was, at fifty-three, some ten years younger than he, but I knew he worked out daily in his gym and always kept himself fit. He neither smoked nor drank alcohol. And yet a mere eight hours of gentle trudging in calf-deep snow had rendered him useless for further progress. Soon the ageing process would drag at me, and I too would gasp for breath, hold up colleagues and wonder whether it was time to learn golf or bridge. I glimpsed the future and did not like what I saw. A life without the prospect of any physical challenge would be no life at all.

For many days Arctic storms blasted Dan's hut. Then the weather cleared up. We spent a number of days and quite a few nights working out how best to progress over deep snow and shiny ice. Whenever we met up with deep soft snow we took the wheels off one by one and replaced them with triangular tracked units weighing forty-five kilos apiece. Even with all four of these mini 'tank tracks' in place we often bellied deep into drifts, whereupon someone had to wade ahead, often waist height, and dig deep channels to fix fast points for the winches. We soon became slick at such drills, and during our second month in Alaska we drove right over the York Mountain range and down to Teller, the first road vehicles ever to do so in winter.

We turned our attention in early May to the arrival of the Arctic spring and the break-up of sea-ice in some of the nearby coastal bays. There was a long spell of calm, clear weather so Mac Mackenney and I went jogging in hills where wolf, bear and wolverine prints criss-crossed those of lesser beasts, partridge and moose. Mac, who did most of our cooking and all of our sponsored food rationing, made friends with many of the Inuit and sensibly exchanged our sponsored tinned rations for fresh food and anything else that we were short of. Our New Zealander, who had strident opinions on many topics, complained in surprisingly angry tones that Mac was abusing both Inuit hospitality and the generosity of our sponsors by using barter simply to help our tight Land Rover budget to stretch further. Mac was taken aback by this verbal venom, but we avoided making an issue of the matter since our inter-team relations had been previously untroubled. But I resolved then and there to re-assess the team make-up before the main journey. After thirty years of travel with small groups, I believed I could spot a likely source of trouble fairly quickly.

In early May I found an open bay only a mile from Dan's house, so we towed the catamaran-shaped pontoon, sledge-like, along the coast behind a Land Rover, and on reaching the belt of rough pressure ice that formed a wall up to four metres high and 300 metres wide between land and sea, we cut open a rough lane using axes.

At some point soon this zone of topsyturvy ice chunks would fracture with no warning and float out to sea, so we advanced with the pontoon pushed ahead of the vehicle until it slid down into the sea, where we moored it to two ice-anchors screwed into the seaward edge of the ice. We lowered the ramps and drove up them from ice to pontoon. There was quite a sea swell, so to watch this, our first launching rehearsal, was tense, especially for the driver.

The vehicle was quickly clamped into the correct position atop the catamaran-shaped hull, and the power take-off spindle, a standard device for farmers in Britain, was clipped into a custom-made box unit which allowed us to transfer from mechanical to hydraulic power, which in turn rotated the twin paddle-steamer blades at the rear of the pontoon's twin hulls. Speed and steering functions were controlled by the driver inside the Land Rover's cab. Sockeye, Mac and I watched with pride as our three mechanics 'swam' the Land Rover far out to sea and dodged between ice-floes. These semi sea-ice conditions were, along with the snow flanks of the Rockies, the most severe obstacles we were likely to meet on our 21,000-mile journey. The trials had proved successful and we returned to Britain to announce that we would set out in the autumn of 1998. Two years of solid unpaid work by all the team, the design engineers and sponsors, had finally paid off.

Our contacts at Land Rover from the very top decision-makers to the shop floor had backed us to the hilt all the way. Then, less than three months before our departure BMW's German headquarters decided to cut various Land Rover budgets. Money was needed to launch a new model, the Freelander, so Transglobal was given the chop. So much wasted time and effort to no avail. In nearly forty years of sponsored projects, I have only suffered from last-minute sponsor-withdrawal once, so I suppose I have been lucky overall.

I had failed in Antarctica, and now with Transglobal. I had to recognise the signs. Ginny was, as always, a sympathetic shoulder to nuzzle against. We went skiing in Courcheval, the activity and the place that we both loved best. We made plans to spend much more time together, although I had learned at least twenty years before never to promise Ginny that I would do no more expeditions.

When I was in Antarctica she had been interviewed by *Woman's Weekly*. The reporter, Sue Pilkington, reported her as saying: 'Of course I worry, but I don't sit here with my head in my hands because that's very negative and doesn't do anybody any good . . . I've never said, "Don't go" and I never will. I'm supportive of everything he does.' Any suggestion that she was being brave was dismissed. 'It isn't brave at all. I was brought up in a fairly strict, old-fashioned, stiff upper lip kind of way where you don't show emotions. You don't just sit down and weep. You have to get on with things. If I hadn't been brought up like that, I might find it very difficult.'

She went on to confirm my own memory of our shared Antarctic winter. 'It was one of the happiest winters of my life . . . a crisp, dry cold not like the miserable damp we get here, and our huts were tough and warm.' When asked if she thought I would ever retire and become a pipe-and-slippers man, she replied, 'He wears bedroom slippers most of the time when he's here, but I can't see him ever retiring.'

After twelve years on Exmoor, Ginny had taken on three local people to help run everything. Gina Rawle organised the office and the lectures, Jean Smith helped out in the house, and Pippa Wood on the farm. My accountant suggested I should ask the Inland Revenue if anyone should be treated as fully employed, so I called some tax lady in Taunton who visited the farm.

'Why,' she asked, 'is your company called Westward Ho Adventure Holidays, although you tell me you have never run a commercial holiday?'

'True,' I agreed, 'but when we married nearly thirty years ago we did intend to and so named the company accordingly. Now we make an income through cattle, sheep, writing books and lecturing, but why waste £100 re-registering the company name?'

She gave no immediate response, but I could sense her bristling with suspicion. She called in two more senior Revenue officers who interrogated both of us and suggested to Ginny that she only farmed as a tax dodge. Ginny was furious and told them exactly where to get off. That started a five-year-long 'tax investigation' into our company and our personal affairs, going back ten years through our accounts and files. For five long years my accountant answered constant Revenue questions, for which he naturally charged us.

Since neither the Antarctic nor the Bering Strait projects had succeeded, my normal post-expedition income sources were not available. There was nothing to write or lecture about. At some point I would need another expedition, and it had better be a successful one, to boost the fairly meagre profits accruing from all Ginny's hard work and perseverance with the farm. The only way I knew to stand a fair chance of expedition success was by keeping fit so, remembering the extreme rigours of Mike Stroud's Eco-Challenge race in Canada three years before, I rang him up. Would he enter a team for another Eco race? And might I join it? Sadly, Mike was too busy, having taken over big responsibilities at Southampton General Hospital, but David Smith, the Exeter cardiologist and good friend of us both who had been with us in Canada, did agree to put together a four-person team and enter the 1998 race which was to take place in Morocco.

We duly arrived in Morocco that summer with a team which included Hélène Diamantides, Britain's fastest female 100 kilometre endurance racer, Steven Seaton, an accomplished marathon-runner and the editor of *Runner's World* magazine, David and me. We had trained hard together at weekends over the previous year, but we were up against the world's best endurance racers, fifty-five teams from twenty-seven countries over a race course of 300 rugged, remote miles. There were no official overnight stops and no sleeping areas, for sleep deprivation is a major feature of Eco-Challenge racing. Lack of sleep cuts in with most racers after three days and nights. But if one of the four of us failed to turn up at the finish in eleven days, the whole team would be disqualified.

In Morocco 220 racers on 220 camels lined up along the beach at Agadir. Mark Burnett, the ex-British Paratrooper whose idea the Eco race was, fired the start gun and pandemonium ensued. Our Hélène fell off at once when her mount's girth rope broke. Minutes were lost fixing it but, through the luck of the draw, we had no single camel that held us back and we had made four pairs of light-weight camel stirrups back in Britain so that we could trot in comfort, whereas a stirrupless trot would quickly become too painful on the backside to keep up. So we finished that fourteen-kilometre leg in fifth place. The next seven-kilometre sector involved a fast run along the coastline in between the advancing tide and the rocky shoreline. Slower teams had ever increasing swimming stretches as the sea reached the cliffs. We all carried heavy rucksacks.

We then reached a beach where two two-seater kayaks were awaiting each team. We launched ours through the pounding surf just as we had been taught by Royal Marines off the Cornish coast. The trouble was that the most ferocious surf back then had been two feet high, whereas in Morocco it averaged thirteen feet. Each time over the next eighty kilometres that we had to call in at an obligatory checkpoint, the surf defeated our attempts to reach the beach unscathed. Time and again both our kayaks were rolled and much of our gear was sodden.

Next came 120 kilometres of trekking and canyoning through the Atlas Mountains, burning hot by day and cold by night. When we came to the clifftop above the Taghia Gorge, lying in nine-teenth position, we found nine teams huddled about their camp cookers in a strong, cold wind. They were awaiting their turns to descend a dizzy 200-metre abseil rope to the gorge below, and a backlog of teams had developed. Most teams were using the respite for a brief sleep.

We sat around our cooker pleased with our recent trek, having overtaken eleven teams en route.

'I'm afraid I have to stop here.' We looked up sharply at David, our team captain. I could not believe my ears: he had been going so well.

'What do you mean? Stop?' I breathed.

'I have a health problem. I can't explain, but I really cannot go further.' He was adamant.

Hélène, a highly competitive person, said, 'If you drop out here, David, I will too. I see no point in carrying on if we are unable to gain a qualified place at the Finish. And teams without all four members do not qualify.'

I looked at Steven. He shrugged. 'I would be happy to keep going, but the safety rules forbid teams of less than three continuing.'

I looked around and it struck me that there might be other teams with similar problems. So Steven and I went from group to group and came upon Team California. They had just suffered the withdrawal of half their number from gastroenteritis. Greg, the team leader, was small and cheerful and had recently won the international Camel Trophy Race, a vehicle-borne form of adventure race, with the US Team. He introduced us to Kim, who was very dark-skinned and six feet tall but was of Chinese American parentage. She was a karate champion in California.

'I limp badly from blisters,' Steven told them, 'and Ran here is past his prime, but we always keep going.'

So the four of us set off. The race computers require that each team has a specific title, and we now raced as Team California. We carried on up the Atlas, slowly gaining height, after leaving David and Hélène at the gorge. Six hours later, Kim collapsed, groaning and retching. Greg recognised the trouble at once and broke the seal on his radio beacon to summon a race helicopter.

'Kim has gastro – same as our other two members,' he sighed. 'It was the water we drank on the third day out, from a harmless-looking pool.'

We waited eight hours until dawn when the race helicopter arrived and removed Kim. Five hours later we reached the riding section. Each of us drew a horse, Berber-Arab cross-blood animals of the Moroccan Army. As we mounted two tall men came up. They had lost the female member of their team, thrown off her horse and badly hurt, and their fourth member, her fiancé, had decided to stay with her. Their race title was Team Germany and they asked if they could join us. Greg had no objection even when they said that we must collectively now become Team Germany or their sponsors back home would be angry. The five of us rode the next fifty kilometres fast enough, mostly in the dark, until Greg began to vomit. He too had gastroenteritis, so we left him at a checkpoint along with our horses.

For ten hours we followed the two Germans up Mount M'Goun (4,071 metres), the second highest peak in North Africa. Here we met a team waiting to be airlifted out as one of them had severe symptoms of altitude sickness. Darkness came as we neared the summit ridge, so our German leader decided we should rest for two hours. I snuggled into my thin race-bag against the cold but, moments later it seemed, I was woken by a choking groan and horrid gurgling sounds.

Our leader, over six feet four inches and an ex-swimming Olympian, had for warmth tied up the ties of his six-foot-long sleep-bag, but was then violently sick and started to drown or asphyxiate, unable to untie the knots above his head.

Steven found a knife and cut the knots of the German's bag. The second German, Soren, activated his rescue beacon and, soon after dawn, the helicopter took away our severely ill ex-leader.

We eventually summitted M'Goun and gazed at the stupendous views of the Atlas Mountains all about us.

'Steven,' Soren announced, 'and Ran. I should tell you in confidence that I am actually Danish and only joined Team Germany because we have no national team of our own at present.' We laughed as we realised that we could not alter our team title. There were no Germans in Team Germany. After an exhausting, sleep-deprived, bloody (due to frequent falls) mountain bike ride of 190 kilometres, we arrived in the centre of Marrakesh, unqualified, bruised, 'German', but happy, for we had beaten the eleven-day deadline by twenty-four hours and seen a wild, untamed part of Africa that we could never have glimpsed as mere tourists. We

finished in twenty-ninth place, but were 'disqualified' since we had
lost two of our original team members.

Apart from the sixteen kayak casualties, fifteen racers were
treated for severe altitude sickness, many for gastroenteritis,
exhaustion, hypothermia and dehydration.

Steven agreed that we should enter the next Eco-Challenge,
wherever in the world it was planned for.

Early in 1999 I was paid a worthwhile amount as a publisher's
advance for an expedition book. An expedition I was to pay dearly
for.

14

Falling Through

Not long after the Bering Strait project was scuppered by BMW, I heard that plans for the coming millennium year were astir in Norway to knock off the Arctic journey which most polar pundits considered the only true polar challenge that still remained. All others had been achieved during the twentieth century and 99 per cent of them by the Canadians, Russians, British and Norwegians.

Børge Ousland, following his Antarctic crossing success, had tried crossing the Arctic Ocean solo, but had to be airlifted over an especially lethal area. However, he had managed to travel solo and unsupported to the North Pole from Siberia via sea-ice floes that drift slowly towards the Pole. Nobody had as yet completed the final polar grail of reaching the Pole solo and unsupported along the North American or direct route, which involved travel against the prevailing currents.

Norway had at the time at least a dozen powerful cross-country skiers with polar experience, each of whom might be preparing for the solo direct route. The rumour mill favoured one Sjur Mordre but, whoever it might or might not be, it was clear that this last of the great polar challenges was about to be broached.

I approached my literary agent Ed Victor who, despite my recent run of failures, was enthusiastic and quickly gained a good contract. So, with Ginny's blessing, I began the search for a sponsor and struck lucky quite quickly with the giant logistics corporation, Exel. They, in turn, chose the Cancer Research Campaign as our charity and Prince Charles agreed to be patron, as he had for all my expeditions for the past twenty-two years. Mac Mackenney, the linchpin of our Bering Strait project, would be Arctic base leader in Resolute Bay, helped by Morag Howell who had become the Base Manager of First Air in Resolute Bay, the air charter company that would fly me to my Arctic start point at Ward Hunt Island. Morag had by then been involved in the polar journeys for some two decades and seen all the developments in radio communication from remote places. Of that period, she wrote:

> We went from Morse Code, which we used extensively in the beginning, to the most highly advanced technical communications system ever used in any polar environment anywhere. And we succeeded. On my last trip with Terry Lloyd we made communications history by sending the first ever same day news report complete with video from Antarctica to ITN in London. Despite extreme conditions. This was the first ever Inmarsat B data transmission used to send our reports . . . We worked with many journalists and film crews over the years, and most were difficult to look after or very demanding. Or they just found the remoteness, the inaccessibility combined with the cold, just miserable. But our Terry [Lloyd] was great. Very demanding. Extremely difficult at times, and he really didn't enjoy the cold, but in all this he was a laugh! His stories, his humour and his resolve were quite unique and a perfect fit for our team.

Flo Howell dealt with all the communications planning. He is separated from Morag now, and they remain on good terms.

Mike Stroud who, as previously, planned special ration packs for me, was interviewed by the *Daily Express* and explained: 'When we walked across the Antarctic continent together, we both ended up losing more than three stone, despite eating 5,500 calories daily. Ran will start out this time eating 4,000 calories daily and slowly increase to 6,000 calories daily as his hunger mounts. We were burning 11,500 calories on many days. The question is: will he be strong enough in the last month or two to get there?' Mike himself gave me only a 20 per cent chance of success.

I had two amphibious sledges made by Roger Daynes of Snowsled, Europe's top sledge-maker, and began an ambitious fitness schedule in mid-1999, seven months before my Arctic start date. This went alongside a diet of half a pound of complex carbohydrates on top of my normal daily intake, usually pasta, brown rice or potatoes.

I ran over the moors for two hours every second day and entered numerous races. I aimed to do the 1999 London Marathon in 3 hours 30 minutes, and only missed out on this by 29 seconds. This was nonetheless an hour faster than my previous best. Then, with Steven Seaton, I paddled the 125-mile non-stop Devizes to Westminster canoe race in under twenty-six hours. In December Steven and I joined Britain's top male and female adventure racers, Pete James and Sarah Odell, for the 300-mile Eco-Challenge race in Patagonia. At fifty-six, I was the oldest competitor among the fifty-five international teams and was twenty-three years older than my three team-mates. Steven, as was his wont, constantly referred to me as 'the old man'. He still does. I got my own back every now and again, including during the seventy-eight-kilometre Swiss Alpine Marathon that year, which took us nine hours. His subsequent report on that race was disapproving:

We did the first downhill 30 kilometres in three hours. Then we started climbing. Ran isn't great on climbs and struggled a bit, so I waited for him at the top of each climb. The final ascent topped out at 9,500 feet twelve kilometres from the finish and all downhill. Ran took off from the top and I didn't see him again until I finished fifteen minutes behind him and a touch cheesed off that I'd waited for him on so many climbs, only to be run out on the final downhill stretch.

Nonetheless, we continued to team up for many races in various parts of Britain and around the world for many subsequent years.

Pete James, our leader on the 300-mile Patagonian Race, wrote for *Trail* magazine:

> The race venue was the Nahuel Huapi National Park, snow-capped peaks, crystal clear lakes, deciduous forests, bamboo groves and dry pampas grassland. The race started with a 90 kilometre canoe paddle. Then horseback across land once owned by Butch Cassidy and the Sundance Kid, then two days of trekking with hours of climbing and traversing fixed rope. We slept as little as possible, perhaps two hours a night. We (Sarah, Steven, Ran and I) had spent months testing and acquiring the best equipment possible, training for at least five different activities (running, horse-riding, sea kayaking, white water canoeing and mountaineering), competing together in shorter races and safe, quick team movement.
>
> One irony of such races is that you pass through the most incredible scenery whilst in a constant hurry, and sometimes in considerable pain and discomfort. We emerged from the bamboo on the morning of our seventh day in 14th place. A good result against a top class field.

I developed big blisters on the balls of both feet. By day five I could only hobble. But by New Year 2000 I felt quite fit. Despite various media innuendoes about my age, I had no qualms, having kept up with world-class athletes in their prime for eight days and nights.

Ginny drove me to Heathrow. A reporter from *Woman and Home* magazine that week asked the same old questions. 'When he's away,' Ginny said, 'I consciously stop if I catch myself worrying . . . I think of Ran as my very closest, dearest friend as well as my husband. It's hell when he's away and he's a wonderful person to be with.'

Each time we parted for such journeys, I hated myself and knew I was guilty of hurting the person I loved most in the world. I was like some smoker, alkie or drug addict who knows he is doing wrong but is too addicted to stop.

Mac and I arrived at Resolute Bay on 5 February, not long after the sun had reappeared there for the first time in five months. Morag met us off the plane and assured us that she had a ski-plane booked to fly me the 600 miles north to uninhabited Ward Hunt Island, the last land before the Pole, from where Mike Stroud and I had made our first foray north in 1986. Meanwhile she had fixed us up with a warm hut with plenty of space to prepare the sledge gear. She drove us through driving snow at −42°C to meet my old friend, Karl Z'berg, the legendary Swiss bush pilot I had first met here some thirty years before. We drank thick Arctic coffee in a canteen where grizzled polar buffs had their own language. 'Jafas with snotsicles', for example, was a suitably derogatory term for the scientific denizen of such a place, jafa standing for Just Another Fucking Academic. A snotsicle, as you might more easily work out, is a long frozen thread of mucus suspended from its owner's nose.

Karl clearly thought I should not set out until early March when the sun would first rise at the latitude of Ward Hunt Island. By my own reasoning that would be too late for me. There are two modes of Arctic Ocean manhauling: very fast or very slow. The Norwegians are the chief proponents of the Speedy Gonzales approach, with light equipment, medium-range calorific intake, superb fitness and, above all, the brilliant skiing technique that comes from cross-country ski-racing since childhood. Such technique becomes useless when towing very heavy sledge-loads, so they keep their loads manageable. At fifty-five I could not hope to reach the Pole in less than the fifty days, which is the sort of time Norwegians aim at. I would take at least eighty-five days and for safety would need ninety days of food. This alone would weigh 230 pounds, with fuel to melt ice to rehydrate it coming to another sixty pounds.

All additional gear – tent, sleep-bag, mat, cook kit, rope, axe, shovel, spare ski, spare clothes, repair kit, medical kit, camera, radio, lithium batteries, fluorescent marker poles, paddle, etc – would add up to another 160 pounds, too much for a single sledge travelling in Arctic rubble ice, so I had to use two sledges. When walking back along my trail to collect the second sledge, I would need a gun, and in the past had had a .45 magnum pistol on my belt. However, thanks to recent Canadian legislation hand guns were forbidden, so I now would have to lug a heavy shotgun back and forth. Altogether I would need to haul 510 pounds and relay two loads which meant every mile gained to the north would involve three travelled on the ground, with the additional hazard of white-outs. In such conditions the need to relay sledges involves a potentially lethal risk – once you have parked the first sledge and set off for your second load, you may never find it. At some point you will decide, because of the cold, to return to the first sledge. But it, too, may be impossible to find. You will then die from the cold.

I had no option but to take two sledges, so my schedule took the extra mileage into account. If I could travel north for ten hours every day for eighty days, with no rest day for injuries, bad weather or watery obstacles, my best progress would be 500 yards a day for the first three days, 1.4 miles daily for the next thirty days, 4.5 miles daily until day fifty-eight and then, with a single sledge only, eleven miles daily to the Pole.

Many unsupported treks towards the Pole have been scuppered by stretches of open water blocking the way north without temperatures low enough to refreeze the sea-water. To avoid such delays I had two buoyancy tubes designed by Snowsled that fastened to either side of my bigger sledge, making it buoyant even when fully laden with me sitting atop its load wielding a paddle. At Resolute Bay I spent a week testing equipment and hauling the sledges over ice-blocks on the sea-ice a mile from the self-catering hut Mac and I rented.

On 14 February we flew through an ever-darkening sky to the most northerly of Canada's meteorological stations at Eureka, where musk oxen and wolves roam the hills around the airstrip.

After refuelling Karl took the plane 300 miles north of Eureka to the edge of the Arctic Ocean and the conical hill at the north end of Ward Hunt Island, starting-point of most North Pole attempts. I threw a 1.4 million watt illuminating flare out of the window, giving Karl four minutes of light in which to spot and land on a flat 400 yards of drift-free snow. With lurching bumps we were down. It sounds simple, but very few pilots in the world could have managed it.

As the door opened I felt the cold of Latitude 84° North in winter. The sun would not show its face here for another three weeks, and then only for thirty minutes on its first twenty-four-hour appearance. Terry Lloyd and cameraman Rob Bowles, friends of so many expeditions, helped Mac unload my gear to the light of three moons. The two false moons, known as moon dogs, were the result of the true and central moon's light being reflected by ice crystals. I shook hands with Karl and the others, gave Mac a note to send Ginny and watched as Karl applied full power. The Twin Otter lurched away in a storm of snow and ice crystals which would remain here as a local dense fog for many hours. I tugged on my dog harness, attached it to the sledge ropes and started to lug the first sledge northwards, not yet on sea-ice, but, for the first few miles over Ward Hunt ice-shelf, land-attached ice jutting out into the Arctic Ocean.

The Twin Otter's lights disappeared, as did the drone of its engines. Silence but for my breath and the sound of my own heart-beat. On my hand compass I set a bearing to geographical north. The compass needle pointed to magnetic north 300 miles west of Resolute Bay and 600 miles south of my position. I had to set a magnetic lay-off of 98°, then wait a minute for the needle to settle in the less than normal viscosity of its alcohol-filled housing. I could not use the North Star as a marker because it was almost directly overhead. Nor, pulling a sledge, could I use my GPS position-finder for direction.

The clothing policy I had evolved over twenty-eight years of polar expeditions was based on non-stop movement and light, breathable clothes. Any halt, however brief, led quickly to hypothermia. Once my metabolism was up and running, pumping blood furiously to my extremities, I took off my duckdown duvet and stuffed it in the sledge next to my Thermos and 12-bore pump shotgun. Now I was wearing only a thin wickaway vest and long johns under a black jacket and trousers made of 100 per cent ventile cotton. Cotton is not windproof so body heat is not sealed in. Alas, no modern clothing is completely breathable so cotton is still in my opinion the best compromise for polar heavy manhaul travel.

My schedule allowed two days to descend the soft snowfields of Ward Hunt Island's ice-shelf to the edge of the sea. But I kept going without a rest and established both sledges at the coastline within seven hours. This boded well, for the sledges were running easily despite their full loads, the low temperature and soft, deep snow.

Geoff Somers, an experienced polar man, had advised me to include a cantilever design in the sledge moulds. Snowsled had done so, and the result was good. After seven hours of hard manhauling, I was cold and tired. I erected the tent in six minutes and started the cooker in four. These two acts, which I had practised thousands of times, are the key to survival, and with two usable hands can be performed easily in extreme temperatures, high winds and blizzards. I got into my sleeping bag, drank energy drink, ate chocolate and set my alarm watch for three hours. The weather was clear when I woke and the sea-ice quiet to the north, a sign that the ice-floes were not on the move.

The moon had vanished behind the hills so I would not be able to differentiate clearly between solid ice and thinly skinned zones, so the overall silence was a bonus. I re-stowed the big sledge, moving rapidly to keep my body core temperature up. I decided to take the smaller sledge first. Its load was 210 pounds, a third less than the eight-foot sledge. The ice-floes that are blown south against this northern coastline of the Canadian Archipelago often shatter against the ice-shelf, and blocks up to thirty-five feet high tumble over one another, often forming huge ramparts that run east-west for miles. Behind them a scene of utter chaos can meet the despairing manhauler, slab upon slab of fractured ice-block as far as the weary eye can see.

Travelling over the past twenty-five years our group had four times broken the current world record for unsupported travel towards the North Pole. Each time the ice conditions north of Ward Hunt Island were invariably bad to horrible. To my joy I saw that, this year, the previous condition of wall-to-wall ice blocks was broken down by a series of crazily laid out but negotiable lanes. The ice 'defences' were split everywhere by recent breakage. In many places, like the cauldrons of witches, thick black fog swirled above new cracks and pools as the 'warmer' water gave up its comparative heat to the supercool air above. This phenomenon is known as frost-smoke or sea-smoke. New ice-floes of twilight grey zigzagged through the stark black outlines of ice obstacles wherever I looked, a fragile highway to the North. My schedule of 500 yards a day for the first three miles from the start began to look pessimistic.

I pressed on over the fissure dividing land from sea and into a broad belt of rubble. One sledge at a time. I took my skis off. For a few hundred yards I would have to haul each sledge over a vista similar to that of post-war Berlin. Between each ice slab soft, deep snow covered the fissures. I often fell into traps, sinking waist-deep into pools of *nilas* slurry, that thin elastic ice crust, a dull grey in colour, which forms on calm sea-water and is easily bent by a wave or mere swell.

I came to a wall of slabs fifteen feet high and, to help haul the sledge over it, I decided to test the simple pulley system devised by Mac. I attached it to the big sledge, which I had hauled first to the wall, and tugged it jerkily up the forty-five-degree slope. With the 300-pound sledge at the top of the wall, I detached the tiny grapnel hook and rolled up the pulley line. Too late I heard movement, and leaped towards the sledge, which quickly gathered momentum in its slide over the edge of the wall. I managed to grab the rear end, but my 200-pound body weight was not enough. The far side

225

of the wall was a sheer fifteen-foot drop on to sharp ice-blocks. I landed hard and was winded but unhurt.

At first the sledge appeared to be undamaged, but closer inspection revealed a thin tear under the bow, presumably where the sharp edge of the ice-block had made contact with the 300-pound falling sledge. I tried pulling the sledge, but snow lodged in the damaged section and dragging it became difficult. Also, the sledge's hull, designed to be 100 per cent watertight, was compromised. There was no course but to head back to the hut on Ward Hunt Island and find suitable materials to effect a repair. In the mid-1980s we had erected a canvas cover over the steel skeleton of a hut long abandoned by scientists and installed a couple of wind-powered generators to provide electricity. With minimal safety gear in a bag, I skied for two hours back up my trail and via the Twin Otter's landing strip about a mile east of the huts. The camp looked ghostly, unchanged over the twelve years since my last visit. After an hour spent digging out the door of our old hut, I gained entry. There were a few tools and canvas materials, so I decided to bring the sledge back to make it watertight and capable of being towed in all conditions. I skied back to the sledges and loaded minimal camping gear on to the smaller one. Then I lashed the damaged sledge on top. Uphill through soft snow was slow going, some several hours back to the hut.

I put my tent up inside the canvas-skinned hut. The temperature had fallen to −49°C and a bitter breeze caressed the frozen canvas. With the cooker on, a hot drink inside me and fully clothed, I began the repairs. Some hours later I was back at the ice edge, happy that my work had made the sledge easy to tow, even in soft snow, and pretty much watertight again.

I found my previous trail easily. I camped on thin ice and woke to hear all manner of noises: cracking and rumbling, then silence. Then a frightening roar that galvanised me into movement from the depths of my four-layer sleeping bag. The moon was full, the scenery startlingly beautiful. Moonshadows played about the upended ice-blocks and the ice shapes took on an uncanny resemblance to animals, castles or giant mushrooms. Fearful of imminent upheaval due to the tidal influence of the full moon, I pressed on northwards. I dared not take either sledge too far because the surface between the rubble fields consisted of very thin ice, through which my probing ski stick sometimes passed with ease into the dark waters below. After eight hours I had moved both sledges more than a mile to the north. My morale was high, for the sledges ran well whatever the surface, far better than any previous design. My mental arithmetic raced ahead and I estimated a Pole arrival in only seventy days.

I kept an eye open for a good campsite. Sea-ice grows at a rate of two to three feet a year. Ice-floes that survive intact for more than two years are easy to identify, for the broken blocks that litter their surfaces will be rounded off by two or more years of summer melt. Floes in this condition are known as multi-year floes. The wind and snow abraid them into hummocks. Such floes can be at least eight feet thick and are more likely to withstand great pressure from neighbouring floes. They can provide good landing strips for ski-planes. Above all, the surface snow will have had most of its original salt content leached away by the sun and so will provide good drinking water. Unfortunately, time passed without the appearance of any floe older than a few months. Indeed, the area began to show increasing signs of recent open water only partially refrozen. My ski stick frequently sank through the surface skin, forcing me to detour to safer ice.

I had been travelling for well over the intended ten hours and making good progress, but was tired and cold. I ate a chocolate bar every two hours to ward off hypothermia, but was still very weary and decided to camp on any surface that looked solid. I came to a zone of interlacing fractures. The moon had vanished and, whenever I stopped, I heard the grumble of ice on the move. I tried to avoid a trench of black water, and mounted a bridge of twelve-inch-thick slabs, buckled by floe pressure. I had the small sledge with me and the big one 500 yards to the south. I clambered over the slabs with my skis on. The sledge followed easily in my wake.

There was no warning. A slab tilted suddenly under the sledge, which responded to gravity and, unbalancing me, pulled me backwards. I fell on my back and slid down the slab. The noise that followed was the one I most hate to hear in the Arctic, a splash as the sledge fell into the sea.

I kicked out with my skis and flailed at the slab with both hands. One ski boot plunged into the sea and one gloved hand found an edge of the slab. Taking a firm grip I pulled my wet foot and ski out of the water. I unfastened the manhaul harness. I was already beginning to shiver. I squirmed around until I could sit on a flatter slab to inspect the sledge in the gloom. It was under water, but afloat. I hauled on the traces, but they were jammed under the slabs. Seventy days' worth of food and thirty of fuel were on that sledge – and the communications gear. Without it, the expedition was over. A nearby slab crashed into the sea: the ice was moving. I had to save the sledge quickly. Soon I would be dangerously cold.

With my feet hooked around a slab, I lay on my stomach and stretched my left arm under the slab to free the sledge trace. I took off my mitt so that I could feel where the rope was snagged. For a minute or so I could not find the underwater snag. Then by jiggling the rope sharply, it came free. I pulled hard and the sodden sledge rose to the surface. My wet hand was numb but I could not replace the mitt until the sledge was out of the sea. Gradually the prow rose on to a slab and water cascaded off its canvas cover. Minutes later the sledge was on 'dry land'. I danced about like a madman. Both my mitts were back on and I used various well-tried cold hands revival techniques to restore life to the numb fingers. Usually they work and my blood returns painfully to all my fingers; this time they did not.

I took the wet mitt off and felt the dead hand. The fingers were ramrod stiff and ivory white. They might as well have been wooden. I knew that if I let my good hand go even partially numb, I would be unable to erect the tent and start the cooker – which I needed to do quickly for I was shivering in my thin manhaul gear. I returned to the big sledge. The next thirty minutes were a nightmare. The cover zip jammed. With only five usable but increasingly numb fingers, precious minutes went by before it was free and I unpacked the tent. By the time I had eased one tent-pole into its sleeve, my teeth were chattering violently and my good hand was numb. I had to get the cooker going in minutes or it would be too late. I crawled into the partially erect tent, closed its doorzip and began a twenty-minute battle to start the cooker. I could not use the petrol lighter with my fingers, but I found some matches I could hold in my teeth.

Starting an extremely cold petrol cooker involves careful priming so that just the right amount of fuel seeps into the pad below the fuel jet. The cold makes washers brittle and the priming plunger sticky. Using my teeth and a numb index finger, I finally worked the pump enough to squirt fuel on to the pad but was slow in shutting the valve; when I applied the match a three-foot flame reached to the roof. Luckily I had had a custom-made flame lining installed, so the tent was undamaged. And the cooker was alight – one of the best moments of my life.

Slowly and painfully some feeling came back into the fingers of my right hand. An hour later with my body warm again, I unlaced my wet boot. Only two toes had been affected. Soon they would exhibit big blood blisters and lose their nails, but they had escaped true frostbite. All around the tent cracking noises sounded above the steady roar of the cooker. I was in no doubt as to the fate of my bad hand. I had seen enough frostbite in others to realise that I was in serious trouble. I had to get quickly to a hospital to save some fingers from the surgeon's knife. I had to turn back.

I hated the thought of leaving the warmth of the tent. Both hands were excruciatingly painful. I battered ice off the smaller sledge, unloaded it and hauled it back to the big sledge. I set out in great trepidation. Twice my earlier tracks had been cut by newly open leads, but fortunately needed only small diversions to detour the open water. Five hours later I was back on the ice-shelf. I erected the tent properly and spent three hours massaging my good hand and wet foot over the cooker.

I drank hot tea and ate chocolate. I felt tired and dizzy, but the wind was showing signs of rising and I knew I should not risk a high wind chill. The journey to the hut took for ever. Once I fell asleep on the move and woke in a trough of soft snow well away from my intended route. Hypothermia is a danger at such times. When I feared its onset I often spoke to myself aloud, trying to enunciate the *My Fair Lady* lines about the rain in Spain, because an un-slurred voice is about the only reliable assurance that I was not on the slippery path to hypothermia and, on a solo expedition, death.

When at length I came to the old hut, I erected the tent on the floor, clumsily started the cooker and prepared the communications gear, which we called a Flobox after Flo Howell. I spoke to Morag in Resolute Bay. She promised to evacuate me the following day on the Twin Otter scheduled flight due to change over the weather men at Eureka.

The fingers on my left hand began to grow great liquid blisters. The pain was bad so I raided my medical stores for drugs. The next day I found an airstrip near the hut and marked its ends in the moonlight with kerosene rags. When I heard the approaching ski-plane I lit the rags and prayed the First Air pilot, not Karl this time, would not funk the landing. He didn't, and some forty-eight hours after my arrival at the hut I was on my way to try to save my left hand. At Resolute Bay Morag did what she could with immediate dressings and took me to a nurse. Morag, who had seen me survive kidney stone cramps and other batterings, understood frostbite at first hand. She later wrote to me: 'I have had some (frostbite) in my time and can relate to the pain. It's awful. All you want is for it to stop. I know that when you froze your hand you bound it tight. I have always believed that you stopped the circulation by that action, and that's what caused you to lose the fingers. There you go, that's my one gripe over twenty years. Mo.'

That night I flew to Iqaluit on Baffin Island where, after intravenous antibiotic therapy, a doctor started to open up the big finger blisters. After transference to the Ottawa Hospital, I was in

the hands of frostbite experts, Doctors Conrad Watters and
Heather O'Brien. Their initial report stated:

> The left hand demonstrates severe thermal injury to all five digits.
> The thumb is blistered from the mid portion and the fingers are
> all edematous throughout the course.
>
> His right foot is remarkable for areas of frostbite covering a
> coin-sized area of the distal great toe and a corresponding por-
> tion of the second toe on the right side. He was unaware of this
> injury prior to changing his clothing to begin hyperbaric treat-
> ment. I am optimistic that he can get some benefit from
> aggressive and immediate hyperbaric oxygen therapy.

Over the next two weeks I spent sixty hours sitting in a long
oxygen tank like a goldfish bowl. A fat Frenchman sat in the far
end of the tank facing me. He had diabetes leg damage. We both
watched videos (in French) on a roof-screen of our container tube.
The Frenchman was constantly and noisily flatulent in the
enclosed tank. When the hyperbaric treatment ended, Conrad
Watters reckoned a few millimetres of my fingers had been saved.
The down side was that I couldn't see properly. Everything
remained out of focus and blurred for the next three weeks.

I called Ginny, whose immediate reaction to my being less able
to help with the cattle was, 'Typical, and we're already short-
handed on the farm.' To a *Times* reporter she commented, 'We
know several people here on Exmoor who have lost bits of fingers
or worse in farm machinery or with ferret bites. As long as Ran
doesn't leave his finger bits on the edge of the bath, as he once did
with a blackened toe, I'll be happy to see him back next week. He
did put on a lot of extra weight for the expedition, so now he'll
have to take it off again. I might hide the farm machinery and give
him a dung fork to clear the cowshed by hand.'

15

Amputations

I returned to Britain with another failure under my belt, a scant amount raised for our charity and a disappointed sponsor. Kidney stones and frostbitten digits are no more acceptable to critics as reasons for failure than are unseasonal polar storms or crevasse accidents. I suppose that, over a twenty-six-year period of polar travel, the frostbite odds were always narrowing. This time they caught up with me, which was a shame because everything was otherwise looking good, the sledge was going well and I was in peak condition.

There is, of course, no point in crying over spilt milk since, if you go for the big ones and you win some in your lifetime, you can be sure you will lose at others on the way. The best course, I've usually found, has been to shrug, note what you've done wrong and apply yourself quickly to trying again. This, my standard policy over the years, sadly did not look like working this time because my damaged fingers were liable to be amputated fairly shortly, which would seriously affect extreme cold projects in the future. One of my firm rules in selecting individuals for polar travel had always been to avoid anyone, however experienced or skilled, who had any history of frostbite damage. Badly bitten noses and ears were okay. Fingers and toes were not.

I also knew that this Arctic failure, coming hot on the heels of the Bering Strait cancellation and the Antarctic solo kidney stones, was asking for trouble from the UK media, who are almost as eager to savage a failed expedition leader as a football manager who has lost a couple of key matches. Most of them enjoyed being witty at my expense. *The Times* offered me solid advice.

It is a reasonable bet that if Sir Ranulph's frostbitten hand allows it, he will be planning to trudge through the snow again. Doggedness and fortitude saved his life on this occasion, but he was fortunate to survive and time is not on his side. The older someone is, the more they are liable to suffer from hypothermia, frostbite and diseases associated with the cold. The reflexes that come into play to protect skin when its temperature is dangerously lowered are less efficient, so corrections to skin temperature may be slow and frostbite more likely. So Sir Ranulph should opt for holidays in Spain.

Media barbs the week after I returned home from Ottawa were easily kept in perspective by the more immediate worry of what to do about my damaged fingers. They throbbed most of the time and complained loudly with needle-sharp pain when brought into contact, however lightly, with any object, even clothing material. To avoid this, especially when trying to sleep, was often difficult. Two of my friends who were surgeons advised speedy amputation of the damaged fingers to avoid complications such as gangrene. After checking the records of a number of specialists, Ginny found a surgeon in Bristol, Donald Sammut, with a history of brilliant treatment of damaged fingers. The south-west of England produces very few frostbite cases, but so what? Damaged fingers are all the same once cut off, whatever the original reason for the trauma, and I was greatly relieved when Donald agreed to deal with my fingers.

A friend from the Institute of Naval Medicine in Portsmouth, for whom I had previously completed cold water research work in his immersion tank, telephoned out of the blue. Under no circumstances, he warned, should I undergo any amputations until at least five months after the date of the accident.

'Why not?' I asked, perplexed.

The Navy surgeon explained that he had seen many divers with toe and finger damage which had been operated on too early before the semi-traumatised tissue that lies between the dead ends and the undamaged stumps had had time to heal properly.

'This is the tissue,' he stressed, 'that will be needed – after the dead finger ends are cut away – to stretch over the stumps. So it must be strong, elastic, healthy tissue; not severely damaged, as it is now. More fingers have been shortened unnecessarily by premature surgery than by the original damage from the bends or from frostbite. So don't you let them cut you up too early, Ran, or you'll regret it. Your new stump material will simply fail to do its job and you'll end up back on the chopping block with ever shorter fingers.'

Donald's own policy on the best timing for the surgery was similar. He advised me 'The best method is to advance the "frontier" skin, which is immediately adjacent to the frostbite and is inflamed. It is crucial that this skin returns to supple normality before any attempt is made to dissect and advance it.'

Throughout this period I took penicillin to keep gangrene from developing in the open cracks where the damaged but live flesh met the dead and blackened ends. Mary Bromiley, the physiotherapist who had over twenty years dealt with my aches and pains, applied laser treatment and electrical stimulation to the stumps. Every three weeks I also drove to Bristol to Melanie Downs-Wheeler, a specialist physiotherapist, who taught me gripping and bending exercises for each semi-mummified finger, and then, the dreaded moment, out came her debridement tweezers and for the next fifteen minutes, which is all I could stand, she picked away at the dead and damaged tissue in the semi-live areas to 'encourage healing there'.

Most days I tried to help Ginny with the cattle and sheep. I bought her two black alpacas for her birthday. She named them Punto and Mucho and they soon became inseparable companions to the black sheep. After their bi-annual shearing they resembled Spielberg's ET, gangly with huge liquid and appealing black eyes.

The tax investigation into the affairs of our company and

ourselves, sparked off by my enquiring back in 1995 about self-employment rules, had been ongoing ever since, at considerable cost in terms of my accountant's responses to the voluminous questionnaires from the Revenue. Since one of the main lines of attack by the taxman was that all Ginny's farming activities were a mere front to offset or avoid taxation, the five-year-long investigation with its often threatening overtones both worried and depressed her. No farmer worked harder or more meticulously than did Ginny, and in weather conditions that were at best sturdy, at worst foul, for Greenlands is, at 1,300 feet above sea-level, one of the highest – if not the highest – working farm in the south-west. Driving sleet and fog off the adjoining moors and the nearby Atlantic were the norm for much of the year. Midnight calving and difficult deliveries in sodden clothes were common every spring, and snow drifts would cut the farm off from the road over the moors, our only access point, for up to three weeks a year. So Ginny did not need officious taxmen telling her that her only aim in life was to defraud the Revenue. We were referred to as 'Registered Investigation Case F18579'. An old expedition friend who had become a part-time tax commissioner in Northumberland advised us to take the matter to our local commissioners. This we eventually did, and finally the adjudicator at the court concluded that the Revenue had handled our tax affairs very badly, should pay the court costs and close the investigation. There was no compensation or apology after five years of worry and doubt.

Our long-time expedition patron, Prince Charles, asked us to visit him at his Highgrove home. He wished me well with my pending amputations and we joked about old times with Dr Hammer. The Prince had been the active and caring patron of all my expeditions for twenty-five years, during which we had raised millions of pounds for the charities he had nominated.

After four months of living with grotesque, witch-like talons, purple in colour, sticking out of my stumps, I could take it no longer and, with another month to go before Donald Sammut was due to cut them off, I decided to take the matter into my own hands. Each and every time over the previous sixteen weeks that my fingers had hit or merely brushed against anything, never mind something hot, I had sworn at the pain. Ginny suggested that I was becoming irritable.

The answer was obvious. The useless finger ends must be cut off at once, so they could no longer get in the way and hit things. I tried tentatively to cut through the smallest finger with a new pair of secateurs, but it hurt. So I purchased a set of fretsaw blades at the village shop, put the little finger in my Black & Decker folding table's vice and gently sawed through the dead skin and bone just above the live skin line. The moment I felt pain or spotted blood, I moved the saw further into the dead zone. I also turned the finger around several times to cut it from different sides, like sawing a log. This worked well and the little finger's end knuckle finally dropped off after some two hours of work. Over that week I removed the other three longer fingers, one each day, and finally the thumb, which took two days.

My physiotherapist congratulated me on a fine job, but Donald Sammut was not so happy. He later recorded my visit: 'Ran appeared one day on a routine appointment and calmly told me he'd chopped off his fingertips. We had quite a heated exchange over this. He risked making it worse.' I apologised to Donald, but felt secretly pleased with myself since life improved considerably once the gnarled mummified ends no longer got in the way. Ginny agreed that I had done the right thing. She no longer had to tie my tie for me, nor put in my cufflinks before I gave a conference talk.

That summer we received an invitation for the Millennium Year meeting of the Fiennes tribe at the family HQ, Broughton Castle near Banbury, in which the family boss has lived since 1377. This clan coming-together involved 200 of us from all over the world and all descended from Frederick Fiennes, the 16th Lord Saye and Sele. James, the 1st Lord, fought at Agincourt and was Treasurer of England. You can catch up with the rest of them in the family tree on page 360.

At least sixteen of us at the castle that lovely summer's day were the progeny of my mother who, at eighty-eight, was the oldest person present. Our host, Nat, had been a pageboy at her wedding. Ginny and I had a great time meeting my sisters' families, including my American nephews and nieces. The castle is surrounded by a wide moat complete with drawbridge and portcullis, and Ginny provided Nat with iridescent Cayuga ducks from our farm that swam around in the Broughton moat weed, out of reach of foxes. My cousin Joseph Fiennes was at the meeting. He was no stranger at the castle, having recently starred with Gwyneth Paltrow in *Shakespeare in Love*, which was filmed there. His brother, Ralph, was unfortunately away in America.

The very first Fiennes who came to England that we know about was Eustache Fiennes, who came from a village called Fiennes in northern France which is now an industrial suburb of Boulogne. According to the historically accurate picture diary that is the Bayeux Tapestry, Eustache arrived at Hastings in 1066 and, commanding the Norman Army, he personally cut off the English King Harold's head with his axe and was given various castles as a reward. One was Herstmonceux just a few miles from Hastings, but subsequent Fienneses sold it. Today, only Broughton, which is open to the public for most of the year, remains. Oliver Cromwell plotted against the Royalists using Broughton as his local base, since most of the Fiennes family were fervent Parliamentarians. Cromwell's war jacket is still on show in the castle.

Before we left Broughton my sisters and I agreed that we should meet up in Lodsworth as our mother was moving, after forty years in the village, including twenty as president of the football club, to a retirement home in nearby Petworth. She was becoming increasingly forgetful and a little lame, so she had decided to make the move whilst she was still physically able. She wanted us all to decide which items of furniture each of us would like, since in her new one-room home there would be no space for most of it. We all sat around the kitchen table and one by one – starting with Sue, the eldest – listed our choice, little knowing that within three years only two of the five of us would still be alive.

Ginny had for years only been able to go on holiday or on expeditions with me by hiring an Animal Aunt, a sort of experienced animal-babysitter, from a company in Sussex. She had often been sent one particular girl, Pippa Wood, who was excellent with the animals. Eventually Pippa, who was self-employed, agreed to work at Greenlands whenever needed, enabling us to enjoy holidays again with old friends like the Gaults and the Bowrings without Ginny constantly worrying about the farm. That summer, unable to race competitively, I had time on my hands and almost learned to relax. We went for long walks with the Black Dogs, Pingo and Thule, great-grandchildren of the original Black Dog Ginny had brought to England a quarter of a century before. We expanded the farm by thirty-five wilderness acres, bought from our neighbour, mostly a place of wild flowers, jack snipe and a tumbling stream. A good place for picnics and bird spotting, with plenty of shelter for the cattle in winter.

Five months after my Arctic accident, Donald Sammut amputated the remaining bits of dead finger on my left hand and folded the previously semi-damaged skin neatly over the newly gaping stumps. He described the operation in simple terms:

Ran's Do-It-Yourself amputations had rather forced the issue, since the resulting raw surface had opened up the core of the amputated bone to the elements and we no longer had the protection of the mummified dead finger tips. The results of his 'surgery' included the middle finger bone being particularly exposed, protruding free well beyond the skin cover. Nevertheless this did not much compromise the eventual surgery, and I operated on 14 July, removing any residual dead tissue and providing skin cover to the tips. This skin cover consisted of islands of skin dissected virtually free on a stalk of nerve and artery advanced to cover the tip of each digit: this permits one to preserve maximum length (and crucial tendon insertions which preserve maximum power) while providing good quality, sensate skin similar to pulp.

So Donald grafted on extra patches cut from the sole of my left hand. He is a superb surgeon and anything I have been able to do since then which involves intricate finger movement is thanks to his meticulous skill.

I spent a post-operative week in hospital doing nothing in between visits by Ginny, various good friends and my cousin Rosalie Fiennes, who gave me a book which appeared from its cover, to be the Works of Shakespeare but which was in reality the first book about the as yet unknown boy wizard, Harry Potter.

'You may think it is a children's book,' Rosalie told me, 'but don't be embarrassed. Nobody will know it's not Shakespeare. I have read it and, believe me, it's brilliant.'

I whiled away the hours with the book and have been a Potter fan ever since.

Back at Greenlands again with time on my hands – one of them gloved after the operation – I was sorting through some long over-due filing when I came upon a box of documents I had forgotten all about. The papers had come a long way. In 1995 when I was working as a lecturer for an Abercrombie and Kent cruise ship, I had found myself in Antarctica and, because that year was unseasonably warm with lots of loose ice the ship was able to visit a scientists' hut on the coast not previously reachable by cruise ships. Our German skipper asked the chief lecturer, Dr John Reynolds, Europe's top polar geologist, to check out the hut's safety before allowing his shipload of mostly American tourists ashore and John asked me to join him.

We beached the inflatable boat close by the hut. The last scientists to have worked there, some thirty years before, had left everything in place – food, equipment, six bunk beds and a great many books, including notes on the very first studies of what later turned out to be the ozone hole. Many of the scientists' notebooks were damp and stuck together, so John decided they should go back to Britain, and when I flew back to London from Chile I handed them over to Dr John Heap, Director of the Scott Polar Research Institute. Two of the notebooks, unlike the rest, were not on Her Majesty's Stationery and, since John Heap did not want them, I took them home and soon forgot about them.

I now found that the pages of one of the books had, over years of damp summer atmospheres presumably, become largely glued into a pulped mess. The other was in better condition and appeared to be a rambling diary written in biro. I could only access forty-five mostly separated and disjointed pages, but the little that I could read was fascinating.

I called Ed Victor, my literary agent, who agreed to approach a publisher, and I phoned Paul Cook, chief paper conservation expert at the Greenwich Maritime Museum, who gave me detailed advice on, and materials for, un-sticking the pages. Using Gore-Tex slips and an iron, I eventually managed to separate and render legible some 60 per cent of the diary, which turned out to be that of a fifty-five-year-old Canadian welfare worker named Derek Jacobs who, during the 1970s, had learned of his family's massacre at the hands of Nazis in 1945.

Determined to locate his mother's murderer, a policeman escorting the Wallern Death March during the last week of the war, Jacobs joined the Secret Hunters, an organisation dedicated to tracking down perpetrators of war-time atrocities. The diary showed that he had eventually traced the man he believed to be his mother's killer to Bermuda where the former Nazi had chartered a yacht to sail to Antarctica in secret quest for a reputed seam of gold. Jacobs had joined the yacht as crew.

When my application to inspect the records of the 1945 Death Marches drew no response, I asked a German friend, Mike Kobold, to trick his way into the archives at the Zentrale Stelle zur Verfolgung von Nazi Verbrechen and photocopy 400 pages of the relevant documents. I also tracked down Prince Yurka Galitzine, the man who had originally set up the Secret Hunters, and I went to visit him at his Mayfair address.

I spent the next eight months checking out most of the events described in Jacobs' diary and travelling the Sudetenland Death March route in Czechoslovakia and East Germany with Mike before settling down to start writing. I intended to produce the full story of Jacobs' life and the horrors experienced by his parents. But at that stage, Mike and I had failed to track down the whereabouts of Michael Weingärtner, the man Jacobs held responsible for his mother's death.

Travelling in Mike's lethally fast Audi on autobahns with no speed limit gave me a taste of Formula One, so when the *Top Gear* TV programme asked me to have a go on their Surrey race track, I jumped at it. They had an instructor named Stig who taught me the rudiments required and my best time, although bettered by Kate Moss, was several seconds ahead of the socialite Tara Palmer-Tomkinson, which was a great relief for my ego.

At the weekends I took time off to show Ginny's best cattle at agricultural shows. I came home from a show one night, well past midnight, and found Ginny sitting in the kitchen with a man. They were both drinking whisky and both were literally covered in blood – recent blood that was still shiny in the lamplight. The scene resembled that of two killers having a drink after committing a murder, but I soon recognised Donald, our local vet of many years, who Ginny had called in to deal with a difficult birth and prolapse. They had just spent an hour together in rain and darkness trying to force the bloody intestines of the mother cow back through her vulva.

Each of Ginny's hundred or so Aberdeen Angus cows had a name and, that year for the first time, I got to know most of them by sight. Ginny specialised in selling her own brand of bulls and, because few fences can keep randy bulls away from cows on heat, she kept all her bulls at a farm several miles away from Greenlands. Sadly bovine tuberculosis, which is endemic in the south-west, struck in the autumn of 2000 and all Ginny's bulls had to be shot by the Ministry. I remember the night before it happened, I came home from a lecture to find no supper but a note from Ginny saying, 'Not sure when I'll be back. Have joined the blockade. Love you, Gin.' I turned on the television news and learned that there was a national fuel crisis, sparked off by the sudden hike in petrol prices to £0.81 per litre at the pump, and groups of truckers, taxi drivers and farmers, including Ginny, were blockading oil terminals. There were pictures of police breaking up demonstrations. Ginny eventually called me on her mobile, not to explain what she was up to nor with whom, but to announce that she'd left me a rice dish in the Aga.

Only five months later, in February 2001, the foot and mouth epidemic was officially confirmed. I shuddered at the thought of how Ginny would react to the prospect of each and every one of her cattle and sheep being shot. If the virus reached anywhere on Exmoor, it would spread like wildfire across the largely unfenced moorlands of the National Park over which red deer and sheep wandered at will for many miles. For months we exercised maximum movement control on and off our farm. We avoided calling in the vet in case he brought us the dreaded bug on his van tyres or his clothing. All our gates were kept closed at all times and buckets full of disinfectant with a hand spray were left by our cattle grid for use by essential visitors like the postman. Every farmer in the area did likewise and prayed hard.

After the tax investigation and tuberculosis, Ginny needed this foot and mouth threat like a sore foot. She did not look at all well over those long summer months as the virus crept closer and closer to Greenlands, eventually stopping, God knows why, approximately twelve miles away.

Ever since the end of the Transglobe Expedition some twenty years before, Charlie Burton, Oliver Shepard, Ginny and I had met from time to time to chat about all those special years we had spent together. We thought of big, tough Charlie as immortal, but in October 2001 he suffered some form of heart attack whilst crossing a road, and then a few months later he died at home one morning, and Oliver rang to tell us. The three of us joined many more members of the Transglobe team and several hundred others for his memorial service at the Royal Geographical Society. I was lucky to have shared so many trials and tribulations over so many years with such a brave and solid man with a huge spirit and sense of humour.

Ginny and I had always slept with one leg or one arm entwined. When we had an argument by day, increasingly rare as the years fled by, this physical contact – which had become virtually sub-conscious like puffing up a pillow last thing – stopped any bad feeling spilling over into the next day. It also led to the likelihood of being struck when the other party was having a bad dream. One morning that June, just before dawn, Ginny went rigid and I woke with a shock.

'What's up?' I asked. 'Are you okay?'

Ginny stared down at me. 'Celia,' she said, 'your sister. You must go and see her. Now.'

'Why?'

'I don't know, but I think she's got much worse.'

My middle sister, Celia, living in Augusta, Georgia, had for a year or so been receiving chemotherapy for stomach cancer. That month reports from her husband Bob indicated that things were not too good, but there was no suggestion that she was dying. However, Ginny had never had such psychic intimations of bad news before, so I caught a flight the very next day, rented a car in Charlotte, North Carolina, and arrived at Celia's home at 6.00 p.m. Bob greeted me at their door with a worried look. He and Celia had gone for a quiet walk together the previous day, but on return she had fallen into a deep sleep, her breathing had rapidly become shallow and she was no longer reacting to normal stimuli.

She opened her eyes when I greeted her and seemed to smile. Her fingers lifted momentarily from the quilt and Bob said he was sure that she knew I was there. But I never heard her speak again. We stayed in relays with her through that night. Bob and her son, my nephew Tony, were both doctors and one of her two daughters, Deirdre, was a nurse. They looked after her beautifully and held a bedside communion service, until at 9.00 a.m. the following morning, with her family all about her, she died peacefully – a lovely person, an active and committed Christian and a perfect sister.

When the following week I drove to see my mother, I found her much quieter than usual. We went out to lunch, as we often did, at the Angel Hotel in Midhurst where, as a teenager over forty years before, I had done the washing up for pocket money. For the first time my mother did not recognise members of the hotel staff she had known for many years. She asked why my fingers were bandaged, a question I had answered her in full many times since the accident. She asked me about Celia, and I stressed that I had been with her as she died peacefully. But my mother did not seem able to take in at all that one of her children was dead.

That summer, back in the village hall of her beloved Lodsworth, my remaining two sisters and I arranged a party for her ninetieth birthday with fifty of her best and oldest friends, plus many of her grandchildren. After various toasts were offered and speeches laughed at, my mother spontaneously stood up and, with a lovely smile, thanked everyone there for all the happiness and fun they had given her down the long years. I loved her dearly and knew no mother could ever have been more loving or caring. She had brought up four young children, for much of the time in a foreign land, with no husband and a domineering mother-in-law. Thanks to her I had never felt any parental void as a child, no need for a father figure, for her shoulder was always there to cry on. I wondered on her ninetieth birthday, perhaps for the first time in nearly sixty years, on whose shoulder she had been able to cry since my father's untimely death.

My father, although I never missed him, has always been one of the three people I have in different ways wished to emulate. I was brought up with stories of his bravery. My other two heroes were Wilfred Thesiger and Wally Herbert. That summer I learned that the former, whom I considered the greatest British desert traveller of all time, was living out his old age in a rest home in Surrey. I had met him, only once, to interview him about one of his travel books thirty years before. He was a craggy, imposing figure, even then, with the face of a hawk. I decided it was time I paid him another visit. I found him resting in a deep armchair in a small room that seemed to imprison him. But he was cheerful.

'I've won at last,' he said with his sun-leathered features

creasing into a smile. 'I've escaped from the mixed wing. No more old ladies blocking up the stairways.'

He levered his long frame out of his chair with two sticks and suggested we venture to the local pub for some lunch. He spurned the offer of a lift in my car and we walked down the road for twenty minutes, resting occasionally as he leaned heavily on my shoulder. The pub turned out to be a sandwich bar. His mind, like my mother's, wandered now that he was ninety-two years old, but I listened spellbound to his stories of the great deserts of Oman, Saudi and the Yemen, and especially of his wanderings, some twenty years before I was there, in the wilds of Dhofar. I had met and worked with perhaps a dozen Dhofaris who clearly remembered Thesiger. They had called him by his Arab nickname of Mubarreq bin Miriam, and all remembered him with great respect. After two hours of yarning he began to doze off, so we walked slowly back to the rest home and I left him alone in his room. He had no family any more, but an unrivalled wealth of memories of people and places, of incredible journeys he had dared and endured, and the inner pride in knowing that he had never given up.

A year later I was lecturing in Kenya when Ginny phoned me to say the Prince of Wales had asked me to represent him at Thesiger's memorial service in Eton's magnificent college chapel, as he would be abroad. If I could taste just a mere fraction of the wonders Thesiger experienced, I would die happy, but I never will, for Thesiger was born just in time to be the last of the Marco Polos, a stranger in strange lands marvelling at weird, often savage, rituals in the harsh badlands of Danakil, among the nomad raiders of the Empty Quarter or the biblical marsh-men of the pre-Saddam Hussein Euphrates marshes. Thesiger's powerfully written and photographed books ensure that neither these people as they used to be nor he who travelled then among them will be forgotten.

The other great traveller whose books I had studied and whose journeys I had long coveted was not acquainted with hot deserts at all, for he specialised in the world's coldest places. In Antarctica and on the shifting sea-ice of the Arctic Ocean, Wally Herbert's great journeys were, through the 1950s and 1960s, the stuff of polar travellers' dreams, especially his 1968/69 first true crossing of the Arctic Ocean. On this expedition a news reporter in his radio base camp overheard Wally describe his expedition's London committee, a group including the most senior polar men in the Establishment at that time, as people who 'didn't know what the bloody hell they were talking about'. As a result, thirty years after his monumental success in the Arctic, Wally had still not been honoured in any way, unlike a number of his direct contemporaries, including Chris Bonington, the mountaineer, and Robin Knox-Johnston, the sailor.

For three years I conducted a fierce correspondence with the Cabinet Office and the relevant civil honours bureaucrats. But Wally's file was clearly blacked, and I got nowhere fast. Eventually, after obtaining letters of admiration for Wally's pioneering achievements from all over the world, the Cabinet Office agreed that Wally should be knighted. He died in 2007, our greatest polar traveller since Scott.

Early that autumn, Mike Kobold phoned from Austria to say he had traced the ex-Nazi policeman who had murdered the mother of Derek Jacobs, as well as some 200 other women. Since neither the Secret Hunters nor the Nazi-hunting services of Simon Wiesenthal in Vienna, who had helped us in our Nazi search for over a year, had been able to trace the man, I was amazed at Mike's announcement. Nevertheless I flew out to meet him at Frankfurt Airport, close to his German home, the following day.

An exhausted Mike Stroud surveys his sledge after its 25 feet fall
into a crevasse. Antarctica is bigger than China and
India put together. But with no shops.

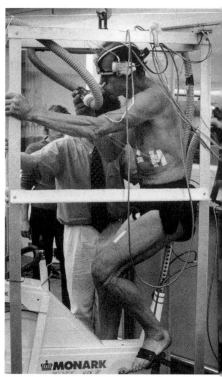

Many things go into making an expedition happen: a supportive sponsor like James Dyson, hours of training and a good relationship with the media – on the left is the late Terry Lloyd who was killed in Iraq, believed to be the victim of American so-called 'friendly fire'.

Then there is the assembly of all the necessary supplies – and if you return safely, a chance to meet interesting characters like Mrs T. This photo was taken five days after the Brighton hotel IRA bombing.

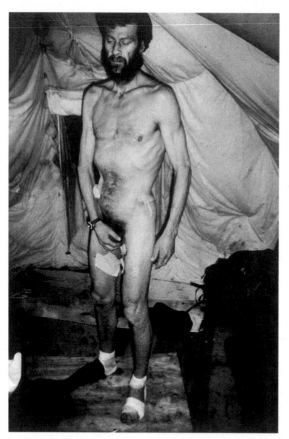

Counting the cost: the author after one of the polar journeys. Such expeditions are hard on the human body, particularly if you don't take in enough calories while you're exerting yourself in what are very unfriendly conditions.

My right hand, photographed (by me) soon after frustration drove me to amputate the mummified ends with a hack-saw.

Over the years I've tried many things to keep in good condition, from camel racing to endurance running – here with Gary Tompsett after winning the Elite Veterans Cup at the two-day Karrimor Mountain Marathon.

Seven marathons in seven consecutive days on seven continents: in the words of *The Times*, 'an inspiration for every runner, every ordinary person, tempted to give up in the face of the impossible'. Clockwise from top left: the first in the Falklands accompanied by penguins, then on to Santiago, Sydney, Singapore, London, Cairo and finally New York (overleaf).

16

Heart Attack

Mike Kobold had trained with the German Traffic Police driving department and as we sped from Frankfurt to Vienna he frequently exceeded 150 mph in his Audi. My feet pressed hard against the footwell, as Mike chattered amiably. I began to understand why Germany produced so many Schumacher-class speedmasters.

Simon Wiesenthal, Mike informed me, had identified the Nazi we were after – Michael Weingärtner – who had never been punished, nor indeed had the vast majority of individuals who had perpetrated acts of cruelty or murder in the name of Hitler. Weingärtner had, according to Wiesenthal's researchers, fled Germany in the sixties, soon after Adolf Eichmann's hanging in Israel and, like many of his ilk, had found sanctuary in Austria. Our discreet enquiries had revealed that he was living in the suburbs of Wels, a prosperous town near Vienna. We drove to Wels and parked close to the house. We both wore suits and carried briefcases. Mike led me up a path through a well-tended garden and knocked on the front door. A small grey-haired woman with tight features stared at us with hostility, if not menace. Mike explained that we had just flown from New York to follow up our newspaper's story about Weingärtner's part in the Wallern Death March of April 1945. We had heard that Weingärtner had somehow saved the lives of three women from murder by his colleagues. Would he please corroborate this?

Frau Weingärtner, for she could be no other, disappeared for a few minutes. An angry male voice sounded from within. Then she returned and told Mike that her husband was watching the F1 Grand Prix, that Michael Schumacher was winning, that it was a Sunday, that we had not deigned to make an appointment and that we should leave their home at once. The door slammed.

We had come a long way, if not from New York, and we conferred on the doorstep. We agreed to wait in the car until the Grand Prix ended. The Audi's radio duly announced that Schumacher had won the event so, assuming that Weingärtner would now be in as good a mood as we would ever be likely to find him, we again knocked on his door. Weingärtner himself answered this time.

He was no bigger than his wife and as unremarkable-looking. His face was certainly hard and his manner ice-cold, but, at first, his tone was polite enough.

'May we come in?' Mike asked.

Weingärtner ignored this. 'You say that I saved the women's lives.' He made a slight shrugging motion. 'Na. Ya. I did my best for them. They were difficult times for us.'

'So,' Mike countered, 'you would disagree with these US 5th Army records resulting from interrogations of the surviving women?' Mike produced a file from his case. 'As you can see, they say that, of the 3,000 women killed or allowed to die on the march, you were personally the killer of at least 200 women, mostly teenage girls, whose photographs are shown here.' Mike pointed at line upon line of women's mugshots.

Weingärtner then clammed up. 'I killed nobody,' he said, and slammed the door in our faces. After a minute, his wife poked her head out and said firmly, '*Das ist alles.*' So ended our attempt at being foot-in-the-door investigative journalists and I was left wondering about such people as Weingärtner who are still to be traced all over the world today, individuals who have caused agony and misery and committed mass murder. To my mind there can be no date nor age beyond which a person guilty of mass murder should become immune to justice. Mike and I sent details of Michael Weingärtner's address to Simon Wiesenthal's office and I subsequently gave talks on our search for the Wallern Death March murderers to groups of Holocaust survivors in Britain. The book about Derek Jacobs and his quest, *The Secret Hunters*, was published in 2001.

My next biography was going to be a very different sort of undertaking. In 1980, when I reached the South Pole Scott-Amundsen Base for the first time, I spent four days there. I helped the inmates with the dishwashing in their canteen and chatted to many of the overwintering scientists. It was interesting to hear their views on various explorers, including Captain Robert Falcon Scott, after whom their polar base was half named. They mentioned to me that the previous year an Englishman named Roland Huntford had published a new book on Scott. Apparently, they said, the whole story about Scott the polar hero was merely old Brit imperialist propaganda which this Huntford guy's book ruthlessly exposed. I meant to buy this book on returning home, but I forgot.

Then, in the mid-1980s, I was reminded about it from an unexpected source – Mrs Raisa Gorbachev, to whom Ginny and I were making a presentation in Moscow on behalf of Dr Hammer. She told me that Stalin had much admired Scott, who had been awarded various Soviet honours, but that more recently Scott had been exposed as a mere fool. I bought the Huntford book and watched a seven-hour ITV documentary film based on it. Both contained much information that my own experiences by then made me find questionable, although I found book and film good entertainment value. The book read like an exciting novel and, not being well versed in polar history at the time, I was impressed by its lengthy acknowledgments and lists of references.

Later, after Mike Stroud and I manhauled across the Antarctic continent in 1993, I saw the ITV film again and this time it rang a very different bell. There were huge inaccuracies and they stemmed from Huntford's book. Over the next decade I read all the books that I could find about Scott, some 112 in all, and I became slowly aware of the magnitude of the change wrought to Scott's reputation by Huntford's book which had by 2003 become the generally accepted view of the explorer. Huntford himself was considered the world's number one polar biographer, although he had never been near either Pole, and his books were treated as reliable history. His fabricated version of Scott would be difficult to expose.

I was not alone in my dismay at the injustice done to Scott. Britain's most senior polar explorer, Sir Vivian Fuchs, dismissed Huntford's book: 'This is one man's interpretation and his inexperience of the conditions he is writing about clearly makes him incompetent to judge them.'

I determined to instigate my own research and reach my own conclusions which were that Huntford had skewed history in his vendetta against Scott and his championing of Amundsen. At least with polar experience on my side I could reinvestigate the facts and contribute something towards restoring historical reality.

As work on my Scott biography was coming to an end I knew I needed a complete break and change of activity. Out of the blue I phoned Mike Stroud and suggested we get involved in another expedition. He was however too busy in Southampton to spare the three months an average expedition would take. His counter-suggestion was that we run seven marathons on each of the world's seven continents in seven days. This was an idea originally proposed by Mary Gadams, his American team-mate on a previous Eco-Challenge race, but she had not managed to get the enterprise off the ground. The idea appealed to me enormously and Mike and I set about getting the sponsorship and logistics in place while training seriously for the running. We would need to start in Antarctica and it would be good to aim to finish by joining an official marathon run somewhere like New York. It was only a case of connecting it all up.

The day after I finished the final corrections to the text of my Scott biography I was due to give a talk to a convention in

Dunblane, so I told Ginny I would see her the following morning and I drove to Bristol Airport, arriving at the departure desk of the no-frills airline, Go, in good time. I boarded the aircraft and settled down to read a magazine. I can remember nothing that happened from that moment for the next three days and nights.

Apparently not more than a few minutes before take off I collapsed noiselessly and was dragged into the aisle, where a passenger with medical training gave me instant mouth-to-mouth cardiac resuscitation. The pilot called the fire service, and the fire engine accelerated across the tarmac to drop off two firemen recently trained in the use of the mobile defibrillator which they carried on board. They applied a powerful 200-joule DC electric shock which passed right across my chest to depolarise every cell in my heart. This caused my natural pacemaker to recover and my heart was once more a regularly beating pump. Deeply unconscious, I was then rushed to a waiting ambulance. Twice more on the journey to Bristol's Royal Infirmary and three more times in the Accident & Emergency unit I lapsed back into fibrillation. The stabilising drugs I was given proved ineffective but the doctors managed in due course to stabilise my condition. Fearful however that I would have further attacks, they sent me to surgery. Within just two hours of my initial collapse, I was on cardiac bypass with a machine artificially pumping and refrigerating my blood.

A consultant cardiologist, Dr Tim Cripps, commented to me much later, 'Out of the hundred thousand people a year in the UK who have a cardiac arrest, the first and only warning they get is the attack itself and only very few are lucky enough to be near a defibrillator and someone who knows how to use it.' After treating me to some examples of others who had not been so lucky, he went on, 'When you arrived in our ICU you were measured at 4 points on the Glasgow Coma Scale. The lowest the scale goes is Level 3, which Richard Hammond of *Top Gear* achieved after his car crash at 260 mph.'

Dr Cripps called the senior Bristol cardiac surgeon, Gianni Angelini, who subsequently wrote:

On arrival RF had a coronary angiography which showed the presence of a large thrombus (blood clot) blocking the left anterior descending and the intermediary artery, two of the most important arteries of the heart.

He was fully anaesthetised, artificially ventilated and taken at once to the operating theatre. I was informed at my home and when I arrived was told the situation was quite bad . . . The situation was so urgent that we decided to go ahead and open his chest even prior to the arrival of the team . . . Two bypass grafts were performed, one using an artery called the internal mammary artery, which is behind the breastbone, the other a long segment of vein from the leg . . . There was serious concern about his neurological state since we didn't know the extent and duration of his cardiac arrest at the airport and thereafter. He was kept sedated for 24 hours . . . Then woken up . . . From then on it became rather difficult to manage him, since he virtually refused any analgesia, saying he did not have a great deal of pain. And that he wanted the tubes and lines removed as soon as possible because he had to walk up and down the corridor. He was discharged five days after surgery.

Ginny had sat by my bedside day and night and watched my tube-fed, artificially ticking body, blood-smeared in places, lying in front of her for more than three days. Every now and again a nurse would enter and thump my knee or foot for a reaction. None came. This could not have been a good time for Ginny. When I eventually came to, we kissed as best we could and she told me that I had had a heart attack. It took a while to work out what she was saying and where I was. My chest had been opened up from top to bottom and later sewn up with silver wire, the knots of which I can still feel jutting proud just beneath my skin.

Leaning on Ginny's shoulder, once the pipes and tubes had all been removed from various places, I managed to walk a few paces but felt extremely sore. Ginny drove me home the next day and put

me to bed with strict instructions not to move. I asked for chocolate, but she said I was never to eat chocolate again.

Why, we both wondered, had I had this attack at all? Some years
later Mike Stroud wrote about my attack and his opinion of it in
his book *Survival of the Fittest.*

Ran smoked enthusiastically earlier in life and never paid much
attention to 'healthy' aspects of his diet. Furthermore, he probably has an inherited metabolic predisposition for heart
problems. In many, this would have been recognised from their
family history – a mother or father having a heart attack at an
early age. In Ran's case, however, this could have been missed. He
knew his mother had a healthy heart to great age but his father's
medical potential was unknown (he died young in the Second
World War). Ran's cumulative risk factors simply overcame even
his level of physical-fitness protection. Of course, the newspapers
had a field day, for the story of Ran's heart attack was of great
appeal. Sir Ranulph Fiennes, the epitome of continued vigorous
activity in middle age, declared various columnists, had clearly
been overdoing it. This annoyed me intensely. I immediately rang
the hospital intensive-care unit to send best wishes to Ran and his
wife Ginny. She must have been incredibly distressed, and she now
faced a future without the man who had matured from childhood
sweetheart into a husband and longstanding expedition partner.
But although concern for them both was uppermost in my mind,
I have to admit that, for me, Ran's condition also raised practical
issues, because with Ran in a coma in intensive care, all thought
and planning that had gone into our seven marathons project
seemed to have come to nought. This did not, however, reckon
with Ran's resilience. On the fourth day after his surgery he rang
me.

'Mike?'

I immediately recognised his voice.

'Ran, how are you? How's Ginny? How's – ' My flurry of surprise was swiftly interrupted.

'Mike, I can't chat for long but I'm fine. Don't cancel anything for now.'

I guessed immediately what he was referring to but I needed to be absolutely certain.

'You mean the marathons?'

'Yes,' he replied. 'I've been told there was a little damage so I don't see—'

'What? You mean your doctors say it's okay?' I interrupted.

'No, no,' he responded, whispering. 'I haven't asked them yet.'

Our conversation ran on for a couple more minutes but at the end I was clear. Ran was in cloud-cuckoo-land and his specialist would soon bring him down to earth.

Then five days later he rang again.

'How's it going? When will you be home?' I started.

'Oh, very soon,' he came back, a slight laugh in his voice. 'I'm just walking off the moor.'

When it came to confessing my future marathon intentions, I had hopes that my surgeon Professor Angelini would be sympathetic. After all, he still held the Italian 800 metres record. However I decided to approach the topic cautiously. Here is his account of his response:

I saw RF in my office for the usual post-operative check-up and he told me it was his intention to run a marathon. He asked my opinion and I said, as much as I liked running myself, I have never had a patient who had asked me a question like can I run a marathon after a heart operation. I told him he probably could, given the fact that his coronary were now pretty well sorted out. However I would advise him not to run in a competitive fashion. What he failed to tell me was that his intention was to run seven marathons in seven days on seven continents. Something which I would strongly advise not to do!

Meanwhile, the cardiologist, Dr Tim Cripps, decided that his colleague, Dr David Smith in Exeter, would be best qualified to decide whether or not I should be allowed to try to run a marathon, since he knew a lot more about sports cardiology. David, who was a frequent running partner and good friend to both Mike Stroud and myself and had been my team leader on the Moroccan Eco-Challenge, checked my post-operative angiograms with care and said it would be okay to run non-competitively provided I kept my heart rate low.

For my own part, I decided to see if the sponsors of our marathon project, Land Rover, would be prepared to postpone everything for a year. They were then owned by Ford who decided that postponement was not on the cards. I must teach myself to run again in three and a half months. The bottom line, I decided, was to give it a go and if I couldn't do it, Mike would have to go solo.

So I started to walk, very slowly, on mostly flat ground, and whenever I became breathless or felt giddy, I lay down on the ground until I felt better. Sometimes, if I tripped on uneven ground, my chest hurt where the rib-cage had been slit open and it felt as though the wire ties had torn.

I took a mobile phone on each outing and kept calling or being called by Ginny. After a while she agreed that I was approaching things in a slower, more controlled manner than she had thought possible and did not seem worried by the marathon plan which, unlike most previous projects with Mike, would only last a week. Our charity, which we chose ourselves this time, was the British Heart Foundation, who support the placement of out-of-hospital defibrillators, like the one that saved me. Mike also decided, with Ginny's enthusiastic approval, to take one with us on each run.

My recovery programme, also carefully planned with Ginny's approval, stated:

3 weeks after op: walk for 5 minutes with stops, lie down when giddy

8 weeks after op: walk for 30 minutes, no stops
12 weeks after op: jog for 60 minutes, no stops
13 weeks after op: jog for 120 minutes, no stops
15 weeks after op: jog gentle (7 hour) marathon
16 weeks after op: start the 7x7x7

A total of 294 kilometres in seven days. The seven marathons would not be at fast race pace but they would not be gentle runs either. We would need to complete each within six hours, including airport customs and security (in and out). Since none of the scheduled jumbo flights could be expected to delay take off by even one minute if we were late, I tried to forsee potential airport security problems by writing to airlines in advance, warning them of Mike's metal detector-alarming medical hand baggage and the defibrillator.

Only eight weeks before departure Mike called me. Bad news. He had been going for a run near his home in Hampshire when his left hip began to complain. He was forced to call his wife Thea to collect him by car to take him home. In a few hours a grapefruit-sized swelling appeared which became a massive, blue-black bruise tracking down his thigh. He had an ultrasound check which showed that a small muscle running from the hip to beyond the knee had torn through. The ripped ends were swimming in a pool of blood. Mike's orthopaedic and sports medicine colleagues' advice was gloomy: he would not be running anywhere for several months, let alone doing a marathon.

Mike said he was not sure he agreed with their negative prognosis and would hope to get training again after a short rest. In fact, he took only twelve days' rest, lots of aspirins, some physio and then a test half-hour outing. His hip was sore, he self-diagnosed, but workable.

Our sponsor Land Rover decided not to announce the event at all unless we could prove we were fit to run at least two full marathons before departure. Mike chose the Cardiff event a fortnight before our start date and a small marathon near Winchester a week later. Land Rover stressed that we must tell nobody at all about the project until after both trial runs were successfully done. So I was extremely worried when the Cardiff organisers sent me my running number to stick on my vest a week before their event. The number was 777! They had obviously found out about our main plan. I called Mike, but he assured me he had not told anyone, and it transpired that the number had been chosen entirely at random. We took this as a good omen.

The Cardiff course turned out to be flat, and Mike, who set the pace, went fast by my standards, finishing in around four hours. I felt drained at the end, but Mike wrote:

In contrast to me, Ran looked pretty fresh at the end . . . despite the ten years' age difference and his enforced, slow training schedule. It was easy to see that he was by far the more natural athlete. But he too had a problem. For many years, his back had been the source of much discomfort, causing considerable grief when he was pulling heavy sledges during some of our polar trips. Sadly, running also made it worse and if one marathon exacerbated the pain, how would it react to the hammering it was going to receive? We were both aware that, determined or not, enough pain could defeat us. I made a mental note to add more pain-killers to the medical kit.

The next marathon, seven days later, took us from Winchester to Salisbury and Mike slowed the pace slightly. We finished in 4 hours 22 minutes. I had taken Ibuprofen tablets and aspirins and felt better than in Cardiff. The Big Seven, we agreed, was at least worth having a go at. We left Heathrow on schedule on 21 October, heading for South America. Land Rover had announced the overall plan of the Challenge the day we left Britain with a simplified summary:

The team will run their first marathon in Antarctica and the 7-day clock will tick from the moment they start. A twin-engine plane will immediately fly them back to Santiago to run the South

American marathon (Number 2). From there to Sydney, Singapore, London, Cairo and finally New York. But they will lose a whole day when they cross the international date line and will have to make this up by running two marathons within one 24-hour period, a morning run in London and another that night in Cairo. If they succeed, the two runners will complete the seven runs in less than 7 x 24 hours and will see only six whole days in terms of sunrises and sunsets.

Put like that it all sounded straightforward enough. We intended to run our first leg, the Antarctic marathon, on the sub-Antarctic King George Island, part of the South Shetlands once administered by the British Antarctic Survey, but now a Chilean airbase. On 25 October we left Punta Arenas and flew over the glaciers and mountains of Tierra del Fuego for two hours. Then our pilot had to turn back due to bad weather. On 26 October, the forecast being better, we again taxied hopefully along the Punta Arenas runway. Rob Hall, our BBC reporter and by now good friend, announced, 'Nothing can stop us now.' A minute later, on sod's cue, the starboard engine coughed, the pilot confirmed engine failure, and our last chance of making the South Shetlands on time was lost.

A rapid conference at the Punta Arenas Airport followed. From long experience I have always believed that if Plan A fails you get going with Plan B. Our Plan B was that we would run our South American leg immediately and here in Punta rather than in Santiago as originally planned. And while we were doing it, our local organiser would try to find another aircraft to take us to another ex-British Antarctic Survey islands group, the Falklands, for the Antarctic leg.

That afternoon we all drove out of town to a long pebble-strewn beach beside the Magellan Strait. At 6.00 p.m. a whistle from a member of our Chilean support team served as our starting gun and off we loped along the coast before, ten miles later, we turned inland and crossed barren moorland where we flushed out startled groups of rhea who galloped off very much faster than we could. I managed to stay close behind Mike's shoulder all the way and our first marathon clocked in at 3 hours 45 minutes. Back in Punta Arenas we were greeted with the news that a twin-engine jet was on hand to take us to the Falklands.

The question has been asked whether the Falklands are genuinely part of the Antarctic continent or not. Well, they aren't part of South America and the *Antarctic Dictionary* assures me Antarctica comprises the continent and its surroundings seas and islands. Support came from quite another direction with the illustrious nineteenth-century botanist Sir Joseph Hooker writing about the flora of the Falklands and South Shetlands in his *Flora Antarctica*. It was good enough for me.

'Look left, Ran.' Mike woke me from sleep on our executive jet and pointed out of one of the portholes. An RAF Jaguar fighter plane cruised a few metres from our starboard wing: the pilot's thumbs-up was clearly visible. We landed at Mount Pleasant Military Base. A giant map of the Falklands hung in the airbase commander's office and we agreed to follow a marathon route he and other officers suggested that led from close to the base to the cathedral in the islands' capital, Port Stanley. We set out with six hours to go before our jet would have to leave in order to connect with the next key flight. We had therefore to run this one in under five hours.

At first we were both painfully stiff. Army vehicles passed by every now and again, the drivers hooting and waving. Our progress was being reported on Falklands Radio. There were long climbs and the pebbly road was uneven. We passed by skull and crossbones signs, warning of twenty-one-year-old minefields beside the track. In dry areas dwarf shrubs known as diddle-dee spread like heather with red berries mixed with an overall dun-coloured grass, white plumed flowerheads and patches of low pig vine. Occasional rook-like birds plunged and soared over the moors. After three hours we passed below Mount Tumbledown, site of fierce fighting during the 1982 conflict, where British paratroops assaulted Argentinian infantry dug into its upper slopes.

My legs began to demand remission. On the uphills as we climbed hundreds of feet, they begged me to stop. I had reached 'the wall' and the time for gritted teeth . . . Fatigue was not my only concern. As Port Stanley grew closer, I kept getting twinges of cramp. These occurred every time we climbed a hill, and this could be serious. You can choose not to listen when muscles cry 'enough' which is just a matter of exhaustion, but the body does have other means of making you stop. Cramp in both legs can't be ignored: it simply takes you down . . . My legs were lead when we crossed the finish line after four and a half hours to be met by Stanley's children, half of the adult population and the Governor of the Islands.

The Governor had laid on tea and sandwiches for us at Government House but there was, unfortunately, no time to observe the diplomatic civilities as an army Land Rover rushed us back to Mount Pleasant and hasty goodbyes to the commandant. We made it to Santiago Airport in the nick of time to catch the scheduled BA flight to Sydney with two marathons under our belt and not yet down and out, just tired and aching all over. Before we left Chile we had pared our luggage down to a single item of hand baggage. As the schedule became tighter, we would have no time to wait for baggage carousels at airports.

We reached Sydney on the morning of 29 October, raced through the airport formalities to face a barrage of questions from a curious but sympathetic media, Australians being keen on any form of sporting activity. Then we changed speedily into our running gear. Land Rover Australia had thoughtfully arranged for members of the Sydney Striders running club to run with us in a pack, which was a big help. They included the Australian Iron Man champion who made sure we did not get lost. The route began near the Opera House, transited the Botanic Gardens and climbed up and then down the impressive Harbour Bridge, a near nine-mile course that we were to repeat three times, thus ascending and descending the bridge's 104 steps six times. Marathons are meant to be flat. So far none of ours had been. I remember feeling drained.

But Mike was feeling much worse. It had started for him in the previous race but now his legs were becoming tighter and stiffer in a way he could not at first understand, and the competitive edge which we used to spur each other on had not kicked in for him this time. The first signs that Mike's problems were not just fatigue appeared before we left Sydney. His urine was mixed with blood and he suffered persistent diarrhoea. This in turn led to the likelihood of dehydration. But when he weighed himself, anticipating severe weight loss, he was shocked to find that he weighed six kilos more than in Patagonia three days earlier. This explained to him that the tightness in his legs was because of the build up of fluid in his muscles caused by damage to the muscle cell membranes due to extreme mechanical overwork. What was going on in Mike's body was the result of the abuse to which he was subjecting it, the actual breaking down of his muscles. Not a happy state of affairs given the fact that he had only run three out of the seven marathons and the worst part of the schedule lay immediately ahead. The hottest, most humid run would be in Singapore. And then two marathons within twenty-four hours and ever increasing jet lag.

We arrived half-asleep and confused at Singapore Airport, and were whisked by our hosts, the Singapore Heart Foundation, to a hotel for one hour's sleep before the press conference they had fixed for 4.00 a.m. We awoke like zombies, stiff as boards all over. I really did not feel like getting up or walking to the bathroom, never mind trying to run somewhere. Failure, I now perceived, was eminently likely. However, a cold shower, a cup of black coffee and a well-attended press conference, at which we were reminded that we represented the UK, made me realise that withdrawal from the nightmare, at least at this stage, was not an option.

So, to the hooting of horns and the cheering of the sixty Singapore runners who were to accompany us, we set out at dawn

261

to thread our tortured way for the next six hours through the parks and skyscrapers of Singapore. The sun rose all too quickly, as did the roar of the rush-hour traffic.

Singapore was a marathon too far for poor Mike. He was peeing blood and reduced to walking the last third on jellied legs. His diary recorded:

> Within an hour of starting the Singapore run I realised that this was the marathon too far. I felt sick and my legs, although still painless, had become utterly useless as the first few miles flew by. The heat was stupefying . . . We had managed little more than a quarter of the course before I drew up beside Ran and told him of my predicament. However much I wanted to go on, it was not within my capability and I explained that for me there was no choice but to give in. I urged him to go on running every step if he possibly could. Feeling pretty dismal I cut back and watched as he and most of our accompanying runners drew slowly away.

I was not much better. After four hours I felt faint, nauseous and could not run in a straight line. A Singaporean Army major from their Special Forces clung to my running vest to steer me. Another runner kept dousing me with water and shouting constant encouragement. He must have said 'Nearly there' a hundred times. But we never were.

My back ached. My neck was shot through with sharp pain from the weight of my hung head. I drank copiously from my camelback container of Science-in-Sport drink. I fought against the ever increasing desire to stop running. I counted my steps. One to a hundred. One to a hundred. Again and again and again. I tried to think of home and Ginny, of the Dhofar war, of Charlie Burton, Ollie Shepard and Anton Bowring on the bridge of the *Benjamin Bowring* in a South Atlantic storm. Of anything that could even briefly take my mind away from the torture of Singapore that morning.

Mike's diary:

Towards the end of our run, the course made a short loop of about three miles with outward and backward paths along the same sector of road. Struggling along, I suddenly realised that Ran was coming the other way. He crossed over and as we approached one another we both raised our hands, which met in passing as the briefest of high-fives. It was a privilege to witness this supreme performance by a man ten years my senior, a man whom so many had recently written off.

Ran went on to finish having run every single step, although he still took five hours and twenty-four minutes. I ended up running about two-thirds of the course and walking the remainder, coming in more than half an hour behind him at just over six hours. I was disappointed, but at least I had done the job.

When the end finally came (on the parade ground where Lord Mountbatten had received the Japanese surrender fifty-eight years before), I simply fell over under the FINISH banner. The time was over five hours, but the time was immaterial. (The results of all seven marathons are in Appendix 3) Paramedics supported me to an ambulance, shoved needles into me and gave me various drinks. A BBC Singapore man with a tape recorder came in and sat on the ambulance bunk. 'Are you giving up?' he asked. He looked blurred to me. 'Yes,' I whispered. 'It would be stupid for me to carry on. But Mike will keep going. I know he will. If one of us can do it, that will be enough.'

Mike said that run was the hardest thing he had ever done. 'I felt like shit from the word go. The prospect of doing this again in London tomorrow is really appalling.'

Three hours later and just before our next intercontinental British Airways flight, we were feted at a Singapore Heart Foundation dinner. A doctor gave Mike the report on our body checks, done at the end of the run. Mike believed we were suffering from something called rhabdomyolysis, which simple tests would confirm by measuring the

263

level in our blood of creatine kinase (CK), which plays an important role in fuelling muscle function. The Singapore report showed that my CK level was fifty times above the norm. I was suffering from significant muscle damage. My disappointment in learning this was soon overshadowed by Mike's exclamation as he studied the report. His own CK level was nigh on 500 times the norm, surpassing by far anything he had feared and indicating massive muscle loss. Mike was still up and running through sheer mental willpower alone. His reaction to the news was typical.

Boarding the plane from Singapore, I seriously considered giving up. If things got much worse, I would be in real danger. The blood test results offered me a get-out, a chance to listen to my body's injuries with little loss of face. But I knew inside that there was another way. The risks were manageable if I had further tests with each subsequent race. Giving up is fine if you really have no choice. But if I stopped when I could have done better, I would regret it for the rest of my life.

We flew on to our next continent, Europe, where London, or rather Heathrow's immediate surroundings, had been the only choice for our fifth run if we were to fit Africa and North America into our remaining forty-eight hours. Even this thought was stressful, and I had been warned 'not to get stressed'.

Our main marathon organiser, Steven Seaton, also our Eco-Challenge companion in years gone by, had arranged for some fifty runners to accompany us on the European leg and our race leader was Hugh Jones, one of the best marathon runners Britain has ever produced and a previous London Marathon winner. He had researched for us the exact route of the original 1908 London Olympics marathon, which began at Windsor Castle and ended at the White City Stadium. Things had changed since 1908 and the morning rush-hour traffic was in full tortoise-like flow when we set out from the castle gates at 7.30 a.m. My thoughts as my back, hips, neck and legs creaked into action were centred around the ghastly proposition that, if we managed to complete this run, we would need to begin our next marathon in Africa that same night.

The Independent newspaper was clearly wary of our challenge. They quoted a Loughborough University sports science professor: 'RF and MS are risking permanent damage and even death by trying to complete their challenge. They could suffer potentially fatal kidney failure because their bodies will have no time to recover between each of their 26 mile runs. They are really punishing their bodies, possibly even to the point of death. We could never get approval from an ethics committee to conduct an experiment on people like this.'

Bruce Tulloch, another racing legend, led the way. We passed by Eton College, where groups of boys in tailcoats cheered us on. I glanced up at the high dome of School Hall and remembered the long ago thrill of night-climbing. Mike, who should have been recovering in a hospital bed, somehow ran for two and a half hours before having to walk intermittently. Friends and relations from all over the UK greeted our arrival at White City before Land Rovers rushed us to Heathrow for our flight to Cairo. Mike had lost a torn toe nail and was hobbling, but somehow he had completed the twenty-six miles ten minutes faster than I had finished in Singapore the previous day.

The wife of President Mubarak of Egypt was hosting our African run and using it to raise funds for one of her charities, Women for Peace. She had organised a press conference at Giza immediately below the floodlit Pyramids, so I answered the press queries in Omani-accented Arabic, which is perfectly understood in Egypt. We set out at midnight, passing the Sphinx and running alongside some sixty local runners through clamorous crowds of residents busy feasting after their Ramadan daytime fasting. There was an atmosphere everywhere of carnival and chaos, but we ran behind a hooting phalanx of police vans and two ambulances. 'One each,' Mike shouted at me.

The roadside crowds cheered and cat-called as we passed, and the route was flat tarmac all the way to the airport. We recorded our speediest time since our first Patagonian run, which completely mystified Mike from a medical point of view. We had just run, after all, two complete marathons in a single day. Circadian rhythm, Mike pondered, might be involved.

We had, by the time we finished in Cairo, chased the sun three-quarters of the way around the globe, creating about eighteen hours of jet lag. In general, Mike knew, the body can recover about one hour a day so, on our sixth day, we were twelve hours out of phase. He theorised that our time-confused bodies, during the London run, must have thought it was midnight when all hormone support is at a low ebb, whereas in Cairo we had woken up and our systems were firing on all cylinders.

We arrived at JFK Airport, New York, on time on 2 November and, with the help of a British Airways special assistant, passed rapidly through immigration and customs. My German friend, Mike Kobold, and Steven Seaton had organised things with great efficiency and we joined some 35,000 other runners at the Verrazano Narrows Bridge for the start of the New York Marathon, a far cry from our first run six and a half long, long days ago in Tierra del Fuego. There, the only other runners in sight had been the odd group of rhea.

Knowing that we would, if still going by New York, be physical wrecks, we had taken the precaution of assigning two strong helpers to each of us for this the last of our seven runs. Mike Kobold would stay with Mike, and so would my American nephew, my late sister Celia's son, who was a doctor and extremely fit. Steven Seaton and a runner friend of his would, if necessary, physically push me for the twenty-six miles through the streets of the Bronx, the concrete canyons of Manhattan, and finally the green acres of Central Park. The excitement of the great human pack surging forward to the boom of a cannon at the start momentarily made us both forget our delicate states of health, but not for long. My own main memories of the day are of fighting off the desire to stop running, bad but not as bad as in Singapore, and Steven was always there with his depth of endurance knowledge and calm encouragement.

I knew that Mike was suffering mental torture to keep going in his physical state, but I remembered many, many days on the ice at both ends of the world and over many years when he had been in dire straits and yet kept going. I felt certain he would make this last run within the rapidly dwindling time reservoir of our seven-day limit, and I was determined that this time we should cross the final line together. So I started running back to find him which other runners must have thought quite mad.

Mike wrote:

Ran was still forging ahead but he soon hit a generous (if painful for him) solution. Unlike previously, he had determined we should cross the line together. Every few hundred yards he would turn round and drift slowly back towards me. Other participants, spotting this figure moving in the wrong direction, must have questioned his sanity. Had they known that this was now his seventh marathon in seven days, he might have been committed.

Even with intermittent walking, I began to wonder if I could finish. My legs at times were literally buckling beneath me and this led to an intermittent sudden stagger. Worse, when I did so, I could not help but yelp with pain.

Central Park was a scene of wonder. Each side of the road was lined with tens of thousands of well-wishers and although we had ended up going slowly there were still thousands of other runners around us. For me, its gentle hills were still utmost tests of resolution, but now there was a difference. From the moment I entered the park gates, I knew for sure that it was all over. Even if I had to crawl, I would cover those final two miles in the two hours that were still left before our clock hit seven full days. I had not done as well as I had wished, for I had not run every single step. But at the outset I did not really think that I would make it at all. Now I was about to complete the undertaking.

And then there was Ran. He had never stopped running, not even for a single step, in any one of the seven marathons. As I saw him waiting, trotting on the spot, a few hundred yards from the finish, I was so grateful. When we finally crossed that seventh line together, it was a moment to cherish. I cannot thank him enough.

We finished 28,362nd out of 35,000 runners. Mike went on to make a very important point:

When, following our success, many experts in both the USA and Britain expressed disbelief at what we had achieved, they did not realise that they could have done it too. The difference is only one of perception. Whereas most people look at very big challenges, whatever the field or their walk of life, and start from the position 'I can't', Ran and I make a simple word substitution and say 'Why can't I?' 'I can't run seven marathons' easily transforms into the question, 'Why can't I run seven marathons?' Once it was asked, we felt obliged to find the answer.

The Times editorial the following day said: 'Both men are supposed to be too old to be running so far and so often. Both ignored medical scares and both kept going not by coddling or psychological bonding but by the abrasive competitive spirit that has marked their friendship and rivalry. Their triumph against all odds is not only a magnificent publicity boost for the charities that they are supporting, it is also an inspiration for every runner, every ordinary person, tempted to give up in the face of the impossible.'

17

Ginny

The day we returned to England, a press conference was held by the British Heart Foundation. I said goodbye to Mike and his family and was given a lift back to Exmoor by a friend. On reaching Exford village, just over a mile from home, I saw a big banner flying high over the road by the village green, and, below it, a crowd of people. We stopped as local folk, many of whom I knew well, surrounded the car and cheered and clapped. The banner was a 'Welcome Home, Ran' sign. I looked around for Ginny and spotted her with our two dogs. She wore her lovely warm smile of welcome, but looked both tired and thin. Later that evening, sitting by the log fire at Greenlands as we had so often done over the past twenty years, she told me her news and my stomach churned with dread. She might have stomach cancer.

The days, weeks and months that followed were the worst of my life. I cancelled everything in the diary except a handful of contracted conference lectures, and I called their organisers with the warning that, should my wife's condition deteriorate, I might not be there. Because we had both paid for private health care insurance for over thirty years, I drove Ginny to the top cancer-care hospital in London the following day, having booked her into a room there and requested an urgent appointment with a relevant specialist.

Ginny had, over many years, had sudden stomach pains at no particular time and for no known or obvious reason. We had both put this down to twisted Fallopian tubes, or some other

269

birth-connected condition. We had seen our doctor and specialists about the pain intermittently after especially bad attacks, but these were thankfully rare, to the point that sometimes a year would pass without one. Or so I assumed. Maybe Ginny did not always tell me when it happened. The doctors never found anything specifically wrong with her. Ginny had suffered two especially bad pains in the lower stomach area whilst I was away on the seven marathons and she had been driven to Taunton Hospital, an hour from home, for a check-up and pain-killers.

Now, at a major London hospital, a place rich in millionaire patients from many countries, with doctors and nurses of similar ethnic diversity buzzing around the plush corridors like white or blue-coated flies, we could find nobody able to deal with the sudden attack of stomach pains that convulsed Ginny in the waiting room. There was no warning. One moment we were quietly chatting; the next she was in agony, clawing at her bowels and moaning aloud, a sound which wrenched at my heart. I rushed into the corridor and approached the first nurse I could find.

'Please come at once. My wife is in extreme pain.'

'I will get someone for you.' She trotted off.

'Somebody is coming,' I told Ginny.

Five hellish minutes later nobody had come.

Ginny, the bravest of people, wept tears of pain, fear and desperation. I ran again down different corridors. I begged four different nurses to come to the waiting room. Ginny looked at me in confusion, hurt that I was doing nothing to help her in her hour of greatest need. I swore to myself that I would never leave her alone here, however magnificent the decor.

A doctor arrived some twenty minutes after Ginny's pains began. He looked impatient at this detour from his programme and gave me a prescription for some form of morphine. I rushed to the basement in-house pharmacy and asked the waiting queue if I could go to the front as my wife was in great pain. A pharmacist took my proffered prescription and returned, after an interminable pause, to tell me that the doctor had not signed the correct spot.

She was obdurate when I begged her for the pain-killers. So I rushed upstairs again and luckily found the doctor who, without apology, scribbled another signature on my docket. Back to the pharmacy and, after some forty minutes of hell and suffering by Ginny, eventually found a nurse who administered the tablets.

Our lifelong friends, William Knight (who had in 1965 been with me at the 'bombing' of Castle Combe) and his wife Sylvia, were true friends to us during that nightmare time, and I spent the next week in London, by day at Ginny's bedside, and by night letting myself into the nearby Regent's Park home of my literary agent and kind friend, Ed Victor.

The specialists confirmed that Ginny had a virulent form of stomach cancer which was spreading fast. She must have chemotherapy sessions every week for at least three months and starting at once. In between them we could live at home.

We spent Christmas on Exmoor with Ginny's family and many of our best friends visiting from time to time. But mostly we just stayed together. I tried always to be in the same room. When we cooked, we both moved to the kitchen. As Ginny became weaker, we made up two beds downstairs. Ginny spoke often to Neil and Ruth, who looked after the sheep and cattle for her. We went for walks and, when the pain attacks came, our doctor or the local nurses made sure Ginny had sufficient morphine. She did not want her family, apart from her sister Abby, told of her illness until the last moment, to shield them from worry.

I will never forget that time. I cannot believe that any human has ever loved another as much as I loved and still love Ginny. I could not remember any time in my adult life when she was not the reason for the glow in my heart when we were together, and the longed-for safe haven during my wanderings without her. I was desperate not to lose her and thankful for any tiny spark of hope that our doctor might murmur.

By the second month, January 2004, Ginny was seldom able to leave the house, other than by ambulance for treatment. We were assigned a doctor in Exeter Hospital who specialised in cancer treatment. But the various chemotherapy treatments did not work and the disease spread. Later that month Ginny moved into an NHS cancer ward shared with some seven other ladies. She made friends quickly with many of them and with many of the nurses. I spent every day at her bedside or wheeling her about in a chair. At night I slept in a spare upstairs room in the hospital. Abby would drive down from Liverpool as often as she could and many friends were frequent visitors, but Ginny's health diminished inexorably as the disease spread into her key organs. She had emergency operations and I sat outside the theatres startled by every unusual noise from within.

Three months after her diagnosis, Ginny was moved to the hospice close to the hospital, and I think she took this as a sign that the end could not be far away. I was allowed to sleep in a spare room in the hospice. Our lifelong friends the Bowrings and the Gaults drove from Suffolk and Kent respectively to visit us. Just before writing this book, I received a note from Anton Bowring taken from his diary of those sad times:

Many years ago, soon after we finished the Transglobe Expedition, I went to hospital with a suspect lump in my throat. I was sitting in bed in the lung cancer ward awaiting surgery the next day and surrounded by very ill people when Ginny arrived out of the blue and announced she was taking me out to supper. We had a wonderful evening and I completely forgot all my woes. Later my lump was found to be benign, but I never forgot Ginny's warmth and thoughtfulness. Nearly twenty years later, Jill and I arrived at the Exeter hospice knowing full well we might not see your Ginny again. The four of us had supper in nearby Topsham, Ginny in a wheelchair, but otherwise just as though we were on holiday at your home or ours. She was so alive and full of her usual fun that it was hard to believe anything was wrong. I remember she had a morphine drip in a floral pattern bag around her neck which alone showed what she was going through. We talked that evening of all the wonderful times we had had together, of Namibia, France, Scotland, and we planned new outings too. We played cards by the fire there and we were together.

The excitement of our outing was maybe too much and Ginny could not see us the next day, so Jill and I bought bird feeders which we hung in the hospice garden outside Ginny's room. You told us then that the specialist had said Ginny's chances were very slim.

The next day, our last down south, we drove Ginny to Teignmouth and you pushed her chair about the crowded town until we found a pub overlooking a small boat harbour at low water. We sat outside and watched the seagulls. After a lovely day we returned to Exeter and said our goodbyes, believing we'd meet up again before long. That was the Sunday evening. The following Friday you phoned us in the evening and told me that dear Ginny had died just fifteen minutes earlier and that she was still in your arms. It makes me tearful, even now, just remembering that moment.

Many friends and Ginny's family came on her last day alive to show their love for her. But her pain became ever worse, and towards evening the nurses had to increase her morphine drip above the previous levels. Abby and my niece Beelie were with me as Ginny faded slowly. I could not control my misery. She died and escaped further pain.

Over the previous week we had sometimes prayed together with the friendly and sincere hospice chaplain. Once Ginny held me tightly and thanked me for our life together, using wonderful words that I will never forget.

Anton and Abby came back to Greenlands and stayed with me. Together we planned Ginny's funeral, memorial service and, months later, a gathering of her friends, over 700 people, at a celebration of her life at the Royal Geographical Society, the place where she had spent many long hours in the dusty archives with maps and books researching for our expeditions. Three of the Black Dogs Ginny had bred were there and a film of her life was shown, put together by her old friend Alex Leger, the long-time producer of television's *Blue Peter* who had, in the 1970s and eighties, often featured Ginny and her Jack Russell, Bothie, on the programme.

Abby was ten years younger than Ginny. She later wrote of her inner thoughts.

It wasn't easy was watching my sister die, too fast and too slowly, of an aggressive cancer that gave her months of excruciating pain. She was fifty-six, fit, strong, tough, and it was Ran who'd had a major heart attack less than a year before. He was the one at risk, not Ginny.

I'd known she wasn't well, but we all thought she needed a hysterectomy, nothing more. Then she phoned me when I was walking into a restaurant one evening in October 2003. She never phoned my mobile; so I knew before she spoke that it was bad news.

I didn't realise she was in hospital till New Year 2004, because she hadn't wanted to worry me. In the end Ran rang, because Ginny couldn't. Her body was packing up and she was in constant pain.

I shot down to Exeter hospital. Ginny was thin and pale, but undiminished: still my big sister. The days I spent with her from then until her death will be some of the most prized of my life. And the hardest. In those few weeks the patina of sibling squabble was scrubbed away and all that was left was love. In February, after three days at home, I got back to find she'd been moved to the hospice. I got there at 2 a.m., and Ran was asleep in the camp bed, gripping his beloved wife's hand. He didn't wake, but Ginny opened her eyes. Her smile terrified me because it was a really lovely, joyful welcome and there was no worry or pain on her face. I just hope she couldn't see the shock on mine. This was the first time I'd been so close to someone who was going to die very soon, and this was the person I loved most in the world. There were black circles round her eyes and her lips were shrivelled in gaunt, waxy cheeks. This change from my big sister, ill but alive, to this shadow creature on the fraying hem of life undid something in me which hasn't been repaired.

Seeing Ran and Ginny together in their last two days you'd think they'd only been married a week, instead of thirty-four years. It hurt badly to watch a true marriage being ripped apart.

I started life without Ginny. At Greenlands, the urn containing her ashes was buried in a garden beside the earlier graves of all the dogs she had owned and Fingal, her cat. Set in a glade of trees she had planted and overlooking the hills and fields where her cattle still grazed, it is my most special place.

On weekdays I busied myself in the office, where Gina and Jill and Joyce were kind and understanding, and on the farm, where Neil and Ruth continued to deal with the cattle and the sheep. Jean tidied the house three times a week, as she always had, and often left a saucepan of rice mixed with sweetcorn, which became my staple diet. At night, alone, I would wander around the cows, especially Ginny's favourites, talking to them and at times crying aloud. Three months after Ginny died I could bear things no more. I was becoming morose, inactive and full of self-pity. I knew I must break out of my own cage of misery and I remembered the Everest climb invitation I had received a year before from Sibusiso Vilane in Swaziland, the first black person ever to summit Everest. I needed a sharp jolt and what could provide one better than facing my greatest, lifelong fear – vertigo. If I went with Sibu to Everest that would surely drag me out of the dark void of my current existence. The highest mountain on earth would surely test my irrational terror of heights.

I wrote to Sibu. He was delighted and accepted the fact that I would first have to learn how to climb. He suggested doing so through a UK mountain tours company called Jagged Globe. I called them at once, but their boss, Simon Lowe, explained they could not take anybody and everybody up Everest and, with due respect, I was 'sixty, cardiac-challenged and missing some digits'. He drove to Greenlands later that week and suggested that I join two of Jagged Globe's mountaineering courses. First there was a ten-day Alpine peaks instructional tour to see if I could cope with the basics of snow and ice climbing. Then, if I received a reasonable report from the Alps guide, I should progress to their Ecuador Volcanoes tour, involving climbs up to 20,000 feet, which would introduce me to the effects of high altitude on my system. This was especially important because of my cardiac history.

Since none of the relevant Alpine or Ecuadorean mountains needed actual technical climbing skills, I assumed that no big drops would be involved.

Many years ago Ginny and I had gone to the Alps with Monty Don, the gardener, and other friends, including Simon Gault and Geoff Newman. We had walked up Mont Blanc, the Matterhorn and the Jungfrau with a guide and had a good time. So I invited Simon and Geoff to join me on the Jagged Globe Alpine fortnight. Both accepted. There were fifteen students on the course, mostly men at least thirty years younger than us, but we all passed the guides' report easily enough. The basic skills we learned involved use of ice-axes and crampons and long snowy trudges. But no actual climbing.

Back home my sister, Susan, ten years older than me, was ill with mesolthelioma or asbestosis. Her husband of over forty years, John Scott, called me, and I joined him and my two nieces, Beelie and Neesh, at the Wiltshire hospital where Sue had been assigned to the cancer ward. She died three months after Ginny, and I lost another wonderful, caring member of the family. My last remaining sister, Gill, and I went to see our mother in the Sussex rest home. Usually we visited her once every month on different dates. She had been getting increasingly forgetful and confused, which was just as well in a way since the news of Celia's death, then Ginny's and now Susan's never really sank in. She kept asking us how they all were long after we had gently told her that they had died.

After her ninetieth birthday party in July 2002, my mother slowly became less interested in the world outside her own little room. Early in 2003 she had a stroke. The last time I took her outside the home, on one of my monthly visits, was soon after

Ginny's death in the spring of 2004. Thereafter we stayed in her room or sat holding hands and saying little on a bench in the garden outside her room. Her best and oldest friend from Lodsworth, Betty Simmonds, visited her every week, as did Judy Tarring, who had once been her professional carer.

In August, when I returned from the Alps, my sister Gill warned me that our mother was fading away and unable to leave her bed. We took it in turns to visit her daily. I stayed in a bed and breakfast near the home and one evening arrived in her room after dark. The nurse said she had been sleeping most of that day. I found her fast asleep and sat by her bed, whispering that I loved her and that she was the best mother in the world. Which she was. Her breathing was shallow. I am not sure if she heard me or not. I fell asleep on the carpet beside her bed and woke some time later towards midnight. I have no idea what woke me, but I held her hand and some minutes later she stopped breathing.

Gill and I followed our mother's wishes and made sure her grave was beside those of her many old friends and fellow parishioners in the village of Lodsworth. Within a stone's throw of our old house, the graveyard overlooked the fields and woods and the River Lod where I had spent so many happy teenage holidays with my sisters and with Ginny.

I tried to lift my head above the deep ache of Ginny's death and tell myself that she would be wanting me to attack life again, to 'get on with it', to 'be dangerous': all her little catch phrases. I still keep a short pencilled note she left me about six months before she died. I can't remember the exact context, but it reads:

My poor, mad, bad, darling man, I didn't realise you were giving a lecture there. PLEASE stay the night with Charles or John. You'll be so tired – and dangerous to drive home. Everything will be OK here and you'll be back on Saturday for a lovely evening. I love you so much and hate to be so worried about you and see you so tired. Please be good.
Your Ginny.

She often, remembering her father's description of me before we married, called me 'mad, bad and dangerous to know'. I found boxes of all the notes and letters she had sent me down the years since long before we married. I read them all again when alone in our bedroom. Then I filed them in boxes and sent them to Abby for safe-keeping because, at the time, I felt and wished that I would die.

Sometimes I would say to myself that everybody will sooner or later lose or be lost by their loved ones, but life has to go on. I would argue to myself that every one of the billions of people who have ever lived has been sad to some degree at some time. I remembered walking with Ginny and Anton and Jill Bowring down the 1.5-kilometre-long death tunnels of the Paris catacombs. We passed by six million neatly stacked skulls. Each and every one had had, during their brief lifespan, the chance to spend time in sadness or in joy. I thought, too, of how lucky I was to have known such love and to have been with Ginny during the last months when she needed me. Now, with Ginny gone, and my mother, and Susan, and Celia, in so short a time, I was still alive, if only just, cardiac-wise, so I must get on with life. Not vegetate for even a moment.

I took on as much work as I could and averaged four conference lectures a week. I loved Greenlands, but the sadness and loneliness returned each time I went back. Ginny had told me many times over the years that, should she die before me, I was to remarry as soon as possible. I had said the same to her. She had also told me that I was to sell her sheep and cattle only to people with whom she had done previous business. Over that summer I sold the majority of the sheep and cows to individuals from Ginny's contact list. A friend and neighbour who had bought many of her cattle took over the rest of the herd and continues to run them, many at Greenlands, to this day.

I flew to Quito in Ecuador and met Jagged Globe's chief guide there. For a week he took our group up minor volcanoes which overlooked the polluted pall of Quito. Then we moved further afield to tackle the two 'big ones'. Cotopaxi is 19,000 feet above sea-level, and the effects of the altitude slowed me down alarmingly. But we reached the top and, being by then the only remaining 'student' on the course, I travelled in guide Pepe Landazuri's car for the four-hour drive south-west from Quito to Mount Chimborazo. I was aware that, if I summitted this last volcano, I would be cleared for Everest with Jagged Globe the following year. We spent the early part of the night in the Carrel Hut at 4,800 metres and immediately below the volcano's steep ascent route. Pepe regaled me with strong coffee and stories of the hut's ghosts. One of his own experiences included a night when a guide friend of his, with a famous Norwegian climber client, briefly met him in the hut but went on up soon after midnight. The next day, some hours after the two men should have come back down, Pepe phoned the local rescue team and went with them to the summit, where they found both men lying dead near the crater rim. The Norwegian's head had a neat round burn hole drilled in it by a lightning strike. His ice-axe and crampons were mere molten metal and the bolt had passed down the frozen rope to kill the guide for good measure.

'Never climb,' Pepe warned me, 'if you have any reason to think there may be an electric storm coming. If you are caught in the open, never lie down. Just kneel with your head low and your hands on the ground. Avoid shallow depressions in the ground, all forms of water or damp ground where you can, and, if it has a metal frame, keep out of your tent. Many people die on our volcanoes from lightning strikes.'

He also warned me that we had to cross a highly dangerous rockfall zone on our imminent climb, so we must ascend in the darkness and reach the summit by a predetermined turnround time. If we had not reached the top by that time, we *must* turn around or risk death by rockfall on the return journey, since the heat of the sun always loosened the rocks. We left the hut at 3.00 a.m.

Pepe climbed slowly but surely over the next ten hours. I lagged behind feeling the altitude and, despite having taken pills, my head throbbed with a dull persistent ache. The Cinderella-hour of Pepe's turnround time arrived when we were an hour from the top, but he was lenient and let me slog on tortoise-like and breathing heavily to the summit itself. I felt nauseous and my heartbeat was well over the 130 beats per minute that Gianni Angelini had warned me to respect. But, once we had descended 1,000 feet, I recovered and thereafter speeded up to cross the rockfall region whilst the cliff faces above were still in shadow.

A week later Pepe's report reached Jagged Globe's UK office, and Simon Lowe officially accepted me for their projected 2005 attempt on Everest via the Tibetan north side.

At that time everything seemed fine with my health, but I had earlier agreed a week's climb on Kilimanjaro with Simon Gault and a friend, Nick Holder, who had been on the Norway and Nile expeditions in the 1960s. A Masai guide took us along the Lemosho trail for four days, climbing slowly to acclimatise. If we tried to quicken the pace, he would sensibly intone, '*Poley, poley*', meaning 'Slow down', but on the last night he speeded up in competition with another group under a rival guide. At one point, not long before dawn, I asked if we could halt briefly so I could take off my fleece. This was not popular. Seemingly I was the only one finding the pace too fast. This was strange since I was normally fitter and faster than Simon. The last 500 feet were unpleasant. My chest grew ever tighter, as though squeezed by an invisible sumo wrestler, and the resulting constriction made my breathing difficult just when I needed maximum lung power.

Simon taunted my slowness in a good-natured way, as was his wont. We had done a great many walks together since first meeting at school forty years before, so I tried hard to keep up with him. I reached the summit ridge, but only just. I was incoherent and could hardly walk straight. Our guide, worried, tried to say I should go back down at once. He knew of my cardiac history from the client forms we had had to sign. I refused, hardly knowing what was going on except that the true summit was further along the rim of the crater. Some time later we arrived there and I rested with my head held low between my knees. Only when we had descended some 500 feet to about 5,486 metres (18,000 feet) did the feeling, by then like a tight band wrapped around my chest, disappear and I immediately felt normal. We walked back down to the base camp in good time where other guides were swapping gossip about their groups. Ours translated for us that two clients from separate groups had died of heart attacks that night on the mountain.

Back in London I had an ECG which recorded no new cardiac damage, so I thought no more about the incident. The British Heart Foundation took on my Everest project as a charity-raising tool, calling it the Ran Fiennes Healthy Hearts Appeal. The aim was to raise £2 million specifically for a new scanner unit for children with heart trouble at the Great Ormond Street Children's Hospital.

I gave a talk after a fund-raising dinner for twelve well-heeled businessmen in a North Yorkshire castle, and the host, Paul Sykes, a fiery Yorkshireman, asked if I was planning any more expeditions. I told him about Everest, and he agreed to sponsor the project financially as he approved of the plan and the charity aim. He had a long history of donating to charities, he liked to keep fit, and we were the same age. Paul was fiercely opposed to the EU and Brussels government, and largely funded the campaign against the single currency and the UK Independence Party election success. He would leave the climbing to me, but would do his best to keep the Heart Foundation working hard to reach our target figure of £2 million.

Late in the winter of 2004 I found myself high up on the Empire State Building, having given a talk at a New York conference. I tried to look down but, in seconds, felt the familiar nausea, the quickly rising terror of vertigo, and had to look away immediately to recover my composure. Vertigo is, I knew, an irrational problem, a mental sickness that is purely psychological. Some people are born afflicted by a deep-seated fear of wide open spaces, and that is just as unreasonable. I did not like living in the knowledge that, aged sixty, I had still not outgrown this problem, but I felt confident that if I could climb the highest mountain in the world, I would gain sufficient self-confidence to lose all fear of lesser heights.

18

Almost

The Ecuador volcanoes and Kilimanjaro were reasonable teasers for Everest but did not help my overall aerobic fitness, so I entered one or two team races in 2004 including, with Steven Seaton from *Runner's World*, the North Pole Marathon in the Arctic spring that year. This was organised by the Irishman, Richard Donovan, the first person to run a marathon at both Poles, and took place at 89.5° North on a floating Russian ice station. The temperature was –28°C and the surface was firm and icy. Due to the usual moving canals of open water between floes, the course consisted of a five-kilometre circuit to be completed eight and a half times.

Entries for the marathon from all over the world were restricted to sixteen, since the two Russian helicopters Donovan had hired each had a capacity for eight passengers. Many of the other runners had very respectable marathon records. Steven and I set out together wearing snowshoes, but after two laps Steven removed his and dropped behind. I gradually moved up the field over the next three hours until, with two laps to go, I was lying second. The leader was a tall, thin American, Sean Burch, martial arts expert and mountaineer, who went on to claim a world speed record, climbing Kilimanjaro in 5 hours 28 minutes.

I tried hard to catch him but failed, and finished a good thirteen minutes behind him in just under four hours. Having run the twenty-six miles with my legs forced apart by the snowshoes, my groin muscles took several weeks to stop aching.

The UK media portrayed the race in a way which must have muddled the minds of quite a few young readers because, in a *Yellow Pages/Daily Mail* survey a few months later, only 30 per cent of the young adults questioned recognised Robert Falcon Scott as the first British explorer to reach the South Pole, with 28 per cent wrongly crediting me. Similarly, only 29 per cent correctly named Sir Francis Drake as the first Britisher to sail round the world, with 36 per cent naming Dame Ellen MacArthur. However, 80 per cent answered correctly when asked the names of the recent winners of *Big Brother* and other celebrity television shows. (I was invited to participate in *I'm a Celebrity, Get Me Out of Here* in a jungle setting somewhere. I said no with alacrity for various reasons, including horror at the thought of having to lunch on live maggots.)

A year to the day after Ginny's death, her sister Abby and I sat together at Greenlands on the hill where Ginny's headstone stands. We remembered our times together with her.

At a lecture I had given to the Chester branch of the Royal Geographical Society the previous summer I had met one of their members, Louise Millington, and had since taken her out when she was not busy with the horse transporting company she had built up based from her Cheshire home. She was thirty-six years old, full of life, mercurial, had a ten-year-old son Alexander, and she jolted me out of my miserable state. We agreed to marry in March 2005 and honeymoon at the Everest Base Camp in Tibet.

Abby, Ginny's closest relative, said to the press:

Ran has been a much-loved member of our family for nearly fifty years and always will be. He and Ginny had an exceptionally happy marriage and were in love with each other for all their adult lives. Ran was devastated by Ginny's illness and death and he has had a desperately long, lonely year without her. To see him happy again with Louise is wonderful. He still grieves for Ginny and nothing will change or diminish his feelings for my sister. But

Ginny wouldn't want Ran to be sad or lonely. She urged him to marry again and everyone in the family is one hundred per cent supportive of his decision. We all wish Ran and Louise every happiness.

Abby's mother Janet had collapsed on her way to Ginny's funeral over a year before and had never really recovered. We went to see her that spring at a rest home in Liverpool, close to Abby's own home, and I sensed that she did not have long to live. A month before I was due to leave for Everest, I joined Abby in fulfilling a promise I had made to Ginny two years before. Her father, who had fought our teenage love for so long, had been buried in a churchyard close by the family chalk quarry in the South Downs of West Sussex. But no headstone had ever been erected at his grave due, in a roundabout way, to a nationwide gravediggers' strike at the time of his death. We had contacted the relevant vicar and, on a cold clear February morning with a group of Tom Pepper's old friends and relations, we prayed by his newly erected headstone.

During the last month before going to Everest, I discovered that I could not properly hold a standard ice-axe in my frost-damaged left hand. So we went to DMM, a climbing gear factory in Wales, where they sponsored me with a special axe with a thin shaft as well as a steel hook for, hopefully, gripping those tiny holds that my half-fingers could not manage. Whilst in Wales we also went with an old SAS friend to the Cardiff Millennium Stadium to watch Wales defeat England at rugby.

No football fan, I had recently acquired a definite appetite for watching the fifteen-man sport at national level after meeting the Irish team in Dublin. Ten days before they were due to fly to Australia for the 2003 World Cup, their manager Eddie O'Sullivan and former captain Keith Woods had me flown out at the last minute to lecture the squad on 'team morale when the odds look bad'. I had talked to the forty-strong group for an hour in a small closely packed hotel room. No smiles. No laughter. Just intense frowns that looked to me like glares. I don't remember ever feeling so much concentrated human *power* in one place before. But when I stopped talking, their enthusiastic questioning went on for a second hour, and Eddie sent me emails of their subsequent excellent progress down under.

My own power during the run-up weeks to Everest was not improved by a severe bout of bronchitis. Louise was worried and booked me to see various lung, chest and heart specialists, starting with my own cardiac surgeon Gianni Angelini in Bristol and progressing to Dr John Costello, a lung expert, in London. An altitude test chamber simulated up to 15,000 feet above sea-level where I had to perform various lung function tests, and then have blood taken. The results, which were quickly available, were disappointing. They showed a limitation of flow in my airways, presumably due to my previous smoking. The flow was 80 per cent of what it should have been for a man of my age and height and, in John Costello's professional opinion, 'would be an important limiting factor in my ability to carry on at 7,000 metres and above'. Additionally, my ability to saturate my bloodstream with oxygen, a key function when exerting yourself at high altitude, was badly impaired. Coupled with my cardiac status which dictated never getting badly out of breath, I was not an ideal candidate for an Everest attempt. Better news was that the organisers of our Everest fundraiser, the Ran Fiennes Healthy Hearts Appeal, had already raised, prior to our departure, more than the entire £70,000 the charity had managed to total following our 7x7x7 marathons.

7 March was my sixty-first birthday. Five days later Louise and I were married, and a fortnight after that we left Heathrow bound for Kathmandu in Nepal. At the airport a reporter from *The Times* interviewed Louise and asked her all the usual questions. She admitted she was worried about the altitude and the strain on my heart. This reminded me of Sherpa Tenzing's account of his wife's reaction when told he was joining John Hunt's attempt on Everest. 'You are too weak,' she said. 'You will get ill again, or you will slip on the ice and fall and kill yourself.' 'No, I will look out

for myself,' he told her. 'Just like I always have.' Adventuring husbands have always been having these prior-to-departure conversations.

Those members of our team we did not meet at Heathrow we caught up with in Kathmandu where we were introduced to our group leader. He was a tall Scotsman named David Hall. His number two, Neal Short from Liverpool, was small and mild-mannered. The rest of the group included my South African friend, Sibusiso, at whose suggestion I had become involved in the first place, and Ian Parnell, a professional freelance climbing photographer, who was covering my climb for *The Times* and, with minimal equipment training, was organising live TV coverage for BBC Breakfast TV.

Ian later wrote:

My first introduction to Ran was when I received a phone call from him pretty much out of the blue in February 2005. 'Ian, would you like to go to Everest with me?' 'Er . . . um . . . well, maybe . . . when?' 'We leave in two weeks, it'll be a ten-week trip.' 'Well I was meant to be travelling to the States to see my girlfriend.' 'Ian, I'm sure she'll understand. If you have any problems, let me have a word. I tell you what, I'll give you twenty-four hours to talk it over with her.' So within two minutes of talking to Ran for the first time, I'd been invited to spend three months with him on the world's highest mountain and had twenty-four hours to make a choice.

My job on the expedition was to facilitate live broadcasts and send back film and still pictures to be used by the BBC and *The Times* newspaper. The fact that over ten weeks this probably only amounted to twenty minutes of footage makes this task seem pretty trivial. However, the reality proved pretty challenging. My first inklings of this reality gap came when I went to Broadcasting House to pick up all the equipment I would be using. The conversation with one technical guy started with, 'Can you get power on the summit?' I wasn't sure how to answer. Was he wondering if there was a mains plug, or something? 'Well, how about getting a generator up there?' he asked. Considering that most people could barely walk at over 29,000 feet and the Sherpas were pushed carrying enough oxygen for everyone, there was no chance. We eventually settled for a relatively lightweight battery-operated set-up. When I say relatively lightweight, I'm talking about an extra twenty-five pounds of equipment.

Problems started early. The laptop computer's hard disk drive gave up the ghost only a week into the trip, while other parts of the set-up needed constant nursing to keep operating. A typical broadcast would involve an hour or so spent locating satellites for the two sat phones in series. Of course, with one sat phone locked in, the other phone would drop its connection, and vice versa – it was a constant plate-juggling trick. Having finally got both phones talking to Broadcasting House, I'd have to fire up the video phone, which unfortunately developed an alarming syndrome of cutting out every five minutes. Each live interview lasted about three minutes, so the timing when to crank up the video phone was crucial. To top it all, I discovered the batteries had a warning that they shouldn't be used below +5°C. Considering that the average temperature at Everest Advance Base Camp hovered around −10°C, we had a constant battle on our hands. The trick, I found, was to get in my sleeping bag and put the batteries on my belly minutes before transmission.

But, as with most things in life, the more effort you have to put in, the greater the reward. So, despite the struggles, we managed not to miss a single broadcast, and the feeling as you listen to a live interview broadcasting from the slopes of Everest all the way back to the UK is one that rivals the feelings I have when I reach mountain summits.

Two other South Africans in our group, Alex Harris and Mark Campbell, were both experienced climbers and good friends of Sibusiso. Tore Rasmussen was a Norwegian businessman, hobby climber and black belt karate instructor. Fred Ziel from California was our doctor. Like Sibu, and indeed with Sibu, he had been on a previous Jagged Globe Everest climb, on the south side, but he had failed, where Sibu had succeeded, and he had suffered frostbite damage to his fingers and nose. Jens Bojen, born in Norway, was now a Grimsby businessman with a lifelong experience of North Sea fishing. Although a year older than me, he was twice as fit and the proud possessor of an abnormally slow heart rate. Rosalind Buckton had once very nearly been the first British woman to climb Everest and, although now in her late fifties, was keen to succeed on this her second attempt.

The general opinion of the more experienced climbers in our group was that our Tibetan northern route was a bigger challenge than the Nepalese southern route, pioneered by John Hunt's British expedition of 1953 which made the first ascent. This was because our route involved more time spent higher than 8,400 metres, in the notorious 'Death Zone'. The twin words 'altitude' and 'acclimatisation' were on our group's lips much of the time. Sensible application of the latter, the old hands constantly assured us, would be our main way of defeating the potentially lethal effects of the former.

The next day we started our drive towards Everest Base Camp 400 kilometres (250 miles) away and at an elevation of 5,200 metres (17,000 feet). We would drive there in stages because we must not rush our acclimatisation process. At Base Camp there would already be just half the oxygen available at sea-level. We travelled north-east towards the Nepalese/Tibetan border in jeeps, our gear on high-back lorries, and we all attempted to drink four litres (eight pints) daily, as advised by David, our leader. The border town of Zhangmu, a place of shabby wood huts on the Nepalese side and ugly concrete blockhouses in Tibet, buzzed with groups similar to ours and all with the same thing on their minds . . . the summit. As we joined various queues in the complex process of passing through Chinese customs, security and immigration, I met nine climbers of different nationalities, some aiming to climb Everest solo but most with commercial groups and street-wise handlers adept at dealing with Chinese bureaucracy.

From Zhangmu the scenery changed from relatively bland to spectacular as our road, evilly potholed and often edged with sheer drops to our immediate left and cliff walls to the right, fought its tortuous way up the sheer and rugged gorge of the Bhote Kosi. A thousand feet below, often immediately below us, roiled and roared the fearsome rapids of the Bhote Kosi heading back south to Nepal. Neal assured us we had already been lucky on two counts when our convoy reached our overnight stop, the raggedy town of Nyalam. Not only had we avoided ambush by Maoist terrorists in Nepal who shot up tourists or merely stopped them and demanded cash, but, secondly, we had to date been spared the avalanches and mud slides which most years plague the Nyalam road. What we could not avoid were the rat-infested, filth-encrusted rooms in Zhangmu and Nyalam. I itched like hell. Louise was fairly stoical but, a migraine-sufferer since her teens, her headaches were exacerbated by the ever increasing altitude. Others in our group also began to complain of lethargy, appetite loss and splitting headaches, and Dr Fred offered us all the altitude sickness prevention drug Diamox.

An hour or so north of Nyalam, our convoy eased into the main Himalayan range between India and Asia, the mightiest geographical feature on the earth's surface. It boasts more than a hundred peaks in excess of 24,000 feet (7,315 metres) above sea-level, and includes all the famed fourteen 8,000ers, the trophy peaks over 8,000 metres (26,247 feet) whose summits are 'collected' by many dedicated high altitude climbers, the first of whom was Reinhold Messner. For hours we travelled on up over the high dusty plateau until we came to a couple of passes, the higher being the Lalung La at 5,125 metres (16,810 feet).

The Tibetan Plateau stretches across south-west China, bounded by the deserts of the Tarim and Qaidam to the north and the Himalayan, Karakoram, and Pamir mountain chains to the south and west. With an elevation of nearly five kilometres above sea-level, this desolate, dry, windswept landscape is the world's highest plateau. Wild yaks were once abundant on the plateau, but in were mostly killed off for meat from the 1950s, when new roads made the area more accessible to hunters.

After Nyalam's concrete scenery, we passed isolated villages the same orange-brown hue as the wide country vistas that rolled away beneath the great clear blue sky. The wind was always blowing when we stopped to leg-stretch, and the spring weather seemed always cold and dry. Our average height now, on these panoramic plains between high crumbly hills, was some 4,300 metres (14,000 feet). The Tibetan herders and farmers were clearly a hard bunch. Their squat adobe huts, isolated or in hamlet clusters, were often close by stone-built ruins of ancient Buddhist monasteries destroyed in the Chinese Cultural Revolution, often along with their inmates. Potato and barley crops showed between intricate irrigation ditches, whilst scraggy sheep, goats and yaks roamed free.

After many hours our road began to turn east and we came to the village of Tingri, built on a hillside with an impressive view looking back to the south of a distant array of snow-clad peaks floating on cloud. This was the great Himalayan range that reached east and west from Everest, mother of all mountains. Our convoy hove to in a dusty football field-sized courtyard with low dormitory blocks on three sides. A canteen and office provided the only facilities, and rooftop squat toilets awaited the growing number of our group with uneasy stomachs. From this fly-ridden base we trudged out of town and climbed local hills to find our feet at our new altitude of 4,390 metres (14,400 feet). I discovered that I could keep up with or ahead of most of the others without undue effort or breathlessness. So far, so good.

From Tingri our group headed east on a switchback drive over the 5,120-metre (16,800 feet) Pang La pass. We stopped at the highest point to take photographs, for the view was impressive. Everest was now clearly visible, crested by a plume of ice crystal 'smoke', indicating violent winds on the summit ridge. The highest mountain on earth was certainly no visual let-down.

The onward road took us through moon scenery with wide river beds now dry but ready conduits for awesome melt-floods. Towering glacial moraines loomed above and twisted spires of rock supported boulders, big as churches, which teetered on the highest ledges and threatened imminent freefall. Some four hours after the Pang La, we came to the Rongbuk Monastery, close to the original Base Camp used by the pioneering British expeditions of the 1920s. It was from here that Mallory and Irvine set out in 1924 never to return. Then we climbed sharply up a narrow valley, the Rongbuk Gorge, which widened quite suddenly to become a bleak, flat plain some 500 metres wide between high hills with Everest dead ahead. This plain, home to the modern Everest Base Camp, was dotted with the colourful tents of at least a dozen expedition groups and was swept by a bitter cold wind from the glaciers above. Everest herself, now only twelve miles away, rose impressively above us, black rock streaked with ice and crowned with snow.

Louise and I shared a two-man tent which was hardly a honeymoon suite. There was a fairly cramped communal tent for meals and various stores tents. David introduced us to our Sherpas, small powerful men with affable features, and we settled down for the night.

Due largely to a Nepalese government clampdown on the number of climbers they allowed annually on Everest, more and more groups and individuals were switching to our Tibetan approach. We learned that at least 400 individuals would be hoping to climb the northern route over the next few weeks. Some years there was enough good weather to allow climbers to sneak briefly on to the summit, other years nobody made it at all, however great their skill and their strength. Most years people died trying. The current death rate was estimated at one in every ten attempts.

We spent two weeks in Base Camp at 5,200 metres (17,060 feet), sometimes trudging a few miles upwards on the Everest trail or back downhill to the Rongbuk Monastery. Acclimatisation was the main aim of our existence. Louise still suffered severe headaches but stayed with me for a fortnight before returning to England just before David decided we were ready to try our first trek up to the Advance Base Camp. Our gear was taken by sixty-five yaks with drivers who whistled and yelled at their animals when the trail was especially narrow or slippery.

The morning before we left Base Camp, a Belfast police friend of mine, Noel Hanna, visited our group tent. I knew Noel from adventure racing in New Zealand. He was one of the fittest men in Britain and had been planning to marry his long-time fiancée on the Everest summit. His group had trudged up to the Advance Base Camp (ABC) a few days earlier, but Noel's eyesight began to trouble him. His group leader diagnosed tunnel vision, but a doctor with an ophthalmoscope later discovered 'pools of blood' behind his retinas where blood vessels had burst. He was now due to head back to Ireland for treatment as soon as possible or, he had been warned, he would risk permanent eye damage and possible blindness.

Following behind Sibu and Alex I began the walk up the Rongbuk Valley from Base Camp on 12 April, often moving off the well-trodden but narrow path to make way for yaks coming back down from the ABC with loads of rubbish or barrels of latrine soil which is sold for crop manure in the valley. Past ecological outcry had resulted in a system of payment to yak drivers for this litter removal service, which was becoming ever more necessary as the annual numbers of climbers increased exponentially.

As we moved up the glacial valley, banks of hardened mud and rock pinnacles, some as high as thirty metres, flanked our progress. Rocks rain down regularly from these walls on to the path below but, thankfully, not while we were passing. After some four kilometres we trudged up a steep scree slope and into a side valley. This, after a few hours, widened out into the corridor of the East Rongbuk Glacier, our highway to Everest.

I knew that all 2005 summit bids had to be completed by the first week of June because that was the annual date for the arrival of the monsoon winds which would make Everest lethal to climbers. I still had about fifty days in which to reach the top and thereby, I hoped, enable the Heart Foundation to raise our £2 million target. I also had a personal pet hope. For twenty-three years I had competed with Norwegians for polar firsts. Now I had a chance of going for another. Only a handful of individuals had managed to cross both Antarctica and the Arctic Ocean. Børge Ousland was one of them, and he had tried to add Everest to his trophy list. Sibu and Dr Fred had been with him when he had decided to turn round not far short of the summit. So I hoped that my heart, my lungs and, remembering Noel Hanna, my retinas would behave themselves for the next fifty days. Weather permitting, I might then raise my £2 million *and* beat the Norwegians. Wishful thinking, I realised, but there was no harm in hoping.

I slept well that night at the first interim camp at 5,500 metres (18,045 feet) en route to Advance Base. I had taken three hours to get there at a slow trudge with a light rucksack, and still had no headache, no sickness and no loss of appetite. Sibu kept telling me to drink more water, and I had done so, mostly to keep him happy as I'm not normally a water drinker despite knowing (and indeed preaching) all the standard dictums on the blessings to be had from H_2O.

Next morning our group moved on up the glacial valley, an ascent of 950 metres with sharkfin pinnacles of ice towering above each side of the trail, known as the Magic Highway. We crossed or skirted lakes of frozen melt-water, great glaciers curved down from high valleys to join ours, but all, we knew, were shrinking, the main glacier by over 100 vertical feet in the past ten years alone. I kept up with the others without trouble, and after five hours came to the tents of the second interim camp at 6,088 metres (approximately 20,000 feet).

I slotted my sleeping bag, boots and rucksack between the two other Brits, Ian and Jens – by chance, not chauvinistic intention – and welcomed a cup of tea proffered by Ian. We were all dog-tired and most of us had headaches since, despite our cautious acclimatisation to date, we were for the first time living and working well above 17,000 feet where the human body starts to deteriorate, indeed to rot. It literally consumes itself for energy. Sleeping becomes a problem, muscle wasting and weight loss take place, and this process of deterioration continues more quickly the higher the altitude. Scientific advice by 2005 strongly recommended that nobody stay at that height for more than an absolute maximum of ten days and that, at or above 26,000 feet, the so-called Death Zone, acclimatisation is not possible.

Ian asked me if I'd like to take over the cooking, for he was dog-tired, having a far heavier backpack than mine due to all his delicate photographic and TV gear. I declined as I was struggling with my first bad headache and felt nauseous, and so did Jens. This naturally irritated Ian who felt he was doing all the work, as though he were a paid Sherpa or guide. In such close quarters when tired, sick, wet and uncomfortable, folk can get easily irritable or offended. Ian did well to hide his annoyance at that time, and I only learned about it two years later in another cramped and difficult night spot.

I lay awake for a while listening to water dripping on to sleeping bags, the distant crackle of moving glacier ice and the muted rumble of some snoring neighbour. Then, with no warning at all and a nasty shock, I jerked up gasping for air with a terrible sensation of suffocation. My heart beat wildly. The phenomenon passed as quickly as it came, and I felt drowsy again. Within minutes, or maybe mere seconds, I was again jumping up in a panic. Again I felt as though I had been throttled. The instant the shock awoke me, my breathing reverted to normal, but as soon as I drowsed off again, the gasping for air routine was back. There was no way I could get any sleep.

Next day, after a sleepless, worried night, I learned from Fred Ziel exactly what my problem was – an ailment known as Cheyne-Stokes periodic breathing which occurs when the system which regulates breathing gets out of sync. The would-be sleeper responds involuntarily to a build-up in carbon dioxide by hyperventilating which in turn leads to the breathing centre responding by shutting off respiration. CO_2 levels then increase and the unfortunate cycle repeats. A standard cure is for the victim to take Diamox tablets just before going to bed. Diamox blocks an enzyme in the kidney and makes the blood acidic, which is interpreted by the brain as a signal to breathe more. Diamox, therefore, enhances the physiological response to altitude by increasing the rate and depth of breathing. However, with my lung problem, I was already taking the maximum advised dose of two 250mg tablets daily. The only answer therefore, Fred advised, was to use oxygen whenever I needed to sleep at or above the height of that camp at 20,000 feet.

Early next day our group pushed on up the Magic Highway until we came to a great bowl of polished blue ice nearly a mile wide and rimmed by steep ridges. The trail then veered farther east, climbed abruptly over rough ground and, rounding a sharpish bend, revealed, all of a sudden, the stupendous mass of Everest's North-East Ridge ever ascending to the wind-driven streamer that raged along the impossibly high summit ridge at a height of 8,850 metres (29,029 feet) where jumbo jets fly.

After an hour I clambered up scree and loose boulders, over small melt pools and past the first outlying tents of the waiting congregation of aspirant summiteers, climbers of varying skills or, like me, none at all, from all over the world. This was Advance Base Camp (ABC), splattered like some multi-coloured rash up the rock-strewn moraine that lies in the eastern shadow of Changtse, a giant feature in her own right but a mere dwarf satellite to her neighbour Chomolungma, the Goddess Mother of the Snows to all Tibetans, Everest to us foreigners.

I caught up with Sibu after a three-hour trudge somewhere in the hugger-mugger labyrinth of tents large and small which stretched for at least 600 metres up the moraine, perched wherever a flat platform could be found or prepared by Sherpas smoothing out rock jumbles.

I was now at 6,460 metres (21,200 feet), higher than I had ever been. So far, I thanked God for small mercies, I appeared to have escaped retinal damage, severe headaches, heart pains, cerebral and pulmonary oedema, tensions with my fellow climbers, and even the hacking Khumbu cough that racked many climbers even down at Base Camp. Periodic breathing or Cheyne-Stokes syndrome would only affect me if I slept or dozed without oxygen, so my summit chances were still intact.

David's plan, now that all the Jagged Globe group, apart from a badly coughing Rosalind, had reached ABC in good condition, was to have us sleep only one night there, then descend all the way back to Base Camp. This was part of the generally accepted acclimatisation policy of 'climb high, sleep low'. We would recuperate for a while at Base Camp, then come back up (in a single day next time) to ABC *and* climb the formidable ice slopes which give access to the North Col. Then back down. And so on until we and the weather were ready for a final four- or five-day push from ABC to the summit. It was the yo-yo principle of bouncing up and down. This is how the body and the brain learn to cope with inadequate oxygen. By pushing the limits, then retreating to safety, repeatedly, human beings can gradually acclimate to the thin air of the high Himalaya. The thicker, more oxygen-rich air down below allows the body to sleep better and recover faster than at the debilitating altitude of ABC. The body's metabolism begins to work more effectively. On returning to ABC, the body is as strong as it will ever be.

David and Neal were sympathetic about my Cheyne-Stokes problem and agreed that I could use oxygen from their precious supply of canisters, but I was to control the usage or flow rate to as low a setting as would allow me to sleep. Later, thanks to a sat-phone facility at Base Camp, I was able to ask Louise to organise an additional supply.

I slept hardly at all that night, finding it difficult to fit the oxygen mask so that it stayed tight when I moved in my sleep. Saliva slowly blocked up the inlet pipe and mouthpiece, which impeded the breathing process and produced a gurgling snore which my tent companion, Ian Parnell, found so distracting, he eventually banished me to sleep by myself. I was not alone in finding control of my oxygen mask difficult to master. No less a climber than Ed Hillary had described the same salivatory problems, I was pleased to discover later.

I was relieved to leave ABC after an early breakfast of cereal. I turned down the Sherpa chef's kind offer of yak stew and set out downhill at a good pace. Alex was the only member of the group faster at descents, and he was a long-time adventure racer for a top South African team. The only obstacles that day, since the trail was obvious enough to preclude any chance of getting lost, were the intermittent traffic jams of yak caravans hogging the narrow mountain paths. The yak drivers were a wild-looking bunch with deeply wrinkled features and sleek black hair of which they were clearly proud, plaited beautifully and braided with precious gems and shiny bones.

My first night back down at Base Camp was blissful now that I knew how unpleasant it was to sleep or even doze using oxygen. On subsequent days I heard the faraway muffled thud of avalanches. Over on the south Nepalese side we heard that Kenton Cool, my erstwhile Alpine instructor and Jagged Globe Everest guide, was doing well with his client group, the mirror image of our own gang. An avalanche had, however, struck at one of the tented camps over there and injured some of the climbers. I knew that avalanches are one of the main reasons for Everest deaths.

Before we left Base Camp for our next upward sortie, David and Neal arranged for a lama from the Rongbuk Monastery to conduct a *puja* or blessing ceremony for our climbers. Prayer flags were strung in long lines from a makeshift stone altar on a hillock, and the ensuing rituals lasted almost an hour with much chanting, hand drum-thumping, bell-ringing, throwing about of tsampa flour and rice, and the eventual handouts of good-symbol-necklaces to help protect us. I took mine but decided not to wear it, since I trusted that my own bog-standard Church of England beliefs would sort out whatever fate had in store for me.

By the time we left Base Camp for the second time, there were few folk still there other than temporary acclimatisers like us, the sick and wounded, and the camp guardians. There were also a few unlucky souls whose arrival had been delayed along the road from Kathmandu by the haphazard ambushes of the heavily armed Maoist rebels whose fight had begun in 1996, killing since then over 3,000 Nepalese and a few tourists.

My second return journey to ABC took a full day with no halts en route and far fewer yak jams to cause delays. After resting for forty-eight hours, I joined David and the others for my first trip from ABC to the North Col. We were starting out from a point already 1,600 feet higher than Mont Blanc (where twenty years before I had been violently sick from altitude) and, within ten minutes of climbing into what Tibetans call 'the poison gas' – the thin air of high altitude – I was already feeling geriatric. It seemed as though, at 21,000 feet, my personal tree-line was broached.

I could never match Alex for speed, but had previously kept up with all the others uphill and well ahead downhill. Now, all of a sudden, I lagged behind everyone, constantly needing to rest my lungs and my legs. It was a novel experience for I normally prized my ability not to need a rest for many hours of adventure racing and ultra marathons in wild country. I felt wretched and, when David dropped back to check on me, I apologised and felt ashamed. He was kind and stayed close as I trudged on for an hour over rocks, ice and snow to the base of the North Col ascent. Fixed ropes were in place all the way from this point to the summit of Everest, put there and maintained by Sherpas from all the groups.

Using a simple hand device called an ascendeur (to grip the rope when tugged downwards but to slide along the rope when pulled upwards), I followed David up a succession of very steep snow slopes. In my free hand I grasped my ice-axe. Everybody climbed in this manner, pretty much all the way up the mountain. You do not need to be a 'proper' technical climber for Everest. But you do need to be altitude-fit, which I clearly wasn't. All the others in the group (except Rosalind who was back in Kathmandu seeing a lung doctor) made it to the North Col that day and spent the night there.

David saw me back down to ABC and gave me a gentle but not too subtle warning that my current form would not see me much higher than the North Col. My speed must improve.

Various other sorties followed, then it was back once more to Base Camp. With time on my hands I took a lift in a jeep down to Tingri, where I stayed for four days at a spa-cum-bed-and-breakfast. I went for a long walk every day and met up with an American climber in Tingri village. In the high street he pointed out two climbers striding past us.

'Those guys,' he muttered, 'are both big US climbers. I mean Number One dudes. Ed Viesturs and David Breashears. Both have been up the Big E several times with and without oxygen. And all the other big peaks too. Hey! Isn't that something?'

I agreed that it was, wishing only that I could make it up the North Col, using plenty of oxygen all the way. A few days later, on 27 April, I did manage the North Col, extremely slowly, but in time to make it in daylight and to spend the night there at 7,066 metres and using oxygen before heading back down to ABC.

After one more spell in Base Camp, we all (except poor Rosalind who had had to return home due to her lung trouble) made our last ascent to ABC by the third week of May and stayed there, with small local excursions from time to time, eagerly awaiting our chance for the final push. We were truly acclimatised, but were also in danger of general deterioration due to spending far too long above the 17,000 feet marker. We were living on borrowed time, according to every high-altitude book on the market.

David allocated a Sherpa to each climber. I was matched with Nima Dorje Sherpa (or Boca Lama), the smallest and most humorous ever-grinning dwarf of a Nepali. He was also a lay-lama which, I mused, must be a plus point in these Buddhist mountains for whoever he worked with. More than half of all Sherpas live entirely off their seasonal tourism and mountaineering incomes. Whether high-altitude guides, cooks or camp staff, they are among the best paid people in Nepal, earning up to eight times the average annual income.

Whilst our group yo-yoed up and down between Base Camp and the North Col, our Sherpas were moving heavy loads up to and establishing the higher camps, often without oxygen. I could imagine the frustration of the many Sherpas whose clients fall by the wayside long before they reach the high camps, never mind the summit. Then their poor Sherpas have to bring down all the heavy gear they have just sweated blood to position at risk to life and limb. In 2005 on our side of Everest only sixty of the 400 climbers who reached ABC actually went on up to reach the summit, so there must have been a good many irritated Sherpas.

The high 2005 failure rate was due to many causes. The weather was average to bad, but altitude sickness, diarrhoea and the Khumbu cough took their regular toll. The dry air at altitude can wreak havoc with even the toughest climber's prospects. Also known as high altitude hack, the Khumbu cough can be bad enough to cause broken ribs. One of the early British attempts to pioneer the northern route involved climber Howard Somervell in 1924. When a coughing fit wracked him just above the North Col, he found his throat was obstructed. He could neither breathe nor call for help, so he sat down to die. Then in desperation, 'I pressed my chest with both hands, gave one last almighty push and the obstruction came up. Though the pain was intense, I was a new man.' He had coughed up the desiccated mucous membrane of his throat.

The two main high-altitude sickness killers, cerebral and pulmonary oedema, are both caused by the body's reactions to lack of oxygen. Many people who travel from sea-level to over 8,000 feet report symptoms ranging from headache to loss of appetite and nausea. Why? As the available oxygen falls, the body responds by increasing the blood flow to the brain, but it can overcompensate, whereupon fluid leaks from the blood vessels into the brain causing it to swell. The victim is then suffering cerebral oedema.

Not surprisingly, the greater the elevation gain, the more severe the swelling. In severe cases the brain can get squeezed down the spinal cord, which results in death. The way to avoid falling victim is to ascend gradually, about 1,000 feet per day over 8,000 feet, which gives your body time to acclimatise properly.

As the body tries to get as much oxygen from the air as it can, pulmonary oedema can result from the greatly increased blood flow through the lungs. The heart increases the flow by increasing the pressure, causing leakage from the blood vessels into the air sacs. It usually takes a few days to develop, and is exacerbated by overexertion. In bad cases, you can hear a gurgling of fluid in the lungs, and the victim brings up bloody sputum. This is a serious condition which can kill in only a matter of hours and again is best avoided by gradual ascent. Treatment is by an immediate descent of several thousand feet and use of oxygen if available.

The body also responds to the lower oxygen levels by putting more red blood cells into circulation. Up to a point, this is a good thing. However, if it goes too far, the blood becomes thick and prone to clotting. Clots which get dislodged float around and can cause strokes, heart attacks and pulmonary embolisms. Due to my own cardiac state, Professor Angelini had upped my daily blood-thinning aspirin intake from 75mg to 350mg whilst I was at high altitude.

The Times journalist who had been sent out to cover the entire climb, wrote cynical articles, humorous in a caustic sort of way, that covered most aspects of life at ABC:

There are normal people on Everest, but the proportion of glory-hunters is abnormally high when compared with that at sea level. As a BBC compère might say: if you liked 'Fame Academy', then you'll LOVE 'Advance Base Camp'. They're all here, the star-struck and the fame-chasers, with their promotional stickers and funny logo'ed hats, their business cards and Americanised pidgin English, and for a journalist there is just nowhere to hide from these people – all want front-page coverage, preferably in *The Times*. So far I have met the sirdar who is to guide Tom Cruise up the mountain next year, the prospective first Punjabi woman and the first Bhutanese man to climb Everest. There is the bloke from

Australia whose aim is to be the first one-armed Australian on the summit and another man who claims that he will be the first asthmatic to have reached the top.

Why do these trophy-hunters annoy me so much? And doesn't Ranulph Fiennes fall into the same category? In answer to question two: absolutely not. Fiennes is one of the most self-effacing, focused people here and is climbing Everest only to raise £2 million for charity: he talks about almost nothing else.

The Times journalist was less enthusiastic about the ABC lavatory facilities, one of which was very close to *The Times* tent. I have experienced many such way-out facilities all over the world. In order of dreadfulness, I would rate the long communal muddy trench with a sit-on-pole down its length, as dug for the annual Karrimor Mountain Marathon in the UK, as winner, a short head in front of the Soviet military bucket squat galley in Sredniy, Siberia. Then came the Everest loos. Rosalind was unlucky enough one night to lose her spectacles (and her head torch, if the camp gossip was to be believed) down one of our loos. As deputy boss, the task of locating and retrieving both items fell to Neal, who did so successfully and without complaining.

On 30 May we were still ensconsed at ABC and still waiting for the high roar of the jet stream winds, up to 200 mph on Everest's upper reaches, to die away and stay away for the five-day period of calm, clear weather that we would need to attempt the climb. Such a break in the jet streams usually comes just before the onslaught of the annual monsoon storms which arrive most years in the first few days of June. Some years the break never comes, and nobody summits Everest. And some years the break only lasts a day or two, catches people out in the Death Zone and kills them.

The group leader has the often extremely difficult task of assessing from met forecasts whether or not to risk the lives of his clients, all of whom will be raring to go, especially if they can see the fatal date of the monsoon's dreaded arrival fast approaching. Many clients will have spent some US$65,000 of their savings and will know they are unlikely to have another chance, so they champ at the bit at the ongoing wimpishness, as they see it, of any group leader who is still refusing to try for the summit with only five or six days left till the monsoon is likely to be due.

At last, on 31 May, half of our group left ABC for their summit attempt. David had sensibly divided us into a fast-moving grey-hound group of Sibu, Tore, Alex and Fred, led by him, while group two, led by Neal, would be Mark, Jens, Ian and me.

On the other side of Everest, only a single day of less strong winds is needed to climb from the South Col to the summit and back. Jagged Globe's group on that side, led by Kenton, summit-ted on 31 May. That same day I made it up to the North Col camp with the rest of group two. Group one were, by then, two camps ahead of us and experiencing high winds. The North Col camp, in the lee of a great snow wall, was the last haven of shelter all the way to the summit, so our group, sleeping with oxygen, stayed there awaiting orders from David to come on up once his group had vacated our tents. This leapfrog shuffle would involve the three camps between the North Col and the summit, positioned at 7,500 metres (Camp Two), 7,900 metres (Camp Three), and 8,400 metres (Death Camp).

We had set out from ABC much later than would have been possible in a normal monsoon year. But in 2005 it was running late, so we just squeezed in. Of the 400 would-be climbers in ABC, about one-third had been forced to give up during the ongoing bad weather in May, due to ill-health, homesickness, flight dates, or visa restrictions.

I was happy to have made it to the North Col Camp at a reasonable rate; slower than the rest, but not by much. I was feeling far better physically than at any time over the past month. The Col is hard grind. I had read descriptions of it by experienced climbers. One, Andy Politz, was part of an earlier group who located Mallory's body. He wrote simply, 'The entire lower half of the Col was an exercise in surviving torture.'

Scaling the Col involves a series of short, nearly vertical steps interspersed with steep snow slopes and twisting crevasse detours. The relief when reaching the last ladders over a wide crevasse, just a few metres from the first tent at the Col Camp, is huge. I tottered into one of the four tents our Sherpas had erected for us, fairly near to the great snow wall that gives protection from the violent west winds and surrounded by some ninety or more other tents. The toilet arrangements were simple. You squatted as near as was safely possible to the edge of the ice precipice on the far side of the encampment. Slipping on the ice there would be a bad idea, for the resulting fall would be over 1,000 feet.

At the Col Camp I spent a lot of time in the tent fiddling with my oxygen system in the knowledge that most deaths on the upper reaches of Everest are the result of oxygen shortage, and the oxygen regulator is the key to survival. New Zealander Russell Bryce, generally accepted as head honcho on the north side, had kindly lent me a spare regulator as all the Jagged Globe spares were already in use. The oxygen systems we used were made by Poisk in Russia, and they had been in use for many years but were prone to failed seals and valves due to grit particles and ice. The smaller orange cylinders most in use gave five or six hours of oxygen if you set a flow rate on the regulator dial of 2.5 litres a minute. The larger 1,000-litre canisters gave ten hours on this setting.

Eventually our number two group set out from Col Camp. The sky was clear and the winds manageable, so we all made good time up the long steep snow ramps to where shattered shale underfoot gradually replaced the snow, and the fixed ropes edged to the right, at first gently then, for the last hour, at quite a steep gradient. This 7,500-metre camp was much smaller than the Col Camp and the few dozen tents there were tattered, in some cases completely shredded. Our own two tents had survived well and we all slept on oxygen. Each time I woke to knock frozen dribble from my mask, I intoned, 'Only two days to the top and two million quid in the kitty.'

From 7,300 to 7,500 metres the wind had picked up and made life quite unpleasant. My oxygen mask kept needing adjustment, my frost-damaged feet spent a good deal of time complaining that my Kathmandu-purchased boots were too tight, and my frostbitten hand needed many halts to force blood back into the fingers during those stretches where I needed to keep the fixed rope on my right-hand side. Let me explain to anyone who is not a climber how Everest hopefuls who are upwards-trudgers like me haul themselves up the many thousands of feet from the base of the North Col, where the fixed rope starts, to the summit where it stops.

You have a climbing harness around your waist and crutch and to a strong point on the belt's front just above your tummy button there is attached a steel karabiner (or krab). A loop or sling is attached to this krab. Another detachable device, also on your sling, is clipped on to the fixed ropes that lead you up the mountain. This is called a jumar (or ascendeur), and has metal teeth. Slide the jumar up the rope and it runs along smoothly, but any downwards pull and the jumar's teeth will clench the rope and stop you falling.

Because there are hundreds of knots and fixed points along the rope line, you always use two of these slings and never unclip one until the other is attached to the rope beyond the obstacle. Many of the bodies lying along the rope line and below it are there because they slipped and fell when briefly unattached to the mountain or a rope. You can't add to the number of corpses who died from that particular fate so long as you always use the two-sling system – *and* so long as the fixed rope does not break or come loose. The older ropes are often cut by falling rocks or chafed through by rubbing on sharp points, so Sherpas assess and, where necessary, renew them most years. But it still pays to keep checking every rope that you intend to rely on.

The 7,500-metre 'camp' was in reality a raggedy series of ledges, anywhere big enough for a tiny tent to be pitched with guy ropes tied mostly around rocks in lieu of tent pegs. The recent big winds that had held up David's group had rendered many of the tents I passed mere skeletal tent-pole hoops attached to wildly fluttering bits of material. Cylinders and food packs and bric-a-brac lay all around. Every so often a couple of climbers would slowly descend, and I would unclip myself to let them pass down the rope. They often moved like zombies and were unrecognisable in their hooded, goggled sameness. One of them was our doctor, Fred Ziel, who had sensibly turned round too sick to continue.

Between the 7,500- and the 7,900-metre camps the going became harder, with many slippery rocks and icy runnels to negotiate. A strong cold wind from one flank had the effect, I am not sure why, of blocking off oxygen, at least partially, somewhere between the cylinder in my rucksack and my mask. This caused constant halts to turn away from the wind and breathe deeply. My hooded down jacket covered parts of the system to stop them freezing up, but in order to reach them or to alter the flow setting, I needed to undo the jacket's main zip. Dribble from the mask often landed on the zip and froze it solid. Should my goggles mist up or move out of place, I again needed to unzip. Whereas these sorts of clothing problems had often occurred on polar expeditions in far colder circumstances, they had not involved the added complications of an oxygen system, nor being attached to a mountainside, nor feeling below par due to the altitude. In the Arctic most travel was at three or four feet above sea-level, and in Antarctica we had suffered from altitude sickness at a mere 11,000 feet up.

I kept checking that my system's pipes were not snagged, nor the mask workings frozen, but I never managed to discover why, every so often in strong winds, the oxygen stopped coming and I had to tear my mouth from the mask and try to gulp in air. I had set out from 7,500 metres an hour earlier than Ian, Jens, Mark and Neal in order to reach the next camp at the same time as them. My driving aim as I toiled up the mountain was to keep ahead as long as possible, growing to dread the moment I heard the crunch of their boots just below me. Halfway through the morning, Mark caught up with me. We lifted tired arms in greeting. There was no point in trying to communicate verbally as the wind tore away the words.

At 7,900 metres the camp was perched on tiny tilted ledges and felt, I thought, unpleasantly exposed. But I also enjoyed a new feeling of anticipation because the summit ridge that, for the past seventy days had seemed so far away and so high as to be unobtainable, now for the first time looked within reasonable grasp. How many other hopeful folk had reached this point and likewise felt they could make it, only to die within forty-eight hours? A good many. At least one out of every ten. The most famous were, of course, Mallory and Irvine.

In 1924 Mallory was on the mountain for a third time. The British were gradually pushing the northern route, experimenting with oxygen, and Mallory was their best climber. That year their colleagues far below spotted Mallory and Irvine on the summit ridge through binoculars, but neither man ever made it back down. To this day it is uncertain if they reached the summit, but in 1999 a group of top US climbers searched for Mallory and Irvine's bodies in the area around and above the 7,900-metre camp, especially the snow basins beneath the steeper rock faces. Bodies dressed in brightly-coloured Gore-Tex jackets were not hard to find. The climbers recorded, 'We found ourselves in a kind of collection zone for fallen climbers . . . Just seeing these twisted, broken bodies was a pretty stark reminder of our own mortality.' Then one of the Americans, Conrad Anker, spotted something different. He thought he had discovered the remains of Andrew Irvine: 'We were looking at a man who had been clinging to the mountain for seventy-five years. The clothing was blasted from most of his body, and his skin was bleached white. I felt like I was viewing a Greek or Roman marble statue.'

Soon the five searchers were crouched around the body in awed silence.

The body itself did the speaking. For here was a body unlike the others crumpled in crannies elsewhere on the terrace. This body was lying fully extended, facedown and pointing uphill, frozen in a position of self-arrest, as if the fall had happened only moments earlier. The head and upper torso were frozen into the rubble that had gathered around them over the decades, but the arms, powerfully muscular still, extended above the head to strong hands that gripped the mountainside, flexed fingertips dug deep into the frozen gravel. The legs were extended downhill. One was broken and the other had been gently crossed over it for protection. Here too, the musculature was still pronounced and powerful. The entire body had about it the strength and grace of a dancer. This body, this man, had once been a splendid specimen of humankind.

Name-tags on the tattered clothing remnants established that this was Mallory, not Irvine. The searchers concluded that:

> George Mallory fell to his death from a spot well down the face of the Yellow Band, tantalizingly close to Camp VI and safety; his injuries are too mild, his body too unmarred, for there to be any other explanation. And he did not fall alone; at the critical moment, he appears to have been roped to his partner, Andrew Irvine. Irvine fell too and was injured, though not as profoundly as Mallory. They did not fall far. They did not fall from the dangerous Northeast Ridge, as had the many badly twisted bodies frozen in agonized death in the great catch-basin of the 'snow terrace'.

The searchers' conclusion was open-ended, but one wrote:

> The route they pioneered to the Northeast Ridge in the 1920s is the one most climbed today on the north side. For the two of them to have gotten as high as they did with the resources they had is truly amazing. Whether or not they made the summit, they will forever hold a place as heroes on the world's highest peak.

If Mallory and Irvine did not summit, it is certain that nobody else did until, twenty-nine years later, a British Commonwealth expedition under John Hunt, an Army colonel, finally placed two of its climbers, Ed Hillary from New Zealand and Sherpa Tenzing Norgay from Nepal, on the summit from the southern side on 29 May 1953. By then, ten expeditions had tried for the summit and failed, and thirteen men had died. The previous year Tenzing himself, with a Swiss climber, had been forced to turn back not far short of the summit. News of Hillary and Tenzing's success was flashed to London just before the coronation of Queen Elizabeth II.

By the end of 2006, records showed that, in the seventy-six years since Mallory's death not far from my 7,900 metres tent, 2,062 climbers had reached the summit and 203 of them died on the mountain. Since there were ten climbers in our two groups, I wondered if any would succumb to this Everest law of decimation. Five climbers had died on the mountain already during the past month, I knew, and maybe more, since there were a number of lone climbers as yet unaccounted for at ABC.

The good weather spell was still with us at dawn on 3 June. Today we would move into the so-called Death Zone, above which the majority of North Ridge climber fatalities take place. Our next camp lay, at 8,400 metres, higher than all but five of the world's mountain summits.

Two hours later, above 8,000 metres (26,246 feet), I was preoccupied with not slipping off the shale and ice, aware of, but studiously avoiding, any glimpse of the sharp drop to my right and focusing on slow but continuous movement to keep ahead of the others in my group. I had, as usual, set out an hour ahead of them and was determined to keep that lead. Luckily I felt stronger than before, probably because the oxygen system was working better because there was less wind.

One of America's most famed modern-day climbers, David Breashears, described the act of upwards movement of the route. 'Our bodies were dehydrated. Our fingers and toes went numb as precious oxygen was diverted to our brains, hearts and other vital organs. Climbing above 26,000 feet, even with bottled oxygen, is like running on a treadmill and breathing through a straw. Your body screams at you to turn around. Everything says: this is cold. This is impossible.'

There were some very steep sections where I had a problem passing other climbers descending in a dazed, clumsy state. I tried speaking to one who knocked his pack hard against me as he slipped down past me, but there was no reply. He looked exhausted. I passed by a climber curled up on a tiny ledge. As I cautiously unclipped to get by him, I asked if he was okay. There was no reply, but his hooded, masked head nodded slowly. It struck me that, if he was dying, I might well be accused of being one of those callous climbers who pass by the near dead without offering aid. But I had passed several such inert individuals and I myself had been passed as I rested, completely winded, on some tiny perch, too tired even to acknowledge a passing greeting.

The media point fingers of guilt in such cases. The following year a Kiwi amputee climber, Mark Ingliss, was interviewed and agreed that, after he had talked to fellow climber, David Sharp, in a bad way some 1,300 feet below the summit and sheltering under a rock, he had moved on upwards, as had others in his group. All agreed that any rescue attempt would only cause more deaths. Many of the forty climbers who passed Sharp by assumed that his own group would save him, whereas in fact he was not with any group. His condition slowly deteriorated as climbers went by him on their way up and, later, back down. His chances of rescue diminished through the day. His legs, feet and fingers became frostbitten and dead, so he could no longer walk or use his hands. His oxygen gave out and he died, as some people do on this stretch of this mountain. When a climber near the summit of Mount Everest reaches a stage of exhaustion and oxygen starvation so severe that he can no longer move on his own initiative, he is typically left to die. It is simply impossible for one climber to descend such treacherous terrain carrying or dragging the inert body of another. The mountain is littered with the bodies of climbers who have simply sat down and died of exposure. Sibu nearly joined their ranks.

Five days after our wedding, Louise and I were in Nepal.

Below the Advance Base Camp: many climbers were already
seriously affected by altitude by this point.

My second attempt to follow David
up the North Col without oxygen:
20% of my lung capacity was shot.

At the North Col camp: from he
I used oxygen all the way to th
'Death Camp'.

With my friend Sibusisu, the first black person ever to climb Everest and
the man who inspired me to make this attempt.

Recreating the last few days of Doctor Livingstone's journey to Victoria F with a team of Zimbabweans and Zambians in 2005.

With Louise at the very edge of the Victoria Falls.

One hundred and fifty years to the after he reached the falls, we unveiled plaque honouring the great explo

The North Face of the Eiger, Tuesday 13 March 2007, day 1.

There's a drop of 3,000 feet from the overnight ledge at Death Bivouac, so sleep-walking is to be avoided.

For five days I tried to avoid looking down.

The Summit Ice Field, where Ian began his fall.

The summit in sight.

On the summit of the Eiger, 10.30am, Saturday 17 March, 2007.

I came at last to the exposed series of ledges at 8,400 metres on which perched a few battered tents. I saw Sibu sitting outside one. I waved to him and he waved back slowly. He looked tired. I assumed he was on his way down from the summit with David and the others. The last fifty metres up to one of the two colour-coded Jagged Globe tents took me twenty minutes, for my oxygen pipe kept snagging on my rucksack but, for the first time, I arrived within a few minutes of Ian, Jens, Neal and Mark. We crawled into our tents tired but exhilarated. After seventy days we were nearly there. The tent was pitched on a slope. The Sherpas had done their best to find a flat spot, but there were none. Ian, my own Sherpa, Boca Lama, and I tried to get ready for our night in the Death Camp, unpacking our rucksacks and checking our oxygen systems without upsetting each other's space, all in a tiny two-man tent pitched on rocks and ice. Any item that escaped through the entry door was liable to slide, then fall for many thousands of feet to the snow terraces and glaciers below. Various dead bodies had been found in the tents here, including an Indian climber the previous week.

Sibu nearly died that day when his oxygen ran out, although we did not know this until the following morning when one of our Sherpas found him slouched beside the ropes an hour or two below the tents. Various stories of recent happenings reached us on the walkie-talkie system or through other climbers. A few days earlier, when a Slovenian died on the summit ridge, a solo climber from Bhutan, close by him, ran out of oxygen and began to hallucinate due to hypoxia. He wandered by one of the old corpses near to the fixed rope, probably the one with green boots that most climbers remember, and thought he saw the corpse pointing at an object nearby. This turned out to be a half-snow-buried orange oxygen cylinder. The Bhutani, to his joy, found that there was still oxygen in it, clipped it to his system and survived to tell his tale to everyone in ABC.

From the Death Camp, the final climb ascends and traverses a steep stretch of striated limestone, known as the Yellow Band, mostly by way of a part-snow-filled gulley where many old ropes can cause confusion, especially since this section must be done at night. However, the great motivating thought is that from the tents to the summit ridge is a mere 300 metres in height.

So why on earth do people want to risk their lives on Everest year after year? George Mallory wrote:

> If one should ask me what 'use' there was in climbing, or attempting to climb the world's highest peak, I would be compelled to answer 'none'. There is no scientific end to be served; simply the gratification of the impulse of achievement, the indomitable desire to see what lies beyond that ever beats within the heart of man. With both poles conquered, the mighty peak of the Himalayas remains as the greatest conquest available to the explorer.

Mallory, in fact, had a very reasonable motive for his Everest trials. Curiosity. Nobody had yet reached the summit. Nobody knew if the human body could survive at that altitude. On a more cynical level another British climber, Stephen Venables, observed, 'Everest is prime *Guinness Book of Records* territory.'

In 2004 150 climbers had summitted Everest in a batch and, had the weather turned nasty at the wrong moment, there would have been dead people all over the Death Zone. Back in 1996 it did and there were. Two world-famous professional guides were among them. Questions were asked about Everest tourism. One amateur climber who survived was journalist John Krakauer who went on to write a bestselling book about the debacle, *Into Thin Air*. In it he apportioned blame and particularly criticised Anatoli Boukreev, an immensely experienced Russian guide who had rescued three people. Boukreev hit back with his own book, and was then killed climbing on Annapurna. The American television talk shows were packed with journalists and with survivors. Discussion forums sprang up on the web, filled with speculation by people who knew very little about it all. It began to rival the assassination of J.F. Kennedy for conspiracy theories. Everest had become a spectator sport.

I struggled into my boots, pack and oxygen system, said good-bye to Ian and the other three and, with Boca Lama a few yards behind, grinning as usual, began the fairly steep climb up the fixed ropes with new batteries in my head torch. The others would start out in an hour at 11.00 p.m. In seven or eight hours, on a fixed rope the whole way, I hoped to be on the summit of Everest. We moved off into the night, pitch black beyond the cone of our torch lights. There were slippery rocks, snow patches and a bewildering choice of upwards-leading ropes, some frayed almost through, others brand new. In the torch light it paid to take time. I found myself panting far more than on the previous climb, despite taking it slowly, perhaps because of the gradient. I felt cold despite the exertion, and I felt dizzy, too. Something was wrong but nothing I could identify, so I kept going in a stop-start way, gasping for breath every few metres. Then, some forty minutes after setting out, my world caved in.

Somebody, it seemed, had clamped powerful arms around my chest and was squeezing the life out of me. And the surgical wire that held my ribs together felt as though it was tearing through my chest. My thoughts were simple: I am having another heart attack. I will be dead in minutes. No defibrillator on hand this time. Then I remembered that Louise had pestered me to carry special pills with me – Glycerine Tri-Nitrate (GTN). You put one under your tongue where it fizzes and causes your system to dilate in all the right places. I tore at my jacket pocket and, removing my mitts, crammed at least six tablets under my tongue before swallowing.

I clung to the rope, hanging out over the great drop and waiting to die. My one glimpse of Boca Lama, who said nothing, was of his usual big grin as my torch light lit up his features. Five minutes later I was still alive. The tablets, I knew, could, if you were lucky, stave off a heart attack and give you time to get to a cardiac unit. They are *not* a means of avoiding an attack in order to allow you to continue climbing. This might not be my own end, but it *was* definitely the signal to descend to lower altitudes at once.

Some twenty minutes later we were back down in the Death

Camp. There was no tent to enter as our group were in the act of booting and kitting up, using all available tent space. So I waited outside with Boca Lama until Ian and the others had disappeared up into the night.

'I must go down quickly,' I told Boca Lama. He shook his head and the grin disappeared. It would, he explained, be too dangerous to descend until we could 'see our feet'. That meant dawn in five hours' time. I knew my best hope of survival, as had been the case on Kilimanjaro, was to lose height rapidly. The tightness had gone from my chest, but the sharp discomfort around the stitch-wires was still there. I contemplated going on down without Boca Lama, but decided against it. Going up an icy, slippery, steep slope in the darkness is a lot safer than descending one. Statistically, the vast majority of accidents happen on the descent. The concentration of going up seems to disappear to be replaced by a weary nonchalance. Nothing matters apart from a longing for warmth and comfort. Lost in these thoughts you become careless. The focus gone and the mind weary, it is all too easy to lose your footing or clip carelessly into a rope. Three thousand metres of void waited directly below our tent.

Nine times Everest climber, Ed Viesturs, has two favourite sayings: 'Just because you love the mountains doesn't mean the mountains love you' and 'Getting to the top is optional. Getting down is mandatory.'

Dawn came eventually and we descended without a break to the North Col, where we rested for two hours, then on down to ABC for the night. My Everest was over. If I had feared a scathing reaction from our *Times* correspondent, I was pleasantly surprised: 'Aborting his climb will be seen by the mountain community as a wise and courageous decision. Duncan Chessell, who has led thirty-five Himalayan expeditions, said, "For a 60-year-old man to make it even this far is extraordinary. You would expect only fifty per cent of climbers to reach anywhere near this high, especially during this season."'

I congratulated my fellow Jagged Globe climbers, especially Sibu, who was the first black person to climb Everest from both sides, and Jens, who was a year older than me. Fred, who had recovered from his illness but still looked weak, assured me that he would be having another go, his third, in a year or so. I thanked David, Neal and our wonderful team of Sherpas, especially Boca Lama, for what had truly been a great experience. Would I try again? Not for a while. Maybe never, but I hate saying 'Never again'.

Within a day, with Tore, Alex and Sibu, I was back down in Base Camp, and forty-eight hours after that I was checked out in Harley Street for new cardiac damage. None was evident, so it is likely that, on Everest and previously on Kilimanjaro, I had mere angina warnings. What would have happened if I had not heeded them or had not had the GTN tablets, it is impossible to know. I learnt later that, on the other side of the mountain a Scottish climber, 49-year-old Robert Milne, died of a heart attack on the same night and at the same height as I had my attack. I assume he had no GTN pills with him.

The tangible declared aim of my Everest attempt, all costs of which were sponsored by the generosity of Paul Sykes, had been to raise £2 million for an MRI Scanner Unit and Catheter Laboratory in the Great Ormond Street Hospital for Children in London. The British Heart Foundation eventually raised the £2 million through the Ran Fiennes Healthy Hearts Appeal, despite my failure on the mountain, and I cut the ribbon to officially open the gleaming new clinic. Its purpose is purely for heart research, and it will enable BHF medical professionals to explore the heart disease that affects children, helping them to develop new interventional techniques with the aim of saving young lives.

Since our 'honeymoon' at the Everest Base Camp had been a non-event, Louise and I took up the kind offer of John Costello, who had checked out my lungs prior to Everest, to stay for a week in his family villa in southern Spain. A couple of months later, Louise told me that she was pregnant and, on Easter Day 2006, our daughter Elizabeth gave her first yell. A month later I was sixty-two years old and changed my first nappy.

19

Vertigo

The Everest experience and the advent of my new family extracted me from my period of misery and hopelessness following Ginny's death. But my irrational fear of heights (or rather drops) was never put to the test on Everest, since the seventy-two days I spent moving up and down that mountain's north side at no time involved any vertigo-inducing moves.

A couple of months after returning to England, I had a letter from Neal Short, who had led our ascent group two. He wrote: 'As you were so close, I often wonder whether you are tempted to give it another go. Maybe you could go from the south side, with Kenton Cool, where they spend far less time above 5,300 metres and where dropping down the valley to lower altitudes for recuperation is an easier option.' Kenton Cool had been one of four mountain guide instructors on my Jagged Globe pre-Everest course in the Alps. He had mentioned during that course that Everest was not a particularly scary feature in terms of sheer exposure, and he should know, as he was to become the first Briton to scale Everest five times. But I had assumed that his definition of scary was light years away from mine and that, since Everest was, after all, the highest mountain on earth, with a menacing casualty rate, it would prove a truly vertiginous experience for a person like me. Perhaps if I had completed the last few hours of traverse along Everest's summit ridge, I would have experienced the 'fearful voids' I had looked for. But, as it was, my seventy-two Everest days had merely provided a long, toilsome trudge along fixed ropes up endless snow slopes with some rocky zones thrown in, plus a huge slice of boredom in high-altitude tents. My vertigo remained unchallenged, apart from by crevasses and school roofs.

Back on that Alpine course, it had been suggested that anyone looking for a *real* test of exposed climbing would be a lot better off in the Alps rather than in the Himalaya, since the daddy of all nasties was ready and waiting a mere three-hour drive from Geneva Airport: the North Face of the Eiger, the notorious Nordwand, the North Wall. In German *mordwand* means 'murder wall' and that is what the face is often called. I had heard various horror stories of this face, and some twenty years before, together with Simon Gault and Geoff Newman, had planned to walk up one of the easier ridges over a weekend with a guide. Those plans had never materialised for Geoff and me, although Simon had managed it and had never since let us forget the fact.

At some point I had tentatively approached Kenton with the suggestion that, if the Eiger was indeed to be a tougher challenge exposure-wise than Everest, would he guide me up it? And, if so, when? I knew that Kenton had climbed the North Wall of the Eiger with two friends and had taken three days and nights to do so. I also knew that he was held in huge respect by Britain's mountaineering community. He was thirty-three years old and supremely fit. He lived and worked in Chamonix, the mecca of Alpine climbers, and did not suffer fools, especially climbing fools, gladly. In response to my Eiger query, he was forthright. He would not even consider climbing the Eiger with me unless he first taught me how to climb to a standard where he was sure he would not be risking his own life.

How long would such an instructional period last, I asked him. 'As long,' he replied, 'as a piece of string. It depends on your ability, determination, strength and how long you're prepared to spend training in the Alps. Have you read *The White Spider*?'

'No,' I replied.

'Well, you probably should. It may put you off before you even think of going anywhere near the Eiger.'

I found a copy of the book, by the Austrian, Heinrich Harrer, one of the team who made the first ascent back in 1938, and noted his comments on some possible motives of a would-be Eiger North Face climber.

With the best will in the world no one could suggest any usefulness to mankind in such a climb. Nor could any material advantages be worth the risks, the indescribable labours and difficulties which demand the uttermost physical, spiritual and mental resistance merely to win fame at the expense of that horrific wall. To do the climb as compensation for an inferiority complex? Any climber who dares to tackle the North Face must have examined and proved himself a hundred times in advance. And how about a climb of the North Face as a counterbalance to hysteria? A hysteric, an unstable character, would go to pieces at the very sight of the Wall, just as surely as any mask would fall away in the face of this menacing bastion of rock and ice.

The White Spider made harrowing reading and explained in detail the reasons for many of the deaths of the highly capable climbers who perished on the North Face. I was impressed and not a little disturbed. Harrer was doing nothing to put my mind at rest, no doubt as Kenton hoped.

The North Wall of the Eiger remains one of the most perilous in the Alps, as every man who has ever joined battle with it knows. Other climbs, the North face of the Grandes Jorasses for one, may be technically more difficult, but nowhere else is there such appalling danger from the purely fortuitous hazards of avalanches, stone-falls and sudden deterioration of the weather as on the Eiger . . . The North Face of the Eiger demands the uttermost of skill, stamina and courage, nor can it be climbed without the most exhaustive preparations . . . The Eiger's Face is an irrefutable touchstone of a climber's stature as a mountaineer and as a man . . . Anyone who makes headway on the North Face of the Eiger and survives there for several days has achieved and overcome so much – whatever mistakes he may have committed – that his performance is well above the comprehension of the average climber.

I assumed that Kenton would, given time, be able to turn me into an 'average climber'. Was that going to be enough? I moved on, depressed, from *The White Spider* in order to find more optimistic advice from equally famous but more contemporary climbers.

Joe Simpson, of *Touching the Void* fame, had written: 'It wasn't the hardest or the highest. It was simply "The Eiger". The very mention of the name made my heart beat faster. The seminal mountain, a metaphorical mountain that represented everything that defines mountaineering – a route I had dreamed of climbing for my entire adult life.' This, from the man famed for rescuing himself from the depths of an Andean crevasse after his partner had thought him lost and cut the rope, was less offputting than Harrer but reassuring.

Jon Krakauer, who had stirred up the Everest '96 hornet's nest, wrote:

The problem with climbing the North Face of the Eiger is that in addition to getting up 6,000 vertical feet of crumbling limestone and black ice, one must climb over some formidable mythology. The trickiest moves on any climb are the mental ones, the psychological gymnastics that keep terror in check, and the Eiger's grim aura is intimidating enough to rattle anyone's poise . . .

The history of the mountain resonates with the struggles of such larger-than-life figures as Buhl, Bonatti, Messner, Rébuffat, Terray, Haston, and Harlin, not to mention Eastwood. The names of the landmarks on the face – the Hinterstoisser Traverse, the Ice Hose, the Death Bivouac, the White Spider – are household words among both active and armchair Alpinists from Tokyo to Buenos Aires; the very mention of these places is enough to make any climber's hands turn clammy. The rockfall and avalanches that rain continuously down the Nordwand are legendary. So is the heavy weather. Even when the skies over the rest of Europe are cloudless, violent storms brew over the Eiger, like those dark clouds that hover eternally above Transylvanian castles in vampire movies . . . Needless to say, all this makes the Eiger North Face one of the most widely coveted climbs in the world.

All this and more in the same vein by other Eiger climbers put me off the whole idea in terms of treating it as a reasonable project. But from the point of view of a worthy vertigo-testing challenge, the mountain seemed perfect.

So I went back to Kenton, who agreed to have a go at teaching me how to climb on mixed rock and ice in the Alps. But because there would be a good deal of plain rock as well as ice on the Eiger, I needed to learn simple rock-climbing as well, which I could do near home on Exmoor, my finger stumps well strapped for protection. A Welsh climber from Cardiff, Haydn Griffiths, started me off on sea cliffs on the Gower Peninsula, various quarry-type cliffs near Cardiff, and the Avon Gorge near Bristol. Whenever I fell off, which was often, he held my fall from above and was always patient. Under his tutelage, I passed from climbs graded as DIFFICULT (meaning Easy) to those graded HARD VERY SEVERE (HVS), but never managed to complete the latter without considerable shouted advice from Haydn en route.

Paul Sykes from Yorkshire had underwritten the Everest project, so I put the Eiger idea to him. This time he was not happy. It all sounded a lot more dangerous and if anything happened to me he, as sponsor, would feel partially responsible. But he did agree to meet up with and quiz Kenton, who talked him round, even if Paul was still dubious about my chances of success.

I looked at various UK charities and ended up deciding on Marie Curie Cancer Care. This was an easy choice for when I had been with Ginny in Exeter Hospital's cancer care ward, we had noticed other terminally ill patients who were never visited by friends or family and, when we went to their bedsides, they confided that they pined for the familiar surroundings of their own home, the friendly face of some pet or other and the memories they associated with their own pictures, ornaments and furniture. But they couldn't afford to pay carers, so they must die, lonely, in an NHS cancer ward. Macmillan and Marie Curie nurses are the best answer to this very real problem and, because I had done some work ten years before for Marie Curie, I called them first. They were enthusiastic and their committee decided that, using my Eiger attempt, they could and would raise at least £1.5 million, and maybe double that figure.

My literary agent Ed Victor signed up *The Sunday Times* to cover the climb exclusively, and I approached old friends at ITV News (the new name for ITN). Sadly, their veteran reporter, Terry Lloyd, who had been on so many of our expeditions in the past, had been killed whilst on ITN duty near Basra in 2003. An investigation was still going on as to the exact circumstances of Terry's death, but the official version was 'caught up in a fire fight between US and Iraqi forces near the Shatt Al Basra Bridge'. However, the Leader of the Liberal Democrats, three and a half years after Terry's death, was still pushing Parliament for justice. 'When,' he asked, 'may we expect the Attorney-General to make an application for the extradition and trial in Britain of those American soldiers against whom there is a *prima facie* case for the unlawful killing in Iraq of the ITN journalist Terry Lloyd?'

ITV News agreed to send a two-man team to record the Eiger attempt and to make clear how viewers could donate to Marie Curie. The new Terry Lloyd was reporter Philip Reay-Smith and his cameraman was Rob Turner. ITV subsequently agreed, with Paul Sykes' help, to produce a sixty-minute documentary film in addition to their sequences for the national news.

Once ITV and *The Sunday Times* were on board, I approached Mountain Equipment, the mountain and polar clothing company I had worked with since 1972, and they agreed to full equipment sponsorship, and the UK Met Office in Exeter and the Swiss equivalent in Berne also agreed to sponsor us. Met forecasts are key to any successful attempt on the North Face of the Eiger, which Kenton assured me would best be made in March when winter temperatures should freeze loose rubble in place and minimise the likelihood of rockfalls.

'Which March?' I asked Kenton.

He smiled. 'That depends on when, if ever, you become sufficiently proficient for me not to consider you the lethal liability that you are right now.'

So month after month through 2006 I flew out to Geneva for five-day training sessions in the Alps, trying to imbibe a basic understanding of the principles of rope-work and how to use an ice-axe (or two) in conjunction with crampon spikes, in order to head in an upwards direction on vertical ice sheets. Not just to help plod up slopes, as on Everest.

The nursery slopes that Kenton initially used were mostly close to Argentière, near Chamonix, but, when the weather was bad, he drove us through the Mont Blanc tunnel to the Italian valley of Cogne, a place of many frozen waterfalls. The basics of ice-climbing, as far as I could see, involved hacking one or both of your axes into the ice-wall above your head, kicking the front-facing spikes on your boots into the ice at about knee-level, then hauling your weight up. You then keep repeating this process until you reach the top of the waterfall.

As we progressed slowly to more difficult waterfalls, variations on this basic theme were introduced, some fairly dicey. When the ice was a mere transparent coating, as though painted on to the rock, bludgeoning your axe into it was useless. In such places it was better to try to be incredibly patient and place your axes' tips with surgical precision into the tiniest indents. That sounds easy, but it's not when your arms are burning or cramping with muscle pain.

Joe Simpson wrote, 'Climbing frozen waterfalls appears to the uninformed observer to be a complicated if somewhat novel form of suicide, and quite often this very same thought worms itself uneasily into the mind of the hapless climber.'

An American climbing journal sent a freelance journalist, Greg

Child, out to Chamonix to record a typical Kenton training day. Greg had himself been a world-renowned mountaineer for many years. He wrote:

We're all clammy with sweat when we reach the frozen waterfall. Ropes uncoiled, ice axes leashed to wrists and crampons clamped to boots. 'Baron von Cool', Ran's pet name for his guide, leads us up a swathe of vertical ice. Ran hacks with his ice axes and Cool pulls the rope in on his waist. Despite his mangled hand and awkward grip, Ran swings his ice tool true and confidently, and judging by our relaxed banter, he's well on his way to conquering his lifelong fear of heights. Cool then belays me up. I find that the cold air has rendered the ice so brittle that grapefruit-size chunks of it are exploding all around me as I hack my ice axes into the cascade. Halfway up to the ledge where Cool and Ran are seated I notice a trail of blood. The droplets lead straight to Ran's nose, which an ice shard has neatly slit. He's unperturbed, and he sits on his perch with a bloody grin.

With Cool in the lead, we start up a rambling ice floe near Italy's Cogne Valley, a grade 4+ named Patri. Mini tornadoes of powder snow sting us whenever the wind feels angry. On a low-angled stretch of the route, Ran steps on the rope in his spiked boots – a climbing no-no.

'Get off that bloody thing, Ran,' Cool barks like a rabid drill sergeant.

Ran smiles at me, and steps aside. For an alpha male accustomed to unconditional authority over his expeditions, his deference to Cool is quaint. It's also pragmatic: he knows he's on a learning curve as a climber, and he's soaking up everything Cool can teach.

That day we completed my first Grade Five waterfall, aptly named the Cascade Difficile.

I got to know the mountains above Chamonix quite well through my training with Kenton. The town is possibly the greatest mecca in the world for mountaineers and is dominated by the great rounded summit of Mont Blanc. On average, one climber dies each and every day in and around Chamonix during the summer climbing season. Helicopters fly overhead on rescue missions, and sometimes come back with a bodybag dangling beneath them.

In November 2006 Kenton finally agreed that I could, if I continued my improvement, set a date of 1 March 2007 for the Eiger climb. Meanwhile there were times when he was busy with other clients in the Alps or Himalaya, so he appointed alternative guides for my tuition. One such was Jon Bracey, another Chamonix-based Brit, who led me to my most difficult ascent at that time, the great tooth-shaped block called La Dent du Géant (the Giant's Tooth), a true Alpine aiguille or needle. We only reached the base of the final 600-foot cliff at dusk, so we dug a bivouac into the snow slope at the very base of the rock and carried on the climb after dawn the next day. I didn't relish the unbroken nature of that stark wall and was extremely thankful for the thick rope which some thoughtful soul had fixed all the way up the cliff face to the vertiginous summit.

Climbing guides like Jon, who live in Chamonix and depend upon the Alpine snows for their livelihood, are worried, as is everyone in the winter sports industry, that the Alps are running out of snow. It is true that during Roman times the Alps were warmer even than they are today, but the current speed of warming is what worries French and Swiss scientists. They estimate that the Alps have lost half their glacier ice in the past century, and 20 per cent of that since the 1980s. Swiss glaciers have lost one-fifth of their surface area in just fifteen years. One side effect is an increased incidence of huge rockfalls and avalanches.

Kenton introduced me to various other individuals who are cult figures in the large expatriate British community in the Chamonix area who pay French taxes. One was the Alpine guide and artist Andy Parkin who had suffered appalling fall injuries on some Swiss rockface. He received surgery to his heart, spleen, liver, hip and elbows but, within months of leaving hospital, he was climbing again on highly demanding routes.

By the end of 2006 Kenton professed himself satisfied that there had been 'improvement'. He was a hard taskmaster, which I liked, especially since I am forgetful and inclined to be vague. I need to be shouted at in circumstances where a single absent-minded action (or lack of action) can kill someone. On two occasions over the months I received a major Kenton bollocking for putting my helmet down during rests between climbs with its rounded top on the ground. That way it could slide the more easily down a mountainside.

One day at the base of the Tournier Spur of the Aiguille du Midi, we stopped to take our crampons off, when Kenton yelled, 'Get down', and flung himself sideways. A rock, slightly bigger than a rugby ball, screamed through the air directly towards us from some distant cliff. I copied Kenton's evasive action with less than a second to spare, and the missile thrummed past the point where our heads would have been.

Five minutes later we had to stop to put our crampons on again, and whilst doing so Kenton took his helmet off. To my amazement and great delight he put it down on the snow *the wrong way up*. I screamed at him, 'KENTON!!' Quick as a flash and thinking another flying rock was about to arrive, he crashed to the ground.

'Kenton,' I said, when he had picked himself up warily, 'you put your helmet down the wrong way up. You should never, ever do that. You might lose it on a slope.'

I cannot remember now whether he said 'You bastard' or not, but he was considerably less bossy than usual for an hour or so afterwards.

Most of my climbing back at home had to be squeezed in between lectures and family activities so, since Bristol was a lot closer than Cardiff, Haydn gave me some pointers to instructors there, and by good fortune I ended up in the capable hands of Paul Twomey, the supremo instructor-cum-manager of Undercover Rock, a former parish church taken over as a climbing school for the young and old of Bristol (including, I noticed, the very young and the very old). The atmosphere was happy, excited and frenetic.

It was fun to watch as well as to participate. Each and every wall and nook of the entire church, including the belfry, was crammed with artificial climbing routes, colour-coded for degrees of severity. Paul taught me many excellent rock-climbing tips in the church, and then drove us out to the Avon or Cheddar Gorge for real climbs whenever the rock there was dry.

One hot summer's day, Ian Parnell took me to Cheddar. I watched every move Ian made in order to copy it when he was ready to belay me. One difficult section was only negotiable by holding a rock bulge from below whilst traversing round it. When I reached this rock, aping Ian's every handhold, the entire rock, all 200 pounds of it, came away, knocking me into space. Ian held my fall and the rock landed several metres away from our car in which Louise, Alexander and Elizabeth were sitting. The same face higher up proved too much for me. A key grip, tiny and all but smoothed away by weather, defeated my stumps. Since I could not use my good right hand anywhere useful and my arms ran out of strength, I fell off again.

'Pull me up, please,' I yelled at Ian, unseen but somewhere high above. Either he couldn't or he wouldn't. I tried again and again to find a way up the tricky bit and kept shouting at Ian. He continued to ignore my pleas. I swore (silently) at him. He was Kenton's climbing partner of many years. Between them they had achieved great new climbs on many sheer remote faces. They were the best in Britain, and Ian had agreed to join Kenton and me on our Eiger attempt. Now, I assumed, he was testing me out in cahoots with Kenton. They had plotted this between them. Damn them. With all my strength virtually gone, I was forced to *think* about the bit of rock that was defying my every effort. I spotted a side hold and two finger-holes that I had previously missed but which made all the difference. On my seventh attempt, I made it. I said nothing to a grinning Ian when I reached him, but made up my mind to learn how to ascend the rope itself in case I again came across rock I couldn't manage.

I knew that Ian's opinions of my ability, or lack of it, would be reported to Kenton, who, despite our tentative March 2007 date, had yet to make up his mind finally about the wisdom of taking me up the Eiger Nordwand. I did later see Ian's summary of the climbing.

His hand, damaged by frostbite, of course proved a real hindrance, and at times his 'stumps' would prove completely ineffective at gripping the rock. I'm sure for Ran this was a real frustration, but he didn't let it show. The real big issue, however, was Ran's vertigo. Again, he would say very little and at times you could forget that he was battling a constant fear of heights, but when things got tricky and he became flustered, his vertigo would begin to spiral out of control. During these moments he'd seemingly lose sight of any alternative foot- or handholds other than those right under his nose. Scrabbling for purchase, his feet would start pedalling as though riding as bike over slippery cobbles and his knuckles would be white as he gripped harder and harder. But he wouldn't give up until his arms were so drained of energy that the holds would just melt through his fingers. I did wonder if Ran's proposed ascent of the Eiger would ever happen.

In order to work on overcoming this Kenton introduced me to a Scottish climbing instructor, Sandy Ogilvie, who took me to Swanage one day on the Dorset coast. Halfway across a sea cliff route called the Traverse of the Gods, I lost a key hold and fell in a long pendulum swing, just missing the tide-free rocks below by a metre. I was left dangling free some twelve feet below the nearest point of the rockface. Fortunately, Sandy had explained how to use prussik loops, small cord slings which form rope grips, and clumsily but successfully, I managed to scale the taut rope itself in order to get back up to the rock and continued the climb.

Soon afterwards Sandy took me and the family to the Orkneys to climb the famous Old Man of Hoy. This sea stack was my first truly exposed climb, with a near 400-foot drop to the sea. What helped me considerably was the presence, as third man on the rope, of the freelance reporter sent by *The Sunday Times*, himself a famous climber and author. Stephen Venables had a great sense of humour and was completely unfazed by the exposure. There were two especially nasty places, both of which Sandy from above and Stephen from below talked me over with clear and patient shouted instructions.

But I did it. Stephen later wrote,

> Ran shoved and grunted, trouser seat scraping one wall, knees the other. It was all brute strength with little finesse, but the cussed determination was impressive. I also had a struggle getting out of the chimney and round the roof, conscious that there was nothing but fresh air between my feet and the sea-washed boulders over a hundred feet below . . . The accident happened on our way back down from the top, during an abseil. 'Keep to the right,' I shouted, as Ran walked backwards down the cliff, over the big ledge. But he didn't move in time. I heard the throaty rattle of a defiant bird standing its ground, then a violent splatter as the aspiring mountaineer was showered with fulmar bile.

The smell was horrible but at least I had a helmet on, though as Sandy reminded me, it was a helmet with ventilation holes. People steered clear of me for a while that day.

Louise had watched the climb from the mainland clifftop. She confessed to Stephen Venables. 'He's away almost continuously. So either I'm left holding the baby or I have to go everywhere with him.' She hadn't developed a very high opinion of my ability to look after myself either. 'On Everest,' she said, 'I had to stick Ran's heart pills up all over the Base Camp mess tent to make sure he took them.'

Louise, Alexander and Elizabeth flew out to Geneva with me a month after the Hoy climb and Stephen came too. This time our goal was to reconnoitre the Nordwand so that I could actually look at the great wall close up for the first time and, if I realised that it would be folly to have a go at such a climb, I could still cancel things without embarrassing our charity. I knew that on his first attempt Joe Simpson had turned back after climbing part way up. If somebody like Simpson could make such a decision, I realised that I must face up to the unpalatable fact that I might be way out of my league. A lot of the problem, I know, would be entirely caused by my over-active imagination. Jon Krakauer, the famous climber journalist, who once managed to climb halfway up the North face, summed up this tendency well: 'The problem with climbing the North Face of the Eiger is that in addition to getting up 6,000 vertical feet of crumbling limestone and black ice, one must climb over some formidable mythology. The trickiest moves on any climb are the mental ones, the psychological gymnastics that keep terror in check, and the Eiger's grim aura is intimidating enough to ruin anyone's poise.'

At Grindelwald Jon Morgan, one of Kenton's guide friends, took charge and Stephen, Jon and I travelled to the base of the Eiger by train, the amazing legacy of nineteenth-century Swiss railway fever which tunnelled into the North Face itself. We got out at the Eigergletscher station and started walking up the gentle south-west flank of the mountain. Stephen takes up the story:

We were still in shadow, following Jon up scree slopes and occasional little rock steps. When it got steeper he stopped to put Ran on a 'short rope', leading him on a 10-foot tether up hard frozen snow, then a little rock overhang, which got us onto classic Eiger territory – downward sloping tiles of grey limestone, littered with rock debris.

Then suddenly it all changed as we emerged onto the crest of the west ridge proper, where the sloping tiles reached a knife-edge between two utterly different worlds – on one side our rambling sunny slope, and on the other an immense sombre abyss.

Jon lobbed off a rock and counted 15 seconds before hearing its distant clatter. The bottom of the north face was 2,500 feet below.

Ran said nothing. Jon got him to crawl along the edge. Then he made him stand up and walk along the edge. Then he anchored the rope, paying it out slowly as he told Ran to lean right out over the abyss.

Like the well-trained former soldier that he is, Ran obeyed orders, brown eyes still inscrutable beneath bushy eyebrows. Then he admitted: 'That is horrible!'

We dangled him there for about ten minutes, then let him back onto the gentle side where he and I sat in the sun, sharing a sandwich. I asked him why he needed this challenge, and he insisted that he just had to overcome his 'irritating' fear of heights.

Somehow that bluff quip didn't quite account convincingly for this non-mountaineer's ambition to attempt the climb which one of the first ascentionists described as the mountaineer's 'supreme test of stamina, skill and courage'.

Dangling over that 2,000-foot sheer void would, I am certain, have made me realise I could not face climbing up to such a place (nor the other 4,000 feet above) *if* I had actually dared to look down. As it was, I had spent the entire ten minutes focusing as hard as I could on watching Stephen and Jon on the cliff edge just *above* me. On reflection, this rendered pointless the whole rationale of the reconnaissance which was to learn whether or not I could stomach full-scale exposure. I had merely put off the day of reckoning.

Back in France, Kenton drove me to a cliff face known as La Fayet, an hour or so from Chamonix, and introduced me to a climbing technique known as dry tooling, which he advised me would be especially useful for the mixed rock and ice conditions he reckoned we would face on the Eiger. He headed up the cliff with only the very tips of his axes hooked into tiny rock holes or over fractional rock ledges. Sometimes just one axe's tip. His legs often hung in space where there was an overhang or the vertical rock offered no purchase point at all for his crampon spikes. I grew really attached to this, to me, new system because it meant virtually no requirement for me to use my stubby left hand to hold and haul up my bodyweight. This gave me the much needed confidence to decide irrevocably to try the Eiger in March 2007. Both Kenton and Ian Parnell wrote off that entire month in their diaries, and the fundraising machine of Marie Curie clicked into action.

Throughout the post-Everest, pre-Eiger months, I had needed to make a living and accepted lectures to business conferences all over the place. We flew everywhere as a family. One lecture, to 9,000 individuals, all members of the Million Dollar Round Table, in a huge theatre in New Orleans, allowed us a spare day in town. So we walked to the banks of the Mississippi and watched the paddle steamers moored close by. Later that week, after we had left, Hurricane Katrina struck the city, and the conference organisers must have thanked the Lord that they had just got rid of their 9,000 millionaire attendees.

We flew all the way to Sioux Falls via Chicago to lecture to just thirty crop-spray manufacturers in the middle of the prairies. My US-based German friend, Mike Kobold, who had so helped me research the Nazi horrors of the Death Marches, joined us there for a three-day drive to the Black Hills of Dakota and the high sculptures of Mount Rushmore.

We went to Cape Town for a forty-minute presentation and, wanting to show Louise my old home in nearby Constantia, took a taxi there. The entire area had altered beyond recognition. Gone were the open vineyards and the dusty roads. Instead, acres of high security fences and tall dense undergrowth lined both sides of the smart tarmac lanes, and this time I failed even to find the home of my childhood. In between the lectures, we managed to slot in brief holidays, including a week in Transylvania with Abby who had bravely bought a derelict cottage in the mountains close by Castle Bran, the original home of the mythical Count Dracula. We trekked along high ridges and saw wolves and bears, but no vampires.

The Allied Joint Force Command in Naples, part of the United Nations force there, asked me to be guest speaker for their Trafalgar Night Dinner, and a Scottish colonel, Jim Hutton, kindly spent the following day in a jeep tracing from archive material he had researched the exact route along which my father and his tanks of the Royal Scots Greys had advanced in 1944 between their landing at Salerno and his death from a German anti-personnel mine just before the relief of Naples. I was sixty-one years old when I stood for the first time in the leafy Italian lane where my father had been mortally wounded, aged forty-four. I would have loved to have told my mother about that day, reliving his last few months, but, as I have mentioned, she had died the previous year, as had two of his four children. I hope there is an afterlife, as I would love to meet my father for the first time.

On our last day in Naples, I joined two bus-loads of soldiers, sailors and airmen for the annual Vesuvius Half Marathon, uphill all the way to just below the crater and won by a very fit Frenchman. At the prizegiving he was reminded in a (half) joking sort of way that the French hadn't done too well at Trafalgar.

The trouble with being post-middle-aged, I found, was that I needed to spend a lot more time trying to keep fit. The most time-effective way of maintaining basic all-round fitness was jogging but, as the years went by, the number of hours needed per week pounding out the miles kept on increasing if I was still to do things that involved fairly strenuous activity. Added to this, I did not really enjoy the training runs as I once had and was often too busy or travelling when I most needed to put in all those boring jogging hours. My old friend Mike Stroud pinpointed my problem:

> Why is exercise so hard to undertake? Boredom, discomfort, fatigue and lack of time must all be contributory, but there is an additional problem. Goals such as good health in old age are far too nebulous to provide the motivation. For that reason, it is often only those with a more definite short-term goal that succeed. People who need to lose weight, for example, are more likely to continue to put in time and effort than those who are not too fat. If you give yourself a definite aim, exercise acquires a purpose. You need to set yourself a challenge.

This is what saw me, especially in my post heart-attack years, entering the succession of races itemised in Appendix 5.

My old nanny from South African days had been a loving

correspondent ever since I was eight, but she finally died aged ninety-five, having driven until she was ninety. Ginny's mother, Janet, died whilst I was on Everest, and my late sister Sue's husband, John, who I had known for over forty years, died suddenly of a heart attack in March 2006. My family and friends had begun to disperse in an upwards direction, which is what can happen with alarming frequency when you pass by the magic year of sixty.

I reacted by passing all my old photos, maps, polar documents and gear from the 1970s and 1980s to the Royal Geographical Society and the Scott Polar Research Institute. To our regimental museum in Edinburgh Castle, I gave my own medals from the seventies for fighting Marxists, my father's 1940s medals for fighting Nazis, and my grandad's (he had by far the greatest number) for extending the Empire and then defending it in the late nineteenth and early twentieth centuries.

In the African summer of 2005, Louise and I interrupted lectures and climbing training to join a team of white Zimbabweans and Zambians on the Zambezi River to recreate the last few days of Doctor Livingstone's journey to the Victoria Falls. We paddled traditional dugout canoes with steersmen from the same tribe as had accompanied Livingstone exactly 150 years before to the day. We passed a great many hippopotami, an unknown number of crocodiles and, on our arrival at the falls, unveiled a commemorative plaque to the great doctor beside the Zambian edge of the mighty waterfall, which truly deserves its position as one of the seven natural wonders of the world.

After this enjoyable journey to honour a great Scottish explorer, I contemplated switching future activities from the cold regions of the world, whether the Poles, the Himalaya or the Alps, to places where cool breezes, eggshell-blue skies and verdant valleys can be savoured. It was a nice idea, but my more pressing concern was the North Face of the Eiger.

20

Murder Wall

On 1 March 2007 I flew to Geneva with the family and drove a rental car to Grindelwald, where we stayed at a family-run hotel, the Grand Regina, with a reputation among British tourists of being the best in all Switzerland. The owner, Hans Krebs, had kindly given us accommodation free of charge because he approved of and wanted to help our Marie Curie aims. The hotel manager, Ingo Schmoll, warned us of the consequences of the mountains not being as stable as they should normally be in mid-winter. The rate of retreat of glaciers throughout the Alps, together with the thawing of the permafrost layer, had created temporary barrages of fallen rock blocking high ravines and creating lakes. Increasingly torrential summer rains then burst the feeble dams of rubble, causing flash floods, mudslides and more loosened rock. The previous autumn the Eiger itself had suffered a major rockfall, a chunk bigger than two Empire State Buildings.

Kenton, in Chamonix, was in touch with Ralph Rickli, the famous Swiss met forecaster in Berne, and with the top European weather bureau, the Met Office in Exeter. We needed a clear good weather window of at least five days and nights on the North Face if a non-skilled climber like me was to reach the summit. Kenton and I cleared the whole of March in our diaries and waited. The ITV crew, led by Philip Reay-Smith, installed themselves in a suite with a balcony looking directly opposite the Eiger which was swiftly transformed into a studio resembling a CIA electronic snooper room, with the intention of transmitting the first ever live news footage from the Norwand. Philip warned me that, once his team was in Grindelwald, we must start the climb. ITV could make no open-ended commitment, since their team had to be on permanent call to go anywhere in the world at short notice. Indeed, Philip sent me an email warning me not to do the climb during the week starting 19 March, because that was ITV's 'Iraq Week' and there would be much less space on the News for non-Iraq-related items.

When I told Kenton this, he snorted, 'If the weather's good for the week of 19 March, and we haven't gone by then, we will set out at once, ITV crew or no ITV crew.' I relayed this back to Philip.

The March days slowly ticked by in Grindelwald, Louise having to return to Britain to take Alexander back to school. I began to find the bulk of the Eiger, looming over the hotel, a touch oppressive. I tried to keep busy. I went for a daily two-hour run out of the village, along hilly lanes and up the glacial ravines. As I ran I heard the intermittent explosions of avalanches from the heights of the Alpine giants all around. After six days of evil weather forecasts, I was padding about Grindelwald increasingly worried that we would never get a five-day clear period in March. Every time I looked out of the window or trudged through the village streets, I found myself looking up at that great black wall, the upper limits obscured in thick fog. One night I couldn't sleep and spotted a single pinprick of light high up on the bulk of the North Face. The very sight of it made my stomach muscles tighten as I imagined having to try to sleep anywhere on that hideous cliff.

I went for a walk to a mountain coffee house and paid £3 in Swiss francs for a 'Rockslide' (coffee spiked with schnapps) named in honour of the recent big Eiger rockfall. I sat there for three hours and frightened myself reading Joe Simpson's Eiger experience in 2002. But at last, our friendly met-experts in Berne and Exeter concurred and a five-day window was forecast for the middle of the month.

Louise and our baby Elizabeth, eleven months old with blonde hair, large blue eyes and a sunny nature, were back in Grindelwald when Kenton confirmed our imminent departure. I tried to hide the fear, almost panic, that surged with the knowledge that we were about to start the climb. Until then there was always the doubt about the weather, the chance that we might not be able to try the climb at least until the following September. But now the die was cast. I did my best not to reveal my wobbly state of mind, especially at the Grindelwald rail station when saying goodbye to my wife and daughter. And later that day, in the hostel at the foot of the Eiger, I needed to work hard to appear unfazed in the boisterous company of Kenton, Ian, the ITV crew and Stephen Venables, who was back reporting for *The Sunday Times*.

We were to leave the hostel for the hour-long snow traverse to the base of the North Face at 4.00 a.m. the next morning and I found sleep elusive that night. I remembered a hundred similar sleepless nights before big moments, but polar fears were something I knew how to handle. Mountain fears were different. I feared my own inadequacies, of being revealed as a coward or, at best, as a wimp. Would the North Face trigger uncontrollable vertigo? Would I freeze to some cliff, unable to move, thereby risking Ian's and Kenton's lives, as well as my own? Never mind the ridicule. And what of a fall? I had by now read all the accounts by far better climbers than myself.

Joe Simpson, survivor extraordinary, wrote about how he felt *as* he fell, apparently towards certain death.

Deprived of the ability to imagine the future, you are fearless; suddenly there is nothing to be scared about. You have no time to ponder on death's significance or fear what it may feel like. In the cataclysmic violence of the accident you lose not only the future but the past as well. You lose all possible reasons for fear, unable as you are to understand the loss of what you once were or what you could become. Time is frozen for you into the present events and sensations, the knocks, and bumps from which you can draw no emotional conclusions. 'I'm crashing. I'm falling fast. I'm about to die. This is it.' In truth you have far too much on your mind for such frivolous luxuries as fear.

One set of fears I had fought against in the 1960s, which had nothing to do with crevasses or frostbite or falling through weak sea-ice, was that of being shot when fighting Marxist terrorists in Dhofar. It was not so much the fear of being killed outright as the thought of some bullet, shrapnel shard or mine blast ripping out my genitals or blinding me. These were the terror images in the mind. To cope, I learned to keep a ruthlessly tight clamp on my imagination. With fear, you must prevent, not cure. Fear must not be let in in the first place. If you are in a canoe, never listen to the roar of the rapid ahead before you let go of the river bank. Just do it! Keep your eyes closed and let go. If the fear then rushes at you, it will not be able to get a grip, because your mind will by then be focusing on the technical matter of survival.

That was all very well when coping with rational fears about what *might* happen. But vertigo is not rational and the trigger likely to set it off was the all too real sight beneath my feet of a great beckoning sickening void. Exactly what would it feel like to spend time cartwheeling, rushing downwards for several thousand feet?

I have been asked, since Elizabeth was born, if I felt guilty risking my life on the Eiger. Perhaps I should, but being aware I could have another heart attack at any moment militates against such guilt feelings. Additionally, I know that Louise is a truly wonderful mother, as mine was, and I grew up without a father. To this day, although I hugely respect his memory, I have never emotionally missed him, for I never knew him, and Elizabeth, not yet one year old at the time of the Eiger, would certainly not remember me. Both Ginny and Louise married me in the full knowledge that I make a living through expeditions and intend to do so as long as I can. So I could feel no more guilt than would, say, a miner or truck driver, both professions with far higher death rates than mine.

Once my alarm went off and I began to check all my gear before a rushed breakfast, the dread thoughts and fears of the night did indeed disperse. We left on time in pitch darkness with Kenton leading. Ian's diary of the week recorded: 'For Ran, although he hid it well, Everest had been a failure. This time round we were to attempt the Eiger North Face, and while we didn't have the barrier of altitude, in my mind this was a much tougher challenge.'

Ian's backpack was heavier than mine, due to all the camera gear, as he was to document the climb and attempt the live ITV News broadcasts. Kenton's pack, also heavier than mine, was festooned with climbing paraphernalia, but I still felt dubious about climbing with a pack that restricted my movement, cramped my arms and limited my ability to look upwards. Dawn crept over the Alps and the mountain tops were tipped with an orange alpenglow. The stars disappeared and the great wall above us came alive. I thought of its German nickname *Mordwand*, or Murder Wall.

Half an hour of trudging along a line of boot prints in deep snow took us to the spot Kenton decided to climb from. We said our goodbyes to Philip and Rob of ITV and to Stephen Venables. They should be able to watch our every move over the next few days, providing bad weather stayed away, through their powerful camera lenses. And at night they should be able to spot the pinpricks of our head torches from wherever we slept.

We fixed on our crampons beneath a feature known as the First Pillar. Many climbers lose the route in this area, but Kenton seemed confident as he stared up at our first obstacle, some 2,000 feet of mixed snow gulleys, loose scree, shiny ledges of smooth, compact limestone and temporarily lodged boulders. Looking away to the flanks of the face, the lofty silhouettes of the peaks of the Wetterhorn and Mittelhorn seemed dwarfed by our own monster.

Few of the infamous Eiger tragedies occurred on this first 2,000-foot climb, but the fallen detritus of many an Eiger incident lay all around us. I remember, from one of the Eiger books, a photograph of climber Edi Rainer's body lying smashed in the scree of this catchment zone. And Chris Bonington, on his Eiger ascent, had among these rubble-strewn lower reaches passed by blood trails and a piece of flesh attached to some bone.

I knew that the world's top soloists, acrobats of the top league, could climb the Nordwand in hours, not days, without ropes, in their sticky-soled rock-shoes, as light as woollen socks. A single slip or false move would see them dead, crushed on the rock, but they survive on the confidence born of their expertise. The mere thought of climbing a single rock pitch unroped made me flinch.

In a few hours, with constant encouragement from Kenton and Ian, I had blundered my way up 1,000 feet or more of the initial rubble slopes. I felt much comforted by the thought that, if my nerve failed as the drop below grew far greater than any climb I had done before, there was a nearby escape hatch, the Eiger tunnel's gallery window or porthole which allows tourists to look out and gasp at the airy void immediately below them.

We must have climbed some 2,000 feet up the mountain when we reached the next recognisable feature, the aptly named Shattered Pillar. I was feeling tired and my neck muscles were aching from the tug of my rucksack harness. But the weather was, as prophesied by the met offices of Berne and Exeter, holding good and clear. Every few hours I tore open a new hand-warmer bag with my teeth and inserted the two tiny pouches into my mitts. They worked well and whenever the sensitive stumps of my amputated fingers began to feel numb with cold, I positioned the hand-warmer pouch over their ends for a while.

I had never climbed on similar rock before, smooth like slate with almost nowhere to provide even the tiniest holding point for the tips of my ice-axes and crampon spikes. At times I had to remove one or other of my mitts with my teeth and use my bare hand to clasp some rock bulge or slight surface imperfection to avoid a fall. This I hated to do, for my fingers, once cold, took for ever to re-warm, even with my heat pouches.

Every now and again I glanced below me without thinking and felt that shock of terror I knew so well which presages the first wave of vertigo. I instantly forced my mind to concentrate on something of interest above me, usually Kenton's progress. On that first day this process worked well for me. I was, due to vanity, keen to prevent Ian and Kenton from glimpsing my fear. With Kenton I may have succeeded, but Ian was a sharp cookie and zealous in his film-making responsibilities. Philip had especially instructed him to record personal emotions and such points of human interest as discord within the group.

At some point on a steep icy slope, to my considerable alarm and dismay, one of my boots skidded off a nub of protruding rock and my left crampon swung away from my boot. Although still attached by a strap, the crampon was useless. Luckily the same crampon had come loose once before, on a frozen waterfall with Kenton a month ago. So I reined in my rising panic and, hanging from one axe and a tiny foothold, I managed, with much silent swearing, to reattach the crampon to the boot.

We came, over 2,000 feet up, to an eighty-foot-high rockface known as the Difficult Crack, which I found virtually impossible, far more technically demanding than any of my previous training ascents, and extremely testing on my puny biceps. To be more precise, my arms felt as though they were being torn from their sockets since, in the almost total absence of any reasonable footholds, I had literally to haul my body and rucksack upwards by arm-power alone. I wished I had spent more time obeying Paul Twomey's instructions to train hard at obtaining some upper body strength. By the time I heaved myself up the last steep and glass-smooth boulder of the Crack, I was on my very last ounce of willpower and wanted only to stop for the day and sleep. Not that there was anywhere remotely suitable in sight to lie down or even sit.

Ian recorded my ascent of the Difficult Crack through the eyes of a top-flight mountaineer who knew I was facing my first big test on the North Face.

Through Ran's two years of training for the route, he proved himself to be a competent and efficient ice and mixed climber, but steep rock tended to bring out his weaknesses. In particular, his ineffectual stumps for fingers on his left hand . . . Ran's worst fear was that he might be forced to climb bare-handed. Luckily he had one big advantage. Whereas Kenton and I spent valuable time fretting and testing the security of the meagre hooks we'd uncovered, Ran, to put it bluntly, was clueless. His technique basically involved dragging his tools down the rock until they somehow snagged, then he would blindly pull for glory. His footwork on rock was similarly polished: a wild peddalling technique that for all its dry tooling naivety was surprisingly effective.

From the top of the Difficult Crack we could look immediately above us at an immense sheer wall, known as the Rote Fluh, smooth, red and infamous for its propensity to shower loose rock-falls on to the face below. A natural desire of all climbers at this point is to ascend as quickly as possible towards the base of this lethal feature, since proximity minimises the danger of being hit. With a bulky backpack, however, speed is not too easy. Balancing like a dainty gymnast in rock-shoes is a far cry from climbing heavily laden with the weight on your back ever threatening to pull your body away from the rock and out into space. From the Crack we still had more than 8,000 feet of climbing, including traverses, on the North Face, much of which, I knew, would be a lot harder and more exposed than had been the eighty-foot-high Crack.

Kenton had planned for us to bivouac the first night at a ledge known as the Swallows Nest. Between the Difficult Crack and this refuge was the infamous Hinterstoisser Traverse, the key passage, unlocking access to the centre of the wall. It was a passage won at considerable cost by its pioneers, two German guides, Andreas Hinterstoisser and Toni Kurz, and two Austrian guides, Willy Angerer and Edi Rainer.

Their story forms a part of the forbidding history of this section of the face. In 1935 a couple of Germans, Sedlmayer and Mehringer, had climbed a record distance up the mountain, but at 3,300 metres they had frozen to death on a ledge. A year later Hinterstoisser and his companions, hoping to set a new record, if not to reach the summit, had reached the ledge of the frozen bodies which with climbers' macabre humour they named Death

Bivouac, only to be themselves turned back by the weather and falling rocks. But fatally they had left no rope in place across their key traverse, and their desperate attempts to reverse their route over this slippery, vertical cliffside all failed. So they tried to rope down to reach the railway's porthole in the rock but disaster overtook them. One fell and dropped free to the valley below, one was strangled by the rope, and a third froze to death. The youngest German, Toni Kurz, dangled from the rope-end a mere 100 metres above the porthole, just out of reach of and conversing with his would-be rescuers. His was a slow, unenviable death.

When we reached their traverse, a relatively new-looking rope, clipped to the rock, disappeared round a bulge at the top of the great slab. My mouth felt dry and my hands weak. This was a moment of truth, and the only way I knew how to face it was by attacking the obstacle in a rush, desperate to keep my mind busy with no tiny chink into which sheer terror could claw, then spread incubus-like and render me a gibbering fool, an embarrassment to myself and to the others. This was my nightmare as I tried to find successive nicks in the glistening rock to place the steel points on my crampons. I gripped the black rope where I had watched Kenton hold it, and edged down around the bulge – and into space. Suddenly, and with a visual impact that took my breath away, there was a panoramic view of the world below. For 2,500 feet under my boots, only the wind touched the plunging rock. My crampons skidded out of their tenuous holds. I gripped the black rope dangling from the rock as my feet scrabbled desperately to find a hold. Into my brain, unbidden, came the picture of my heavy body tearing Kenton off the cliff, and then the deadweight of us both pulling Ian away, and the rush of air as we cartwheeled through space. *Will I scream*, was my main worry, strangely enough.

The first team to climb the North Face had used this same route, and the author of their story, Heinrich Harrer, wrote, 'The rocks across which we now had to traverse were almost vertical plunging away beneath into thin air. We were full of admiration for Hinterstoisser's brave achievement.'

My own memory of that traverse is thankfully confused. I know that I swore to myself again and again that this was my last climb. I also recall, at some point during that fearful move, focusing on a sudden whiteness in the black rope, the rope upon which I was, in my mind, utterly dependent each time my crampons slipped away from the face. Somehow the rope had become frayed at this point to a single fragile strand.

When I eventually came to the far side of the traverse, Ian recorded:

Ran emerged near the end looking by his standards pretty nervous – not one to shout his complaints, his eyes which were wide open and out on stalks betrayed what he was really thinking. I kept the ropes tight but couldn't pull him up the final few feet. So, when he started slipping down, his cramponned feet pedalling for purchase on blank rocks, sparks flying, I think he felt desperate measures were needed. The nearest thing at hand to assist him was his ice-axe, so he took an almighty lunge up at the ropes and pulled himself to safety. The only problem was that his 'safety' was reliant on the one centimetre thick cord of nylon he had snagged with his razor sharp axe blade and which secured *me* to the belay.

I clambered past Ian's body and savoured the blessed relief of a solid six-inch ledge under one crampon. I rested on it and felt a wave of exhaustion pass through me. So had I conquered my fear of heights? Had I vanquished my sixty-two-year-old bogeyman of vertigo? I *had* crossed the Hinterstoisser Traverse on the great North Face of the Eiger, so surely I *must* have become a 'proper climber'. And proper climbers surely don't fear heights. Yet I suspected that nothing had really changed. There had been no actual confrontation within myself. No fearful struggle I had bravely and finally won. My only victory thus far had been to prevent the creeping angst getting a grip on me. Day one on the Eiger was almost over without a disaster. Three or four more days, ever higher, lay ahead.

From the end of the traverse, we inched up a seventy-foot

vertical crack to an eighteen-inch-wide ledge beneath an overhang, the Swallows Nest. A scab of frozen snow was stuck to the ledge and we used our axes to flatten this out, giving us some four feet of width and almost standing up space. Ian clipped my waist harness to a rock bolt, and Kenton melted snow over a tiny gas stove. Our bivouac was comfortable but, for me, ruined by the knowledge that, as I lay with my nose up against the rock wall and my knees curled up for warmth in the lightweight sleeping bag, my backside protruded over the edge of our ledge and over the void below.

The world-famous climber, Walter Bonatti, pioneer of some of the hardest cliffs in the Alps, wrote of his own Swallows Nest visit in the 1960s:

I was not the first man to tackle the Eigerwand alone. Two others had tried in recent years, but both had died in the attempt. The aura of fatality and blood that hangs over this killer mountain seemed painfully distinct to the eyes of a solo climber, restoring it to the atmosphere of the early years.

I appeared on the first snowfield simultaneously with the first thundering salvo of boulders, and I just had time to dodge smartly back into the Swallows Nest before they came shooting by. The incident did not surprise me; it is natural on a face like this that as soon as the upper snow slopes are touched by the sun they should start to unload their wares, and it was by chance that with the whole wide face available they had fallen exactly where I happened to be.

When Joe Simpson and Ray Delaney had bivouacked here seven years before us, two other climbers (Matthew Hayes from Hampshire and Phillip O'Sullivan from New Zealand) had fallen off, roped together, from an icy slope higher up and dropped past this ledge. Simpson had written: 'I thought of their endless, frictionless fall, numbed in their last moments of consciousness by the full enormity of what was happening . . . I stared down thinking of them lying there tangled in their ropes, side by side . . . We didn't hear them go. They didn't scream.'

That could have been their epitaph, I thought. 'They didn't scream.'

During the night a breeze blew ice-dust down the neck of my jacket, and small stones clattered by. I resisted the temptation of rolling over to sleep facing outwards. The clear night sky was crammed with stars, mirrored by the pinprick lights of Grindelwald in the dark valley below. Kenton woke us before dawn. He passed me an empty cloth bag which I filled with snow blocks that I cut, reluctantly, from the end of my sleeping platform. Ian asked me for some item and, unthinkingly, I threw it along the ledge to him, forgetting for an instant where we were. This deserved and got a mouthful of abuse from the others. '*Never*,' they cried in unison, 'throw anything. Pass it over with care.' Ian went on to warn me about my boots and crampons. 'Put them on carefully. It's all too easy with cold hands trying to force a cold foot into a rigid boot to lose your grip and then, before you know it, a boot is gone – a long way. Then you are in *serious* trouble.'

Answering the call of nature during the first day's climb was something I had successfully postponed, but the moment of truth arrived on the narrow ledge. There was a sharp breeze and I felt cold. Squatting between the rock face and the void, I was thankful for the small mercy that I was up one end of the ledge and not, like Ian, in the middle. Luckily I had an empty polythene bag to hand as a receptacle. Nonetheless, I did begin to wonder how climbers cope on big mountain faces having to drink water from the soiled snow floors of oft-used ledges. But then I remembered that the London sewage system provides Londoners with oft-recycled drinking water without even the safeguard of its being boiled on Kenton's gas stove.

Shortly before sunrise, Kenton disappeared upwards from the Swallows Nest. Soon after I followed his lead on to the ice slope above our bivouac, there came an awkward leaning move over the face of a smooth rock. For a while I was flummoxed, but, stretching the axe in my good hand fully upwards, I felt its spike lodge in some unseen nook. Such moments require a blind hope that your sole hold on life will be a reliable one when you make the next

move. If it isn't and your sudden bodyweight dislodges the ax
placement, you will plummet downwards hoping not to drag yc
colleagues with you.

Once over the rock I was on to a long steep icy slope known
the First Ice-Field, and here I heard the whistling thrum of so
matter falling past us, whether ice or rock, I'm not sure. The c
before, a small stone had struck Kenton's helmet, and at the ba
of this First Ice-Field, arrowing upwards at some 55°, a larg
lump of ice caught Ian on the helmet.

With careful axe work, I crawled up two steep slopes of mix
rock and ice with extreme caution, for there was a deal of loc
rubble just itching to respond to the call of Isaac Newton. Af
200 feet negotiating this unstable zone, we scaled the first real i
field, which I found less difficult than anything to date. It ended
too quickly at the bottom end of a 300-foot-high near-verti
gulley of part-iced rock known as the Ice Hose. I definitely d
liked this section which, as an amateur, I find difficult to descri
But I took some comfort from Harrer agreeing with me: 'th
isn't a cranny anywhere for a reliable piton, and there aren't a
natural holds. Moreover, the rock is scoured smooth by falli
stones, bread-crumbed with snow, ice and rubble. It isn't an in
tation to cheerful climbing, it offers no spur to one's courage
simply threatens hard work and danger.'

More stones whistled by as I inched up the Hose but, althou
I found myself flinching and ducking, none made contact, and t
next time I reached Kenton's belay position, he looked hap
clearly pleased we had reached the Second Ice-Field intact. T
was the great white sheet easily identifiable from Grindelwald.
some point as we axed our way up it, Kenton saw an ice-axe wh
tle by us on its way down the face. We never did identify its own
I shivered at the thought of trying to climb any distance at all
such a mountain with only one axe. The wind picked up on t
wide open flank of the ice-field. An explosion sounding furtl
down the face, as we learned later from Philip and his film cr
came from an avalanche of rock and ice roaring down the Ice Hc

that we had earlier scaled. The ice climb seemed to go on and on and our ropes were usually slack between each other to the extent that I felt as though I was almost free climbing un-roped. On the many soft snow patches, I took special care to dig in my spikes and axes as deep as I could.

Philip had hired a helicopter to film our ascent of the ice-fields, and he needed to collect all the film Ian had taken with the hand-held videocam. The helicopter dropped a steel hawser down towards us with a black bag on its hook. But the angle of our slope was too steep, so Ian cramponned down and then out towards the centre of the ice-field. Perched on a rock, with no apparent regard for the huge drop below, he attached his film container to the swinging hook. Simply watching him made my blood run cold.

The helicopter disappeared way below us, and we finally reached the upper edge of the ice slope, following it to the left. At this point a difficult rock pitch leads up on to a triangular rock buttress called the Flat Iron. In 1961 two British climbers, Brian Nally and Barry Brewster, were progressing below the buttress when Brewster was hit by a rock and injured. Chris Bonington and Don Whillans abandoned their own ascent to attempt a rescue, but the already unconscious Brewster was swept to his death by rockfall before they could reach him, so they led a seriously dis-oriented Nally to safety.

Kenton, seeing that I was flagging badly on a difficult section to access the Flat Iron, had pointed upwards. 'Only two or three pitches to Death Bivouac,' he assured me. The name of the place was hardly reassuring. Just then, however, Kenton's promise of its proximity did make it sound a very welcome spot. Again we dug away at a snow-clogged ledge and cleared enough space for the three of us to lie head to toe. I slept well at Death Bivouac for I was tired, but some climbers have found its atmosphere oppressive. The legendary French climber, Gaston Rébuffat, wrote of his time there: 'On this sinister, murderous face, the rusty pitons and rotten ropes dating from the early attempts, the stone wall which sur-rounded us as we ate, and which sheltered Sedlmayer and

Mehringer before they died, all combined to remind us that t
moment you cease climbing toward the summit, success and saf
itself are compromised.'

That night my right arm rested on the very edge of a 3,500-fc
drop, and Kenton's pan of breakfast muesli tasted none the wo:
for his half-joking warning that some previous climber had us
his end of the ledge, from where he had scooped our brew-
snow, as the Gents.

As before, Kenton set out at dawn. He led some pitches a
handed over to Ian for others. I remained always in the midd
Since I was by far the most likely to fall, this system would ho]
fully minimise the chances of my body dragging both the oth
off the mountain with me. That, of course, assumed that neitl
of *them* were knocked off by a rock first.

That day, our third on the Eiger, began badly for my men
state because, expecting to continue heading in an upwards dir
tion, we actually had to move diagonally downwards across
extremely steep slope, known as the Third Ice-Field, to the base
a crucial feature known as the Ramp. This 700-foot-high le
slanting gash overhung by walls of limestone contains many na
surprises, and was graded in 1997 by two skilled Irish climbers
'a solid VI.6', a grade more difficult than I could climb withou
number of falls when attempted during my British climbing o
ings. However, I had not used axes or crampons in Britain, s
hoped that they would make a key difference. (For comments
the severity of grading the North Face, see Appendix 4.)

I had read much about the Ramp, which some Eiger pund
describe as the most technically difficult section on the w:
Harrer, one of the first group to try it, wrote, 'The "Ramp" – w
it fits that Face, on which everything is more difficult than it loo
You cannot run up it, for there are no rough slabs, no good fo
or hand-holds. Here too the rock-strata slope outwards and dov
wards, and the crannies into which a piton can be driven can
counted on one hand.'

Twice over the next few hours, inching up the central chimney the Ramp, I came within an ace of falling, but on each occasion, my axes caught hold on some tiny unseen nub and halted my downwards rush. There were icy chimneys, awkward rock slabs, tricky and frightening overhangs, side-pulls, hand-palming off sloping holds, and the occasional hand-jamb, all techniques I had been taught by Paul Twomey on his Bristol church climbing walls. Near the upper reaches of the great gully there were two or three stretches of rock that nearly defeated my every attempt. Looking down at any point during the Ramp climb would have been a big mistake, as the airy ice-fields immediately below had a hypnotic effect. Looking up was not to be recommended either in the Ramp's narrower reaches, for then my rucksack lid's contents would jab the back of my neck.

Somewhere on the Ramp in 1961, an Austrian climber with a brilliant repertoire of ultra severe Alpine ascents, the twenty-two-year-old Adolf Mayr, came to grief attempting the first ever solo ascent of the face. Down in Grindelwald, queues of tourists waited their turn to gawp at 'Adi' through the hotel telescopes. Somewhere in the mid-section, at a spot named the Waterfall Chimney, he needed to traverse across wet rock. Watchers below saw him hack at a foothold with his axe. Then he stepped sideways, missed his footing and fell 4,000 feet to his death.

Above the Ramp there were sections of slippery ice and treacherous patches of soft snow into which neither my axes nor my crampons could be trusted to hold firm. By always checking I had three reasonable holds before advancing a leg or arm to a fourth higher hold, none of the many slips that I made proved disastrous, merely heart-stopping at the time.

Unbeknown to me, both my companions had been concerned that the Ramp might prove too technically difficult for my meagre rock-ability and that the expedition would end there. Ian recorded on his camera tape that evening:

The Ramp is about three pitches high, or three rope lengths high, and the most difficult bit is the final rope length. There is no ice which would give good purchase for the axes, it's only rock. It's

349

very steep in places and it's also overhanging. That pushes you out and, with the rucksack, all the weight is on your arms. You're looking for features either side on the wall and they are pretty smooth in places, so you are scratching on tiny holds to get up. Ran is doing excellently; today was probably the point at which he could have failed. He managed to do it very well, so we were very pleased.

At one belay I met up with Ian just below a single boulder the size of half a standard UK red postbox. As we conversed a rock struck the boulder and shattered into shards, one of which struck me hard on the helmet. The rest passed harmlessly over our heads. Just above the boulder, Kenton traversed to the right of the straight-to-heaven route we had been following for 700 feet up the gulley of the Ramp. Here we ran out of ice at a place of much loose slate aptly named the Brittle Ledges.

For a while I could find no way up one layer of slate, for every rock I tried to use for a hold simply broke off. My axes were no help. Eventually I had to remove my mitts and bury my bad hand deep into a vertical cleft to achieve the needed purchase. This move coincided with the failure of my last available hand-warmer pouch. Resupplies were unobtainable deep in my rucksack, and my hand soon grew numb with cold. This was bad timing because, above the Brittle Ledges, Ian led up a vertical wall of slate about ninety feet high. Maybe I was too tired to think clearly, or perhaps my cold, numb left hand, incapable of gripping anything but my ice-axe (and that thanks only to the crutch of its wrist loop), left me pretty much one-armed at the time.

Whatever the reason, I worked harder and with greater desperation on that single ninety-foot wall than on any previous part of the North Face. Despite the brittle nature of the rock, the first few metres up from a little snow-covered ledge on to the Brittle Crack are really overhanging. The upper twelve feet involved an appallingly exposed traverse around a corner with space shouting at you from every direction. The tiny cracks and sparse pitch placements available for my axes disappeared as I neared the top

All apparent handhold bulges were smooth and sloped down-wards, and my bare fingers simply slid off them. My arms and my legs began to shake, my biceps to burn. Pure luck got me to the ice patch that capped the wall, into which I sank an axe with great relief and hauled myself up, a wreck, to the tiny snow ledge where a grinning Ian was belayed.

'This is it,' he said. 'We spend the night here. Lovely view.'

A bit of axe burrowing formed a fairly comfortable ledge for the three of us, and again the mental stress and physical toil of the day overcame my worries about that drop a few inches away from my sleeping position. I lost a mitt off the ledge during the night, but I had a spare immediately available. The stumps of my left-hand fingers ached, but far less than all ten fingers had hurt on most polar trips. I felt fine as I fell asleep, worried only by tales I had heard of two of the obstacles to be faced the next day, the hugely exposed Traverse of the Gods and the technical problems of the final Exit Cracks, rated more difficult than the Ramp. I had just spent hours ascending by far the most difficult climbing of my admittedly short climbing life, and yet, by repute, the worst lay ahead.

Ian recorded his night perched above the Brittle Crack, during which he was scheduled to conduct a live interview. This, according to our ITV friends, would – if it worked – be the first time ever that anyone had managed a live interview on the national news from somewhere as remote as the Eiger Nordwand. A digilink was used in order to achieve this, utilising microwaves to send high-quality television images through the air so that Philip and the ITV crew at the base of the mountain could see and talk to me. Ian recorded:

I knew the film crew were getting my footage from the helicopter long line pick-ups of my tapes, but I really wanted to make a breakthrough and manage a live broadcast with Ran being inter-viewed on the face. I'd painstakingly shivered through the hour of preparation and tested both previous evenings, but first commu-nication problems scuppered things and then a breaking story of a stabbed Welsh vicar knocked us off the News roster. This time, as I knelt on the edge of the drop, camera held out in one hand and the broadcast antennae in the other, I felt a muscle begin to spasm in cramp. 'Three minutes to go', and the cramp starts an inexorable rise up my back. 'Two minutes, could you hold the camera steady, Ian', and my neck has joined the knot. I try to meditate and breathe through pain. 'Thirty seconds, keep the light on Ran', and I'm gasping for air now. Must try to stop breathing. 'So, Ran, could you tell us how you keep your spirits up in such hostile terrain?' It's happening, we're live! 'Excellent chaps, you can relax now. London says it's some of the best footage they've seen all week.'

On the morning of our fourth day on the face, I woke with a dry mouth and butterflies fluttering about in my stomach. Simpson's professional description of the Traverse of the Gods was clear in my mind. 'For 400 feet the points of protection weak, damaged pitons, battered into shattered downward-sloping cracks – are marginal to say the least. Most climbers would prefer not to weight such pitons statically, let alone fall onto them and the drop beneath the climber's feet is 5,000 feet of clear air. The hardest climbing comes right at the end of the traverse around a protruding prow of rock and close to the edge of the Spider.

In the valley below, Stephen Venables, who had climbed North Face over twenty years before, watched our every move through binoculars. He wrote: 'Taking crampons repeatedly and off is not an option, so Ran had to tread with steel points snow, ice and bare rock. Terrified of damaging the shortened fingers of his left hand, he kept his mitts on, gripping as best could. He knew that if he fell, he would go for a huge swing over the void before the rope held him.'

Stephen was assuming that the rope would hold me, but, having just come away from the unreliable region of the Brittle Crack envisaged the scenario of a pendulum plunge with my full weight tearing out the feeble flaky placements, together with both Kenton and Ian who were attached to them.

The Irish climber, Paul Harrington, who had climbed the Traverse of the Gods at exactly this time of year, had observed: 'Everything revolved around balancing crampon points on snow-covered ledges. There were no positive handholds. Only rock that could be pushed down upon to take some weight off the feet. It was a psychological passage.' Ian was behind me as I stepped out along this hellish cliffside. He described his thoughts. 'It's dramatic, nervy climbing for experienced climbers, but for someone like Ran who suffers from vertigo, it can easily become a complete nightmare. The rock here is loose, covered in verglas in winter and frighteningly exposed. In fact, at one point your heels overhang the whole drop of the wall to the snows of Kleine Scheidegg below.'

Suddenly, well ahead of me and appearing to be glued to the sheer wall merely by his fingertips and booted toes, Kenton disappeared around an abrupt corner. For no good reason this unsettled me badly. Behind me, Ian observed my reactions:

He is no drama queen, so I didn't expect him to break down sobbing, but by the methodical and calm way he worked across the first half of the traverse, he looked to be in complete control. Once he'd disappeared out of sight, I packed up my cameras and began climbing. It soon became evident that all wasn't as well as it seemed on the surface. I can't repeat Kenton's comments here, but it was a classic example of what is known in British alpine circles as a 'Kentrum' – the toys were well outside the pram. The issue seemed to be that, caught out of rope, Kenton had been forced to take a belay on two pathetic rotting bits of tat. Ran, swinging round to the second half of the traverse, felt the full impact of the sickening exposure and suffered an attack of the vertigo he'd so far successfully kept at bay. Reeling in their own worlds, a frank exchange of views followed.

Ian's interpretation of events was close to the mark. Something snapped as soon as I rounded the sharp bend in the wall. I may have inadvertently allowed myself a glimpse downwards beyond my normal carefully regimented focus point – my crampon points and not an inch beyond them. The onrush of sheer terror that this error sparked coincided with a tightening of the rope between me and the still invisible Kenton.

'Give me slack,' I shouted.

I had the rope back to Ian jammed behind me round an ice nub. I had to retreat a metre to loosen it. I was teetering on my front points on a mere rock scratch. I was terrified. My voice rose to a bellow.

'GIVE ME SLACK!'

This brought a furious response from my unseen leader. Furious, but to me unintelligible, so I had no idea what his problem was, no idea that his position was precarious. He knew that, if I fell at that moment, he was unlikely to be able to maintain a hold on the mountain. He was desperately doing his best to screw ice-screws in to improve his belay point. The last thing he wanted to do was to give me slack.

Fortunately, my instant reaction to the angry tone of his voice was to get angry myself, and that eclipsed the power of the vertigo attack. I controlled myself, closed my eyes, thought of a huge plate of steaming porridge laced with maple syrup and clung to the miserable rock face. After an age, or so it seemed, I felt slack rope from Kenton, reached back to flick Ian's rope free, and crept onwards above that sickening drop until I could see the still muttering Kenton perched on a patch of naked ice. I joined him and stayed silent as he berated me for my impatience, knowing that his moods of thunder never lasted long and were usually well deserved. There was nobody, not even Ian, who I trusted so completely in what, to me, was the most frightening environment on earth. Without Kenton, I could never have even contemplated setting foot on the Eiger's North Face.

'Lighten up,' Ian advised Kenton. They knew each other well.

We moved fairly quickly up the steep hard ice of the White Spider, so called due to its shape – a blob of white ice with white gulleys stretching up and down from its centre for hundreds of feet. In bad weather detritus from above can turn the Spider into a death zone for any climber caught on its face. Above and just to the right of the Spider was another, smaller ice-field, the Fly.

I crawled up the Spider. I felt really tired; perhaps due to the stress of the Traverse of the Gods or because the previous three days of climbing had slowly taken their toll on my reserves of fitness. I was also getting clumsy in a place where this was inadvisable. The sun beat down from a clear sky and the extreme exertion of hauling myself and my rucksack ever upwards made me sweat. Kenton, at a belay, helped me take off my windproof jacket, but I fumbled and lost my grip on it. A breeze grabbed it and, in an instant, it slid away down the slope, gathering speed. A bad item to lose at that height on the Eiger. We still had 1,000 feet to go straight up a maze of intricate gulleys, the notorious Exit Cracks, the final chimney of which included two rope-lengths up a near vertical ice staircase with the treads all sloping the wrong way.

From the White Spider on there were many obstacles that would, back in the Avon Gorge or on the Welsh sea cliffs, have been too much for my inadequate technical skills and lack of upper body strength. But this was the last rock problem I would face. The summit was tantalisingly close, so I attacked each new problem as though my life depended on it. Perhaps it did. The walls on both sides of various grooves and chimneys were smooth, featureless and often at eighty degrees. I remember a whitish wall called the Quartz Crack which looked evil but turned out to be merely nasty. And a smooth walled runnel which nearly stopped me and where Kenton pointed to a tiny ledge. 'Corti Bivouac,' he said, and I remembered Harrer's tale of this Italian wrongly accused of cutting his companions' rope.

Corti and Longhi had joined up with two top German climbers in 1957 down near the Hinterstoisser Traverse. They later missed the Traverse of the Gods altogether and tried to reach the Spider by a far more perilous route. Longhi fell 100 feet on to a ledge, where he sat for five days before he died. His body dangled on the rope for two years, ogled by telescope tourists. High in the Exit

Cracks Corti took a bad fall, so the Germans gave him their tent and key supplies and climbed on, hoping to raise help. Corti camped on a tiny ledge, the one Kenton showed me, until he was eventually rescued by the pioneering use of a winch cable from the summit. Longhi was too far below to be saved. The Germans disappeared and Corti was suspected of being responsible for their deaths until, four years later, their bodies were found. They had reached the summit, but died of exposure on their subsequent descent down the western flank.

I had reflected more than once on our climb how often Ian and Kenton must secretly have dreamt of cutting their ponderous client off their rope, since I knew they could both move like ballerinas over ice or rock as a team of two. Mountaineering was their passion and their profession and they had reached the pinnacle amongst their brilliant international peers.

The nightmare of the Exit Cracks ended with a great pendulum traverse, way to the left of our previous axis of ascent, a long icy shute and a treacherous bulge of mixed shale and snow, both ingredients being unpleasantly loose underfoot. The evening sun was welcoming as we emerged from the last of the gullies. I craned my neck, arching my back, and saw a wonderful swathe of open sky where for four long days I had seen only the ever-rising, dark wall of the Eiger. Above us now was only a steep wall of snow and ice leading up to a knife-edge, the summit ridge. This sharply angled snow wall was the reservoir, the source of the avalanches that sweep down the North Face. New, often wet, snow that settles here frequently fails to cohere firmly with the névé and ice beneath and sloughs away in lethal waves down the Exit Cracks, out over the Spider and beyond.

Ian led up this last steep climb, taking his time with care and caution. From an ice-screw belay I paid out Ian's rope. I could see the outline of his rucksack high above as he fixed another screw into the snow. He straightened up to move off and I felt the rope go taut. I obviously had him on too tight a leash. I quickly paid out more rope, looking down at the coils to check against knots forming. At the same moment, Ian, caught off balance by the taut rope, had slipped, fallen over on to his back and begun to slide head first down the Eiger.

He wrote later: 'I began to head down towards Grindelwald. Kenton luckily heard my screams, saw that Ran was paying *out* the rope and yelled at him. This seemed to reawaken Ran to the appropriate rope procedures and, thankfully, my downwards journey was brought to an abrupt halt.'

By dusk we had reached the knife-edge snow cornice of the summit ridge, but were still some thirty minutes and 300 metres below the actual summit further along the Mittellegi Ridge. So Kenton selected a nook on the far, southern side of the cornice, where we spent an hour digging out a platform for the sleeping bags. Ian's notes recorded: 'We had an awful night. There was no reception on the mobiles, so we couldn't communicate with anyone or do the live broadcast. Then I dropped the ITV camera over the edge – but we were so knackered and it was so cold. It was a spectacular ridge to the summit, so it was a really nice finish. I'm pretty proud of what we had done. Particularly for Ran.'

We spent eleven hours in the snow dugout, and I remembered, nearly two years before, thinking I had a good chance of summitting Everest because Ian and I had spent that last pre-summit night at some 400 metres below Everest's summit ridge. Almost there. And I never made the summit. Now here we were again, a mere 300 metres below another summit. Ian considered the Eiger North Face a far more difficult ascent than Everest's North Ridge, but this time I had no cardiac troubles lying in wait, for we were at a mere 14,000, not 28,000 feet.

We left the bivouac at 9.30 a.m. and threaded our way towards the summit along a classic knife-edge ridge. Ian wrote: 'Kenton led us with Ran in the middle and myself last in our little line. I was acutely aware that if Ran began sliding down one side of the ridge, it was my job to throw myself off the opposite side of the mountain, arresting our fall in a seesaw effect.'

At 10.00 a.m. on the fifth day of our climb we reached the

summit. Thanks entirely to the brilliance and the patience (usually!) of Kenton and Ian. Within half an hour of our arrival there, an evil-looking cloud bank raced over the mountain ranges to the south, soon to envelop the Eiger. Our weather forecasters had got it dead right. As we descended down the easy side of the ridge I felt deliriously happy to be back on comparative *terra firma*. I made up my mind to steer clear of all mountains in the future . . . probably. It was great to learn that within a week of our return, our friends at Marie Curie Cancer Care had already raised £1.4 million towards our £1.5 million target, with hopes that our Marie Curie Eiger Challenge Appeal would top out at well over £3 million before it closed down.

The climbing training over the last two years has resulted in a lot less running, so I must try to get fit again. And expeditions, whether polar, archaeological or up mountains, do not provide any personal income, so I need to get back on the lecture circuit, along with the US ex-presidents and failed *Big Brother* contestants. As for the next expedition, that depends on who comes up with what suggestion, who agrees to sponsor it and which charity wants to benefit from its proceeds, should it succeed. I would love to reach the figure of £15 million raised for charities before I die, for that is a good sounding round figure to aim for, and I am two-thirds of the way there to date.

For a great many years I have been lucky with the very best of families, friends and good fortune at dicey moments. The future may still hold interesting times. Only yesterday, on 20 July as I finished writing this book, I received an email from Mike Stroud . . . 'Any wild ideas for a trip together would be very much welcome.' I do have an idea or two to put to him.

Appendix 1

I believe we are each very much congenital victims or beneficiaries. Of course there are twists of fate whereby the occasional house-painter's bastard becomes a Führer or a grocer's daughter an Iron Lady, but in the main we run life's course the way we do because of our hereditary make-up. We are each the sum total of a chain of ghostly sires, generation upon generation of evolving characters, of actions good or evil, the vibrations of which pass silently on, foetus to foetus, until there is you and there is me.

On the pages that follow is a family tree of my ancestors. They have owned land in southern England since the days of an Ingelram Fiennes who lived around AD 1100. His family became anglicised and have lived here continuously since 1260. Earlier they were based in the village of Fiennes, which lies between Calais and Boulogne in France.

There, of course, many members of the family, dead and still alive, not included on this simplified family tree.

KING CHARLES the GREAT
AD 800
(EMPEROR CHARLEMAGNE)

His daughter, BERTHE

The Dukes of PONTHIEU

EUSTACHE FIENNES
(died 1144)
Fought for the Normans at Battle of Hastings, 1066, but other Fiennes family members fought on the English side. Eustache was given English land by William the Conqueror. His brother-in-law founded Beaulieu Abbey.

INGELRAM FIENNES

married SYBIL de TINGRIES, heiress to the Dukes of Ponthieu. Through Sybil's dowry, the Fiennes family inherited English manors at Martock, Wendover and Carshalton, all of which they lost in the Hundred Years' War. Ingelram was killed at the Battle of Acre in 1189, as was his cousin Tougebrand Fiennes, close companion to King Richard Coeur de Lion. Another cousin killed in the Crusades, John Fiennes, donated his heart to the citizens of London along with a burial plot, still known as Finsbury Square.

ENGUERRAND FIENNES
Married the daughter of King Alexander of Scotland. Enguerrand, Lord of the Fiennes clan in Artois, was responsible for the Wars of the Roses since his direct descendants included the main protagonists, Edward IV, Richard III, Henry IV and Henry V, Henry Stafford, Duke of Buckingham.

ENGUERRAND FIENNES
Married Isobel, daughter of King Edward III.

WILLIAM DE SAYE I
(died 1144)
Moved from Saye, Normandy, to England. Fought with the Earl of Essex against King Stephen.
Killed at Burwell.

WILLIAM DE SAYE II
(died 1177)
Captured seven knights single-handed at the Battle of Lewes. At the Battle of Saintes, he fought with King Henry III against the barons.

His brother
GEOFFREY DE SAYE I
(died 1214)
Helped ransom King Richard I from the Germans. He was one of the twenty-five barons to sign Magna Carta.

GEOFFREY DE SAYE III
(died 1321)
Fought for King Edward II vs. the Scots and the Earl of Lancaster. In 1318 he was jailed for consorting with the outlaw Robert Coleman.

GEOFFREY DE SAYE I
(died 1359)
Fought at Crecy, 1346. In 1339 as Admiral of the Fleet, he captured the French fleet at the battle of Sluys.

JEHAN FIENNES
Fought against King Edward III's English. Jehan was one of the five famous 'Burghers of Calais' who offered their lives in exchange for a promise not to massacre the citizens.

His son, an MP, married MAUDE MONCEUX.
Fiennes family inherit Herstmonceux.

JOAN SAYE married WILLIAM FIENNES

ROGER FIENNES
A constable of the Tower of London. He married the heiress of the Dacre family, so this branch became the Lord Dacres of Herstmonceux.

THOMAS FIENNES, LORD DACRE
Imprisoned for collusion with thieves.

THOMAS FIENNES, LORD DACRE
Courtier of King Henry VIII. On jury of Anne Boleyn's trial. Bore canopy at Jane Seymour's funeral. Hanged at Tyburn for poaching neighbour's deer.

JAMES FIENNES, 1st LORD SAYE AND SELE
Because the male descendants of the Sayes died out, their grandson James inherited. He was born in 1395 at the dawn of the Civil War. Created a baron in 1447, he chose the title Saye and Sele after a Benedictine Priory which he owned. He became Lord High Treasurer but, in 1459, things went sour. For years, with his son-in-law the Sheriff of Kent, he had practised large-scale extortion in Sussex and Kent, to the fury of the locals, including various Fiennes cousins. Now, an angry mob of southern gentry and clerics, including several Fiennes cousins, went to London and demanded retribution from King Henry VI. Their leader, Jack Cade, lived at Herstmonceux and may even have been a member of the Fiennes family, since Cade is known to have been an alias. Cade had James Fiennes beheaded in 1450.

WILLIAM 2nd LORD SAYE AND SELE
Married the heiress of William of Wykeham and inherited Broughton Castle near Banbury. As a soldier in France he was twice taken prisoner and ransoms forced him to sell the Knole estates in Kent. During the Wars of the Roses he fought for Earl Warwick, the King Maker, at the Battle of Northampton, where King Henry VI was deposed. At the Battle of Towton in 1471 he fought for the Yorkists while his cousin, Ranulph Fiennes, a Lord Dacre, was killed fighting for the Lancastrians at the Battle of Barnet.

GREGORY FIENNES, LORD DACRE
Queen Elizabeth I restored the Dacres' lands confiscated after his father's disgrace.

(This branch of the family died out.)

NATHANIEL FIENNES
Roundhead Colonel.

CELIA FIENNES
Famous traveller who rode around England on horseback annotating everything she saw. A nursery rhyme about her survives to this day: 'Ride a cockhorse to Banbury Cross to see a Fiennes (fine) lady upon a white horse . . .'

WILLIAM FIENNES, 8th LORD SAYE AND SELE
Founded a settlement along the Connecticut River which he called Saybrook. With Hampden and Pym he plotted against King Charles I, although he was not in favour of regicide. When war broke out in 1641, William and his four sons raised a cavalry regiment. Prince Rupert's Royalists routed the Fiennes troops at Edgehill and King Charles's troops captured Broughton Castle. William became known as 'Old Subtlety', for he managed to retain the trust of both sides throughout the Civil War. After the restoration, Charles II elevated William to Lord Privy Seal.

JAMES FIENNES, 9th LORD SAYE AND SELE
Hero of Baroness Orczy's novel The Honourable Jim.

Daughter CECIL TWISLETON, BARONESS
married COLONEL TWISLETON

Daughter CECIL TWISLETON, BARONESS
SAYE AND SELE eloped, aged fifteen, with her cousin GEORGE TWISLETON

GEORGE FIENNES TWISLETON, 11th BARON SAYE AND SELE
Fought with Duke of Marlborough. Adjutant-General during Quebec Campaign.

JOHN FIENNES, 12th BARON SAYE AND SELE
Constable of Dover Castle.

GREGORY TWISLETON FIENNES, 14th BARON SAYE AND SELE
Lived to be the 'Oldest Whig in the House of Lords'.

William Fiennes, 15th Baron Saye and Sele

Friend of the Prince Regent. He once left a note to his valet: 'Put 6 bottles of port by my bedside and call me the day after tomorrow.'

Frederick Fiennes, 16th Baron Saye and Sele

Archdeacon of Hereford. His mother's second cousin was Jane Austen. By Royal Licence, this Baron restored the old family name to make him Twisleton-Wykeham-Fiennes.

John Twisleton-Wakeham-Fiennes, 17th Lord Saye and Sele

His horse Placida won the Oaks.

Geoffrey Twisleton-Wakeham-Fiennes, 18th Lord Saye and Sele

Eustace Twisleton-Wakeham-Fiennes

After three years as a fur-trapper and later as a Canadian Mountie, he travelled widely in Africa and fought in the Boer War. Became Private Secretary to Winston Churchill and served in Gallipoli during the First World War. Was later created Baronet of Banbury, Governor of the Seychelles and, later, the Leeward Islands.

Ivo Twisleton-Wakeham-Fiennes, 20th Lord Saye and Sele

Lt. Col. Sir Ranulph Twisleton-Wakeham-Fiennes, Baronet

Commanded Royal Scots Greys 1942–3. Died of wounds in Italy 1943.

Nathaniel Fiennes, 21st Lord Saye and Sele

Current incumbent of Broughton Castle, open to the public.

The Author married Virginia Pepper 1970.

Nathaniel Fiennes, 21st Lord Saye and Sele

Current incumbent of Broughton Castle, open to the public.

Appendix 2

The individuals involved with the travels I have enjoyed over the years include:

Norway 1961
Simon Gault, Maggie Raynor

Pyrenees Crossing by Mule 1962/63
Hamish Macrae, Pat Offord, Maggie Raynor

Norway 1967
Peter Loyd, Simon Gault, Nick Holder, Don Hughes, Martin Grant-Peterkin, Vanda Allfrey

Nile 1969
Peter Loyd, Nick Holder, Charles Westmorland, Mike Broome, Anthony Brockhouse; UK: Ginny Pepper

Norway 1970
Roger Chapman, Patrick Brook, Geoff Holder, Peter Booth, Brendan O'Brien, Bob Powell, Henrik Forss, David Murray-Wells, Vanda Allfrey, Rosemary Alhusen, Jane Moncreiff, Johnnie Muir, Gillie Kennard; UK: George Greenfield

Canada 1971
Jack McConnell, Joe Skibinski, Stanley Cribbett, Ginny Fiennes, Sarah Salt, Bryn Campbell, Ben Usher, Richard Robinson, Paul Berriff, Wally Wallace; UK: Mike Gannon, Spencer Eade

Greenland/North Pole 1976/78
Oliver Shepard, Charlie Burton, Ginny Fiennes, Geoff Newman, Mary Gibbs; UK: Mike Wingate Gray, Andrew Croft, Peter Booth

Transglobe 1979/82
Oliver Shepard, Charlie Burton, Ginny Fiennes, Simon Grimes, Anton Bowring, Les Davis, Ken Cameron, Cyrus Balaporia, Howard Willson, Mark Williams, Dave Hicks, Dave Peck, Jill McNicol, Ed Pike, Paul Anderson, Terry Kenchington, Martin Weymouth, Annie Weymouth, Jim Young, Geoff Lee, Nigel Cox, Paul Clark, Admiral Otto Steiner, Mick Hart, Commander Ramsey, Nick Wade, Anthony Birkbeck, Giles Kershaw, Gerry Nicholson, Karl Z'berg, Chris McQuaid, Lesley Rickett, Laurence Howell, Edwyn Martin, John Parsloe, Peter Polley and others; UK: Anthony Preston, David Mason, Janet Cox, Sue Klugman, Roger Tench, Joan Cox, Margaret Davidson, Colin Eales, Elizabeth Martin, Sir Edmund Irving, Sir Vivian Fuchs, Mike Wingate Gray, Andrew Croft, George Greenfield, Sir Alexander Durie, Peter Martin, Simon Gault, Tommy Macpherson, Peter Windeler, Peter Bowring, Lord Hayter, Dominic Harrod, George Capon, Anthony Macauley, Tom Woodfield, Sir Campbell Adamson, Jim Peevey, Eddie Hawkins, Eddie Carey, Peter Cook, Trevor Davies, Bill Hibbert, Gordon Swain, Captain Tom Pitt, Alan Tritton, Jack Willies, Graham Standing, Muriel Dunton, Edward Doherty, Bob Hampton, Arthur Hogan-Fleming, Dorothy Royle, Annie Seymour, Kevin and Sally Travers-Healy, Jan Fraser, Gay Preston, Jane Morgan, Jack Willes

North Pole 1986/90
Oliver Shepard, Mike Stroud, Laurence Howell, Paul Cleary, Beverly Johnson; UK: Ginny Fiennes, Alex Blake-Milton, Andrew Croft, George Greenfield, Perry Mason, Dmitry Shparo, Steve Holland

Ubar 1991
Juris Zarins and team, Nick and Kay Clapp, Ginny Fiennes, Ali Ahmed Ali Mahash, Ron and Kristine Blom, Trevor Henry, Andy Dunsire and team

Alaska, Arctic and Antarctica 1993/2000
Gordon Thomas, Dmitry Shparo, Laurence Howell, Morag Nicolls, David Fulker, Bill Baker, Graham Archer, Charles Whitaker, Granville Baylis, Steve Signal, 'Mac' Mackenney, Steve Holland, Mike Stroud, Oliver Shepard, Charlie Burton

Seven Marathons/Seven Days/Seven Continents 2003
Mike Stroud, Steven Seaton, Mike Kobold, Tony Brown, Giles Whittell, Gill Allen, Robert Hall, Julie Ritson. UK: Ginny Fiennes

Everest 2005
Paul Sykes, Sibusisu Vilane, Ian Parnell, Neal Short, Jens Bojen, Mark Campbell, 'Boca' Lama (Nima Dorje), Louise Fiennes

Eiger North Face 2007
Paul Sykes, Kenton Cool, Ian Parnell, Louise Fiennes

Major Financial Sponsors
Pentland, Damart, Dyson, British Aerospace, British Airways/ Terry Beuacqua, Occidental Oil, Land Rover, Excel, Paul Sykes

Charity Beneficiaries
The Multiple Sclerosis Society, Breakthrough Breast Cancer, Cancer Research Campaign, British Heart Foundation, Marie Curie Cancer Care
(Total raised by 2007: £10 million plus)

Note

A book about the *M.V. Benjamin Bowring* by Anton Bowring, telling the full story of the Transglobe voyage, is expected to be in bookshops in 2008/09.

The original film of the Transglobe expedition is now available on DVD. The three-year, 52,000-mile journey across deserts, oceans, the North West Passage and both Poles was recorded on film by Armand Hammer Productions. Written, produced and directed by William Kronick, the film is narrated by Richard Burton, with a music score by John Scott. It is available (on DVD region 2, UK & Europe only) for £20 from the Transglobe Expedition Trust, c/o 30a Broad Street, Bungay, Suffolk NR35 1EE (Tel. 01728 604434). For further information and details about the Transglobe Expedition Trust, see the expedition website www.transglobe-expedition.org or email TGExpedition@aol.com.

Appendix 3
Land Rover 7x7x7 Challenge
(Route as planned by British Airways)

The results of the challenge raised large sums for our charities in the relevant countries and by 2007 had not been successfully repeated. The timings were all under 5 hours, except for Singapore and New York. The schedule was in outline:

Date	Location	Completion
27 Oct	Patagonia, S. America Through the Passage of the Great Explorer	3 hrs, 45 mins
28 Oct	Falklands, S. Antarctica Islands Through the hinterlands of Castle Falklands, past mine fields, to Government House	4 hrs, 41 mins
29 Oct	Sydney, Australia, Australasia Over Sydney Harbour Bridge, past the Opera House and through the Botanical Gardens – six times	4 hrs, 41 mins

30 Oct   Singapore, Asia   5 hrs, 24 mins
Cordoned off route through the parks
of Singapore and the central business
district

31 Oct   London, Europe   4 hrs, 40 mins
The Olympic marathon route of 1908
from Windsor Castle to White City

1 Nov   Egypt, Africa   4 hrs, 19 mins
From the Sphinx to the Pyramids from
midnight till dawn

2 Nov   New York, North America   5 hrs, 23 mins
Through the streets of New York
finishing at Central Park as part of the
annual New York City marathon (we
finished 28,362 out of 35,000 runners)

THE TIMES 21/10/03

183.4 MARATHON ULTIMATE TEST

GRAPHIC: HELEN SMITHSON

RUNNING ROUND THE WORLD IN SEVEN DAYS

1

ANTARCTICA
Running on snow, rock and ice, Fiennes and Stroud will also have to keep 25 metres clear of King George Island's nesting southern giant petrels in accordance with the 1994 Antarctic Act

2

SANTIAGO
At the foot of the snow-capped Andes, Santiago's location is spectacular but its smog could be a problem for the runners

3

SYDNEY
The course takes in the Opera House but also over 600 steps in six crossings of the Sydney Harbour Bridge

4

SINGAPORE
Hoping for a monsoon downpour, the runners will otherwise face temperatures of around 30C despite starting at dawn

5

LONDON
The run starts at 8 am on Friday Oct 31st on Castle Hill in Windsor, leads through Fiennes old stomping ground of Eton and ends at the BBC headquarters in White City

6

CAIRO
The Africa run starts at midnight, ending at dawn at Pyramids. Time is so short runners may use motorbikes get back to the airport

7

NEW YORK
Fiennes and Stroud will be near the back of the official New York marathon field, but triumphant if they finish by 8 pm

London
Singapore
New York Marathon
Cairo
Santiago
Sydney
Antarctic

All times GMT

	October 26	October 27	October 28	October 29	October 30	October 31	November 1	November 2
	START			SLEEP	SLEEP			SLEEP
		FLY	FLY	FLY	FLY	FLY	FLY	FLY
	RUN Antarctica	RUN Santiago		RUN Sydney	RUN Singapore	RUN London	RUN Cairo	RUN New York

6pm 9pm 12am 6am 12pm 6pm 12am 6am 12pm 6pm 12am 6am 12pm 6pm 12am 6am 12pm 6pm 12am 6am 12pm 6pm 12am 6am 12pm 6pm 12am 6am 12pm 6pm 8

© The Times/Helen Smithson (graphic) 21 October 2003

Appendix 4
Endurance Running

The last year when I can remember feeling reasonably fit was the year after my finger amputations in 2000. I was fifty-seven and averaging three 2½-hour runs most weeks of the year. I ran the London Marathon in 3 hours 39 minutes, some nine minutes slower than my best time in 1999, and, after many years of failing to complete either the Karrimor or the Lowe Mountain Marathons, I entered both with a top adventure racer, Gary Tompsett from Edinburgh. His memories of the Karrimor 2001 were: 'We surprised everyone and ourselves as we survived the attrition of the terrain with our diesel-powered legs and good navigation, whilst the Ferraris around us fell apart, including the Swedish teams who made good scalps. We were 12th in the Elite. This dispelled the myth that you couldn't complete these events.'

Later in 2001 we teamed up again for the Lowe Mountain Marathon, targeting the Veterans' Trophy in the Elite grade. We had to overcome the age handicap system by a long chalk. We did, coming 12th overall in the Elite and first in the Vets.

In the winter of 2002, with top British endurance racers Ski Sharp, Steven Seaton and Anna McCormack, I entered the Southern Traverse adventure race based from Queenstown in New Zealand. Steven and Anna had to drop out for health reasons three days into the race, so Ski and I joined up with the remnants of another team. Together we ended up in 14th place. This race was extremely demanding, with long stretches of cross-country running, high mountains, bogs, devilish mountain biking, and lots of rough water for the canoe stretches. Ski and I agreed to try again the next year, and to that end I trained hard throughout 2002. An outline timetable was:

January	In the UK Mud Race, seven miles of mud and sweat and obstacles, I came 238th out of 2,500
March	The High Peak Marathon: a 40-mile night race in a team of four. Peter James led. We came 4th out of 40. Gary Tompsett's team beat us by a short head
March	The Grizzly 2002: I came 334th out of 1,306. If I had been 9 minutes quicker, I would have come in 208th! The 20 rough miles took 2 hours 49 minutes
April	London Marathon: 3 hours 38 minutes
May	ACE Race, Thetford Forest: 10th out of 72 teams, with Sean Fishpool
May	Devizes–Westminster Canoe Race: 125 miles and 76 locks. 48th out of 88 teams in 25 hours 28 minutes, with Steven Seaton
July	Alpine Marathon: 78 kilometres. 297th out of 780 men in 9 hours 10 minutes, with Steven Seaton
September	ACE Race, Ullswater with Ski Sharp. 1st in '2 males class', and 6th overall out of 189
October	The Southern Traverse 2002, back in New Zealand, was by far the toughest adventure race I've taken part in. Ski Sharp was leader. We were in 10th position when a checkpoint error caused us a 5-hour delay, and we ended up 13th

I entered the High Peak Marathon again in March 2003, this time with Yiannis Tridimus, a top UK veteran endurance runner, and two others. We came in 3rd overall in 11 hours 25 minutes. That year I had the heart attack and ran the seven marathons, but twelve months later I was back with Yiannis and his team. This time (2004) we came in 3rd in 10 hours 51 minutes and won the Veterans Prize.

Ginny died that February and, in a kind attempt to help keep my mind occupied, Steven Seaton entered me for the 26-mile North Pole Marathon, which I have already described.

In June with Yiannis we won the Veterans Elite at the Lowe Mountain Marathon, and came in 10th Elite overall in 11 hours 7 minutes.

In July, in John Houlihan's team of three, we came 5th out of 110 teams in the 100-kilometre two-day Edinburgh Rat Race, the first urban adventure race in Britain.

In December, to pay back the Singapore Heart Association for their help during the 7x7x7 Marathons, I ran in the Singapore 2004 Marathon, being crewed by Louise, and completed the course in 4 hours 29 minutes. Slow in the humid heat, but an hour quicker than the previous year.

In August 2005, again crewed by Louise, I ran the Tour du Mont Blanc Ultra Marathon, taking 38 hours to complete the 158 kilometres of mountain trails, including 8,500 metres of climbing. I was 358th out of 2,000 runners.

In March 2006, crewed by Louise and running once more with Yiannis and his usual team in the High Peak Marathon, we again won the Veterans Trophy and came in 6th overall in 12 hours 14 minutes. The temperature en route dropped to $-13°C$.

In June 2006, Yiannis and I dropped out of the Lowe Alpine Marathon on Mull, having failed to find a checkpoint.

My last race prior to attempting the Eiger was the Karrimor Mountain Marathon (renamed the Original Mountain Marathon) in October 2006, aged sixty-two years. My team-mate and leader was Jon Brooke. We missed the last checkpoint on Day One, but completed the whole two-day course and came in 23rd in the Elite class, five places behind Gary Tompsett's team. Jon was honest at the end of this race. He needed to race with somebody a lot faster than I now was. I was racing in Britain's top endurance grade and had kept up after a fashion for quite a few years, but in 2005 and 2006 I had spent too much time trying to learn how to climb, at the expense of keeping up my running hours.

By the summer of 2007 I was struggling to jog for more than three hours non-stop and failed to complete a single long-distance race. So, I was happily surprised to be nominated Great British Sportsman of the Year 2007 by the ITV awards against the likes of the boxer Joe Kalzigi and Formula One driver Lewis Hamilton. At 63 years old I felt a bit of a fraud. At the awards Louise sat immediately behind David Beckham and was fascinated by the butterfly tattoo that she said was to be found on the back of his neck.

At the time of writing, I have entered the 2008 40-mile High Peak Marathon with the Yiannis team and will see how things go. But even if I continue to drop down the endurance race rankings, I will still take on team challenge events of some sort, just to keep my feet out of the grave as long as possible.

I have found the ageing process can be slowed down by running for at least two hours every other day or, at worst, every third day. A route including reasonably demanding uphill stretches is important. Entering a team race at least once every three months gives a solid purpose to keep the mind focused. Any period of 'no running' causes ever increased difficulties when you get back in your trainers. At sixty-three I find I have to accept that I'm slower than at sixty, but I can still compete at a slightly lower level.

Appendix 5
The Eiger North Face – 1938 Route

Grading any climb for difficulty is always a controversial issue, so I have chosen a fairly typical assessment of this route by the Irishman Paul Harrington, who led a two-man rope up the standard route at more or less the same time of year (i.e. late February/early to mid-March) in 1997.

Both Paul Harrington and Russian climbing instructor Andrey Kosenko (who led the route in late February 2007) have considerable experience of Scottish Grading. Andrey summarised his Eiger climb as, 'I have onsited various Scottish Grade VII climbs and found some parts of the Eiger route as demanding as them, when in poor condition.'

The Harrington Grading was given when the 1938 route was 'less ice than normal, but with no fresh snow lying around and perfect weather'.

The Entry Chimney: (IV,4)

From the triangular snow slope up to the fixed ropes below the Difficult Crack: (V,4)

Fixed ropes below the Difficult Crack on the Hinterstoisser Traverse and between the First and Second Ice-Fields: Ungradable, but if the ropes were not there, you can be sure that in typical winter conditions you would be talking about no less than Scottish winter Grade VI

Difficult Crack: (V,5)

The first pitch off the end of the Second Ice-Field: (V,5)

The Ramp from the bottom up to the snow slope before the Brittle Ledges: (VI,6) and A1

Brittle Ledges: (IV,3)

The eighteen-metre vertical access pitch to the Traverse of the Gods: (V,6) and A1

Traverse of the Gods: (V,4)

Exit Cracks: (VI,5) and A1. This is assuming the easiest route is taken and it is possible to tension traverse into the middle gully. If one of the other variations had to be climbed, you're probably talking about (VI,6), or maybe even (VI,7)

Appendix 6
Organizing a Polar Expedition –
Some Outline Tips

Antarctica is expensive and difficult to reach, which is why, blocked by the roughest seas in the world, nobody penetrated its interior until just over 100 years ago. Scott, Amundsen and Shackleton struggled over the Ross Ice-shelf and on to the vast inland plateau; while the Arctic Ocean, peopled by the Inuit who, for centuries, have survived along its coastlines, is infinitely more accessible to travellers. Sledgers who cross Greenland, the Canadian north and Svalbard often describe themselves as polar travellers, using the Arctic Circle as their yardstick. Thus there are a great many more veterans of the Arctic than of Antarctica.

Travel in the remote polar reaches of the Arctic Ocean itself and the high plateaux of Antarctica demands careful preparation and constant wariness due to unpredictable weather and local hazards which can rapidly prove lethal. On the other hand, during the summer season, polar travel can be easy and almost temperate on windless days and away from problem areas. I have travelled to both poles, often without suffering unduly from the cold, yet I lost part of a toe from frostbite during a weekend Army exercise in Norfolk. A need for wariness is not a uniquely polar prerogative but, due to the remoteness of many polar objectives and the potential hazards involved, the organisation for any polar expedition must be especially meticulous.

You may travel by a wide variety of methods and there is not room here to cover all of these. Dog teams, microlights, snow machines, hot air balloons or even motorbikes have been used, but the most common form of travel at the time of writing, and for adventurous activities, is that of manhaul sledging.

In 1993 Mike Stroud and I suffered considerable physical damage crossing the Antarctic continent by manhaul and minimal use of old-style sails that could only use following winds. Our sledge loads, each in excess of 215 kilograms, required brute force to shift, and 16 kilometres a day was a fair average manhaul stint, costing a daily deficit of 8,000 calories and leading to slow starvation.

In 1996, again towing a load of nigh on 225 kilograms, I deployed a 4.5-kilogram kite and managed up to 190 kilometres a day with minimal physical effort and correspondingly less calorific expenditure. My sledge load could be halved in terms of fuel and food. What had previously proved remarkably difficult was now comparatively simple and, in my opinion, could hardly be described as 'unsupported'.

Polar travel has been truly revolutionised by such wind devices. It is now possible to cross Antarctica in under two months. Of course the element of luck can still play tricks. Broken equipment, unusually bad weather, sudden illness and well-hidden crevasses can all prevent a successful outcome, but at least the reality of polar travel is now within the grasp of the many, not just the few.

To give any practical advice on the organisation of a polar journey would be difficult without lists. Those that follow are the result of a dozen polar journeys in many regions and with differing purposes. I have spent more days and nights out on the Arctic pack and Antarctic plateau than anyone alive, but my kit lists and general tips are by no means infallible. They will not prevent you falling into the sea or an ice crack. You may still become hypothermic, snow blind or lost or be eaten by a polar bear, but I hope they will at least help you get started as a polar traveller of reasonable competence.

First of all, read as much available literature by previous travellers in the area of your chosen trip as you can. Study the annexes at the rear of expedition books. Lists of sponsors and manufacturers are often quoted and can save you time.

Then apply, ideally through the Royal Geographical Society's Expedition Advisory Office, for information on expeditions currently planning to go into your area of interest. It will help if you have a skill to offer (cook, communications, photographer, mechanic, etc).

Go on other people's trips to Greenland, Svalbard, Iceland, Norway, anywhere with snow and ice, to gain experience before progressing to the deep south or north and to leading your own projects, eventually to and across the poles if that strikes your fancy.

Here are some guidelines. Feel free to ignore or alter them wherever you can garner more appropriate updated advice.

Equipment

Clothing

1 Fleece jacket with hood.
2 Ventile outer trousers with braces and long-length hooded anorak (baggy).
3 Down duvet jacket with hood attached (for periods when not manhauling).
4 Wick-away underwear (long sleeves and legs).
5 Meraklon headcover.
6 Duofold balaclava with mouth hole.
7 Separate lip protector mouthpiece with elastic to hold in place
8 Ski goggles and ski glacier glasses with nose-protecting felt pad glued in place.
9 1 pair thick wool socks.
10 1 pair thin Helly Hansen socks.
11 1 pair vapour barrier socks.
12 1 pair Dachstein mitts.
13 1 pair Northern Outfitters heavy gauntlets.

14 1 peaked cap, kepi-style and with under-neck strap.

15 1 pair thin working gloves.

16 1 pair vapour barrier mitts (optional). Some folk swear by them.

17 Footwear, as advised by polar travellers of your acquaintance (or from their books!). There are too many alternatives to be specific here. Correctly fitting boots are of great importance.

18 For polar work when using snow machines, skis or dogs, shops specialising in the relevant sports gear will be able to advise you best.

Note: The heavier the weight you tow when manhauling with no wind support, the more difficult the selection of clothing, as you will sweat, despite the cold, when working and various parts of your body, especially feet and crutch, will suffer if your clothing choice is not excellent. Ensure your initials are clearly printed on each item unless you travel alone.

General Items

1 Geodesic dome tents are best (two- or three-man), but beware of the elastic holding the poles together. When cold it loses elasticity so, if you have room on a sledge, keep as many of the pole sections permanently inserted together as possible. Black tents make the most of the sun's heat and can be seen nearly as well as fluorescent colours.

2 Sledge harness and traces (solid traces are best for crevassed areas). In the Arctic Ocean pack-ice, your sledge should be amphibious. Dry suits can be used to swim over open leads.

3 Skis, skins, ski sticks and relevant spares. (Make sure your ski bindings mate well with your boots.)

4 With your sleeping bag and tent, use stuff sacs that don't need too much effort to squeeze in. The best custom-made down gear in the UK comes from Peter Hutchinson Designs in Stalybridge.

5 MSR (Mountain Safety Research) cooker. Coleman fuel is best in extreme cold. (Be sure to get a secure cooker fitting

fixed to the lid of the box you carry your cook gear in.) Clip the MSR fuel bottle into it firmly before priming. You need a firm base. Take a spare MSR and bag of spares, especially a pricker. (Ensure your MSR fuel bottle tops have winterised washers if you intend to use them in extreme temperatures.)

6 Brush to clear snow (hard bristles).
7 Insulated mug and spoon. Set of cooking pots and pot holder.
8 Zippo lighter and spare flints. Use Coleman fuel.
9 Spare lighter. (Keep warm in trouser pocket.)
10 Silva (balanced) compass and spare compass.
11 Reliable watch and spare.
12 Optional: a light rucksack.
13 Optional: windsail kit and spares in bag (unless travelling 'unsupported by wind').
14 2 ice-screws, 1 pair jumars with loops.
15 Ice-axe (very small, light model).
16 16-metre length of para cord.
17 30 metres of thinnest relevant climbing rope.
18 Optional: foldaway snow shovel.
19 Karabiners.
20 Karrimat.
21 Sleeping bag with inner (and optional outer) vapour barriers.
22 Pee bottle (Nalgene or Rubbermaid).
23 PLB (Personal Locator Beacon) and spare lithium battery.
24 GPS (Global Positioning System) and spare lithium battery.
25 Optional: HF radio and ancillaries (or Global Satellite mobile phone).
26 Video and still camera kit. Polythene bags to avoid misting up.
27 Steel Thermos.
28 Rations (high-calorie and low-weight). Pack as for a twenty-four-hour day per tent.
29 Personal bag. This may contain: small adjustable spanner, pin-nose pliers, dental floss, needles, thin cord, Superglue, wire, diary and pencil, Velcro, charts and maps, Swiss Army knife (with all necessary tools) and spare underwear (optional).

Medical Kit

This should include all that polar travellers advise, and may well include:

- *Pain*: paracetamol for mild pain. For more severe pain and when inflammation is involved, use Ibuprofen. For severe pain, mst tablets or Buprenorphine or morphine (on prescription). Voltarol suppositories are a good additional pain-killer. Be sure to study the instruction paper that comes with each of the above.
- *Infections/Antibiotics*: Augmentin for dental and chest infections. Ciproxin is excellent for severe spreading infections of skin or gut or anything non-responsive to Augmentin. Cicatrin powder for dressing superficial cuts and rashes. Chloromycetin for eye infections. Flucloxacillin is powerful. Good for painful frostbitten toe areas.
- *Wounds*: for deeper wounds, take threaded surgical needles. Take Lignocaine for self-injection for local anaesthetic. Use Steristrips for smaller wounds. For open blisters, burns and frost injuries, Flamazine cream is effective. Take alcohol swabs to clean wounds. Tegaderm second-skin dressings are useful. Granuflex dressings are good for open blisters and frostbite areas. Canesten powder for crutch fungal infection.
- *Sickness*: Immodium is best for diarrhoea. If not effective, use Ciproxin. Buccastem is good for nausea (absorb in mouth, don't swallow).
- *Sunblindness*: take Amethocaine drops.
- *Teeth*: take oil of cloves. Also dental cement pack.
- *Other*: Jelonet dressings for burns/scalds. Rolls of sticky plaster and gauze dressings. Bonjela for mouth ulcers. Neutrogena for hand sores. Anusol for haemorrhoids. Compeed for smaller blisters.
- Treatment for your own personal health needs.

Other Considerations

Remember that insurance, fully comprehensive and including possible search and rescue costs, is mandatory and always sensible.

In Antarctica the best air charter company, Adventure Network International, will give you all the necessary advice on every side of your expedition. In the Canadian Arctic, First Air is the best (based at Resolute Bay, NWT). Remember that your cargo will cost a great deal at both ends. (In Antarctica, count on an extremely large cost per kilogram above your basic allowance to get you there from Chile.)

You can usually locate the very cheapest but suitable flights to Santiago or Cape Town (if Antarctic-bound) or various Canadian/Russian airports (if headed to the Arctic) through the London offices of WEXAS (World Expeditionary Association).

Final Advice

Always train hard and, where possible, with your prospective expedition colleagues to ensure that everybody involved has as much experience as possible. (It is best to be sure that first-time members of your team really are as good as their CVs state, since you will only progress as fast as your slowest member.)

Don't go to Greenland, Iceland, the Arctic or Antarctica to do difficult journeys with folk you don't really know. They should be reliable, easy-going and experienced. You can get to both poles by paying expert guides to help you there. Some are to be avoided. Others are excellent. All are expensive. Pay more and an aircraft will take you all the way to either pole and allow you an hour or two there, before whisking you back to warmer climes.

Never leave litter nor harm life in any form while you are there. Some Everest climbers have polluted their grail. Keep our poles clean.

Plan with great care and never rely on gizmos working, plbs and gpss for instance, or count on immediate rescue, since storms can keep search planes away for days, even weeks, so play safe.

If you aim to join the 'way-out' section by bicycling across Ellesmereland or 'collecting' different poles (geomagnetic, magnospheric, lesser accessibility, etc) then plan accordingly. For example, if you intend doing the South Pole on a pogo-stick, don't forget lots of low-temperature grease and your haemorrhoid cream. Have fun and stay cool.

Picture acknowledgements

Colour inserts, pages 1 – 32

Author's collection: 1 – 7, 9, 10 above, 11 below, 12 above, 13, 18 above left, 20 below, 21 above, 22 above, 23 centre and below. Additional sources: © Ian Bannister 28. © Neil Barnes 15. © Alex Blake-Milton 14 above. © Anthony Bowring 12 below. © Bryn Campbell 8, 11 above. © John Cleare 18 above right. © Fiennes/Stroud/Howell 16, 17, 19 above, 20 above. © Mike Hoover 10 below. © Rob Howard 21 below. © Morag Howell 18 below. © NI Syndication/The Times 22 centre and below, 23 above, 24. © George Ollen 14 below. © Ian Parnell 25, 26, 27, 29, 30, 31, 32. © John Whitbourne 19 below.

Index

Figures in italics indicate maps.

Index

389

KU-338-438

AIRPORT IMMIGRATION
TRIVANDRUM
27 JAN 1990
ARRIVAL - 1

DEPARTMENT OF IMMIGRATION
PERMITTED TO ENTER
AUSTRALIA
on 24 APR 1986
For stay of 12 Month
SYDNEY AIRPORT 54

IMMIGRATION DIVISION BANGKOK THAILAND
A 72
DEPARTED
- 6 FEB 1988
SIGNED

IMMIGRATION & ETHNIC AFFAIRS
..........Person
30 OCT 1989
DEPARTED
AUSTRALIA
SYDNEY 32

THE INSIDER'S GUIDE TO

INDIA

中华人民共和国
广东省公安厅

上陸許可
ADMITTED
15. FEB. 1986
Status: 4-1- 4
Duration: 90 days
NARITA(N)
Immigration Inspector
日本国

ADMITTED
20 OCT. 1988
Status: 4-1-16
Duration 180 days
Port: HANEDA
Signature

№ 011278

THE UNITED STATES
OF AMERICA
NONIMMIGRANT VISA
ISSUED AT
U.S. IMMIGRATION
170 HHW 1710
JUL 20 1983

...SED Air Port

HONG KONG
(1038)
- 7 JUN 1987
IMMIGRATION
OFFICER

THE INSIDER'S GUIDES
JAPAN • CHINA • KOREA • HONG KONG • BALI • THAILAND • INDIA • NEPAL • AUSTRALIA
HAWAII • CALIFORNIA • NEW ENGLAND • FLORIDA • MEXICO
THE SOVIET UNION • SPAIN • TURKEY • GREECE
INDONESIA • KENYA

The Insider's Guide to India
First Published 1990
CFW Publications Ltd, 5th Floor, 11 Wing Lok Street, Central, Hong Kong.
Fax: (852) 5438 007

© 1990 CFW Publications Ltd

ISBN: 962 7031 46 1

Created, edited and produced by CFW Publications Ltd
5th Floor, 11 Wing Lok Street, Central, Hong Kong

Editor in Chief: Allan Amsel
Original design concept: Hon Bing-wah
Picture editor and designer: Michelle Chan
Text and artwork composed and information updated
using Xerox Ventura software

All rights reserved. No part of this publication may be reproduced, stored in
a retrieval system, or transmitted in any form, or by any means,
electronic, mechanical, photocopying, recording, or
otherwise, without the written permission of the publisher.

Printed by Samhwa Printing Co Ltd, Seoul, Korea

THE INSIDER'S GUIDE TO

INDIA

by Kirsten Ellis
Photographed by Robert Holmes

CFW GUIDEBOOKS
Hong Kong

Contents

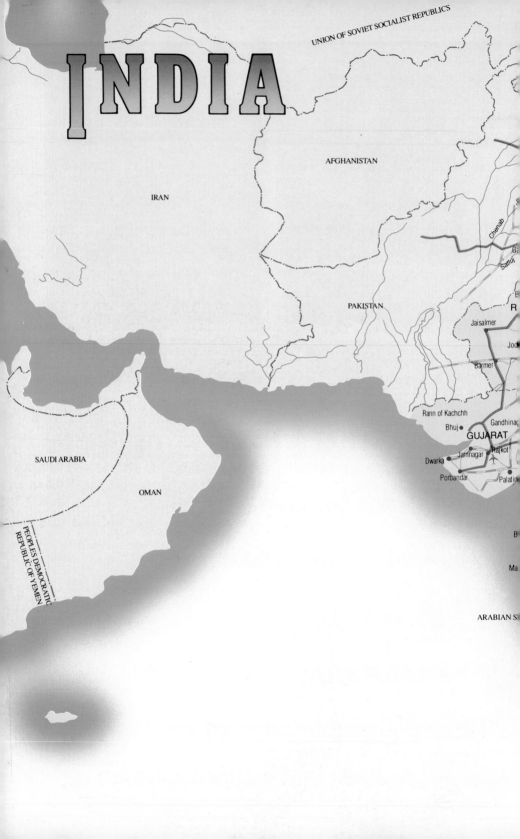

INDIA

UNION OF SOVIET SOCIALIST REPUBLICS

AFGHANISTAN

IRAN

PAKISTAN

SAUDI ARABIA

OMAN

PEOPLES DEMOCRATIC
REPUBLIC OF YEMEN

Chenab

Sattuj

Jaisalmer

Jod

Barmer

Rann of Kachchh

Gandhinag

Bhuj

GUJARAT

Rajkot

Dwarka

Jamnagar

Porbandar

Palatin

ARABIAN S

The Indian Experience

A PERSON who tells you they found what they expected in India is probably not telling the truth. No traveler is ever fully prepared for the first experience of India, nor leaves feeling untouched. Many approach their arrival with excited anticipation — for here, they have been told, exists all that is most extraordinary and shocking, most marvelous and bizarre.

The first glimpse of the vast subcontinent is very often misleading. This is the India revealed in the bright fluorescence of its international airports, where jet-lagged newcomers usually land during the early hours of the morning — the arrival time of most international flights. As the doors of the air-conditioned airport close behind them, they feel enveloped by waves of sticky heat and pungent, unfamiliar scents from the darkness — and unsteadily step into what seems a flickering Hades of shouting Indians, bundle-like pavement sleepers, car horns bleeping in unison and urgent scrums of taxi touts pulling at your shirt sleeves. Most travelers feel being instantly caught off guard, catapulted into confrontation with a strange alien land.

Yet India has many guises. India offers its visitors majestic temples and tombs, erotic sculptures, forlorn royal palaces, fabled mountains and great natural beauty.

A tour through this ancient, vast and crowded land is always an authentic adventure — sometimes daunting, often moving, but always stimulating and memorable. This colossal pendant-shaped continent is a place where breathtaking extremes are accepted almost as commonplace, and where the traveler learns to expect the unexpected.

India covers a land mass roughly the size of Europe and is home to one fifth of humanity — more than 800 million people — who form a diverse multitude of cultures, languages, religions and dress. Its domain extends 3,300 km (2,000 miles) from the northern snow-capped peaks of the Himalayas to the steamy palm-dotted plains of the southern tip of Kanniyakumari, and sprawls for 2,700 km (1,700 miles) between the mountainous frontiers of China and Burma to the arid desert wasteland at the borders of western Rajasthan. Its people speak a total of 1,652 dialects, of which only 15 are officially recognized. It has a present-day society with a paradoxical inner core: while it prides itself as the world's largest democracy and a leader of the Third World, it remains overwhelmingly a peasant nation rooted in often brutal traditions that have barely changed for centuries. It is the cradle of one of the greatest ancient civilizations — and during its heyday, one of the wealthiest — with a history that spans more than 4,000 years and that today offers its visitors a glimpse of an infinitely diverse, rich cultural heritage.

Above all, India is a flesh and blood encounter with the Indian people — for no country can ever be judged by its spectacle alone, nor can a traveler be insulated from its ocean of faces. It is they who will reveal India to you in all its baffling, rich, and often exasperating complexity. There will be moments on your travels when you will feel intoxicated by the diversity and splendor that India has to offer, and others when you just want to fly home as quickly as possible. India demands much patience and tolerance from its visitors. It can seem just too big and overwhelming to understand.

In a headlong rush to get visas and immunization jabs, many tourists overlook two very essential items of luggage for travel in India: an open mind and a well-developed sense of humor. If you manage to keep these intact throughout your stay, you will have mastered the knack of appreciating India.

While you'll probably never see the entire country, or ever completely understand it, you'll come away with an enduring fascination, exerting a pull that may bring you time and time again. Memories of India's pageant-like streetlife, teeming with endlessly moving crowds and infused with dust-laden light, vivid flashes of color and spicy scents, and its landscape layered with majestic relics of lost empires, leave an indelible impression, touching a human hunger for all that is most exotic, bizarre and elusive.

PLANNING FOR DEPARTURE

India offers something for everyone all year round. However it is virtually impossible for the visitor to "do" India in a limited period of time. Each state offers its own unique attractions and rewards. Clearly you will need to be ruthlessly selective about your priorities. The destination you chose should take into consideration India's climatic extremes, how much time and money you want to spend, and what sort of experiences you imagine are most going to enthrall you.

More than half of all visitors to India do not stray beyond the well-trodden tourist triangle of Delhi, Agra and Jaipur. Although these places are as worth visiting, India has much more to offer.

Glossy tourist pamphlets and the anecdotes of India-traveled friends often help sway the balance in choosing between, let's say, going to Kashmir for houseboats, *shikara* rides across Dal Lake and trekking in the Himalayas, or to Rajasthan for fortress cities, palace hotels and camel odysseys across the desert. Other pleasures can

OPPOSITE: India's trains, TOP, at a remote hamlet in Rajasthan and BOTTOM, the *Dehradun* refuels while villagers scavenge for unburnt coal.

seem equally enticing: to south India for languid palm-lined waterway tours and ancient Dravidian temples, to Goa for sandy beaches amid vestiges of Portuguese colonialism, or to Varanasi for spectacular devotional pageantry.

This guide's purpose is to present the most worthwhile and accessible Indian destinations, and help plan your itinerary within a broad framework of travel options. Whether you are backpacking, traveling in luxury, or taking a midway compromise between the two, this guide contains up-to-date information on hotels, restaurants and transport to help you fully appreciate each place.

Unless you plan to stay for several months — and there are plenty of enthusiastic travelers who end up staying in India for years — you'll need to be very selective in your choice. It is usually best to focus on one or two main regions, rather than attempting a crammed all-encompassing tour of India, a nation best appreciated on a loose schedule. An itinerary that looks good on paper may not account for ever-lurking complications of traveling in India, such as an odd "off-key" day due to a bout of the notorious "Delhi-belly", or missing a crucial connection due to an unforeseen act of God.

To do justice to the country, an Indian expedition should be at least three weeks long. Most people take at least three or four days to acclimatize after arrival, not just from the usual jet-lag, but to the overwhelming "strangeness" of India's climate, pace and culture. Many who undertake a flying visit have a frantic encounter with a country that yields richer and more varied experiences the longer one stays, when a certain buoyant adventurousness takes root. Conversely, few newcomers to the subcontinent tend to stay longer than six weeks. Most people find it both exhilarating and exhausting, a place that rivets the senses and triggers such a complex array of reactions to its varied sights that one can feel rather mentally pommeled. Experiences are foisted upon travelers as it is not a place where one can just drift through passively, expecting things to function as elsewhere. Responding to India's idiosyncrasies — as baffling or downright frustrating these may be at the time — is what makes the country such a special destination. If you maintain a fairly relaxed attitude, plenty of fresh enthusiasm and enough sang-froid to put it all down to experience, than you will most certainly love India, and have some of the most fantastic and unforgettable experiences of your life.

Hardy but fun-loving Rajasthani nomads of the arid Thar desert, swaddled against the sands in colorful camel-hair rugs.

The
Historical
Legacy

TO VISIT INDIA is to be given a tantalizing glimpse of one of the world's most ancient and complex cultures. The 4,000 to 5,000 years of India's recorded past have seen its soil annexed countless times by history's shifting fortunes. Dynasty has usurped dynasty, empire has followed empire, and the lives of ordinary people have been plunged into suffering and turmoil from one century to the next. India's civilization has been of crucial importance to world history and culture, particularly within the context of central and south-east Asia. Westerners may find it hard to believe, but India's creative and intellectual tradition has produced more major works than the entire European tradition — even more impressive considering its extraordinarily destructive tropical climate which has devoured vast quantities of sculpture, painting and manuscripts.

A holidaying traveler, whose interest in India's history is often sparked by a desire to learn more about the people he has begun to encounter, or about the awe-inspiring relics of fallen empires that stand before him, may find that trying to understand India can be a maddeningly elusive occupation. Even if you travel from the proverbial "Kashmir to Kanniyakumari"; pride yourself on taking the rugged trail through the "real" India of mud-hut villages and earthy peasants, or arrive well-primed by novels and history books, you'll probably find India still skittishly defies comfortable definition. Perhaps in the end, only a lifelong scholar of things Indian could come to grips with the question: What makes India, India? The best that can be done in a book such as this is to give India's past a comprehensible perspective. The history as recounted here deals not just with India's present boundaries with Pakistan and Bangladesh, but with the entire subcontinent.

ECOLOGY IS HISTORY

Just as some people hold that biology is destiny for individual human beings, so too it may be said that ecology has determined the history of India. The story begins with the Indus river, the very lifeblood of prehistoric India, from which the country's name is derived. Along its lushly forested banks, the early Indus Valley civilization flourished more than four thousand years ago. The early settlers — and many future conquerors — were lured by the region's fertile soil: the legacy of the physical forces that shaped the surfaces and the climate of the subcontinent long before man existed. Nature bequeathed India with the mighty 2,692-km (1,600-mile) -long chain of the Himalayas, the "resting place of the snows", without which the land would

be little more than a desert. The Indus and northern India's other two great river systems, the Ganga–Yamuna and the Brahmaputra, all fed by Himalayan glaciers, still continue to sweep vast quantities of sedimentary topsoil downstream to form rich alluvial valleys and plains right across the northern plains. Worshipped as goddesses by Hindus, these formidable rivers gave rise to India's greatest ancient cities. Their inhabitants were able to tap the river waters to irrigate a crop-growing hinterland and also to set off on them to distant destinations for trade. It was in the most bountiful region, watered by five upper tributaries of the

Indus, and hence called "land of five rivers" (Panch-ap, or Punjab) that the immigrant Aryans composed India's first ancient literary work, the Rig Veda, some 3,000 years ago.

India's destiny was shaped by the idiosyncrasies of its geographical isolation. It was cut off from its Asian neighbors by the sea around its coasts, by the protective natural barriers imposed by the Himalayas in its northern frontier with Tibet and China, and by the vast stretches of virtually impenetrable jungle-clad hills blocking contact with Burma. In the south, the spine-like wall of the Vindhya and Satpura mountain ranges presented another barrier to easy communication between north and south India, encouraging the development of almost completely independent cultures and empires. Even today, few people in the Tamil-speaking south can speak Hindi, the national language, for example. But most significantly, India's earliest migrants and invading armies swept in from its most accessible corner — and its historical Achilles' heel — the northwest frontier. They came along a series of well-known passes — the

ABOVE: Sunset over Dal Lake in Srinagar, Kashmir. OPPOSITE: Shy village belle stands in the courtyard of a temple in Khajuraho, Madhya Pradesh.

Khyber, the Bolan and the Khurram — now shared by Afghanistan and Pakistan. For this reason, India's northwestern corner has always been the most turbulent historical battleground, with each invasion sowing fresh seeds into India's ethnic patchwork — whether zealously spurred on by visions of conquered wealth and glory — or more recently, by the zeal of Islam or Christianity, or by profits of commercial enterprise and power.

ANCIENT INDIA

Evidence suggests that pro-human life existed in India during the Paleolithic Age when nomadic tribes of primitive men first began drifting across the subcontinent, leaving stone implements and crude hand axes as the only clue to their existence. A sketchy evolutionary trail, fueled by finds in the Sind province of Pakistan of terra-cotta pots, mother goddess figurines, phallic symbols, fragments of bronze as well as copper, suggests that some sort of village culture might have developed as long ago as 4000 BC. Exactly how long it took for India's early villagers to make the extraordinary leap to urban settlement is not known.

Although a lot of India's early history lies in legend, it's not disputed that its earliest major civilization was established in fertile, forested pockets beside the Indus River, and that it thrived for at least a thousand years from around 2500 BC. Its people were thought to be Dravidians, whose descendants still inhabit the far south of India today. The ruins of its major cities — located at Harappa (Hara is one of Shiva's names) and Mohenjo-daro ("Mound of the Dead"), now in present-day Pakistan, and to a lesser extent at Lothal and Kalibangan in Gujarat, Ropar in Punjab — all indicate highly rigorous town planning. As many as 70 unearthed sites have also been found right across the northwestern region of Punjab and Sind. Informed speculation has it that some buried cities still await discovery beneath Indian soil.

Archaeologists compare the systematically laid-out sites to what has been unearthed at Pompeii. Excavations reveal that large-scale commercial operations flourished in these ancient cities. Their citizens, who enjoyed a hitherto unknown high standard of living, subscribed to religious beliefs and had some knowledge of script. Kiln-baked bricks, as opposed to simple mud bricks, were the standard building material. (In contemporary Mesopotamia in Egypt, kiln-baked bricks would have been regarded with fascinated awe). Mining and working of several metals such as bronze, copper, lead and tin were undertaken. Some cities, like Mohenjo-

daro must have existed for centuries, as nine layers of construction were unearthed. Streets and lanes were laid out according to an axis grid running from north to south; houses were spacious units based around a central courtyard that ensured privacy; a bathroom and kitchen were de rigueur; evidence of stairs suggests double stories. Well-covered sewage drains existed, both inside private homes and on the streets, as did hot and cold public baths, deep wells, public buildings, trading posts and harbor ports. Indeed, Lothal, now in southwest Gujarat, was once a port, whose inhabitants bartered with their northern neighbors at Harappa and Mohenjo-daro, as well as the Persian Gulf and Sumeria (Iran), in the Indian currency of the day — ornamental conch shells, bone inlay goods, cotton, pearls, and possibly even in peacock feathers and apes.

Discovery of these ancient ruins came relatively late in the mid-nineteenth century — when India's history was commonly believed to have begun only from the time of Alexander the Great's invasion in the fourth century BC. British engineers laying a railway between the Punjab and Karachi observed that local laborers seemed to have an unlimited supply of bricks with which to build the track's foundations. The time-worn bricks remained an enigma until the 1920's when archaeologists explored the region and changed history books with uncovering of Mohenjo-daro along the Indus and Harappa on the Ravi.

Surviving artifacts offer intriguing glimpses into the art and culture of the Indus people. Perhaps one of the most famous finds is that of a bronze naked dancing girl striking a provocative pose. Large numbers of excavated female figurines with their overemphasized hips, protruberant breasts and pudenda seem to indicate fertility worship. Among the discoveries are hundreds of small, ornately inscribed steatite seals with pictographic portraits of Brahmanic bulls, "unicorns" tigers and other animals, and also pictographic signs, thought to have been used by merchants to brand their wares, as an early form of trademark. Despite extensive on-going research, comparatively little is known about the Indus Valley civilization's development and eventual decline, nor has their script ever been able to be deciphered. The current theory has it that sometime after 1750 BC, the efficient, wealthy settlements at Harappa and Mohenjo-daro suffered a series of earthquakes and floods, spelling complete disaster. Evidence at Mohenjo-daro suggests that, as with Pompeii, homes were hastily abandoned, cooking pots scattered across kitchen floors, and crushed skeletons of people attempting to flee have been found caught in the debris of walls and ceilings.

THE ARRIVAL OF THE ARYANS

Sometime after 2000 BC, semi-barbaric tribes of fair-skinned Aryans swept into India, probably from northeastern Iran and the region around the Caspian Sea. By 1500 BC they had snatched control from the Harappans, whose developed way of life had all but collapsed, and had become well ensconced in the Punjab. The Aryans were a pastoral race, who had stormed the fortified cities of the Indus wielding bronze axes and riding in horse-drawn chariots. Unlike the Harappans, they lived in tribal villages with their migrant herds, and these dwellings, made from bamboo or light wood, have not survived the ravages of time. The Aryans became known as Hindus, from the word "Indus" and they worshipped a pantheon of gods, most of them nature's elements, such as the sun, wind, water and fire. These gods did not replace the mystical fertility or earth gods of the Dravidians — both found room within the same evolving religious faith that eventually became Hinduism.

It's thought that Aryans were the original architects of the caste system, invented to ensure that their racial distinctiveness was kept "pure". Early Aryan society was broadly divided into four hereditary social strata, called *varna* or "colors". The priestly Brahmans, were the aristocrats of the social pyramid. Next came the Kshatriyas, the warriors, whose duties involved warfare and government, and the Vaishya, who tended to be farmers, merchants or skilled artisans. At the bottom were the Sudras, the menial laborers. Beneath them were the indigenous dark-skinned slaves, scoffed at by the sharp-featured, fair Aryans as the "noseless ones". Each *varna* was associated with a distinguishing color: white for Brahmans, red for Kshatriyas, brown for Vaishya and black for Sudras.

Along with their Caucasian genes, the Aryans brought with them a new, rich and precise language: Sanskrit. This was a branch of the Indo–European family of languages and it was later perfected to express in literary form the hymns and epics of the Vedas, the Upanishads and the Bhagavad Gita. These huge compilations of myth and folklore were the seminal religious texts of virtually the whole of Indian thought to follow. Even the unorthodox religions, Buddhism and Jainism, were influenced by the Vedas to some extent. Before Sanskrit was written, however, the Aryans had to rely for a long time entirely on rote learning of hymns and rituals by the priestly caste, the Brahmans. From the epics written by these Vedic Aryans, it seems they were an earthy bunch, who adored gambling, music and large quantities of *soma*,

an alcoholic drink heavily laced with hashish, as well as war and chariot racing. The Mahabharata, whose epic core is thought to reflect Indian life at about the time of 1000 BC, starts with King Santanu's obsessive love for the beautiful goddess Ganga, whom he "marries", symbolizing the Aryan advance east across the Ganges river.

At about this time too, the Aryans had mastered the art of smelting iron ore for tools and weapons and had ventured further inland — perhaps lured there by rumor of large iron ore deposits — to Uttar Pradesh, Bihar and Orissa. New cities rose to prominence: Indraprasatha, (site of present-day Delhi), Kashi (Varanasi) and Pataliputra, (Patna in Bihar). All this eastward colonizing meant that they failed to maintain their crucial hold on the north-west frontier. Inevitably this led to invasion and yet further cross fertilization of cultural influences.

THE WESTERN CHALLENGE

The first invaders were Persians under Cyrus, followed by Darius (521–485 BC) who occupied the Indus Valley region of Punjab and Sind. They later recruited Punjabi soldiers who fought with Darius' son Xerxes in the Persian invasion of Greece (479 BC). Fantastic tales of India had been circulating ever since the return of their first official envoy, Scylax, a decade previously. Darius the Great, Emperor of Persia had deposited him near the head-waters of the Indus and instructed him to sail down the river to its mouth and make his way home by the Red Sea. In so doing, Scylax was to follow the same route as the Phoenicians of the Levant who traded with Western India as early as 975 BC and went on forays for ivory, apes and peacocks. Scylax's account of his adventures (were) taken up by Heredotus who had a great deal to tell about India at the time: for instance, that there were two races, the dark aboriginals and the fair Aryans, "white like the Egyptians". He told of "gold-digging ants who labored in gold-strewn plains"; of the crocodiles of the Indus, the extremes of temperature in the Punjab, and the novel cotton clothes of the Indians. He also described a religious sect which ate nothing which had life and lived on grain — a reference perhaps to the Jains. Scribes also described the existence of marriage markets, where impoverished parents sold their daughters, and the practice of immolation of widows on the funeral pyres of their dead husband — the economically motivated tradition known as suttee.

No wonder the world's greatest young general, Alexander the Great of Macedon was spurred to lead his armies, estimated at some

25,000 to 30,000 men, on his epic march from Greece to this exotic, distant land across the Indus in the spring of 326 BC. Alexander first occupied Taxila, now in Pakistan, then usurped the Persians and proceeded further inland, defeating the Aryan King Porus and his vast army of elephants. Following this crushing defeat, no Indian ruler seriously contested Alexander's advance, but the further inland he moved, the more mutinous his travel-weary army became. Drunk on conquest, Alexander was anxious to venture on to the "Eastern Sea", which may have been the Ganges river, but was forced to accept the will of his men. Leaving behind a few officers as petty princes in the Upper Indus Valley, the Greek army turned back to the homeland that Alexander himself never lived to see again. He died in 323 BC at the age of 36 in Babylon. Despite the sowing of seeds into India's gene pool by his soldiers (still said to be the cause of blond hair and blue eyes among children in the upper Himalayas), Alexander's most lasting legacy to India was the development of Gandharian art, a mixture of Roman–Hellenic artistic ideals — including the draped toga-like garments and the bare torso — and Buddhism, the emerging "radical" religion of the time.

THE GROWTH OF RELIGION

The Aryan epoch marked the emergence of Hinduism, the subcontinent's greatest religion, and the two born in revolt against it: Buddhism and Jainism. Few religions in the world can claim such an ancient tradition as Hinduism. Its essential beliefs can be traced to the Indus Valley civilization, when it is thought that Shiva was revered by lingams, or phallic stones, excavated at Indus sites. It was left to the nature worshipping, priest-dominated Aryan society to lay the framework for the development of Hinduism. They wrote their sacred religious text, the Vedas, written around 1500 to 1200 BC, which is thought to refer to actual historical events. This epic tells of the victory of Brahma over Indra, the god of thunder and warfare — a fable that is thought to refer to the revival of Brahmanism (the Indus Valley's embryonic form of Hinduism) in the wake of the Aryan invasions.

The majority of Indians today still believe in the idea the Aryan priests formulated of karma, meaning "one's deeds", with its notion of cause and effect in the reincarnation of the soul — what is done in one life has direct repercussions

OPPOSITE: Procession of high-ranking Hindu priests during the Kumbh Mela, India's holiest and most spectacular religious gathering, which is held every four years.

for the next, for better or for worse. This posed a Catch 22 situation to society's underdogs, since any protest about oppression or injustice in one's present life could be easily attributed to bad behavior in one's past life, for which punishment was required to earn a better life in the next.

In the sixth century BC two contemporary figures emerged — first Mahavira, then Buddha — both challenging orthodox Vedic solutions to the question: Why is there so much suffering in life? Buddha, like Mahavira, was born into the Kshatrias, the warrior class, which permitted religious learning, but precluded priesthood. Both these two great religious reformers rejected Hinduism's central ethos and its rigid caste system, but from this point their paths diverged: Mahavira's led to Jainism, a relatively hermetic faith; while Buddhism emerged as a formidable religious force, supplanting Hinduism as the official religion under Emperor Ashoka, and gradually adopted throughout Asia. At this time Hinayana, or "lesser vehicle" Buddhism was in vogue, in which the image of Buddha himself was never revealed, in case it inspired physical desire, thus causing attachment to life on earth and distracting from the striving towards nirvana (release from the cycle of birth and rebirth). Instead, Buddha was alluded to through such symbols as stupas, footprints, trees or animals. The more populist, less monkish schism, Mahayana, or "greater vehicle" form of Buddhism, (which exists more or less in its original form among Buddhists today), emerged several centuries later, with its more tactile images of Buddha's various incarnations, from animal to human, as well as to Bodhisatta, the potential Buddha.

THE MAURYAN AGE AND ASHOKA

The departure of Alexander the Great left a power vacuum that was rapidly filled by India's first imperial family, a mighty Aryan clan who used the peacock as their totem. These were the Mauryas, (326–184 BC) who rose to prominence under the leadership of Chandragupta, perhaps inspired by Alexander's catalytic invasion of the Indus. From their capital at Magadha, built on the site of ancient Pataliputra and present-day Patna in Bihar, they were to unify the warring kingdoms and tribes along the Ganges under a single imperial umbrella for 140 years.

A fascinating insight into the contemporary Mauryan society and India's earliest foreign policy ploys was given by the contemporary Greek ambassador, Megathenes at the court of Chandragupta's son, Bindusara. He cites a rather amusing correspondence between Bindusara and the Greek ruler Antiochus I: the former had apparently requested Antiochus not only to send him samples of Greek wine and raisins, but also philosophers to teach him the art of arguing. Antiochus replied dryly that the wine and raisins had been dispatched, but that the Greeks drew the line at trading in philosophers.

THE BIRTH OF BUREAUCRACY

It's thought that the genius behind the Mauryan throne was Chandragupta's chief minister Kautilya Chanakaya, who wrote the *Arthashastra*, or *"Science of Material Gain,"* a treatise on the art of government and taxation written around 250 BC. He was diabolical and shrewd enough to have given even Machiavelli a few pointers. Kautilya realized that the path to a powerful empire lay in a strong civil administration and punishment of those who trespassed its laws — he also introduced a state tax on everything from land and harvested crops to gambling and prostitution.

Mauryan society marked a unique transition from a rural monarchy to a strictly enforced civil administration — an indication that bureaucracy took indigenous root in India then and not after the arrival of the British, as it is commonly argued. Megathenes noted seven "classes" within Mauryan society, the highest class being royal councilors, whom he ranked above the priests or Brahmans. The others were agriculturists, soldiers, artisans, police (including spies) and last but not least, the bureaucrats. At the peak of Mauryan power it is thought that more than a million men acted as imperial administrators, soldiers and spies. The Mauryan state controlled all the major industries — everything from wine-making to road-building — with strict pay-scales and taxes imposed on artisans and professionals alike. The great Magadhan capital was administered by the traditional *panchayat* (five member) council of elders, a structure that was repeated throughout the Mauryan empire to govern India's villages, guilds and castes as well as towns and cities. Even today it remains a strong force in modern Indian villages.

THE ENLIGHTENED EMPEROR

The Mauryan empire reached its zenith under Chandragupta's grandson, the legendary Ashoka, "Sorrowless One". During his reign from 269 to 232 BC, Ashoka emerged as India's most powerful and possibly, most enlightened emperor. In its heyday, Ashoka's empire ruled over

more of India than any other invader until the British some 2,000 years later, claiming revenue from Kashmir to Mysore and Bangladesh to Afghanistan. Only three Dravidian kingdoms — Kerala, Chola and Pandya — remained independent in the far south.

Following the advice of the *Arthashastra*, which instructed that "any power superior in might should launch into war", Ashoka invaded the frontier tribal kingdom of Kalinga to the south, in modern Orissa, subduing it after the bloodiest war of his era. The sight of the battlefield's terrible carnage was to haunt him for the rest of his life, causing him to renounce violence as an instrument of policy. He became a Buddhist, and spread his faith by inscribing some 5,000 words of moral advice across 30 pillars (of which only 10 survive) and 18 rock faces across his enormous domain, notably in Orissa, Gujarat, Delhi, Sarnath and Sanchi. The most famous of his pillars, adorned with lions, has now been adopted as the symbol of modern India.

Ashoka's reign is best distinguished by his paternalistic toleration to his subjects of every faith and tongue. He abandoned the traditional annual royal hunt in favor of a *dharma yatra* or "pilgrimage of religious laws", which involved long journeys throughout his realm. An offshoot of this was that India gained an early network of tree-lined highways, leading from the capital. Ashoka is said to have informed his subordinates that wherever he was, whether eating or in his harem, he was always "on duty" to carry out the business of the state. His Mauryan capital Pataliputra became Asia's foremost center of art and culture, while Mauryan administrators were posted to every far-flung region of the empire, rotated regularly to avoid corruption — a system with many similarities to the way British "collectors" later operated.

Under Ashoka, Buddhism spread throughout the society — his own son Mahendra became a monk and took the gospel of Buddha to Ceylon, now Sri Lanka. Another by-product of Ashoka's conversion to ahimsa or non-violence, was that vegetarianism was adopted by the masses.

POST-EMPIRE OPPORTUNISM

Fifty years or so after the death of Ashoka in 232 BC, the Mauryan empire had collapsed. Some historians would have it that his pro-Buddhist stance led to insidious resistance from power hungry Brahman priests, while others believe that his pacifist ways allowed the military strength of the empire to wane leaving it highly vulnerable to fortune hunters from central Asia. Possibly it might just have been that Ashoka's successors were weak and ineffectual, lacking what it takes to hold a vast empire together.

Whatever the reason, the Mauryan Empire had collapsed by 184 BC. Confusion and warfare reigned as various triumphant central Asian and Persian tribes warred to take advantage of the political void. For more than five centuries, from 232 BC to AD 320, power shifted from one dynasty to another, ushering in half a millennium of unsettled, often barbaric rule which largely undermined the great civilization and unity of the Ashokan era.

First had come Alexander the Great's successors, the Bactrian Greeks. They captured Peshawar in 190 BC, and a decade later, with the collapse of Mauryan rule, established control throughout the Punjab. Many of these Greeks accepted Indian religions, the most famous conversion being that of their powerful king, Menander (circa 150 BC) who embraced Buddhism. The most enduring legacy of this Bactrian bridge between east and west can be seen in their distinctive classical Buddhist art, known as the Gandhara school, examples of which can be seen in many of India's national museums. Then, around 50 BC, the Greek Bactrians fought in vain against a double-pronged attack by two foreign nomadic tribes: the Scythians, or *Sakas* over the Kabul Valley in the north, and the Parthians, or *Pahlavas* over the Bolan Pass further south, who both managed to win solid power bases in the Indus Valley in the following century. Neither proved a match for the next spate of invasions by the more powerful central Asian Kushan warriors. The Parthians fell in battle, while the Scythians simply melted away inland, adopting Kshatriyan names and becoming Indianized.

The Kushans (circa AD 50–240) sent their armies along the Ganges as far as Benares, now Varanasi. Their most famous king, Kanishka had a utopian fantasy that his dynasty would rule forever. He gave India a new calendar, intended as a historical *tabula rasa* that began with the year he commenced his reign in AD 78. Like Ashoka and Menander, Kanishka converted to Buddhism, and he hosted the Fourth Great Buddhist Council in Kashmir, which gave rise to the radical new schism of Mahayana Buddhism. During Kanishka's reign, the very first carved images of Buddha began to appear.

Meanwhile, against this backdrop in the north, Brahman rulers had established themselves further south-east in the Indo-Gangetic plains; the former Mauryan domain in Bihar had been directly inherited by the Sungas (184–70 BC), while the central Deccan was ruled for four and a half centuries after 230 BC by the Telugu-speaking Andhras.

Although for some five centuries, post-Mauryan era India was thrown into political fragmentation, many impressive artistic and scientific contributions emerged at this time. Foreign influence—in the form of the Bactrian Greeks—allowed Hellenistic ideas to percolate into Indian thinking, and vice versa. In particular, medicine and astrology flourished. In medicine, India was already rather advanced, being based on the ancient Hindu science of ayurvedic medicine, with its many herbal medication and "magic" potions, was widely accepted in India. Interesting enough, during Ashoka's reign, yoga gained imperial patronage—an indication perhaps of how seriously longevity was taken in those days. In astronomy, the solar calendar, with its seven day week and the hour, seem to have been Hellenistic imports, along with the zodiac, which the Indian adopted zealously.

This was also an era of greatly expanded trade via the sea and the fabled Silk Road, the long and often perilous overland trading route traipsed by merchants, camels, oxen and donkeys that crisscrossed the subcontinent. It began near what is now the port of Tyre in Lebanon and crisscrossed through what is now northern Iran, Afghanistan, Soviet Central Asia, and China, making India the economic center of Sino-Roman trade. Increased trade and wealth inspired Indian thought and art in various ways. Indian merchants, who set aside some of their fortunes as donations to religious orders, usually Buddhist, in the belief that such piety would be well rewarded in the next life, or preferably by attaining blissful "ultimate release" or nirvana from life's cycle of re-births. Consequently virtually all the great artistic and architectural remains from this period are Buddhist. The Buddha image, which first emerged under Kanishka under the new Mahayana sect, sparked an artistic religious fervor to represent the Enlightened One in all his many guises and symbolic poses with varying hand gestures (*mudras*) to depict his various messages, including his most famous gesture of reassurance, the "forget fear" gesture, which Gandhi later adopted as one of his favorite symbols. This prompted Buddhist monks to raise monasteries, temples and beautifully decorative stupas, of which the most famous can be seen at Sanchi with its gateway of voluptuous *yakshi* (mother-goddess figures), dancing elephants and other carved figures intended to depict stories of the Buddha's previous incarnations.

Perhaps the most extraordinary Buddhist legacy can be seen in a series of great monolithic rock-hewn temples throughout the Deccan, the most magnificent of which are hewn from crescent-shaped ridges at Ellora and Ajanta, near Aurangabad in Maharashtra state, where the earliest temple caves date back to 200 BC. The tradition of creating these fabulous cave grottoes was to continue over the centuries until the thirteenth century. Yet it was during the imperial reign of the Guptas that artisans working here executed the most ambitiously monumental temples together with the most exquisite relief sculptures and large-scale fresco paintings, all constructed for the greater glory of Buddha.

THE CLASSICAL AGE

India's greatest Hindu dynasty, the Guptas (320–700) is noted for its grand cultural con-

tribution to Indian history. Under its auspices, the arts blossomed as never before, while Sanskrit poetry and literature reached celebrated heights of sophistication. The Guptas, like the Mauryas, established their base of imperial power in Magadha, in present-day Bihar, where they controlled rich sources of iron ore. The dynasty was founded by Chandragupta I, and although their empire never matched that of the Mauryan's, these powerful rulers lost no time in usurping pettier princelings and could soon claim a territorial triangle extending from Punjab to the north, Bengal to the north-east and the southern Deccan plateau, with imperial cities rising throughout the domain, most importantly at Ayodhya. Soon, Kashmir too was claimed — a rare and highly coveted jewel in the Gupta crown.

With the Guptas on the throne, India entered its so-called "classical age", a golden epoch of peace, prosperity and stability. This era produced India's "Shakespeare", the brilliant court poet-playwright, Kalidasa, whose seven major Sanskrit classics marked the flowering of purely secular literature. Many new theories in

Dravidian women walk bare-footed through the ancient temples of the Five Rathas in Mahabilpuram, Tamil Nadu.

algebraic mathematics and astronomy also surfaced. Ironically, the Guptan astronomer Aryabhatta I, who calculated that earth moved around the sun and not the other way around, as was commonly believed at the time, was completely ignored. Royal patronage was tolerant, extending to Hindu, Buddhist and Jain faiths, as can be seen in the cave art and sculpture perfected at Ajanta. However, the Guptas artistic effort reached in culmination in the classical architecture of the Hindu temple.

Importantly, the Guptas brought about a wholesale revival of Hinduism. Its popularity had sagged in the post-Mauryan era, when

upper castes to stand clear in order to avoid being "polluted" by their presence. Another important social change under the Guptas concerned the status of women. The Guptas were the first to legalize the practice of arranged marriages, and codified a system which had existed for centuries, making women legal wards under the power of fathers, husbands, sons and brothers.

Perhaps one of the most fascinating windows on the world of the equivalent of the upper castes during this time is the *Kama Sutra* by Vatsyayana, referred to by the Guptas as a classic textbook on the art — and gymnastics — of love. It also describes the highly hedonistic

Buddhism predominated amid a bevy of other fashionable "alternative" sects, ranging from fatalistic determinism to ritualized human sacrifice — with everything else in between. The rise of Hinduism automatically reconditioned the caste system, tightening up the social hierarchy and regulating its conduct. Untouchables and slaves became little more than two-legged chattels. They were confined to the outskirts of towns and villages, and designated the "unclean" menial jobs of scavenging, cleaning, tending the dead and making leather goods. Even accidental contact with an untouchable by a high-caste person was a contamination and required ritual cleansing. The visiting Chinese Buddhist pilgrim Fa-hsien, who traveled though India for six years at the beginning of the fifth century was rather taken aback to find that untouchables carried gongs to warn passing

lifestyle a wealthy young man of the time might well pursue for the benefit of his education. According to the Kama Sutra, days should also be spent appreciating poetry, music, sculpture and painting and delectable food, all in a haze of delicate perfume, fresh flowers and elegantly coiffeured young women. However, it's important to stress that the *Kama Sutra* dealt with only one aspect of a courtier's life — the period of being a "good householder" — sandwiched in between "celibate studenthood" and "sagacious old age!"

Ultimately, the Gupta empire was weakened by invading barbaric White Huns. By the sixth century they had gained control of Punjab and Kashmir and splintered the former Gupta stronghold across north India into a number of separate Hindu kingdoms which would not be united again until the coming of the Muslims.

THE LEGACY OF THE SOUTH

Few of the political intrigues occurring in north India had much, if any, bearing on the contemporary political climate of the south. At this time the south was divided into three major ancient Tamil "kingdom," the Cholas on the east coast at Tanjore near present-day Madras, the Cheras, or Kerala, in the west, and the Pandyas in the center, based at Madurai with a domain reaching down to Kanya Kumari in Tamil Nadu. Madurai, still one of south India's greatest temple cities, was the center of Tamil literary culture with its prestigious *sangams* or academies where some 500 poets are reputed to have congregated, also attracting philosophers and artists.

In the face of attacks from the north, these three Tamil kingdoms formed political alliances, but during rare moments of peace they schemed and plotted against one another. Early in the fourth century, another Tamil dynasty appeared on the scene, the Pallavas ("robbers") who managed to oust the Chola monarch from Kanchipuram, and set about leaving an incredible architectural legacy, as the vast *goporams* or gateways so distinctive of the south testify.

Unlike the Aryan caste system, the Tamils had their own pyramidal social structure, divided into "castes" that were really a kind of geographical identity, for instance, hills people, plains people, and forest, coastal and desert dwellers. Within each of these five groups were divisions relating to employment, including pearl divers, fishermen, boat-makers and boatmen. At society's apex sat the supreme ruler, the monarch who was considered part-deity. These Tamil Dravidians also had a tradition of matrilineal succession — which survived right up until the nineteenth century. They also had the custom of cross-cousin marriage — and were repelled by the northern practice of arranged marriage to "strangers."

This was a prosperous and cosmopolitan region, with well established seaborne trading links with other civilizations, notably the Romans and the Egyptians, and later Bali, Sumatra and Java. Spices, teak, ivory, exotic birds, onyx, precious gems, cotton goods, silks, and even Ayurvedic medicine were bartered for gold coins, while India's art, philosophies and religions were inadvertently exported into the bargain.

A new and important foreign influence in the south was Christianity, brought by St Thomas the Apostle when he arrived in Kerala in AD 52. He was said to have been martyred at Mylapore, a suburb of Madras in AD 68, and ever since, Christianity has retained a foothold in India's deep south. The tiny Jewish community of Cochin is also thought to have been founded in the first century.

THE IMPACT OF ISLAM

The First Muslim Invasions

The Muslim conquest of India had the most profound impact on the political, social and culture life of the country. Islam spread like wild fire, and India was never the same again. With Hinduism and Islam being as incompatible as fire and water, the blend of religions was far from amicable. To somewhat puritanical

Muslim eyes, the whole Hindu way of thinking was suspect. Hindus were seen as caricatures: caste-bound cow-worshippers, with a slavish devotion to thousands of different gods who they worshipped in the form of idols — anathema to followers of the monotheistic Islam. Hindus, on the other hand, saw Muslims as gross over-simplifiers, with a doggedly single-minded perception of a complex elemental cosmos. They saw no need to recruit fresh converts, since anyone not born a Hindu was automatically excluded from the faith. Conversely, Muslims were great proselytizers. Proselytizing was not always peaceful, as Muslims not only brandished the Koran but battle swords as well. Islam did not acknowledge that any person was better than another by reason of race, skin color or social class, although women did not enjoy the same status as men. Evidence given by a woman, for example, was (and still is today in Islamic countries), only half as credible as that given by a man.

The first Muslims to arrive were peaceable Arab traders who landed on the west coast from

OPPOSITE: Lonely, boulder-strewn moonscape surrounding the Thikse monastery in Ladakh.
ABOVE: Detail of the Taj Mahal, considered the most sublime architectural achievement of the Mughal Emperors.

what is now Saudi Arabia as early as the seventh century, not long after the death of the Prophet Muhammed, the founder of Islam, in 632. Although Muslim merchants returned home laden with exotic imports and tales of India's wealth — creating the impression that the country was ripe for plundering — more than two centuries passed before Islamic armies launched a full-scale invasion. This was left to Mahmud of Ghazni, "the Sword of Islam," who mounted 17 separate attacks between 1000 and 1027, leaving a bloody trail as he and his Turkic hordes zealously smashed countless Hindu temples to dust and descending upon India's cities in a frenzy of murder and rapine. His most successful campaign netted him so much booty from the holy Shiva temple at Somnath, on the Arabian sea in Gujarat, that not even a giant caravan of elephants, camels and mules was able to carry it all away. Mahmud's court chronicler may have exaggerated, but he recorded that more than 50,000 Hindus were slaughtered that day. Certainly his credo was convert or die, for in his opinion, Islam tolerated no rivals. Vanquished Hindu chieftains were lucky if Mahmud spared them their lives — and even if he did, he was known to severe their fingers as trophies for his ever-growing collection. As much as he enjoyed these periodic sprees of acquisitive mayhem, Mahmud was a bandit at heart, and had no great political designs on India.

It was not until 1192 that Muslim power took firm root in India, this time with another fierce Turko-Afghan Muslim warlord at the helm, Muhammed Ghauri. Within a decade, his armies had forced the Hindu kingdoms of the Gangetic valley to collapse, one by one, like dominoes. Only the valiant Rajputs never completely surrendered, although they suffered horrific losses. During this expansion, Buddhists were especially vilified, with monasteries destroyed and thousands monks sent fleeing to Nepal and Tibet. Exiled from the land of its birth, Buddhism was not to be restored in any significant way in India until the twentieth century. Subjugated Indians were treated as second-class citizens, and were forced to pay their new rulers hefty tax. The Muslim title, *zaminder* or landlord dates from this period of feudal rule.

After Ghauri's death in 1206, his slave lieutenant, Qutb-ud-din-Aibak, declared himself the Sultan of Delhi, commemorating the event with a towering victory tower, the Qutb Minar, and what is supposed was India' first mosque — symbolically constructed from the remnants of 27 Hindu temples. His Sultanate is also known as the "Slave Dynasty" referred to martial slavery, which allowed ambitious low-born young men an opportunity to rise above their status. During the 320 years of its existence the throne

of the Delhi Sultanate changed hands among six successive Turko-Afghan dynasties. Next came the Khilji monarchs, notably Ala-ud-din-Khilji, (1296–1316), whose reign spanned 20 years, and together with his general, Malik Kafur, not only conquered the Deccan, but also the kingdoms of south India — although these did not stay subjugated long. Despite their iconoclastic and almost wholesale destruction of Hindu architecture, these Muslim sultans imported the imposing building styles of Central Asia, introducing two features without which Islamic architecture would later be unrecognizable: the minaret and the dome.

The Delhi Sultanate was beginning to weaken by the fourteenth century, during the reign of the next Turkic dynasty, the Tughlaqs, who ruled 1320–97. The first of Tughlaq rulers was Muhammed bin Tughlaq, who was notorious for his insane zealousness, a sort of Indian "Grand old Duke of York" who first marched his subjects to his new capital in the Deccan, then marched them all back again. Discontent and rebellion pock-marked the 26 years of his reign, and two southern regions of his Sultanate broke away and formed independent kingdoms in the north of present-day Karanataka, one Hindu, one Muslim. The Hindu Vijayanagar kings built a magnificent capital at Hampi, forming a united Hindu front against the flood-tide of Islam in the north. Meanwhile the Bahmani Muslim empire emerged, later splitting into the warring provincial kingdoms at Berar, Ahmednagar, Bijapur, Golconda and Ahmedabad, all leaving behind impressive medieval fortresses.

The waning Delhi Sultanate proved an irresistible lure to one of the most dreaded names roaming the wilderness beyond the north-west frontiers, the ruthless warlord Tamerlane or "Timur the Lame." His devastating raid across the Punjab to Delhi in 1399, left "towers built high" of severed heads and mutilated bodies, and Delhi itself laid waste with famine and pestilence. His invasion resulted in a catalytic shift of power — severing India once more into two parts. The north reverted to the Turkic Afghan princes, while the south one more regained its independent status as a conglomerate of Hindu kingdoms. Slightly more than a century later, Timur's great grandson, Babur, an Uzbek prince, would return to found his Mughal dynasty on the same site.

POWER AND DECADENCE

No other age in India's history has ever been as dazzling, as affluent or ultimately as decadent as that of the Mughals, a two-century-long era of six major emperors that reached its zenith while Elizabeth I ruled in England. The period saw a remarkable blend of Indian, Persian and Central Asian influences, manifested in an impressive legacy of magnificent palaces, forts, tombs and landscaped gardens, including India's most famous building, the Taj Mahal.

Mughal is a corruption of *Mughul*, the Persian word for Mongol, since the Mughal rulers were partly descended from the great medieval Mongol leaders, Genghis Khan and Timur. But the Mughals were more Persianized Turks than Mongols, and they spoke a language among themselves known as Turkic.

The Mughal chieftain Babur in 1526 swept down on the Hindu plains from current-day Afghanistan and at the Battle of Panipat his army killed Ibrahim Lodi and 20,000 soldiers, laying open the road to Delhi where the young warlord proclaimed himself emperor.

"Do not hurt or harm the flocks or herds of these people, not even their cotton ends or broken needles", Babur was recorded as telling his soldiers. "Beware not to bring ruin on its people by giving way to fear or anxiety. Our eye is on this land and on this people. Raid and rapine shall not be."

Babur dispatched his son, Humayan, to capture Agra, where the conquerors acquired the fabulous Koh-i-noor diamond from the disintegrated armies of the Lodi dynasty. Babur's legacy in Agra is the Ram Bagh garden, where the emperor liked to compose poems. Despite his success, Babur disliked India and the Indians, writing in his diary: "Three things oppressed us in India, heat, violent winds and dust." All he found to praise was India's countryside, its monsoon and its gold. He died, homesick for the cool fragrant air of Kabul, where his body was later taken for burial.

Humayan succeeded Babur at the age of 23 but was a natural recluse who lacked his father's military skills and acumen required to hold together the new empire. He preferred to study languages, mathematics, philosophy and astronomy, and was also fond of illuminated manuscripts and opium. Humayan was ousted in 1540 by a brilliant Afghan commoner, Sher Shah Suri, who captured Delhi and slaughtered 8,000 Mughal soldiers. While Humayan skulked in exile in Persia, Sher Shah earned popularity during his five-year reign for impressive civil policies; the construction of Delhi's sixth city, Shergarh, numerous state highways, and for active promotion of Hindu employees and Rajput soldiery.

Humayan recovered sufficient experience in statesmanship during his 15-year exile, and in 1556 he again brought Delhi and Agra back under Mughal rule. His taste of victory was to be brief. Just a few weeks after reinstating himself in Delhi, he died from a fall down some stairs, aptly enough in his library. Humayan's contribution to Mughal architecture is his impressive name-sake tomb in suburban Delhi that strongly resembles the Taj Mahal.

Akbar, destined to be mightiest emperor, was only 13 when he succeeded his father in 1556, although he took six years to shake off power-hungry guardians. Born of exiled parents, Akbar's unsettled childhood denied any chance of a formal education and he remained illiterate throughout his life, yet he was soon able to memorize vast tracts of Persian and Arabic poetry, displaying the brilliant intellect that later earned him the sobriquet "Akbar the Great". Historian Philip Mason wrote that Akbar "tried to give India the unity she had nearly attained under Ashoka, and once again under the Gupta dynasty; his was the third attempt and the fourth was to the British."

Akbar, through a series of military campaigns, pushed the borders of the Mughal empire three-quarters of the way across the subcontinent, always creating an efficient bureaucracy in conquered areas. He encouraged harmony between Hindus and Muslims, setting an example by marrying a Rajput princess from Jaipur and appointing her Hindu kinsmen to powerful positions. He patronized the arts on a grand scale and had such a fascination for other religions that his courtiers privately expressed doubts that he was a Muslim at all. He devised his own faith, the Din-i-Allahi, a mélange of Islam and Hinduism and other dogmas with himself as the supreme god-head. This enlightened experiment proved short-lived, but its memory is preserved in Akbar's greatest architectural achievement, his beautiful city of Fatepur Sikri, abandoned just 14 years after it was built 37 km (23 miles) from Agra.

When Akbar died in 1605, his powerful empire passed to his son, the despotic and frequently drunk Jehangir, who expanded his domain with calculated brutality. He once coolly calculated that his hunting exploits had killed a total of some 17,000 animals and 14,000 birds. Yet at the same time, he was an aesthete whose patronage of painters produced gauche miniatures illustrating court life, love life and natural history of unsurpassed delicacy. He also built exquisite marble tombs, mosques and Mughal gardens, but did not share his father's vision for a united, secular India.

The fifth Mughal, Shah Jehan executed all possible rivals as soon as he sat on the throne in 1627, and further unraveled Akbar's achievements by destroying sacred Hindu temples and waging brutal wars against the Hindu Rajputs and the Deccan Muslims. Yet now he is remembered for the elegant beauty of his architectural

masterpieces; the infamous Taj Mahal, the Pearl Mosque in Agra Fort and the Jama Masjid and Red Fort in Old Delhi. His colossal expenditure on grandiose architecture became so profligate that his son Aurangzeb finally locked him up to save the dynasty from financial ruin. Shah Jehan spent his last years imprisoned in Agra Fort, where from his quarters he could gaze across the Yamuna River to the Taj Mahal.

Aurangzeb took the throne in 1658 and his 51-year-long reign is remembered for fanatical imposition of Islamic orthodoxy. He aroused the hatred of his Hindu subjects by making them second-class citizens, building mosques

The lakeside Shiv Niwas Palace and City Palace complex in Udaipur. Of all the ruling Rajput clans, only the Udaipur Mewars managed to remain virtually independent of the Mughal yoke.

with the rubble of their holy temples. Although he extended the Mughal empire's boundaries to their furthermost, he also paved the way for its eventual collapse by alienating the rulers from the ruled. Aurangzeb lived frugally, never touching opium or visiting his harem, and banning dancing girls and musicians from his court. His paranoia about losing power led him to systematically exile, imprison, and in some cases execute his male relatives. He even imprisoned his favorite wife and daughter and had them deliberately insulted by eunuchs. Aurangzeb died in 1707 and his grave is a spartan affair covered only with earth and open to the sky at Khuldabad, near Aurangabad.

After Aurangzeb, the Mughal dynasty fell into slow decay. Eleven successive kings ruled over its dwindling fortunes, each as ineffectual and profligate as the last. Fresh contenders for

inence under the low-caste warrior Shivaji. Villagers in present-day Maharashtra state still relate anecdotes of Shivaji's daring military exploits. The Marathas gradually controlled most of north India except Punjab. They were soon to face a challenge by new and unexpected rivals from across the seas, and one that would eventually prove more formidable than the declining Mughals — the British East India Company.

THE ARRIVAL OF THE EUROPEANS

A PROFITABLE TRADE

The European vanguard arrived even before the Mughals, when adventurous Portuguese explorers made forays into India in the late fifteenth century. Six years after Christopher Columbus discovered America, Lisbon's own Vasco da Gama landed at modern day Kerala in 1498, succeeding in his dream to rediscover the fabled Indies related by Marco Polo 200 years previously. His men set about zealously converting Indians to Christianity and sending home ship-loads of exotic spices, which reaped colossal profits in European markets. The Portuguese enjoyed a century-long monopoly on this lucrative trade before other European powers followed suit and began to sail East. Pepper became known as "black gold" and spices in Europe were highly valued as preservatives and flavoring. The Portuguese established bases at Damen and Diu in Gujarat, and made their headquarters at Goa, an enclave captured in 1510 and kept under Lisbon's rule until 1961.

The Dutch inadvertently brought about the British Raj, as Elizabethan Englishmen grew envious of their coastal neighbor's success in the Indonesian spice trade and resolved to compete for the booming markets in the East Indies. A series of bruising battles forced them to retreat to India, where they were enticed by tales of the decadent Mughals' treasures. Stories percolated back to England of kings who weighed themselves in gold, of stores of silver, silks and jewels in ornate palaces filled with dancing girls, eunuchs and exotic animals such as peacocks and elephants.

Queen Elizabeth I in 1600 granted the British East India Company a trade charter, and eight years later the corporation of wealthy English merchants landed a vessel at Surat in Gujarat during the reign of Emperor Jehangir. The Portuguese, Dutch, French and Danes were all active in the East during this period but it was the English who were fated to found an Indian

power sensed that the Mughals were on their last legs, and the first serious body blow came in 1739 when the Persian king Nadir Shah stormed Delhi. He slaughtered more than 30,000 people and returned home with 1,000 elephants, 7,000 horses and 10,000 camels laden with booty, including the symbol of Mughal power, the fabulous Peacock Throne.

DECLINE AND TRANSITION

The seams of the Mughal empire were splitting, and by the middle of the eighteenth century, India had seen numerous shifts in power and influence, with many regions falling to strong Hindu rulers. Some subject Indians revolted, such as the Sikhs and the Jats, but the most formidable were the west-Indian Marathas, the militant anti-Muslim group that rose to prom-

empire. By the end of the seventeenth century, the Company's various settlements were dominated by three Presidencies: Madras, founded in 1640, Bombay in 1668, and Calcutta in 1690.

The British East India Company expanded during the next 250 years, exporting cotton, cloths, silks, saltpeter and indigo, and opium from poppies, which was sent to China in exchange for that other valuable commodity, tea. From the outset the Company had a structured hierarchy upon which the Indian Civil Service was gradually superimposed. At the bottom were the "writers", or clerks whose starting salaries were £10 a year, the minimum age a young man could come out from England being 16. At the top were governors, who ruled like mini-emperors from palatial mansions. In order to bolster official salaries, private enterprise flourished and created the breed of social-climbing Company-men known as "nabobs" who accumulated vast fortunes and returned to England to build themselves country estates, hobnob with aristocrats and often, to enter Parliament.

By mid-eighteenth century, tensions between England and France were simmering in Europe when the War of Austrian Succession began, followed by the Seven Years War. Hostilities broke out on Indian soil in 1746 when a French army based at the trading post of Pondicherry captured British Madras, only to lose it back to the East India Company three years later. Tension between French and British posts remained long after peace returned in Europe, and both sides frequently provided local Indian rulers with arms, supplies and expertise in attempts to hasten each other's end.

The Company's first full-scale military intervention in Indian politics was both accidental and decisive. Bengal was one of the several independent kingdoms that arose as the Mughal empire disintegrated, and in 1756, its nabob, Suraj-ud-daula, captured the British garrison at Calcutta and the infamous Black Hole incident took place (see CALCUTTA, page 225). One year later, Robert Clive's forces easily defeated the nabob and his French supporters on the field of Plassey, and finding himself in control of Bengal, Clive put his own candidate, Mir Jafar on the throne. In the south, the so-called "Tiger of Mysore", Tipu Sultan and his father Hyder Ali inflicted a series of defeats on the British, but were overcome in 1799, opening up the region for British exploitation. In the west, British forces defeated the Marathas in 1803, and after two Sikh Wars left Punjab in British hands in 1849, the Company had become the effective sovereign of most of India. English armies also defeated Nepalese troops and annexed Burma.

THE BIRTH OF THE RAJ

British domination of the subcontinent by the late eighteenth century stemmed both from timely opportunism as the Mughal empire collapsed and their pragmatic policy of toleration towards the conquered, indirectly employing the same rules Akbar had employed so successfully. The British initially made no attempt to interfere with Indian religions, customs and culture, and made it clear that their interest in India was making fortunes, not conversions.

With British muskets at their throats, so to speak, local rulers saw no choice but to accept British suzerainty. For the next 50 years, the British focused their attention on gaining complete political control. In 1803 the blind Moghul emperor Shah Alam was formally taken under British protection. Deference continued to be paid to him as the Great Mughal and it was officially he who ruled an empire but in reality he was a puppet of the British Resident in Delhi. Disgust with the Mughals was no secret among the British. Lord Thomas Macaulay derided Aurangzeb's heirs as "a succession of nominal sovereigns, sunk in indolence and debauchery, sauntering away life in secluded palaces chewing bang, fondling concubines and listening to buffoons."

The British froze the borders of numerous Indian kingdoms, ranging from the largest and grandest, like Hyderabad and Kashmir, bigger in area than many European nations, to smallest and most insignificant enclaves. On the up side of the coin, rulers of these so-called princely or native states enjoyed a security of tenure that their predecessors had never enjoyed. The aristocratic Rajput maharajas, the Muslim nizams and nabobs, and the few remaining Maratha generals were obliged to swell British coffers with generous annual revenues and acknowledge British paramountcy, but were otherwise autonomous in the administration of their territories.

Company agents were amassing enormously inflated personal fortunes, often by highly unscrupulous tactics. Tales of greedy excess filtered back to London, resulting in the India Act in 1784, which established the British government's control over the Company, although the Company was retained as a full partner in trade. London appointed a Board of Control to supervise all civil, military and revenue matters, and the body was presided over by the Company's Governer-general, the first being Warren Hastings who ruled from 1774 to 1785.

The British poured their mercantilist energies into large-scale iron and coal mining, developing tea, coffee and cotton production, and creating a vast network of railways, highways, postal and telegraph services, irrigation and agricultural programs. English was the official language of the civil service and education, and still remains the lingua franca among India's administrative classes. By the mid-nineteenth century, some 1,000 Englishmen governed the affairs of some 221 million people. The British never allowed Indians into the upper government echelons, but they established numerous schools and universities that led to the birth of an educated Indian elite.

Governor-general William Bentinck, influenced by philosophies of humanitarian liberalism fashionable in London in the 1830s, for the first time introduced laws against certain Indian cultural practices. He outlawed human sacrifice; the practice of suttee, or the ritual suicide of widows upon the death of husbands; and took actions against the Thugs, a secret society estimated to have strangled some 30,000 travelers a year in obeisance to the Hindu goddess of destruction, Kali. Not all British reforms were destined for success, and their tactics of delegating responsibility had dubious success in many rural areas. They bestowed administrative powers on *zamindars*, local land-owners who generally abused their authority and forced many peasants into bonded labor in order to pay exorbitant taxes. The short-sighted policy gave birth to a class of impoverished landless peasantry, whose plight of living in near-slavery is still rife across India.

THE SEPOY REVOLT

British missionary zeal in reforming India led to considerable Hindu and Muslim antipathy, which in 1857 and 1858 took the conquerors completely by surprise. The revolt of the sepoys, British-employed foot-soldiers, is called the "Indian Mutiny" in the West, but titled the "War of Independence" in modern Indian school primers. Either way, both sides spilled much blood. The rebellion's unlikely symbolic figurehead was the last Mughal emperor, Bahudur Shah II, whose talents were more suited to perfecting poetry than revolutions.

The rebellion began in Meerut, near Delhi, where sepoys were incited by a rumor that new bullets being issued were greased with animal fat from pigs, which are deemed unclean to Muslims, and cows, which are sacred to Hindus. In the space of an afternoon, 47 battalions mutinied and began a spontaneous bloody trail of destruction across the north, killing every *feringhi*, or foreigner, they could find. A cheering mob proclaimed Bahudur

Shah II the Emperor of Hindustan, and reinstated the octogenarian Mughal in Delhi's Red Fort.

The British contained the rebellion to the northern plains by disarming sepoys based in other areas, and recruiting Sikhs and tribal irregulars to assist them in reasserting control. The campaign was marked by extreme brutality on both sides, and it took the expeditionary force six months to reach numerous besieged garrisons and eventually recapture Delhi in January 1858. Bahudur Shah was banished to Burma, signaling the final defeat of the Mughal Empire.

THE SEEDS OF REBELLION

The traumatic experience of the mutiny made London reassess its position in India. The Company was abolished in 1858 and its authority replaced by the British Crown. Queen Victoria was proclaimed Sovereign Empress of India, where a Viceroy would be her representative and chief executive. The industrial revolution was in full swing in England, and India — the "jewel in the crown" — became a key source of raw materials for the "workshop of the world".

From 1858 until 1900 was the full-blown era of the Raj, Hindi for "rule". Ironically, British-founded educational institutions created an Indian intelligentsia, who justifiably became incensed that principles of democracy fastidiously upheld in the United Kingdom were not applicable to Indian subjects.

National pride was also fueled by a growing awe for India following numerous revelations on its grandeur and complexity as the site of ancient civilizations. Archaeologists unearthed cities

ABOVE: Shah Jehan's Red Fort in Delhi, which saw the dethronement of the final Mughal emperor, Bahudur Shah in the aftermath of the 1857 Mutiny.

twice as old as Rome and discovered that Buddha was an Indian. Scholars deciphered ancient Sanskrit texts that revealed several millennia of formerly unknown kings and emperors. They pieced together the significance of coins, paintings and sculptures, and uncovered long-lost philosophical, artistic and literary achievements.

The Hindu renaissance and will for social reform was spearheaded by a handful of modern-thinkers: Ram Mohan Roy, Ramakarishna, Swami Vivekanda, Dayanada and even the English Annie Beasant, president of the Theosophical Society and founder of the Central Hindu University, which later became Benares Hindu

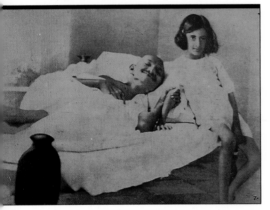

University. They preached a common philosophical ground between modern Hinduism and Western thought, and called for the religion to break away from its domination by high-caste Brahmans.

The movement found its voice in the Indian National Congress, started in 1885 from the efforts of another reformist Englishman, Allan Hume. The Congress gradually came to articulate Indian desires for self-rule, and its creation led to the 1906 birth of the All-India Muslim League, whose founders derided plans of an India dominated by Hindu "Brahmans, moneylenders and shopkeepers", and called for separate political representation.

Violence flared between the two communities and intensified under Lord Curzon's ill-conceived plan to divide Bengal into eastern and western administrative zones respectively dominated by Moslems and Hindus. The British also passed, in 1909, the Morley–Minto reforms, which called for separate electorates for Hindus and Moslems. Clashes between Moslem separatists and mostly Hindu unionists prompted

Curzon in 1911 to reverse his Bengal partition plan, but the two British schemes, intended to placate the demands of the two communities, had instead exacerbated the rift.

GANDHI AND INDEPENDENCE

Self-rule demands widespread at the turn of the century, were temporarily abandoned during World War I. Thousands of Indians served the British with honor and wanted their loyalty to be recognized by an act of imperial generosity granting similar terms to India as Australia and Canada, which enjoyed considerable self-rule as dominions within the empire. When London offered nothing in 1918, disillusionment among educated Indians turned to anger.

Congress began to expand its appeal, largely due to the inspiration of Mohandas Karamchand Gandhi, a young lawyer who returned to India in 1915 fresh from campaigning for human rights in South Africa. Gandhi called for the Congress to broaden its attitudes and membership, and include the rural classes and the illiterate poor. He realized the near-impossibility of ousting the British through armed might, and instead insisted that all agitation by based on *ahimsa* or non-violence, and *satyagraha*, or passive resistance. Gandhi's inspired views earned him the title of Mahatma, or "Great Soul", and he undertook a series of famous fasts to urge Hindus and Muslims to lay aside their differences and create a national unity that would cut across caste, community and religious barriers. He insisted on the dissolution of untouchability, and called upon Brahmans to remove their sacred threads that symbolized their place in the elite caste.

Gandhi dreamed that India would once more be Rama Raj, a mythical golden age under the benign Hindu god, Rama, when food was abundant and all people lived in peace and equality. He wanted the Indian flag to bear the spinning wheel, the symbol of his philosophy, and hoped that once the British left, India's economic future would be assured through small-scale cottage industries in which the rural masses could happily produce handicrafts, enjoying the utility derived from their labor.

With Gandhi's prompting, Indian women first began to involve themselves in politics and social movements. One of the most effective tactical weapons he used against the British was the ancient Hindu custom of *hartal*, or boycott, in which the daily functioning of the government ground to a halt due to nationwide strikes affecting all sectors of the economy.

A horrifying event in 1919 proved catalytic to the independence movement. General

ABOVE: Two icons of twentieth century Indian history: A fast-weakened Mahatma Gandhi with Nehru's daughter Indira, who later succeeded her father as prime minister of India.

Reginald Dyer ordered his Gurkha troops to open fire on a peaceful but illegal protest meeting in Amritsar, killing 379 people and wounding 1,200 others in the sealed courtyard of Jallianwala Bagh. Sikhs, whose loyalty to the British had remained steadfast even throughout the Indian Mutiny, largely changed their alliance to Congress. Gandhi shrewdly began campaigning against products and practices that made the British presence in India profitable. He agitated against taxes on Indian-produced salt and urged boycotts against British manufactured textiles, symbolizing his protest by learning to spin cotton thread and by wearing only handwoven cloth, or *khadi*.

Although Gandhi spent several years in jail for his efforts, the British gradually accepted they must relinquish India, but plans for their departure were complicated by their official control being over about three-quarters of the subcontinent. Roughly one fifth of the population lived in some 600 princely states, whose rulers mostly did not relish the thought of sacrificing their typically lavish lifestyles.

Confrontations escalated between the Congress Party led by Jawaharlal Nehru and the Muslim League's leader, the sharp-witted Muhammed Ali Jinnah, who rallied the large Muslim minority behind his call for independent Islamic homeland.

Viceroy Lord Wavell further infuriated Indians by announcing without consultation that they would fight for the empire in World War II, but many rallied to the cause and fought in Africa, Europe and Asia against the Axis. The war stymied the independence movement, but peace was marked a new wave of Congress civil disobedience marked by mass arrests, riots and bloodshed.

All parties now conceded that independence was inevitable, but Gandhi's call for the British to "Quit India" was now matched by Jinnah's slogan "Divide and Quit". The results of central and provincial elections in India — as well as intensifying bloody clashes between Hindus and Muslims — made it clear that India's future lay either with partition or a possible civil war.

A new British Viceroy, Lord Louis Mountbatten, was charged with the responsibility of handing over full control of India and the date was set for midnight, 14th August 1947. Both Nehru and Jinnah preferred partition to the alternative of a loose federation which had been proposed by the British as early as 1945. Jinnah in particular refused to budge, proclaiming, "I will have India divided or India destroyed." Only Gandhi remained unmoved by the mood of jubilation, believing that India should be fully united.

Princely states were released from British sovereignty and obliged to decide which nation to join. The evacuation of some 200,000 British Sahibs and Memsahibs in India was surprisingly smooth, almost anti-climactic as India exploded with celebrations to mark its newborn freedom. However, the euphoria was soon overshadowed by the holocaust of partition.

The subcontinent was sliced into two new nations, its geographical boundaries imposed by religion. Pakistan was comprised of two completely separate regions; West Pakistan, which included half of the fertile, affluent Punjab, Sind province and several mountainous tribal states; and more than a thousand miles away, East Pakistan, made up of the eastern half of Bengal, which has became Bangladesh. At the time of partition, India was home to 35 million Muslims, while the newly-created Pakistan housed millions of Hindus. In the months-long upheavals triggered by partition, more than ten million people migrated in each direction across the divided Punjab—the largest human exodus in history. The price of the operation was to be paid in frenzied communal bloodshed and suffering. Estimates of how many people, mostly villagers, died in the terrible slaughter range between 200,000 and one million. Communal violence between Hindus, Sikhs and Muslims spread so fast and so far that the Indian Army without the aid of British troops was quite unable to contain it. Trains were found in the middle of nowhere, their carriages spilling with mutilated corpses. Convoys of trucks were ambushed, and entire villages wiped out to last man, woman and child.

So extreme was the murderous madness that Jawaharlal Nehru, India's first prime minister, saw no option but to hand back responsibility to Mountbatten, who had by then become the first Governor-General of the independent nation. Gandhi came to Delhi and went on a prolonged hunger strike for reconciliation and an end to communal violence. His assassination by a Hindu fanatic, on January 30, 1948, so shamed the nation that the blood-letting ceased. "The light has gone out of our lives", Nehru announced in a voice choked with grief. The impact of Gandhi's assassination was national psychological shock, sapping the will for communal violence and allowing Nehru time to turn his attention to the task of building a new India. One of his most pressing concerns was resolving the status of the 362 major princely states. Kashmir, the last state to join India, had at its helm a vacillating Hindu maharaja governing a predominantly Muslim population, who refused to make his mind about which side he wanted to go. His decision was made for him when the strategic state was invaded by Pakistan-backed tribals in October 1948, and he was forced to seek help from the Indian Army. New

Delhi's forces halted the invaders, but lost about one third of Kashmir, which is now divided by a U.N.-mediated frontier.

AN INDIAN DYNASTY

The 1950s were the golden years of Indian independence, during which Prime Minister Jawaharlal Nehru formed what he hoped would be the guiding principles of his modern nation — secularism, democracy, social justice and political non-alignment. His great personal charm and integrity, his intellectual stature and his westernized sophistication singled him out as the leading international spokesman for newly-independent Third World nations. A Socialist, but not a Marxist, Nehru's goal was to create a modernized, self-sufficient India that would never again be beholden to another power. Nehru's socialist stance softened somewhat after consultations with the industrialists and Congress-backers, J.R. Tata and G.D. Birla, the Indian equivalents of Ford and Rockerfeller. He established a protected and centralized economy through a series of Five Year Plans aimed at encouraging massive industrialization and agricultural reforms.

Despite Nehru's policy of non-alignment, India increasingly found itself linked to the Soviet Union — partly in response to its month-long rout by China in 1962, and America's increasing support for its arch foe, Pakistan. Gandhi's belief in peaceful neutrality was laid to rest when Beijing's forces poured across their mutual Himalayan frontier, and relations between the world's two most populous nations remain bedeviled by disputes over two border areas.

Nehru died in 1964, and one year later his successor, Lal Bahudur Shastri, successfully repulsed Pakistan's twin attack on India — in the Rann of Kutch and in Kashmir. In January 1966, Shastri died, and Indira Gandhi, Nehru's daughter and no relation to the Mahatma, won a landslide victory at the polls to replace him. Skeptics darkly predicted that Indira would share the fate as India's only other woman ruler, the thirteenth century Muslim Slave Queen, Razia, whose three and a half year-long reign ended with a palace coup and her murder at the hands of her armed protectors.

With her election slogan "India is Indira and Indira is India", she was to prove them all wrong. During her 15 years in power she was both revered and severely criticized. Writer Salman Rushdie observed, "Her use of the cult of the mother — of Hindu mother-goddess symbols and allusions....was calculated and shrewd." Mrs. Gandhi's most trying problem was sectarianism, in the form of Congress Party splits or conflicts with neighboring powers. Agitation in East Pakistan against subjugation of the Bengali population by Islamabad erupted in 1971 into a civil war, that culminated in Indian involvement. New Delhi's troops fought Islamabad's forces in both Kashmir and East Pakistan, from where nine million refugees flooded into India. After 12 days of fighting, Islamabad yielded its shaky hold over its eastern section and sued for peace, resulting in the creation of the independent nation of Bangladesh.

Mrs Gandhi's travails were by no means over. National debt, caused by the war and the refugee crisis, mounting inflation and unemployment caused popular opposition to her rule. Sensing that the tide was turning against her and prompted by a low-level indictment that she had used government money for electioneering, the prime minister imposed an 18-month-long state-of-emergency involving suspension of civil liberties and imprisonment of thousands of her political opponents. India ceased to be a democracy during this period. Indira's zealous son, Sanjay, who she was grooming as her successor, incensed the populace with radical programs of forced sterilization of more than 11 million villagers and clearing slums with bulldozers.

Mrs Gandhi called an election in 1977 under the misguided belief that she remained popular, and was ousted in a wave of support for the newly-formed Janata Party, largely comprised of disgruntled, Congressmen. Its elderly, pedantic leader, Moraji Desai, is remembered largely for his idiosyncratic habits of drinking urine, protecting cows and banning alcohol and Coca-Cola, than solving India's pressing economic problems. After their brief honeymoon, the Janata Party crumbled into squabbling factions, and a 1980 election placed "Mrs G" back on her pedestal in the nation's hearts and on its ruling seat.

Mrs Gandhi valiantly tried but failed to conquer escalating economic and social ills, as well as bitter inter-communal unrest. Extremist Sikhs began agitating for the creation in northern Punjab of a theocratic nation named "Khalistan", or "Land of the Pure". The radicals began stockpiling arms in Amritsar's Golden Temple, Sikhdom's holiest shrine. Mrs Gandhi retaliated in June 1984 with "Operation Bluestar", a massive week-long army assault on the shrine that left some 600 people dead, mostly Sikhs.

The carnage and desecration of the shrine enraged Sikhs and led to the Oct. 31, 1984 retaliatory assassination of Mrs Gandhi by two of her Sikh security guards. Communal violence raged across northern India, where an estimated 3,000 Sikhs died at the hands of Hindu mobs. The mantle of the Nehru dynasty was passed onto

Mrs Gandhi's oldest son Rajiv, a former Indian Airlines pilot inducted into politics since the death of Sanjay in a 1980 plane accident.

Rajiv Gandhi called elections in December 1984, and was swept to power in an unprecedented wave of popularity that gave him an 80 percent standing in Parliament. The 40-year-old leader began his term with radical plans to liberalize the Indian economy, but many of his ideas have run into opposition from the entrenched bureaucracy. In November 1989, Rajiv Gandhi unceremoniously lost his mandate to the opposition, and Vishwanath Pratap Singh, leader of the National Front, became Prime Minister.

INDIA TURNS FORTY

Take a glance at the front page of any Indian newspaper for stories of mayhem and excess matched by few other nations. Political unrest could come from any region — perhaps from Sikh separatists in the Punjab, from the remote northeast, where there are several tribal insurgencies, from near-feudal Bihar, where peasant militia clash with private armies funded by land-owning families, or anywhere where the centuries-old enmity between Hindus and Moslems may flare.

In the capital, headlines may cry of corruption in high places, prompting opposition members to walk out of Parliament, "amid uproarious scenes". Farmers, lawyers or students may have called for hunger-strikes, processions or sit-ins that have brought the nation's businesses grinding to a halt. There may be another of God's terrible acts — drought or floods, ferries overturning or buses plunging off ravines. There may be bizarre stories of a child being revered as a God, a movie star turning to politics, a widow throwing herself on her husband's funeral pyre, girls cutting off their tongues to honor Lord Shiva, or an elephant stampede destroying a remote village.

However startling to a Western eye, none of these yarns mean India is falling apart. The nation still lives in the shadow of the utopian dreams of Gandhi and Nehru, whose legacy lives in the yet unshaken ideals of unity, secularism and social justice, maintained imperfectly perhaps, but nonetheless cherished as necessities. Beyond the story of sectarian violence is the telling fact that Hindus, Sikhs, Muslims, Buddhists, Parsis, Jains and many other groups have lived together in India's nearly 600,000 villages for many centuries. Hinduism, the nation's most pervasive religion with some 600 million adherents, exerts a strong binding moral and spiritual force. Its central world-view is of flexibility and absorption.

India can point to impressive economic modernizations, but it can not shake the growing burdens of the rural poor or its mountain of untrained and unemployable people flooding the cities. In a nation of 800 million people there are only 24 million wage-paying jobs. Seventy per cent of Indians live in the villages, yet their water supply is barely adequate, and they have no electricity, nor can many of them read or write. One statistic simply speaks for itself: one in every ten people who walk on this earth is an illiterate Indian.

But the single-most problem facing the nation today is its ever-growing population. India's

population is estimated to be about 800,000 million, and with one baby born every two seconds, it adds an Australia to its ranks each year. Demographers say the next generation has already been born, and nothing can halt the population reaching 1 billion by the year 2000. But they warn that steps must now be taken to stop an extra 200 million people being born by the year 2000.

India is very proud of its scientific community, the world's fourth largest, be it locally-made space rockets, battleships, atomic power stations or India-assembled sophisticated fighters from the Soviet Union, its main arms supplier. They also glow about India's position as a leading member of the Non-Aligned Movement and its status as a regional superpower.

And they are sure that India, with its massive population and resources, is well on its way to being a leading power on the world stage comparable to China. At the same time India's burgeoning middle class — an estimated 80 million people — is regarded as one of the world's last great consumer markets.

ABOVE: Dapper regiments at the annual Republic Day in New Delhi when India proudly shows off its latest military hardware and martial might.

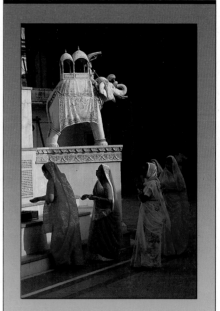

India
and her
Culture

THE ARTISTIC LEGACY

India's spectacular artistic heritage began 6,000 years ago when ancient tribesmen began fashioning buxom mother goddesses from clay: the earliest surviving artifacts to have been dug up at the Indus Valley sites in present-day Pakistan. It was not until the Mauryan age in the third century BC that India experienced a burst of artistic brilliance, notably in Buddhist art during the reign of Ashoka. The remarkable stone-carving of this period can be seen at its most impressive at Sarnath and Sanchi, in Madhya Pradesh. Succeeding dynasties — the Sungas and Satavahanas — adapted Mauryan motifs and techniques and were very keen on using symbols to indicate Buddha's all-seeing eye, such as a footprint, the sacred wheel and the stupa.

The next artistic wave was Alexander the Great's legacy from his subcontinental foray near present-day Peshawar: Gandharan art was classic East meets West, a mixture of Greco-Roman know-how and Buddhist inspiration. Gandharan art is recognizable by its classical Grecian-style torsos, draped toga-like folds that are thought to be the inspiration behind saris and *dhotis*, and its "avant-garde" depiction of Buddha in human form. At the same time, a major school developed in Mathura, mid-way between Delhi and Agra, that reflected the revival of Hinduism and also featured busty *Iyakshinis*, or nymphs who were the dumpy forerunners to the sophisticated ladies of Khajuraho.

During the "golden age" of the Guptas (AD 320–600), an artistic renaissance created the so-called classical style of Indian art. The paintings and sculpture of this time have a fluid and sensuous look, with a consummate fascination for detail yet contriving an effect of utter simplicity. During this period images of Buddha's stylized attitudes, clothing and hand positions evolved to perfection, and are today mimicked by modern mass-produced images in Buddhist countries. Just as the Guptas were taking Buddhist art to its zenith, Dravidian craftsmen in the south were developing a strongly Hindu tradition with new sculptural forms crafted in stone and bronze.

The next millennium saw a steady evolution from stylized, rather static Buddhist art towards almost decadent freneticism as the medieval Hindu revival entered full swing, perhaps best illustrated at the rock-cut caves of Ajanta and Ellora in modern Maharashtra. By then, sculpture had become an inseparable part of architecture, with every surface dripping with carved activity — as seen at the Hoysala temples at Karanataka, the Sun Temple at Konarak, and the celestially carnal temples at Khajuharo.

The arrival of the temple-bulldozing Muslims undoubtedly wiped out great chunks of the Hindu artistic tradition. In their zeal to build empires these early invaders had little time for art, and only under the Mughal Emperor Akbar did a truly creative style of art emerge. This was miniature painting, concocted from a blend of Islamic and Persian styles, and primarily depicting portraits, courtly life, battles and under Jehangir, exquisite wildlife and nature studies were produced. An artist's palette included malachite, lapis lazuli, gold, silver and an ingenious substance called peori, a yellow dye extracted from the urine of cows fed

on mango leaves.

Throughout the Hindu states of north India, artists were quick to take their cue from the Mughals, combining their own religious and artistic traditions with those established by the Mughal school. Provincial styles differ greatly and are divided into different schools, notably Rajastani or Mewar, Jammu or Pahari, Basolhi and Kangra, all former hill states of the Punjab.

Although best remembered for their remarkable architecture, the Mughals represent the last great period of exclusively Indian artistic

ABOVE: Stylized stone carving dating from the Hoysala dynasty (1006–1310) who marked a peak in Dravidian temple architecture that can be seen at Somnathpur, Belur and Halebid. OPPOSITE: A towering *goporum*, or gateway, typically adorns the giant temple complexes of South India.

activity. During the British Raj, the British East India Company commissioned Indian artists to paint picturesque landscapes in oils and water-colors, and this became known as the Company school. Modern Indian painting gained impetus in the 30's with the so-called Bengali school, a distinct style of painting developed by a group of artists who took inspiration from traditional water-color techniques and folk art motifs. India's most famous twentieth century artists include Amrita Shergill, M.F. Husain and Krishen Khanna, whose work is rooted in the Indian tradition, yet reflect western influences.

THE SACRED FLAME

THE RELIGIONS OF INDIA

The nation's founding Prime Minister, Jawaharlal Nehru once described India as "a madhouse of religions". He was only half in jest. Religion is the heart-beat of the nation, and its influence, symbolism and superstition pervade every facet of life.

Four of the world's most influential religions — Hinduism, Buddhism, Islam and Christianity — have flourished on Indian soil, the first two born in India. In addition, India also saw the rise of Jainism, Sikhism and countless minor sects and tribal cults, as well as playing host to Judaism and Zororastrianism.

India has long been perceived as a land of mystic wisdom and spirituality, standing in

The spectrum of faith in India is as infinitely varied, startling and mysterious as the country itself. ABOVE: Totemic image of Kali, the fearful Hindu goddess of destruction. OPPOSITE TOP: Sikh clerics within the exquisitely ornate sacred citadel of the Golden Temple at Amritsar. OPPOSITE BOTTOM: Unorthodox Hindu temple with Belgian chandeliers and slumbering devotees in Goa.

contrast to Western society with its emphasis on material gain. Yet outsiders often find it near bewildering to grasp how important religion is to the average Indian — as sustaining and inseparable to their existence as air, water and food. As casual spectators to this fairground of faiths, tourists will catch glimpses of its influences almost every day they spend in India. Glittering ornate temples are found even in the most remote villages, some ancient and exquisite, others modern and gaudy, but always atmospheric — busy with devotees making *puja* offerings to brightly painted deities, chiming temple bells, and filling the nostrils with wafts of incense and marigold blossoms. In the courtyard, sacred poems are read, hymns are chanted, dances are performed. Just as noticeably, on Fridays, the Muslim Sabbath, the nation's mosques throng with white-capped Muslims who chant verses from the Koran, bow and cup their hands to Allah. Drivers adorn their dashboards with incense sticks, flowers and the images of their faith — Sikhs enshrining the image of Guru Nanak, their religion's founding father; Hindus painting swastikas, the ancient Aryan symbol around gaudy pictures of favorite gods or goddess. Many homes have shrines, or even a room set aside for worship. The Indian calendar is peppered with religious festivals, some of them drawing pilgrims by the million. The Hindu religion has the most — 360 with an average of a festival a day. Just as important are the innumerable commonplace rites and observances performed almost unconsciously each day — a Hindu's pre-dawn *puja*, a Muslim's Mecca-facing five prayers, a Sikh piling up his hair and re-winding his turban.

Indian society is dominated by Hindus, who make some 83 percent of the population; Muslims comprise some 10 percent; Sikhs and Christians combined make up a further 5 percent, while a handful of other minorities, namely Jains, Parsis and Buddhists, make up the remainder.

HINDUISM

The world's most ancient living faith, Hinduism is not so much a religion as a system of philosophy. It has more adherents than any other religion in Asia: more than 500 million Indians are Hindus.

Although its origins can be traced back to the fertility cult of the Indus Valley civilization, Hinduism formally emerged as a distinct religious tradition with the Sanskrit-speaking Aryans invaders some 3,500 years ago. It is rare among major religions since it neither claims a specific founder nor can point to a single "holy book" as its ultimate spiritual reference. Instead it has many — the earliest being the four sacred

Vedas, notably the Rig Veda, composed between 1600 and 1000 BC, formally marking the birth of Hindu mythology. Other scriptures include the Upanishads, the Bhagavad Gita (described by Mahatma Gandhi as his "spiritual dictionary"), the Puranas, and two remarkable epic poems, the Mahabharata and the Ramayana — written in a tradition that would later be echoed in Homer's Iliad and Odyssey.

Hinduism has survived numerous periods of both prosperity and decline, demonstrating a resilient capacity to absorb and assimilate opposing faiths, rather than forcefully seeking converts. Its central view of religious tolerance was en

capsulated in the Upanishads, (800–400 BC) which states: "The Great God is One, and the learned call him by different names." Far from diluting itself out of existence, Hinduism seemed to gain strength from its flexibility and religious synthesis. It allows an astonishing freedom of worship. Under its umbrella can be found monotheists, polytheists, pantheists, totemists, animists, agnostics and even the odd atheist!

Despite its inherent pluralism, Hinduism has several essential beliefs that tie the various creeds together. The ultimate objective of life is essentially life's renunciation of life by achieving moksha, or perfection, thus breaking the soul's cycle of birth and re-birth. The passage leading to this desirable state is determined by an individual's karma, which roughly translates as "actions", but meaning a law of cause and effect whereby a person's deeds in this and previous lives tally up to influence their status in the next life; and dharma, an individual's moral duties to perform in life. Both are inextricably bound up with the concept of reincarnation, which offers both solace and hope in the belief that present troubles are the wages of a former life's sins and that pious and unselfish actions hold the key to a better life in the future.

The rules for reincarnation can be extraordinarily complex. Some 2,000 years ago, the great

legal scholar Manu wrote learned treatises codifying ancient precepts of law and sacred duty — then punctuated them with digressions on what kind of rebirth is punishment for which sin. For example, if a man steals silk he becomes a partridge; if he steals cotton cloth he becomes a crane; if linen, a frog, and so on.

Although the larger esoteric concept of attaining an unblemished soul is important, Hinduism has its feet firmly on the ground, and encourages its adherents in kama, or earthly pleasures, including sex, and artha, or prosperity and material wealth. According to Hindu beliefs, life passes through four stages — the stage of the learner, demanding self-control and abstinence; the stage of the householder, when kama and artha are healthy pursuits; the stage of detachment or gradual turning away from worldly things; and the stage of ascetic renunciation, when a person becomes devoted only to spiritual meditation and yoga, preparing for moksha.

An interesting feature of Hinduism is its cult of its peripatetic sadhus or holy men, who are rarely seen outside their mountain retreats where they endure great hardships to show renunciation of the material world, occasionally congregating at large religious festivals. Foreign visitors to India have for centuries been mystified by sadhus' bizarre acts, such as lying on beds of nails and being buried for weeks on end. Many deliberately cultivate their bedraggled appearance by smearing their half-naked bodies with ash and growing their hair and beard in matted dreadlocks. Many brandish tridents in obeisance to Lord Shiva to whom they ritually smoke hashish.

A Pantheon of Gods

Hinduism recognizes an ultimate omnipotent force, known as the Supreme Universal Soul, or Parabrahma, who has three physical manifestations — Brahma, the Creator, Vishnu, the Preserver and Shiva the Destroyer. All three are represented with four arms, while Brahma also has four heads to depict his all-seeing wisdom and he is said to have delivered the four sacred Vedas from each of his mouths.

Orthodox Hinduism is divided into two main sects: Shaiviam, comprised of those who worship Shiva, and Vaishnaiviam, comprised of those who worship Vishnu. Unlike these two, the other member of holy trinity, Brahma has almost no temples, save for a unique shrine at Pushkar, where you can see his "stead" or so-called vehicle, the sea turtle. This trinity symbolizes the main basic stages of life — birth, life and death — and presides over a vast pantheon of some 330 million Hindu gods. Despite such a profuse array of gods, most people concentrate their devotional energies on just a select few.

48

Vishnu, the most revered of the gods, possesses cosmic powers more formidable than Einstein's Theory of Relativity: when Vishnu sleeps, the universe goes into spasms of agitated flux that only normalize when he wakes up again. Vishnu is usually depicted sitting on his vehicle, a human-faced eagle called a "garuda". Vishnu has already visited earth in nine incarnations (*avatars*); as a fish, a tortoise, a boar, a half-man, a beggar-dwarf and as the axe-wielding Parasurama, and is scheduled to return once more as the horse-headed Kalki. On his seventh call, he came as Rama, with his Herculean mission to destroy the demon king

incarnation was Buddha himself, apparently the result of an inventive ploy to lure breakaway Buddhists back to the Hindu fold.

Shiva's main symbol is the cobra, the deadly snake of death and destruction, and he usually rides around on the bull Nandi. He is worshipped as the Lingam, the phallic symbol of creativity and fertility. Shiva's formidable temper resulted in the odd appearance of his elephant-headed son Ganesh. When Shiva returned from many years absence, he hoped to surprise his beloved wife Parvati in her bedroom. Instead he discovered her talking to a young man—imagining himself cuckolded and

of Ravanna of Lanka (Sri Lanka). The remarkable story of his success, aided by the faithful monkey-god Hanuman became one of India's greatest epics, the Ramayana. Vishnu made his eighth visit as Krishna, the handsome blue-skinned cow-herder god, who like Christ is said to have lived on earth in human form. Unlike Christ however, Krishna was something of a Casanova, who decked himself out in yellow silk, peacock feathers and jasmine-bud garlands. He was the heart-flutter of all the Mathura *gopis* (milk-maids), whom he married en masse after delivering them from the clutches of the demon king Naraka. Krishna is said to have had some 16,000 girlfriends, but Radha was his favorite and their romantic love was woven into Hindu myth to symbolize the relationship between the human soul with the Divine Spirit. Vishnu's ninth and most daring

not recognizing his own son, he furiously swiped off Ganesh's head with a sword. Mortified to discover that he had decapitated his own child, Shiva replaced the severed head with that of the first creature he could find — an elephant. Thus "lucky" Ganesh re-emerged as one of the most popular of all deities, affectionately known as the "Divine Remover of Obstacles", whose animal vehicle is the bandicoot or rat.

Each of the Hindu trinity has a consort, representing the feminine side of their powers. Brahma is married to his own daughter, Saraswati, Goddess of Knowledge, who travels about

ABOVE: This pilgrim takes elaborate measures to preserve her precious cargo of water from the Ganges River in Varanasi, which Hindus believe has the power to cleanse the soul. OPPOSITE: Restoring the frescoes of a Rajput temple requires both skill and a certain religious fervor.

on a swan. Vishnu's consort is the gorgeous Lakshmi, the Lotus Goddess of wealth and prosperity, Shiva's first wife was Sati, but after her tragic demise as India's first suttee victim, he married the beautiful Parvati, Goddess of Cosmic Energy, whose soul splintered into innumerable incarnations — Kali, the terrifying Goddess of Destruction, capable of inflicting disease and misery, but also to heal and bless, depicted with a necklace of writhing snakes and skulls; Durga, the Slayer of the Buffalo Demon, a female warrior usually depicted riding around on a tiger and waving weapons from each of her ten hands; and Shakti, the Goddess of Cre-

ative Energy. As well as Ganesh, Parvati had another son by Shiva, the six-headed god of war, Kartikeya.

Modern-day Hinduism is steeped in elaborate legends about the courageous exploits and playful idiosyncrasies of these flamboyant, larger-than-life gods and goddesses, as well as heroes and demons. Mythology is inseparable to all Indian art — sculpture, paintings, classical music and dance — and the tradition continues to be kept alive today through fairs, festivals and folk songs.

Caste

One of the most pervasive aspects of Hinduism is caste, the schematized division of society into four castes or *varnas*, or "colors": Brahmans, (priests and teachers), Kshatriyas (leaders and warriors), Vaishyas (merchants) and Sudras (farmers, craftsmen and laborers). Caste was invented as a form of social apartheid by the fair-skinned Aryans, (see THE ARRIVAL OF THE ARYANS, page 23). A more romantic explanation for the system is that the four castes sprang from the mouth (Brahmans), arms (Kshatriyas), thighs (Vaishyas) and feet (Sudras) of the creator, Brahma. Over the centuries, these four categories of caste splintered into thousands of sub-castes or *jatis*, so that their original job-defini-

tions have lost their meaning. Only the Brahmans, by virtue of their high-caste status, have preserved their exclusivity, and regardless of their profession, they tend to occupy privileged positions within society.

Inextricably bound to the notion of caste are the concepts of purity and pollution. Higher castes, especially Brahmans, have their lives regulated by a bewilderingly complex laundry list of prohibitions. Cardinal "don't do's" include the eating of beef and any contact with lower-castes or items of food, water or objects touched by them. High-born castes often refuse to perform tasks that is deemed polluting. This is why many Indian households employ a bevy of servants — a Brahmia cook, a Sudra sweeper, and sub-Sudra toilet cleaner and so on. To transgress these rules requires rigorous ritual, such as bathing in holy waters, and extra time spent at the temple. However the most infamous aspect of the caste system lies outside its boundaries — untouchability. Traditionally, untouchables have always been considered social pariahs, and designated tasks considered lowly and contaminating to all other castes, such as sweeping houses and streets, cleaning sewers and removing corpses. Since independence, the new constitution abolished untouchability, renaming members of the out-caste, harijans or "children of god" and giving them full democratic and human rights.

However breaking customs that have existed for thousands of years is difficult. Caste still determines the kind of work a man accepts, the woman he will marry, the people he will and won't mix with and the type of religious observances he will perform.

Religion in Revolt

From Hinduism emerged two different breakaway ideologies — one propounded by Gautama Buddha and the other by Vardhamana Mahavira, each opposed to extravagance, hierarchical rule and violence. Both philosophers were Kshatriyas, who stood against the complications and in-built prejudices of caste and advocated a return to a simpler, more direct lifestyle, and boundless compassion for all beings — an ascetic approach focused on the belief in the "One Soul", namely the belief that everything that exists within the material world lives on an equal plateau.

JAINISM

Jainism was the first major sect to rise in rebellion from Hinduism and was founded around 500 BC by Vardhamana Mahavira, an older contemporary of Buddha and the last of the 24th Jain saints or *tirthankaras*. He rejected the Hindu gospel that a Supreme Creator had engineered the universe, believing instead that it was infinite and eternal. Mahavira preached the complete renunciation of desire and the material world as the most direct path to spiritual salvation, encouraging his adherents to follow the path of asceticism, austerity and non-violence. Jain monks became noted for their extreme asceticism, many of them adopting the habits of the Hindu sadhus or holy men, taking to the road dressed in just a loin-cloth with just a begging bowl and a stave as possessions. The Jain's cardinal doctrine of ahimsa, non-injury to any living creature stems from their belief that all matter is eternal and that every object has a soul, even pebbles or a grain of sand. Plants and trees have at least two souls, while animals are thought to have three. This leads some of them to wear thin muslin masks over their mouths to prevent them from breathing in small insects. These devotees do not eat after dark in case insects should accidentally fall into their food and die. Many sweep the ground before them as they advance to avoid treading on small creatures.

The Jains are just as preoccupied as Hindus with the theory of rebirth, and becoming a monk is thought to provide a fast track to release. Lay Jains traveling the slower route, try to refrain from telling lies, being devious and from indulging in sensual pleasures.

In the first century AD the Jains split into two sects: the white-clad Shevetambaras and the misogynist, sky-clad Digambaras. The latter were literally "sky-clad", so zealously disdainful of possessions that they refused to don clothes at all, and also regarded women the scourge of humanity, whose charms were evil temptation to those trying to tread the path of straight and narrow. Jain temples are frequently exquisite, with ornately carved marble pillars and sculptures. The most impressive of these can be seen in Rajasthan (Mount Abu), Gujarat (Palitana and Junagadh) and Bombay, the three main Jain centers. The Jains have more than three million adherents in India today. Despite their ascetic beliefs, the Jain community has a strong presence in the business world as traders, bankers and philanthropists, and run rest houses for pilgrims, homes for widows and orphans and even hospitals for sick birds.

BUDDHISM

The Buddhist religion was the second religious schism to emerge from Hinduism, and proved far more influential. The Lord Buddha was born Siddhartha Gautama, the son of a local prince, between 563 and 556 BC in what is now Nepal. Living at first in luxury, he had married and

fathered a son before at the age of 29, he left the palace to embark on a long quest for truth, human mortality and suffering. After several years of rigorous asceticism, he sat down under a bo tree at Uruvela, near Gaya in Bihar state, and achieved "enlightenment" or nirvana. He spent the next 45 years of his life preaching his new philosophy. His message was that everyone, not just priests or ascetics, was capable of aspiring to enlightenment in their own lifetime, without having to passively await a better incarnation in the next life.

Gautama's answer to the problem of suffering was contained in his "Four Noble Truths".

In this doctrine, he offered the diagnosis, that human suffering is rooted in terminal dissatisfaction and insatiable desire, and the solution, that in order to remove suffering you must escape desire, and that the way to escape desire is to follow the Eight-fold Path. This path details the ways to become disentangled from all desire for worldly gratification.

At Sarnath's Deer Park near Benares (Varanasi) Gautama met five Brahmans who became his disciples. Called the "Buddha" or the Enlightened One, Gautama reputedly died at the age of eighty, having eaten poisoned food.

ABOVE: An infamous Indian "sacred" cow, elaborately clad for the harvest festival of Pongol in South India. OPPOSITE: An elephant fresco in Shekhavati district, Rajasthan.

Buddhism was clearly a radical departure from Hinduism or Jainism, which held that rebirth, rewards and deliverance came after death. Instead Buddhism renounced the need for extreme asceticism, and instead emphasized living in the present.

Buddhism at first flourished in India, adopted by the great Emperor Asokha (231–198 BC). It was carried to every part of his extensive empire, and spread in time to Burma, Thailand, Sri Lanka, Korea, China, Vietnam, Nepal, Tibet, Central Asia and notably in present-day Japan.

Buddhism was soon divided by a schism, leading to two main schools of Buddhist thought. The Hinayana or "lesser vehicle" held that enlightenment was an individual pursuit and referred to Buddha in external symbols (the lotus for his birth, the bo tree for his enlightenment, the wheel of law for his first sermon, and the stupa for his enshrinenment). The Mahayana or "greater vehicle" held that it was a collective one, with the ultimate aim of bringing humanity to salvation, who took Buddha's last words as gospel, "Be a lamp unto yourselves, be a refuge unto yourselves, seek no refuge outside of yourselves".

Buddhism later waned in popularity in India, the land of its birth, largely because of the challenges it faced from Hinduism and Islam. Although Hinduism and Buddhism were almost diametrically opposed theories, these religions and Jainism still co-existed relatively peacefully for many centuries until the advent of Islam.

ISLAM

Muslims are the largest religious minority group in India, with more than 95 million adherents, almost the same as that of Pakistan. They are mainly scattered throughout northern India. Only in Kashmir are they a regional majority. The Muslims first came to India as powerful, iconoclastic conquerors, making the bulk of their converts from low-caste Hindus. Today the most visible legacies of Islam can be seen in the nation's Mughal forts, mosques and domes, in the Mughali cuisine and art.

Arab traders sowed the first seeds of Islam in India when they beached their sailing vessels along the southern coast during the seventh century AD — bringing news of the recently-founded faith of the Prophet Muhammed. They also brought the Muslim canon, the Koran, a collection of messages from Allah (God) spoken to Muhammed. The overwhelming feature of Islam was its forceful zeal to spread the word — by the sword if required. Beginning in Arabia, Islam spread east over the centuries and eventually took firm root in three continents. Unlike the Hindu religion, which requires its adherents to be born Hindus, conversion to Islam is easy — to become a Muslim merely requires saying the words "There is no god but Allah and Muhammed is his prophet."

Early in its history, Islam experienced a schism that remains to this day. The majority of Muslims are Sunnites, whose allegiance is to the descendants of Muhammed's direct successor, the Caliph — while other Muslims are Shias or Shi'ites who follow the descendants of the prophet's son-in-law, Ali. Both aspire to make a pilgrimage to Mecca — the prophet Muhammed's birthplace in AD 570—and become a haji.

SIKHISM

The Sikh religion is fairly new, having broken away from Hinduism in the the sixteenth century. Sikhs became increasingly martial towards the end of the seventh century due to Muslim persecution. The Mughal Emperor Aurangzeb so detested the Sikhs that he offered a reward of gold coins for any citizen who brought him a severed head of a Sikh. Provoked by this, the sixth Guru of the line, Guru Gobind Singh (1675–1708) turned the Sikh religion into a military brotherhood, whose members all took the surname Singh or "Lion". He enjoined male Sikhs to observe and wear "the five K's" or *Kakkari* (symbols): *kesh*, uncut hair (normally wrapped in a turban) and beard; *kara*, a steel bangle; *kachh,* short boxer shorts; *kangha,* a wooden or ivory comb and a *kirpan,* a dagger.

Although Sikhs make up only two percent of the population, with some 14 million adherents, they are a very proud and visible community in India. Sikhism grew in response to frictions between Hindus and Muslims in the Punjab, and was founded by Guru Nanak (1444–1538). Sikhism originated as a bhakti or pacifist caste-rejecting movement, seeking to fuse the best from both Hinduism and Islam. It is based on the teachings of ten gurus and contains its essential message in the Sikh Bible, the Granth Sahib. The Sikhs have one god, have temples known as *gurdwaras*, and have had a total of 10 gurus whose collected writings, as well as various Hindu and Muslim scripts form the Granth Sahib. The holiest Sikh shrine is the Golden Temple in Amritsar, in northern Punjab state.

Sikhs are notable for their pragmatism, their earthy good humor, capacity for hard work and skill in mechanical matters.

ZOROASTRIANISM

The tiny community of Zoroastrians, more popularly known as Parsis, are mostly concentrated in Bombay, and are thought to number around 10,000. Their religion is one of the world's oldest, founded by the prophet Zoroaster in modern-day Iran around 800 BC. After the Islamic conquest of Iran many intrepid Zoroastrians left their homes and sought refuge in India. The first group is said to have reached Diu, in Gujarat around AD 766. There was no tension or religious conflict probably because they made no attempts to convert. They were considered desirably fair-skinned and they were astute — as they are still considered to be — in business and intellectual matters.

Their scripture is the Zend-Avesta, which describes the on-going battle between good and evil, and their god is Ahura Mazda, who is symbolized

century of Christ's own lifetime. St Thomas, one of the Disciples, arrived in Kerala in AD 54, and spread the Syrian Christian faith, so that Christianity was by no means unknown when Catholic and Protestant missionaries made converts from various Portuguese, Dutch and English settlements during the sixteenth century, mainly amongst low-caste Hindus. Today India has some 18 million Christians, many of them living in the ex-Portuguese enclave of Goa, as well as a quarter of the population of Kerala. Two small north-eastern states — Mizoram and Nagaland — were also sufficiently impressed by intrepid Christian missionaries to convert in large numbers.

by fire. Parsis worship nature's elements and are fire-worshippers, keeping the symbol of their belief burning in their temples. They are probably best known for their rather macabre habit of leaving their dead in "Towers of Silence" to be devoured by vultures, thus avoiding polluting the sacred purity of the elements — fire, earth, water or air —by burying or cremation.

The numbers of Parsis are on the wane today due to intermarriage becoming more common. Indira Gandhi was married to a Parsi but her son Rajiv could not be a Parsi even if he wanted to — it takes two to tango and two Parsi parents to make a Parsi child.

In Kerala again, the Jews of Cochin should get a special mention — their ancestry dates back to 973 BC when King Solomon's merchant fleet began trading for spices and other fabled treasures. Scholars say that the Jews first settled in Craganore, along Kerala's Malabar Coast, soon after the Babylonian conquest of Judea in 586 BC. The immigrants were well received and the Dravidian king of Cochin granted a title and small principality to one Joseph Rabban, a Jewish leader. Although only a handful of so-called White Jews remain in Cochin, it's possible to see their synagogue, which is the oldest in the Commonwealth.

CHRISTIANS AND JEWS

Many people are surprised to learn that Christianity first took root in India within half a

ABOVE: A diptych of elderly bibliophiles. LEFT, A monocled Sikh huddled over the holy Granth Sahib and RIGHT, a Rajput gent lost between the pages of his yellowing book.

INDIAN PLEASURES

FESTIVALS AND FAIRS

The Indian calendar brims with thousands of festivals and many fairs all year round. For its most special days, India explodes with dazzling color, religious pageantry, trumpets, fireworks, tinsel, feasting, glorious costumes, brocade-showered idols, and magic outdoor processions of caparisoned elephants. There are festivals to celebrate everything under the sun, from

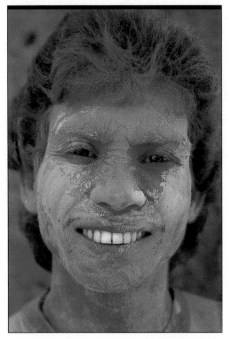

the latest military hardware to the arrival of the monsoons, even festivals to honor sacred cows and cobras. There are Muslim, Sikh, Buddhist, Jain, Parsi and Christian festivals. But the infinite pantheon of Hindu gods generate the most. Every temple has its own special festival, often occasions when its deities take a bath, require a ritual anointment, or are re-united with a spouse.

In a nutshell, Indian festivals are an excellent excuse for most Indians to put their work aside, forget their hardships, dress up and have fun. The major arts festivals attract the country's best performers of classical and folk dance, music and theater. Many attract thousands of pilgrims, strolling players, and the merely curious, from all over India. The party spirit extends to all aspects of Indian life — from cities to villages, from the annual Republic Day parade to individual wedding celebrations.

The dates of most festivals are calculated according to the Indian lunar calendar, and can be determined only by around October the previous year. At this time your nearest Government of India tourist office should have the full list of upcoming festival dates.

The most interesting and worthwhile festivals and fairs, together with their approximate dates and the best place to see them are listed below. You'll find more details in the relevant section covering the destination.

JANUARY

Pongol, or **Sankranti,** is south India's most exuberant harvest festival. It lasts three days and is best seen in Tamil Nadu and Karnataka. Villagers decorate cattle with fragrant blossoms, ghee, and mango leaves, feeding them "pongol", or sweet rice, and parade them in lively processions with drums and music. Its highlight is a sort of Dravidian rodeo, when local lads try to wrest bundles of currency from the horns of ferocious bulls.

Republic Day, on January 26, is an important national festival celebrated in all over India, but the most spectacular is in New Delhi: a magnificent military parade with regiments in full dress, bands, richly caparisoned camels and elephants, floats and colorful folk dancers rolling along Rajpath. It is followed by a two-day festival of music and dance, and culminates with the famous dusk "Beating the Retreat" held on January 29 at Raj Bhawan.

JANUARY/FEBRUARY

Vasant Panchami honors Saraswati, the Hindu goddess of knowledge, and is celebrated with colorful processions and kite-flying, best seen in West Bengal. Paint-brushes, ball-point pens and musical instruments are reverently placed at Saraswati's shrine, as if to encourage continued creativity.

Float Festival is held in the famous temple town of Madurai in south India, marking the birth anniversary of Tirumali Nayak, the city's seventeenth century ruler.

Desert Festival, Jaislamer's popular three-day festival coincides with the full moon and brims with a carnival Rajput atmosphere. Highlights include camel polo, camel races, turban-tying competitions, desert music and dance. (see page 138.)

Nagaur Livestock Fair, located half a day's drive from Jodphur, rewards adventurous travelers with four days of camel races, livestock competitions and colorful Rajasthani dancing and singing. Old India hands rate it just as highly as its better known cousin, the Push-kar Fair.

Goa's Carnival (see page 202) is no longer as exuberantly spectacular as in former days, but still attracts devotees for its free-flowing feni and party atmosphere.

FEBRUARY/MARCH
Shivrati marks the day when Hindus across India pay their respects to Shiva, the religion's father figure. The most colorful pageantry occurs at the largest Shiva temples at Khajuraho,

foreigners may not enjoy the experience of being sloshed with buckets of paint from rooftop pranksters. Go prepared like everyone else by purchasing plenty of powder, paint and water-pistols, and wear clothes that can be thrown away the next day. Don't despair — you may resemble a walking artist's palette for days, or even weeks later — but the color will eventually come out!

Khajuraho Dance Festival is held early March in the famous temple, with a week-long program of evening performances by the country's best artists to a backdrop of flood-lit temples and glittering stars.

Varanasi, Mandi, Chidambaram and Kashmir. Devotees fast for a day, then fall upon dates, fruits, nuts, sweet potatoes and rice — Shiva's favorite snack.

Holi is India's color-doused version of April Fools day. Spring is celebrated with explosive Bacchanalian, paint-sqirting revelry that breaks down all traditional barriers of caste, religion in an atmosphere of playful flirtation. Picasso never visited India, but he was so impressed by the idea of Holi that he once staged it at his Spanish villa. It's best to soak up the carnival atmosphere of a "real" rural Holi in one of the smaller Rajasthan towns, where you'll be drawn into exuberant folk dance, music and gentle pelting with clouds of saffron, emerald, turquoise, pink and red powder. Large cities are often not so much fun — and unwary

MARCH/APRIL
Gangaur is best seen in Rajasthan, especially Jaipur and Udaipur, West Bengal and Orissa. It pays tribute to Shiva's wife Parvati, in her incarnation of Gangaur, goddess of marital happiness, abundance and fertility. *Gauri* means yellow, the color of ripened wheat. In Jaipur, idols of Shiva and Gangaur are paraded on floats pulled by caparisoned horses and elephants, amid trumpeting and singing. Everywhere else, marriage parties add to the atmosphere.

Festival fun. ABOVE: Sikhs LEFT don traditional attire to celebrate the birthday of Guru Gobind Singh. RIGHT: At Pushkar Camel Fair. OPPOSITE: A smiling paint-splattered youth after a busy morning of Holi festivities. OVERLEAF: Dazzlingly colorful elephant parade in Jaipur.

Mahavir Jayanti is a Jain festival dedicated to Mahavira, the 24th Jain Thirthankara or saint, best seen at Jain shrines at Jain centers in Gujarat or at Mount Abu in Rajasthan.

APRIL/MAY
Urs Festival Ajmer Held for six days in April to May, the Urs Festival is a dramatic annual display of *quwwali* singing, exuberant fairs and feasts (see page 130).

Baisakhi celebrates the beginning of the Hindu solar New Year. Hindus throng to the sacred Ganges River to bathe and worship, since the

goddess Meenakshi and Shiva with ten days of non-stop revelry in the courtyards of the famous Meenakshi Temple. Artists dance, priests chant, children dress as gods, and musicians play enchanting devotional music.

MAY-JUNE
Buddha Purnima celebrates Buddha birth, death and enlightenment, and is best at the famous Buddhist centers of Sarnath and Bodhgaya.

Hemis Festival is held at the largest monastery in Ladakh, and celebrates the birth anniversary of the Guru Padmasambhava. Masked dances,

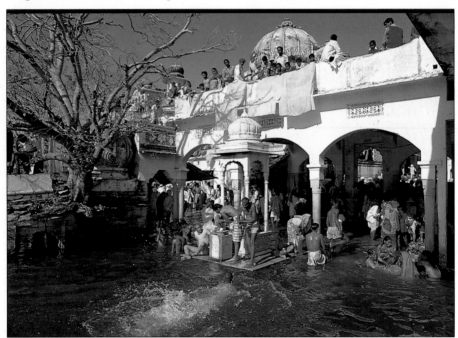

goddess Ganga is thought to have descended to earth on this day many millennia ago. Festive processions are best seen in the holy cities along the Ganges river in north India, as well as in Srinagar's Mughal Gardens and in Tamil Nadu. Sikhs also celebrate it to commemorate the day in 1689 that Guru Gobind Singh founded the Khalsa or militant brotherhood of the Sikhs. In Punjab farmers start harvesting and perform the *bhangra* dance, as wild and vigorous as that of the cossacks.

Pooram in Trichur, Kerala, is one of India's temple festival highlights with its 30 decorated elephants, dhoti-clad priests, trumpets and fireworks (see page 329).

Meenakshi Kalaynam in Madurai, celebrates the annual mock-marriage of the "fish-eyed"

fairs and the ornately-dressed Ladakhis are the highlights (see page 181).

JUNE/JULY
Id-ul-Fitr, also known as **Ramazan-Id**, is a major Muslim celebration which marks the end of Ramazan, the Islamic month of fasting. Thousands of devout Muslims stream into the major mosques to pray, then rejoice and feast. It's best seen in Delhi, Lucknow, Hyderabad and Calcutta.

Rath Yatra, held in Puri, Orissa, is the most spectacular of all temple festivals, with cast of devout thousands, like an Indian version of a Cecil de Mille epic. Held in honor of Lord Jagannath, three enormous temple chariots carrying the idols of Jagannath and his siblings, Balabhadra and Subhadra, are dragged by sweating devotees (see page 252).

JULY/AUGUST

Naag Panchami is held in honor of Naga, the great thousand-headed serpent on which Vishnu reclined in contemplation. It's most dramatic in Jodhpur, where giant colorful effigies of Naga are erected, and women worship visiting snake charmers for fertility. Throughout India, cobras are fed with milk and sweets.

Teej celebrates both the onset of the monsoon and the reunion of Shiva and his wife Parvati, (Gangaur). Nubile girls dress up in tinsel-fringed saris, jewelry and bright green veils, playfully

ful pageantry takes place in Kulu, Mysore, and West Bengal. In Delhi and Varanasi it is known as **Ram Lila**.

Diwali, or the "festival of lights" traditionally takes place on the full moon night after Dussehra. It's the gayest and most riotous of all Indian festivals, with a night-long display of fireworks, illuminations and general pageantry. Throughout India, houses are cleaned and repainted to honor Lakshmi, the goddess of wealth and the home, then bedecked with hundreds of oil-lamps. It's best seen in north India and at Mysore in the south.

push each other on garland-bedecked swings, and pray for a faithful loving husband. It's best seen at Jaipur, where gaily, vividly dressed villagers swarm to see the pageantry as caparisoned elephants, dancers and musicians escort the Parvati idol from her parent's home into Shiva's waiting arms.

Independence Day on August 15, is celebrated all over India, notably in New Delhi.

SEPTEMBER/OCTOBER

Ganapati (Ganesh Chaturthi) honors the elephant-headed god of good luck inspires grand processions everywhere, but especially in Bombay (see page 197).

Dussehra is a 10-day festival celebrated with performances across India, but the most color-

NOVEMBER/DECEMBER

Pushkar's Cattle Fair. A definite "must-see" tourist highlight (see page 130).

Christmas Day, December 25. Exotic piety is most spectacular in Goa, where glorious sixteenth-century cathedrals stage candle-lit mass, hymns and pompous religious celebrations.

Madras Dance and Arts Festivals lasts from mid December to early January and offers a potpourri of excellent performances by the nation's best artists.

OPPOSITE: Villagers undergo a ritual bath in the holy lake at Pushkar. ABOVE: Naked Naga sadhus, clad only in marigold garlands and Rastafarian dreadlocks converge at Hardwar for the Kumbh Mela.

FESTIVAL FOOTNOTE

India's **Kumbh Mela** is the most ancient and spectacular religious carnival on the planet, revealing to astonished Western eyes all that is most mysterious, bizarre and awesome about Hinduism, a faith that was born some 3,000 years ago. It is held every three years consecutively in one of the four places: Allahabad (Uttar Pradesh), Nasik (Maharashtra), Ujian (Madhya Pradesh) and Hardwar (Uttar Pradesh). Ancient legend relates that demons once stole sacred nectar of immortality from the gods in a

kumbh, or vessel, and during the ensuing battle between the gods and the thieves, the nectar spilled at 12 spots in the universe — eight in the heavens and four on earth — forming the four most sacred Indian cities. The Kumbh Mela begins when the astrological positions of the sun and moon are most auspicious, and millions of pilgrims and thousands of holy men (sadhus) of every order descend in order to bathe in holy rivers, believing the holy rivers suddenly run with life-preserving nectar. Ash-smeared, leopard skin-clad "gurus" preside over captive audiences; "god" children bestow regal blessings; naked ascetics perform miraculous feats of endurance amid a temporary city erected from tents on huge sand belts near the river. The holiest of all, the Kumbh Melas occurs every 12 years at Allahabad, the confluence of the Ganges, Yamuna and the mythical Saraswati rivers. The next Kumbh Mela will be held at Nasik in 1992.

DANCE AND MUSIC

India has extraordinarily rich traditions of both classical and folk dance and music, woven inextricably together. It also offers a wealth of gifted artists, and performance festivals, some-

times against the original backdrops of ancient temples. In the large cities, five-star hotels often lay on performances in their restaurants as an extra draw for tourists, but more authentic happenings can be found by scanning details of events in the English-language newspapers.

There are several well-defined classical dance forms, each having evolved from a particular part of the country. All are rooted in the ancient religious tradition of dance as a form of worship, and their themes tend to concentrate on Hindu myths and the legendary exploits of the gods. In fact dance is said to have originated with Lord Shiva, who in the form of Nataraja, the Lord of the Dance, performed the energetic *tandava* or cosmic dance.

The most ancient classical form is BHARAT NATYAM, performed for centuries by *devadasis*, girls who were dedicated to Dravidian temples in Tamil Nadu. It is performed solo by a woman, who begins with *alarippu*, a dance symbolizing that she is offering her body for the pleasure of the gods. The fluid, sensuous style combines *nritta*, or "pure dance" with expressive facial and hand movements, as well as jingling ankle bells, to depict maidenly love, accompanied by musicians.

KATHAKALI, literally "dance-drama" comes from neighboring Kerala, is derived from a form of strenuous yoga. It is easily the most spectacular of all India's dances, always performed by males in outrageously burlesque Mikado-like costumes that require hours of preparation.

ODISSI, from the eastern state of Orissa, is the most lyrical, erotic of all devotional temple dances.

KUCHIPUDI, from southern Andhra Pradesh is a form of decorative dance dramas.

KATHAK, from northern India is a fast-paced Muslim-influenced north Indian dance with complicated footwork, whirling pirouettes and rhythmic sensuality — performed by *nautch* or dancing courtesans in the Mughal court.

Apart from these main styles are many regional folk dances, tribal martial art and drama traditions. such as Manipur's graceful Manipuri style, Bengal and Orissa's tradition of *Chahau* masked dance. There are many others — ritualist dances to welcome the birth of a child, or chase away demons — and some involving balancing tricks with jugs of water or juggling knives.

Dance in India is unthinkable without music and song. According to legend, *nada* (sound) was the cosmic boom that accompanied earth's creation, while musical, rhythmical chanting of holy scriptures is as old as India's earliest civilization. Classical Indian music and its accompanying singing has a timeless, spiritual quality that must be experienced to be understood.

Broadly speaking, it can be divided into two distinct styles; northern Hindustani and southern Carnatic, the former being more earthy and improvisational, steeped in Muslim and Persian influences, while the latter is more melodic and devotional. The music has two basic elements, the *tala* and the *raga*. Tala is the rhythm and is characterized by the number of beats, while the *raga* provides the melody. Best known of the Indian instruments are the sitar and the tabla. The sitar is the large stringed instrument popularized by Ravi Shankar, while the tabla, a twin drum, is rather like the western bongo. Other less known instruments include the stringed *sarod* and *sarangi*, the latter played with a bow, and the reed trumpet-like *shehnai* and *tampura*.

ELEPHANTS AND MAN-EATERS

India offers the chance to walk on the wild side, to see and photograph some of the world's most majestic creatures — tigers, lions, elephants, rhinos, leopards and wild bears — getting as close as you dare to be in their natural habitats. India has a rich variety of wildlife — over 350 species of mammals, 900 species of reptiles, 2,000 species of birds and over 30,000 varieties of insects and butterflies, to be exact — enough to fascinate serious naturalists and casual tourists alike.

Although aristocratic maharajas and topeed British colonialists adored shikar, the sport of tiger shooting and netting countless mounds of dead animals and birds, conservation of wildlife actually has a very long history in India. It began over 2,000 years ago when Emperor Ashoka forbade his subjects to destroy forests or slaughter wildlife. He called forests "abhayaranya", meaning places "free from fear" — an ethic that anticipated the wildlife sanctuaries of the modern era. Ancient Aryan nature worship wove animals into Hindu myth, legend and religious belief. Animals were the sacred steads of the Hindu gods, on which they could roam the universe. Lord Shiva, god of creation, rode about on a Nandi or bull, Saraswati, goddess of knowledge on a swan, Vishnu, god of preservation, on a garuda, a sun bird with golden wings. Others were part-gods themselves, like the elephant-headed Ganesh, god of wisdom, or the monkey god Hanuman. Today, something of this ancient harmony between man and nature endures with the Bishnois community in west Rajasthan, who have a remarkable rapport with the black buck antelope, believing the animals are their reincarnated ancestors.

Presently, India has 20 major wildlife sanctuaries, 121 national parks and nine bird

reserves, scattered from Ladakh in the Himalayan mountains to the southern tip of Tamil Nadu, and covering a combined total of 90,000 sq km (35,000 sq miles), some three percent of India's total land. They are vital to the conservation of endangered species, such as the Bengal Tiger, the Asiatic Elephant and Lion, the Snow Leopard and the Siberian Crane. India's most successful conservation effort is Project Tiger, launched in 1973 by the government and the World Wildlife Fund to create strongholds for the tiger, the very symbol of India, when the beast was on the edge of extinction. There are now 15 of these through-

out the country, and some 4,000 tigers. The most famous (and accessible) of all Project Tiger reserves is Corbett National Park, an six hour drive from Delhi on the edge of the Himalayas.

Sanctuaries offer rewards of great natural beauty as well as magnificent wildlife. They all seem to have good lodges — particularly located within former princely hunting reserves — facilities, adequate restaurants and almost always offer excellent tours for visitors, often with the option of hiring jeeps, tame elephants or in some cases, boats for exploring. Each sanctuary usually has a Forest Department with a raft of local guides and trackers. If arranged in

OPPOSITE: A master musician instructs his pupils in a Madras school. ABOVE: A lone tiger in Rajasthan's Ranthambhore National Park.

advance, it's possible to stay in the Department's rest-houses and hideaways, usually tucked within dense forest — marvelous for safe, comfortable "spying" at very close quarters. You will almost never be allowed to meander off into the jungle without an experienced guide.

Go well-prepared with binoculars, a good camera (preferably with a wide-angle and zoom lens), rolls of camera film, plenty of mosquito repellent and / or a mosquito net for slumbering comfort in jungle lodges. Camouflage clothes — olive green, khaki, and dull brown colors — are in lurid Hawaiian shirts, transistor radios, strong after-shave and loud conversations are definitely out — they'll send most wildlife running for cover.

WILDLIFE DIRECTORY

Delhi and the North
UTTAR PRADESH   Corbett National Park (see page 89), Dudhwa National Park.
MADHYA PRADESH   Shivpuri Wildlife Sanctuary, Bandhavgagh National Park, Kanha National Park, Panna Wildlife Sanctuary.

Rajasthan
Keoladeo National Park, Bharatpur (see page 102), Ranthambhore National Park (see page 128), Sariska Tiger Reserve (see page 122).

The Mountain Trail
KASHMIR   Dachigam National Park (see page 172).

Bombay and the West
GUJARAT   Sasan-Gir (see page 201).

Calcutta and the East
ASSAM   Kaziranga Wildlife Sanctuary (see page 251, Manas Wildlife Sanctuary (see page 251).
WEST BENGAL   Sunderbans Tiger Reserve, (see page 242), Jaldapara Wildlife Sanctuary, Sajnak-hali Bird Sanctuary (see page 242).
BIHAR   Hazaribagh and Palamau Sanctuaries
ORISSA: Simliphal Reserve.

Across the Deccan
KARNATAKA   Bandipur and Nagarhole Wildlife Sanctuaries (see page 285), Ranganathittu Water Bird Sanctuary.
TAMIL NADU   Mudumalai Wildlife Sanctuary (see page 288).

The Deep South Trail
TAMIL NADU   Vedanthangal Water Bird Sanctuary, Point Calimere Bird Sanctuary.
KERALA   Periyar, Thekkady Wildlife Sanctuary (see page 318), Mundanthurai Tiger Sanctuary, Anamalai Tiger Sanctuary.

SPICY PLEASURES

INDIAN FOOD AND DRINK

Visitors soon awaken to the fact that Indian food is infinitely more than merely curry. The word is an English mispronunciation of *kari* or spice sauce. In fact curry is only one of many techniques used in India's countless kitchens. Housewives from Kashmir and Kanya Kumari are further apart cuisine-wise than those from Scandinavia and Spain. Even curry itself is more than its seems. The Indian cook uses an enormous armory of more than 30 freshly ground spices like an artist's palette to make endlessly inventive combinations of marsala sauces, which like each basic ingredient, varies from region to region.

The fabled furnace-like heat of Indian food, particularly in the South — causing the unwary eater to turn bright red and blink back tears — can be an occupational hazard of experimentation, better soothed by *raita* (yogurt side-dish) or coconut milk than water. How Indian stomachs cope with this everyday is a mystery.

India's great religions — Hinduism, Buddhism and Jainism — have long advocated vegetarianism, and this has led to the development of what is surely the world's most delicious vegetarian cuisine. In Gujarat, the Jains refuse to eat meat (even insects) and even shun the color of blood. Although not all Hindus are vegetarian, you will probably end up eating more vegetable dishes during your stay, particularly in south India. Table manners in India dictate that if you adopt the local custom of eating with your fingers, you do so only with your right hand, the other being considered "unclean" and used for something completely different altogether. There is always somewhere to wash, and many restaurants bring finger-bowls to the table.

Broadly speaking, the cuisine of India divides the nation.

Northerners, whose paunches tend to be more developed, adore their traditional rich Mughali cuisine, redolent of yogurt, fried onions, saffron and nuts — brought by the Mughals from Persia in the sixteenth century. *Rogon josh*, (curried lamb), *gushtaba* (spicy meat pounded to paté-consistency, formed into balls and simmered in spiced yogurt) and *biryani* (chicken or lamb in orange-flavored rice, sprinkled with rose water, almonds and dried fruits) are well known. The world-renowned clay oven-baked tandoori cooking (chicken, meat or fish marinated in herbs and baked in a clay oven) and charcoal-grilled kebabs also hail from north India. *Naans, paratha*, stuffed *kulcha*, and hankerchief-thin *romali roti* breads are served alongside.

India and her Culture

Longevity-conscious southerners, who are almost exclusively vegetarian, traditionally serve an array of light, but fiercely hot curries with steaming rice, chutneys, pickles and *puris* — either on a well-washed banana leaf or on a *thali*, a large round metal tray filled with little bowls that are constantly refilled. Other specialities include the breakfast staples — the popular *dosa*, a form of crepe made from lightly fermented rice flour and stuffed with spiced potato, and steamed rice-cake *idlis*, both eaten with fresh coconut chutney and *sambhar*, a chilli-laced lentil soup.

There are several staples without which no meal on the sub-continent would be complete. A day without bread for most Indians would be unthinkable—like a Frenchman without his baguette. Certain unleavened breads such as the common *chapati*, *roti* and millet *paratha*, originated 4,000 years ago and these slapped to the side of a tandoor oven or fried over charcoal braziers, still dominate most meals. Dairy products are liberally used in both the North and South — so that it is not difficult to understand why the Indians regard the cow as sacred.

Desserts are mainly very sweet milk/curd-based puddings and confections like mouth-watering *kulfi* ice-cream, flavored with cardamom, pistachio nuts and saffron, *rasgullas* (cream cheese balls in rose syrup), and *burfi* halva sweets, covered in wafer-thin silver paper. *Gulab jamun* (spongy ground almond balls), and *jalebi* (cartwheel-shaped sweets), both come dripping with honeyed syrup.

There is a spectacular variety of fresh fruit — mangoes, pomegranates, melons, pineapples, fig-like pitchouts, bananas, coconuts, Kashmiri apples and tangerines—found right across India, most of it extremely cheap. Always buy complete fruits and peel them yourself. If grapes and tomatoes look appetizing, wash them in sterilized water first.

It's common to end your meal by chewing palate-cleansing handfuls of *sof*, or aniseed. The mildly addictive *paan* is also served—a mixture of betel nut and spices wrapped in a betel leaf —and the cause of all those red-stained lips and teeth.

India's national drink is *chai*, the army-style brew made from boiled up tea, buffalo milk and spoonfuls of sugar, served at every railway station and *dhaba* or roadside café, usually in red clay cups which are supposed to be shattered afterwards. If you ask for "tray tea", it is served the conventional way. If you don't like sugar, ask for *"ek chai neh chini"* (one tea, no sugar). Local south Indian coffee is excellent, and is available from the extensive network of Indian Coffee Houses in most cities and towns.

For thirst-quenchers, *nimbu* or lime soda, served sweet, salt or plain, or freshly squeezed juices are the most refreshing "safe" beverages. Yogurt-based *lassis* and milk straight from the king coconut are also very cooling and cleansing. Fizzy bottled soft drinks — with improbable names such as Limca, Thrills, Campa Cola and Thumb's Up — can be bought virtually anywhere and consumed with relative safety, but are very sickly. A bag of oranges are probably a healthier, more satisfying alternative. Bottled mineral water is widely available, but check first that its seal has not been tampered with.

Imported wine and spirits is available in top

hotels, but is very expensive, which is why bottles of Scotch are so gratefully received as presents in India. Indian alcohol is cheaper, craftily confusing matters by its name: Indian Made Foreign Liquor or Foreign Liquor for short. Indian-made beer, wines and whiskey are not terribly memorable (except the morning after) and are served in most hotels except in "dry" Gujarat and Tamil Nadu states, where liquor permits must be collected from the nearest tourist office. Popular brands of beer, good for drinking along with spicy curries, include Golden Eagle, Punjab, Kingfisher, Rosy Pelican and London Pilsner. Bangalore has excellent draught beer served on tap in many English-style pubs. In the ex-Portuguese enclave of Goa, coconut and palm-leaf *toddy*, and cashew-nut *feni* make an piquant, interesting variation—and goes down very well with fresh grilled seafood on a tropical star-filled night.

ABOVE: Chefs display tantalizing Mughali fare at the famous Rambagh Hotel in Jaipur.
OVERLEAF: Communal bread-baking at a Sikh festival in the Punjab.

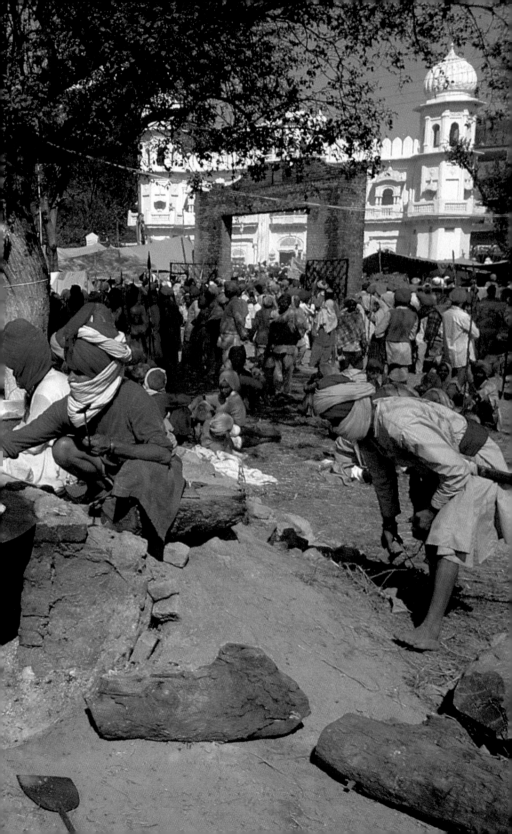

Delhi
and
the North

THE CAPITAL: A TALE OF TWO CITIES

New Delhi, India's capital and its third largest city, plays host to the nation's political elite, influential tycoons, *dhoti*-clad bureaucrats and Mercedes-driven diplomats. It is the political and administrative powerhouse of the world's largest democracy, grafted on an ancient relic-dotted hinterland that once formed the seat of the mighty Mughal empire. Its origins are thought to extend as far back as 1200 BC, and since then, no less than seven cities have risen and fallen, phoenix-like from the abandoned ruins of the last. Across Delhi's skyline, centuries-old monuments, lapis-domed mosques, and magnificent forts are surrounded by elegant Raj-era architecture, modern government blocks, embassies and stark concrete tenements.

Visitors to Delhi are immediately struck by the immense contrast between its ancient and modern character, for it is really two distinct cities merged into one. The more historic, medieval Old Delhi was built by the Mughal emperor Shah Jehan, drawing tourists to its imposing seventeenth century Red Fort, the Jama Masjid mosque and network of tangled bazaars. It is an oriental hubbub laced with dust and sneeze-inducing spices, teeming with both human and animal life. Here pavement earcleaners ply their trade; squads of *burqa*-clad women move like shiny black shadows into narrow secret lanes; strings of sure-footed coolies strain under giant sacks; and indolent merchants sell everything from brass utensils to wedding turbans.

To the south of the old city lies **New Delhi**, which was laid out during the early twentieth century by the British as an imperial capital from which to direct affairs on the subcontinent. This spacious eighth Delhi was designed by British architects Sir Edwin Lutyens and Sir Herbert Baker, and is dominated by a vast sandstone presidential palace, larger than Versailles, which is linked to the Arc de Triomphe-like India Gate by a sweeping ceremonial avenue, called Rajpath, or King's Way. From these pompously grand architectural icons radiate concentric rings of wide, well-paved tree-lined boulevards, flanked by handsome white bungalows and landscaped gardens. Completed at the tailend of the British Raj in 1931, New Delhi was a ready-made capital inherited by India's new leaders 16 years later. It still manifests a perceptible hangover from the Raj-era, not only in much of its old-world architecture, but in the British systems of parliament, law and bureaucracy which survive more or less intact, albeit idiosyncratically. An early illustration of this,

just after India became independent in 1947, was when many of the original 6,000 servants who kept the Viceroy's Palace pristine during the Raj, and lived behind the palace in a township of their own, were first dismissed in a show of egalitarianism, but soon asked to resume up their old jobs in the newly-named Rashtrapati Bhawan. These days New Delhi's colonial architecture has a seedy, decaying air, seen everywhere but most noticeable in the central spoke-like Connaught Place where the once-grand colonnaded arcades have become dirty, peeling pissoirs, covered with crow-infested *tatties* or giant rattan curtains to shield shops from sun

and rain. Fast-food parlors and handicraft emporiums ensure a steady flow of tourists who learn to negotiate pavements covered with blood-like betel stains spat from pedestrians, child beggars and prowling touts hawking extraordinary junk.

The social life of Delhi's rich and powerful is played out against a backdrop of genteel clubs, five-star hotels and Raj-era bungalows, where gossip is spiced with the latest wafts of scandal and sycophancy. On the flip-side, Delhi also houses thousands of homeless on its streets, many of them Rajasthani villagers fleeing the ravages of drought to find work as laborers on the city's

ABOVE: Lutyen's India Gate remains the emblem of British-built New Delhi. Beyond stands the empty Rajput-style *chhatris* where a statue of King George V used to stand before it was removed after Independence.

numerous construction sites. After a day or so in Delhi, you'll see these hordes of gaunt workers, who look like sun-blackened skeletons draped in bright rags, who balance impossible loads on their heads on sites resembling biblical epics. At night, you'll see their makeshift cardboard hovels go up on pavements and traffic islands next to slumbering cows, barely a stone's throw from the capital's luxury hotels and embassy colonies.

Delhi can be a rather deceptive introduction to India — with its built-up urban sprawl, large influx of foreign tourists and sten-gun toting security patrols — but its historic sights merit a

stay of at least four or five days. Of all the large Indian cities, it offers the most gentle transition to life on the subcontinent with some of the country's best hotels and restaurants. It's also the most efficient center from which to make bookings and gather information, and a convenient base for exploring northern India, with easy access by air and train to the ever-popular "Golden Triangle" route of Agra and Jaipur; to the rest of Rajasthan; to Varanasi and Khajuraho, and to Kashmir and Ladakh.

THE NORTHWEST CITADEL

Historically, Delhi represented a crucial foothold on the subcontinent that none of India's prospective invaders could afford to ignore. It commanded the strategic north-eastern routes from Central Asia and the high valleys from Afghanistan, where Delhi's early conquerors came from — many of them in the footsteps of Alexander the Great — and provided a bastion for plundering the rich lowlands of the Ganges delta.

Competition for the mastery of Delhi began in the eleventh century, much of it marked by gruesome Oriental despotism and valiant victories — the city was raised, fought over, destroyed, deserted and re-built no less than seven times,

although archaeologists argue that as many as eight other cities existed, and also put forward the hypothesis that idol-smashing Muslims may have wiped out remnants of ancient Hindu settlements.

The antiquity of Delhi may be traced to the legendary city of Indrapratha, the capital of the Pandavas, the mythical heroes of the Maharabharata epic. Legend has it that their city was founded on the banks of the river Yamuna over 3,000 years ago, although archaeologists trace the earliest settlements in Delhi to 1200 BC. Indrapratha was said to be located where the sixteenth century Purana Qila now stands — where shards of fine grey earthenware have been found that seem to give substance to this myth.

Invading Rajput dynasties were responsible for the first "Dillis", whose decaying ruins can be seen 10 km (about six miles) south of the Connaught Place near the Qutb Minar. Of these, the first was Lal Kot, built by the Tomar Rajputs in AD 1060, who brought with them the mysterious Iron Pillar with its fourth or fifth century Sanskrit script, said to be more than 2,000 years old and made of such pure iron that it has never rusted. Even more enigmatic than the origin of the Iron Pillar, is the only great ancient Hindu shrine left intact in Delhi's environs, 17 km (10.5 miles) south of Delhi, known as Suraj Khund. Thought to have been constructed by the Tomar Rajputs, it is a pool surrounded by wide amphitheater-like steps, with the remains of a large temple nearby dedicated to the sun-god, Surya.

Feudal battles ensured that Lal Kot soon fell to another Hindu Rajput clan, the Chauhans, in the twelfth century. They considerably expanded this original domain, re-naming it Quila Rai Pithora.

Then in 1206, Delhi trembled to the rumblings of India's "Spartacus", the former Turkic slave, Qutb-ud-din-Aibak who became Delhi's first Muslim Sultan. He pounded his predecessor's cities to rubble before laying the base for Delhi's second city with his two significant edifices: — the Quwwat-ul-Islam, one of India's first mosques, built from the remains of 27 Hindu temples with the looted Iron Pillar given pride of place in its courtyard — and his famous tower of victory, the Qutb Minar, situated south of New Delhi and celebrating the Muslim defeat of a Hindu king.

The line of the so-called Slave Kings ended with assassination in 1296, when Sultan Ala-ud-din of the Afghan Khiljis stormed through India, capturing the Rajput fortress of Chittaugarh and founding Siri, Delhi's second city, leaving a magnificent sprawling fort that visitors will find surrounded by encroaching modern tenements in the present-day Hauz Khas suburb.

By 1321, the Afghans, were ousted by the Muslim Tughlaqs, a formidable Islamic warrior dynasty, who constructed no fewer then three cities here during the fourteenth century, The first, Tughlaqabad, built by Ghiyas-ud-Din, is now a ruined ghost fort city, dotted with tombs and fortified by massive sloping walls, 10 km (about six miles) southeast of the Qutb Minar. Whether or not the city is haunted — as the story goes — by the ghost of a vengeful saint, is a matter for speculation, but it was abandoned only five years after its construction due to a shortage of water. Today it is inhabited only by the Gujars, a gypsy tribe. The second city, Jehana-panah, was also rapidly deserted. Its founder was the mad quixotic Sultan Muhammed Shah, an Indian "Nero", renowned for fiendish ways — among his many exploits, the most vicious was crushing his elderly father to death beneath a specially-constructed "ceremonial welcome" archway. Acting on imperial whim he decided to quit his father's domain, and force-marched his subjects 1,100 km (563 miles) all the way to his new capital at Daulatabad, near present-day Aurangbad. According to an eye-witness ac-count, two subjects attempted to evade the Sultan's Long March, and suffered the ruler's wrath. The first, a cripple, was butchered, and the other, who was blind, was prodded all the way to Daulatabad by soldier's lances. It was later observed that only the poor man's severed leg, a macabre trophy, eventually arrived. Seventeen years later, the Sultan grew tired of debauched amusements at his Deccan fortress, and marched his subjects all the way home to Delhi again.

Delhi's fifth city, was the final and most impressive achievement of the Tughlaq rulers, founded in 1351, by the Sultan Muhammed's considerably more tolerant cousin, Feroz Shah. His 37 year-long reign was relatively peaceful, and he was able to indulge his hobby for build-ing, and repairing the existing buildings of the Qutb complex. Today visitors explore the crum-bling ruins of his historic capital's core in the site known as Feroz Shah Kotla, just to the south of the Red Fort, where you can see one of two ancient third century pillars which bears the edicts of the Emperor Ashoka in the Brahmanic script deciphered by James Prinsep in 1837.

After Feroz's death, confusion about the succession of the Tughlaq line weakened the kingdom, and when in 1398 Timur the Lane, the dreaded Tamerlane, the emir of Samarkand and conqueror of Persia, Afghanistan and Mesopo-tamia, invaded India, he met with only slight resistance. But after two weeks sacking the city, Timur led his armies back to Samarkand, taking 120 elephants as useful booty, but not bothering to set himself on Delhi's throne. The last of the Tughlaqs died in 1414, and power passed to the

Sayyids, descendants of the Prophet, who barely made a dent in Delhi's history, and to three generations of Pathan Lodhi kings, who built a necropolis of tombs and mosques but little else, and moved to Sikander, just outside Agra in 1504.

The first of the Great Mughals to arrive in Delhi was Babur, a feudal overlord from Samar-kand who claimed the blood of both Genghis Khan and Timur ran in his veins. He swept through Delhi briefly before marching his ar-mies onto Agra, where he acquired the Koh-i-noor diamond and founded the Mughal dy-nasty before dying in 1530. His son Humayan

moved north to Delhi, building a fort-capital, known as Purana Qila on the banks of the Ya-muna river, where his magnificent tomb stands today. Humayan called his capital Din-Panah or Asylum of the Faith, but had to flee to Persia (using the Koh-i-noor to bribe his way out in safety) when an Afghan adventurer, Sher Shah Suri arrived on the scene in 1540. The usurper was able to add several impressive monuments to what became Delhi's sixth city, Shergarh, before Humayan reclaimed his throne with a vengeance in 1555.

From then on, into the seventh century, Delhi and Agra became twin jewels in the

ABOVE: Mahatma Gandhi depicts the "Father of the Nation" in a characteristically stalwart pose.
OPPOSITE: Decaying colonial colonnades in Connaught Place.

Mughal crown, and not until 1638 did Humayan's great-grandson, Shah Jehan transfer the seat of his empire to Delhi. Completed over a decade, the seventh Delhi, Shahjahanabad, became India's regal center. It was dominated by a magnificent euchre sandstone walled fortress, now called the Red Fort, the giant Jama Masjid mosque and the broad processional avenue, Chandni Chowk, or "moonlight bazaar", named for a wide canal which once ran down its center. Chandhi Chowk was described by the contemporary American traveler Robert Minturn as the "gayest scene in India" filled with "scarlet ladies" and gloriously-clad "natives" gadding about on howdahed elephants and Arab steads. With this in mind, it's easy to picture the pride of Mughal Delhi's architect Shah Jehan, who inscribed his famous claim: "If there is paradise on the face of this earth, it is here, Oh! It is here!" in gold above his marble audience hall in the Red Fort.

However, the Mughal empire was fated to fall into decay, and a century later in 1739, Delhi's prized gem-studded Red Fort fell to the plundering Nadir Shah, the emperor of Persia.

By this time the weakened Mughals were no match for the British, who had long ago established footholds in Madras and Bengal. By 1803, the British placed under their yoke the last Mughal, the blind old poet, Bahudur Shah, who was in reality only a puppet king. All that remained to him was his title, palace and a pension bestowed by the new rulers. But the British suffered a severe setback with the year-long Indian Mutiny in 1857 — sparked in Meerut by protesting sepoys, or native soldiers, whose principal objection seems relatively straightforward in retrospect — pig and cow fat to grease Muslim and Hindu cartridges. The British reaction was one of classic hubris, and the enraged sepoys went on a murderous spree, arriving in Delhi after a day's gallop to bayonet every European in sight. The sepoys secured the reluctant support of their symbolic emperor, Bahudur Shah in their bid to oust the *feringhi* or foreigners. The insurgents were later strung up by avenging British troops, so incensed at the sight of their mutilated womenfolk and children that they not only blew up mutineers by placing them over the mouths of their cannons, but seriously debated blowing up the Jama Masjid too, with the notion of raising a Christian cathedral in its place. At Kashmir Gate, slightly north of the Red Fort, you can still see the pock-marks of shot and shell, where the dwindling number of British were forced to retreat to defend themselves. Bahudur Shah was packed off in disgraced exile to Rangoon, but a

vigilante British officer "bagged" the last Mughal's sons for the greater glory of Empire during a spate of cross-firing at Humayan's Tomb. Delhi remained a provincial town set amid hyena-infested wilds and magnificent relics, until 1911, when for the first and only time, a ruling English monarch came to India to be crowned Emperor in Delhi at the Coronation Durbar. This was where the new King George V broke the news of the shift of India's imperial capital from Calcutta to "this beautiful and historic city". His words so traumatized the British in Calcutta that they omitted to print the numbing news in the next day's newspapers, fearing perhaps that their new Emperor was suffering from a bad bout of sun-stroke.

VISITING DELHI

New Delhi's grid-like boulevards are relatively easy to find your way around — roads are well signed and all the street names uniformly belong to the post-Independence era — but the city is very spread out, leaving many travelers with the impression that they've spent much of their time in Delhi just getting from one place to another. To a large extent, whether you stay in Old Delhi or New Delhi has a significant effect on which aspect of the city you end up experiencing.

Travelers tend to concentrate their sightseeing efforts in three major areas: in and around the central hub of **Connaught Place** and **Janpath** where you'll find all the banks, shops, emporiums, tourist and airline offices, and many tourist-orientated restaurants and budget hostels — near the **Red Fort** for exploring the old walled city's bazaars and sights, which is located close to Old Delhi Railway Station, and a little further north, the Interstate Bus Terminal near Kashmiri Gate — and around the **Paharganj** area, situated two kilometers (a mile and a quarter) north of Connaught Place next to New Delhi Railway Station with a reputation as a back-packer's haunt for its cheap accommodation and cafés. Unless you are staying at one of the five-star hotels within Lutyen's residential New Delhi to the south of the city, it's often easy to neglect this exceptionally pleasant area, but it's well worth making time to explore the tranquil Lodhi Gardens, the tombs of Safdarjang and Humayan, and the imperial

The best time to visit Delhi is between mid-September and March, when the days are crisp, fine and sunny and the evenings cool. Winters can be surprisingly chilly — so if you plan to arrive between December and January, you'll need woolens, socks and sweaters. Winter is also India's marriage season — a good time for seeing

---

OPPOSITE: Humayan's Tomb, the majestic prototype of the Taj Mahal, is one of Delhi's best preserved monuments.

spontaneous processions of brocade-clad tur-baned grooms resplendent on white horses and their glittering brides with an entourage of drunken guests, lamp-wallahs and trumpet-tooting bandsmen in old epauletted uniforms. Delhi has a fleeting but beautiful blossoming splendor during the spring months of February and March.

One of Delhi's most spectacular annual festivals is Republic Day, held on January 26th, when India displays its martial might along the Rajpath with parades of dapper regiments (including the famous Camel Corps), brass bands, folk dancers and India's latest military hardware. Don't take along any thing valuable, as all baggage has to be left with security. At dusk, crowds watch silently as camel-mounted soldiers perform their ritual for Beating the Re-treat. Delhi is also particularly lively during the 10-day Ram Lila (Dussehra) festival in October. Continuous plays, marathon readings, music and dance are performed by weird and wonder-fully dressed actors on chariots in Old Delhi, recounting episodes from India's epic poem, the Ramayana, which tells the story of the god Rama's victory over the Lankan demon king Ravana and the rescue of Rama's abducted wife Sita. The festival culminates in a procession of immense, firework-padded, brightly painted effigies of the evil ten-headed Ravana and his henchmen to the Ram Lila fairground (located where Old Delhi ends and New Delhi begins), where they are set ablaze to the roar of thousands of onlookers. The Muslim festival Bakr Id in April is also very dramatic, with hundreds of thousands of devotees kneeling in prayer out-side the Jama Masjid. The only festival you might want to avoid in Delhi is Holi in March — which is possibly India's most delightful festival in small villages or amongst friends — but can turn nasty in big, impersonal cities, when gangs of young men use it as a excuse to pelt unwitting passer's by, particularly young women and tourists, with paint, colored water, stones or even kerosene and battery acid.

GETTING AROUND

Of all the Indian cities, Delhi's varied and spread-out attractions require you to be selective and organized about sightseeing. It helps to have a good city map so that you have at least some idea where your driver is supposed to be taking you, otherwise you may find yourself being taken for a ride! You can begin on a city-wise note as soon as you arrive in Delhi's airport terminal by heading for the "Pre-Paid Taxi" booth, and utilizing the no-hassle system on paying your fare in advance, with the rate cal-culated against your desired destination. The fare from the airport to Connaught Place is around Rs 80.

It might take a while to adjust to the anarchic haphazardness on the capital's roads, where a combination of relatively well-paved roads and erratic horn-bleeping driving often proves fatal. According to statistics, Delhi's roads are the second most dangerous in the world after Nairo-bi, and there seems every indication that they will stay that way. You'll need to adopt a little Hindu fatalism to stay cool, but you'll soon get used to seeing lurching over-crammed sardine-can buses or snail's-pace motor-scooters atop which an entire family have arranged them-selves. After a few days of observation on Delhi's roads, you'll come away with some new dis-coveries about the Average Indian vs. the Law of Physics and some new ideas about different ways of utilizing vehicles. You should have learnt how to detect subtle suicidal urges in potential auto-rickshaw or taxi-drivers. For in-stance, glazed blood-shot eyes are tell-tale signs that they have recently been sipping *bhang*, which is a marijuana-based concoction, to which many drivers are addicted It's also worth noting that it's not always wise to follow-up your driver's invitation to change money on the black mar-ket, as a good number of them are paid as police informers. Just put it all down as good character assessment practice for being out in the "field"!

You may wish to ride a Delhi bus just for the experience, and for Rs 1 a shot you can hardly complain about the price. But they are very crammed and often downright unpleasant, particularly for women. It's far more fun to watch the macho sport that young Indian men seem to regard as a sort of rite of passage — they'll go to astonishing lengths to self-con-sciously loiter until the bus has begun to accel-erate, then sprint after it for a highly competitive (highly amusing) last-ditch effort to hurl them-selves aboard, often left desperately half-dan-gling to the cheers of watching onlookers!

Auto-rickshaws provide the cheapest, most convenient way of negotiating short distances in Delhi. They tend to be slow and kidney-rat-tling, and so are obviously less practical for longer distances, like going out to the airport or to the Qutb Minar.

With any motorized transport, always agree on the price first (this deflects the driver's incli-nation to waste his petrol on driving you around in circles) or make sure that the meter is being used. The current rate for taxis starts at Rs 3.50, then Rs 2 per kilometer, while auto-rickshaws start at Rs 2.30, then Rs 1.20 per kilometer. Drivers will wait quite happily if you want to retain them, while you hive off for an hour of so of sightseeing or shopping — but you must agree on the waiting charge — usually about Rs 15 an hour for taxis. Taxi-drivers are legally entitled to charge you 25 percent "night charge" after 11 pm, but their "ten percent extra charge" story is bosh at all other times. You're free to tip drivers liberally if they have been particularly helpful. In Old Delhi, you can get about the bazaars by cycle-rickshaw or horse-drawn tonga — both are good for laid-back, open-air sightseeing.

HOTELS

Delhi is one of India's busiest entry points for foreign visitors, expatriates and business people. It has a fleet of fine international-standard five-star luxury hotels, most of them hastily built to house athletes and politicians for the Asian Games in 1982 and the Non-aligned Movement conference a year later. Even so, few travelers stay longer than a few days in Delhi before heading off for their chosen destinations. One reason for this is that, by Indian standards, hotel rates are expensive — beginning at around Rs 1,250 (US$100) a night in most of the top tourist and business class establishments. Facilities in the five hotels are top-notch, with a range of excellent restaurants, 24-hour coffee shops, recreational facilities and swimming pools (a definite plus during summer), business desks, travel agents, shopping arcades, bakeries, bars, astrologers and discotheques.

Most of the luxury hotels are miles away from the center of town (close to the city's Fort Knox grid of diplomatic embassies at Chanakyapuri), which makes sightseeing less much less spontaneous in sprawling Delhi. It's always essential to advance-book five-star accommodation, especially so during the peak season months between October and March. In the range of US$100 and up you can take your pick of the following luxury hotels:
Maurya Sheraton (Welcomgroup), ✆301-0101, Diplomatic Enclave.
Taj Mahal Hotel, ✆301-6162, 1 Mansingh Road.
The Taj Palace Hotel, ✆301-0404, 2 Sardar Patel Marg.
The Oberoi, ✆363030, Dr Zakir Hussain Marg.
Hyatt Regency Delhi, ✆609911, Bhikaji Cama Place.
The Holiday Inn, ✆332-0101, Connaught Plaza.
Le Meridien Hotel, ✆389821, Windsor Place, Janpath.
Ashok Hotel, ✆600412, Chanakapuri.
Centaur Hotel, ✆545-2223, Delhi Airport.

Several impeccably-kept colonial hotels offer less expensive elegance with plenty of period flair as well as efficiency for those arriving in Delhi to embark on their Indian adventure: The fairly central **Claridges**, ✆301-0211,

12 Aurangzeb Road, price: moderate; the delightful, pukka Georgian-style **Oberoi Maidens**, ✆252-5464, 7 Sham Nath Marg, built in 1900 just north of Old Delhi in the former Raj-cantonment of Civil Lines, and where Lutyens stayed as he planned his new city with spacious comfortable rooms. price: moderate; and the **Hotel Imperial**, ✆311511, a peaceful garden retreat right on central Janpath, with quirky, recently refurbished 1930's decor, a good shopping arcade, swimming pool, period bar and pretty terrace and lawn for al fresco meals and afternoon teas, prices: moderate to expensive. The Imperial Hotel, like the Ashok, Claridges, Maurya and the Kanishka hotels, allow non-guests to use their pool for around Rs 30 to Rs 50.

Comfortable inexpensive priced hotels that are relatively convenient to the city include the **Hotel Ambassador**, ✆690391, Sujan Singh Park, with air-conditioned rooms and the advantage of having New Delhi's best South Indian restaurant downstairs; **Lodhi Hotel**, ✆619422, also in south Delhi on Lala Rajput Rai Marg has comfortable rooms and an excellent restaurant; **Nirula's**, ✆352419, L Block, Connaught Place is as central as it is possible to be, located right next to one of New Delhi's most popular restaurant complexes. Continuing anti-clockwise is the **Hotel Marina**, ✆344658, G 59 Block, with quiet, clean rooms. A cheaper central option is the ITDC-run **Ashok Yatri Niwas**, ✆344511, 19 Ashok Road, a giant 556-roomed complex with basic but adequate rooms and a good South Indian restaurant.

The most popular of Delhi's four "Y's" is the **YMCA Tourist Hostel**, ✆311915 near the Regal Cinema on Jai Singh Road, which offers excellent value comfortable single rooms with hot and cold water in the cheap to very cheap range, a good restaurant, gardens, and room rates include breakfast. If this is full, try the similarly priced **YWCA International Guest House**, ✆311561, in Parliament Street (also known as **Sansad Marg**), where you'll be given basic clean rooms, or the lesser-known **Blue Triangle Family Hostel**, ✆310133, on Ashoka Road just off Parliament Street, where rooms with attached bath and including breakfast are fall within the cheap range. All the "Ys" will accept a Rs 5 temporary membership fee and they take both sexes.

There are plenty of budget (cheap to very cheap) lodges scattered around Janpath, but few are reliably clean, friendly or reasonable — in fact, most are downright grim, and over the decades have fueled thousands of traveler's tales about disastrous encounters with the subcontinent. However, there is one worthwhile lodge to try in Janpath, **Roshan Villa Guest**

House, ℭ331-1770, at 7 Babar Lane, which offers basic, well-kept rooms, plus Rs 20 for an attached bath, and there's also a Rs 30 dormitory. Otherwise take yourself down to the Paharganj area near New Delhi Railway Station, which is a rabbit warren of very cheap (and often nasty) lodges in and around the Main Bazaar Road. If you have a definite aversion to creepy-crawlies this may not be the place for you, but if there's any reasonable accommodation under Rs 100 to be had in Delhi this is where you'll find it. It's really a matter of combing through several such places yourself since one man's squalor can be another's mansion. But one seems to get consistent praise from back-packing tourists: **Vivek Hotel,** ℭ523015, at 1541-50 Main Bazaar, where rooms have an attached "bath" (euphemism for "tap" and "hole!") where the natives are friendly and helpful!

RESTAURANTS

As the nation's cosmopolitan capital, Delhi offers some great eating experiences. You can either dine at its luxury hotels which employ top chefs and usually have a varied range of Indian, Western and Chinese restaurants and coffee shops, or there's a wide choice of well-established eating houses scattered across town.

Delhi is probably the best place in the world to sample delicious, authentic north-Indian Mughali food. This strongly meat-based cuisine is very rich, redolent of thick yoghurt, onions and exotic spices which the Mughals brought with them when they quit Persia in the sixteenth century. It's served with a variety of breads to mop up its sauces, most popularly the delicious fluffy, yoghurt-leavened *naan* which is baked clinging to the side of a tandoor clay oven; whole wheat *rotis*; *roomali* (handkerchief) *rotis* or parathas, layered and stuffed with minced meat or *paneer* cheese, and really a meal in themselves. Tandoori mutton, poultry and fish are a famous Mughal speciality, and these dishes attain their distinctive succulence from being marinated in a mixture of yogurt, crushed garlic, tumeric, sometimes papaya pulp and salt, and then skewered over the tandoor's glowing coals. Don't be alarmed by the fiery red of your tandoori chicken — the color comes from the marinade, not from being smothered with chilies! Then there's the classic *biryani* of *basmati* rice and spiced meat cooked with saffron to sticky, fragrant perfection in a sealed pot, or popular chicken Mughali which has a thick creamy sauce with onions, cashews and raisins. Mughali vegetable dishes tend to be equally sumptuous. Try *dal makhni*, rich spiced lentils with coriander, *shahi paneer*, cheese in cream

and tomatoes, *khatte alloo*, spiced potato, or *baingan mumtaz*, stuffed eggplant. Desserts are generally prepared from milk or Indian cottage cheese flavored with cardamom or saffron. *Firni* is the most popular, a kind of exotic rice pudding served in earthenware bowl. There's also *kheer*, a rich thickened milk with raisins and nuts, and a summer favorite is *khulfi*, Indian ice-cream accompanied by transparent sweet vermicelli called *falooda*.

Foreigners and diplomats who live and work in Delhi swear that the major hotels offer the best cuisine — and they rate the Maurya Sheraton and the Oberoi Intercontinental as two of the very best. Arguably, these two hotels offer the most memorable Mughali cuisine in town: the Maurya Sheraton's very elegant **Dum Pukht** for aristocratic sixteenth century Lucknowian specialities cooked by India's most famous chef, Muhammed Imtiaz. Also at the Shereaton is the popular **Bukhara** — renowned for its delicious north-west frontier dishes, notably its succulent *raan* or roasted spiced lamb, chicken *tikka* and charcoal-grilled kebabs, all served in mock-rustic surroundings where guests are invited to slip on aprons, eat with their fingers like baronial Mughals, sip frothy Indian beer from pewter goblets, and watch chefs deftly gouging rows of skewers behind huge glass windows. This place is so popular, they don't take bookings after 8:30 pm.

The Oberoi's **Kandahar** has similar excellent fare served in classic European surroundings where the tone is set by bow-tied waiters, subdued lighting and elegant silver platters, although true to Mughal form, you'll find no knives or forks on the table. Although these restaurants are fairly expensive by Delhi standards, at around Rs 200 per head (including liberal quantities of beer), it's absurdly good value if you consider what a comparable meal would cost at home. It's only when you start ordering imported wines or spirits at hotels that you'll really start paying through the nose. Delhi, like the rest of India, only sells foreign liquor in hotels, priced up to four times more than their original value. Another pointer — it's also advisable to advance-book at any of the main hotels, as all the popular restaurants are lionized by socializing Delhites.

You'll also find classic, hearty Mughali fare at the Taj Mansingh's **Haveli**, where classical dancers and musicians perform while you eat; at Claridges' **Dhaba** which has a real-life truck incorporated into its decor; and the Hotel Ashok's **Frontier** which has strumming minstrels who doggedly serenade your table (something you either adore or suffer). More authentic restaurants outside the hotels tend to have unpretentious surroundings, but can be surprisingly good. Try especially the **Khyber**, ©252-0867, 1514 Kashmiri Gate, for good, reasonably priced Afghani dishes, and ring in advance to order their excellent *raan*, and both branches of **Karims**, the more classy air-conditioned one at Nizamuddin West, ©698300, or the other located on the south side of Jama Masjid along Motia Mahal, which is more popular with locals. (As with any eating house in Old Delhi, if you're there later than 9 pm, you'll observe rows of urchins patiently congregating outside — after the last diner has left, they'll be given the night's scraps!)

For exceptional south Indian food, (which

South Indian Boarding House, opposite Shankar Market.

If you're in Connaught Place on the prowl for a solid meal, try one of Delhi's oldest, most eccentric haunts, **Gaylord**, 16 Regal Building, Connaught Place, (it began in the early 1950's, and still retains the original waiting staff, damask tablecloths and chandeliers), or **Kwality**, just around the corner on Parliament Street — both are air-conditioned havens where you can feast on good Indian food for about Rs 100 for two. Or go to the **Imperial Hotel** where you can sit under umbrellas on the lawn for a lunch of chicken *tikka*, *naan* and sip *nimbu* soda for Rs 35.

tends to be much lighter on the palate if you're still adjusting to the Indian diet), head for **Dasaprakash**, located in a cavernous, lamp-lit dome in the lobby of the Ambassador Hotel, and always crammed with avidly eating locals. Their three-course *thali* meal costs Rs 30, and waiters are always hovering to refill your platter with varieties of *subze*, or spiced vegetable dishes and puffed *puri* bread — as much as you can put away. Fresh grape juice, *lassis* and creamy mango milk shakes are the house specialities. Other good places include Delhi's branch of the famous **Woodlands** chain of restaurants at the Lodhi Hotel; the **Coconut Grove** for delicious non-vegetarian South Indian and Bengali dishes at the Ashok Yatri Niwas Hotel; at **Sona Rupa**, 46 Janpath, good for sampling a typical Madras-style breakfast of steamed *idlies* (rice cakes) in spicy *sambar* gravy, and at the very cheap, prompt

Unlike most other Indian cities, Delhi also has a rash of pseudo-American fast-food parlors, complete with french fries, "buffalo" burgers, thick-shakes and ersatz pizzas — great if you need a complete change from Indian food. They're also the "in" place with gum-chewing, jean-clad Indian yuppies, and the place to meet other hungry tourists. Best of all is **Nirula's**, located in L Block, Connaught Place, where there's also a popular Rs 27 vegetarian lunch buffet. The complex also includes Delhi's oldest Chinese restaurant, a cake and pastry shop, an ice-cream parlor and two popular stand-up fast-food annexes, selling everything from *dal* and *chapatis* to pizzas and India's very own

ABOVE: Tea House of the August Moon at the Taj Palace is typical of elaborate restaurants in Delhi's five-star hotels.

Campa-Cola and **Thumbs Up**. Another novelty is the subcontinent's only **Wimpy Bar** in Connaught Place, just along from the Tourist Office at 5 Janpath, which serves burgers made from almost everything except beef, but still taste okay. Numerous snack bars in the city serve local favorites: *khulcha bhatura*, a soft doughy bread eaten with spicy chick-peas; the South Indian *dosa*, a crisp rice pancake often with a mashed potato filling served with *sambhar*; *pakoras* or fruit *chaat*, prepared by roadside vendors and made up of potato, papaya, apple and tomato chunks, tossed with piquant chutney, lemon juice and salt.

It's possible to dine well on Chinese food in Delhi — virtually all the main hotels employ Chinese chefs, who usually hail from Calcutta where most of India's Chinese community live, and the best restaurants will send to Hong Kong for essential ingredients. For stylish and fairly authentic fare, try the **Tea House of the August Moon** at the Taj Palace, which has eye-catching decor mocked up like a pagoda garden, good *dim sum* and a variety of regional dishes; the Oberoi's **Taipan**, the Hyatt's **Pearls**, and the Taj Mansingh's **House of Ming**. For something a little different, you might try classic French cuisine at the Oberoi's pricey **La Rochelle**, where you can dine on quails, oysters and steaks and imported wines, or to the Maurya's **Bali Hi** for good Polynesian, and South East Asian dishes, stunning rooftop views and live band. The ultra-smart **Valentino's** at the Hyatt has an Italian chef behind its excellent pasta creations and *zabaglione* and there's Mediterranean food at the Ashok Hotel's **Taverna Cyprus**. If you yearn for seafood in land-locked Delhi, **Fisherman's Wharf**, ©698123, at A-1 Moolchand Shopping Complex, Defense Colony, is one of Delhi's few exceptional independent eateries, and probably the best place to satisfy cravings for fresh fish, king prawns, mussels and lobster. Standards of hygiene (you can never be too fussy about seafood!) and preparation are high — and their tandoori pomfret, sold at seasonal cost price, is a real winner.

The truly adventurous will enjoy a visit to the **paratha-wallah gully** or "the alley of bread sellers", which is wedged in Chandni Chowk's lanes. Originally established in 1875, this row of historic "cafés" is run by high-caste Brahmans, employing Fagan-like urchins as adept street "chefs", and over the decades has catered to everyone from colonial British administrators to jailed opposition party leaders. Its fame rests on its fresh unleavened *paratha*, sprinkled with cumin, sesame, caraway, or stuffed with peas, onions or potato. While the restaurants barely conform to Western standards of cleanliness, you'll dine extremely well here on insatiable amounts of sizzling, fragrant *parathas*, all served with rounds of delicious, freshly cooked *subze* (spiced vegetable) banana chutney and curd for less than Rs 10. It's Chandni Chowk's most popular lunch-time spot, and has an enthusiastic clientele of travelers disillusioned with the expensive, less authentic fare of New Delhi's five-star hotels. No one I know has ever got "Delhi-belly" here! Here's how to find it: start with the Red Fort behind you, walk a hundred yards or so up Chandni Chowk's boulevard until you see a large State Bank of India building on the other side of the road. This is your cue to turn left into a lane directly opposite and this should lead you directly to the spice-smelling cul-de-sac of your search. Don't worry if you seem to be getting impossibly lost — everyone in Chandni Chowk knows "paratha wallah gully" and should be able to point you in the right direction.

NIGHTLIFE

While Delhi is not as lively as cosmopolitan Bombay, top classical dancers and musicians perform here far more regularly. If you're determined to experience at least something of India's dazzling cultural heritage — be it dance, drama or music — scan the morning's *Times of India* or *Indian Express* for their daily listing of what's on, the *Delhi Diary* sold at most newsstands, or consult the tourist office's fortnightly *Program of Events*. Performances tend to start around 6:30 pm and there's a central ticket office at Cottage Industries Emporium, Janpath. One regular event to catch is the Dances of India program at the **Parsi Anjuman Hall**, ©275978, Bahadur Shah Zafar Marg, Delhi Gate, a popular showcase of *bhavai*, *kathak* and *bharat natyam* styles, and starts at 7 pm every night, at Rs 25 a ticket. If you want to experience the technicolor thrills, wet saris and outrageous fortunes of Hindi movies, join the scrums of flared-trousered youths at the **Regel Cinema** complex in Connaught Place or the modern **Sheila** opposite New Delhi Railway Station.

At night, you can always try the city's discotheques — dark, flashing pits full of bebopping turbaned Sikhs, African students, and other night lizards dancing to the latest pop music. The best is the **Ghungroo** at the Maurya, but the Taj Mansingh's **Number One** has a regular following amongst Delhi's moneyed young. The Hyatt Regency has a flashy basement disco, but is open only to members or guests — visitors to the other two pay a cover charge of Rs 100 to Rs 150.

SIGHTSEEING

Most travelers are still working off jet-lag when they arrive in Delhi, and need time to ease into ambitious sightseeing. Besides, it's often interesting enough just getting acquainted with the Indian sights, sounds and smells of your immediate neighborhood. If you feel you're not quite in a mood to go charging off into the Old City, or scrambling over ramparts out at Tughlaqabad, then you might like to try the tourist office's four-hour morning conducted tour, which whisks you about to many of Delhi's far-flung places of interest, so that you get to see a good deal of the city and many of its most famous sights without much effort or expenditure on your part. (See GENERAL INFORMATION, page 89) on where to book conducted tours). If you want to tackle Delhi's sights at your own pace, then the suggested routes below should serve as a useful framework, best spread over three or four days.

OLD DELHI: MOSQUES AND MONEYLENDERS

Make **Shah Jehan's Medieval Walled City** your first sightseeing stop in Delhi for a taste the "real" India — a total contrast to Lutyen's spacious green city — of vibrant color, tangled alleys, pungent scents and frenetic crowds. Here you can linger in Chandni Chowk's bazaars, visit Jama Masjid and old Delhi's majestic centerpiece, the Red Fort — and this one combined destination will probably fill an entire day.

Old Delhi is dominated by the gigantic rust-colored **Red Fort**, or Lal Qila, which looms 18.5 m (60 ft) at its highest watchtowers, and is enclosed by nearly two and a half kilometers (one and a half miles) of snaking battlements. The fortress-palace became the courtly hub of the Mughal empire when Shah Jehan decided to shift the seat of power from Agra to Delhi, sparking a construction boom between 1638–48 to create his new capital — Shahjahanabad. The emperor-architect prided himself on the unequaled grandeur of the Red Fort — no small thing for the man who designed the Taj Mahal — and tantalizing reports of his precious gem-studded palace, pieta dura inlay, marbled fountains, ceremonial pomp, and above all, his solid gold jewel-encrusted Peacock Throne, spread the Red Fort's fame. Shah Jehan was soon deposed by his fanatical son, Aurangzeb who was the last of the Great Mughals to rule from Delhi. Shah Jehan's palace, once considered a symbol of monumental wealth, now has a desolate, plundered look — all its precious gems, gilt and silver were plucked bare in the aftermath of the 1857 mutiny.

Entry is through the massive **Lahore Gate**, so-named because its faces Lahore in what is now Pakistan, which leads you into the vaulted shopping arcade known as **Chhatta Chowk**, formerly where royal memsahibs would inspect the latest creations of court goldsmiths, jewelers and weavers, but today full of "antiques" (usually "aged" by pros down in the old city) tourist junk and frantically gesticulating touts. At the end of this is the two-storyed **Naubat Khana**, where court musicians used to serenade passing nobles on their way across the garden to the colonnaded **Diwan-i-Am**, or public audience hall. This was a sort of impromptu law

court where any commoner had the right to plea their case before the emperor, who gazed down from an ornate palanquined platform. Beyond lies a large formal garden and six palace *mahals*, through which ran the network of lotus-shaped marble fountains Shah Jehan named Naher-i-Bahisht or "Stream of Paradise", which has sadly been allowed to fall into disrepair. To the far right is **Mumtaz Mahal**, now a museum open from 9 am to 5 pm, and close to it is Rang Mahal, once an elaborate painted boudoir. As you move left, you'll pass through the emperor's former trio of apartments known collectively as the Khas Mahal. The palace's citadel was the

ABOVE: The emperor's marble canopied throne in the Red Fort's Diwan-i-Am. OVERLEAF: Impregnable and forbidding, the Lahore Gate looms at the entrance to the Red Fort, flanked by crenelated battlements.

adjoining **Diwan-i-Khas**, the majestic private audience hall, where the emperor received his most important visitors seated on his priceless Peacock Throne. This was given its name from two peacock forms outlined in jewels forming the main part of the design. After the plundering Nadir Shah took it back with him to Persia, it was broken up and so no longer survives. Shah Jehan's famous inscription can still be seen above the entrance to the hall. Close by are the *hamams*, or baths, where royal parties took hot saunas and perfumed baths and could cool off by parading down the fort wall, which overlooks the Yamuna River. Aurangzeb's Moti Masjid, or Pearl Mosque was built in 1622 for his own private worship. It's worth returning for the excellent sound- and light-show dramatizing the Red Fort's history held at 8:30 to 9:30 pm within the central courtyard.

Directly opposite the Red Fort sprawls **Chandni Chowk**'s arterial row of bustling bazaars. It was laid out in 1648 by Shah Jehan's daughter Jehanara Begum with a central canal flanked by merchants and nobles' mansions. If you took away the multitude of jangling cycle-rickshaws and humpbacked Ambassador cars, you'd swear that little had altered its inexorably oriental character for centuries. Residents know its web of narrow alleys like an intimate secret — but newcomers often get lost quite happily for hours, fascinated by its explosive street life, wafting smells and bizarre sights, every second humming with activity in every directions. Scrawny coolies weave in and out like human oxen here, pavement barbers lather and snip there. Street photographers huddle in Victorian cameras to immortalize clients against surrealistic landscapes, while matrons scrutinize silver jewelry for timid brides. Wobbling rickshaws pull wooden cages of giggling kohl-eyed schoolchildren, while ash-smeared ascetics trudge through with tridents and begging bowls. Almost everything can be found here, but the historic lanes are most fun to browse — **Pul-ki-Mandi** for flowers, **Dariba Kalan** for moneylenders, weight-priced gold and silver, **Kinari Galli** for wedding garb, tinsel and turbans, and Nai Srak for perfume. Don't forget **Paratha-Wali-Gali** (see RESTAURANTS, page 76) if all this walking has given you an appetite. The moment you start to feel slightly fractious having to sidestep speeding rickshaws, clumsy cows and bubbling vats of ghee, climb aboard a cycle-rickshaw — it's exactly the right pace, and it enables you to see far more without constantly glancing behind or beneath you.

At the top of the Chowk is the seventeenth century **Digambar Jain Mandir**, better known by tourists for the **Bird Hospital** within its grounds, where hundreds of sick birds are ad-

ministered splints and medicine and even given ceremonial cremations on the banks of the Yamuna if they die. Non-vegetarian birds, like vultures, are considered spiritually unclean, and are only allowed in as "out-patients!" Visitors are welcome and donations help keep the birds in grain. From here, just let your feet wander — but landmarks include the seventeenth century **Sikh Gurudwara Sisgani**, dedicated to Tegh Bahudur, a Sikh guru beheaded by Aurangzeb and the *Kotawali* (police station) where mutineers were hung by the British after the 1857 Mutiny. Make sure you pay a visit to the lively **Spice Market** at the end of the Chowk near Fatepuri Masjid.

It's impossible to miss the tapering minarets and onion domes of the **Jama Masjid**, India's largest mosque opposite the Red Fort. Built predominantly from red sandstone and white marble, and adorned with exquisite Mughal inlay, it was commissioned by Shah Jehan in 1644 and completed by Aurangzeb 14 years later. There are three main gateways, each approached by steep flights of stairs — the magnificent eastern gate reserved for the Emperor riding in magnificent procession to attend Friday prayers. It's the epicenter of India's Muslim community — you'll notice black flags which mourn the death of Muslims in communal violence — and on Fridays and Islamic festivals thousands of white-capped devotees prostrate themselves in its central courtyard — which accommodates up to 20,000. A small booth at the entrance sells tickets to the 46-m (150-ft) -high **South Minaret**, where a 122-step climb earns you one of the best views across the old city. Women must be accompanied by "responsible family members" — a rule imposed after several incidents of molestation up in the tower. Within the courtyard is a small marble crypt containing various treasures — an alleged whisker from the Prophet's beard, the imprint of his foot at Mecca, and ancient Urdu parchments.

CIVIL LINES: THE CUSP OF OLD AND NEW

Civil Lines was the British cantonment in Delhi before New Delhi was dreamt up. North of the old city near Kashmiri Gate, the area is dotted with crumbling historic homes — the scene of brutal murders of Europeans during the 1857 Mutiny — worth a stroll if you are especially fascinated by the Raj era in India. Places of interest include the Greco-colonial **St James Church** (consecrated in 1836), built by the larger than life Sir James Skinner, the son of a Scotsman and his Rajput mistress, who founded the Indian Army's yellow-clad Skinner's Horse Cavalry Regiment. Inside are beautiful stained-glass windows, oak pews and fascinating plaques to a deceased "Who's Who" of nineteenth century Anglo-Indian families, swarms of whom perished at the sepoy's hands. Skinner's own tomb is by the altar — and his many family members were buried outside — when he died 64 men contested his estate claiming they were his sons. Sunday services are held in English, but at all other times, between 8 am and 5 pm, a church attendant should be on call to let you in with a key. Nearby also see the nineteenth century **Lothian Road** and **Nicholson Cemeteries** and the once select, now seedy **Raj-era Mall** near Kashmiri Gate.

On Rani Jhansi Marg which winds uphill onto North Ridge, you'll see the **Mutiny Memorial,** known as "Jeetgarh," or victory fort which looks like a lopped-off Gothic cathedral spire. It marks the spot where the party of cholera-stricken, beleaguered British, Gurkha and Sikh soldiers camped out for several weeks before mounting their assault and commemorates those who died in the attempt. Further up the road on your right is a motley-looking **Ashokan Pillar,** (273—236 BC) patched up after being broken in many pieces, with most of its Brahma script worn away. It was brought to Delhi by Feroz Shah Tughlaq, a Sultan of the fourteenth century. **Flagstaff Tower** stands on the crest, slightly off the road, with a gate entrance. Terrified British memsahibs and children fled here on May 11th 1857, as sepoys began rampaging in Civil Lines. The nearby **Oberoi Maidens Hotel** is a good place for a tea break.

Several other Raj-era treasures lurk nearby, difficult to hunt down unless you are especially zealous. Closest are the **Old Secretariat,** just north of here, and the once-magnificent **Metcalfe House** located not far from Delhi University at the northern end of Mahatma Gandhi Marg. Built in 1835, it was the museum-piece home of Sir Thomas Metcalfe, British Resident of the Mughal Court, who transferred all his family art treasures from England to India. Metcalfe died in this house in 1853, which was later occupied by his nephew, Sir Theophilus, Joint Magistrate and a key figure in rousing Delhi's Europeans to arms against the mutineers.

NEW DELHI: IMPERIAL INHERITANCE

Start with **Connaught Place,** built to commemorate the Duke of Connaught's visit in 1920. This paint-splintered ring of ever-widening colonial arcades is lined with dusty-shop fronts, airline offices, restaurants and squatting merchants selling everything from piles of books to (inexplicably) whips and knuckle-dusters. Other eccentric Raj-era oddities can still be fossicked out, like solar topees, military attire and old regimental silver — or you can pick through Janpath's overflowing Tibetan market — and there's plenty to occupy an entire morning.

Leaving Connaught Place, turn down Parliament Street to arrive at the **Jantar Mantar,** the astronomical observatory of Maharaja Jai Singh I of Jaipur. Built of sandstone and marble in 1724, this was the experimental prototype of five similar structures scattered across India, the most famous of which can be seen in Jaipur. It comprises four "instruments", including the huge "Prince of Dials" sun-dial, each designed to exactly measure the position of sun, planets and stars, as well as to predict eclipses. Set in pretty gardens, it's open from sunrise to 10pm daily.

Hail a rickshaw to visit the garish elaborate **Laxmi Narayan Temple,** on Mandir Marg, west of Connaught Place, built by the industrialist Birla family in 1938, and usually referred to as the **Birla Temple**. A "modern" Hindu, Birla wanted his temple to symbolize unity of faith, so he broke all the traditional rules and caste barriers and came up with something completely different. Constructed from a medley of different stones instead of the usual sandstone or marble, it is a mixture of many different types of Hindu architecture, but more radically, it's open to all Hindus, including harijans, or untouchables, and instead of being dedicated to just one god, it not only worships a whole gamut, but incorporates icons of other religions too — Buddhist and Sikh wall frescoes and a giant Chinese Buddhist bronze bell. The main attraction is Krishna's mirrored shrine, designed to reflect the deity's face from which ever way you look at it.

It's a short rickshaw hop to **Sansad Bhawan**, the circular colonnaded house of parliament designed by Lutyen's colleague, Sir Herbert Baker. Originally created for the Chamber of Princes, the Council of State and the Legislative Assembly, it now houses the Rajya Sahba (Upper House) and Lok Sahba (House of the People). It's quite easy to arrange a visit to watch India's political turbines churning — sessions are often, in *Times of India* parlance, "uproarious", and when tempers run high, certain members of parliament have been known to hurl their shoes in rage. Contact your embassy or the tourist office for details on acquiring a pass for front row seats.

Beyond is Lutyen's magisterial Indo-Baroque **Rashtrapati Bhawan,** the former Viceroy's Palace now used as the official residence of India's president and flanked by imposing secretariat blocks, both inaugurated in 1931. As pompous and awe-inspiring as this sprawling apparatus of empire was, the British proved only temporary tenants and its keys were handed to

India's politicians only 16 years after its inauguration. Somewhere beneath the palace lies a foundation stone originally laid by King George and Queen Mary at a site at some distance north which was later deemed impractically far away from the old city, so, to save face, the stones were secretly exhumed at night and carted off to the new site. Lutyens never really forgave his collaborator, Sir Herbert Baker, for miscalculating the steep gradient of the slope upon which this complex stands — the result of which obscured the view from India Gate up to Lutyen's Rashtrapati Bhavan. You can wander through the main entrances of Baker's secretariat buildings, now North and South blocks, where crucial executive decisions are made in an ambience rendered eccentric by nesting pigeons, aged shuffling tea "boys" and huge stacks of yellowing files. Curious tourists aren't allowed inside Rashtrapati Bhavan (where servants still use bicycles to get from one wing to another) but you can visit the adjacent four-hectare (10-acre) **Mughal Gardens** between February and March when they are gloriously in bloom.

At the end of stately Rajpath is **India Gate**, the 42-m (138-ft) -high memorial arch with its "eternal flame" built by the British in memory of the 90,000 Indian soldiers killed during the First World War and in the ill-fated 1919 Afghan expedition. After the 1971 war with Pakistan, Indira Gandhi added a smaller arch for more war dead. Enveloping it is the **Maidan**, the imperial village green, mowed by oxen and a magnet on hot summer nights for ice-cream wallahs, lolling families and courting couples.

THE HISTORIC TRAIL

Delhi's most famous landmark, the **Qutb Minar**, is best visited in the sunlit peace of early morning (avoiding scrums of tourists and irritating "hullooing" touts). Located about nine and a half kilometers (four miles) south of New Delhi, this "tower of victory" was the Empire State Building of ancient India — and at 72.5 m (239 ft) high it's still the country's tallest man-made tower. It was built by the Turkic "Slave king" Qutb-ud-din-Aibak in 1199 to celebrate his victory over Delhi's last Hindu ruler. Modeled on the tower at Ghazni, and adorned with Islamic arches, motifs, bold script, the red sandstone and marble five-storied structure has survived lightning and earthquakes (which destroyed the topmost cupola in 1803, at that time enjoyed by Europeans as a surreptitious picnic spot). After a gruesome

accident with many killed in 1981, visitors are not allowed up its tower stairway for spectacular views. Within the Qutb complex lies Delhi's first mosque, the Quwwat-ul-Islam or the Might of Islam. Begun in 1193, it was modeled on the Prophet's house in Medina and built with many decorative remnants from 27 demolished Hindu temples — figures of gods and goddesses which the Muslims found offensive were defaced and turned inward. Within the mosque's courtyard is the Iron Pillar, erected here in the fifth century. According to lore, if you can stand back against the pillar and clasp your hands, your wish will be granted. See also the richly carved tomb of Aibak's son-in-law, Iltutish, built in 1235, and the structures erected by the Khilji ruler Alu-ud-Din, the architect of Delhi's second city at Siri: the Alai-Darwaza (south gateway) the vast base and unfinished 27-m (88-ft) -high Alai Minar tower — intended as a sequel to the Qutb Minar, and his own tomb amid the rubble of his college for Islamic studies.

From here you can either drive eastwards to the rampart ruins of **Tughlaqabad**, (from which the huge amphitheater at Suraj Kund is a convenient detour south), or head back into residential New Delhi to browse through a cluster of forlornly beautiful monuments and tombs, built at different stages of the city's history, There's no need to tackle them all at once — in fact it's best to leave these until you feel in the mood for a quiet garden stroll away from the hectic bedlam of Delhi proper. Like all Delhi's historic places, they are open from sunrise to sunset. Perhaps start with **Safdarjang Tomb** at the end of Lodhi Road, built in 1753 to 1754 for the second Nabob of Oudh, Safdar Jang, its wistful charms enchained as the last of the great garden tombs constructed by the waning Mughals. Just south is Safdarjang Airport where Indira Gandhi's son and Rajiv's brother, Sanjay, crashed his plane in 1980.

It's barely two minutes stroll to the **Lodhi Gardens**, a picturesque necropolis of over 50 large octagonal-shaped, blue-domed tombs of the Sayyid and Lodhi dynasties (1451–1526) set amid a leafy park. School-boys play cricket on the green, retired civil servants read Hindu epics to rapt cross-legged illiterates, *ayahs* wander about with toddlers in tow, and MPs and diplomats jog breathlessly here. Tombs are everywhere, often sadly debauched with graffiti and sure signs of inhabitance, but look especially for the Bara Gumbad with its large dome, the Sheesh Gumbad which still has much of its blue-tiled roof intact and exterior inlay floral designs, and Muhammad Shah's tomb erected in 1450, one of the earliest prototypes of Mughal design.

A far more sophisticated version of this basic design can be seen at **Humayan's Tomb**, located at the very end on Lodhi Road (half-an-hour's

---

OPPOSITE: The twelfth century Qutb Minar, with its intricately fretted and embellished tower, seen through the archways of India's oldest mosque, the Quwwat-ul-Islam.

stroll) at the crossroads with Mathura Road. Flanked by four impressive archways and four garden squares, this black and white marble and red sandstone tomb is considered the architectural precursor to the Taj Mahal — with its octagonal base plan, grand arches, lofty double dome and fountains in a central canal. It was built in 1555–69 by Humayan's senior widow, known as Haji Begum, nine years after the emperor's death. Her tomb lies here, along with those of other Mughal royals, including that of Dara Sikoh, Shah Jehan's favorite son. It was at Humayan's Tomb that the last of the Mughals, Bahudur Shah Zafar, hid then gave himself up

courtyards, stalls are a jumble of perfumed rose water, embroidered caps, freshly slaughtered buffalo and hookah pipes. To reach the shrine, take the narrow path near the police station on Mathura Road. Along with Ajmer in Rajasthan, Nizamuddin attracts flocks of pilgrims for the Urs festival (dates vary from year to year) with poetry readings, fairs and performances of Khusrau's *qawwalis* or mystical verses.

From here, it's a 10-minute rickshaw ride north along Mathura Road to **Purana Qila**, which is said to straddle the legendary city of Indraprasatha. The walled fort's original structure was initiated by Humayan, but the Afghan Sher

to the British — his two sons were killed here by a trigger-happy officer. The Lodi-style tomb outside belongs to the nobleman Isa Khan, built in 1547, and the Mughal-style one to Khan-i-Khanan, a military general under Akbar, built in 1627. Across the road, explore the fourteenth century Sufi village of **Nizamuddin** which is still an exclusively Muslim precinct which grew up around the *darger* (shrine) of the Sufi saint Sheikh Nizamuddin Christi. He died in 1325, aged 92 and his tomb is the most famous of several in the Muslim cemetery here, including those of renowned Urdu poets, Amir Khusrau and Mirza Ghalib, and Shah Jehan's daughter, Jehanara, who loyally stayed with her father when he was imprisoned in Agra by Aurangzeb. Here life follows a medieval pattern, shimmering with heat, dust and flies; women live in strict purdah, goats are tethered in mud-bricked

Shah expanded it during 1538–45 in the interim decade before the ousted emperor returned from exile to wrest Delhi back. Two main gateways still stand — the northern Talaqi Darwaja or "Forbidden Gate" and the southern and Lal Darwaza which overlooks Delhi's Zoo. Inside, look for the Sher Mandal, a two-storied octagonal tower which Humayan converted into his library. A year later he stumbled on the stairs in his haste to attend the muezzin's call to prayer, dying from his injuries three days later. Just beyond is Sher Shah's **Qila-i-Kuhran** mosque (1541), and an interesting museum housing the site's archaeological finds which date back to 1000 BC.

Purana Qila is flanked on the right by the **Zoo**, India's largest and notable for its rare white tigers of Rewa and open-plan (water canals instead of cages) and open daily except Fridays from 9 am to 5 pm; and on the left by the **Pragati Maiden** exhibition grounds built for the Asian Games in 1982, which is worth visiting for its excellent **Crafts Museum**. This displays traditional icons, rare religious wooden figurines, tribal *bhutas* (folk deities) of Karnataka, terra-cotta figures from Tamil Nadu, textiles, brass crafts and utensils. Outside is a "village" collection of rustic huts peculier to each Indian state, and a courtyard where village artisans are invited to demonstrate how traditional Indian crafts are made. You can buy Rajasthani fabrics, terra-cotta pottery, bronze miniatures, Hyderabadi *bidri* ware and many other crafts very reasonably. It's open 9:30 am to 6 pm, and the crafts demonstration program lasts from October 1st to June 30th.

Slightly north-east of this area on Mathura Road is Delhi's fifth city, **Feroz Shah Kotla**, built during the fourteenth century by Emperor Feroz-shah Tughlaq. Much of it was wrecked to build Shahjahanabad, but its ruins are still impressive and contain one of Ashoka's inscribed pillars which dates back to the third century BC. (See THE NORTHWEST CITADEL, page 70). From here it's a 10 minute walk north-east down Mahatma Gandhi Road to **Raj Ghat** on the banks of the Yamnua River. A simple black marble slab marks the place where Mahatma Gandhi was cremated following his assassination on Friday, 31 January 1948. Members of India's ruling Nehru dynasty have had their funeral pyres here: Jawaharlal Nehru, India's first prime minister in 1964, his grandson, the hier-apparent, Sanjay Gandhi in 1980 and most recently, Indira Gandhi in 1984. Various dignitaries have planted trees here — most recently Russia's Mikhail and Raisa Gorbachev: Others include Queen Elizabeth II, Gough Whitlam, Dwight Eisenhower and Ho Chi Minh. Opposite Raj Ghat is the Gandhi **Museum**, open 9:30 am to 5:30pm except Mondays.

MUSEUM ROUND-UP

If you have time, Delhi's lesser-visited sights are very worthwhile. The **National Museum**, on Janpath, just below the Rajpath intersection, contains one of the largest and most precious collections of Indian art and artifacts. It houses many key finds from the Prehistoric and Indus Valley civilizations, terra-cotta figures dating to the seventh and eighth centuries, miniature paintings, and sculpture from the Maurya, Gandhara and Gupta periods. Central Asian antiquities are well represented, (with some Tibetan objects secretly smuggled out of Lhasa during the Younghusband mission in 1904) and there's a new wing devoted to folk, classical and tribal music instruments. The museum shop offers cheap replicas of famous sculptures, and shows good films at 2:30 pm on Saturdays and Wednesdays, and is open daily except Mondays from 10 am to 5 pm.

The **Indira Gandhi Memorial** at Number One, Safdarjang Road, the residence of India's former prime minister is preserved as a museum with many of her personal effects and a photographic display, after she was was assassinated in December 1984 while strolling through her garden by two of her own bodyguards, both Sikhs. Her recorded voice follows visitors through the garden, and the site where she fell is covered by glass, her bloodstains preserved. For another chapter in India's modern history, go to the **Nehru Museum** on Teen Murti Road,

near Chanakyapuri, where the residence of India's first prime minister has been converted into a fascinating repository of documents and photographs about his life. There's a sound-and-light show every night about Nehru and the independence movement. To see where Mahatma Gandhi was killed, visit the **Gandhi Smriti Museum** in Tees January Marg. All are open from 10 am to 5 pm and closed Mondays.

Rail-buffs won't need encouragement to visit Delhi's interesting **Rail Museum** in Chanaky-apuri, (behind the Bhutan Embassy) where highlights include an 1855 steam engine, a 1908 Viceregal dining coach and a museum stuffed with fascinating rail-lore, with its most eccentric exhibit the fractured skull of a wild elephant which charged a Calcutta-bound rail train in 1894. Original sepia plates of trains are also on sale for around Rs 400 to Rs 1,000, and the museum is open from 8:30 am to 11:30 pm and 4 to 7:30 pm (April to June) and 10:30 am to 5 pm (July to March).

Other notable museums are the **Doll's Museum** with over 6,000 dolls from 85 different

OPPOSITE: Dawn breaks over the medieval Jama Masjid, casting its distinctive silhouette across old Delhi's skyline. ABOVE: Itinerant street performers entertain in one of Delhi's shantytowns.

countries on Bahudur Shah Zafar Marg, the **National Museum of Modern Art** on Dr Zakir Hussain Marg, and **Tibet House**, 1 Institutional Area, Lodhi Road, which displays ceremonial items brought out of Tibet when the Dalai Lama fled the Chinese invasion. Tibetan handicrafts are sold, and there are often lecture and discussion sessions that visitors are welcome to join.

SHOPPING

If you plan to return home laden with exotic purchases, then Delhi is the best place for seri-

ous shopping. As India's competitive marketplace, its shops are overflowing with goods from all over the country. Hard bargaining pays off in Delhi, where prices are often hugely inflated for the tourist market—but often dropped just as quickly for the citywise. The biggest center is **Connaught Place**, and the best place to start browsing are at the fixed price **Government Emporiums**. Even if you don't buy anything here, you'll gain an insight into the range, quality and price of goods to expect in bazaars and shops elsewhere. The two-storied, merchandise-crammed **Central Cottage Industries Emporium** on Janpath has a fine range of fabrics, crafts, furniture, pottery, carpets, dhurrie rugs and jewelry. On the other side of Connaught Place on Baba Kharak Singh Marg you'll find the long row of government state emporiums, each specializing in the crafts of a single

state — they make a fascinating morning's excursion. Especially good are **Tamil Nadu** for colorful applique lantern and umbrellas, giant terra-cotta animals, bronzes and papier mâché masks, **Bihar** for fine raw silk, **Nagaland** for tribal woven rugs and bamboo baskets, **Orissa** for unusual *ikat* fabrics and toys and **Gujarat** for fine weaves, embroidered fabrics and lacquered furniture. The only drawback with the state emporiums (open 10 am to 6 pm) is its archaic system of sale (bills in triplicate done at one counter, collection at another). Just opposite is the **Regal Building Complex**, where it's worth visiting the **Khadi Gramodyog Bhawan**, which specializes in *khadi*, the coarse fabric that is spun, dyed, woven and printed by hand as opposed to handloom fabrics which are millspun, then hand-woven. Prices are government subsidized to promote cottage industry, and the whole place is festooned with pictures of Mahatma Gandhi, who as part of his Quit India campaign urged all Indians to burn British clothes and adopt khadi as a symbol of independent India. In the same block, is **The Shop** on Parliament Street for high quality leather goods, stylish linen, hand-printed fabric and pottery. Also in Connaught Place, comb through the underground **Palika Bazaar**, a warren of 300 stalls, and the **Tibetan Market** along Janpath, good for cheap clothes, ethnic jewelry, bronze, carvings and bric-a-brac.

Aside from Chandni Chowk's curio shops, (clustered around the Jama Masjid), it's fun to witness the lively Sunday market along Mahatma Gandhi Road, known as **Chow Bazaar**. Originally started during the Mughal period, this Indian version of London's Portobello Road is has an extraordinary assortment of old and new, and also crowds to see itinerant circus performers doing death-defying stunts. For essential oils, rose water, henna and ornate sandstone-carved bottles — all perfect for gifts — visit the unique **Chhabra Perfumery** at R-Expo, 1115 Main Bazaar, Paharganj.

For antiques and curios, you need go no further than **Sunder Nagar Market**, located near mid-way between the Oberoi Hotel and Purana Qila on Dr Zakir Hussain Road, with some 40 antique and art shops. If you're unsure about the authenticity of an antique or item of jewelry, you and the shop-owner can always pay a visit to the National Museum or to the Government Gem Laboratory in Barakhamba Road. For the best books, head for **Khan Market** (near Lodhi Gardens) Delhi's "prestige" market, which has **The Bookshop** for up-to-date book releases, or **Oxford Book and Stationary Company,** Scindia House, in Connaught Place. All the main hotels have shopping arcades, but the best are found at the Taj Group's **Khazana** shops, at the Maurya and the Imperial. For the finest Indian tea, also prettily gift-wrapped, go to the **Tea Room Aap Ki Pasand**, Netaji Subhash Marg, opposite Golcha Cinema, Old Delhi. Stop here after exploring the old city and for delicious iced lemon tea. Shops, in general, are open from 10 am to 6 pm daily except Sundays.

GENERAL INFORMATION

Consult the monthly Delhi Diary for its extremely useful directory that covers all the information centers, travel reservation offices, restaurants, theatres, embassies, hospitals etc that you could possibly need.Delhi is the place to stock up on information for your next destinations, as well as doing as much advance-planning and booking as possible to save hassle later. The main **Government of India Tourist Office**, © 332 0005 and 333 0008, at 88 Janpath is open from 9 am to 6 pm daily except Sundays offers answers to queries about all Indian destinations, and usually stock a good map of Delhi. This is where you book conducted tours for New Delhi (morning) and Old Delhi (afternoon), run by both ITDC (Rs 20) and DTDC (Rs 14). See also TRAVELERS' TIPS for addresses of appropriate Government and State tourist offices.

CORBETT NATIONAL PARK

India's most famous, gloriously scenic and well-organized tiger sanctuary is 267 km (140 miles) north-east of Delhi, in Uttar Pradesh is easily reached in six hours by car, or by rail to Ramnagar, the nearest station, 50 km away. It's named after Jim Corbett who spent a lifetime hunting down man-eaters and leopards in these parts from 1907 to 1939, and whose ripping yarns and instinctive understanding of these mesmerising beasts spawned a series of books, notably *The Man-Eaters of Kumaon*. Corbett Park has crocodiles, elephants, leopards, Himalayan black bear, hog deer, chital and spectacular bird-life (585 species). But it is the lure of seeing a tiger that draws visitors here. Stay at one of the many forest lodges, all comfortable and inexpensive with modest menus, but with confusingly identical names. In Dhikala, the main entrance to the park, there's a choice between the "luxury" New Forest Rest House and Annexe, New Forest Rest House, Old Forest Rest House and individual cabins. To add spice to tiger-watching, there are numerous lodges in the park, notably the Khinanauli Forest Rest House. For information and bookings contact the Reservations Director, Project Tiger (UP), PO Ramnagar, District Nanital or the UP Tourist Office,

© 322251, Chandralok Building, 36 Janpath, New Delhi. You can explore by elephant and jeep, or hide out in machans (watch-towers). The park's Ramganga river brims with trout and mahseer, and you're free to go fishing as long as you have a permit from the Dhikala Game Warden. Best season to visit is between November and May, with the park most beautiful between January and March.

PUNJAB

Tourists are now free to travel through Punjab

state, as the Indian government lifted its ban on foreign visitors citing a decrease in terrorist violence. In **Amritsar**, see the famous sixteenth century **Golden Temple**, the holiest of holy Sikh shrines. It was consecrated by the fifth Sikh Guru, Arjun, but the Sikh ruler, Maharajah Ranjit Singh created its grandiose marble structure and smothered its domes with 400 kg of gold. The city is named after its sacred pool — *amrit* (nectar) *sar* (pool). Make sure your head is covered and your feet bare, try not to swallow too much of dubious sweet *prasad* which temple attendants will encourage you to eat as a sign of good-will, and join the throng of pilgrims within the temple complex and see especially the **Akal Takhtor** "Throne of the Timeless God" facing the Golden Temple. Also seek out **Jallianwala Bagh**, 100 yards away from the temple complex's main entrance, where on 13th April 1919, General Dyer ordered his Gurkha troops to fire on peaceful protestors. Over 300 people died and the massacre ignited anti-British hatred in the struggle for independence.

OPPOSITE LEFT: A *paan*-wallah awaits customers in Chandni Chowk. ABOVE: Sikhs in ceremonial costume guard the sacred pool lake precincts of the Golden Temple complex at Amritsar, the holiest of all Sikh shrines.

Agra
and India's
Heartland

AGRA AND THE TAJ MAHAL

Agra is the medieval Mughal city of the famous Taj Mahal, the creation of a dynasty that dedicated its spoils to building architectural masterpieces. Its origins are recounted in the epic *Mahabharata* — as "Agrabana" or "Paradise", it was a strategic Aryan stronghold some 3,000 years ago. Agra first rose to prominence as the capital of Sikandar Lodi during the early sixteenth century, soon usurped by the Mughals, and both Babur and Humayan made some early efforts to establish it as their power-base. In 1566, the 24 year-old Akbar ordered the construction of his red sandstone fort beside the Yamuna river, and the city of Agra grew up around its lofty crenellated battlements, massive watch-towers and giant gateways. It was the dynasty's first major architectural venture, and it remained the center of imperial activity during the early years of Mughal rule. At is peak, tales of Agra's splendor and the lavish patronage of its powerful rulers lured emissaries, traders, missionaries, musicians, scholars, artists, physician, philosophers and craftsmen from practically every civilization, ushering in a period of creativity comparable to the Italian Renaissance. The mightiest of the Mughals, Akbar not only established control across almost three-quarters of the sub-continent, but also created an efficient bureaucracy and fostered the arts on a grand scale. His rule was marked by religious tolerance towards the people he had subjugated, and he set an example by taking a Hindu wife, Jodhai Bai from Amber, and raising her Rajput kinsmen to positions of eminence. His vision of creating a secular state prompted him to devise an eclectic faith, the Din-i-allahi, or "Ultimate Religion of God", combining what he considered the best elements of Islam, Zoroastrianism, Hinduism, Jainism and Christianity into a single, unifying religion, with himself as the divine god-head.

Akbar's legacy also included the nearby city of Fatehpur Sikri, described by author Geoffrey Moorehouse as "the most enduring, elegant ghost town than man ever abandoned" from which he ruled between 1570 and 1585, before quitting, apparently due to poor water supply.

It is Akbar's grandson, Shah Jehan, (ruled 1627–58) whose name is most romantically linked to Agra. He was a compulsive builder, addicted to monumental architecture inlaid with jewels and semiprecious stones (as well, apparently for his harem, whose population numbered some 5,000). He created the Jami Masjid and an array of lavish marble palaces, pavilion gardens and an exquisite mosque within Agra Fort — all executed with such finesse it was said of the Mughals that they "designed like giants and finished like jewelers". By far his greatest contribution however, was the Taj Mahal, the elaborate mausoleum for his beloved Empress Mumtaz Mahal, whom he called "The Light of the Palace" who died at 39 after delivering him his 14th child — only half of whom survived to adulthood. "Empire has no sweetness, life itself has no relish left for me now", Shah Jehan was said to have mourned when he heard the news. Although he was to outlive his wife by 35 years, Shah Jehan became progressively reclusive and devoted himself to what, apart from Mumtaz, had always been his passion — architecture.

As the "seventh wonder of the world", and perhaps its most enduring symbol of human love, the Taj Mahal is still India's most popular tourist attraction. For many it is one of the main reasons for visiting India, usually inspiring even the most seasoned traveler. Yet Shah Jehan grew restless at Agra, and by 1648 he had prepared his magnificent new capital of Shahjahanabad, now Old Delhi, as the new seat of Mughal power. However, Shah Jehan was fated never to reign from his imposing Red Fort in Delhi — within a decade he was deposed by his own son, the fanatical Aurangzeb, and spent the rest of his days confined to royal quarters in Agra Fort, from which the imprisoned monarch could gaze across the river to his finest creation, the Taj Mahal. Under Aurangzeb, the Mughal empire fell into slow decline, suffering random sieges by local Marathas and Jat forces, who wrecked havoc, even pillaging the Taj Mahal. By 1803, the British had marched their troops in, establishing their capital of the North-Western Province (now Uttar Pradesh). Their stately cantonment town, to the south of Agra fort, is now known as **Sardar Bazaar**, is now an oasis of peaceful bungalows and gardens, but was the scene of violent battles during the Mutiny in 1857.

Few visitors seem inclined to linger long in Agra, which despite its historic Mughal monuments, is also regarded as a tourist trap, swamped with assertive touts, beggars and tourist shops. It's worst at the Taj Mahal, where droves of prospecting con artists swarm up waving soiled testimonials, a bundle of smudged postcards or a mangled limb or two, and turn sightseeing into a mixture of the sublime and the ridiculous. Just when you're lost in the Taj's milky, mirage-like beauty, some smirking commission agent may sidle up, offering you anything from a cheap and nasty "light-up" Taj Mahal socket plug or an invitation to buy yourself a wife. Studious refusal to stop and converse, and sharp "no

OPPOSITE: Glowing like an opalescent pearl, the marble surface of the Taj Mahal with its floral inlaid motifs and stylized calligraphy is a masterpiece of exquisite ornamentation.

thank-you's" are the only tactics to ensure relative peace at the Taj Mahal. Rising at dawn helps too, and it's worth allowing time to view the Taj's chameleon-like guises in different light. You'll enjoy Agra's sights much more if you spend two or three days, rather than day-tripping from Delhi and also to cover surrounding sights such as Sikandra, Fatehpur Sikri and Bharatpur bird sanctuary. Other easily accessible destinations from Agra include Jaipur in Rajasthan and Gwailior, Datia and Orchha in Madhya Pradesh.

Like Delhi and most of central India, Agra is at its optimum best during October to March, when days are warm, nights just cool enough for a sweater, and the landscape filled with exuberant bursts of bright bougainvillea and mustard flowers. Attempting sightseeing during high summer entails distinct discomfort — temperatures can soar as high as 50 °C (122 °F) and choking dust storms, or *simoons*, sweep across the plains.

ACCESS

Located 204 km (126 miles) southeast of Delhi, Agra is conveniently reached by direct daily flights from Delhi, Khaju-raho, Varanasi, Jaipur and Bombay. Few travelers take the half-an-hour flight from Delhi, preferring to take the

Taj Express, which departs daily from New Delhi station at 7 am daily and returns from Agra at 7 pm, with a travel time of three hours each way — a convenient day trip if time is short. The Shatabdi Express also goes directly from Delhi to Agra, ending in Gwalior. It leaves New Delhi station at 6:30 am, arriving in Agra at 8:30 am, and returns the same night from Agra at 8:10 pm, arriving at New Delhi station at 10:15 pm. Its air-conditioned first-class cabins are usually luxurious, with free packed snacks and coffee. One-way fares range from air-conditioned first class at Rs 63, and Rs 27 for second class. It certainly works out cheaper, and often faster traveling by air, since flights are often delayed. A word of warning however — be wary of extra-chatty young men and pick-pockets — touts and thieves manage to make canvassing this popular tourist route worth

their while, and many have quite ingenious ploys all figured out. It's a five-hour journey by bus, with hourly departures from the main Delhi inter-state bus stand, and deluxe buses leaving daily at 7 am, from the ITDC Transport Counter, L-Block Connaught Place, costing Rs 40. At Agra railway station, day-trippers may want to join the excellent daily government-run tour of Agra's key sights, including Fatehpur Sikri, Agra Fort and the Taj Mahal in air-conditioned comfort with an articulate guide for Rs 35, with timings linked to train arrivals and departures. Tickets can either be purchased on the Taj Express or from near the Platform 1 inquiry window. The state tourism bus leaves the railway station at 10:30 am for Fatehpur Sikri, returning at 6:30 pm.

HOTELS

Agra's constant floods of tourists ensure that hotel rates remain India's highest. Rooms with a vista across the Taj (for moonlight gazing) are highly coveted, yet ironically, most of the luxury hotels who boast the superiority of their "Taj Views" are several miles away — you'll often find the best balcony seats in the

The Taj Mahal, the most enduring symbol of India, seen from the monsoon-swelled Yamuna River.

"front-row", the less-than-basic budget hotels clustered around the back of the Taj's South Gate.

Agra's top hotel is the five-star **Mughal Sheraton**, ©64701, Fatehbad Road, a design award-winning marble edifice with cascading fountains, terrace swimming pool and landscaped gardens. As far as the locals are concerned, this is Agra's real "Taj Mahal", a mecca of chic restaurants and tourist-crammed "atmosphere", and, for Agra socialites where they like to see and be seen. It certainly offers some of the city's best Mughali food, accompanied by Indian musicians, as well several good restaurants and may be the only hotel in India with a resident elephant, camel and mongoose. Rooms are in the expensive range.

The **Taj-View Hotel**, ©64171, is moderately priced, located just down the road. There's a good restaurant, swimming pool, travel desk and shopping arcade, and rooms cost from Rs 650 to Rs 850. Other "luxury" hotels are the **Clarks Shiraz**, ©72421, 54 Taj Road, situated within the leafy cantonment area, just next to the Indian Airlines office. It has a popular rooftop restaurant, swimming pool and comfortable "Taj-View" and the **Agra Ashok**, ©76223, The Mall, both moderately priced.

In the cheap range, try either the three-star **Hotel Mumtaz**, ©64771 or the slightly cheaper **Hotel Amar**, ©65696, both on Fatehbad Road with comfortable air-conditioned rooms, and less expensive "fan-cooled" singles. Two Raj-era options in this price range have more faded charm: the **Grand Hotel**, ©74014, 137 Station Road in the Agra Cantonment area with air-conditioned rooms, and the **Hotel Lauries**, ©72536, MG Road whose eccentric High-Raj atmosphere was profiled by one of its room guests, J.G. Farrell, author of *The Siege of Krishnapur*, as "a little island of English peace" with enormously high ceilings, non-flushing toilets, lizards, and "a dining room with a horde of waiters dressed in elaborate cummerbunds and turbans serving Queen's pudding, creamed rice and jam and egg-white...".

Back-packers tend to zero in on the main cluster of budget lodges around the back of the South Gate, just outside the precincts of the Taj Mahal. The area is riddled with prowling touts, tourist shops and cheap cafés — all of whom deluge you with offers of cheap accommodation. Check out the current travelers' favorite, Shanti Lodge, which offers Taj "special single cheapies", and clean doubles with roof-top views. Nearby, other good very cheap lodges that get consistent praise from tourists, are the **Agra Lodge**, the **Shah Jehan Hotel** and the **New India Hotel**.

RESTAURANTS

As well as its legacy of Mughal architecture, Agra also offers a chance to sample fine Mughali cuisine, refined by court chefs to tantalize the taste-buds of emperors. For stylish authentic fare, try the Mughal Sheraton's **Nauratna** restaurant, excellent for succulent spiced tandoori *burra* kebabs, *rogan josh* (curried lamb), mutton *biryani*, (mutton in saffron flavored rice), and rich *rasgulla*, (cream cheese balls soaked in sugared rose water). Or opt for a Rs 65 *thali* platter, either for lunch or dinner, which has a delicious selection of meat and vegetable dishes. Musicians and *ghazal* singers entertain while you eat. Also within the hotel complex, you'll find Agra's best Chinese Szechuen restaurant, and an outdoor garden café for barbecue dishes. The Clarks Shiraz has good-value Rs 65 dinner buffets at its **Rooftop Restaurant**, with a choice of Indian, Chinese and Continental dishes.

Outside the hotels, try **Kwality Restaurant** at 2 Taj Road, near the tourist office, for reasonably priced, promptly served Indian food. Nearby, for excellent cheap South Indian vegetarian food, try **Lakshmi Vilas** in Sadar Bazaar, popular with locals for Rs 7 breakfasts of fluffy *idlis*, *vadas* and banana *lassis*, but open all day, and Agra's local cheap Chinese restaurant, the **Chungwah**. Near the main entrance to the Taj Mahal, the ITDC-run **Taj Restaurant** is good for lunch or afternoon teas after sightseeing, with a pleasant outdoor annex. Otherwise you'll find plenty of cheap cafés catering to Western tastes jumbled around the tourist lodges near the back of the Taj Mahal's South Gate.

At night, the hotel-lined Fatehbad Road transforms into a long strip of alfresco food *dhabas* or sidewalk stalls, all lit by hissing gas lamps and doing a roaring trade in meat and vegetable curries, griddle-hot chapatis, and stewed, sugary *chai*. It's very basic — with knee-high tables, rickety stools and tarpaulins overhead — but always full of appreciative locals and street-wise tourists. The best to try is the **Amar Dhawa**, near the Raj Hotel.

SIGHTSEEING THE TAJ MAHAL

Described by Rudyard Kipling as "the embodiment of all things pure, all things holy and all things unhappy", the Taj Mahal is India's ultimate symbol. The so-called "Crown of Palaces" has been eulogized by poets and artists countless times, so much in fact that when Mark Twain visited in 1897, he felt himself "drunk on someone else's cork", but like him, most visitors still feel that the vision of its fabled splendor is more than ample compensation for traveling around the globe.

The Taj was Shah Jehan's greatest architectural project, completed in 1659 after 22 years of construction with some 20,000 artisans on the site — including many from Iran, France, Italy and Turkey. Beneath its tons of seamless white marble lies plain red sandstone, wrought to jewel-like brilliance by exquisite pieta dura inlay of precious stones and Urdu verses from the Koran, fretted marble kiosks, and bulbous domes. The marble came from Makrana in Rajasthan, and over a thousand elephants were required to transport it and work construction pulleys. Its cost in those days was well over five million rupees, and it is priceless by today's standards. Pollution smudges have done little to diminish the majesty of the building, perhaps the most photographed in the world. The Taj is ever elusive, its Macarana marble taking on different hues with changing light, emanating a ghostly phosphorescent glow in moonlight, a oleander-pink glow at dawn and dusk, and a blindingly white glare in the heat of the day.

Like lifting the veil from a beautiful woman, it was designed to tantalize the viewer with a series of coquettish glimpses as you pass through the courtyard leading to the huge red sandstone entrance gate, when all its splendor is revealed. Raised on a central marble plinth, flanked at each corner by minarets and silhouetted against the sky, the huge domed mausoleum gives the illusion of "hovering" above its reflected image in the central watercourse. Classical Mughal symmetry is achieved by precisely laid-out formal gardens and water pavilions, and by balancing the great tomb with two subsidiary buildings; one a mosque, the other an assembly hall. As remote as it might seem today, during the early years of the Agra cantonment, the early British once held moonlit balls here — although after the Mutiny in 1857 this was deemed a tad too inflammatory for local sensibilities!

As with any temple or mosque, you're required to take off your shoes before entering the cenotaph chamber — or opt to rent a pair of peculiar regulation canvas "slippers" to fit over your shoes — while they're guaranteed to make you feel like a shuffling yeti, they're a practical concession to the multitude of tourists who are sometimes (quite naturally) wary of entrusting their footwear to the official "shoe minding" service. The entrance level contains false tombs of Mumtaz and Shah Jehan, who actually were laid to rest in precise duplicates in a lower-burial vault, surrounded by a superbly fret-worked marble screen decorated with thousands of inlaid semiprecious stones. Once there was a golden screen around them, but in the eighteenth century, this was looted by the Jats

of Bharatpur, who also took away original silver entrance doors. The tombs are engraved with floral patterns of jaspers, emeralds, sapphires and other precious stones. But Mumtaz's sarcophagus is more elaborate, in line with an order from Shah Jehan, who wanted his wife's grave continually covered in flowers. The screen and the dangling Cairine lamp was donated by former British Viceroy, Lord Curzon in 1909. If you listen to the Indian guides, they'll tell you the story that Shah Jehan planned to build an identical tomb in black marble on the other side of the Yamuna, joining the two with a bridge. As fanciful as it sounds, this seems to be more legend than fact. It is true that on the other side of the river from the Taj, large quantities of old brickwork have been unearthed, which gave substance to the story — but they were later identified as the remains of walls and pavilions in one of Babur's gardens. Another lesser-known rumor concerns the late Shah of Iran's tour of India during the '70's, and whether or not Indira Gandhi granted his private request to be able to spend a night in the Taj Mahal with his wife, in the hope that she might conceive an heir.

Purists say the Taj Mahal is best seen in the moonlight, but after random incidents of vandalism, it's now open to the public only from dawn to dusk. The only way to see the Taj at night is to book a hotel room with a view directly overlooking it.

THE FORT

Built by Akbar between 1566 and 1573, **Agra Fort** was created as his much-needed military stronghold from which to govern the burgeoning Mughal empire. Determined at any cost to have an impregnable citadel, Akbar ordered it encircled by nearly two and a half kilometers (one and a half miles) of monumental 15-m (50-ft) -high turreted walls and wide moats, constructed from sandstone slabs so skillfully joined that Akbar's court historian wrote that even "a hair could not fit between them". Aside from Akbar's sturdy earth-bound battlements, few of his original buildings remain, for his son Jehangir and grandson Shah Jehan replaced them with their more opulent structures. Most of the fort's interior belongs to Shah Jehan's reign, whose residential jewel-encrusted palaces are linked by pavilions and terraces from which to gaze across at the Taj Mahal and the plains beyond.

Entrance is through the main southern Amar Singh Gate, named for the Maharaja of Jodhpur who was killed near the gate after coming to blows with Shah Jehan's soldiers in the Diwan-i-Am in 1644. It's emblazoned with the words Allah-o-Akbar, the Islamic call to prayer, which means "God is Great". Within, the first buildings visitors see were built by Akbar; the **Akbari Mahal**, Akbar's former quarters, and his son's Jehangiri Mahal, unusual for its Hindu decorative motifs. Look for the stone pool nearby in which Jehangir's wife Nur Jehan ("Light of the World") used for her rose water baths. Within the center of the fort is Shah Jehan's **Diwan-i-Am**, the hall of public audience, a pavilion supported by 40 carved pillars where the emperor once sat in state, consulting with officials and receiving petitioners. No ordinary citizen was permitted to venture further. Beyond lies the **Moti Masjid**, the pearl mosque, where the em-

pavilions, linked by colonnaded terraces set amid a formal garden. An adjacent sunken courtyard once served as a pool stocked with exotic species of fish, for emperor was fond of angling. Look especially for the **Sheesh Mahal**, the royal bathing quarters, where the light of a single lamp is reflected in thousands of tiny mirrors embedded in the walls and ceiling. Water cascaded down marble chutes into vast intricately-carved Turkish-style tubs. Within the courtyard stairs lead up to the octagonal **Mussamamman Burj**, or **Jasmine Tower**, named for its adornment of mosaics, flower-wreathed columns and beautiful marble filigree screens. It was here that Shah

peror, his family and attendants gathered for private prayer. From its domed ceiling once hung a huge priceless pearl. Near the mosque are a group of arcaded sandstone structures, the site of the annual New Year Meena Bazaar when the aristocratic ladies took on the role of flirtatious purveyors, selling exotic wares to the princes, nobles and even the emperor himself. As a local guide pamphlet rather graphically puts it, "Emperor Akbar used to attend in feminine disguise so that he could mix up with the female sex!" It was here that Shah Jehan, then a prince, met and fell in love with Mumtaz Mahal. The fort's true citadel of power was Shah Jehan's **Diwan-i-Khas**, or private audience hall, which glittered with solid gold, silver and precious stones. Here the emperor would receive important dignitaries or foreign ambassadors. Close by are the **Khas Mahal**, Shah Jehan's private

Jehan spent the last eight years of his life as a prisoner, dying in 1666. Like most of Agra's monuments, the fort is open from sunrise to sunset.

Agra Fort's **Delhi Gate** directly faces the squat domed Jami Masjid, built by Shah Jehan in 1648 and dedicated to his daughter Jehanara Begum, who loyally stayed with her father during his imprisonment.

From here, hire a taxi or auto-rickshaw for the 15 minute ride across to the opposite bank of the Yamuna River, about a kilometer (two-thirds of a mile) north-east of Agra Fort, to the **Itmad-ud-Daulah**, known as the **"Baby Taj"** — less frequented, smaller and yet somehow more delicately beautiful than its grander famous cousin. Completed in 1628, it is the resting place of Nur Jehan's father Mirza Ghiyas Beg (alias Itmad-ud-Daulah, the "Pillar of the State").

The story attached to Ghiyas Beg is fascinating, for his family became intimately entwined with the fortunes of the Mughals. The Persian noble fell out with the Safavid king Abbas of Persia, and fled to India with his wife and small daughter, but the journey was so difficult, and money and morale so low, that they decided to abandon the little girl to speed the journey. Allah intervened, or so it seemed, when a caravan traveling behind the penniless couple, found the child and returned her to her parents. Ghiyas Beg soon rose to prominence in the Mughal court, and his rescued daughter, Mehrunissa, became the beautiful young wife of a Persian general. On her husband's sudden death in 1607, the 30 year-old, Mehrunissa returned to Agra and became a lady-in-waiting to one of Akbar's widows. Here she was spied by the young Emperor Jehangir, who made her his Empress Nur Jehan in 1611. Despite being in purdah, Nur Jehan wielded formidable power and as her frequently drunken husband became increasingly ruled by his three main passions — art, hunting and his harem — she proved herself an exceptional administrator. Many of her family members rose in the Mughal ranks, including her niece, Mumtaz, the woman who inspired the Taj Mahal.

Itmad-ud-Daulah was the first Mughal tomb to incorporate the Persian technique of *pieta dura*, the inlay of semiprecious stones in marble that was later popularized by Shah Jehan in the Taj. A feminine touch prevails in its intricate geometric and floral mosaics and lace-like pierced screens, similar in style to the tomb Nur Jehan built for Jehangir, near Lahore in Pakistan.

Further north, you'll see the **China-ka-Rauza**, the "China Tomb" notable for its giant enameled dome, constructed for posterity by Afzal Khan, a noble in Shah Jehan's court. Continuing two kilometers (one and a quarter miles) north along the riverside lies **Emperor Babur's Ram Bagh Garden**, laid out in 1528 and presently being restored to its former glory. It's said that Babur was temporarily buried here before being permanently interred at Kabul in Afghanistan as was his wish.

Finally, visit **Sikandra**, 10 km (six miles) north of Agra, to see Akbar's vast beautifully carved, but ravaged red-ocher sandstone tomb set in a lush garden and completed by his son, Jehangir in 1613. Guarded by four monumental gateways, its architecture blends Muslim, Hindu, Sikh and Christian designs, reflecting Akbar's secular faith, with the lavish, more typically Mughal *pieta dura* inlay work added out of filial duty by Jehangir. Sikandra is quite a distance — taxis are more practical and cost about Rs 60, auto-rickshaws charge anything from Rs 25 to Rs 40.

SHOPPING

Agra brims with handicraft shops and emporiums, and is famous for its *pieta dura* marble inlay work, embroidery, carpets, and jewelry. It's also notoriously touristy, with plenty of shabbily-produced goods pumped out for impulse-buyers. Every taxi or auto-rickshaw driver will spin a story about their "brother's" shop, but if you take up their offer of visiting a certain shop, they're liable to rake up as much as 40 percent profit on anything you buy, meaning the overall price is inflated. As with most large Indian ci-

ties, make the government emporiums your first stop, so that you'll be able to compare quality and prices when picking through curio shops later. Good shopping areas include **Sardar Market**, near the Mall, and further up Balu Ganj, where hundreds of "factories" churn out marble inlay goods, painstakingly fitting in mosaic patterns in a process little changed since the days when the Taj Mahal was built. The easiest way to tell bone-fide marble from inferior soapstone or alabaster is to scratch it surreptitiously: alabaster marks, marble remains clear.

EXCURSIONS

For an adventurous, unforgettable day, combine Agra's two most compelling surrounding sights — **Fatehpur Sikri** and **Bharatpur Bird Sanctuary** for a single day's excursion. By far the most pleasant way to do this is to hire a taxi the day before, agreeing on the rate for a round-trip beforehand — usually in the range of Rs 400. If so, arrange to leave about 4:30 am (you'll soon nod off in the taxi!), and arrive at Bharatpur by

ABOVE: Detail of surface exterior at Itmad-ud-Daulah's tomb. OPPOSITE: Mughal columns within the Diwan-i-Am at the Red Fort.

sunrise to see all its exotic birdlife swoop and dive, fluttering brilliant plumage against the soft dawn sky. The return journey is then broken with an afternoon ramble through Fatehpur Sikri, and you'll arrive back in Agra around 5 pm in time to catch on-going connecting flights or trains. If you've more time to spare, it's much cheaper to make the hour-long bus trip to Fatehpur Sikri from Agra's Idgah bus station, and continue onto Bharatpur that afternoon for an overnight stay. From Bharatpur, which is located in Rajasthan's south-eastern corner, direct twice daily trains run to Agra, Jaipur and Delhi.

ABOVE: The magnificent citadel of Fatehpur Sikri with its stately arrangement of palaces, pavilions, gardens, shrines and administrative buildings, all in cinnabar-red sandstone. The world may not contain a larger, more beautiful and more perfectly preserved ghost city than this.

FATEHPUR SIKRI

This gigantic, forsaken sixteenth century city looms high above the dusty tableland 37 km (23 miles) southwest of Agra. It was the Mughal empire's most fleeting capital, and perhaps its most magnificent, still almost perfectly preserved. Emperor Akbar conceived it as a "modern" utopian city — a meeting place of enlightened scholars, philosophers and statesmen — and its distinctive architecture reveals far more of this ruler's brilliant and enigmatic personality than his enormous palace complex at Agra Fort.

For all his pragmatic hardheadedness, Akbar was inspired to build Fatehpur Sikri in a fit of romantic superstition. As the story goes, the emperor was is his late twenties, possessing as

began in 1565, and for a decade the site teemed with the empire's best architects, masons, stone-cutters and sculptors, as well as some ten thousand coolies to help build what came to be known as Fatehpur or "City of Victory", named for Akbar's victory over Gujarat in 1573. Even by the heroic and decadent standards of the Mughals, Akbar's magnificent sandstone metropolis must have seemed a sumptuous court, filled with palaces, pleasure domes, mosques, gardens, courtyards, bathhouses and stables, enclosed within a circumference of some 14 km (nine miles). A contemporary English traveler, Ralph Finch, wrote: "The king hath in Agra and Fatehpur Sikri 100 elephants, 30,000 horses, 1,400 tame deer, 800 concubines and such other store of leopard, buffaloes, cocks and hawks that it is very strange to see. Agra and Fatehpur Sikri are very great cities, either of them much greater than London". Yet by 1586, Akbar was forced to abandon Fatehpur Sikri, apparently when the water supply dried up, prompting a mass migration back to Agra.

Akbar's elegant inner citadel remains strongly evocative of his cultured Mughal court. His graceful buildings seem barely touched by the ravages of time, although only ruins remain of the original town on the periphery. There are two entrances to the city — the official one through the **Shahi Darwaza**, where licensed guides can be hired for several hours strolling, the other up majestic steps to the monumental 54-m (177-ft) -high **Buland Darwaza**, or "Gate of Victory", visible for miles, and bearing a Koranic inscription that was to prove strangely prescient for Akbar's city: "The world is a bridge: pass over it but build no house upon it. He who hopes for an hour, hopes for Eternity, for the world is but an hour." It leads into an enormous congregation courtyard, containing the **Friday Mosque**, or **Jami Masjid**, said to be a copy of the main mosque at Mecca, and the tiny white marble jewel-like tomb of Sheikh Salim Chisthi, ornamented with latticed screens and serpentine brackets. The holy man died in 1571, but the tomb was completed some years later on the orders of Akbar, and given much of its exquisite pieta dura work later by Shah Jehan as an act of piety. It was built on the site of the Sheikh's favorite meditation place. Childless women of all religions come to pray at the Sheikh's tomb for his blessings. The mosque and shrine are cloistered outside the city's main secular enclosure and must be visited separately.

much territory and wealth as a monarch could ever hope for, yet despite his many wives (and his extensive 800-strong harem) he lacked a legitimate male heir. Apparently the problem lay not in his fertility, but in the fact that his male children failed to survive. Akbar sought the advice of a Sufi Muslim saint, Sheikh Salim Chisthi, who successfully prophesied that the emperor's wives would soon produce three healthy male children. Sure enough the next year Jodhai Bai, one of Akbar's Rajput wives and the daughter of the Maharaja of Amber, gave birth to a son. He was named Salim in honor of the holy man, and became the future emperor, Jehangir. (The other two sons followed soon after.) Overjoyed that his line was secure, Akbar announced his intention to move his royal capital from Agra to a brand new city built at Sikri, the home of the holy man. Work

To the left of the Buland Darwaza is a very deep well filled with murky water into which local lads dare to dive if you give them a few rupees. From here it's a five minute stroll to the Shahi Darwaza. Within this royal citadel past the royal stables, stretch seemingly endless palaces, each more majestic than the last. First looms the casket-like palace that belonged to Raja Birbal, Akbar's brilliant Brahman prime minister, one of the "Nine Jewels of Akbar's Court".

To your right lies the principal harem wing for the Hindu wives, over which Akbar's Wife No.1, the Rajput princess Jodhai Bai presided imperiously from her spacious purdah-screened salon. Within the zenana (harem) were spacious gardens, fountains and a mosque, and privacy was ensured by solid gates guarded by eunuchs. Two favorite wives had separate abodes: Akbar's Christian wife from Goa, Maryam, lived in the so-called Golden Palace, named for its gilded interiors; and his Turkish wife, Sultana Begum, (who was, it is said, his favorite, despite her inability to provide him with a son) was the envy of all the harem for her elegant marble pavilion, once studded with precious jewels.

Look especially for the **Panch Mahal**, a five-storied architectural marvel and Akbar's personal citadel of pleasure, where he would wile away his evenings in the company of his harem. Close by, you'll see two of Akbar's quasi-bureaucratic chambers, the **Astrologer's Seat**, a ornamented pavilion where the resident astrologer played an important role in day-to-day court life, and the **Treasury**, or the **Ankh Michauli** (Hide and Seek) building, nicknamed for Akbar's favorite game in the harem, but functioning as the imperial repository of gold and silver.

This section leads onto the **Pachesi Courtyard** where Akbar and his courtiers used slave girls attired in brilliant dresses of different colors as pieces to play *pachesi* (a game similar to ludo), moving when ordered on a giant marble board, a notion that inspired India's famed film-maker Satyajit Ray to create his classic *The Chess Players*.

Akbar's private quarters flanked those of the Zenana, screened away from the courtyard, and his richly embellished "House of Dreams" or bedchamber is on the first floor.

Across the royal courtyard is Fatehpur Sikri's architectural gem, the **Diwan-i-Khas, (Hall of Private Audience)**. This single vaulted chamber is dominated by its massive central Lotus Throne Pillar, which supported Akbar's throne and is linked to the upper-level gallery by four suspended gangways. The central pillar is tiered with eclectic carved motifs of a potpourri of religions, reflecting the universal outlook of Akbar's faith. It is simultaneously the Hindu tree of life (of which the *bodhi* tree of the Buddhists is a version), the lotus flower stretching to the heavens, and the royal umbrella that protects the king and his subjects. Akbar's throne itself was designed to represent the nail of the river-god Indra, in an unmistakable allusion to the Hindu concept of the cosmos: the emperor in the middle

and the universe radiating around him. Within this resplendent honey-comb chamber, Akbar would conduct philosophical debates with adherents of diverse faiths, some Hindu, some Muslim, others mystics of no particular persuasion, and even missionaries from the Portuguese trading posts on the south-western coast of India.

Climbing to the roof of Diwan-i-Khas, you'll get a good view of the octagonal Elephant Tower to the north. Spiked with masonry "tusks", this tower is the tomb of Akbar's favorite elephant, Hiran "The Golden One". Even in Akbar's relatively tolerant court, Hiran was often called upon to perform one of the more gruesome punishments meted out by the Mughals. Convicted criminals sentenced to be "Crushed by Elephant" were placed strategically beneath his feet, whereupon he was usually ruthless. If the elephant seemed indifferent, and refused to squash the victim three times in a row, this was considered divine intervention and the happy criminal would be set scot-free. Further north, lie the remains of the caravansary, where visiting traders would stay; the Elephant Gate, (one of nine gates that dot the massive city walls), as well as the imperial workshops and market.

Coming out of the south door of the Diwan-i-Khas, you'll follow Akbar's route along a raised pavillion to the colonnaded **Diwan-i-Am**, designed for large public gatherings. Akbar sat at the center (flanked by unseen wives behind a carved *jami* screen), dispensing justice and hearing litigation. According to his biographer Abul Fazl, Akbar was "without harshness or ill-will", but if you examine the center of the lawn, you'll see the sickle-shaped stone where Hiran the elephant trampled convicted criminals to death.

You'll need a map, and may wish to hire a licensed guide — both available at the Shahi Darwaza entrance. If you're keen to stay overnight in Fatehpur, try the **Archaeological Survey Rest House**, where basic rooms cost Rs 20, bookable through the Survey's main (informative) office at 22, The Mall, Agra.

KEOLADEO NATIONAL PARK, BHARATPUR

Located in Rajasthan's eastern corner, 17 km (10.5 miles) from Fatehpur Sikri, Bharatpur is an ornithologist's paradise: one of the world's finest bird sanctuaries with over 29 sq km (11 sq miles) of fresh water marshland, originally developed by the Maharaja of Bharatpur for his legendary duck shoots. The sanctuary was established in 1956, when it had been a royal hunting domain for more than 200 years. During British colonial times, English aristocrats and their supporting casts of young subalterns never refused an invitation to a shooting spree. Sepia photographs in the old hunting lodge, now a tourist guest house, record arch-imperialists, Lords Kitchener and Curzon at at shoots in 1902, but it was Lord Linlithgow, a former viceroy, whose Bharatpur record remains unbroken and caused the demise of 4,273 birds on November 12, 1938.

Thankfully, today the park's 370 species of birds live in lushly beautiful, protected peace. The sanctuary is open from September to February, but best visited from November to January, when about 150 different types of migratory birds wing in for a temperate winter, usually from China, the Arctic Circle, Afghanistan and Siberia. Bharatpur's most famous residents are rare Siberian cranes, often as many as 40 out of some 2,000 believed to exist in the world. They take just under a week to reach India from Siberia. You'll see the Indian sarus, dazzling white egrets, hunch-back herons, water-dancing Chinese coots, gliding eagles, extravagantly-colored storks poised on treetops, lapis-blue kingfishers, and many others, dipping, diving and spiraling.

Arriving at dawn, (armed with binoculars, camera, a jersey and mosquito repellent) is an absolute must, when the mists rise and the sanctuary's feathered occupants stir into life with the first sun's rays, sending stereophonic bird-song echoing across the water. At the Forest Office at the main entrance, where Rs 10 tickets must be purchased, you can arrange bicycle (best for covering plenty of ground) and rowboat hire (for punting across the marshes), as well as hire one of their excellent guides, who are usually trainee ornithologists with a genuine enthusiasm for their subject. It's enticing to meander off the well-designated roads and marshland embankments — for there are plenty of established forest tracks, where you may encounter Indian antelopes and the odd wild boar, who tend to sprint away from human foot-falls. Cobras inhabit a small breeding patch within the park, and their mid-morning wriggle in the sun has become a small tourist attraction in itself — but it's wise to let your guide approach first! If you want to bone up on birdlife, take along Salim Ali's *Book of Indian Birds*. Jeeps and taxis can pick up passengers at a halt zone about eight kilometers (five miles) into the sanctuary.

After a morning's scout, you can proceed for a hot brunch at the **Forest Lodge**, the Maharaja's former hunting lodge and the sanctuary's nicest accommodation option, in the cheap range. Airconditioning is available but usually not required in winter. To book, call ©2322 or contact the Forest Office. Another in-park option is the quaint **Shanti Kutir Forest Rest House,** the former maharaja's old hunting lodge, perfect for secluded bird-watching. It's best to book in writing. In Bharatpur town, opt for newly refurbished old-world palatial charm at the Golbagh Palace Hotel © 3349, Agra Road. This former palace guest house brims with trophies, collector's item photographs and faded frescoes. Meals are excellent, with vegetables picked straight from the garden. Rates are inexpensive. Other good options can be found in Bharatpur town, otherwise try the RTDC-run **Saras Tourist Bungalow,** © 3700, on Agra Road, with practical, clean rooms, hot showers and a basic menu, (very cheap). Aside from the sanctuary, there's plenty to see in Bharatpur, a former British cantonment town. Its most impressive sight is

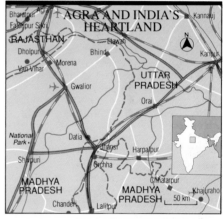

the eighteenth century **Lohagarh (Iron) Fort**, built by the Jat ruler, Maharaja Suraj Mal, the founder of Bharatpur, and named for withstanding numerous attacks by the British. There's an interesting museum displaying artifacts from the region, open from 10 am to 5 pm, closed on Fridays. It's also worth cycling to see the Jat dynasty's imposing palace and museum, where family heirlooms are displayed. Locals describe with relish how the present Maharaja's grandfather was renowned for his eccentric manner, and how he used to don his flying goggles and take off in his World War I biplane, laughing maniacally as he strafed "moving objects" in the fields below!

KHAJURAHO

The famous erotic sculptures of Khajuraho display the most sensuous and vivacious motifs of all Indian temple architecture, ranking close to the "Golden Triangle" of Delhi, Agra and Jaipur as a major tourist destination. Built between AD 950 and 1050 by the rich and powerful Rajput Chandella rulers, these temple sculptures with their countless scenes in praise of earthly passion are the very antithesis of India's modern, more censorious sexual mores. Situated in the middle of Madhya Pradesh's dry rural plains, Khajuraho was once a magnificent temple city, clustered with some 85 spire-peaked temples, of which today only 22 remain, seeming all the more extraordinary in their desolation.

A thousand years ago, Khajuraho was encircled by a fortress-like wall with eight gates, each flanked by two gilt date palms — inspiring the Chandella's to call their capital "Khajurvahika" or "city of the golden dates". The surviving temples are remarkably intact, revealing this ancient civilization's zeal for life it all its forms: spiritually, sexuality, music, hunt-

ing, and martial conquest. They probably owe their continued existence to their remote location, therefore escaping the destructive fury of icon-smashing Muslim armies as they swept across northern India during the eleventh century.

Why the Chandella kings — who claimed descent from the moon god, Chandra and worshipped Lord Vishnu, God of Preservation — decided to build their capital in such a remote barren spot remains a mystery. The pure technological feat of constructing these architectural marvels is impressive. The sandstone was dug from the Ken River 20 km (12 miles) away, and chiseled to crisp perfection by a laborious method involving cutting and carving every stone individually, then assembling it like a giant three-dimensional sandstone jigsaw. Believing that temple-building ensured a place in heaven, this dynasty erected the bulk of their temples in an intense burst of creative energy between the tenth and eleventh centuries. Five hundred years later, the Rajput Chandella empire was on the wane, and their fabulous capital became obscured by undergrowth, and the region notorious for its ruthless *thugs* or Kali-Worshiping bandits. The temples were recorded with dispassionate, if somewhat dismissive accuracy as "ruins" by a British military official surveying the region in 1819, leaving the discovery of Kha-

juaraho's wonders to the more adventurous Captain T.S. Burt in 1838. However his excitement at uncovering such ancient masterpieces was tempered with the realization that "the sculptor had at times allowed his subjects to grow a little warmer... than there was any absolute necessity for doing so", perhaps the most classic understatement of the Victorian era.

Today visitors are awed by the sheer intricacy, workmanship and optimism of the temple carvings. From a distance they resemble a kind of tiered, variegated beehive, but at close range, they depict a universal hierarchy seething with mythological gods and goddesses, warriors, seductive celestial nymphs or *apsaras*, animals and changelings. Certainly you will find countless loving couples locked in sexual union, *mithuna*, fondling each other, engaged in oral sex, (and even indulging in the odd bout of bestiality), yet this is presented as a natural and integral part of human nature. Above all they celebrate man's union with the divine and the pleasures of the material world.

During the British Raj, unwitting young memsahibs reportedly fainted away when faced with the more lurid of Khajuraho's couplings. Just after India's independence, when politicians were doing much soul-searching about their national heritage, they actually contemplated screening off "offensive" portions of Khajuraho's temples from public view, and classifying their famous ancient treatise on the art of sex, the Kama Sutra, as obscene literature — taking a stance towards there earthy ancestors that astonish any Western reared on notions of the "Wisdom of the East". For India is the heir to a religious tradition that took unashamed delight in sexuality, even adopting the phallic lingam and the female genital-shaped yoni as its most widespread symbols of worship.

Various theories have been put forward about the purpose of the sculptures. One story has it that the copulating couples were a test of the monk's celibacy, another that the figures were a graphic reminder to the worshipers to leave all earthly thoughts behind before entering the temple's hallowed inner sanctum. The most outlandish explanation was that the temples were built for purposes of sex education when the population was in serious decline!

Avoid Khajuraho's blistering summer, and arrive between November and February for cool comfort.

Khajuraho's highlight is its annual week-long Dance Festival, held during early March, when India's top classical dancers and musicians perform every evening against the flood-lit backdrop of ancient temples, rekindling the traditional practice of the *devadassis* (girls dedicated to Indian temples), and an unforgettable experience for performers and audience alike. Tickets range from about Rs 10 to Rs 50 per "seat", (a cushion space), and this is the time you'll need to advance book hotels and flights. While Khajuraho is small enough to see within an afternoon, it's best to plan to spend at least two days to appreciate its temple architecture by leisurely bicycling, returning for the charmed light of dawn and dusk.

ACCESS

Khajuraho is small enough to cover in a day and many visitors fly in on the shuttle flight from

comparable accommodation, and also has a good swimming pool and shopping arcade. The best cheap range option with air-conditioned rooms is the **Khajuraho Ashok**, ©24, slightly north of town. Of the array of budget (very cheap) lodges clustered around the town center try the **Rahil Hotel** ©62, which has clean rooms, as well as dormitory beds and communal showers, or the newly refurbished Tourist Bungalow, ©64, with rooms in the very cheap to cheap range for air-conditioned doubles. Otherwise try Hotel **Sunset View, New Bharat Lodge** or **Jain Lodge**, (very cheap) are all popular with back-packers, clean and within a min-

Delhi in the morning, and return the same evening. Daily flights also link Khajuraho with Agra and Varanasi. Arriving overland can be problematic — the most convenient railhead is Jhansi, 175 km (108 miles) away, for trains to and from Delhi, Bombay and Madras, while Satna, 120 km (74 miles) to the nearest railhead for trains from Calcutta and Varanasi. Regular bus services link Khajuraho with Agra, Jhansi and Satna.

Hotels

There are two top-class luxury hotels, both excellent, set in large gardens and convenient to the airport, located four kilometers (two and a half miles) away from the temples. The Taj-run **Chandella**, ©54, has moderately priced rooms, an idyllic swimming pool, excellent health club and serves an array of Indian, Chinese and continental food. The **Jass Oberoi**, ©66, offers

ute's walk from the Western group of temples.

Restaurants

The two leading hotels offer a range of excellent Indian restaurants with Western-style coffee shops. Beyond that, locals have cottoned on to foreign tastes and set up a row of open-air cafés near the entrance to the Western Temples, prettily lit up at night with fairy lamps. The best of these is the Swiss-run **Raja's Café**, good for full Rs 12 breakfasts of eggs, toast and coffee, and popular for its cheap, delicious Indian meals as well as its apple pancakes and banana fritters. Other highly patronized spots include the

ABOVE: The variegated surface of Khajuraho's beehive-shaped temples teem with countless *mithunas* or love-making scenes. OPPOSITE: An amorous couple entwined in one of Khajuraho's less explicit, perfectly chiseled embraces.

Safari Restaurant with good-value Rs 10 *mewari thalis*, the Madras Coffee House and the all-vegetarian Gupta Restaurant.

SIGHTSEEING

The Temple Tour

For easy reference, Khajuraho's medieval temples are divided into three main areas, the most famous of which are the Western group, located at the center of town and fringed by tourist cafés, lodges and shops. The Eastern group lies one and a half kilometers (just under a mile) away near the old village, while the

copy of Krishna Devi's informative pamphlet sold at the museum.

As a general introduction, the temples follow a distinct pattern, externally resembling a sort of giant textured beehive, tiered with rising spires or *shikaras*. Each is a compact mass of five parts, with an *ardhamanadapa* or entrance porch leading onto a pillared *mandapa* hall, then a *antarala* or vestibule, and finally an enclosed corridor, or *pradakshina* revolving around a central inner sanctum, or *garbhagriha*. The temples can be divided into two groups — those dedicated to Vishnu, Lord of preservation; and those dedicated to Shiva, Lord of destruction. Traces

Southern Temples is located some four kilometers away. The temples are open from sunrise to sunset, and it's possible to explore them in about five to six hours, best on a cycle hired from town; by auto-rickshaw, or a taxi for longer excursions. Enjoyment of the temples is definitely enhanced by the service of well-informed guide — you can always return to appreciate them alone. Bear in mind that the Archaeological Survey conducts free lecture tours of the Western group twice daily except on Fridays and holidays, leaving the main entrance at 9:30 am and 2:30 pm. Otherwise make your way across the road to Raja's Café, where talented graduate guides rent themselves out for about Rs 35 for half a day, or Rs 50 for a full day, as well as lunch allowance and "language allowance" if you happen to be French, German or Japanese. It's well worth getting a

are also found of Buddhism, Jainism, sun-worship, animism and various other cults that indicate the eclectic tastes of their architects. They also stand on high platforms, some two and a half meters (eight feet) above the ground, causing speculation that the Chandellas may have flooded these enclosures to create the illusion of a lake of floating temples.

Start with the famous Western group, first visiting its fascinating Archaeological Museum, located just outside the enclosure. It contains a rich collection of relics found within this area, and is open from 9 am to 5 pm daily except Friday. Remember to keep your ticket (with its strategic rip!) which also allows you to enter the Western group of temples. Just next door you'll see a shrine dedicated to the region's former ruling Maharaja Sri Pratap Singh Dev, touchingly laid out to recreate his personal bedroom, complete with a blown-up photograph of the deceased ruler and many personal effects.

Set within beautifully maintained gardens, the Western group represent the zenith of Chandella art. Just to the left, stands a quartet of early temples, all dedicated to Lord Vishnu. The **Lakshmana** (circa AD 930–50) is covered in rampaging sculpture, eulogizing the marital might of the Chandellas, and also notable for fine figures of *apsaras* with numerous erotic scenes on a frieze running around the temple base. Two small temples stand nearby, **Lakshmi** and **Varah**, the latter bearing a huge statue of Vishnu in his incarnation as a boar. Slightly south of the enclosure is the Matangeswara Temple, the fourth of the group, with its giant lingam This is Khajuraho's most popular "living" temple, and on festival days comes alive with clanging bells and vividly dressed villagers laying flowers and sweetmeats around its central shrine.

Walking westwards, you'll find the **Kandariya Mahadev** (circa 1025–50) the most artistically magnificent of all Khajuraho's temples, teeming with over 900 sculptured figures, its spectacular main spire soaring to a height of 31 m (108 ft). Friezes depict deities on their cosmic plateau, observing the activities of mere mortals beneath, swarming into epic battles with phalanxes of elephants and dragons (the symbol adopted by the Chandellas), or reclining with curvaceous young women on their return home. Every detail of contemporary life is captured here, portrayed with exuberant realism and humor. Above all they celebrate the idealized woman, with her hour-glass waist and high provocative breasts, smoldering with saucy sensuality in countless poses and moods. As if caught unseen, these seductive creatures go about their toilette, combing their hair, applying eye-shadow, preening in the mirror or perhaps joyfully entwine with their lovers. Here are found Khajuraho's most energetic and explicit *mithunas* (love-making scenes), graphic illustrations of the Kama Sutra. Just north is the small **Dev Jagdamba** temple, thought to have been dedicated to Goddess Parvati and on close inspection, filled with formidably athletic orgiastic sequences.

In the northeastern corner is the **Chitragupta Temple**, dedicated to Surya, the sun god, portrayed driving his chariot drawn by seven horses. There are interesting exterior reliefs of hunting scenes, dancing nymphs, rural processions, and fights between incensed elephants. Inside look for the 11-headed Vishnu in the central niche, each head representing his various incarnations. Completing the temple circuit is the **Parvati Temple**, notable for its inner frieze of the Goddess Ganga using a crocodile as a carpet, and the **Vishvanath Temple**,

dedicated to Shiva, and flanked by a large Nandi bull.

It takes about 15 minutes to cycle to the Eastern group of temples, following the dirt road to Khajuraho's medieval village. This walled enclosure is more evocative of the sedate influence of Jainism, lacking the frenetic erotic fervor of the Western group. The largest and finest of these Jain temples is the central **Parsavanath Temple**, with its elegantly chiseled *apsaras* engaged in prosaic day-to-day activities: fondling a child, writing a letter, applying make-up, removing a thorn from feet. Within the inner shrine stands an ornamental throne and ornate carved

bull, the emblem of the first Jain Tirthankara, the saint Adinath. Just outside is a circular museum which houses a find collection of relics, columns and broken-off friezes from the site. The Eastern group's Hindu temples are actually scattered in the surrounding fields nearby: the **Javeri**, dedicated to Vishnu, located near the village, the **Vamana**, 200 m (217 yds) north dedicated to Vishnu's incarnation as a dwarf and notable for its bands of dazzling maidens in a variety of come-hither poses, and the **Brahma Temple**, one of the oldest at Khajuraho. Nearby, you can't miss giant luridly orange statue of Hanuman, the monkey god, guarding a modern

Despite its popularity with tourists, Khajuraho remains very rustic and unspoilt, with an unhurried pace of life. ABOVE: An old man soaks up the morning sun. OPPOSITE: Bullocks being used to draw water in Khajuraho village.

Agra and India's Heartland

temple on the road out to the Jain enclosure. For more, temple addicts can venture out to the Southern group, four kilometers (two and a half miles) away to admire the two interesting temples, the **Duladeo** and the **Chaturbhuj**.

A highly rewarding day excursion is out to the fantasy tree-house built by Khajuraho's lovable eccentric, Gilles Bohnenblust, a Swiss who considers India his adopted home, and runs the Raja Café with his English wife Betty. His designer tree-abode has to be seen to be believed, perched high above the gushing torrents of the Ken River in Panna District, 23 km (14 miles) away. Among those eager to stay and experience life among the leaves have been actresses Julie Christie and Vivien Leigh. It's certainly a pleasant place to linger — they have possibly the world's most unique bar — and Gilles and Betty are about to offer guests the opportunity to experience luxurious tree life. If you're curious to see and possibly stay, contact the staff at the Raja Café.

GWALIOR

Located only 118 km (73 miles) from Agra (with regular trains and buses plying to and fro), and connected by daily flights from Delhi, Gwalior attracts few tourists, yet it offers one of India's most spectacular Rajput forts and is a good base for exploring two fabulous, deserted medieval cities nearby — Datia and Orchha.

Gwalior Fort, a colossal honey-colored sandstone citadel set some 91 m (300 ft) along a crest-like rock face, is the city's principal lure. Akbar was said to have been influenced by it when building his own Fatehpur Sikri. According to legend, the fort's history began in the fourth century AD when a sun-worshipping, but leprous Rajput chieftain named Suraj Sen encountered a faith-healing ascetic called Gwalipa on the fort's site — and after experiencing a miracle cure built the first fortress in gratitude. The ascetic also prophesied that if Suraj Sen took the name "Pal", his line would reign successfully in Gwalior. Suhan Pal and 83 of his successors did indeed rule after him, until Tej Karan failed to comply with the hermit's prerequisite for power. The Tomar king, Man Singh (1486–1516) built the six-towered Man Singh Palace, considered to be the finest example of Hindu architecture extant in India. Fresh usurpers have ensured many bloody battles for its possession, first Sikandar Lodi, then Moghul Emperor Babur, then the Marathas, whose descendants are now Gwalior's ex-First Family. Their ancestors battled with the British twice, and were twice returned to the throne. During the 1857 Mutiny, the ruling Maratha king at Gwalior was loyal to the British — but his 18,000-strong army

was not. They went to war independently with the British under India's Joan of Arc, the legendary Rani of Jhansi. She was slain alongside her troops in 1858, and the British moved into the fort, finally returning it to the Scindias in 1885.

You'll need at least a full morning or afternoon to do justice to this magnificent Boy's Own fortress, whose rambling battlements wind a five-kilometer (three-mile) -long circle. Approach it by the south-west Hindola Gate, passing the giant Jain statues craved from the rock faces (whose faces were defaced by Babur in a fit of pique). Inside is Man Singh's palace, a quintessential Oriental "wonder", with its six onion-dome cupolas, and myriad rooms adorned with dazzling lapis lazuli tiles, encrusted with broken jasper and emerald mosaics, a menagerie of carved gargoyles and peacocks, and even a natural air-conditioning system. The subterranean quarters beneath were used by the Mughals as dungeons, notable as the place where Aurangzeb hanged his brother, a possible successor to his throne. Also see the cluster of marble palaces built by the Mughals; the two eleventh century **Sasbahu Temples**, literally "mother-in-law" and "sister-in-law" temples along the eastern wall; the ninth century **Teli-ki-Mandir**, a curious temple built for newly-weds, with erotic sculptures which instruct young brides in the art of pleasing their husbands. There's an excellent museum housed in the fifteenth century **Gujari Palace**, just inside the Hindola Gate, with a fascinating collection of inscriptions, carvings, Gupta sculptures and miniature paintings. As at **Amber** (near Jaipur), caparisoned elephants carry passengers up to the fort's gate. The entire complex is open daily except Mondays, from 8 to 11 am and 2 to 5 pm. From April 1 to September 30, the schedule is 7 to 10 am, 3 to 6 pm.

Other sights in Gwalior include the ornate Italianate **Jai Vilas Palace**, built in 1872 to 1874 by the madly decadent Maharaja Jayaji, whose tastes ran to "see-through" glass furniture, gilt brocade, kitchy amusing erotica (see Leda in a loving embrace with a swan) and tiger-head trophies, Built during 1872 to 1874 while the British still occupies Gwalior Fort, it was designed by one Lieutenant Colonel Sir Michael Filose of the Indian Army as a princely showpiece for the Prince of Wales to sojourn in during his tour of India. Its gem-like **Durbar Hall** contains two immense chandeliers, reputed to be the largest in the world. Each is nearly 13 m (42 ft) high, carries 248 candles apiece, and weighs three tons. Before they could be hung, three elephants were hoisted to the roof to make sure that it was going to stand the strain. Not to be out-done, the next successor, Madhav Rao Scindia, built a silver train set that chugged its way around the dining table delivering mutton *vindaloo*, port and cigars. This gleeful Maharaja charmed the pants off the British — as legendary for his school-boy pranks and unerringly accurate water pistol attacks as for enthusiastically modernizing his state. He also staged perhaps the most elaborate tiger shoots in India for the benefit of the British aristocracy. One observer estimated that if the all the Maharaja's combined kills were laid out, they would stretch for more than two and a half miles — in the days when tiger slaughter was all the rage. Even more eccentrically, he managed to be the only Indian to fight with the British expeditionary force against the Chinese in Peking at the time of the Boxer uprising.

Also in town, you'll find the tomb of Tansen, the brilliant bard whom Akbar made Master of Music at his court in 1562, and according to local lore, chewing the leaves of the tamarind tree nearby gives you a mellifluous singing voice.

Stay overnight in Gwalior at the Welcomgroup's **Usha Kiran Palace**, ©23453, Jayendragunj, a stylish palace guest house crammed with 1930's furniture, set within well-maintained grounds. Air-conditioned singles are moderately priced, with slightly cheaper fan-cooled rooms. Otherwise try the government-run **Tansen Hotel**, ©215688, at 6 Gandhi Road, which has very cheap, comfortable rooms with hot water, or cheap rooms with air-conditioning.

DATIA AND ORCHHA

It's worth visiting Gualior just to make the memorable day-trip to the hauntingly forlorn palace-cities of **Datia** (69 km or 43 miles) and **Orchha** (129 km or 80 miles) — almost completely untouched by visitors. Regular buses ply from Gwalior to the city of Jhansi, 11 km (nearly seven miles) from Orchha, but hiring a taxi makes for speedier, more relaxed sightseeing. It's nicest to leave at dawn, driving past tiny hamlets and fields of swaying wheat, arriving at Datia in the morning cool. At Datia, the seven-story hill-top **Gobinda Palace** (1614) awed even Lutyens (who failed to be moved by many Indian buildings), who went as far as calling it "one of the most interesting buildings architecturally in the whole of India". The palace is a fabulous maze of latticed corridors, verandahs, pillared cupolas and fresco-covered rooms, once studded with semiprecious gems. It's to the west of the surrounding town, encircled by a seventeenth century stone wall.

Both the Datia and the Orchha palace-complexes were financed by Raja Bir Singh Deo, a Bundela Rajput ruler based in Jhansi during the seventeenth century. This rather Machiavellian character won sway and great wealth in Jehangir's court, rewarded for his services to the em-

peror when he was still Prince Salim and plotting to depose his father, Akbar. As one of Jehangir's side-kicks, the Raja was entrusted with the task of murdering one of the heir apparent's key rivals — Akbar's personal friend and chief advisor, the influential Abul Fazal, who was also an outstanding writer whose voluminous works provide an intimate account of India under the Mughals.

Up until the 1930's Datia was a standard spectacle included in viceregal itineraries — hosting the British Governor-General Lord Hastings in 1818 and the Viceroy Lord Curzon in 1902. Today it is a forgotten masterpiece, and gypsies camp in its decaying ruins with herds of goats. Continuing onto Orchha, the most magnificent and least spoilt of the two fort cities, with its palaces and temples rising from overgrown foliage, inhabited by deer and nesting birds. It's perfect for a quiet picnic and undisturbed exploring. Tucked away at Orchha's fringes is a tiny village with small shops and tea-stalls — connected to the medieval palace by an impressive stone seventeenth century bridge. Orchha's monuments are a rich amalgam of different architectural styles, with incorporating Mughal, Jain, Persian and even European features. Its most impressive structure is the perfectly symmetrical **Jehangir Mahal**, combining lofty walls with the fragile delicacy of numerous *jali* screens and ornate carvings. Close by is **Raj Mahal**, the royal chambers connected by a maze of colonnaded corridors lined with silver doors and exquisite wall paintings, even along the curving ceilings. Other palaces are linked by crossing Mughal style gardens with pavilions and fountains serviced by underground pipes. Orchha also has some beautiful and unusual temples. The **Laxmi Narain Temple**, dedicated to the goddess of wealth, Lakshmi, is covered in paintings depicting the pomp of Orchha court life, sadly defaced by graffiti, and the large **Chatturbhuj** temple dedicated to the four-armed Vishnu, with a layout that visually reproduces each of his four limbs. Along the Bewa River are rows of domed cenotaphs housing the ashes of Orchha's former rulers. The booklet *A Study of Orchha*, should be available from the Archaeological Survey Office or from the Madhya Pradesh tourist office in Jhansi. You can actually stay within the palace quarters, partly converted into the delightful **Hotel Sheesh Mahal** by Madhya Pradesh tourism authorities. Its most beautiful deluxe suite has its own sun-filled courtyard and large marble bathroom with a wall-size mirror. Suites and double rooms are in the cheap range, all with running hot and cold water and attached bathrooms — food is extra and perfectly adequate for a day or so. Book through the Madhya Pradesh Tourist Office, 19 Ashok Road, New Delhi ©351187.

VARANASI (BENARES)

CITY OF LIGHT

Varanasi, as Mark Twain put it in 1896, is "older than history, older than tradition, older even than legend, and looks twice as old as all of them put together." The spiritual heart of Uttar Pradesh state, it is one of the world's oldest continuously inhabited cities, and was a bustling metropolis when its main counterparts were the ancient centers of Thebes, Ninevah and Babylon.

Hindus flock to Varanasi for purification and death, to bask in the *Kasha*, or divine light that they believe emanates from the ancient holy city thousand or more temples clustered along the Ganges river. Washing in the sacred waterway is said to cleanse away all sin. To die next to the river and have one's ashes scattered into the water is the goal of every devout Hindu, who hold that this guarantees release from the eternal cycle of birth and rebirth.

Every dawn in Varanasi involves spiritual devotion on an epic scale. As temple bells peal across the city, thousands of pilgrims throng the ghats, or stone waterside steps, leading down to the khaki-colored sacred waterway. Bearing ritual brass vessels, marigold garlands and earthen oil lamps, they immerse themselves in the Ganges and reverently cup water to their lips as the sun rises. In soft, almost evangelical light, Varanasi's teeming river-front canyon of spire-topped temples, decaying eighteenth century palaces and ashrams, presents a haunting, unforgettable sight. Behind the ghats lies a medieval maze of tangled alleys crammed with glittering bazaars, ascetic priests, dusky-skinned urchins, tumeric-smeared fakirs with rope-like hair, white-clad widows, chanting mendicants and plump painted cows.

Hinduism's umbilical attachment to the Ganges river is thought to have begun with the Aryans, who understood that the waterway saved much of north India from being a barren desert. The 2,525-km (1,565-mile) -long river begins as a spring at Gangotri in the Himalayas and snakes through the northern plains into a mammoth delta of fertility before flowing into the Bay of Bengal. With its current it carries the hopes, the prayers and, in death, the ashes of millions of Indians. Other holy towns in Uttar Pradesh also line its banks: Allahabad, Rishikesh and Hardwar. Although Ganges water is sacred and countless people drink it, the river is severely polluted by millions of liters of raw sewage and industrial waste pumped into it each day. The problem is compounded by the Hindu practice of forbidding cremation of children, holy men and disease victims, who comprise the estimated 60,000 corpses annually thrown straight into the Ganges.

Archaeologists believe the city's mythological name, Kashi, probably derived from its earliest inhabitants, the aboriginal Kashia tribe, who settled by the river some 3,000 years ago and eked out a living by bartering woven matting made from local grass and known as *kushasans*. The mats are still made and used as umbrellas to shield meditating holy men from the often fierce sun.

The Hindu Aryans occupied the site around 800 to 900 BC, and the city soon became a magnet for philosophers, poets, mathematicians and pilgrims. Buddhism began at nearby Sarnath, where Prince Siddartha preached his first sermon in the sixth century BC after he found enlightenment by sitting under a tree.

Varanasi emerged as a prestigious and wealthy metropolis of gilded temples and shrines dedicated to the city's special deity, Lord Shiva. Local rulers constantly contested the right to claim its considerable revenue, and plundering northern invaders periodically laid siege. Varanasi's attraction had lain in more than mere intellectual or religious curiosity: its rich silks, brocades, cotton textiles and woolen cloth were coveted from China to Rome. Muslims frequently held the city to ransom from the eleventh century onwards, but the most ruthless destroyer of Hindu temples was the Mughal Emperor Aurangzeb, who converted into a mosque the Lord Vishwanath Temple, said to be the original home of Lord Shiva, god of creation and destruction. Hindu Rajas came to power in 1738, giving Varanasi a spell of local rule until it was ceded to the British in 1775.

Benares was the British corruption of a Mughal version of the old Hindu name. The ancient Hindu name Varanasi — a compound of the nearby Varuna and Asi rivers — was restored after independence.

The city has long been renowned for as a center of creativity and culture, and is still the best place to hear the graceful *thrumri* and *dadra* melodies of Indian classical music. Spectacular enactments of Hindu epics have been performed since the seventeenth century, and the Benares Hindu University founded in 1916 by the nationalist Madan Mohan Malviya is now India's premier school for Sanskrit and Hindu studies. Internationally renowned musician Ravi Shankar hails from Varanasi, as do many of the country's most talented sitar and tabla players.

OPPOSITE: Pilgrims throng Varanasi's ghats or steps to bathe and pray beside the Ganges River, which devout Hindus believe has the power of cleansing away cumulative sins.

Tucked away in the city's medieval old center are thousands of families, many of them Muslims, engaged in making Varanasi's famous silks and brocade fabrics, intricately carved wooden toys and carpets.

WHEN TO GO

Every day in Varanasi is dedicated to one of the gods in the Hindu pantheon, and pilgrims ensure that the city is lively all year around. But the weather is best between October and March as the monsoon swells the Ganges between mid-June and September. Varanasi stages during

September to October India's most flamboyant festival, the Ram Lila or Dussehra, a 10-day extravaganza of pageants, dance and music performances. Music festivals are the best showcase for Varanasi's extraordinary talents, the best being held at the Sankat Mochan Temple in early April when top musicians perform for four to six nights as a tribute to the Monkey-God Hanuman. Others to watch out for include the Lalit Sangit Parishad in December; the Rimpa in January and the Dhrupad Mela in late February. Admission is free, but bring a blanket to wrap yourself in as evening concerts often end at dawn.

HOW TO GET THERE

Indian Airlines connects Varanasi with flights from Delhi, Bombay, Agra, Khajuraho, Hyderabad, Calcutta, Lucknow, Allahabad and Patna,

and there are also connections to Kathmandu. Vayudoot flies from Delhi and Agra. A regular bus links the airport to the city, and the 22-km (13.6-mile)-long route costs about Rs 100 in a taxi.

Northern and North-Eastern railways link Varanasi to major cities, and overnight sleepers from Calcutta (12 hours) and New Delhi (17 hours) are the most comfortable rail option.

WHERE TO STAY

Varanasi's few luxury hotels are frequently over-booked, so try to reserve well in advance. Top of the range is the **Hotel Taj Ganges**, (©42480, rates: moderate). Opt for a high-storey room with a view across the leafy garden, swimming pool and the adjacent Nadesar Palace of the former Maharaja, where the Queen and Prince Philip stayed in 1955. Facilities include several excellent restaurants, a shopping arcade and travel desk. Two less expensive but comfortable options are the **Varanasi Ashok**, ©42550-59, and the **Clarks Varanasi**, ©42401, 42406. All these hotels are centrally located in the Raj-era Mall area and also will allow non-guests to swim in their pool for a nominal fee.

Hotel de Paris, (©42464-6; rates: inexpensive) is opposite, located halfway between the old St Mary's Church and the Tourist Office. A former guest house of the Maharaja of Benares, it has eccentric, natty charm, with a huge garden filled with hammocks and deck chairs, and a dining room crammed with sepia photographs and deer heads. Another good economy option is the popular **India Hotel**, (©42634, 59 Patel Nagar).

Budget travelers will find affordable space and peace at the **Tourist Dak Bungalow**, (©42182, rates: cheap). It's rooms are set in pretty gardens, but the food is dreadful. Backpackers tend to stay in the rock-bottom priced lodges clustered at the heart of the atmospheric old city. The **Trasmati Lodge** and the **Yogi Lodge** both have very cheap, crash-pad style accommodation right opposite the Golden Temple. You'll awake just before dawn to the sound of temple gongs, and the scent of incense and *parathas*.

WHERE TO EAT

Clarks Varanasi probably has the best restaurant, and it is pleasant to have pre-dinner cocktails in the garden before tasting their superb Mughali, Lucknowi or Chinese food that costs around Rs 80 per head. Lunchtime poolside barbecues are also popular. The **Taj Ganges** offers similar fare, as well as garden buffet dinners.

Locals swear by the generous portions and reasonable prices of the less glamorous **Dia-**

mond **Hotel** at Belapur, especially good for splurging on rich Mughali cuisine, fluffy *naans* and *kulfi* ice-cream. For light, nourishing south Indian food, seek out the **Kerala Café,** also at Belapur, open all day and excellent for lightly spiced *dosas,* lunch-time *thalis* and aromatic Mysore coffee. Other popular eateries can be found in the central Lohurabir area, including the **Tulasi Restaurant** for simple Indian cuisine. Nearby, **Kwality** has an extensive menu of Mughali, Chinese and Continental food.

Varanasi is famous for its sumptuous sweet-meats — *rasgulla, chum-chum* (oval-shaped, sprinkled with desiccated coconut and stuffed

stand view of the magical light filtering across one of the most spectacular scenes of devotional pageantry on earth. Rise at 4 am — you can always have a siesta — and take a cycle-rickshaw to the central **Dasaswanadh Ghat,** where you'll find plenty of boatmen willing to ferry you around at reasonable rates. A good introductory hour-long tour is to go upriver to **Asi Ghat,** and then return and proceed downstream to **Panchganga Ghat.**

You will see the faithful throng the water's edge, perform Hindu rites and energetically lather themselves with suds from head to toe. Young men strut about and limber up with

with *malai* cream), *kheer-mohan, pista burfi,* and others — best sampled from stalls in **Thatheri Bazaar** in the Chowk area. Residents often start their day with *thundai,* an aromatic concoction of milk, saffron, almonds, black pepper and ground-up marijuana or bhang. Many people are addicted to the brew, and also consume bhang in their *paan* mixtures.

THE GHATS

The city's life revolves around its seven-kilometer (4.3-mile) -long sweep of about 100 bathing ghats which skirt the west bank of the Ganges. Most were built in the eighteenth century, along with palaces and temples constructed by Hindu maharajas of Varanasi, Jaipur, Udaipur, Gwalior and Mysore. No visitor should miss taking a boat ride along the ghats at dawn for a grand-

exercises before making dare-devil dives from temple spires. Women surreptitiously bathe in their saris. Brahman priests hold court on plinths beneath palm umbrellas and give sermons about the Hindu epics. Pavement barbers shave heads of their penitent customers, dhobi-wallahs process mountains of soapy cloth and half-naked yogis sit frozen in contorted positions. Wrestling is a favorite pastime, and crowds cheer as they watch combatants tussle in a special pit in contests to clamber up a *malkham,* or smooth wooden pole.

Most travelers return from Varanasi with graphic tales of the city's death industry. Your boatman will no doubt take particular pleasure

ABOVE: Early morning activity on the ghats. OPPOSITE: Passengers ferried across the Ganges River silhouetted by sunset.

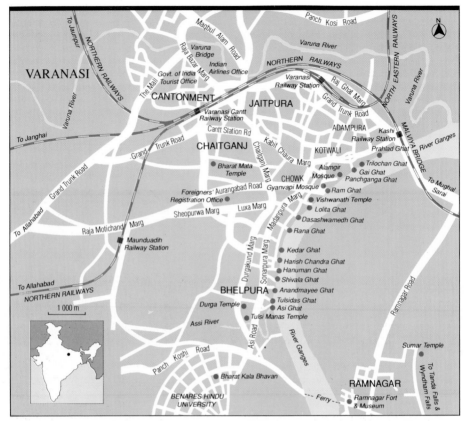

in pointing out "Ganga people," the whitened rubbery corpses which float downstream accompanied by marigolds and plastic bags. Locals shrug these sights off with Asiatic calm and humor, regarding them as all part of the flotsam and jetsam of Varanasi's great spiritual recycling of life and death. Some startled tourists may be instantly converted to vegetarianism. However, most find that fascination wins over squeamishness.

The busiest cremation or "burning" ghats are Manikarnika and Harishchandra. Corpses are wrapped in white muslin cloth and covered with orange marigold flowers, before being borne on bamboo stretchers to the pyres on the water's edge, traditionally set ablaze by the deceased's eldest son. Varanasi's caste of undertakers are the untouchable "doams," recognizable by their shaved heads and loin cloths. The Doam Raja is their hereditary leader who is held in great awe since his blessing is said to ensure a superior reincarnation. He surveys his domain from a house above Manikarnika Ghat that is decorated with two life-size plaster tigers symbolizing death's imminence.

The doams dispatch the dead with alacrity, building pyres, sloshing wood with inflam-

mable cooking oil, and enthusiastically swinging ceremonial staffs to burst open flaming skulls and ensure the soul escapes from the body. At Manikarnika Ghat, wealthy families vie to have their relatives cremated on the Chandrapaduka slab that is believed to be marked with the footprints of the god Vishnu. Grief is rarely evident as Hindus believe that once the soul is released, the body is just a discarded shell. But do not try and photograph the proceedings, as this greatly offends the participants and has caused numerous brawls between mourners and unwitting tourists, sometimes resulting in cameras being hurled into the Ganges.

During your boat trip, make sure you see the five most sacred ghats, the Asi, Dasaswanadh, Manikarnika, Panchganga and Raj. Pilgrims who bathe in each one consecutively believe their prayers will be fulfilled.

The furthermost upstream is **Asi Ghat,** which marks the confluence of the Ganges and the Asi rivers. Next is **Tulsi Ghat** which honors the poet Gosain Tulsi Das who translated the Ramayana and died here in 1623. The city's sewage pumps out under **Janki Ghat,** and nearby is the government's first electric crematorium, an experiment which pits faith against modernization, since it de-glamorizes an event most Hindus consider sacred. **Bachra Ghat** is used by Jains, and has three Jain temples. Beside it is the ornate **Shivala,** or **Kali Ghat,** the most impressive royal ghat still used daily by the former Maharaja of Benares and distinguishable by its huge Shiva lingam. **Hanuman Ghat** attracts hordes of devotees paying their respects to the monkey-god. Nearby, the **Dandi Ghat** is used by ascetics, fakirs and yogis. Past Harishchandra's smoking pyres is **Kedar Ghat** with its fine temples. **Mansarowar Ghat** is named after a Tibetan lake at the foot of Mount Kailash, Shiva's Himalayan home. **Someswar,** or **"Lord of the Moon" Ghat,** is said to have magical healing powers and attracts droves of hopeful lepers, cronies and terminally ill. Next is the ghat of **Ahalya Bai,** an eighteenth century queen of Indore.

Dasaswamedh Ghat is Varanasi's liveliest bathing place, named to honor the site where Brahma sacrificed (*medh*) ten (*das*) horses (*aswa*). One of its many temples is dedicated to Sitala, the goddess of smallpox. Nearby is the grand **Man Mandir Ghat** and an observatory built by Jai Singh in 1710. Mir Ghat leads to a Nepalese temple which is decorated with erotic paintings, and further inland is the **Golden Temple** (see below), Varanasi's most sacred shrine. Nearby are the two holiest burning ghats, the **Manikarnika** and the **Jasain,** a favorite cremation spot for India's elite.

At the northern is **Dattatreya Ghat,** named after a Brahman saint, Panchganga Ghat, where India's five holy rivers are said to merge, **Trilochan Ghat,** marked by its two turrets, and **Raj Ghat,** the final goal of pilgrims.

THE CITY

Back on land, it's most fun to comb the city's atmospheric medieval gullies, or lanes, seeking out bazaars and temples, peering into decaying palaces and emerging at the river-front. No accurate map exists of this remarkable web of stone-paved corridors, barely more than an arm's span wide, often dark and slippery, both enchanting and claustrophobic at the same time. Getting lost is all part of the fun. If all fails, locals claim that following a sacred cow will lead you to the river.

Start from the old city's main forum, the Dasaswamedh Ghat/Chowk area, and take a stroll down Vishwanath gully which leads to the famous **Golden Temple.** Hindus believe Shiva lives here, so it's far too holy for non-Hindus to view, although tourists can peer inside from the old house next door. The original temple built in 1600 was destroyed by the Mughal Emperor Aurangzeb, who, in a display of dominance over his Hindu subjects, built his Gyanvapi Mosque

on top of the site. A Maratha queen, Ahilya Bai, in 1776 reconstructed next door the present shrine dedicated to the god held by Hindus as the lord of the universe. The solid gold plating on the towers were given by the Maharaja Ranjit Singh of Lahore in 1835. Stalls along the lane sell flowers by the kilo, horse-hair fly-whisks, religious paraphernalia, ornate toys, glass bangles and filigreed jewelry.

To the south is the red-ochre **Durga Temple,** built in the north Indian Nagara style by an eighteenth century Bengali Maharani. It is dedicated to Durga, a fearsome incarnation of Shiva's wife, Parvati. She is placated by periodic

goat sacrifices, and the temple is renowned for its resident tribe of stroppy monkeys that often whisk away visitor's glasses and handbags.

Nearby is the modern shikara-style Tulsi **Manas Temple,** engraved with verses and scenes from the Rama Charit Manas, the Hindi version of the Ramayana written by the medieval poet Tulsi Das.

Further south is the **Benares Hindu University,** situated 11 km (6.8 miles) from the city center. It is open daily except Sundays from 11 am to 4 pm, and has an excellent miniature painting and sculpture collection inside its Bharat Kala Bhawan.

From here, you can either take a ferry or taxi to reach the eighteenth century **Ramnagar Fort** across the river, 16 km (10 miles) from the city center. The ex-Maharaja still lives here in a splendid suite overlooking the Ganges, although part of his ancestral home is now a well-organized museum with liveried guards and eccentric treasures giving a whiff of former glories: gem-encrusted weapons, moth-balled howdahs, palanquins, astrological clocks, decadent Kashmir vestments, ostrich eggs and vintage cars. It is open from 10 am to noon and 1 to 5 pm.

ABOVE: Faded clothes being hung out to dry at the Washing Ghat, Varanasi.

SARNATH

Sarnath is a serene Buddhist pilgrimage center about 10 km (six miles) from Varanasi that was the deer park where Buddha preached his first sermon around 528 BC to his five close disciples after receiving enlightenment at Bodhgaya in Bihar. His speech titled "Setting in Motion the Wheel of Righteousness" laid down the Buddhist doctrine of the "Middle Way," which pledged the path of righteous moderation in order to attain spiritual salvation, or nirvana.

Sarnath probably derived its name from one of Buddha's titles, Saranganath, Lord of the Deer. It became a monastic center, gaining official patronage as the capital of the Buddhist religion under Emperor Ashoka (circa 269–232 BC), the warlord turned pacifist who erected several

memorial towers or stupas and one of his famous pillars here. The Chinese Buddhist pilgrims, Fa Hsien and Hsuan Tsiang, who respectively visited in the fifth and seventh centuries, both recorded impressions of their stay. The latter wrote of Sarnath's vast monastery with 1,500 monks, the Ashokan pillar, lakes, gardens and magnificent giant stupas. Over the centuries Buddhism lost its initial momentum, and successive Muslim invasions in the twelfth and seventeenth centuries destroyed much of Sarnath's fabled grandeur, although the sprawling remains of this religious capital are still impressive. The huge swastika-covered **Dhamekh Stupa** dates from around AD 500, and is thought to mark the place where Buddha gave his sermon.

The excellent **Archaeological Museum** is open 10 am to 5 pm, except Friday. Its prize

are called *kinkhab,* and are highly decorative tapestries threaded with pure gold and silver and patterned with delicate motifs. Saris, stoles and cloth woven by craftsmen can cost up to Rs 20,000 a piece, but there are plenty of perfectly exquisite, much cheaper ones. For browsing or buying, you can view the finest selections at **Brij Raman Das** and **Ushnak Malmulchan** in the central Chowk area. The **Silk Corner** next to the Indian Airlines office in the Mall has a large range of reasonably priced good quality silks sold by the meter, as well as silk boxer shorts, cushion covers and ties.

The bazaars offer a plethora of goods, and it is easy to compare prices and bargain. The main **Chowk** and **Godowlia** areas are good for silks, brocade, perfume, paan and carved walking sticks; **Vishwanath Gully** for painted toys and images of gods and goddesses; **Thatheri Bazaar** for ornamental brass work and lacquered glass bangles; **Satti Bazaar** for saris.

Varanasi is also the best place in the world for sitar shopping. Serious students are welcomed by the senior sitar-maker, **Radhey Shyam Sharma,** who is a disciple of Ravi Shankar and has a workshop at 52/34E Luxmi Kund behind the New Imperial Hotel. A fine quality instrument costs around Rs 1,000 to Rs 3,000. Cheaper varieties priced around Rs 300 to Rs 800 can be found in **Nichi Bagh** off Chowk.

GENERAL INFORMATION

There are two main tourist offices: the Government of India Tourist Office (©43189) at 15B, The Mall, Cantonment; and the Uttar Pradesh State Tourist Office (©43486) Parade Kothi, opposite the railway station. Both are very ready with advice on city sights, shopping, music, dance and festivals, and are able to provide knowledgeable guides. At either you can buy Rs 10 tickets for daily morning and afternoon conducted tours — the Dawn river trip, temples, Benares University (5:30 am to noon), or Ramnagar Fort and Sarnath (2:30 to 6:30 pm).

The Indian Airlines Office (©43116) in Mint House, Cantonment, runs a bus shuttle to the airport, but the service can be erratic if you are in a hurry. The *Northern India Patrika* newspaper has good entertainment sections. The best local guide books are *Glimpses of Varanasi* by K. Jaycees, or *Benares* by S.N. Mishra. *Benares: City of Light* by Diana Eck (Princeton University Press) has detailed information on each ghat and temple in particular, as well as Hinduism in general.

exhibit is the four-faced lion capital which originally crowned the Ashoka pillar and is now the official symbol of modern India. It is a treasure-house of sculptures from the major periods of artistic activity at Sarnath — Mauryan, Kushan and Gupta — as well as later Hindu images from the ninth to twelfth centuries.

Sarnath's annual fete is Buddha Purnima, which commemorates Buddha's birth with a colorful fair and procession of his relics held on the full moon of May.

SHOPPING AND CRAFTS

Varanasi's famous silk and brocade fabrics are used by leading American and European designers, and have always been valued by wealthy Indians as wedding attire, to be passed down as heirlooms. Quality hand-woven silk brocades

Varanasi's riverside ghats stretch along the river's edge for nearly seven kilometers like a medieval canyon of plaster-peeling residences, eighteenth century palaces and ornate temples.

Jaipur
and
Rajasthan

VIBRANTLY exotic and colorful, Rajasthan — the "land of the rajas" — is in many ways India's ultimate destination. It is both a barren and an inhospitable land, laid bare to a blazing sun and shifting desert sands, and a fantastic time-worn realm of medieval fortresses. Yet everywhere throbs with a rich diversity of life and color. Rajputs are proud, handsome people. Lithe and graceful, clad in vibrantly colored cloth and glints of silver, they seem to the visitor's eye almost absurdly picturesque. In Rajasthan, one barely feels in the twentieth century at all.

JAIPUR

Known as the "Pink City", Jaipur is the bustling capital of Rajasthan. Nestled amid the rough-hewn Aravalli Hills, Jaipur was founded in 1727 by the brilliant astronomer-king Jai Singh II to replace his ancestral hill fortress of Amber, 11 km (seven miles) away. By the time Jai Singh II came to power at the age of 13, his family had earned the dubious distinction of being the first Rajput power to win sway with the Mughals by marrying one of their princesses to Emperor Akbar. Jai Singh proved a formidable statesman, and the Mughal alliance brought peace and privilege to his domain.

A man of his times, Jai Singh was an enthusiastic student of contemporary sciences. He laid out Jaipur on a grid system consisting of seven rectangular blocks of buildings fronted by seven magnificent gates, and precisely criss-crossed by broad 33.8-m (111-ft) -wide arterial avenues intersecting at the city's core — the City Palace — in keeping with the principles of the ancient Hindu architectural treatise, the *Shilpa Shastra*. In the new city, traders and artisans under court patronage were given their own lanes, a tradition that persists today. Until town planners went on a demolition binge after Independence, the city's encircling walls were completely intact — sadly, only portions now remain.

But the city retains a fairytale exuberance with its courtly palaces, colorful bazaars, and nearby fort. Its streets are spice-scented bedlams massed with bobbing turbans, cocooned women in tinsel-fringed scarlet clutching kohl-eyed babies, gamboling monkeys, camel-drawn carts, and jingling cycle-rickshaws. It's still the "highly ornamented curiosity... all in the soft, rich tint of strawberry ice-cream" described by Mark Twain when he visited the city in 1897.

Actually, Jaipur's overall "pinkness" was then only a recent phenomenon, dating from 1876 when the city was painted up for the visit of the Prince of Wales, later King Edward VII. Today, every shop-owner within the historic "Pink City

Boundary" is required by law to maintain his shop's façade.

As the final destination in the tourist's popular "Golden Triangle" of Delhi-Agra-Jaipur, the city is well endowed with hotels, restaurants, and shops — but also, unfortunately, with pushy touts and con-artists. Watch out for over-pricing and over-booking. Jaipur — indeed, all of Rajasthan — is best visited during October to February, when the days are sunny and crisp and the evenings cool. Jaipur celebrates all the major festivals, but it's especially worth visiting during *Diwali* in November, and the elephant processions and exuberant color-throwing mayhem

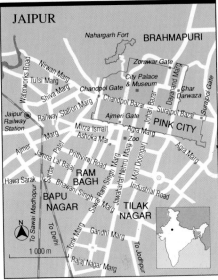

JAIPUR

during March and April, when both *Holi* and the Rajasthani *Gangaur* festivals take place. Also during March, polo fever hits Jaipur, with tournaments of elephant, horse, camel, and even bicycle polo being staged.

ACCESS

Indian Airlines operates two flights daily from Delhi to Jaipur, which is also linked by direct flights to Jodhpur, Udaipur, Ahmedabad, Bombay, and Aurangabad. Vayudoot offers an alternative flight from Delhi to Jaipur en route to Jodhpur, Jaisalmer, and Bikaner. From Delhi, the *Pink City Express* departs daily at 6 am, reaching Jaipur, via Alwar, at 11 am and returns to Delhi at 5 pm, arriving at 10:20 pm. Another late-evening train leaves Delhi and arrives in Jaipur around dawn. You'll avoid last-minute confusion if you remember that all Jaipur-

OPPOSITE: A crow's eye view of Jaipur, with vistas across to the surrounding Aravelli Hills.

ABOVE: Horses graze in the lake beneath the majestic
Amber Palace, the former capital of the royal Jaipurs.

bound trains leave from the Old Delhi railway
station. From Agra, both the *Superfast Express*
and the *Hawa Mahal Express* depart from Agra
Fort Station for Jaipur each day, via Bharatpur,
making daily return circuits. From Delhi and
Agra, there are regular departures of both luxury
air-conditioned and express buses from the
main interstate bus stations.

Jaipur is a perfect staging post for exploring
the rest of Rajasthan by train or bus, and has
direct rail links to Alwar (for visiting Sariska
Tiger Reserve), Sawai Madhophur (for visiting
Ranthambhore National Park), Ajmer (for Pushkar), Jodphur, Udaipur, Abu Road, and Ahmedabad, and Bikaner (via a stop at Sikar to link up
with the Fresco Trail).

HOTELS

Jaipur offers a broad range of hotels, ranging
from pure princely splendor to budget-priced
hostels. Top of the market are three royal palaces
— all run by the Taj Group. The most magnificent
is the five-star **Rambagh Palace**, ©75141, Bha-
wani Singh Road, the late-nineteenth-century
former official palace of the polo-playing maharaja Man Singh II — the world's only private
residence with its own polo ground. Set amid
manicured gardens, this marble palace offers
royal suites with period furniture, four-poster
beds, and art deco marble bathrooms. The Polo
Bar — judged one of the world's most famous
watering holes — and cane chair-strewn veranda are Jaipur's most relaxing oases at sunset.
Facilities include an excellent health club with

squash courts, a beauty salon, an excellent shopping arcade, a delightful 1930's pavilion-enclosed marble-lined swimming pool, and a jacuzzi, the latter open to non-residents for Rs 50. Modern rooms have standard five-star décor and are in the expensive range, but suites offer the proverbial lap of luxury for upwards of Rs 2,500.

Smaller, more secluded, almost as delightful and significantly cheaper (in the moderate range), are two other palatial royal mansions: the **Jai Mahal Palace**, ©73215, in Jacob Road, Civil Lines, and the more period-flavor **Raj Mahal Hotel**, ©61257, set in rambling gardens off Sardar Patel Road, a former British Residency later taken up by Jaipur's First Couple after they left the Rambagh. Prince Philip came here in 1965 and was introduced to the joys of *Holi* when he was showered with colored water by Jaipur's maharaja. All three can be booked through any Taj Group Hotel or Utell worldwide. The **Mansingh Hotel**, ©78771, on Sansar Chandra Road, lacks character but has modern amenities and is reliably efficient and centrally located. efficient and centrally located.

Jaipur has a number of quaint mansions belonging to ex-nobles which have been converted into guesthouses, all set amid peaceful gardens. The most charming of these is **Narain Niwas**, ©65448, Kanota Bagh, Narain Niwas Road, built in 1881. Its decadent suites are a repository of faded finery — four-poster beds, Afghan carpets, old lithographs, and flayed tiger skins — and prices are moderate. There are two little garden cottages, and simpler comfortable rooms for Rs 145. Breakfast on the terrace, with preening peacocks strutting past, is as relaxed and pleasant as Jaipur ever gets. All are well-priced and well-located, with friendly, if erratic service. Meals are prepared only to order. Also highly recommended are **Samode Haveli**, Gangapole (©42407) located north of the old Pink City walls, beautifully maintained and furnished with a large peaceful garden; **Haveli Hotel**, Statue Circle, (©75024), a 1940's style *haveli*, or mansion, with period furnishings, spacious lawns and swimming pool. **Bissau Palace**, ©74191, Chandpole Bazaar, a charming and peaceful refuge in the heart of the old city. Guests can browse through a beautifully kept library, peer at heirlooms, cool off in a backyard pool, and sip tea on the veranda. Excellent Western breakfasts are served. Single rooms to well-furnished suites are within the inexpensive range, all with air-conditioning. Right next door is **Khetri House**, ©69118, a 1930's-style bungalow with pleasant and cheap rooms. Other cheap mansion options are **Achrol Lodge**, ©72254, Jacob Road, in quiet Civil Lines, with spacious, quirkily old-fashioned rooms overlooking the lawns; and **Khasa Khoti**, ©75151, Mirza Ismail Road (known as M.I. Marg), which has comfortable rooms and a tourist office on the premises. Other hotels include the RTDC-run **Gangaur Tourist Bungalow**, © 60231, on Mirza Ismail Road and **Teej Tourist Bungalow**, ©74373, Collectorate Road, Bani Park, neither exceptional but clean and well-priced.

RESTAURANTS

Of the four leading hotels, the Rambagh Palace offers the most spectacular candlelit dining experience at its huge Italian marble-lined **Savaran Mahal**, which has rococo cherubs and pudgy maidens daubed on the ceiling. Regally attired waiters serve excellent Mughali dishes — although it's possible to pitch for less exotic Chinese and Western dishes — and there's an evening accompaniment of musicians and folk ballads. Dinner for two costs about Rs 300. The Mansingh's rooftop **Shiver** attracts scores of Jaipur businessmen for its superb Rs 75 lunches, and has good views and evening music.

Of the dozens of restaurants clustered along Jaipur's main M.I. Marg, the best are **Niros**, **Chanakya** (for vegetarian Rajasthani dishes), and **Kwality**, all reasonably priced with prompt service. For Sino-Indian fare — "masala-style", no chopsticks — try the **Golden Dragon**, just off M.I. Marg. One place where you can be assured of good food, fast service, and a friendly atmosphere without overstretching your budget is the **LMB Hotel** in the old city near Johari Bazaar. It is always packed with discerning backpackers for its delicious vegetarian dishes, *kachori*, savoury puffs served with hot chutney, and milk-based desserts of *rasmalai* and *halwa*. To round off a splash-out meal, Jaipur's best ice-cream counter is just outside.

Sightseeing

Jaipur's sights are concentrated within the old city in and around the City Palace complex. You can spend the best part of a day seeing them at your own pace, enjoying the colorful bazaars and street life in between. When this gets tiring, climb aboard a cycle-rickshaw and be whisked down Jaipur's wide boulevards — the best way to get around and still feel part of the color, scent, and activity all around you. Watch out for glint-eyed auto-rickshaw and taxi-wallahs, particularly those who besiege befuddled tourists emerging from the railway station. They have a pathological dislike of using their meters, so always agree on the fare in advance. The going rate for taxis should be no more than Rs 3 per kilometer (0.62 mile).

Jaipur has plenty of bike-rental places, including a rank outside the rail station. Enthusiasts rave about winding up the steep Aravalli ridge on the Jaipur–Delhi Road to Amber, 11 km (seven miles) away, stopping halfway to admire the eighteenth-century **Jal Mahal**, or "Water Palace", originally used by the maharajas as a summer residence.

You'll need at least two full days to see most of Jaipur's richly diverse sights and to poke through its bazaars for shopping bargains. The RTDC morning conducted tour is a good time-saver, with comfortable buses and English-speaking guides. The full-day tours can be exhausting, and the independently inclined may strain at the leash in a chronic case of too much, too quickly. Tours leave from the RTDC Tourist Office, ©69714, Gangaur Tourist Bungalow.

The Old Royal City
Start just outside the City Palace complex, with Jaipur's famous **Hawa Mahal**, or "Palace of the

Winds". Named for the cool westerly winds which blow through it, this five-tiered pink façade is ornamented with delicate overhanging balconies and gilded arches, yet this unique structure is only one room deep. It was built in 1799, so that veiled royal women could peer down through its 593 stone screens unseen by the world. You can climb to the top for a purdah-view of Jaipur, between the hours of 10 am and 4:30 pm daily. There is also a good "Jaipur Past and Present" display. On the pavement outside, Jaipur's famous "psychic parrot" will tell your fortune for Rs 5.

Behind the Hawa Mahal, a large square

filled with *chai* stalls and fluttering pigeons leads to the oleandern-pink **City Palace**, the symbolic heart of the capital. It is still used as a royal residence and as a backdrop for special state festivals. Jai Singh's eighteenth-century palace is an enchanted miniature metropolis in itself, occupying one-seventh of the entire old city area. The complex — with its confection-like pink façades edged with delicate lacy white borders, arched pavilions, and marble courtyards — has been described by architecture buffs as India's "most daring and successful synthesis of Mughal and Rajput styles". The palace courtyards are full of indolent, picturesquely dressed guards with flowing red turbans, many of them old retainers of the former maharaja.

Just within the entrance courtyard of the City Palace stands the dazzling white **Mubarak Mahal**, or "Palace of Welcome". Built in 1900, it was used first as a guesthouse, then as the Royal Secretariat; now it houses part of the City Palace museum, displaying a fine collection of antique textiles and royal costumes. Among the extensive displays of Rajput weaponry are such curiosities as gold daggers with crystal handles, guns tailored for a camel-back rider, and gruesome instruments designed to spring open in the unfortunate victim's abdomen. To your right is the ornate **Singh Pol**, or Lion Gate, with its guardian marble elephants, which leads into a magnificent courtyard flanked by tiered buildings of oleander stucco, and a marble **Diwan-i-Khas**, or "Private Audience Hall", at the center.

Sanskrit and Quranic manuscripts. Royal palanquins, gilt-studded ivory howdahs, and one of India's largest chandeliers complete the collection. The City Palace is open daily from 9:30 am to 4:45 pm, except on public holidays and festivals.

Directly opposite the City Palace is Jai Singh's fascinating astronomical observatory, the **Jantar Mantar** (see also page 83). Jai Singh's obsession for astronomy inspired him to pore over ancient texts, to ponder the calculations of Euclid and Ptolemy, and to pick holes in contemporary European theories of astronomy. He was the first Indian astronomer to emphasize scientific ob-

The two silver urns here, said to be the world's largest, were made to store six months' supply of Ganga water for a Jaipur maharaja who attended King Edward VII's coronation in London.

On your left, a gateway leads to the "Peacock Courtyard"; its four gateways are studded with glass mosaics and polished brass, each depicting one of the four seasons. Nearby is the seven-tiered **Chandra Mahal**, or "Moon Palace", the maharaja's personal abode. Its mirror-decorated topmost chamber affords fine views across the Jai Niwas Gardens, the eighteenth-century Sri Gobind Dev Temple, and the towering Clock Tower. Back in the main courtyard, the facing gateway leads to the **Sawai Man Singh II Museum**. On display here are some magnificent medieval carpets, most of them from Afghanistan and Pakistan, and some of the collection of Jaipur and Mughal school miniatures and rare

servation rather than theory, and he went on to revise the Indian lunar calendar and astrological tables. The observatory is open from 9 am to 5 pm daily.

One final place to visit in town is the grand nineteenth-century Indo-Saracenic-style **Central Museum (Albert Hall)**, south of the walled city in the sprawling Rang Niwas Gardens, which also contains a small zoo. This vast eccentric collection includes a fascinating display of Rajasthan's tribal groups, lore, costumes, and

ABOVE: The five-story pyramidal Hawa Mahal, (Palace of the Winds) in Jaipur is a classic example of traditional Rajput architecture with its *chhatris* domes, curved arches and latticed windows giving the effect of architectural embroidery in cinnabar and white.
OPPOSITE: Detail of a typically ornate façade in the so-called "Pink City" of Jai Singh's time.

arts. Among its more bizarre exhibits are 100 wax models of gruesomely contorted G-string-clad yogic sadhus or holy men, an Egyptian mummy, many bald stuffed birds, snakes rotting in bottles, hundreds of Austrian rock samples, some very decrepit stuffed crocodiles, and one inexplicable display: an ancient fish dangling in a case, with a tag marked "Fish" tied around its belly — definitely worth a giggle or two!

Amber

Few visitors fail to be moved by the dramatic Rajput grandeur of Amber, the hilltop fortress-palace 11 km (seven miles) north of Jaipur. Surrounded by fortified battlements, it straddles two sepia-hued tundra ranges in the Aravalli Hills overlooking Maota Lake. Higher still, the summit is crowned by a craggy fortress bastion, and the surrounding hills are latticed by sprawling crenellated walls. This was the citadel of the powerful Rajput Kachchwaha kings, whose illustrious descendant, Jai Singh II, founded Jaipur. Although they had ruled the region since the eleventh century, Amber palace was not built until the late sixteenth century, by which time the Kachchwahas had risen to power and wealth. You can either walk up the steep cobbled ramparts to the fort-palace complex or take the popular (but overpriced) ride on a caparisoned body-painted elephant. Passing through the main entrance gate, you'll step into a small courtyard containing the marble-pillared **Kali Temple** which has solid silver doors.

The multi-pillared **Diwan-i-Am** (Public Meeting Hall) nearby leads to Jai Singh's magnificent ceremonial **Ganesh Pol**, or "Elephant Gate" — an ornamental masterpiece of intricate inlaid mirror mosaic, fresco, and scalloped stucco-work. It leads into a charming garden courtyard flanked by royal apartments, many with elaborate frescoes, stained-glass windows, mosaics, plaster reliefs, and mirror-studded alcoves. The main attractions are the fountain-cooled **Sukh Niwas**, or "Hall of Pleasure", the glittering **Sheesh Mahal**, or "Mirror Palace", and the **Jai Mandir**, Jai Singh's royal abode, with glass and precious stones studded into a shining surface of powdered marble, egg-shells, and crushed pearls. Behind the garden court lies the elaborately latticed zenana, where each of Jai Singh's wives had a separate suite.

Amber is best visited in the crisp cool of early morning, allowing plenty of time to wander through the labyrinthine passages leading to the servants' quarters, watchtowers, and dungeons. Bring bottled water and a packed lunch and do what few tourists do — clamber up the steep, boulder-strewn slopes to the fortress ramparts, where you'll find an interesting museum, cool drinks, and sublime views in all directions.

Amber's fort-palace is open from 9 am to 4:30 pm daily.

On the way back to town you can stop at **Gaitor,** the cremation grounds of the Kachchwaha clan, to see the white marble *chhatris* or cenotaphs of Jaipur's rulers. Jai Singh II's is the most magnificent, supported by marble pillars and covered in ornamental friezes. Follow the steep road up the ridge to **Nahargarh** (Tiger) **Fort,** at the top, built by Jai Singh II in 1734 to defend his new city. Alternatively, it's a one and a half kilometer (just under a mile) climb up a paved pathway northwest of the City Palace. Either way, it's Jaipur's loveliest sunset spot.

SHOPPING

Jaipur has the most colorful variety of things to buy in all of India, ranging from enameled blue pottery, exquisite gem-studded, enameled jewelry, and traditional block-printed fabrics to brightly patterned dhurrie rugs. It is tempting to forsake Jaipur's other attractions and spend hours poking about in the spice-scented lanes, drinking sickly-sweet tea and chatting with artisans working at traditional crafts. The bazaars are concentrated to the south of the old city, while many of the modern shops and all the state emporiums are on M.I. Marg and Agra Road.

You can find the most famous of Jaipur's wares — polished gems, semi-precious stones, and exquisite enameled jewelry — in wide-open **Johari Bazaar,** near the Hawa Mahal, and in an opposite lane called **Gopalji Ka Rasta. Bapu Bazaar** and **Nehru Bazaar** are the places to find traditional tie-and-dye *bhandhani*-work and hand-printed textiles, as well as embroidered camel-skin *mojadis,* or slippers, and local perfumes.

ABOVE: Outmoded underwear fashions in a Jaipur shop. OPPOSITE: Chulgiri Temple TOP and Ranaji Ki Nasia BOTTOM, in Jaipur.

Along **Tripolia Bazaar's** long arterial boulevard are endless rows of brassware, terracotta pots, and the famous Jaipur "blue" pottery, and **Chaura Rasta** is crammed with costume jewelry and bangles.

For quality gems and jewelry, there are two particularly good shops to visit — bearing in mind that bazaar jewelry is not always "pukka": **Gem Palace** and the **Jewels Emporium**, both on M.I. Marg. **Anokhi**, on Tilak Marg, opposite the Udyog Bhawan, is easily India's best shop for a large range of traditional hand-block printed cottons and stylish European-style dresses (it has a cult following with Delhi's diplomatic wives). There's another outlet in the Rambagh Palace Hotel, and opposite Delhi's Ashoka Hotel. To see craftsmen making block-printed fabrics, marbled paper, and Jaipur blue pottery, make an excursion out to the charming village of **Sanganer**, 16 km (10 miles) south. The village is also noteworthy for its palace ruins, imposing antique *toranas*, or gateways, and several ornate Jain temples.

GENERAL INFORMATION

Of the six Rajasthan Tourist Offices around town the one at the Railway Station, ©69714, is particularly useful and offers good local information, maps, guide services, and reasonably priced car rental for out-of-town excursions.

SAMODE

If you can spare a night away from Jaipur, make a detour 42 km (26 miles) north to Samode, where there is an enchanting eighteenth-century palace built by Jai Singh II's finance minister, and now run by his descendants as a hotel. Surrounded by barren scrubland and crowned by the battlements of an old fort up on the ridge, it has exquisite jewel-box interiors, fine murals, gilded and painted surfaces, and *meenakari*, or inlay of mirrors and stones, as fine as that of the Sheesh Mahal at Amber. It's splendidly romantic, with a grand central courtyard, carved old furniture, faded courtly photographs, old retainers, and posing peacocks. Evenings are spent in the fine Durbar Hall, being served Rajasthani cuisine and entertained by musicians. The rooms are furnished simply and well. The bathroom shutters open to reveal spectacular views. Prices are in the cheap range.

At Jaipur's railway station tourist office you can hire a RTDC car to take you there for Rs 250 for the round trip. Local buses ply there from outside the RTDC Teej Bungalow, with a change at Chomu village. It's conveniently en route to Shekhavati. Book by writing, Hotel Samode Palace (©34), Samode 303806, District Jaipur, or contact Samode Haveli, ©42407, Ganga Pole, Jaipur.

RANTHAMBHORE NATIONAL PARK

Set between the Aravalli and Vindhya hills, Ranthambhore's 411 sq km (156 sq miles) of dry deciduous forest is tiger territory, full of picturesque pavilions and ruined temples with a thousand year-old fort silhouetted against the hilltop skyline. Since the eighteenth century, the area served as a hunting ground for the Maharajahs of Jaipur, who built a series of artificial lakes as vital watering holes for wildlife. The Project Tiger park also has leopards, hyenas, jungle cats, sloth bears, sambhar, chital, nilgai and chinkara. Marsh crocodiles and monitor lizards can be seen slumbering on lake-banks, and the park attracts many migrant water birds.

Ranthambhore lies 162 km (100 miles) from Jaipur, and can be easily reached by car or train. The nearest station, Sawai Madhopur, is only 13 km (eight miles) away from the park entrance. From Delhi, Ranthambhore is directly accessible on the Delhi-Bombay line. Stay at the ex-royal **Maharaja Lodge** or the RTDC-run **Castle Jhoomer Baori Forest Lodge,** ©620, both in Sawai Madophur or stay in the park at Jogi Mahal. Bookings can be made through Jaipur's RTDC offices, or the Field Director at Ranthambhore. Best season to visit is from November to May.

ALWAR AND SARISKA WILDLIFE RESERVE

A train halt lying 143 km (90 miles) northwest of Jaipur and halfway from Delhi, Alwar has a gruesome martial past, yet today is a languid town dotted with palaces and lakes, dominated by a 300-m (1,000-ft) -high battle-scarred hilltop fortress hewn from the jagged Aravalli Hills. It was founded as an independent princely state late in Rajasthan's history in 1776, but quickly made up for lost time with constant bouts of brutal warfare with Delhi's Mughals. Following an alliance with the British, Alwar's rulers concentrated their efforts on building pleasure palaces and staging extravagant tiger shoots.

Alwar makes a picturesque staging post for a visit to **Sariska Tiger Reserve**, 34 km (21 miles) away, staying overnight at either the **Sariska Palace**, ©22 (Sariska), one of the largest hunting lodges in India, or the RTDC-run **Lake Palace**, ©3764, which overlooks the beautiful Siliserh

Lake and wooded hills. There's plenty to see in town, starting with the opulent 105-room **Vinay Vilas Palace**, built in 1925. In its prime, its stables accommodated 3,000 thoroughbred horses and a herd of royal elephants. To the right of the palace is the magnificent two-story gilt carriage designed to straddle the backs of four elephants and carry 50 people off on a tiger shoot. Among the highlights in its fascinating museum are a cup carved out of a single emerald, enemy-scuttling weaponry, and a rich display of eighteenth- and nineteenth-century Mughal and Rajput paintings. It's open from 10 am to 5 pm, closed on Fridays and public holidays. Clamber up to the fort for an eagle's view of the **Pujan Vihar** garden and summer house, the royal *chhatris*, temples, and pavilions near the tanks.

A former royal hunting ground, the **Sariska Tiger Reserve** spans 800 sq km (300 sq miles) and is one of India's most beautiful tiger sanctuaries. You'll get as close as you would ever want to get to tigers by driving in jeeps or hiding in little *machan*-huts above the reserve's well-patronized waterholes (especially at dusk), and see plenty of leopards, sloth bear, hyenas, nilgai (blue bull), chinkara, four-horned antelope, and various birds. Stay at the **Tiger Den Tourist Bungalow**, ℂ42, with rooms in the inexpensive range, and a good restaurant. The season is from February to June.

THE FRESCO TRAIL

In Rajasthan's northwest corner, the dust-drenched, fresco-filled region of Shekhavati lies within easy reach by road or train of Jaipur, Bikaner, and Delhi. From the fifteenth century, when Rao Sheka defied the rulers of Amber, the area remained a semi-independent collection of *thikanas*, or fiefdoms. But it is the more recent painted walls in Shekhavati that draw visitors to this exotic backwater. It was once the heartland of the wealthy Marwari merchants, from near Jodhpur, who created townships clustered with ornate walled *havelis*, or mansions, which look rather like tiny medieval fortresses but are covered in elaborate life-sized paintings. Most of the frescoes date back to the mid-eighteenth century, worked in a technique similar to that developed during Renaissance Italy of working rapidly on wet plaster — a method that has kept many of them very well preserved. The earliest frescoes are loving depictions of popular gods, martial lore, and elephants — but the later works feature such startlingly quirky subjects as a mourning Queen Victoria, the visit of King George V and Queen Mary to India, podgy

pinstriped Indians waving farewell from a train, and even the Wright brothers in their odd-looking airplane.

You'll find the largest concentration of these beguiling creations within the districts of Jhunjhunu and Sikar at three major fresco centers: **Mandawa**, **Dundlod**, and **Nawalgarh**, each within an afternoon's driving and inspection distance of reasonably priced (Rs 250 to Rs 350) and charming palace-hotels. Of the three, try **Castle Mandawa**, ℂ24, Located 168km (100 miles) from Jaipur, 35 km (22 miles) from Sikar. Built in 1775, it is the most special — particularly when its courtyard throbs with unbelievable

pageantry during the festivals of *Holi*, *Gangaur*, and *Teej*. From the moustached Rajput guards at the entrance to the brilliant peacocks fluttering across the rooftops, it offers a splendid base from which to explore the surrounding villages. At the end of the day, return for a hot shower, a good meal, and a delightful room with original furnishings, either in the castle or in the converted stables. The same family run a Desert Camp, perfect for large groups with its deluxe Rajput huts (with attached modern bathrooms!) and village atmosphere, located just two kilometers (a mile or so) from Castle Mandawa. Both can be booked through: Old Mandawa, Sansar Chandra Road, Jaipur 302001, ℂ75358. The other excellent accommodation options are **Castle Dundlod**, ℂ61611, located 150 km (94 miles) from Jaipur, 25 km (15 miles) from Jhunjhunu, 14 km (9 miles) from Mukundagh. Built in 1756. Can be booked through Dundlod House, Hawa Sarak, Civil Lines, Jaipur, ℂ66276., and **Roop Niwal Haveli**, ℂ75358, located 28 km (17 miles) from Sikar. The best way of exploring these fresco towns is by jeep or car. If you arrive at either Sikar or Fatepur by train, there are plenty

ABOVE: Close-up of a fresco painting in Shekhavati district.

of drivers willing to bargain on rates for driving you around.

You can get there by taking the Shekhavati Express, which runs between Delhi and Jaipur daily and stops at Jhunjhunu, Mukundagh and Sikar, or opt for the erratic bus services linking Shekhavati's towns with Sikar and Jaipur.

AJMER AND PUSHKAR

Located within central Rajasthan, 130 km (80 miles) west of Jaipur and 198 km (123 miles)

east of Jodphur, the walled lakeside city of **Ajmer** is a curious Muslim toehold in a region dominated by Rajput Hindus — for it is India's most famous Muslim pilgrimage center, with its shrine of the Sufi saint Khwaja Muinudin Chisthi (1142–1256), a direct descendant of Muhammed's son-in-law, Ali. Its early history was scarred with bloody rampaging assaults by the Mahmud of Ghazni in 1024 and Muhammed Ghori in 1193, but it later became an important religious and strategic oasis town for the Mughal emperors. It was annexed by Akbar

Rajput villagers ABOVE gather for the annual Pushkar Cattle Fair. OPPOSITE TOP: Children dressed in Rajput finery for the Pushkar fair. OPPOSITE BOTTOM: Beasts of burden and labor, camels are prized for their endurance in the harsh, sun-baked tracts of the Rajasthan desert.

in 1556, who built a fort-palace which has now been turned into a museum. After 1818, it was ruled by the British, who founded the Mayo College, the first-ever Indian public school for young princes.

The city is strewn with historic Islamic architecture, most notably the **Adai-din-ka-Jhonpra,** the remarkable mosque built by Muhammed Ghori's armies in just two days on the ruins caused by an orgy of destruction that razed an ancient Sanskrit college and 30 Hindu temples; and the **Dargah,** a grand shrine built by Humayan, containing the relics of the Sufi saint. The Dargah is the scene of Ajmer's spectacular annual festival of *Urs,* commemorating the saint's death. Held for six days in April or May, the festival draws thousands of pilgrims. Curious tourists go to witness the dramatic spectacle of continuous *quwwali* singing, exuberant fairs, and feasts cooked in iron tureens so vast that people dance in them. You can stay overnight at the RTDC Khadim Bungalow, ©20490, moderate, or head northwest to the tiny temple-dotted township of **Pushkar,** 11 km (seven miles) away across the Nag Pahar, or Snake Mountain. Hindus believe Pushkar's beautiful lake to be sacred, second only to the Ganges River in purifying those who immerse themselves in it. According to legend, the lake was formed when Lord Brahma dropped a lotus flower while searching for a suitable place to do his *yagna,* or sacrifice. Pushkar also boasts the only Brahma temple in India.

But for most visitors, Pushkar means only one thing — the exuberantly colorful 10-day **Camel and Cattle Fair** staged in November, when this tiny oasis town is suddenly crammed with up to 200,000 Rajput traders and 50,000 cattle for an endless round of livestock-dealing, camel racing, fairs selling silver jewelry, embroidered shoes, camel-skin items, and woolen rugs, folk-dancing, music, and itinerant entertainers. You'll never have seen anything like it — the horizon massed with splay-legged camels and blazing with the most riotous bursts of color imaginable. It is a pageant of Rajput women in their swinging, multi-colored *ghagharas* skirts, tie-dyed blouses embellished with silver tinsel, and bedecked with silver jewelry, and turbaned men. Pushkar's modest accommodation facilities are swamped, and the RTDC sets up an amazingly civilized tented village for tourists, with a choice of double tents with shower and lavatory or communal tents, with food included in the tent price. At other times, stay at the Maharaja of Jaipur's former palace, the chaotically RTDC-run **Sarovar Tourist Bungalow,** ©40. Ask for the good air-cooled rooms. Rs 15.

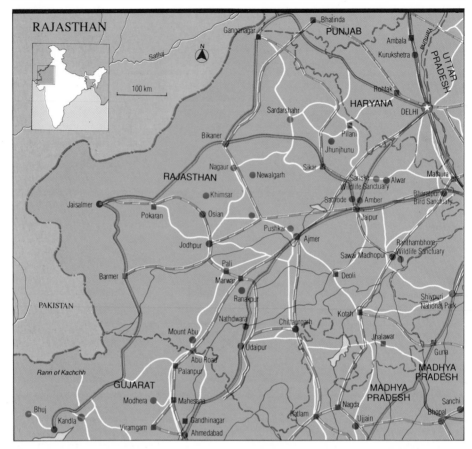

JODPHUR

Lying on the edge of the Thar Desert and dominated by its medieval fortress citadel, this flat, sandy, leisurely paced city was the former capital of the arid, drought-prone principality of Marwar, or "Land of Death".

The city was founded in 1459 by Rao Jodha — attracted by the natural defenses provided by its massive 125-m (400-ft) -high steep scarp — although his clannish Rathore Rajput forefathers had ruled the surrounding terrain since the twelfth century. Jodphur's rulers rapidly amassed vast wealth as a trading post on the main camel caravan routes, and its merchant class — known as the Marwaris — are still renowned in India for their mercenary prowess. Jodphur's main attraction is its extraordinary fifteenth-century fort, encircled along with its old city by a snaking 10-km (six-mile) -long stone wall punctuated by eight monumental gates. This fortress proved invulnerable even to the Mughals, who finally compromised by signing treaties with Jodphur's rulers, exchanging wealth

for military assistance to win Gujarat for the Mughal empire. The patronage of the Mughals reached its height in the mid-sixteenth century, when Jodphur's Rao Udai Singh married his sister to Emperor Akbar and his daughter to the emperor's son, Jehangir. Akbar may have secretly regretted the alliance — his Rajput wife, Jodhai Bai, managed to increase considerably the powers of the Jodphurs, but more importantly for Akbar she made him give up "beef, garlic, onions and the wearing of a beard", according to a court chronicle.

Mughal patronage turned sour when Jodphur's Jaswant Singh backed the losing side in a Mughal dynastic tryst for power between the waning Shah Jehan and his formidable son, Aurangzeb. One of the first commands given by the new emperor Aurangzeb was for the murder of Jaswant Singh's posthumously born boy heir to the Jodphur throne, who was then conveniently at the royal court in Delhi. The attempt failed (the boy was hidden in a basket of sweetmeats and whisked away to safety), but Aurangzeb wreaked his revenge in 1678 by sacking Jodphur and plundering the prosperous towns of Marwar.

Ajit Singh, the boy-prince, recaptured his kingdom after an interval of 30 years, becoming in the process one of Jodhpur's greatest heroes.

Jodhpur was then thrown into a century of dynastic disarray and bloody battles with neighboring states; by the end of the eighteenth century, it was seized first by the Marathas and then by the British. During the early twentieth century, Jodhpur was ruled by the quixotic and powerful Maharaja Umaid Singh, who left the remarkable Umaid Bhawan Palace, one of the world's largest private residences, as his legacy. The palace was built to keep 3,000 of his starving population employed following a devastating famine in 1923. It was completed in 1945, just before the maharaja had to cede his princely state to a new independent India.

Jodhpur remains curiously unappreciated by many travelers, who glimpse it only in passing, usually en route either to Jaisalmer, further west, or Udaipur in the south. But old-India hands rate its charms highly, for as well as its wealth of historic attractions and colorful bazaars, Jodhpur is a place where you can stray off the beaten track for a glimpse of village India.

ACCESS

Some 336 km (208 miles) from Jaipur, Jodhpur has direct flights to and from Delhi, Jaipur, and Udaipur. Unless you're on a fly-by-night tour, Rajasthan is perfect for train trips, with the overnight sleepers providing just the right degree of novelty without being unduly tedious. Good "overnighters" ply to Jodhpur from Delhi and to the main Rajasthan centers of Jaipur, Jaisalmer, Udaipur, Abu Road, and Bikaner, as well as to Ahmedabad.

HOTELS

The magnificent oleander-colored sandstone **Umaid Bhawan Palace**, ©22316, 22516, residence of the former maharaja, is now India's most extraordinary luxury hotel, superbly maintained and run by Welcomgroup. Irrepressibly romantic, swathed in marble, gilt, and rich brocades, this vast 347-roomed palace is eccentric opulence on a grand scale. Massive crested brass doors usher visitors into an art deco lobby leading to spectacular soaring double-domed inner courtyards, the first with stuffed leopards poised on its sweeping twin marble staircases, the second with European gilt furniture and tiered spiraling stairwells leading up to a whispering gallery. Directly below is the basement swimming pool, and from the central courtyard branch trophy-crammed billiard rooms and libraries. It's all so grand, formal, and vast that guests feel dwarfed

and almost chastened. Equally, once settled into their spacious suites and after a few moonlit courtyard barbecues, many guests simply never want to leave. Much of the palace is given over to the hotel, while the uppermost wings are inhabited by Jodhpur's former royal family. The main reception halls hold the palace museum, with its rare antique clock and watch collection, Rajput Mughal miniatures, armor, *objets d'art*, and ambitious painted murals (open 9 am to 5 pm).

Each room is different, but all are spacious and decorated with original period furnishings. The suites are positively splendid — with up to six rooms apiece and balconies overlooking the peacock-inhabited garden pavilions — and are comparatively reasonably priced. There's even a novelty suite created to resemble the interior of a ship, but by far the grandest are the two Regal Suites, formerly occupied by the maharaja and his maharanee, with mammoth beds, interior fountains, chandeliers, and glorious art deco marble bathrooms.

Evenings are best spent on the moonlit terrace, where turbaned musicians play every evening against a magical backdrop of pavilioned gardens and the illuminated fort. The excellent five-star facilities include squash, tennis, and badminton courts, with croquet and golf on request.

Ajit Bhawan, © 20409, near Circuit House, is Umaid Bhawan's closest rival. Built for Umaid Singh's younger brother, this bougainvillaea-covered ancestral mansion has been transformed into a charming hotel brimming with family heirlooms, Raj-era bric-à-brac, hunting trophies, and a friendly atmosphere. It is run with great aplomb in the guesthouse tradition by a raconteurish descendant of Ajit, Maharaj Swaroop Singh — the uncle of Jodhpur's present maharaja — who cuts a dashing figure in riding breeches, cravat, and turban. There's a choice of 25 air-cooled double rooms within the mansion, or any one of the stylish cottages scattered around the pretty gardens, each designed like a traditional village hut but with very pukka tiled bathrooms. Room prices are inexpensive. Additional quirky glamor is provided by Ajit Bhawan's staff, all startlingly authentic in their Rajput costumes, with little English but ready smiles. Excellent breakfasts and home-cooked dinners are served in the garden or the courtyard. Golf, squash, camel rides, and excellent village tours (see page 135) can be arranged. The maharaja is definitely the man to talk to about acquiring a pair of Jodhpur's classic jodphurs.

Another mid-range accommodation option is the **Hotel Kalrni Bhawan**, ©20157, Defence Lab Road. This modern hotel with good amenities offers inexpensive, comfortable rooms, with a pretty breakfast courtyard. Budget travelers can take their pick of a handful of cheap, reliable lodges. The RTDC-run **Ghoomar Tourist Bungalow**, ©21900, on High Court Road near the Ajit Bhawan Gardens, is a popular travelers' halt. It also houses the Tourist Office, the Indian Airlines desk, ©20909, and a cafeteria. Rooms are shabbily worn, but clean, and quite acceptable for a night or so and there are very public-looking dorm beds at next to nothing. Otherwise try the more central **Adarsh Niwas Hotel**, ©23936, just near the rail station which has clean rooms and a popular courtyard cafeteria.

RESTAURANTS

Try to dine at least once at both Umaid Bhawan Palace and Ajit Bhawan, for each offers a unique style, spectacular settings, and good food. Highlights at **Umaid Bhawan** include the excellent blow-out Rs 130 buffet lunches in the grand Marwal Hall, with its dangling chandeliers, polished mirrors, and stuffed tigers, and afternoon teas on the terrace. **Ajit Bhawan** is perfect for sampling authentic West Rajasthani dishes in a prettily illuminated garden or courtyard — or, during Jodphur's bitterly cold winter nights, around a blazing fire — very reasonable at Rs 50 per head. In town are two popular eating houses: the vegetarian **Pankaj** at Jalori Gate, and the **Kalinga** restaurant near the rail station, which is good for reasonably priced

Mughali dishes and as a place to linger before catching an overnight train. Don't miss out on the famous Jodphur treat, Makhania *lassi*, a divine concoction made from whipped-up cow's milk, butterballs, and cardamom — one taste and you're hooked. It's served all over town for about Rs 3, usually in suspiciously grimy glasses, with a lump of ice added for good measure. The **Sri Mishra Lal Hotel** at the main Sardar bazaar gateway serves the nicest and most hygienic of the genre, and are perhaps telling the truth when they claim to sell 1,000 glasses a day. Another decadent Jodphuri dessert is *mawakikachori*, a baklava-like pastry stuffed with caramelized nuts and coconut, served smothered in syrup.

SIGHTSEEING

A novel, but slow, way to get around is by nag-drawn tonga or the ubiquitous cycle-rickshaw. But take a taxi or motorized rickshaw up the winding road to Jodphur's main attraction, the magnificent **Mehrangarh Fort**, five kilometers (three miles) from the town center.

From Jai Pol (Victory) Gate, continue the steep climb on foot past cannon-scarred battlements and the souvenir shops with busking musicians. Commissioned by Rao Jodha in 1459, this fortress eyrie is a masterpiece of medieval defense. It is said that after it was completed, its unsuspecting architect was ordered buried alive so that he could not reveal its secrets.

Another grisly relic of the feudal past is in the forlorn plaster row of delicate sati palm prints beside Lohapol (Iron) Gate, marking the spot of self-immolation by women whose husbands died in battle. Sati was idealized as an act of romance, sacrifice, and devotion, so that a king's prestige was quite literally measured by the number of women who elected to throw themselves on his funeral pyre. Of all Jodphur's rulers, Ajit Singh was to claim the greatest "honor" by having his six queens and 58 concubines share his fate of flames in 1731.

Rudyard Kipling was suitably impressed by the fortress-palace, describing it as a creation of "angels, fairies and giants", though this seems too saccharine a description of the full-blooded, larger-than-life Rajputs. The complex is beautifully maintained as a museum, and houses 18 different sections, each full of carefully displayed antiquities. Open 9 am to 5 pm daily, the Rs 10 entrance fee includes the very useful services of a very knowledgeable English-speaking guide. Elderly royal retainers usher visitors through cordoned passages with a proprietorial air. Within lies a maze of interlocking palace interiors, inner marble courtyards, audience halls, exquisite latticed zenana chambers, and the *pièce de résistance* — the royal boudoir, an Arabian Nights fantasy of exotic paneling, dangling colored balls, mirrored and mosaic walls with swings for romping with his favorite concubines, and an enormous bed upon which generations of Jodhpur's maharajas indulged their peccadilloes. Another highlight is the eighteenth-century Dancing Hall, the ceiling of which is plastered with 80 kg (176 lb) of pure gold.

The museum rooms house a richly diverse collection of weaponry, including the swords of Akbar and Timur, gem-encrusted gilt elephant howdahs, royal cradles, rare miniatures, and many traditional Rajasthani musical instruments, many of which have now disappeared from common use. But pride of place is taken by a huge portable tent-palace, used by Emperor Shah Jehan on his tours.

Beyond the palace lie the fort's craggy ramparts, strewn with antique cannons. The view from the edge is unforgettable, like being atop Mount Olympus and spying on the activities of the world below. From the city rises the hum of massed humanity, with stray shouts, dog's barks, and snatches of song lifted suddenly with almost unnatural clarity.

As you drive down the fort road, you'll see the dazzling white marble **Jaswant Thada**, the cenotaph to Maharaja Jaswant Singh built in 1899. He was the first of the Rathore rulers not to have his cenotaph erected at Mandore, the historic capital. It's worth finding the *chowkidar* to let you inside to see the portraits of all the Rathore rulers.

In town, wander through Jodhpur's colorful marketplace which spans out around the **Clock Tower** square until late in the evening. It's too narrow for cars, but big enough for swarms of jingling bicycles, cows, carts, and camels. This is the fabled Old Market, now known as **Sardar Bazaar**. In the general market, cows doze lethargically under giant tarpaulins, dhoti-clad merchants sprawl like odalisques amid pyramids of millet, women squat like monkeys discarding wheat from chaff, and swarms of flies and giggling children simply cannot be shaken free. Depending on which direction you take, you'll be plunged into anything from a locksmith's cul-de-sac to one stacked with oozing raw jaggery, silverware, sweetmeats, flower garlands, or medical textbooks. Good finds in Jodhpur include wooden puppets, painted horses, ivory-work, tie-dyed *bandhana* fabric, and embroidered slippers.

Tranquil strolls can be enjoyed in the leafy, well-kept **Umaid Public Gardens and Zoo**, full of bougainvillaea, mango, and rose bushes. To the northwest of the gardens is the **Government Museum**, a taxidermist's nightmare with its balding, silverfish-infested stuffed menagerie, reminiscent of the famous Monty Python "dead

parrot" skit. Other exhibits include antique Indian sculpture, scrolls, royal treatises, and a decorated Durbar Hall. It's open from 10 am to 4 pm daily except Fridays.

It's worth reserving a morning or afternoon to see **Mandore**, the ancient capital of the Rathore Marwars, eight kilometers (five miles) north of town. It's a picturesque necropolis set in a lush, leafy garden, strewn with the *chhatris* of the Jodphur rulers. The maharanees' *chhatris* are more desolately elegant, standing amid boulders along the hilltop ridge and reached by a steep winding path to the right of the garden.

Make sure you see the eighteenth-century

Hall of Heroes, a gallery of 16 life-sized gods, goddesses, and Rajput warriors carved from a single rock.

VILLAGE SAFARIS

Between tours of princely palaces and marble mausoleums, many visitors to India lament that they missed a glimpse of the real India — the rural villages where people still live by their ancient customs. Maharaja Singh of Ajit Bhawan offers a unique one-day safari aboard a 1942 U.S. Army jeep through the villages in the near-desert terrain surrounding Jodhpur. His

ABOVE: A Rajput patriarch and his grandson. OPPOSITE: The circular dome within the monumental Umaid Bhawan Hotel, originally an Anglophile maharaja's fantasy palace built entirely of red sandstone in the 1920s.

fascinating firsthand insights into Rajasthani rural life won glowing praise from Geoffrey Moorehouse, author of *India Britannica* and *Calcutta*.

"Everything in towns is evil", explains Singh. "It is on the farms, the uncorrupted areas away from electricity and telephones that the real beauties of life can be found."

The vestige of his previous role still exists, for at each stop the villagers offer an enthusiastic greeting, and still turn to him for guidance, to mediate disputes, and even to conduct wedding ceremonies. The maharaja and his small group of visitors are met by a beaming white-haired

desert's deepwater wells, the significance of turban colors, and local courtship rituals. Visitors are shown how villagers make dhurrie rugs in dug-out huts, and are encouraged to try their hand at making pots, grinding grain, and firing slingshots. The tour costs Rs 250 per person and is an unforgettable experience.

The Umaid Bhawan Palace can also arrange trips to these surrounding villages by putting you in touch with the energetic young men of a local Rathore noble family. Although their tours lack the vigorous personality of Maharaja Singh, they are cheaper at Rs 50 and the pageantry of village life remains as fascinating. They are most

patriarch dressed in white, and clusters of curious, brightly clad tribeswomen laden with chunky silver jewelry and ivory bracelets up the length of their arms. Visitors are asked to take off their shoes before walking across the surprisingly pleasantly textured "protective" ring of mixed dried cow dung and urine around the hut — an ancient practice to ward off snakes and harness the "generative energy" of the cow, a sacred creature to the Hindus. Over spicy ginger tea — and sometimes a draught of *afion* opium, taken infused in water from the cupped hand of the host — Singh holds court on subjects as varied as the plight of the Untouchables, the

worthwhile if combined with a night or two at the delightful sixteenth-century **Rohet Castle**, 42 km (26 miles) from Jodphur, a mini-fortress stronghold of the region's ruling Rathore clan overlooking an oasis lake. Here you'll be well looked after by the present *thakur* (ruler), Siddarth Singh, and his charming family, fed mouthwatering Rajput cuisine, and if you are part of a small group, you'll be given a truly memorable welcome, ending with an uproarious dance on the lawns with infectiously gleeful Rajput villagers. Rooms look out on to the garden and are inexpensive. Or you can opt to spend a comfortable night on the roof under a brilliant canopy of stars. For bookings, contact Rohet Castle, P.O. Rohet, District Pali ©306421, Rajasthan, or Rohet House, ©21161, P.W.D. Road, Jodphur.

If you're getting about Rajasthan by hired car, Castle Rohet can be a good place to break the trip

ABOVE: The magically medieval fortress city of Jaisalmer sits on a rocky promontory on the edge of the Thar Desert, with its amber turrets turning golden in the dusk light.

to see **Ranakpur**'s wondrous fifteenth-century Jain temples, 116 km (72 miles) away. Intricately sculpted from rose marble, these 29 halls form India's most complex and extensive group of Jain temples, covering over 3,600 sq m (40,000 sq ft) and containing 1,444 ornate pillars, each unique and covered with carvings. From Ranakpur, Udaipur is only 60 km (37 miles) away.

KHIMSAR, OSIAN, AND NAGAUR

On the desert route between Jodhpur and Bikaner, 240 km (150 miles) away, are three sight-

seeing "musts". The journey is best made in a hired jeep, though local buses can be taken. Some 100 km (62 miles) north of Jodhpur, nestled near the (real) sand dunes of the Thar Desert, lies the fifteenth-century oasis stronghold of **Khimsar**. Its moated, fortified **Royal Castle**, (℄28 via Nagaur exchange) is a delightful hotel — a mix of medieval architecture and 1920's decor, taken over by the Welcomgroup and run by its ancestral owner and Rajasthan M.P., Onkar Singh, and his family. The rooms are pleasant, with very modern amenities. Evening barbecues and delicious authentic Rajput dishes are served in the ramparts of the old fort. The surrounding plains and sandy dunes are filled with romping nilgai, chinkara, desert fox, and the Great Indian Bustard, with partridges and imperial sand grouse often ending up as Royal Castle fare. For bookings, write to Onkar Singh,

Royal Castle, P.O. Khimsar, District Nagaur, or contact the Umaid Bhawan Hotel in Jodhpur.

It's 65 km (40 miles) to the ancient town of **Osian**, worth seeing for its cluster of 16 ornate Hindu and Jain temples dating from the eighth to the eleventh century. Also see **Nagaur**, 110 km (68 miles) from Bikaner, a medieval town with a very fine partridge-infested, twelfth-century Mughal fort. It's perfect for picnics and for clambering through. The zenana quarters have frescoes painted with crushed emeralds, pearls, and egg yolk; there are also mossed-over swimming pools and a mosque built by Akbar. So few visitors ever explore this remarkable fort that the guard beams with joy when they do appear, proudly producing a musty Visitors' Book for them to sign. On the full-moon cusp of January and February, Nagaur attracts thousands of Rajput villagers for its camel fair — bigger and less of a tourist trap than Pushkar — with camel races, folk dancing, strolling players, and mongoose fights.

JAISALMER: FORTRESS OF GOLD

Nothing quite prepares the traveler for the first breathtaking glimpse of **Jaisalmer**, the remote fortress city on the edge of Rajasthan's Thar Desert. (*"Thar"* means "abode of death".)

It's customary to make the journey by train, Jaisalmer's main link to the outside world. As the trip unfolds, vegetation and life are replaced by the hot and barren desert wasteland. Suddenly the walled city appears, seeming to hover above the tundra and shale. The twice-daily *Jaisalmer Express* is ingeniously timed to arrive at dawn or dusk, an hour of unsettling beauty in the desert light.

Jaisalmer, which lies 287 km (178 miles) from Jodhpur at the edge of India's western border with Pakistan, is the most magically medieval of Rajasthan's desert cities, and certainly the most extraordinary, since all the buildings — from the humblest shop to the palace and temples — are carved from a burnished golden-yellow sandstone. Even today, houses are built in the medieval manner to merge in with the old.

The Bhatti Rajput chieftain Rawal Jaisal deserted his former capital of Lodurva, 17 km (10.5 miles) away to found Jaisalmer in 1156, attracted by the site's large oasis and the natural defense provided by Trikuta (three-peak) hill. It was also a tryst with destiny — for centuries ago, Lord Krishna was said to have predicted that a distant descendant of his Lunar clan would one day rule from here. Jaisalmer's ruling family, who claimed both Lord Krishna and the moon as ancestors, kept only silver furniture in their palace quarters, believing that the moon-like color would give them talismanic strength.

Protected against the shifting sands and feudal marauders by a steep, double-tiered ring of giant stone ramparts, Jaisalmer became a prosperous, coveted stronghold on the great Spice Route from Persia and Afghanistan. It became a city of caravanserais, large buildings surrounding a central courtyard in which the merchants took shelter.

The early Muslim king of Delhi, Ala-ud-din Khilji, laid seige to the city at the end of the thirteenth century when one of his particularly well-laden caravans was pillaged by the Jaisalmer ruler. The siege lasted eight years, and in a bizarre twist of fate, the young Jaisalmer prince, Rattan Singh, befriended the enemy general, Nawab Mahboob Khan. The two were inseparable companions, and would meet to play chess until the war-horn sounded them into battle. Finally, in 1295, the Rajput clan knew that defeat was imminent. While Rattan Singh's sons were secretly delivered into the safe care of the Nawab, Jaisalmer's entire community of women and children committed *johar*, or mass suicide, as their menfolk, clad in ceremonial saffron and delirious with opium, fought to the last.

The warlike Bhattis were soon back in their citadel, waging vendettas against neighboring tribes and spinning webs of intrigue and treachery. Jaisalmer entered a more peaceful era as part of the Mughal empire in the late seventeenth century, prospering as a trading post for silks, spices, indigo, and opium. Hindu and Jain merchants, bankers, and artisans settled here, and built magnificent *havelis* mansions with elaborate honeycomb-like balconies.

Jaisalmer's fortunes dwindled with the opening of the Bombay port in the eighteenth century, but it suffered an even worse crisis in the aftermath of Partition in 1947, when the time-honored trade routes to Pakistan were suddenly deemed illegal. Only when it became an important military base during the 1965 and 1971 Indo-Pakistan wars did Jaisalmer emerge from its almost medieval seclusion to be connected by road and rail to the rest of Rajasthan.

Today, Jaisalmer's main sources of revenue are tourists who, since its "discovery" in the early seventies, go on camel safaris and buy the beautifully-woven local embroidery; the military, who linger in the bazaar smoking cheroots during periods of leave from border patrol duty; and a burgeoning illicit trade of black market goods, smuggled by camel drivers across the dunes separating India and Pakistan.

ACCESS

Indian Airlines flies to Jodphur, the nearest airport, 287 km (178 miles) away. There is also a small light aircraft service three times a week to Jaisalmer run by Vayudoot Airlines, which can link with Jaipur, Jodphur, and Bikaner.

There are twice-daily trains from Jodphur; the overnight sleeper (departs 10:15 pm, arrives 6:30 am) is the most popular, and comfortable, option. Take plenty of water, oranges, and an engrossing book for the arduous 10-hour day journey, which passes through flat and monotonous desert, with gnarled fist-shaped trees, nomadic camels, and graceful lines of *paniharis*, women water-carriers. Hard-seat second-class carriages are the most entertaining, as they fill up suddenly at desert halts with spectacularly attired Rajput villagers who seem preserved from another age: tall, sinewy men jaunty in scarlet onion-dome turbans, glinting earrings, and ingeniously tied white *dhotis*; and women covered in silver jewelry and *chaori*, bracelets of ivory or bone which are worn from the shoulder to the wrist as a symbol of marriage.

Jaisalmer has become an extremely popular destination, and competition for the coveted overnight sleepers can be fierce, so it's essential to reserve tickets as soon as you reach Jodphur.

It's possible to steam across the sands in full-blown sumptuous style — for a suitably sumptuous price. The Maharaja of Jodphur's two white carriages, emblazoned with his coat of arms, are available for hire; one contains seven ornate coupés with baths and dining quarters for 14 people at a cost of Rs 50,000; the other is smaller, although no less modest, and fits six people at Rs 9,000. Prices include two nights (there and back to Jodphur), cooks, butlers, escorts from the Umaid Bhawan palace, and all meals in Jaisalmer.

Jaisalmer is connected by bus to Jodphur, a 10-hour trip, and Bikaner, 280 km (174 miles), about 8 ½ hours. These are not exactly pleasure rides; train travel is vastly preferable.

WHEN TO GO

Ideally, visit Jaisalmer from November to February when the days are warm, the skies clear, and the nights cold enough for a driftwood fire and a warm sleeping bag. Avoid the summer months, when the temperature shoots up as high as 53°C (127°F) and the raging *simoon* (duststorm) turns Jaisalmer into a virtual ghosttown. Jaisalmer is most popular during its annual three-day **Desert Festival**, which coincides with the full moon in February and March. It's a lively jamboree of camel polo, acrobatics and races, sword-swallowers, traditional Rajput *ghazals* (songs) and dance performances, turban-tying, and "Best Dressed Rajput" contests. Villagers from all around throng to Jaisalmer's bazaar to sell silver jewelry and hand-wovenwares. Prices for necessities such as mineral water, toilet paper, and beer suddenly soar, and accommodation and train seats are hard to come by. Many hotels solve the problem by erecting impromptu canopied rooms on their roofs, and a "tourist village" of basic tents and bathroom facilities is set up on the plateau beneath the fort in a style similar to that at Pushkar's Camel Fair.

Jaisalmer is still one of the best places to witness the spectacle of **Holi** (February/March), a day of mock color battles and giggling powder-besplattered chaos. On this day, villagers cram into Mandir Palace, where they playfully pelt the ex-maharaja's family, and the courtyard fills with the sound of the reedy pipe *sheenai*, folk songs, and the clapping rhythm of swirling Rajput dances. All the important Rajasthan festivals—Dussehra, Diwali, and Gangaur—are celebrated here in the traditional exuberant way.

HOTELS

Hotel Narayan Niwas, ☏108, is Jaisalmer's most stylish hotel. A converted caravanserai with 24 rooms, the hotel is quaintly romantic, but simple, with a deep open hall where the camels used to sleep but where guests can now recline on striped cushions and listen to the traditional Rajasthani musicians in canopied culs-de-sac each evening. There's an attached restaurant with a good evening buffet, and highly exotic performances by dancers, sword-throwers, and musicians. Rooms are well-furnished, air-conditioned and moderately priced, and during the Desert Festival, colorful canopied tents, complete with beds, fresh linen, and toilets, are available.

Outside the town walls, the **Jawahar Niwas**, the ex-maharaja's former guesthouse, is now a hotel of faded charm. It has a pleasant veranda and a large billiard room. Rates: inexpensive.

Jaisal Castle, ☏62, an old 11-room courtyard house tucked into the fort's topmost ramparts, has less panache but is inexpensively priced. You'll find it — after asking for directions many times — by weaving up a sloping bottleneck of cobbled alleys. The views at sunset compensate only somewhat for the abysmal service and food — tea is served in chipped, stained cups, and the promised fresh sheets, soap, and towels never seem to materialize.

Close by is the **Sri Palace Hotel**, for highly authentic atmosphere in an old merchant's *haveli*. Its cramped but quaintly furnished rooms are very cheap.

The new **Hotel Neeraj**, ☏142, set slightly outside the city walls, is the best cheapie option and far preferable to the poorly run RTDC **Moomal Tourist Bungalow**, ☏92, which is at an

inconvenient distance (two kilometers, or just over a mile) from town, and has a choice of rooms ranging from air-conditioned "deluxe" doubles to basic singles and a dormitory for budget travelers. Jaisalmer's Tourist Office is located here, but it is not terribly helpful. You'll find more enthusiastic English-speaking guides, who claim to be part of the town's "Guide Association", at the entrance gate to the fort; they will show you every place of historical interest for about Rs 35 a day.

Jaisalmer has become a rabbit warren of small family-run lodges that offer very cheap accommodation (including rooftop mattresses), basic local fare, and all the local information you

Jaisalmer's maze of sheltered lanes are surprisingly cool, lined with merchants *havelis* with façades of honey-colored sandstone carved to weblike delicacy.

need, as well as reserving train tickets and organizing camel treks, all with smiling desert hospitality. By far the most popular is **Fort View Hotel**, ©214, which has spartan doubles (no bathroom), a clambering waiter who serves guests their meals on the rooftop, and an endearing manager whose "no-frills" camel safaris are extremely popular. Other backpackers' havens within the fort town and worth investigating are the **Swastika Guest House**, opposite the State Bank of India, with clean, doubles with bath, the **Sunil Bhatia Rest House**, the **Hotel Pleasure**, and the **New Tourist Hotel**, all with very basic rooms and rock-bottom prices.

RESTAURANTS

You'll dine both deliciously and inexpensively if you stick to Jaisalmer's traditional desert fare, with its simple round of spiced vegetables, robust millet *rotis*, and curd. **Hotel Narayan Niwas** has an excellent evening buffet with local specialties such as nut-textured *kar-sangria*, made from dehydrated desert shrub beans, and *bajra ka sohita*, an unusual combination of ground millet and spiced mutton. Local sweets include *halwa*, made of lentils, and *ghewar*, a sugar-coated ball with a rich milky filling.

Clustered quite close together, Jaisalmer's other reliably good restaurants are **Kalpana's**, **8th of July Restaurant**, and **Gaylord Restaurant**, which all serve good Indian, Chinese, and Continental food. Otherwise you can take your

pick of the dozens of small family-run budget eating places which have mushroomed around the market square. Some are very unhygienic-looking, but are usually safe for simple vegetarian dishes and spicy-sweet *chai*.

SIGHTSEEING

Fort and City Tour

A good walking tour begins at the fortress gate, from where a steep slope branches into a tangled maze of roughly cobbled, dim, and winding passageways. Here the bustle of life seems centuries old. Camels are herded into the shade of overhanging balconies while their owners crouch nearby over a pot of syrupy tea; goods ranging from ornate curled slippers to cartloads of fresh figs are hawked on the cobbles; and villagers, dressed in vivid Rajput costume, haggle over spice trays.

Amidst this mêlée, walking is really the only practical means of getting around, although Jaisalmer is so small and contained it can be enjoyed at a leisurely pace in a morning.

It's a 10-minute walk to the **Gadisar Tank**, the large natural oasis just below the city walls to the southwest. The lake that led Jaisal to found his city is full only in the monsoon months, but there are many temples and shrines around it to explore. The beautiful carved archway leading to the tank is supposed to have been built by Telia, a well-known *nautch* courtesan, for her Bhatti prince lover. She slyly added a Krishna temple so that the monarch's disapproving royal matrons, who refused to use the gate, could not pull it down. For glorious early morning views of the turreted fort, clamber up on to the temple roofs.

A short distance north is the **Fort** by the Gadisar Gate. This majestic sandstone fortress buttressed by 99 cone-shaped bastions is perched high on Trikuta, or "three-peak" hill. It is the second-oldest fort in Rajasthan, after Chittaugarh, and its cannonball-scarred battlements remain mute witness to several bloody conquests over the centuries, most notably by the Tughlaqs and the Mughals.

Just inside the thick gateway of the fort is the ornate seven-story city palace, which rises up from the traditional "blind" zenana ground floor to a riot of carved porticoes; and the four other *mahals* (palaces) which housed the royal queens and concubines. After a short stroll up the steep cobbled path, you'll enter a spacious square, dominated by a magnificent marble throne, the **Diwan-I-Am**, where the maharaja used to preside over public meetings, entertain visiting royalty, and celebrate weddings. It was also within this courtyard that *johar* took place.

Just beyond, past a low arched gateway, are the **Jain Temples**, an elegant group of seven interconnecting temples built by wealthy Marwari traders between the twelfth and fifteenth centuries and dedicated to the Jain saints Sambhavanathi and Rikhabdevji. Each temple is a marvel of elaborate design and intricate carvings; exteriors festooned with mythological deities and coy, curvaceous *apsaras* (celestial nymphs); and incense-laden chambers lined with rows of meditating white marble *tirthankaras*, or Jain saints, whose eyes flicker eerily with precious gems — all 6,666 pairs of them. Look especially for the priceless emerald icon of the Jain deity in the temple devoted to Mahavira.

Within the temple complex is an ancient library, the **Gyan Bhandir**, with a rare collection of manuscripts, miniature paintings, and books. The temples are only open in the morning from 9 am to noon, and only between 10 and 11 am on Sundays.

Follow the path left of the temples and you'll come to the nearby **Dop Khana**, or "place of the cannon", which offers the best views across the maze-like walled city to the desert plains below. It's an enchanting place to return to at dusk, when you see what looks like a row of bobbing glow-worms in the darkness of the surrounding desert — the lantern trail of long chains of nomads astride their camels, arriving laden with goods for Jaisalmer's markets.

Havelis and Palaces

Descendants of the wealthy traders still live in some of these beautiful *havelis*, some of which are centuries old. Jaisalmer is full of these magical eighteenth- and nineteenth-century mansions, their surfaces covered with intricate filigree carvings skillfully created by Muslim *silavats* (stone-carvers) for Hindu traders. The sandstone surface of the buildings crumbles slightly to the touch, creating an odd sensation of having breathed, for a moment, the dust of Jaisalmer's vanished opulence, the scent of silks, rich brocades, and thick incense.

Start your *haveli* tour with the **Salim Singh Haveli**, which is slightly north of the central market. Salim Singh was a despotic prime minister in the late seventeenth century who built himself this Arabian Nights-style *haveli*, with its impressive peacock-motif arched roof and unique sky-blue cupolas, to outshine the mansions of other nobles. Renowned for his cruelty, he once had 3,000 people from a nearby village massacred in order to win sway with the ruling maharaja. According to local lore, he tried to build his *haveli* as high as the monarch's palace, and even planned to build a connecting bridge to the royal chambers, but Rajput courtiers persuaded the king to destroy this skyscraping

rival, and its upper stories were blown to bits. Although its façade is stunning, the interior has been left ransacked and spartan.

Close by is the vast late-nineteenth-century **Mandir Palace**, built outside the city walls by the Maharawal Salivahan of Jaisalmer in the belief that a curse on the old city palace was killing off his family members in droves. It's unlike any other building in Jaisalmer — an Indo-Saracenic extravaganza, with fluted pillars, domed turrets, tiered filigree-work façades, and interiors of silver furniture.

In a cul-de-sac just north of the palace is the most spectacular of all Jaisalmer's beautiful

havelis, the **Patwon-ki-Haveli**, the collective name for five houses built between 1800 and 1860 by the wealthy Patwa brothers (who dabbled in opium dealing and gold smuggling, as well as trading precious gems). Two of the houses are museum showcases (open daily 10:30 am to 5 pm), one is rented by a shopkeeper who seems quite happy to show people through, and the remaining two are private residences. And do not miss **Nathamal-ki-Haveli** nearby, a late-nineteenth-century prime minister's house, with a marvelous fretted frontispiece flanked by sandstone elephants. You can ask to see the first floor, with its intricate painted walls and murals.

Spice, Slippers, and Silver

One of the most enjoyable things to do in Jaisalmer is to wander the alleys seeking out the bazaars, where fossicking can uncover some wonderful treasures, often more unusual and of better quality than those geared for the mass market in Jaipur.

OPPOSITE: Women knitting in the afternoon sun within Jaisalmer's walled town. ABOVE: Balconies of delicate lattice patterns jut out from Jaisalmer's *haveli* walls, under eaves that provide protection from the savage sun.

Camel Safaris

Not least of Jaisalmer's attractions is the romantic lure of the camel safari. This has to be one of India's unforgettable, once-in-a-lifetime adventures: a camel trek across the desolate wastes of the Thar, the monotony broken by sudden magnificent glimpses of an age-old desert culture — encounters with nomadic tribes dressed like theatrical troubadours, ancient palace ruins etched against an azure sky; and swift packs of chinkara antelope racing across the horizon.

In tiny niche-like shops tucked up crooked stairwells, or in *haveli* basements, you'll find colorfully embroidered and mirror-inlaid cloths, decorative banners, and blankets. Jaisalmer is an excellent place to buy woolen dhurrie rugs, which are produced locally in many traditional designs and sizes. To get an idea of the selection, quality, and price, it's worth first taking a look at **Marudhar Handicrafts** in Patwon Haveli and **Kamal Handicrafts Emporium**, just near the the the Jain temples in the fort.

Along **Manik Chowk**, the main market square at the entrance to the fort, dozens of small stalls provide the perfect props for a swashbuckling Rajput-style desert adventure: brightly embroidered, curving camel-skin *mojadis*, or slippers; camel saddles and whips, 14-m (45-ft)-long turbans, and huge gathered *ghagras*, or skirts (taking up to 7 m, or 7.5 yds of cloth). Small items like embroidered camel-leather belts and bags make wonderful gifts, but if you're looking for exotic trophies to take home from Rajasthan, this is the place to browse for unusual antique silk, heavy silver Rajput jewelry, and the unique wall-hangings patched together painstakingly by village women with fragments of embroidery.

Whether you make it an afternoon's camel jaunt or a full-fledged three-week "Lawrence of Arabia" epic journey is up to you. For most people, a single night spent by a thorn-tree fire under a dazzling umbrella of stars, with a glorious desert sunrise, and two days of a camel's odd, lolloping gait, with earthy meals of *dahl*, millet *chapatis*, and *aloo choli* (spicy vegetables), is usually long enough to absorb the spirit of desert travel.

Virtually all Jaisalmer's hotels and guesthouses can arrange camel and jeep safaris for the most popular two-day trail which does a circuit of local places of interest. For practical advice on camel travel, pay a visit to the affable Mr Vyas of the Fort View Hotel, Jaisalmer's walking encyclopedia on the subject, and take a look at his book of tourists' comments. His well-organized tours include interesting sights, mattresses, food, potable water, and the lively company of rakishly turbaned camel drivers who sit behind you, gather firewood, prepare all the meals, and

Few sights are as arresting in Rajasthan as the spectacle of its vivid and picturesquely dressed inhabitants. ABOVE: Four faces of Rajasthan: A young musician and a Rajput beauty, her arms covered in ivory bracelets, signifying her married status. OPPOSITE: A nomadic camel driver, a gypsy tribeswoman,

croon desert ballads — all for the modest fee of Rs 60 per person each day.

The Hotel Narayan Niwas offers a deluxe version more suited to those seeking the comforts of the Raj. The party consists of camels (one each, plus one for luggage), a cook, bedding, World War II-style tents, hampers packed to one's predilections, filtered water tanks, onions to keep the snakes away, nightwatchmen, and wireless contact with the police. You can even request folk dancers to entertain the party in the evenings around the campfire. Prices are considerably higher, ranging from Rs 250 to Rs 375 each per day.

Essentials for a camel safari include a pair of sunglasses (for the intense desert glare), an individual water bottle, sunburn lotion, chapstick, mosquito-repellent, a bag of oranges (great thirst-quenchers), all-encompassing light cotton garments, strong comfortable shoes, protective headwear, and Lomotil tablets for emergency cases of diarrhea. A good book and a torch

to read it with, and plenty of camera film complete the ideal list.

If you're planning a long camel safari of around two weeks, it's only really practical between November and January when the desert is at its coolest and most enjoyable, but Jaisalmer's camel safari season runs from October to March.

Short two- or three-day tours from Jaisalmer usually visit a handful of several ancient monuments in the desert. A short distance north is

Bada Bagh (Big Garden), the cremation ground of Jaisalmer's rulers, dating back to the twelfth century. Here stand tiered canopied rows of marble *chattris*, or memorial cenotaphs, each carved with bas-reliefs. It's the perfect spot to take sunset photographs of Jaisalmer, blazing saffron-pink against the horizon. **Lodurva**, 16 km (10 miles) northwest, is the archaic eighth-century Rajput capital, with fine ruins and an ornate Jain temple complex. One traveler reported stepping into this temple without taking his shoes off, and being astonished to hear a voice exclaim in plummy Oxford vowels: "I say, old chap — you simply musn't wear shoes here, you know!" The owner of this astonishing voice turned out to be a scantily-clad, tumeric-smeared fakir squatting in a darkened niche! Other stops on the trail include **Amar Sagar**, six kilometers (3.7 miles) northwest, where a beautiful Jain temple stands near a dried-up oasis, and **Mool Sagar**, nine kilometers (5.6 miles) directly west of Jaisalmer, a garden and large tank. In between you'll pass many small villages of beehive-shaped mud and cowdung huts and grinning desert dwellers who find the sight of sunburned foreigners atop cantering camels as funny as a Marx Brothers comedy.

Longer treks include the **Sam** sand dunes, 40 km (25 miles) away — where you'll see the true Sahara-like desert landscape of Rajasthan —and the exotic fortress city of Bikaner, 280 km (174 miles) away, which takes about 11 days.

Another popular excursion from Jaisalmer is **Khuri**, 40 km (25 miles) southwest of Jaisalmer and very close to the Pakistan border. Like the Sam, its chief attraction is its "real" desert landscape of smooth tidal waves of golden sand, which seems much more authentic desert than the empty scrubland surrounding Jaisalmer. If you want to see the *real* Rajasthan, where people still live by their ancient customs, visit Khuri. The charming Rajput Sodha family — the rulers of this region for over 400 years until Independence in 1947 — run excellent camel safaris between October and March and also accommodate tourists in small, spotless mud

guest huts in the village for about Rs 40 a day, which includes three delicious traditional meals of homemade cheese, a wide range of breads, vegetarian dishes, and non-stop cups of sweet cardamom tea. The Sodhas are dignified, warm-hearted hosts, and the two sons, Bhagwan and Tane Singh Sodha, make articulate, humorous escorts whether on a camel safari or a tour of the village.

To get to Khuri, either hire a jeep or take the early morning bus from Jaisalmer. Bhagwan Singh is always there to meet visitors when the bus arrives.

BIKANER

Situated in the northern Thar desert, Bikaner is an ochre-colored sandstone fortress city surrounded by high medieval ramparts. It is famous for its distinctive Rajput architecture, martial camels, and exotic inhabitants. It was founded in 1488 by Rao Bikaji and his band of 300 loyal followers. Lying at the crossroads of the great medieval caravan routes, this prosperous stronghold became renowned for its military strength in withstanding a centuries-long vendetta — and many spectacular battles — with the ruling Jodhpur clan.

Like many Rajputs, the Bikaners adored indolent pleasures — and court archives note their excessive consumption of opium and the aphrodisiac *asha*, a potent brew of powdered gold, silver, ground pearls, and goat brains. During the nineteenth century, Bikaner began to curry favor with the British, donating 200 camels to the Afghan Campaign in 1842, and offering shelter to many European refugees during the Great Mutiny of 1857.

Present-day Bikaner owes many of its finest buildings to one remarkable man, the late Maharaja Ganga Singh (1880–1943), who single-handedly transformed his backward feudal domain into Rajasthan's chief granary by building the Ganga Canal to transform the surrounding desert into green fields, and by constructing a railway. This flamboyant monarch founded India's most prestigious military unit, the Camel Corps, and staged spectacular annual shoots for imperial sand grouse, complete with fleets of Rolls Royces and vast banquets. The Prince of Wales attended the shoot held in 1905. Ganga Singh's fantasy nineteenth-century Lallgarh Palace, built in rose sandstone, is now a luxury hotel and looms on the edge of the desert like a vast mirage from *Brideshead Revisited*.

ACCESS

Vayudoot operates regular flights to and from Bikaner, via Jaipur from Delhi, landing at a small airstrip 13 km (eight miles) out of town. Bikaner is also conveniently reached by twice-daily express trains — preferably by sleepers on the overnighters — which take between eight and 12 hours from Jodhpur (240 km, or 150 miles), 10 to 11 hours from Jaipur (354 km, or 220 miles), and 12 hours from Delhi (510 km, or 317 miles), arriving at Bikaner's station just as the dawn sky turns rosy. "Express" bus trips from these main cities, as well as to Jaisalmer (320 km, or 205 miles), take a little longer — mainly due to long halts at shanty tea stalls while the driver has a rollicking time with his mates — and are rather more grueling. Luxury air-conditioned coaches offer more comfort, but run only from Delhi and Jaipur.

HOTELS

Bikaner's grandest hotel is the **Lallgarh Palace**, ©3263, run by members of Bikaner's former royal family. Much of it remains uninhabited, as if magically deserted. Peacocks and squirrels make themselves at home in the echoing, marble-balustraded courtyards; the state rooms are swathed in dustcloths; and in the corridors are mounted trophies and exquisite *jali*-screened alcoves. The hotel rooms are delightful; straight out of the 1930's, they have canopied twin beds, gloomy drapes, and mahogany furniture. Rates: inexpensive. Guests are informed that the staff are at their service should they wish to go clay-pigeon shooting or play croquet! There is also a golf course, squash courts, and bougainvillaea-dotted gardens. The hotel's **Palace Museum** is brimming with royal memorabilia, including many stuffed trophies, *objets d'art*, various military outfits worn by the portly maharaja, and a massive carpet woven by Bikaner's prisoners. There is a particularly fine photographic gallery for a fascinating close-up inspection of virtually all of India's princes,

"Plane Tost"! For those with a sweet-tooth, Bikaner's famous *ghaver*, caramelized fudge, and the town's distinctive combination of hot milk, curd, and sugar, frothed up by sidewalk vendors with theatrical sloshes into brass beakers, can quickly become addictive.

SIGHTSEEING

As with most of Rajasthan's smaller centers, transport around town is mainly by foot or pony-drawn *tongas*, although a few unmetered auto-rickshaws and taxis operate from the railway station. The city is dominated by its impos-

stiff-collared viceroys, and their formidable vicerines. The museum is open daily except Wednesdays, from 9 am to 6 pm. The management can arrange for you to stay at **Gajner Palace**, ©3239, 32 km (20 miles) away, an elegant royal hunting lodge set on the lake of a wildlife sanctuary full of gazelles, wild boar, black buck, sambhar, and imperial sand grouse.

For cheaper accommodation, avoid the cluster of squalid lodges near the railway station; head instead for the state-run **Dhola Maru Tourist Bungalow**, ©5002, which also houses the friendly and informative Tourist Office.

Amber Restaurant, on Station Road, is recommended for delicious, cheap vegetarian *thalis*, creamy *lassis*, and curd. Try their unusual "Amber Special Dosa", stuffed with cashew nuts and fruit and served with fresh coconut chutney. They also serve early-morning "Brake Fast" and

ing medieval **Junagarh Fort**, built entirely with red-ochre sandstone and marble between 1588 and 1593 by Raja Raj Singh, one of Akbar's generals. Successive rulers enlarged and embellished the fort over the next 400 years. With its massive battlements and moat, it is one of the few forts in India never to have been conquered, although it was often attacked. Beyond the main **Suraj Pol**, or "Sun Gate", you can see the silver-fringed sati handmarks left by queens and concubines over the centuries. Inside is a magnificent Mughal Durbar Hall and a maze of no less than 37 ornate palaces, with marble pillared halls, delicately painted chambers, mirror-encrusted ceilings, and ivory and wood carvings.

ABOVE: Dawn silhouette of *chhatris* spires, Bikaner. OPPOSITE: Pastel-hued walls in a quiet alley, Bikaner.

The most sumptuous of all these palaces are the **Chandra Mahal**, or "Moon Palace", a jewel-box of delicate paintings, mirrors, and carved marble panels, and the **Phool Mahal**, or "Flower Palace", filtered with stained glass and studded with mirror mosaics. Other notable places to see within the fort include the Karan Mahal, Rang Mahal, Bijai Mahal, and the Anup Mahal palaces, the latter opposite the Har Mandir temple where royal marriages, births, and the annual Gangaur festival are still celebrated. The fort museum brims with fascinating heirlooms, including rare manuscripts, jeweled weaponry, gold howdahs, hookahs, and a number of oddities including two decaying World War biplanes purchased by the patriotic Ganga Singh. The fort is open daily, except Fridays, from 10 am to 4:30 pm, and also houses the Tourist Office.

Bikaner's old walled city has an equally medieval flavor. It is fun to spend an afternoon combing the filthy, chaotic bazaars clustered around **Kote Gate**, full of turbaned desert nomads, colorfully clad women, and pigeon-hole stalls hawking everything from antique doors and cauliflowers to lacquer-work, camel-skin lampshades, and ivory bangles. The **Ganga Singh Golden Jubilee Museum**, in Gandhi Park near the Tourist Bungalow, is well worth visiting for its rich collection of pre-Aryan archaeological finds, antique Indian sculpture, and fine Bikaner school miniatures. It's open from 10 am to 5 pm, and closed on Fridays and public holidays.

If **Bikaner Jail**'s Superintendent J.K. Sharma is in an affable mood, he will allow you to tour through this massive nineteenth-century stone prison, where some 400 inmates — a mixture of petty thieves and *dacoitish*-looking murderers — create Rs 50,000 worth of carpets annually in a system first begun by Maharaja Ganga Singh during the 1920's. The prison yard presents an unforgettable Kafkaesque spectacle: hundreds of surly calico-clad men sit in dug-out troughs amid a 40-m (130-ft)-long mesh of foot-pedalled pulley contraptions and water wheels which process raw wool into clean threads for the weaving looms — all beneath the burning sun under the watchful eye of a pockmarked Tamburlaine-like jailor. Hand-knotted carpets can be purchased from the prison storeroom.

Out of town, don't miss a visit to the state-run **Camel Breeding Farm**, 10 km (six miles) west of Bikaner, home to about 300 gambolling baby camels and their parents. India's regimental Camel Corps plucks the best and brightest among them. Here you can go for a ride, chat to the traditional clannish keepers, the *Rebaris*, about camel lore, and sample still-warm camel milk. The farm welcomes visitors

only between 3 and 5 pm. At Deshnok, 33 km (20 miles) south of Bikaner, stands the **Karni Mata Temple**, dedicated to the fifteenth-century mystic who prophesied Rao Bika's successes, but more famous as the "rat temple", where swarms of "sacred" rodents are protected in the belief that they are shortly to be reincarnated as gifted humans. Lured in with grain and sweetmeats, hundreds of rats squeak and scurry across the marble shrine — and over the bare feet of devotees. It's not for the squeamish, and visitors are given stern warnings not to stand on one accidentally. Curiously, even the temple priest and his assistant have rather rodent-like features. The beautiful royal *chhatris*, or cenotaphs, at Devi Kund, eight kilometers (five miles) from Bikaner, are interesting memorials to the dead of the princely Rathores of Bikaner.

UDAIPUR

Udaipur—a languid lake city strewn with marble palaces, hibiscus-massed gardens, fountain pavilions, and cobbled medieval bazaars — is one of India's most romantic destinations. It offers a dramatic contrast to the desert-bound fortress towns more commonly associated with Rajasthan.

Udaipur, the "city of sunrise", was founded in 1567 by Maharana Udai Singh, on the advice of a sage who told him that if he built his new Mewar capital here it would never be captured. It was timely advice, for his ancestral fortress kingdom at Chittaugarh had just been dealt a fatal blow by Akbar's army.

As Rajasthan's most ancient ruling family, the Mewars bore the title "maharana", or "light of the Hindus", and felt themselves more distin-

guished than mere maharajas, claiming descent from the sun god Rama. (The royal escutcheon is a defiant-looking sun face.) The proud Mewars suffered the yoke of no foreign power for long, and nursed a bitter grudge against those Rajput clans — most particularly Jaipur's Mansingh — whose kingdoms fell into the hands of the Mughals.

Udaipur had no sooner been founded than Akbar's armies laid siege to it, but despite formidable odds, Udai Singh's heir, the legendary Pratap Singh, kept them at bay for 25 years before finally being overpowered. Successive maharanas were involved in an almost constant round of feudalistic battles and intrigues, and Udaipur achieved a lasting peace — albeit

ABOVE: The cupolas of the Shiv Niwas Palace provide quiet outlooks over the ancient town of Udaipur.

maintained with a superior aloofness — only in 1818 when it came under British control and was rescued, along with the rest of Rajasthan, from the clutches of the Marathas.

Udaipur's most prolific builder was Maharana Jagat Singh, who during the seventeenth century built much of the majestic City Palace. It straddles a sheer natural rock palisade almost 1.5 km (a mile) in length overlooking Lake Pichola, and is a vision of Rajput grandeur with its riot of kiosks, projecting balconies and turrets, and topped by a gold *kalash* (spire), the symbol of gods or independent kingdoms. Successive rulers kept adding wings until it became the

fanned breezes, Udaipur is one of Rajasthan's most beguiling cities. You should plan to spend at least four days visiting its many sights and attractions, including several historic temple complexes nearby. Udaipur is at its most beautiful between September and March, and just after the July monsoons.

ACCESS

Indian Airlines links Udaipur with Delhi via Jaipur and Jodphur, and with Bombay via Aurangabad. The Indian Airlines office, ©23952, is at LTC Building, Delhi Gate, and the airport is

largest and most imposing palace complex in Rajasthan. At the same time, Jagat Singh created an exotic lake citadel — now the famed Lake Palace Hotel — on the island of Jagniwas. He also built the forlornly beautiful palace on the opposite island of Jagmandir, which was later used as an abode-in-exile by Jehangir's rebellious son Shah Jehan; it was from here that he proclaimed himself emperor when his father died. It was on Jagmandir, too, that several British families were given shelter following the Indian Mutiny of 1857.

With its tranquil atmosphere, glittering array of palaces, garden pavilions, and cool lake-

24 km (15 miles) from town. By rail, the daily *Chetak Express* takes 21 hours to reach Udaipur from Delhi, via Jaipur and Ajmer. The *Ahmedabad Mail* makes the eight-hour journey to and from Gujarat's capital, and also halts at Abu Road Station, about five hours from Udaipur, for those traveling on to Rajasthan's hill station. Daily luxury or RTDC express buses ply to Ahmedabad and all major Rajasthan centers from the main bus stand near the railway line opposite Udai Pole. There are also frequent bus services to surrounding historic attractions such as Eklingi, Ranakpur and, slightly further afield, Chittaurgarh.

HOTELS

The glorious **Lake Palace**, ©23241-5, rises from Pichola Lake like a marble confection. Built by Maharana Jagat Singh in 1746, it is now run by

ABOVE: At the Karni Mata Temple at Deshnok, near Bikaner, a Rajput girl LEFT observes a "sacred" rat nibbling her proprietary offering of *prasad* or sweetmeats. RIGHT the keeper of the so-called Rat Temple seems unaware of a new addition to his turban.

the Taj Group as a luxury hotel, complete with shopping arcades, coffee shops, and standard modern rooms, so that only the husk of its original medieval structure remains. Five royal suites, complete with stained-glass windows, glittering mirrored and painted surfaces, and antique furniture, have been painstakingly restored and cost upward of Rs 2,000. Pretty interior courtyards and terraces, and a spectacular little marble swimming pool are illuminated at night. A restaurant serving standard five-star fare draws those who aren't guests for sunset drinks and good Rs 150 buffet dinners. Gondoliers dressed in fraying navy-blue tunics ferry guests and visitors back and forth from the marble steps of the Lake Palace to the shore. The locals have never quite gotten over the excitement of having the James Bond movie *Octopussy* filmed here. The Lake Palace operates one-hour boat tours across to Jag Mandir Palace at 5 pm to coincide with dusk's charmed light. These are well worth the Rs 55 cost.

The **Shiv Niwas Palace**, © 28239, is an extravagantly elegant five-star hotel — part of a grand eighteenth-century addition to the vast, rambling City Palace. It has served as a royal guesthouse, accommodating the likes of Queen Elizabeth, Jacqueline Onassis, and the Shah of Iran. Massive entrance doors open on to a dazzling courtyard with a clear blue marble Grecian pool. The royal suites, furnished with Belgian chandeliers, four-poster beds, and surplus treasures from the City Palace, range from Rs 1,800 to Rs 3,000, while the "ordinary" rooms range from Rs 500 to Rs 1,500. Bookings can be made through the Taj Group of Hotels.

For less-expensive period elegance, try the IDTC-run **Laxmi Vilas Palace Hotel**, ©24411-3, on Fateh Sagar Road. Another former palace guesthouse, it has a swimming pool overlooking Fateh Sagar Lake. The neighboring **Anand Bhawan Circuit House,** ©23256, set on the periphery of a delightful park containing a statue of Maharana Pratap astride his favorite charger, Chetak, has pleasant inexpensive rooms.

Perhaps the best choice for those who don't feel the need for luxury surroundings, but require clean, comfortable, and cheap accommodation, is the **Rang Niwas Hotel**, ©23891, Lake Palace Road. Located in the shadow of the City Palace, it is another former mansion guesthouse, run with boundless enthusiasm by the extremely affable Mr Singh and his two sons. You can arrive at any time of the day or night and be assured of (at least) a Rs 15 stretcher bed in the ping-pong room; or choose from modest but clean Rs 60 rooms (supplied with buckets of hot water) or charming Rs 125 to Rs 200 "suites" with nice old furniture, hot water, and mosquito nets. Other attractions are a useful information board in the lobby, a sweet little courtyard, and Udaipur's best rooftop café. Mr Singh is a great organizer — he'll warn against "fiendish" commission-seeking auto-rickshaw wallahs, hire out bicycles, and help coordinate out-of-town tours with other guests to save on taxi fares.

Udaipur also offers two excellent mansion "retreats", both set amid leafy forest at a slight distance from town. **Hotel Shikarbadi**, ©5321, five kilometers (three miles) away, is a delightful nineteenth- century trophy-stuffed royal hunting lodge, with a swimming pool, old retainers, and leafy gardens. It's good for an overnight stay, and for horse riding at dawn. Rooms are moderately priced and can be booked through the Lake Palace Hotel. Cheaper, and rather more eccentric, is **Pratap County Inn**, ©3638-9, at Titadhra Village, six kilometers (3.7 miles) from town. Set amid lovely surroundings and there are free horse- and camel-rides.

RESTAURANTS

Udaipur's two fantasy palaces both have pleasant bars and coffee shops and stage excellent candlelit dinners with a choice of Rajasthani, Indian, and Continental dishes, often preceded by puppet shows or musical performances. The Lake Palace offers excellent Rs 75 *thali* lunches. The sunny rooftop café at the Rang Niwas Hotel is open all day, with modest but well-prepared food and prompt service. Newspapers can be rustled up along with excellent Rs 20 Western-style breakfasts (with perfect two-minute eggs, warm toast, and creamy fruit *lassis*). Main meal dishes offer a choice of Indian, Chinese, or Western food, and are reliably generous and cheap. Another traveler's favorite is the **Mayur Cafe**, opposite the Jagdish Temple down from the City Palace. The excellent cheap food is served promptly by an expert 10-year-old waiter. Highlights here include "Rajasthani Pizza" made with delicious local cheese, "France Frice", "Think-Shakes", and home-baked chocolate cakes. Also try the modern A-framed, aptly-named **Feast Restaurant**, opposite the Saheliyon-ki-Bari Gardens, for pleasant decor, well-dressed waiters, and classic Mughali fare cooked up by the former chief chef at the Lake Palace Hotel. Downstairs is Udaipur's highly popular fast-food parlor, **Eat-Me-Up**, which serves non-stop *dosas*, hamburgers, french fries, and milkshakes.

SIGHTSEEING

Udaipur's palaces and gardens clustered around the long lakeside boulevards make for a perfect day's cycling or walking. Bike-hire places are found along Lake Palace Road, and usually charge about Rs 8 to Rs 15 per day. Otherwise you're at the mercy of taxi and auto-rickshaw drivers, who don't use meters and are prone to causing scenes, or tongas drawn by rather feeble-looking nags.

The **City Palace** houses a museum open daily from 9:30 am to 4:30 pm. Visitors pass through an enchanting multi-tiered labyrinth of royal apartments, zenana quarters, courtyards, terraces, and pavilions. Every inch of wall and ceiling has been decorated — much of it by Hindu artisans who came to Udaipur after being expelled from Delhi's Red Fort by the sectarian Aurangzeb — with jewel-colored mosaics, inlaid Chinese tiles, mirror-work niches, and fine paintings. In one of these rooms, the beautiful Mewar princess Krishna Kumari drank poison and saved the kingdom from the wrath of her two rival suitors from neighboring states. Clamber up to the roof gardens and overhanging terraces for views of the lake. There is another interesting museum near the main palace entrance, with fine Rajput miniatures, toys, and royal *objets d'art*. It is worth buying the museum guide for the detailed information it gives on each room.

Nearby is the eighteenth-century **Tripolia Gate**, with its eight carved marble arches under which the ruler was weighed on his birthday and his weight in gold distributed to his people. Directly behind are the steep stone elephant-steps leading to **Jagdish Temple**, a fine Indo-Aryan temple built by Maharana Jagat Singh in 1651 and notable for its black stone image of Vishnu as Jagannath, Lord of the Universe. You'll emerge into the cobbled Bara Bazaar, which winds its way down to the larger Bapu Bazaar, east of the City Palace, both colorful mêlées overflowing with wooden toys, perfumes, silver trinkets, *pichwai* (cloth paintings), decorative earthenware pots, and giant troughs of bubbling sweetmeats.

To round up, visit the glorious **Gulab Bagh**, or Rose Gardens, laid out in 1881; cycle to the north of the city to see the ornamental **Saheliy-onki Bari** gardens created for the royal concubines, then glide along the **Lake Fateh Sagar** esplanade, stopping to have tea at **Nehru Park**, a garden island with a restaurant, reached by boat; and visit the fascinating folk museum, **Bhartiya Lok Kala Mandal**, near Chetak Circle, which displays tribal art objects, puppets, masks, dolls, folk deities, and musical instruments and stages an excellent "puppet circus" from 6 to 7 pm. You can also make a pleasant excursion by bicycle to the beautiful royal Mewar *chhatris* at **Ahar**, three kilometers (just under two miles) east of town, where an interesting museum houses archaeological finds. For evening entertainment, traditional Rajasthani dances are performed from 7:30 pm every Tuesday, Thursday, and Saturday at the **Meera Kala Mandir**. ℂ 23976 for more information.

GENERAL INFORMATION

The main Tourist Information Bureau, ℂ23605, is located at the Kajri Tourist Bungalow. Their daily city tours leave from here at 8:30 am and 1:30 pm. There is also an afternoon excursion to **Haldighati** (40 km, or 25 miles away), the site of an historic battle between Maharana Pratap Singh and Akbar; the sacred eighteenth-century shrine to Lord Krishna at **Nathdwara** temple (48 km, or 30 miles away), and the large eighteenth-century temple complex of **Eklingi**, 22 km (13.7 miles) from town. This five-hour tour leaves at 2:30 pm and costs Rs 30. There are also tourist offices at the airport and railway station.

CHITTAURGARH

Some 115 km (72 miles) east of Udaipur, the ancient Mewar capital of Chittaurgarh is the most famous and hallowed of all Rajasthan's fortress citadels. Situated on a 180-m (590-ft)-high precipice, this sprawling, battle-scarred, ghost-ridden fortress was sacked thrice, and thrice won back by the courageous Mewars. With its cannon-shattered battlements, carved marble memorials, and myriad sati palm prints, it is the very symbol of stoic Rajput heroism and sacrifice.

According to legend, the fortress was built by Bhim, one of the five Pandava heroes in the Hindu epic the *Maharabharata*. From the seventh century it was the capital of the Mewars, effectively becoming the ruling seat of Rajasthan and thus coveted by prospective invaders. Its long and traumatic history was a litany of brutal assault during which capitulation to the invading enemy was marked by grisly sacrifice. Preferring death to subjugation, its men drank draughts of opium, donned the saffron robes of martyrdom, and rode off for a final orgy of killing known as *saka*, while their women and children committed *jauhaur* — mass immolation on giant pyres. Yet great care was always taken to preserve the royal lineage so that the ruler's son and heir could return to lead a guerilla war against the usurpers of the Mewar domain.

The Muslim Sultan of Delhi, Alu-ud-din, was the first to sack Chittaurgarh in 1303, in his frenzied desire to abduct the beautiful Chittaur queen Padmini after having seen her unveiled

The towering Jai Stambha, or "Tower of Victory" in Chittagurh.

face in a pool reflection. But his was a bitter victory, since the heroic queen threw herself into the flames beside her Rajput sisters. Chittaurgarh was plundered again in 1535 by the Gujarati sultan, Bahudur Shah; 32,000 Rajput soldiers died in battle, and 13,000 women immolated themselves. Just 30 years later, Chittaurgarh was crushed once more, this time irrevocably, by Akbar's armies, compelling Maharana Udai Singh to found his new capital of Udaipur.

Many visitors find Udaipur a convenient base for a visit to Chittaurgarh, rising early to catch the 5:30 am train, and returning either by express bus or train the same day. Since Chittaurgarh has good rail and bus links, it is also a convenient stopping-off place on the rail journey to Jaipur (320 km, or 200 miles) via Ajmer (187 km, or 116 miles) and on the bus trip to Bundi (156 km, or 97 miles). If necessary, stay at **Panna Tourist Bungalow**, ©273; it's close to the railway station.

You'll need at least three hours to explore the rambling ruins, which need an experienced guide to bring them alive. Either take the local tour, which starts at the Tourist Office in Janta Lodge at 7:30 am and lasts until 2:30 pm, or hire an approved guide from Chittaurgarh's fort-based Archaeological Survey Office to lead you through the main interest points — starting with their "office", the former **Fateh Prakash Palace**, a large wing of which has been converted into a museum with a rich collection of sculptures from Chittaurgarh's temples and buildings.

See the ruined fifteenth-century **Rana Kumbha Palace**, which houses a Shiva temple, elephant and horse stables, and vaulted underground cellars, in one of which it is thought Maharani Padmini committed *jauhaur*. Also see the Jain and Hindu temples, the beautiful seven-meter (23-ft) -high **Jai Stambha**, the "Tower of Victory" to the south, built to mark Kumbha's victory over the Sultan of Malwa in 1440, and the smaller, squat **Kirti Stampha**, "Pillar of Fame". Husks of ruined palaces are found everywhere, including **Padmini's Palace** at the eastern end of the fort.

MOUNT ABU

Mount Abu is an anomaly. It is Rajasthan's answer to Shimla or Ooty, a lush nineteenth-century hill station dotted with date palms and royal summer palaces, nestled 1,200 m (4,000 ft) up in the craggy, almost biblical-looking, landscape of the Aravallis, the home of the colorfully-clad tribal Bhils. It is also an important center for Jain pilgrimage, with an exquisite temple complex dating back to the eleventh

and thirteenth centuries. During the mid-nineteenth century, it suddenly came into vogue as a princely retreat, sprouting stately mansions; later, during the First World War, the British transformed it into a military cantonment, primarily for recuperating shell-shocked soldiers and TB patients. All these influences — as well as its burgeoning popularity as a honeymoon destination for Gujarati Indians, with its rash of kitsch "love hotels" — make it an eccentric, beguiling place to visit.

The origins of Mount Abu are steeped in Hindu lore — it gets its name from "Arbuda", the serpent son of the Himalayas who supposedly rescued Shiva's bull which was stranded in a chasm here; it is also where the gods scooped out the oasis-like Nakki Lake with their "nakks" or nails. Mount Abu is as important to Rajput Hindus as Mount Olympus is to the Greeks for, according to myth, this was where the sage Vashisht lit a sacrificial fire from which the original Rajput warrior clans first emerged.

Like any Indian hill station, Mount Abu is at its most pleasant during the high summer months of March to June. During winter, when the rest of Rajasthan is at its best, Mount Abu can be downright freezing, so be sure to bring sweaters and socks.

ACCESS

Mount Abu can be a convenient place to stop before continuing on to Ahmedabad and Gujarat state. From Udaipur, 185 km (115 miles) away, it can be reached by train or by morning express bus — departing from Udaipur at 8 am and arriving at 2 pm. Book at Udaipur's bus stand or through Taldar Travels, ©28160, Taldar Building, opposite the Town Hall, whose agents wear stetsons and reflective sunglasses — the height of Udaipur fashion! If you arrive at Abu Road by train, you can either hop aboard a local bus or hire a jeep to make the 27-km (17-mile) winding journey up to Mount Abu. On arrival, you'll find yourself surrounded by pram to pushing "porters", all vying for the task of shunting your luggage to your hotel for a few rupees. Get around locally on foot, by the local "jeep" service, taxi, or by pony (Rs 20 per hour).

RTDC-conducted morning and afternoon sightseeing tours leave from the Youth Hostel.

HOTELS

Like other hill stations, Mount Abu's hotels offer off-season discounts of up to 50 percent before Indian tourists start arriving in mid-April. Mount Abu has several "luxury" hotels, notably the five-star **Hotel Savera Palace**, ©254,

Sunset Road, and the three-star **Hotel Hilltone,** ©137, located right near the bus station, but these are geared to the "flashy" tastes of Indian tourists. Foreign visitors tend to find the faded, slightly Gothic, elegance of former palace retreats more to their taste. However the nicest place to stay is **Hotel Bikaner Palace,** ©21, Delwara Road, set amid leafy grounds with tennis courts and a private lake. Quaintly furnished rooms have nine-meter (30-ft) -high ceilings, hot showers, and are inexpensive. Very large Anglo-Indian meals are available in the former dance hall (look for the purdah slats above), and there is a billiards room in the lounge. **Connaught House**, Delwara Road, is the delightful former summer house of the British Resident attached to the ex-princely state of Marwar (Jodhpur). Owned by the Maharaja of Jodhpur, it has bougainvillea-sprayed bedroom cottages, each with complete privacy, good basic amenities, and simple Indian food. Rates: inexpensive. To book, write to the General Manager, Connaught House, care of Umaid Bhawan Palace, Jodhpur. A homely guesthouse option is the **Mount Hotel,** ©55, Dilwara Road. Run by friendly Mrs Bharucha and her son, it serves good authentic Parsi and Indian dishes. If you're determined (and brave enough) to experience the interior of an Indian "love hotel", ask for a honeymoon suite at **Hotel Samrat,** ©73, near the taxi stand, and revel in nylon leopard-skin sheets on a bed shaped like a chariot, "his" and "hers" heart-shaped pillows, Khajuraho-motif tiles, curtains, and bath-towels, and non-stop Hindi movies on TV!

Outside the hotels, it's worth sampling the best of Mount Abu's goldmine of excellent Gujarati fare. The town center is full of *thali*-cafés, whose generous platters cost between Rs 6 and Rs 15. One of the best of these is **Kanak Dining Hall**; otherwise stick to the string of friendly open-air eating places near the bus-stand, where barefoot boys in oversized jackets wait on tables. These places are good for spicy sweet ginger tea, *thalis*, *dosas*, and the addictive *pau bhaji* — a steaming hot mixture of pulverized potatoes, vegetables, garlic, ginger, and chillis served with a fried bun.

SIGHTSEEING

North of town, the **Dilwara Jain Temples** are the main attraction. Set on a hill in a mango tree grove, and built between the eleventh and thirteenth centuries, the temples are famous for their complex and intricate marble carvings. It's no exaggeration to say that these carvings alone are worth the journey to Mount Abu. They are so perfect, it is almost impossible

Jaipur and Rajasthan

to believe they were crafted from a sculptor's chisel. The temples, which deserve several visits, are most beautiful just before dusk. The temple complex is open to non-Jains only between 12 noon and 8 pm; leather items — shoes, belts, bags, watch-straps, etc. — and menstruating females (as a bold sign declaims) are not permitted inside.

Otherwise, Mount Abu is a picturesque place for walking and relaxing. There are wonderful views from **Guri Shikar**, 15 km (nine miles) at 1,725 m (5,660 ft), the highest point in Rajasthan. At **Achalgarh**, 11 km (seven miles), there is an intriguing Shiva temple, with three

stone buffaloes; and the rock-chiselled **Adhar Devi Temple** is reached by a flight of 200 steps. Closer to town are Sunset and Honeymoon points for stunning views and Nakki Lake for boating. The town itself is interesting to stroll around. The Tourist Office, ©51, is opposite the bus station. Its opening hours are rather strange — from 7 to 10 am, 12 noon to 2 pm, and 5 to 8 pm — perhaps because there is a Retail Beer shop nearby selling every type of Indian beer to thirsty refugees from "dry" Gujarat.

Entrance hall of the exquisitely carved Dilwara Jain Temples at Mount Abu.

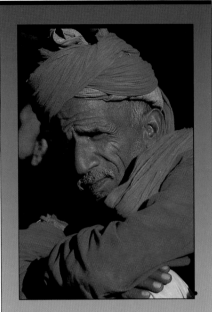

The
Mountain
Trail

SHIMLA

The former summer capital of the British Indian empire, Shimla has colonial ghosts, nineteenth-century cottages with potted geraniums, beautiful alpine scenery, crisp pine-scented air, and monkeys. It sprawls along a 12-km (7.5-mile)-long ridge, 2,200 m (7,218 ft) high in the northwest Himalayan foothills.

The setting for Rudyard Kipling's *Plain Tales From the Hills*, Shimla is thought to have derived its name from "Shamla", a title of the goddess Kali who is revered by local hill people. British officers stumbled on its exceptional scenic charms when driving invading Gurkhas from the region in 1819. Then, in 1822, one Major Kennedy started a trend by constructing permanent residence in Shimla.

The British developed an attachment to this remote Himalayan town that amounted almost to an obsession. During the summer months on the northern plains, government officers would develop a condition known as "Punjab head". The heat was so intense that efficient work and accurate decision-making became well-nigh impossible. Shimla soon became a glamorous summer bolt-hole for the Anglo-Indian elite, the heat-weary, and the invalid, complete with a busy social round of dinners, whist parties, picnics, amateur theatricals, and furtive assignations between young officers and so-called "grass widows", whose husbands labored on the burning plains below. Shimla gained respectability in 1864 when the viceroy Lord Lawrence visited and pronounced it the official summer capital, observing rather soberly, "I believe we shall do more work in one day here than five down in Calcutta". Thus began the great annual exodus of the viceroy with his guards, private staff, and public attendants, along with his secretariat, army headquarters, Foreign Office, the representative of the Indian princes, and a vast entourage of cumbersome file-cases hauled up by pony-drawn tongas, memsahibs, children, and traders. By 1904, the construction of the Kalka–Shimla railway finally provided easy access to the hill station.

Shimla's tiered ridge soon resembled a semi-suburban jumble of fanciful Anglo-Indian architectural styles — red-roofed Swiss chalets with names like Fairy Cottage and Windermere, Tudor and Georgian-style mansions, the Gothic tower of Christ Church with a bell made from a mortar captured in the second Sikh War, and palatial government buildings such as Barnes Court, Kennedy House, and Gordon Castle. The Viceregal Lodge was so luxurious — with a staff of 300 domestics and 100 cooks — that it was said Indian income tax had been invented to pay for it. No carriages (excepting those of the viceroy and his retinue) were allowed in the center of town, known as the Mall, so residents were carried about in *jhampans*, curtained sedan chairs, or four-man rickshaws by hardy coolies. When Sir Edwin Lutyens, the architect of imperial New Delhi, went to Shimla in 1913, he was apparently appalled, and said, "If one was told the monkeys had built it all one could only say: What wonderful monkeys — they must be shot in case they do it again...."

Shimla, now the state capital of Himachal Pradesh, has changed surprisingly little in appearance since the days when memsahibs gathered to gossip at Scandal Point. The town itself is very busy, lively and nostalgically "English", with quaint Raj-era hotels and buildings, and beautiful walks through Himalayan mountains thick with oak, deodar, and pine trees. It's a perfect place to indulge in fantasies of the Raj.

The best time to visit is from mid-April to October, the fragrant summer season when hyacinths, rhododendrons, violets, and lilies fill the meadows. Winters are bitterly cold and Shimla is carpeted in snow between December and March. Whatever the time of year, the nights are chilly.

ACCESS

Shimla's nearest airport is at 1,372 m (4,500 ft), and above a sheer drop, at Juberhatti, 22 km (14 miles) away. Vayudoot operates regular flights to and from Shimla from New Delhi. A good alternative is to take the daily Indian Airlines flight, a train, or a bus to Chandigarh, then proceed the 110 km (68 miles) to Shimla by the charming narrow gauge *Kalka Mail* "toy train", which departs from Kalka, 24 km (15 miles) north of the Haryana state capital. The scenic six-hour journey winds up the original steep track that was built in 1903–1904, and is a collector's item for rail buffs. Shimla's station looks straight out of the series of children's book, *Noddy* with its pretty flower-boxes, gleaming brass, and spic and span coolies in bright red jackets. Several state and luxury coaches run from Delhi and Chandigarh daily, and the trip takes 10 and four hours respectively.

WHERE TO STAY

Shimla attracts droves of holidaying Indians and has a good range of hotels, lodges, and facilities. Accommodation rates drop by 30 to 50 percent during the cold off-season months between November and mid-April.

OPPOSITE: Onion-dome of rustic mosque in Srinagar's old district on the banks of the Jhelum River.

Stay at a choice of old Raj-era hotels which offer a delightful blend of colonial grandeur, eccentric service, and fussy decor with stunning views. In the top bracket, stay either at the **Oberoi Clarkes**, ©6091-5, or the **Hotel Cecil**, ©2073/6041-4, both moderately priced and located on the Mall. The Tudor-style **Woodville Palace Hotel**, ©2712, is very charming — my personal favorite — surrounded by pine trees right on the edge of town. It was used as a set in *The Jewel in the Crown* series adapted from Paul Scott's *Raj Quartet* by Granada Television. It has moderate rates, spacious period suites crammed with curios and mahogany furniture, plenty of

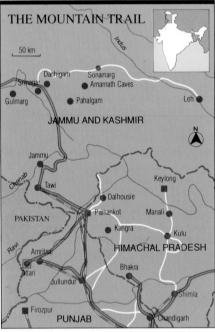

THE MOUNTAIN TRAIL

hot water, and a pretty garden for afternoon teas served by waiters in cummerbunds. Breakfasts are good, but if you value prompt service at other mealtimes, take a stroll down to the Mall to avoid tiresome waits in the dining room for tepid nursery-style Raj food. The inexpensive **Chapslee Hotel**, ©3242, is another time-warp gem, located in Lakkar Bazaar.

Cheaper accommodation is much less memorable, and tends to be filled with rowdy Indian honeymooners. Both the **Hotel Holiday Home**, ©6031, on Cart Road and the **Hotel Mayur**, ©6047/8/9, behind Christ Church, have inexpensive, comfortable rooms.

OUT AND ABOUT

Shimla is a charming place, with plenty of atmosphere and invigorating country walks. Its

main forum is the crescent-shaped **Mall**, lined with stylish English buildings, ice-cream stalls, and souvenir shops, where everyone goes strolling. You can peer at sepia photographs in musty shop-fronts of 1930's Shimla debutantes and bristle-mustached officers, buy ornately carved walking sticks, Kulu shawls, discarded solar topees, or boxes of faded "at home" cards as souvenirs, and stop for refreshments in one of the many cafés and restaurants. The **South Indian Coffee House** serves excellent snacks and aromatic Mysore coffee.

At the top of the Mall, near the Ridge, is the Gothic **Christ Church**. Built in 1857, it is the second oldest church in northern India. Inside are beautiful stained-glass windows, murals, old oak pews, and fascinating plaques to commemorating deceased army regiments. Sunday services are worth attending, just to see the resident organist furiously pounding out *We Plough the Fields and Scatter*. See the mock-Tudor **Gaiety Theater**, where Gilbert and Sullivan tunes were de rigueur, and the grand Scottish Baronial-style **Municipal Buildings**. The church is next to **Scandal Point**, the large open square which got its name 50 years ago when a dashing young Indian prince eloped with a young British memsahib from this spot on horseback. Steep terraces lead down to the crooked, zigzagging levels of **Middle** and **Lower Bazaars**, which brim with local handicraft stalls, cafés, and swarthy-featured Pahari hill tribes.

Visit the **State Museum** for good Pahari-school miniature paintings, costumes, textiles, jewelry, wood-carvings, bronzes, and stone-sculptures. It's open 10 am to 5 pm daily except Monday and every second Saturday. Also see the huge six-storied **Viceregal Lodge** on Summer Hill, which once hosted ceremonial balls and festivities and now houses India's Institute of Advanced Studies, with a fine reception hall and library.

For the best view of Shimla, make the exceedingly steep climb up to **Jackoo Hill** at 3,438 m (11,280 ft), which takes anything from 40 minutes for strapping mountaineers to two hours for mere mortals. At the top is a little temple dedicated to the monkey god Hanuman, presided over by its resident ash-smeared sadhu and his tribe of monkeys. In 1874, Shimla's Victorian society was appalled when a young aristocrat, Charles de Russeth, became a disciple of the Jackoo sadhu, spending his time chanting to monkeys. Known as the "leopard fakir" for his fur head-dress and loincloth, he was India's very first hippie.

Other pleasant walks include **Glen Forest**, four kilometers (two and a half miles) away, a pretty picnic spot with a waterfall near the Annandale racecourse and cricket ground;

Chadwick Falls, two kilometers (one and a quarter miles), for a 67-m (220-ft) waterfall; **Summer Hill**, five kilometers (three miles), to see the elegant Georgian house of **Rajkumari Amrit Kaur** that Mahatma Gandhi stayed in during his visit to Shimla; and **Prospect Hill**, five kilometers (three miles) away.

Good excursions by car or bus include **Wildflower Hall**, 13 km (eight miles), built by Lord Kitchener in 1903 to rival the Viceregal Lodge, and used as a peaceful hotel; **Kufri**, 16 km (10 miles), a modest winter ski resort with equipment for hire; and **Chail**, 90 km (56 miles), with its summer palace of the Maharaja of Patiala, now run as a hotel, bird-sanctuary, and the world's highest cricket pitch.

GENERAL INFORMATION

The Tourist Office, ©3311, is located on the Mall and runs useful tours out to surrounding vantage points. The National Book Depot, just up from the Tourist Lift, sells the excellent *Tourist Guide to Shimla*, full of useful information.

THE KULU VALLEY AND MANALI

Kulu Valley, 205 km (127 miles) from Shimla, is famous for its beautiful scenery, apple orchards, and lively tribal music and dances. Enclosed by the last snow range of the Himalayas, with the Dhauladhar and Pir Panjal ranges running parallel to the south, the narrow terraced valley runs north from Mandi through Kulu and Manali all the way up to the Rohtang Pass, at 2,000 m (6,562 ft). The Beas River flows through its fertile, flower-strewn meadows. It's an excellent base for walks, trout fishing, and gentle treks up through pine and cedar forests. Gregarious local hill people dress in traditional home-spun shawls, Kulu caps, wool jackets, and moccasins — all of which make wonderful purchases in the bazaar. They like to work hard, pray hard, and play hard. The region boasts more than 6,000 carved wooden temples, and religious festivities involve much merry consumption of *chang* (the local rice beer) as temple deities are dressed up and borne on elaborate palanquins in torchlight processions.

It's worth making a special trip to the Kulu Valley to see the most exuberant of all Kulu's festivals, Dussehra (September/October), 10 days of exuberant revelry, folk dances, and music played on hill instruments such as *karnal, narsinghas, dhoi*, and drum. All over India, Dussehra is celebrated to commemorate Rama's victory over the demon king of Ravanna. But in Kulu, the god Raghunath is the victorious one who is the focus of the festivities. Some

200 gods from neighboring villages are carried here on palanquins and chariots to pay him tribute, followed by nightly folk-dancing competitions.

You can reach Kulu's Bhuntar airport, 10 km (six miles) away, by regular Vayudoot flights from New Delhi and Chandigarh. Otherwise, fly to Chandigarh, then make the long 270-km (167-mile) — but exceptionally pretty — journey by road. From Shimla, three buses daily make the hair-raising 205-km (127-mile), eight to nine-hour trip past exhilarating views, perilous drops, and alarming road signs: "Arrive Late In This Life, Not Early In The Next", "Over-

takers Will Meet Undertakers", and "Married Couples, Divorce Speed".

Kulu has few lodging places and restaurants. Both the ITDC **Traveler's Lodge**, ©79, and the **Kulu Valley Resort**, ©223 offer moderately priced and comfortable rooms with attached bathrooms and good restaurants. Many travelers prefer to base themselves at **Manali**, a small, picturesque hill station, 42 km (26 miles) — two hours — from Kulu, with better accommodation. The top-bracket hotels include the **Ashok Traveler's Lodge** (©31, rates: moderate), **Log Huts** (©39, rates: moderate), **Hotel Highland** (©99), and **John Banon's Guest House** (©35, rates: moderate), with well-furnished suites, good food, and wonderful mountain views.

In Kulu, there are pleasant walks to the main seventeenth-century Raghunathji Temple, the Vaishno Devi Temple, and the Bijli Mahadev Temple. There is a good Himachal Pradesh State Museum. Also see two former Kulu capitals, one at Naggar with a castle (now a rest-house) and Jagatsukh, the earlier capital, with many temples.

ABOVE: These Kashmiri schoolgirls seem to require little distraction to be lured away from their studies.

While in Manali, see nearby **Old Manali Village** and the fourteenth-century wooden **Hadimba Devi Temple**. The Himalayan Mountaineering Institute can offer advice for treks and has equipment for hire and Sherpas to guide. Trout-fishing licenses are issued through the Tourist Office from the Director of Fisheries, Dehra Gopipur. Good two-day trekking excursions include Hanuman Tibba at 5,929 m (19,452 ft) and to the Rohtang Pass at 4,000 m (13,123 ft). Other worthwhile treks are to Malana, Parbati, Solang, and Seraj valleys and up the Deo Tibba, at 6,000 m (19,685 ft). Beyond the Kulu Valley is the Kangra Valley, with its impressive Kangra fort; further on is Dharamslala, where the Dalai Lama lives in exile with a community of Tibetan refugees.

KASHMIR

Ever since the Mughal emperors made the Vale of Kashmir their summer haven, successive conquerors have fallen captive to the legendary beauty of this land. Nestled high in the Himalayas in India's far north, this lake-studded valley was the "Pearl of Hind" to the Mughals and the playground for the British Raj — a land of lofty snowcapped peaks, alpine forests, lily-strewn waterscapes, orchards of spring-time blossoms, and patchwork meadows of riotous wildflowers.

Kashmir's spectacular natural scenery and bracing alpine climate attract travelers all year round to indulge in nostalgic memories of the Raj on Srinagar's houseboats, or for trekking, trout fishing, and skiing in the Himalayan mountains. Jawaharlal Nehru, himself a Kashmiri, wrote of the land's "strange enchantment" and "fairy magic", and certainly Kashmir feels less like a part of India than a strange Oriental fable.

Nothing gives this impression more than the Kashmiris themselves. Men wear wide-cloaked *chogas*, which in the cold season conceal *kangris*, the small wicker-work baskets of burning coals. Sturdy barefoot urchins rattle their horse-drawn tongas through the poplar-lined avenues. And young women wearing brightly patterned layers of garments and candelabra earrings can be startlingly beautiful, with almond-shaped eyes and Tartar cheekbones.

Jammu and Kashmir state is made up of three distinct areas, each very different not only in landscape but also in the heritage, language, and religion of the people.

In the very south, at the periphery of Punjab's hot plains before the foothills of the

OPPOSITE: Moored *shikaras* on the glassy surface of Dal Lake, Srinigar.

Himalayas, lies Jammu city, once the stronghold of feudalistic Hindu and Sikh Dogra rajas, and now a winter capital. To the north, across dense, forested ravines and steep mountain passes, lies Kashmir Valley, an oval plateau 1,500 m (5,000 ft) above sea level, framed by three massive Himalayan ranges — the Karakoram, Zanskar, and Pir Panjal. Srinagar, the state's summer capital, is nestled amid the valley's lakes, meadows, and floating gardens. The third main part of the state, the remote and arid region of Ladakh, is at the northeastern border with China where the 7,000-m (23,000-ft) -high peaks of the Zanskar Range are found. Sometimes referred to as "Little Tibet", Ladakh still looks and feels like a medieval, hermetic Buddhist kingdom, with ancient monasteries hewn into the mountain crags, legions of red-robed monks, and prayer flags fluttering everywhere.

Jammu and Kashmir is 94 percent Muslim, and the residents hold that their cultural links to Central Asia, Afghanistan, Persia, and the Middle East are stronger than those to mostly Hindu India. The area's rich history as a major trading center along the ancient Silk Road is reflected in the potpourri of appearances: sharp — almost Semitic — profiles, fair skin, tawny hair, and hazel eyes.

The region's recorded history stretches back to the early second century BC, when it was renowned as an ancient land of scholars and mystics. Emperor Ashoka (269–232 BC) converted its inhabitants to Buddhism, and Kashmiri missionaries were largely responsible for spreading the doctrine across the mountain passes of the Silk Road to Central Asia, China, and Tibet. A Hindu heyday followed in the seventh and eighth centuries with a line of Karkota kings who gave Kashmir its first impressive monuments and cities. But from the tenth to the fourteenth century, Kashmir entered a dark epoch of feudalistic disarray, in which power passed from a line of ruthless commanders to a Muslim Tibetan prince. When the prince died in 1338, Shah Mir usurped the kingdom and founded the Sultan dynasty. The eighth and most celebrated sultan was Zainul-Abidin — known as Badshah, or Great King — who encouraged studies in Hindu and Buddhist philosophy and patronized literature, dance, and music. Every Kashmiri artisan regards Badshah as a kind of patron saint, for he introduced new arts such as shawl embroidery, carpet making, papier mâché, silver work, and carving, and invited entire guilds of craftsmen in Persia and Samarkand to settle in the valley.

The Mughal emperor Akbar conquered the region in 1857. Declaring Kashmir "my private garden", he amused himself by boating, water-fowling, and indulging in eccentricities such as seeing how many of his valets could fit inside a hollow *chenar* plane tree — 34 was the impressive total! Four generations of Mughal emperors made Kashmir their summer idyll, creating elaborate pleasure gardens, delicate marble pavilions, and intricate irrigation systems still in use today, and eulogizing the vale in poems, songs, and paintings. In the meantime, they brought nearly all of the population under the Muslim faith.

As Mughal power waned in the eighteenth century, Afghan warlords occupied the area from 1752 to 1819, when they were ousted by Ranjit Singh, who conquered the valley and annexed it to his Punjab kingdom. After losing the first Anglo-Sikh war in 1846, the Sikhs could not afford the indemnity of £500,000 imposed by the British, and instead offered them Kashmir. The Dogra Maharaja of Jammu offered London twice the amount, and became the ruler of the combined states of Jammu and Kashmir. His descendants ruled under the British until Independence in 1947.

The strategically situated state has been a battleground in 1948, 1965, and 1971 between India and Pakistan, who still contest Kashmir's sovereignty. Troops from both sides frequently exchange gunfire at the restricted frontier areas, and a tense stand-off is in force at Siachen Glacier, the world's highest battleground at 5,800 m (19,000 ft). At the same time, a section of Kashmir near Ladakh is under dispute between India and China, and is another source of regional tension.

SRINAGAR

Visitors who arrive by air from India's hot and dusty plains often find Srinagar's cool alpine air, chenar-shaded meadows, and soaring snow-clad mountains nothing less than a revelation. With its lake-moored houseboats, Mughal gardens, mosques, and the lure of the nearby Himalayan mountains, Srinagar is easily the most popular destination in northern India and the perfect base from which to explore the rest of Kashmir.

Srinagar, or "city of beautiful scenery", is thought to have originated some 2,000 years ago as a hamlet founded by emperor Ashoka when his daughter Charumati took a fancy to Dal Lake during a pilgrimage to the area. The present city was established in the sixth century by the feudal king Raja Pravarasen II, who created many of the serpentine waterways that still wriggle through the city like backdoor entrances to the sprawling Dal Lake and the smaller, more secluded, Nagin Lake.

Srinagar's old quarters on the banks of the Jhelum River, with their labyrinthine alleys and crooked, Tyrolean-looking houses, appear little changed since the reign of the Mughals.

ACCESS

Most travelers prefer to fly directly to Srinagar, as the overland routes can be arduous. The valley is also a convenient starting point for trips to Ladakh in the northeast and to the trekking trails and hill stations of Himachal Pradesh in the southeast.

Srinagar can be reached by direct flights from Delhi, Ahmedabad, Amritsar, Bombay, and Leh. The Srinagar—Leh flight, which operates twice a week, is one of the world's most spectacular short plane rides, as it glides across snowcapped Himalayan summits. A daily flight service connects Srinagar and Jammu, 293 km (180 miles) away. Srinagar's airport is 18 km (11 miles) out of town, and taxis charge about Rs 80 each way.

Srinagar's nearest railhead is Jammu, which has direct connections with all parts of the country. Four trains run daily to and from Delhi. The 720-km (450-mile) -trip takes from 10 to 13 hours; a comfortable overnight sleeper is recommended.

There are plenty of "luxury video" buses from Delhi, but this 30-hour marathon must rate as one of India's most grueling journeys. The bus journey between Srinagar and Jammu takes between 10 and 14 hours and has a notorious record of bad accidents. Before departure, it's common to see a skimpily-clad fakir with his holy oil-lamp sprinkle protective water and blossoms on the passive-faced passengers, and place a garland of fresh flowers around the gaudy portraits of Hindu gods on the dashboard. Happily reassured, the driver flicks on his static-laden transistor to its full, mind-numbing, volume, slams his foot down on the accelerator, and takes off on a kamikaze joyride past stunning scenery and ominous road signs — "Is Your Honeymoon Worth Death?" and "Don't Drive So Fast, Your Life Is Waiting." The alternative is to take a taxi, although this works out much more expensive than the Rs 240 airfare.

State buses leave Srinagar and Jammu early each morning. These vary from Rs 120 "super deluxe" to Rs 50 ordinary class. During the peak season, these buses are often sold out days in advance, so try to pre-book seats through the Tourist Reception Centre.

WHEN TO GO

Unlike most of India, Kashmir is transformed by each passing season: harsh snowbound winters, abundant springs, idyllic hot summers, and mellow autumns ablaze with burnished copper, scarlet, and golden-brown leaves. Kashmir is at its most beautiful between April and May, when the melting snow cleanses the lakes, the flower-carpeted meadows are drenched with color, and the almond, walnut, apple, pear, cherry, and apricot orchards burst into fragrant blossoms. The best months for trekking, trout fishing, and water-sports are June and July. In August, Srinagar's lakes are covered with water lilies, the blooms of which are known as "Buddhist flowers". It is scarf-and-sweater weather by mid-October and the winter ski season lasts from December to February.

HOUSEBOATS

By the late nineteenth century, the British had come to regard Kashmir as their cool Himalayan retreat during the furnace-like heat of the Indian summer. But the ruling maharaja balked at this seasonal invasion of his earthly paradise and prohibited the British from owning or building houses on his land, hoping that this would stem the flow of officers, crinolined memsahibs, and entourages of swaddled infants, nannies, and servants. With inventive literal-mindedness, the British created a floating colony of luxurious, carved mock-bungalows on Srinagar's Dal and Nagin lakes, thus launching the fashion for houseboating.

From these drifting cedar-scented Victorian parlors, they issued "at home" cards, drilled their Kashmiri cooks in Mrs Beeton's gastronomic legacy, and went for pleasure cruises in *shikaras*, the hand-paddled, canopied taxi-gondolas with curtains and mattress-sized cushions on which to recline. Few of the earliest British houseboats survive, but there are many dating from the 1930's, with scrupulously preserved walnut-wood furniture, faded brocade draperies, and biscuit-tin landscapes hung on gingerbread paneling. Most of the houseboats cramming Srinagar's bustling waterways are modern and roomier imitations, with more dependable electricity and plumbing and, during winter, better central heating than the old ones. Their owners compete to woo tourists with colorful awnings, bright flower baskets, and outlandish names such as *Texan Dream, Love-in-the-Mist, Little Dubai,* and *HMS Fairyland* tacked to the roof.

At secluded moorings in the mossed backwaters of lovely Nagin Lake just west of Dal Lake or at the north end of Dal, languid houseboating is a holiday in itself, with somewhat idiosyncratic service provided by the Kashmiri owner's family who live a few steps away in another boat or on the shore. Houseboats range from five-bedroom "five-star deluxe" palaces to modest one-bedroom boats suitable for a couple or a lone traveler. A typical houseboat has two or three bedrooms with attached bathrooms, and dining and lounge rooms fronted by a cupola-style veranda; the more elaborate boats have gaily caparisoned sun decks with chairs, tables, and umbrellas.

There are more than 1,300 boats scattered across the lakes (950 of which are officially approved), so finding one to your taste is not difficult. Travel agents can arrange bookings for a room on a houseboat, or set up special package deals at fixed rates, in which case someone

Road and hire a *shikara*; simply ask the boatman to stop at any houseboat that catches your eye, preferably with a "To Let" sign slung across its balcony. Decide first which of the two main houseboat areas you prefer: the livelier and more congested flotilla in lower Dal Lake, running parallel to the Boulevard and just a short *shikara* hop from the city, or the serene isolated setting of Nagin Lake. On Dal, the most pleasant location for houseboating is along the east-facing backwaters some distance offshore behind Nehru Park. The best location on Nagin is the eastern shore, which has spectacular sunsets and views across snowcapped moun-

will meet you at Srinagar's airport and whisk you to your destination with minimal fuss. But this method requires you to rent a houseboat unseen, which is much more of a gamble than booking a hotel room because a holiday aboard a houseboat involves being on fairly intimate terms with the owner, the staff, and often other guests as well, as the living rooms are frequently communal. For this reason, you may prefer to make the choice yourself.

Srinagar's houseboat touts are notoriously pushy, and even turn up at Delhi's airport to accost Kashmir-bound tourists. It is best to consult the Tourist Reception Centre's houseboat bureau to view a list of recommended boats, from deluxe to D-class *doongas*. The office also provides rental rates and a local map which is a useful guide to Srinagar's liquid highways and land layout. Then proceed to Boulevard

tains to the west.

During your houseboat "inspection tour", you'll meet enough houseboat owners, staff, and other guests to gain a strong sense of which arrangement is likely to suit you best, as well as some idea of the prevailing rates.

Welcomgroup's five-star houseboats on Nagin Lake are expensive with a choice of rooms and suites, all plushly furnished. The Welcomgroup Gurkha Houseboats can be booked though any Welcomgroup hotel or through PO Box 57, Nagin Lake, ✆ 75229.

Officially, room rent aboard a deluxe boat costs about Rs 335, but you'll probably pay Rs 500, which includes three meals plus "bed" and "four o'clock" tea, as well as free use of the houseboat's *shikara* and dugout canoe.

If privacy is the most important consideration, you may wish to rent a more modest, often equally comfortable, B-class boat, some of which have only one bedroom, but are inexpensive and perfect for a couple. For travelers on a tight budget, D-class houseboats offer comfortable rooms for as little as Rs 40, and every impish *shikara* boy will know where to find one.

Before you agree on a price with the houseboat owner, make sure that you both understand the terms so as to avoid ill-feeling if mysteriously inflated bills are produced at the end of your stay. Make sure the rate includes ship-to-shore *shikara* rides and, if desired, three meals a day, on the understanding that missed lunches

to persuade the maharaja to accede to India upon Independence, shocked the palace servants by sunbathing nude here. The maharaja capitulated only when Pathan tribesmen from newly created Pakistan stormed the valley in 1948 and Srinagar was about to fall. As he awaited deliverance by Indian troops, he passed the time by ordering a particularly extravagant meal. As he wandered off for a siesta, he nonchalantly instructed his aides, "If they are not here by three, please shoot me." Luckily, he was saved just in time!

The stately 1930's mansion seems to sprawl endlessly, tempting more than one guest to

or dinners will be deducted from your bill. Finally, don't let the houseboat owner cajole you into paying in advance, which can put you at the mercy of lackadaisical service or mediocre cooking—pay only by the day. Spring, summer, and autumn are the months for delightful, scenic houseboating — not Kashmir's bitterly cold winters, when the houseboats become ice-palaces wedged amidst gray slushy snow.

WHERE ELSE TO STAY

If you sleep easier knowing there is solid ground beneath you, the **Oberoi Palace**, ©75651-3, is the grandest of all Kashmir's hotels. The former maharaja Sir Hari Singh's palace is set in eight hectares (20 acres) of blossoming gardens with panoramic views across Dal Lake. Mountbatten, during a visit

contemplate bicycling down its hallways. The renovated rooms have a comfortable colonial atmosphere, but are expensive — doubles, including breakfast, cost Rs 1,310. Afternoons on the front lawn are the Oberoi's forte — perfect for sipping tea and nibbling delicious macaroons from tiered trays while watching bright-orange *shikaras* ripple the lake's mirrored surface. The dining room is Srinagar's best, serving Mughlai, Chinese, and European cuisine, and Kashmiri dishes on request. The charming Harlequin Bar is perfect for sundowners. Tucked within the green rolling lawns are a six-hole golf course and a swimming pool.

ABOVE: Experiencing domestic bliss aboard a luxury houseboat is one of Kashmir's most profound pleasures. OPPOSITE: Elaborate gingerbread façades characterize Srinagar's houseboats.

The **Centaur Lake View Hotel**, ©75631-33, is a massive, haphazardly designed five-star complex set among five hectares (13 acres) on Dal's lakeside, about a half-kilometer (one-third of a mile) from the Oberoi. During the peak season, it is filled with affluent Indian families who are attracted by its recreational facilities —water-skiing, windsurfing, tennis, swimming pool, table tennis, and a private jetty for speedboat and shikara rides — and its secluded holiday camp atmosphere. The restaurants serve Indian and Chinese cuisine. Avoid the coffee shop with its team of absent-minded waiters. The lakeview rooms are best. Rates: moderate.

The **Hotel Broadway** is in the center of modern Srinagar on Maulana Azad Road, a short walk from the Tourist Centre and the city's shops, banks, and offices. It's more suited to business travelers than tourists, and is efficient and comfortable with two decent restaurants, one opening on to a secluded garden with a pool. Rates: moderate.

Along Boulevard Road is a row of clean, utilitarian hotels, like Korean lodges, with uniform rooms at roughly similar prices. Try **Hotel Shahenshah Palace**, **Hotel Tramboo Continental**, ©73914, or **Zamrud Hotel**, ©75263. **Hotel New Shalimar**, ©74427, with its rose-trellis archway and café-restaurant set on reclaimed land facing Boulevard Road, is reached by *shikara* and is a good cheap budget hotel option.

The **Hotel Dar-Es-Salam**, a delightful lime-white two-story villa set in a restful garden on Nagin Lake's secluded shore, is a restful oasis much favored by vacationing diplomats. There are 14 spacious and comfortable double rooms with lake views. Rates: inexpensive. To reserve, write to Hotel Dar-Es-Salam, Nagin Lake, Nandpora Rainawari, Srinagar 190003.

Welcomgroup's has recently renovated the Raj-era **Nedous Hotel**, near the Golf Club on Maulana Azas Road. The russet-colored manor held afternoon quartets and ballroom dances during its heyday in the 1930's, and rivals the new five-star Oberoi Palace.

GETTING AROUND

Nothing is more restful than a *shikara* ride for exploring Srinagar's lakes and winding canals. Or you can borrow your houseboat's canoe and paddle about on your own.

On land, Srinagar is too spread out to be explored conveniently on foot; bicycles are an excellent way of getting around. It is a real pleasure to cycle along the wide lakeside avenues lined with tall chenar trees, past lush paddy fields to the Mughal Gardens, or along the narrow causeway from beneath the Hari Parbat Fort which cuts right across Dal Lake to the Nishat gardens. The many bicycle-hire shops in the Dalgate and Boulevard Road area charge about Rs 8 to Rs 20 for daily hire. Avoid the near-suicidal route through the central city, with its traffic snarls and pollution.

The ubiquitous auto-rickshaws are easy to find and the best option for short city hops, as taxis are more than three times the price. Both rickshaws and taxis are un-metered, so it's necessary to haggle over the price before setting off. Official taxi fares are listed at most taxi stands, as well as at the airport and the Tourist Reception Centre. For excursions out of Srinagar — to Pahalgam, Gulmarg, Sonamarg, Jammu, or even Leh — use a taxi, or for a fraction of the cost, take a bus tour organized by the Tourist Reception Centre.

SRINAGAR A LA CARTE

The rogue-faced *khan-samah*, or cook-boy, who shuffles on to your houseboat at mealtimes can produce perfect breakfasts of fresh crusty Kashmiri bread, boiled eggs, and coffee, but most other meals consist of bland Raj-era, Anglo-Indian fare. If this begins to pall, try to persuade the cook to prepare Persian-influenced Kashmiri food — rice *biriyanis* perhaps, or cigar-shaped shish kebabs marinated in spices and grilled over a makeshift charcoal fire. Given advance warning, some cooks will serve a few of the 36 or so meat courses that make up the Kashmiri *wazwan*, the ceremonial Kashmiri feast prepared for births, circumcisions, weddings, and religious occasions. *Wazas* — chief cooks who get their huge copper cooking pots from an area called Wazpura — pound meat into sausage-like pulp for the popular meatball sized *guzhtaba* and *rista*, served respectively in a creamy sauce and a pepper-red curry. Other favorites include *dhaniwal korma* (mutton rubbed with coriander and cooked in yogurt) and *tabaq-mazh* (grilled spare ribs cooked in yogurt, cashew nuts, poppy seeds, and onions). Try *phirni*, a dessert of vermicelli, crushed almonds, and milk, and the honey-sweet Kashmiri tea known as *kahwa*, flavored with saffron, almonds, and cardamom.

You can sample these specialties ashore at the **Oberoi Palace** (where lunch or dinner for two will cost about Rs 250), at the **Hotel Broadway**, or the popular **Mughal Darbar** restaurant near the GPO on Shervani Road. **Adhoo's**, one kilometer (half a mile) down the road towards the city, was once famed for its authentic Kashmiri cuisine, but it has become distinctly shabby of late.

Srinagar has few proper restaurants outside the hotels, but there are plenty of excellent, and cheap, café-style eateries along Boulevard Road. The **Kashmir Darbar**, towards Dalgate, is a favorite tourist's haunt with its frothy cappuccinos, cheese-dripping pizzas, and apple pie, as well as Kashmiri *wazwan* dishes.

The place to try Kashmir's unusual hybrid Chinese cuisine, influenced by nearby Ladakh and Tibet, is **Daitchi**, a gem of a restaurant on Boulevard Road, which serves delicious fried *mo-mo* pastries, Chicken Hong Kong, shredded lamb with hot garlic sauce, and dessert pancakes. It's run by a dedicated Tibetan family who whisk steaming platters on to the table with astonishing speed. A full three-course meal, with rice and Chinese tea, costs around Rs 90 and is incredibly good value. **Lhasa's**, off the main road close by, also serves good Chinese food; its outdoor garden is packed every night.

For good cheap food, try the **Hotel Paradise Restaurant**, also off Boulevard Road, for excellent South-Indian snacks and Rs 20 Gujarati *thalis*. The **Dal Rock** restaurant at Dalgate serves reliably good Mughlai, Kashmiri, and Chinese dishes, although the dark mirrored interior with its modern flashing lights — ultrachic by Srinagar's standards — is rather gloomy and cave-like.

Tao's alfresco café is a charming oasis just off the city's Bund promenade on Shervani Road. In this leafy cul-de-sac, you can slump in colorful cane chairs in a garden filled with flowering shrubs, and order cold drinks and snacks. Chinese dishes, notably Manchurian soup, sweet and sour chicken with pineapple, and chow mein, are also served.

The **Lake View** cafeteria is in a picturesque location at the foot of the lakeside Shankaracharya Hill, opposite Nehru Park. Refreshments are served all day on its umbrella-shaded veranda and in the large garden, where groups of devout Muslims gather to pray at twilight. Just opposite is **Nehru Park**, a small island restaurant lit up prettily at night.

Fluffy fresh macaroons and biscuits are a special treat in Kashmir, and there's a score of good bakeries near Dalgate; two of the best are **Jan's Bakery**, beneath the Dal Rock restaurant, and **Moonlight Confectionery**, opposite the Dalgate bridge. Buy a bagful of their specialty,

meringue-topped date slice, to eat with your afternoon tea on the houseboat.

SIGHTSEEING

Shikara Rides and Floating Gardens

Srinagar's pleasures are concentrated on its placid, spring-fed Dal and Nagin lakes, where *shikara* rides prove an addictively indolent form of transport. Spend an hour or two combing the city's backwaters, a network with watery tentacles all along the Jhelum River. The meandering canals are crossed by small Mughal bridges which wobble with the overhead traffic and are flanked by medieval-looking, half-timbered houses buried in bulrush thickets.

Off these liquid corridors are the backwater bayous, where the local river families live in clusters of derelict *doongas* (plain wooden housebarges) with toddlers, mongrels, and chickens scrambling beneath the lines of washing hung on the decks. Gypsy-featured locals dart about in narrow skiffs like dragonflies, collecting water weed, fishing for carp, and stopping to gossip awhile at tiny shops raised on stilts.

ABOVE and OPPOSITE: Cruising by *shikara* provides the most romantic form of transport across Dal and Nagin lakes.

You can turn a *shikara* outing into an all-day expedition by crossing Dal Lake to the **Shalimar Bagh Gardens**. Then paddle across to the southern shore past the **Floating Gardens**, where the thick, buoyant mats of bulrushes are covered with earth and anchored by poles in the deep water. Here you can watch the locals leaning out of their dinghies to harvest cucumbers and melons from these floating beds. The trip takes five or six hours. A *shikara* can be hired at the bottom of the Boulevard for about Rs 125.

If you have another full day to spare, hire a *shikara* to take you across to the secluded bird sanctuary on the northwest side of Nagin Lake, where Himalayan dippers, golden forktails, and golden orioles circle above the endless banks of flesh-colored water lilies amid dramatic views of the mountain-flanked valley. Go well prepared with a packed lunch, binoculars, and plenty to read, as it takes six hours to reach your destination and three hours to loop back to Dal Lake.

Try to wake early, at about 5 am, to catch the dawn before heading by *shikara* for the floating fruit, flower, and vegetable market where most of Srinagar's fresh produce is bartered and sold. It's a churning riot of activity, with echoing shouts and curses as wizened figures strain to maneuver skiffs loaded with vast stacks of green turnips, wispy yellow mustard-seed plants, and scarlet aubergines. Flowers give this market a festive charm — fragrant bundles of fresh dew-sprinkled wildflowers, hyacinths, and tulips destined for houseboat drawing rooms.

Until your *shikara* reaches upper Dal or secluded Nagin, you'll find that wily merchants are constant companions, deftly nosing their well-laden boats alongside. Hesitate for a second too long and you'll be at the mercy of a well-practiced sales patter — in pidgin French, Italian, German, or Japanese — and held hostage by sinewy arms unraveling carpets or dangling necklaces. All sorts of things turn up on these *shikara* shops — ethnic jewelry, cheap trinkets, Tibetan prayer wheels, precious stones wrapped in chamois, embroidered cloth, carpets, papier mâché boxes, flower seeds, saffron — as well as on the floating supermarkets manned by young urchins with sing-song cries of "cash-shoe-nuts, chocy-ice, flute-juice"! Although it's fun to browse, you'll need to bargain hard.

Mughal Gardens

The pleasure gardens left by the Mughal emperors are as evocative of these legendary rulers as the more famous Red Fort in Delhi or the Taj Mahal in Agra. Kashmir was their summer playground, where they could breathe rose-scented air, gaze across the lake to the snowcapped mountains, frolic with an en-

tourage of saffron-skinned maidens, and — like lotus-eaters — banish thoughts of the hot and dusty plains below.

Scattered alongside upper Dal Lake, the two most beautiful gardens are the Shalimar and the Nishat Bagh, both pavilion-pieces with fountains, water-channels, cascades, and formal quadrangles of terraced wildflowers. By far the most rewarding way of exploring these gardens is by bicycle, which enables you to admire the picturesque scenery at your leisure. Set out in the quiet cool of early morning, when the lake's glassy surface shimmers with diving kingfishers. Glide along the Boulevard, and then simply follow the curving avenues which skirt Dal Lake, past fruit orchards, fields of the bluish spinach-like *haq*, and tiny villages with waving urchins. Alternatively, Shalimar-bound buses leave from Dalgate's main bus-stand — an enjoyable and erratic half-hour journey with villagers, baskets of vegetables, and chickens for company.

The **Shalimar Gardens**, 15 km (nine miles) away, were built in 1616 by the emperor Jehangir as a "garden of love" for his beloved wife, Nur Jehan.

There is a pleasant café in the gardens, where you can watch photographers transform day-tripping city honeymooners into giggling Kashmiri rustics by draping them in traditional wedding finery for coveted family album pictures. In the evenings from 9 to 10 pm during May to October, there is a *son et lumière* show which recounts in English the romance of Emperor Jehangir and Queen Nur. Like all gardens in Srinagar, it is open from sunrise to sunset.

If you're on a bicycle, you will already have passed the second garden, **Nishat Bagh**, or "garden of bliss", five kilometers (three miles) back toward the city. This larger and more ambitious version of the Shalimar was laid out in 1633 by Nur Jehan's brother, Asaf Khan, two years after Nur's death. Set on the lakeside slopes of the Zabarwan mountains, it has steep flights of terraces, leafy walkways, waterfalls, and pavilions. In the distance you'll see Hazratbal Mosque's shimmering marble-white dome against the mist-wrapped Pir Panjal mountains.

These gardens have formed the backdrop to countless Hindi blockbuster movies, which usually manage to include a scene where the heroine — a chaste, doe-eyed starlet in a flowing sari — strikes soulful poses in a leafy bower.

Unfortunately, the oldest garden, **Nasim Bagh**, or "garden of the morning breeze", planned by Akbar in 1586, has become rundown, and few people bother to travel the extra 12 km (7.5 miles) to see it.

Toward the Oberoi Palace lies **Cheshma Shahi**, or "royal spring". The smallest of the gardens, it was begun by Jehangir and completed in 1632 by Shah Jehan, who added vineyards, fountains, and tanks. Its spring is believed to produce waters with magically tonic properties. Set in the slopes above are the ruins and gardens of **Pari Mahal**, once a Buddhist monastery and later converted into a school of astrology by Shah Jehan's son, Dara Shikoh. Stroll here at dusk when the ruins are illuminated, the gardens are at their most picturesque, and the resident peacocks begin their mournful chorus.

Mosques and Monuments

Srinagar's chaotically picturesque old city looks barely changed since the Middle Ages — a jumble of cobbled bazaars, almost Tudor-style multistoried houses built of withered timbers held together by sun-dried mud, and antique wooden mosques. Auto-rickshaws are best for negotiating this Muslim quarter, as would-be cyclists in pursuit of mosques in these twisting alleys risk collisions with impassive cows, a bevy of *burqa*-clad matrons, or stacks of Kashmiri turnips.

If you can, visit Srinagar's mosques on a Friday, the Muslim holy day, when they are full of Muslim men reciting the scriptures of the Koran. Stop first at the city's oldest mosque, within the heart of the old city on the banks of the muddy Jhelum River about six kilometers (a little less than four miles) from Dalgate. Situated within a peaceful graveyard, the **Shah Hamdan Mosque** has an extraordinary exterior of ornate carvings and painted papier mâché. Built between 1373 and 1398, it is named after a prominent Sufi from Persia, whose influence led to the peaceful conversion of millions of Hindus to Islamic mysticism during the fourteenth century.

Like a fanciful illustration for an exotic fairy tale, the mosque's interior glitters with still-bright seventeenth-century papier mâché lacquered colonnades, latticed stairs, whimsical stained glass, and European glass chandeliers. The building signifies the five daily prayers offered to Allah, having five walls, five arches, and a repetition of the number five throughout. Burqa-covered Muslim women file into the screened purdah quarter adjacent to the mosque to whisper their prayers, but neither they nor any non-Muslim are allowed inside — so you will have to content yourself with peering through the doorway, although it's worth visiting regardless.

By rickshaw, the **Jamia Masjid** is less than five minutes away, the largest and most popular mosque in Kashmir. Giant speakers strapped to its square-shaped minarets send the muezzin's cry booming to the faithful across Dal Lake.

Originally built by Sultan Sikandar in 1400, and expanded by his son Zain-ul-Abidin, it was razed to the ground by fire three times and rebuilt each time, although it still retains the original immense deodar pillars, 15 m (50 ft) high, carved from whole trees.

Today's Indo-Saracenic structure can accommodate up to 10,000 worshipers in its peaceful inner courtyard during the main Muslim festival, Id-ul-Fitr, which celebrates the end of Ramadan fasting. Clamber to the top of the minarets for a muezzin's-eye-view of the city.

Along the towering ridge of nearby **Sharika Hill** are the crumbling ruins of the eighteenth-

century **Hari Parbat Fort**, built by Atta Mohammad Khan, an Afghan governor. Legend has it that the hill was formed after the goddess Parvati threw a pebble from the heavens, which grew as it fell to crush the wicked water demon, Jalobhava, who dwelt in the depths of a huge lake. Villagers claim that the stones strewn across Hari Parbat are all incarnations of gods from the almost-limitless Hindu pantheon. The emperor Akbar built the surrounding ramparts from local gray limestone in the late sixteenth century, beautifying them with fragrant groves of almond trees. It's worth the invigorating climb for its heady vista across the Kashmir Valley, but there's little to see here. The fort is now an Indian Army watch post, and you'll need

ABOVE: Spring blooms at the Shalimar Gardens just outside Srinagar.

permission from the Director of Tourism to visit.

Continuing along the Sharika hillside and proceeding down the long Gurudwara Naidyat Road, you'll emerge on Dal Lake's western bank. You'll see the elegant white marble **Hazratbal Mosque** in the distance, its Ottoman-style dome flanked by a single minaret like a finger pointed heavenward. Built on the site of the original 600-year-old shrine, it contains the valley's most sacred possession — a strand of the Prophet Mohammed's hair, or the *Moe-e-Muqaddas*, brought to India in 1635 from Medina. The Holy Hair disappeared in December 1963, and black

flags flew from houses across the valley. The ensuing riots held the state government to ransom, and calm was only restored five weeks later when the relic was mysteriously restored. On certain Muslim festivals, it is displayed to massed crowds of pilgrims in the outside courtyard.

Back along the Boulevard, just opposite Nehru Park, is the hill path leading to the oldest Hindu shrine in the valley, the **Shankaracharya Temple**, which stands 300 m (1,000 ft) above the city on a hill known as **Takht-I-Sulaiman** (Throne of Solomon). It is thought that the temple was originally built by the emperor Ashoka's son, Jaluka, in around 200 BC, and later enlarged by an unknown Hindu sage in the reign of Emperor Jehangir. A walk (or sprint) up to the shrine, with its superb panoramic views, is a good way to beat houseboat lethargy.

City Walks

Enjoy a sunny morning's walk along the **Bund**, the narrow, poplar-lined, Raj-era promenade near Zero Bridge in the modern city. It's a Kipling's mall of mock-Tudor buildings and musty antediluvian shops with faded adver-

tisements for outdated products, some with gilt porticoes that still bear the insignia of the British crown. On one side of the Bund is the Jhelum River, with steps leading down to parked *doongas*, some of which have been transformed into floating travel agencies, and *shikaras*. Take a *shikara* from the stand opposite Grindley's Bank building and float across to the **Sri Pratap Singh Museum**, housed in an old palace in a quiet backstreet. There's an eccentric collection of stone sculpture from the fourth to the twelfth century, stuffed trophies "bagged" at the turn of the century, old coins, tapestries, and an extensive stamp collection.

If you stroll the Bund's full length, you'll see the old Srinagar Club and the former **British Residency** building, set in well-kept gardens and now used as the Government Arts Emporium.

Heading west, you'll soon find yourself in bustling **Lal Chowk**, Srinagar's business and commercial center, where Kashmiri salesmen shout over the deafening amplified music to try to lure passers-by into their shops. A mêlée of shops sell Kashmiri crafts, cheap trinkets, garish mirrored pictures of mosques, and lorry loads of almonds, pomegranate seeds, walnuts, cashews, and dried apricots.

Heading back toward Dal Lake, as you cross the Jhelum River into Srinagar's old city, you'll see the white Regency-style **Baradari Palace**, a former summer palace of the Dogra Maharaja. Deserted and forlorn now, the Baradari once epitomized regal splendor. The maharaja would arrive for his annual visit to the summer capital in a pageant-like river procession, flanked by epauletted oarsmen, gaily caparisoned boats, and a water-borne cabinet.

SHOPPING

Srinagar is a tempting treasure house of Kashmir's traditional crafts — hand-knotted silk or wool carpets, unique feathery *pashmina* and *shahtush* shawls, exquisite embroideries, ornate papier mâché, and walnut-wood carvings — as well as tailor-made fur coats, leather ware, and saffron.

But be a discerning and hard bargainer. Srinagar breeds money-hungry sales touts like rattlesnakes, and has a surfeit of mass-produced bric-à-brac aimed at the tourist market. To get an idea of what the legitimate prices are, go first to the **Government Arts Emporium**, Residency Road, or the **Government Central Market**, Exhibition Ground, both open 10 am to 5 pm daily, to see the range of handicrafts sold in Kashmir and the official fixed prices. You'll then be better prepared for browsing in the shops along Boulevard Road and Lal Chowk,

ABOVE: Detail of ornately hand-painted Kashmiri papier mâché box.

and at the better-quality shops along the Bund. Commission sharks who lead you to a particular shop and then loiter inside expect a cut from any purchase you make, which adds to the price considerably.

The most coveted of all Kashmiri handicrafts are the exceptionally fine handmade **carpets**, usually woven in old Persian designs in varying combinations of silk and wool to create a special weave which looks dark from one side and light from the other. They are usually produced on large wooden looms by teams of young boys, and depending on the size and quality can take between six months and four years to complete. Because they are so popular, Srinagar's shops are flooded with inferior mass-produced carpets — particularly those made with cotton-derivative "staple" yarn, which imitates the appearance of silk but is far less durable.

You need to be very careful when choosing a carpet. Check the content and knot of the carpet — regardless of what the salesman tells you. A silk carpet will weigh at least two kilograms (4.5 lb) less than yarn staple or wool. But the true test is to pluck a knot out and burn it — staple yarn ignites instantly, but pure silk smolders. Another test is to check the number of knots per square inch on the reverse of the carpet. A good silk or wool carpet should have around 360 knots per square inch, but the finest carpets have as many as 700 knots. Make sure that you scrutinize the carpet for any design or color faults, and that you are given a certificate of origin to save possible customs duty or VAT payments on your return home. If you want to ship your carpet back, you might feel happier if you make the arrangements yourself. If you don't have time, photograph or mark the carpet under the unfazed salesman's eye. That way he's less likely to send you an inferior or different "replica" of the one you purchased!

Far less expensive are the *namadas* brightly chain-stitched rugs made from pounded fleece, or the unusual and decorative **crewel-work floor coverings** with an underside of white cotton fabric.

Then there are the legendary **Kashmiri shawls**, prized for centuries by Mughals and maharajas, who employed hundreds of skilled craftsmen to produce the *pashmina*, *shahtush*, and exquisitely embroidered *jamawar pashmina* shawls, the latter taking as many as 20 years to complete. Akbar launched the practice of giving shawls to foreign dignitaries, and by the late eighteenth century, as trade increased with Europe, they became an item of aristocratic fashion in France. The French empress Josephine possessed between 300 and 400 of these shawls. According to one story, Napoleon — who liked to see her shoulders bared, while she preferred them decoratively draped — would dramatically whisk off her shawl and fling it into the fire, whereupon the empress would calmly send for another one.

By the mid-nineteenth century, the inexpensive mass-produced English imitation Paisley wool and silk shawls almost destroyed the market for exotic, hand-woven Kashmiri shawls. Today, there are efforts to keep the craft alive, and shawls of all qualities are made.

Shahtush shawls are the most legendary of all. Spun from fleece gathered from the throats of ibex goats in Ladakh and Tibet, they are so airy and feathery they can be drawn through a ring, and so warm they can cook a wrapped egg after five hours. Unlike woolen and *pashmina* shawls, *shahtush* is seldom dyed or embroidered. The rare 100 percent pure shawls are mousy brown in color and highly sought after, costing around Rs 12,000.

Kashmir's **papier mâché** goods can be found all over India, but only in Srinagar can you find the most delicate work etched with real gold, not bronze dust or gold poster paint. The making of papier mâché is a laborious process: pulped paper is first soaked in adhesive fluid, dried in a mold for at least a month, then painted with bright designs before being coated with varnish. Traditionally, men and boys do this work, and still use natural extracts for color: coral is ground for red, lapis for blue, charcoal for black, and cardamom for yellow.

Srinagar is also the best place to buy precious pure red **saffron**, which is harvested each autumn from violet-blue crocus flowers just outside the city at Pampore. It is one of only two places in the world where saffron is grown, the other being Spain. Sealed jars of the spice, with the government laboratory's stamp of approval, are available all over Srinagar. When buying loose saffron, one strand only needs to be sampled to judge its quality, for the flavor and fragrance of saffron are unmistakable.

Aside from the state emporiums, the following places located close together on the Bund are good shops and showplaces for contemporary handicrafts. All are run by descendants of the original craftsmen under royal patronage and maintain a deep pride in the quality and tradition of their work. If you would like to see artisans using traditional methods to produce Kashmiri crafts without feeling any pressure to buy, these are the best people to arrange it.

Sadiq's Handicrafts, at Cottage Chinar, next to the GPO, is the place to browse for high-quality shawls, embroideries, *pherans*, crewel work, floor rugs, and tapestries — mostly made with antique designs.

Make sure you visit the establishment of papier mâché artist **Suffering Moses**, nicknamed in the old days by the British, he says, because of his fastidious workmanship. His family established the shop in 1840, and today it contains a small museum of antiques as well as papier mâché of exquisite quality and design, wood carvings, shawls, and embroideries.

Asia Crafts has an excellent collection of fine Persian, Iranian, and Kashmiri carpets, and the upper story is devoted to papier mâché goods.

SRINAGAR AFTER DARK

Kashmir has a unique and particularly vibrant heritage of satirical folk theater, dance, and music. However, these performances are held as part of village fairs and festivals, so tourists generally never get to see them. Only during the Kashmiri marriage season, from October to December, do exuberant wedding processions and hired performers spill out on to Srinagar's streets.

Kashmir's professional entertainers traditionally come from a community known as the Bhands, whose lifestyle is much like that of medieval Europe's strolling players. Their earthy folk plays are potted histories of Kashmir, handed down from generation to generation and filled with slapstick, outrageous costuming, and bawdy puns.

Most hotels and houseboats can arrange for classical musicians and dancers to perform, and for guests to sample a delicious *wazwan* feast aboard the barge-like *doonga* boats which can be hired out for the evening for large parties.

The **Sufiana** *kalam*, the classic devotional music of the Sufi Muslims, is an unforgettable experience. Often performed by master musicians as an integral feature of important Muslim festivals, this mesmerizing combination of Persian verse and exotic lulling sounds is part worship, part musical frenzy.

Its origins are tied to the cult of Muslim mysticism which took lasting root in Kashmir during the fourteenth century. Sufiana *kalam* is usually performed by three or four musicians who intone verse to the *santoor* (a trapezoid zither), a pair of *tabla*-like drums, and the *saz-i-Kashmir* (a plucked string instrument). Sessions (at which much hookah pipe-puffing is done) last for hours, often until dawn. Devout Sufis believe that these harmonious sounds can send them into a trance-like communion with God. This "music of mystic content" may not whisk casual observers across the great divide, but it is certainly captivating.

A performance of Sufiana Kalam is rarely advertised in advance; it is usually held for small audiences in private houses. The best way of finding out about a performance is simply to ask around, although the Tourist Reception

Centre is unlikely to be of much help. If your houseboat owner can't help, ask at Asia Crafts, Sidiq's Handicrafts, or Suffering Moses.

GENERAL INFORMATION

Srinagar's **Tourist Reception Centre** (TRC) ©74259, 72644, 76107, and after office hours, 77303, 77305, is just off Maulana Azad Road near Dalgate. It provides virtually all the services you're likely to need during your stay — houseboat and hotel reservations, an Indian Airlines office (©73270, 73538, 76557), the Railway booking office, the Post Office, a very useful branch of the State Bank of India which stays open from 4 to 7 pm, a bookshop with local maps, and a State Road Transport Corporation bus counter with adjacent depot. It's open 24 hours a day for general information and assistance, but is more efficient during regular office hours (10 am to 5 pm).

There's a camping shop for route information, trekking maps, and equipment — ground sheets, tents, sleeping bags, and trekking boots hired out by the day or week at modest prices. Here also are the departments of Fisheries and Wildlife for information and permits. You can inquire here about accommodation at Dachigam National Park, 22 km (13.6 miles) from Srinagar. This former royal game reserve is notable for its hangul, the Kashmir stag which is related to the Scottish red deer, and Himalayan black and brown bears. Passes to Hari Parbat, and temporary membership of the Kashmir, Srinagar, and Nagin golf clubs is also issued here. There's a restaurant and cheap hostel-style accommodation at the back. The TRC run daily city sightseeing tours, as well as tours to Gulmarg, Pahalgam, Sonamarg, Daksum via Achabal and Kokernag (Rs 45), and the Mughal Gardens (Rs 24). Westland 15-seater helicopters can be hired from here to ply between Srinagar, Gulmarg, and Pahalgam, as well as around the city. Round trips to Gulmarg cost Rs 500, and to Pahalgam, Rs 700. The TRC also have a bureau at Srinagar's airport which is useful for houseboat information but little else.

For trips further afield, both **Sita World Travel**, ©78891, Maulana Azad Road, and **Mercury Travels**, ©78786, in the Oberoi Hotel, are reliable and efficient.

If you're planning to go to Ladakh, or are interested in adventurous trekking, white-water river rafting, or trout fishing in the Himalayas, it's worth investigating two of India's top adventure travel agencies, both of which offer flexible package deals that include guides/gillies, trained staff, camp facilities, all meals, and transport. **Tiger Tops Mountain Travel** has a Srinagar office at Houseboat Star of Zanzibar, near Zero Bridge, Jhelum River. Their head-quarters in New Delhi, ©521932, 771055, are at 1/1 Rani Jhansi Road. **Tiger Paw Adventures**, ©616137, is at D-383 Defence Colony, New Delhi.

MOUNTAIN RETREATS

GULMARG

Amid the towering pine-forested Pir Panjal mountains about two hours' drive (52 km, or 32 miles) from Srinagar, Gulmarg is renowned for its spectacular alpine scenery and spring wildflowers which carpet the valley in a solid mass of color.

Gulmarg is both a summer and winter resort. Apart from its exhilarating mountain walks, treks, and pony-rides, it has the world's highest golf course at 2,650 m (8,612 ft) and during winter offers the best skiing on the sub-continent.

Originally called Gaurimarg (after Lord Shiva's wife), Sultan Yusaf Shah renamed it Gul (flower) Marg (meadow) in 1581. But for the muezzin's cry echoing across the valley and its swarthy Muslim hookah-smoking inhabitants, Gulmarg looks like a pastoral Swiss landscape.

Gulmarg's warm season lasts from mid-May to mid-October (May to June for spring flowers) and the peak skiing season is in January to February, when the valley is covered in thick, crunchy snow.

Taxis provide the most comfortable means of enjoying the climb up the mountain slopes along the poplar-lined road with glorious vistas across the Kashmir Valley. The round trip costs about Rs 300 (few drivers will agree to take you unless you cover their return). For a fraction of the price, take one of the beaten-up buses which leave the Srinagar bus depot next to the TRC.

During the winter months, when the passes are often blocked by snow, buses operate only up to Tanmarg, eight kilometers (five miles) from Gulmarg, and most people cover the final stretch by hired jeep. Even if the pass is open, you might prefer to hire a pony for an hour's ride through the magical hush of the snow-laden forest.

Gulmarg is preparing for a major onslaught of ski enthusiasts with the recent completion of the five-kilometer (three-mile)-long Poma gondola ski lift. An ITDC five-star hotel and at least three large lodges now under construction will dramatically change Gulmarg's accommodation facilities. For the moment, the best choice for a relaxed stay is **Hotel Highland Park**, ©230, 291, which has tiered luxury cottages set amid pretty sloping gardens with reliable hot water and central heating. Rates: expensive. Its fire-side bar has an unbeatable view across the valley, but the mock-Bavarian dining room serves bland set meals. Facilities include a sauna, jacuzzi, and car rental. In the spirit of *après-ski*, the waiter claimed there was a "live disco", but on inspection this appeared to double as a table tennis room!

Hotel Apharwat has very comfortable pine-wood-walled double rooms with hot water and heaters plugged in with copper wire by dotty, but well-meaning, staff. Somehow their cook succeeds where all of Gulmarg fails, and serves

excellent Kashmiri, Chinese, and Mughal food as well as great mountain-climbing breakfasts. Rates: inexpensive. Other good mid-range options include **Pine Palace**, ©266, **Nedous**, ©223, and **Ornate Woodlands**, ©268. The **Government Tourist Huts** are quaint wooden chalets, each complete with linen, hot-water bottles, and a smoke-stack *bukhara*. These vary in size (a one-bedroom hut will cost Rs 140) and bookings can be made through the TRC in Srinagar. Alternatively, the state-run Tourist Bungalow atop the hill near the town has simple cheap rooms and an atmosphere of rustic lunacy. I don't think I will ever forget the look of wounded dignity on their aged staffer's face when I suggested he remove an unwelcome mouse: "We don't have that kind of rodent here. That was a rat!"

It's worth staying for at least a couple of days to explore Gulmarg's mountain trails, either on foot or by pony. Start with the **Outer Circular Walk**, an 11-km (6.8-mile) road which weaves through pine forests and has breathtaking views down to the Kashmir Valley and up to Nanga Parbat (the world's fifth-highest mountain at 8,137 m, or 26,700 ft), Harmukh, Sunset Peak,

ABOVE: Enticing sign for trek-weary travelers in the hill-station town of Pahalgam.

and Apharwat Ridge. It's an invigorating hour's climb past rippling snow-fed streams and dense cedars to **Khilanmarg** (six kilometers, or just under four miles), a small flower-strewn plateau with stunning views across the mountains and Wular Lake, the largest freshwater reservoir in India. Just across the Apharwat Ridge is **Alpather Lake** (13 km, or eight miles), a deep turquoise lake flecked with floating ice even in high summer. Other good walks include **Ningal Nallah** (eight kilometers, or five miles) and the Muslim shrine of the **Ziarat of Babareshi** (five kilometers, or three miles). For trekking, you can hire a guide/porter from the Tourist Office at about Rs 90 a day for the three-day hike to the beautiful meadow of **Tosha Maiden** (50 km, or 31 miles), an idyllic camping spot. Start the trek from **Ferozepore Nallah**, five kilometers (three miles) from Gulmarg, which teems with plump rainbow trout and makes a peaceful picnic place. To win a trout for your pine-cone fire, first get the necessary permit from the TRC in Srinagar.

Gulmarg's 18-hole golf course was recently re-laid according to international standards. The small club house issues immediate temporary membership and hires out clubs, shoes, and ball-boys.

During winter, Gulmarg is India's most popular ski resort, and offers a variety of graded slopes of beginner to intermediate standards. Facilities include one chair lift, two rope tows, and two T-bars, as well as heli-skiing up to Khilanmarg which costs Rs 250. Once the gondola is operating, there will be runs for advanced skiers. High-quality European ski equipment can be hired for modest sums, along with toboggans and ice-skates for Gulmarg's rink.

PAHALGAM

Pahalgam is a charming sleepy valley 96 km (60 miles) from Srinagar, set 2,130 m (7,000 ft) high among snowy peaks and forests of pine, conifer, and sycamore and crisscrossed by the Lidder and Shashnag rivers. Once a lonely shepherd's hamlet, Pahalgam has become a popular hill resort with numerous lodges and rows of shops selling Kashmiri handicrafts. It also serves as a starting point for several major treks across the Himalayas. Here you can angle for trout in the clear, glacier-fed Lidder River, play golf on a nine-hole course, and take long mountain walks and pony-rides.

If you've hired a taxi from Srinagar, it's worth loitering at several places of interest en route: for the heady sensation of walking through fragrant fields of purple saffron flowers at **Pampore** (13 km, or eight miles), and to see the historic ruins of **Avantipur** (29 km, or 18 miles).

This ancient capital of Kashmir, built by King Avantivarman (AD 855–883), has two ninth-century temples dedicated to Vishnu and Shiva. Beyond the Pahalgam turn-off is **Achabal**, a Mughal garden laid out by Shah Jehan's daughter, Jehanara. Nearby is **Kokernag**, famous for its curative springs and, more recently, it's Indo-Danish trout hatchery which provides many of the plump fish that end up on the tables of India's luxury hotels. Back on the Pahalgam route, high on a plateau you'll see the ruins of **Martand**, the huge Sun Temple built by the sixth-century king Lalitaditya.

At Pahalgam you can hire tents, pack-ponies, and trekking and camping equipment, or equipment can be pre-booked at Srinagar's Tourist Office. Rugged individualists will balk at the government-run tent colony with its military rows of tents complete with cots, hot-water bottles, and electricity. For log stoves and cozy rooms with mountain and river vistas, stay at the well-established, moderately priced and fairly luxurious **Hotel Pahalgam** (©26, 52, 78). Good mid-range accommodation is provided by the **Woodstock Hotel** (© 27) and the **Hotel Hill Park** (©79). The recently opened alpine-style **Kolahoi Kabin** offers by far the best value for the budget-minded and its restaurant serves good, cheap Kashmiri and Mughal fare. There are several state-run tourist lodges and numerous tourist huts scattered across the valley, some very secluded. Bookings can be made through the Srinagar Tourist Office.

With Pahalgam as your base, there are plenty of walks and treks to explore in every direction, ranging from scenic strolls to tough six-day treks.

Good short excursions include **Mamaleswara**, a small twelfth-century Shiva temple just one kilometer (a little over half a mile) downstream, and a hike or pony-ride to **Four Points**, a winding route via the scenic Nehru and Shail parks to the "four points" from which there are splendid views across the valley. Even more spectacular is the view from the Hindu temple up on top of the ridge, reached by pony-trail via the Chikarwada Bridge. **Baisaran**, five kilometers (three miles) from Pahalgam, is a picturesque meadow with clusters of yellow mustard-flowers and beautiful views across the valley and the Lidder River. A further 11-km (seven-mile) climb brings you to **Tulian Lake**. At 3,353 m (11,000 ft), the lake is a giant ice-block for most of the year.

Every year, to coincide with the full moon of July/August, thousands of pilgrims from all over India descend on Pahalgam to make the four-day, 47-km (29-mile) journey to the **Amarnath Cave**. At a height of 3,888 m (12,760 ft), the cave is sacred as the house of Shiva. The god of creation is worshiped in his ice-phallic form as *shivling*, a massive stalagmite that waxes and wanes with the moon. The pilgrims are dwarfed by an awesome primeval landscape of vast slate-gray snowcapped peaks and glaciers that shimmer in the moonlight.

Of all Pahalgam's trails, the four-day trek to the base-camp of the 3,600-m (11,800-ft) -high **Kolahoi Glacier** and back (36 km, or 22 miles) is the most popular. Camps are made at **Aru** (11 km, or seven miles), a small sheep-station, and **Lidderwat** (12 km, or 7.5 miles) alongside rushing glacial streams. Instead of returning to Pahalgam, a further three days' trekking will take you to **Sonamarg** in the Sindh Valley, the smallest, and some say the loveliest, of Kashmir's hill stations. Trekkers often pass through Sonamarg en route to the Zoji La Pass on the arduous 10-day trail to Ladakh across the main Himalayan range. Sonamarg is also a good base for several short treks: to **Thajiwas Glacier** (three kilometers, or just under two miles), and the scenic high-altitude, trout-filled lakes of **Vishansar** (4,084 m, or 13,400 ft), **Kishansar** (3,810 m, or 12,500 ft), and **Gangabal** (3,658 m, or 12,000 ft). This region is a paradise for anglers during August and September, when there is plenty of trout and mahseer.

JAMMU

Few of Kashmir's fabled charms are found in Jammu, the state's bustling commercial winter capital, with its ungainly urban sprawl across the banks of the Tawi River against a backdrop of sandstone foothills, small lakes, temples, and a ruined fort.

Little is known of the city's early history. According to legend, it was founded by the ninth-century king Jambulochan, who built his monumental Bahu Fort overlooking the Tawi. In 1730, the region fell under the control of the warlike Dogra Rajputs, whose descendants retained power over the merged Jammu and Kashmir state until Independence. During the eighteenth and nineteenth centuries, Jammu was the center of a minor artistic renaissance, and its artists created the exquisite court miniatures known as the Pahari school.

Most tourists regard Jammu merely as a stopover after a long bus or train journey on their way to Kashmir Valley, Ladakh, or the hill stations of Himachal Pradesh. But Jammu has several interesting places to visit and it's worth staying at least half a day.

HOTELS

Jammu has only two well-established "luxury" hotels, both moderately priced. The four-star **Asia Jammu Tawi**, ©43930, 43932, is some distance from the city center at Nehru Market, but near the railway station and airport. The staff are friendly and efficient, and facilities include a swimming pool, health club, beauty parlor, J&K Tourist Office, travel counter, and a good restaurant. Double air-conditioned rooms are Rs 450, or you can opt for "fan-cooled" rooms which are just as comfortable but half the price. **Hotel Jammu Ashok**, ©43127, 43864, opposite the Amar Mahal Museum, is a slightly cheaper option.

In the mid-range bracket, the **Hotel Mansar**, ©46161, at Dennis Gate, is inexpensive and is centrally located with a decent restaurant.

Jammu's lodges have a reputation for being cheap and awful. They're clustered mainly around the Tourist Reception Centre (TRC) in Mir Chowk. The best of this fairly motley crew is **Apsara Hotel**, on Shahidi Chowk, which has clean doubles at Rs 35, or **Tawi View Hotel**, ©43752, at Maheshi Gate, with doubles with bath for Rs 45.

The main Jammu TRC, ©5421, on Veer Marg in Mir Chowk, offers basic rooms, very cheap, with attached baths but no air-conditioning in bunker-style blocks, and the smaller tourist office at the railway station has several retiring rooms — useful for an early morning train journey.

RESTAURANTS

Both the Asia Jammu Tawi and Ashok hotels have excellent and reasonably priced Indian restaurants — and both offer good breakfasts of fruit juice, eggs, toast, and coffee for Rs 25. Elsewhere, head for Veer Marg, Jammu's main restaurant "strip" which is cluttered with small *chai* and *thali* stalls. Tucked away here are **Dragon**, Jammu's only Chinese restaurant; **Kwality**, with its tri-cuisine menu and reliably good Mughal fare; and **Silver Inn**, for "multi-cuisine".

The **India Coffee House** (open 8:30 am to 5 pm) in the exhibition grounds serves freshly brewed coffee and delicious South Indian snacks.

SIGHTSEEING

Make time for Jammu's two art galleries. The best is the **Dogra Art Gallery**, Gandhi Bhawan, facing the New Secretariat. Set up in 1954, it houses nearly 600 paintings, as well as terracottas, medieval weapons, sculpture, and ancient tar-leaf manuscripts. Many of these exquisite Mughal miniatures were commissioned by Dogra kings, whose patronage led to the development of the local Pahari and Basholi schools. The gallery has only a selection of its full collection on display; to see more, approach the curator. Open every day except Monday, 11 am to 5 pm during winter and 8:30 am to 1:30 pm in summer.

The **Amar Mahal Museum**, overlooking the Tawi River, was built for Raja Amar Singh in 1907. This extravagantly turreted mock-French chateau now displays the royal collection of rare Pahari miniatures and manuscripts. The imposing ancestral portraits of the Rajput Dogra kings convey much more of the region's history than any book: a heavily-jowled race of flint-eyed monarchs whose plump jewel-

bedecked hands never stray far from their swords. Open every day during winter from 10 am to noon, 3 to 5 pm, and from 5 to 7 pm in summer, with half-days on Sundays.

From here it's a 10-minute auto-rickshaw ride to the historic remains of the **Bahu Fort**, located five kilometers (three miles) above the town. Its ramparts swarm with devotees of the evil-eyed, black-faced goddess in the small Kali temple. Beneath the fort are the sloping terraces of the Bagh-I-Bagu Gardens, a pleasant spot in which to stroll and take tea at the small pavilion restaurant with a view across Jammu and the Tawi River.

Make a last stop at the **Ragunnath Temple**, dedicated to Lord Rama, the interiors of which are coated with gold. Built in 1835 by Maharaja Gulab Singh, it is the most impressive of a cluster of nineteenth-century temples located within the lively and colorful bazaar area in the city center, just five minutes' walk from the tourist office.

ABOVE: A remote hamlet is tucked amid dramatic mountain scenery in Ladakh. OPPOSITE: Gorgeously-hued prayer flags fluttering from Leh Gompa. OVERLEAF: Street scene in Leh town.

GENERAL INFORMATION

Jammu's main Tourist Reception Centre, ©48172, is in Mir Chowk near the main bus-stand and is open 10 am to 5 pm. There's a second, and rather chaotically-run, office in the railway station, where the Post Office is also located. Neither office runs sightseeing tours or offers city maps, which have been declared a security risk. The Mir Chowk TRC houses the Indian Airlines office, ©42735, 47577. The main shopping areas of Jammu are Veer Marg, where there's a well-stocked Government Emporium, Raghunath Bazaar, and Hari market.

LADAKH

Ladakh, or "Land of the Passes", is a region of stark beauty north of Kashmir that remains an unspoilt citadel of Buddhist religion and Tibetan culture locked within a snowy fortress of Himalayan gorges. Travelers have titled the area "Little Tibet", "the Moonland", and the "Last Shangri-La" — all with some degree of truth. Leh, the area's ancient capital, sits on a 3,555-m (11,663-ft) -high plateau in the Indus Valley, and is dominated by a royal palace reminiscent of the Potala in Lhasa. The city is dwarfed by the ocher-hued crags of the mighty Karakoram mountains, and is largely populated by Tibetan refugees who fled their homeland after China invaded in 1959.

India, China, and Pakistan all have contesting claims over parts of Ladakh, which for centuries served as a strategic junction on the medieval Silk Road between Sinkiang (Xinjiang) in China and routes to the Indian plains and Persia. Ladakh was virtually closed to the outside world for most of the post-Independence period, until New Delhi in 1974 decided for reasons of tourism to open up the region. But the area still remains virtually untouched, retaining much of its character as a hermetic kingdom where a "divine" monarchy and powerful priests ruled over nomadic tribes who eked out a living from farming yaks, goats, juniper berries, and barley crops.

Sparsely vegetated and as ruggedly inhospitable as the Sahara, Ladakh is home to the legendary snow leopard. Tibetan eagles soar across the sky, while herds of wild Zanskari horses run in herds across the plains. Its tough, Tartar-featured inhabitants have imbued the landscape with the colorful legends and tantric cults of Tibetan Buddhism. The religion is thought to have been first brought to Ladakh in the third century by missionaries sent by Ashoka, and the doctrine became mingled

with the indigenous animistic Bon faith and ancient Hindu tantric cults. Prayer flags flutter from every household rafter, *chortens* or shrines of holy relics dot the wayside, and villagers carry prayer wheels about with them like fetishes. The region is famous for its perilous cliff-top *gompas*, or Buddhist monasteries, which are brightly painted with murals of tantric gods and laden with gilded gem-studded statues of Buddha, religious icons, carvings, and scroll paintings or thangkas. Many have in recent years been restored and refurbished from donations by tourists, some of whom serve among the red-robed monks.

gar to Leh takes two days and allows time to acclimatize to Ladakh's rarefied altitude. The road is open between June and October and crosses the Kashmir–Ladakh boundary at Zoji La (3,529 m, or 11,578 ft), winding through the Zanskar Range through the Namika La (3,718 m, or 12,198 ft) and Fatu La (4,094 m, or 13,431 ft) passes. Overnight halts are best made at the Muslim hamlet of Kargil, 230 km (143 miles) from Leh, where comfortable accommodation is offered by the Welcomgroup-run Hotel Highlands (©41, rates: moderate) and the Hotel D'Zojila, two and a half kilometers (one and a half miles) from town. This is sensitive

ACCESS

Reaching Leh is an experience in itself. Ladakh is open to visitors only for six months of the year, as winter freezes the region into isolation. Indian Airlines runs regular flights from Delhi via Chandigarh and Srinagar, with spectacular aerial views across the snowy Himalayas. For seven months a year, Leh airport is Ladakh's only link with the outside world. The unpredictable, high-altitude weather sometimes results in canceled or aborted flights. Make sure your schedule is flexible enough to accommodate an extra day or two to return, just in case you are left stranded waiting for the next available flight.

For variety, fly one way and drive the other. The 430-km (267-mile) -long road from Srina-

border territory disputed by India, Pakistan, and China, with armed guards preventing you from going more than two kilometers (one and a quarter miles) north of the Srinagar–Leh road. It's preferable to make the trip by six-seater jeep or car/taxi, allowing you to stop en route to admire the views and monasteries, particularly **Lamayuru**, the most hallowed and architecturally impressive of all Ladakh's *gompas*, with 400 monks, 124 km (77 miles) from Leh.

GENERAL TIPS

Ladakh's high altitude and very thin air mean that you'll need to take it very easy for the first few days after arrival. This is when you are most vulnerable to dizziness, headaches, insomnia or nausea, particularly if you fly direct to Leh

The Mountain Trail

from Delhi. If the problem persists, consult a doctor immediately. People with heart or lung conditions should take special care. Severe altitude sickness can be fatal, but it is more likely to affect overly active trekkers. The only cure is to descend to a lower level as soon as possible.

You should also go prepared for freak temperature changes, bringing light cotton clothes for warm summer days, woolen clothes for nippy nights. Lip salve, sunscreen, sunglasses, hats, and strong walking shoes are essential for all travelers. Binoculars and extra film also come in handy. Local agencies provide

fore arriving in Leh, where both banks and small change are rare.

Finally, you can win big grins from the Ladakhis by peppering your speech with a few local words. *Jullay* is an all-purpose greeting that means "hello, goodbye, how are you" all in one. *Katin chey* means "please", while *thukje-chey* means "thank-you".

WHEN TO GO

Religious festivals add special gaiety, color, and excitement during visits to the *gompas*. While most festivals occur during the winter

tents, mattresses, sleeping bags, and basic utensils for trekkers. The Tourist Office (©97) in the Dak Bungalow can give maps and helpful advice for visiting monasteries, trekking, and the current half-day and day rates for hiring jeeps.

A powerful flashlight comes in handy when studying the interiors of dimly lit monasteries. Smoking in the *gompas* is considered very rude, as is touching art objects. While you are free to photograph in the *gompas*, Indian soldiers tend to get very excited when tourists take innocent holiday snapshots near bridges, airfields, and military installations, and the ensuing drama and confiscation of film and even cameras is not worth the trouble.

Make sure you have encashed your travelers' checks and foreign currency and have plenty of small denomination rupee notes be-

months, summer visitors have the opportunity to see the spectacular Hemis festival of masked dances and drama performed by monks held during June and July at **Hemis Gompa**, 40 km (25 miles) from Leh. All *gompas* have large courtyards where these religious festivities take place, but Hemis stages the most impressive of the genre. Dances are heralded by the discordant crescendo of three-meter (10-ft)-long brass trumpets, drums, and clashing cymbals played by red-robed acolytes in tall hats. Other monks are transformed into

ABOVE: Breathtaking vistas across serrated mountain ranges in Ladakh.
OPPOSITE: Cliftop apartments of Leh Palace, now an impressive museum of palace treasures, chapels, shrines, libraries and tombs.

demons and gods by ornate padded costumes and garish masks, and they twirl, lunge, and shimmy while holding icons of Bon, Buddhism, and Tantra to enact tales from the scriptures. The victory of good over evil tends to be the basic theme, signifying the destruction of baser characteristics such as greed, lust, and anger, but sometimes monks enter trance-like states and act as oracles, making predictions and answering questions. But the greatest spectacle is seeing thousands of Ladakhi villagers arrive in traditional dress bearing brass samovars containing yak tea. The women wear elaborate robes with long felt head-

Meanwhile, Leh has a range of hotels, lodges, and guesthouses, many of the latter private homes which rent rooms out to foreign visitors. Prices vary a great deal, dropping to half the peak-season rate in the off-season, with many places closed during the winter.

Upmarket hotels are all moderately priced, and the best and most convenient are the **Kang-Lha-Chhen** (℡39) and the **Lha Lha-Ri-Mo** (℡101). You could also try the **Hotel Shambala** (℡67), located toward the edge of the valley, or the **Hotel Indus** (℡166), out of town on the Hemis Road.

Tiger Tops Mountain Travel's **Ladakh Sarai**

dresses studded with turquoise and heavy silver jewelry, and the men are swaddled in quilted goncha coats tied with colorful cummerbunds.

Archery contests coincide with every religious festival, and visitors are welcome to try their hand and to join in the music, dancing, and drinking. Check whether your trip coincides with a game of local polo—played at a fast and furious pace on local wild Zanskari ponies on the highest and most spectacular polo ground on the planet.

River rafting in the Indus River can be arranged during the summer (see below).

WHERE TO STAY AND EAT

With more tourists attracted to Ladakh each year, accommodation facilities are improving.

(11 km, or seven miles) offers comfortable Mongolian-style yurt tents pitched amid willow trees near the old Ladakhi village of Stok, famous for its royal summer palace and archery contests. The circular furnished tents are very cozy, with efficient solar-powered showers and modern toilet facilities. Lighting is provided by lanterns and candles so that the meadow's tranquillity is not spoiled by the sound of generators. Good Western and traditional Ladakhi cuisine is served in a separate dining tent. The Sarai is a good base for trips to the monasteries, short treks, and river rafting on the Indus. Most travel agents can book through the London, Delhi, or Srinagar offices. The same company organizes trekking and rafting in Ladakh.

Ladakhi food does not constitute one of the world's most exciting cuisines. Ladakhis consume lots of roasted barley meal, *tsampa*, as well as quantities of salted yak butter tea and *chang*, a potent barley brew. The better hotels and restaurants serve a choice of Indian, Chinese, and Tibetan dishes. Local chefs excel at delicious *mo mo* steamed dumplings, chow mein, and various other rice and noodle dishes, particularly good at **Dreamland Restaurant**, close to the center of town. Others to try are **Chopstick, Potala**, and **Hill Top**.

LEH TOWN

Start your sightseeing with a visit to the abandoned **Leh Khar Palace** (open 6 to 9 am and from 5 pm to 7 pm) which sprawls across Tsemo Hill. It was built by King Singe Namagyl in the sixteenth century, taking its cue from Lhasa's Potala Palace, and still belongs to Leh's royal family who now live in another palace at Stok. Despite its many wall paintings and royal *gompa*, it has a desecrated, pillaged look that dates from the Kashmiri invasion of Ladakh last century. The main attraction is the superb views from its top windows across Leh's fluttering prayer flags. In town, visit the lively marketplace to see elderly Ladakhi women in traditional attire selling vegetables and household goods, spinning, and knitting.

GOING TO THE *GOMPAS*

Sightseeing in and around Leh largely involves scrambling up steep lanes to see cliff-top *gompas*. The drab baked mud exteriors of these monasteries hide colorful tantric frescoes, silk or brocade thangkas, and exquisitely carved statues. *Gompas* are places of worship, isolated meditation, and religious instruction for young monks, as well as the repository of Ladakh's wealth. The approach to a *gompa* is heralded by votive shrines known as *mane* walls and *chortens*. Outer walls and entrances are lined with cylinders of wood or metal mounted vertically on spindles and placed in alcoves which are rotated for prayers.

In Leh, visit the fifteenth-century **Leh Gompa** with its large Buddha (open 7 to 9 am, and 5 to 7 pm) and **Shanka Gompa**, with its gold statues, located two kilometers (one and a quarter miles) away. It takes several days to see the important *gompas* outside town, using a jeep or taxi. Buses run out to most places, and it is sometimes possible to stay overnight in the monastery. The closest are **Spituk** (eight kilometers, or five miles), with fine Buddha icons, masks, and thangkas, and **Shey** (15 km, or just over nine miles), the ancient seat of the pre-Tibetan kings with a 7.5-m (25-ft) -high

copper statue of Buddha. Also see **Phyang** (19 km, or almost 12 miles), a sixteenth-century *gompa* which belongs to the Red Camp sect of Buddhists, and **Thikse** (19 km, or almost 12 miles), a twelfth-century, 12-story clifftop *gompa* with 10 temples full of statues, images, stupas, and wall-paintings and with views across the green Indus Valley. **Stok Palace** (16 km, or about 10 miles) is the home of Leh's royal family. **Hemis Gompa** (40 km, or about 25 miles), built in 1630, is the wealthiest, best-known, and biggest *gompa* in Ladakh. Its popularity stems from its annual festival which honors Guru Padma Sambhav's birth anniver-

sary. It has Ladakh's most extensive collection of wall-paintings, statues, and thangkas, including the world's largest, which is unfurled every 12 years (the next time in 1992).

ABOVE: Worn, rugged features of an old Ladakhi woman wearing a traditional turquoise necklace. OPPOSITE: The twelfth century Thikse Gompa, one of Ladakh's most important monasteries.

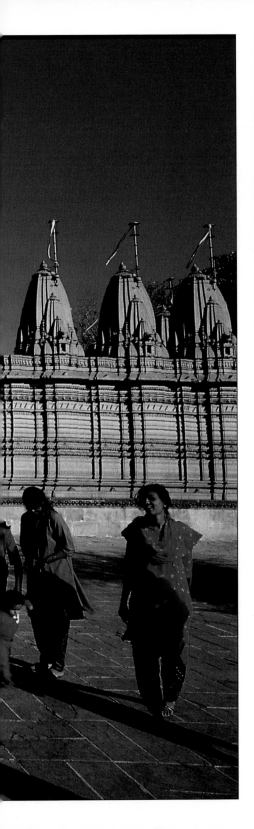

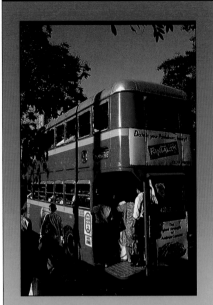

Bombay
and the
West

BOMBAY

Bombay is a flamboyant and cosmopolitan city, with its fortune barons, chic socialites, movie magnates, street-smart hustlers, and above all, its diverse mixture of races and traditions.

The capital of Maharashtra state, on the west coast, Bombay is India's financial, industrial, and trading center, with a prosperous skyline of gleaming skyscrapers, office towers, and five-star hotels. Bombay strikes a balance between a sort of worldly sangfroid and swaggering vulgarity. There's a fleshy, over-ripe veneer to the place — echoed in the lurid cinema billboards of paunchy villains and voluptuously sequinned heroines that mushroom across town to advertise the latest Hindi *masala* extravaganza. This is where India manufactures her dreams, and cinema-hungry audiences worship stars like demi-gods: Bombay is the single-largest producer of films in the world, with about 800 movies in 12 languages completed in its studios each year.

Every aspect of Bombay is influenced by its mélange of migrant communities. Like New York and Sydney, Bombay's dynamism lies in its mixture of imported cultures — and the adroit pragmatism of its communities of Hindus, Muslims, Parsis, Sikhs, Arabs, Jains, and Jews, many of whom originally settled here several centuries ago. Today the lure of work and wealth is just as strong, drawing thousands of refugees who drift in from the impoverished countryside to construct makeshift *bustee* hovels on any available space in the great beehive. Despite the extreme poverty, Bombay is a beacon of the progressive elements in Indian society and has surpassed Calcutta as the nation's leading city. Its port handles 40 percent of the country's maritime trade, it sports a host of secondary and heavy industries, and its inhabitants provide nearly one third of India's entire income tax revenue.

First-time travelers to India often find Bombay the best choice as a starting point — its relaxed social mores, numerous international-class hotels, thriving nightlife, and its shops and restaurants make it easier to adjust to life on the subcontinent. It is also the gateway to western India, and the ideal starting point for journeys to Goa, Maharashtra, and Gujarat. Virtually all of India can be reached by air or rail connections from Bombay.

A PORT CITY'S PAST

Bombay has been an important trading city with strong links to the West for more than three centuries. Portuguese adventurers in the sixteenth century coined and adapted a native name for the original seven swampy, malarial islands of "Buan Bahia", or "good bay". The name has stuck, but the islands were long ago reclaimed and transformed into the isthmus upon which now sits one of the world's largest cities. The small archipelago was the base for a succession of Hindu dynasties that ruled until 1348, when Muslim invaders based in Gujarat overran the area. It changed hands again in 1534, ceded by the Islamic conquerors to the Portuguese in exchange for protection from Lisbon's forces against the mighty Mughals of northern India. The Portuguese built

several churches and large fortifications, but little remains of these earliest European occupiers, excepting the walled city at Bassein, still largely intact, some 50 km (31 miles) from Bombay.

Britain entered the scene in 1662, when Catherine of Braganza married Charles II and gave as her dowry the largest island, Mumbade-vi. The six other islands were ceded three years later when the Portuguese retired to the coastal reaches of Goa. Samuel Pepys recorded that the marshy site was "but a poor place, and not really so as it was described to our King." The archipelago was leased out to the East India Company in 1668, which soon capitalized on its worth.

Movie stars achieve the status of demi-gods with Indian audiences. Bombay alone produces some 800 movies a year — a world record.

Scores of Gujarati, Parsi, Arab, Jewish, and Armenian traders and artisans were soon lured to the town, and salt flats around the islands were quickly transformed into a thriving center for trade in spices, silk, precious metals, cotton yarn, and opium. The upsurge in cotton prices during the world shortage caused by the American Civil War, and the opening of the Suez Canal were catalytic events for Bombay. The surplus funds prompted Governor Sir Bartle Frere to undertake a series of ambitious rojects. He reclaimed land to link the islands into a single land mass, upon which were built dockyards, railways, spacious boulevards, and grand edifices in the Victorian-Gothic style. Bombay became a true city of Empire.

Early this century, Bombay became the center for the "Quit India" movement led by the leaders of the nationalist movement, Mahatma Gandhi and Jawaharlal Nehru, who became the first Indian Prime Minister after India was made independent in 1948.

EARLY SETTLERS

Most notable of Bombay's many immigrant communities are the Parsis, whose ancestors fled Persia and the religious persecution by the Muslims and migrated to India in the seventeenth century. A formidably successful community that includes many of Bombay's most influential families, the Parsis are Zoroastrians, who venerate fire, water, and earth. Believing the elements too sacred to pollute, the Parsis have a somewhat eerie practice for the disposal of their dead: at the "Towers of Silence" on Malabar Hill (just next to the Hanging Gardens), the dead are left in open wells to be consumed by vultures. Parsis tend to be tolerant in outlook, but generally remain a hermetic community, seldom marrying outsiders. However, Parsi traditions seem to be slowly dying out.

THE CITY

Bombay faces the Arabian Sea, and the original seven islands retain their names as the suburbs of Colaba, Mahim, Mazagoan, Parel, Worli, Girgaum, and Dongri. Metropolitan Bombay comprises five square kilometers (1.9 sq miles) at the tip of the peninsula, into which is squeezed many of the city's 10 million people, its main administrative and commercial offices, docks, and factories. Behind it lies the residential area, covering 22 sq km (8.5 sq miles).

OPPOSITE: A red double-decker bus passes in front of a magnificent Victorian-Gothic municipal building in downtown Bombay — reminders of the city's lasting British legacy.

CLIMATE

Bombay's climate, along with that of most of the western region, is at its best from October to February when the air is fresh, the days balmy, and the nights cool. In March, it becomes appreciably hotter and humid until summer reaches its sizzling zenith in June. Heavy monsoon rains often follow, frequently causing floods. During the cool peak season, and particularly just prior to and during the annual Derby (February to March), Bombay's hotels are thronged with travelers. It can prove extremely difficult to make short-notice connections to other cities, especially Goa, at this time, so it's wise to have all your hotel and travel connections reserved in advance.

TOURING BOMBAY

Getting around metropolitan Bombay is surprisingly straightforward, with most of the essential facilities — ticketing offices, post offices, hotels, restaurants, and shops — located in the thin three-kilometer (two-mile) strip between the Taj Mahal Hotel and Nariman Point. Bombay's meandering inner-city boulevards, narrow alleyways, bazaars, and its invigorating seafront are best explored on foot, but take a taxi to each area of interest and walk about from there. Compared to Delhi, Bombay's taxiwallahs are models of propriety — they usually take you directly to your destination and use their meters, which are outdated and show a fraction of the real cost. You are wise to look over the driver's shoulder when he is scrutinizing his official "correction rates" card to check the additional amount you need to pay.

Bombay has a rapid electric train system servicing its outer suburbs. Hundreds of thousands of people cram into its open-air cabins each day, burrowing through the human mass when it is time to disembark (a mere 30-second halt at each stop). It is also a pickpocket's paradise, and so crowded during rush hours that commuters scale the sides and cling to the roof — predictably resulting in several fatalities each day. Bearing this in mind, it is quite an adventure to rattle through Bombay's urban landscape, loitering first to admire the clustered gargoyles and Gothic magnificence of the Victoria Terminus, but one recommended for Sundays only when the carriages are virtually empty. Trains leave for the western suburbs from Churchgate and for the eastern suburbs from Victoria Terminus.

Auto-rickshaws cluster around the suburban train stations, but are a rarity in the city center. Along the Apollo Bunder and both ends of

Marine Drive are the vintage "Victorias", horse-drawn carriages perfect for dusk promenades to Chowpatty Beach. Local buses cost virtually nothing but require much patience as the destinations and numbers are marked in Hindi script.

HOTELS

Good accommodation in Bombay can be fiendishly hard to find in the peak January/February season if you arrive without advance bookings. The best hotels are often overbooked, so it's wise to have your reservations confirmed well in advance.

which provides five-star comfort but lacks the characterful grace of the old wing. It's wise to book well in advance for the old wing's spacious seaview rooms and delightful period suites.

There's a good range of restaurants and bars, notably the Apollo Bar for "designer" cocktails and a view across the Arabian Sea, and the stately Sea Lounge, where the well-heeled discreetly arrange marriages over tiered trays of cucumber sandwiches. It has a superb bookshop, health club, and swimming pool, a resident astrologer, and its shopping arcades make interesting browsing. Rates: very expensive; the modern annex prices are a little cheaper.

The world-famous **Taj Mahal Hotel**, ©202-3366, opposite India Gate, is the haunt of Bombay's glitterati and probably the best icon of the city's affluence, blending Rajput, Renaissance, and Gothic architecture. Industrialist Jamshetji Nusserwanji Tata constructed the hotel in 1903 largely as a reaction against British colonial rulers who barred Indians from their clubs. The Taj opened its doors to all, provided they were well-dressed, and epitomized fin de siècle splendor in its chandeliered salons, protruding bay windows, and marble Turkish baths. Attached to Tata's edifice is its modern multistoried annex, the Taj Mahal Intercontinental,

The recently completed **Oberoi Bombay Hotel**, ©202-5757, is the Taj's nearest rival, a monolith of black marble and glass at Nariman Point that outshines the neighboring Oberoi Towers hotel. The Oberoi offers the most modern suites and sea views in Bombay, stylish service, and reputedly the finest dining experiences in town. Rooms are also the city's most expensive, with singles at Rs 1,850, and doubles Rs 2,000 a night. Next door, at the **Oberoi Towers**, ©202-4343, rooms are from Rs 1,500. Both hotels have a varied range of restaurants, bars, coffee lounges, health clubs, and shops, but the new Oberoi is undeniably more elegant and more suited to business travelers.

The **Hotel President**, ©495-0808, 90 Cuffe Parade, is a Taj-group five-star hotel with an excellent round-the-clock Italian trattoria. Rates: expensive. **The Ambassador Hotel**, ©204-

ABOVE: One of the world's legendary hotels, the Taj Mahal, boasts spacious suites and rooms overlooking the ocean and its large pool, as well as first-class restaurants and modern amenities.

1131, on Veer Nariman Road, Churchgate, has distinctive 1930's decor. **The Fariyas**, ℂ204-2911, off Arthur Bunder Road, Colaba, the **Natraj Hotel**, ℂ204-4161, 135 Marine Drive, and the art deco-style **Ritz**, ℂ222294, Jamshedji Tata Road, Churchgate, are all pleasant hotels in the moderate to expensive range.

The **Grand Hotel**, ℂ268211, 17 Sprott Road, Ballard Estate, is the best of the inexpensive hotels. A pleasant vintage hotel, it has a relaxed atmosphere and a central courtyard. Otherwise try the **Sea Green Hotel**, ℂ222386, 145 Marine Drive, with views of the Arabian Sea and spacious, comfortable rooms. There's a less expensive annex next door, the **Sea Green South Hotel**, ℂ221613.

The **Chateau Windsor Guest House**, ℂ204-3376, next to the Ambassador Hotel, is reliably clean and friendly, and a good economy choice with rooms from Rs 150. Manager Ashok Aggarwal doubles as a travel agent and is very helpful about any travel plans. The modern **YWCA International Guest House**, ℂ202-0445, 18 Madame Cama Road, is open to both men and women. Its Rs 70 to Rs 138 rooms are such good value they are frequently booked in advance. Non-YWCA members can pay a "transient membership" fee of Rs 10.

The best of the other very cheap hotels is **Whalley's Guest House**, ℂ234206, 41 Mereweather Road, in the Colaba area, a slightly frayed, endearing establishment with huge rooms and balconies.

Both Bombay's airport terminals — the Sahar (international) and Santa Cruz (domestic) — are situated at least an hour's drive from the city. Travelers who prefer a quick getaway can stay directly opposite at the five-star **Leela Penta Hotel**, ℂ636-3636, eight kilometers (five miles) from the terminals at Welcomgroup's **Searock Hotel**, ℂ642-5421, at Lands End, Bandra, but ask for a high room facing the sea. There are six restaurants and an elaborate health club. It's worth exploring Bandra itself, which during the days of the Raj was an exclusive British preserve, and to wander through the nearby Linking Road night market.

RESTAURANTS

No other Indian city can rival the quality and diversity of Bombay's restaurants. Here you can find excellent Portuguese-Goan, Iranian, Chinese, Italian, even Polynesian food, as well as every regional cuisine in India. No less exotic are Bombay's own specialties, such as Bombay Duck — feather-light, dried bummelo fish served crisp from a hot griddle. The famous Parsi *dhanshak* dish, made with fried rice and a chicken or mutton *dhal*, the local pomfret, and

the concoctions of *ragada, bhel-puri*, and *pau bhaji* on Chowpatty Beach have also found their way into Bombay's culinary mythology.

There is an almost unlimited variety of restaurants in Bombay — from the most exclusive haunts of the top hotels and glitzy society havens to the proletarian Irani cafés and the city's renowned nocturnal street chef, the Bade-Miyan (meaning "big old Moslem"), who produces delicious brazier-hot kebabs and eggrotis from his cart behind the Taj Mahal Hotel until one or two in the morning.

For truly exquisite dining, the Oberoi is a sure winner. The sumptuous **Kandahar** restaurant serves faultless North-west Frontier food; the pool-level **La Rotisserie** is excellent for French cuisine, specializing in prime and imported meats; and La Brasserie, open from dawn to midnight, has breakfasts (fresh croissants, perfect freshly squeezed juices) to inspire deep sighs of content from homesick Europeans. Next door at the Oberoi Towers, try the city's only Polynesian restaurant, **The Outrigger**, for seafood specialties.

The Taj Mahal's **Tanjore** restaurant is the best in town for regional Indian cuisine, particularly Hyderabadi, Mughlai, and Punjabi specialties, as well as for its evening program of classical Indian dance and music. (Second choice goes to the Oberoi Towers' **Mughal Room**.) Also excellent is the **Golden Dragon**, for authentic Szechuan food.

Outside the hotels, there are literally hundreds of restaurants from which to choose. Currently in vogue with Bombay's glitterati is **China Garden**, ℂ828-0842, Om Chambers, 123 August Kranti Marg, Om's Corner. This exceptional restaurant serves a variety of regional Chinese cuisine. Locals swear by the **Delhi Durbar**. The upmarket, air-conditioned branch opposite the Regal Cinema in Colaba, ℂ202035 is popular with affluent Indians for the city's best *biryani* and *dabba gosh* (spicy meat, offal, and onions baked in an earthenware pot). The original **Durbar**, ℂ359086, in the red-light district of Falkland Road, is easy to find because every taxi-driver knows it.

Good Punjabi fare can be found at the **Sher-e-Punjab** on Bhagat Singh Road, a Sikh enclave where drying turban strips hang from the upper stories, with delicious northern specialties and a distinctive spinach dish made with rye and mustard seeds.

A host of unpretentious vegetarian "clubs" serving the food of South Gujarat, Kutch, and Rajasthan can be found in the central Kalbadevi district. The most famous is the rather basic **Ram Club**, opposite the Cotton Exchange and up a dark staircase, for its Rajasthani *thalis*. Close by are **Thakker's Club** and the **Friend's**

Union Joshi Club, where the kitchens are part of the dining room, so that you can see your *subze* (vegetarian curries) being assembled. To dine like a true sweet-toothed Gujarati, try Samrat, ℃220942, J. Tata Road, where dessert precedes the 10-bowl *thali* meal.

The New India Coffee House, Kittridge Road, Sassoon Dock, is the place to try authentic Keralan food, and Woodlands, Nariman Point, ℃202-3499 (there are two other branches in Bombay), has delicious south-Indian mealtime *thalis*.

For Portuguese-Goan lunchtime fare (superlative fish *vindaloo* and, for adventurous palates, chili-hot pork sorpotal), try either

Martin's at Colaba or the Cafe Kitchen in the Fort Market — both are equally good.

You can take your pick of any number of Chinese restaurants, the best among them being Chopsticks, ℃537789, on Veer Nariman Road, with an atmospheric outdoor café extension, and Nanking Chinese Restaurant, ℃202-0594, Phiroze Building, Shivaji Maharaj Marg, which is especially good for succulent steamed crab, prawns, and lobster at reasonable prices despite its popularity.

For pure idiosyncratic charm, nothing can match Bombay's Irani cafés, the dwindling legacy of the many hundreds founded by staunch Zoroastrian immigrants at the turn of the century, with their marble-topped tables, spindly-legged wooden chairs, salon-style swing doors, illustrated mirrors (often with spidery portraits of the Shah of Iran, George VI, and his Queen Elizabeth), and elderly, white-capped waiters who scuttle around like lizards with a dish in one hand and a tea-towel in the other. Irani cafés are all-day affairs, starting with *brun-maska* hard crusts of buttered Irani bread eaten dipped in *phudhina*, mint tea made with milk and sugar. If Brain Fry In Eggs, or Chicken Dress Gravy seem best left to the imagination, ask for a *dibbe wala* meal of chicken or mutton instead. The oldest and most famous of the cafés are Kyani

and Bastani, at Dhobi Talao toward the north end of M.G. Road; otherwise try the Regal Restaurant and the Byculla Restaurant, both of which are near the Byculla railway station, near Victoria Gardens.

Finally, go to Badshah, directly opposite Crawford Market, for the best rendition of *falooda*, the multicolored vermicelli and ice-cream drink, fresh grape and pomegranate juice, and the addictive *chikku* (fig) milkshake. And don't miss the Leopold Cafe, down the road from the Regal Cinema in Colaba. It's a tropical beatnik haunt with well-thumbed menus, cheap and hearty meals (full English breakfasts for Rs 10), and chilled beer (try the state-brewed London Diet or Pilsener brands).

NIGHTLIFE

Bombay is the brightest beacon in the largely teetotal subcontinent. Of all Indian cities it has the most thriving array of bars, restaurants, nightclubs, and theaters. It has its fair share of glitterati — land barons, movie producers, starlets, and chic socialites — and is an exciting place to be out on the town.

Of all Bombay's night-time entertainment, to miss seeing a Hindi film would be like going to Stratford-on-Avon without seeing a production of a Shakespeare play. There are literally hundreds of cinemas here, showing a variety of films in Hindi, Marathi, and English. They usually screen at 3, 6, and 9 pm, with a few extra matinees at odd hours. To get acquainted with Bombay's insatiable fascination for celluloid, buy one of the "screen gossip" rags sold at every newsstand (*Star and Style* is especially salacious) and then find out from the local newspaper listings what's showing where. It's most fun to go to one of the old "talkies" cinemas with ornate façades dating to the 1930's: the Eros on J.N. Tata Road, Churchgate, the Metro on 1st Marine Drive, and the pretty (but run-down) Opera House, opposite Chowpatty Beach, are popular and centrally located. If your taxi/auto-driver doesn't know them he's not worth his salt. Otherwise, opt for modern air-conditioned comfort at one of the three cinemas directly opposite Victoria Terminus — the Excelsior, the Empire, and the Sterling.

For the city's best cocktails, jazz, and stunning views, the Oberoi's elegant Bayview Bar is a winner. Other haunts for enjoyable sun-downers are the neighboring Oberoi Towers' Supper Club, with nightly cabaret shows and dancing; the Taj Mahal's Apollo Bar, on the 24th floor, with its spectacular views, swaying Goan musicians, 1960's decor, and flared-trousered businessmen clinching deals; and the Ambassador Hotel's revolving Rooftop Restaurant.

Bombay's nightclubs start opening their doors at around 10 pm, but don't really get going until past midnight, especially on Friday and Saturday nights. Virtually all are housed within five-star hotels, meaning that unless you are a guest or can sweet-talk your way past the bouncer, you'll need to pay an entry fee. Once inside, drinks — local liquor, unless specified — tend to be expensive.

The best is **1900**, at the Taj Mahal Hotel, a belle époque-style haunt for Bombay's young, fashionable in-crowd, enlivened by the appearance of models and rising film stars. With teased hair and dangling earrings, girls from the wealthy upper class dance like pouting marionettes in the latest Western fashions. At the bar, a few heavy-jowled men wearing gold medallions drink neat whisky in silence, tapping snake-skin shoes in time with the beat until closing time. Open from 9:30 pm, to 3 am, cover charge: Rs 150.

The **Cellar**, at the Oberoi Towers, is decorated to resemble an Austrian taverna, with waiters clad in alpine breeches. It fails to attract much of a fashionable following. Open from 9:30 pm to 3 am, cover charge: Rs 50.

A half-hour drive north of Bombay is **Juhu Beach**, a mini-Malibu dotted with the kitch mansions of film stars. Palms fringe an unswimmable beach, but at night it looks suitably romantic — a glittering stretch of cafés, neon lights, and carnival-like stalls along the sands. You'll find **Xanadu**, the most popular of the Juhu clubs, down a narrow staircase next to the Hotel Horizon. Its dark, strobe-lit interior makes the grinning barmen look like they've used Chernobyl toothpaste. Proletarian disco tunes keep this place packed to the rafters on Friday and Saturday nights. Open 9:30 pm to 3 am, cover charge: Rs 50.

Nearby, the Holiday Inn and the Airport Plaza Hotel have standard discotheques, patronized mostly by airline crews on their stopovers.

Not far from Juhu is the Searock Hotel's **Cavern** nightclub in **Bandra**, a 45 minute drive from inner-city Colaba. It has a fake Ali Baba-style interior, dangling camouflage nets, and loud disco medleys. Like 1900, this is a popular place for aspiring starlets in Madonna outfits. Aging talent scouts prop themselves against the bar like corpulent lizards. Open from 9:30 pm to 3 am, cover charge Rs 80.

Back in the city, it's fascinating to glimpse the seamier underworld of Bombay's so-called "Cages," the lively brothel area located in Colaba's Maulana Shaukatali (Grant) and Falkland Roads, named for the grilled windows through which the painted ladies peer. It's better to drive rather than walk late at night. You could make one last stop at Chowpatty Beach, at the north end of Marine Drive, which is still lively at one or two in the morning. It's a drifting circus of

hawkers selling king coconuts, giant balloons, and piping-hot midnight snacks; parents trailing small toddlers; and eccentric sideshows on the moonlit sands.

SIGHTSEEING

City Strolls

You could start your day with a swirled cappuccino and the Bombay edition of the *Times of India* at the Taj Mahal before crossing the road to the **Gateway of India.** This was where King George V and Queen Mary stepped ashore in 1911, en route to make the startling announcement at the

Delhi Durbar that New Delhi was to replace Calcutta as the capital of India. In Bombay, they were welcomed by a hastily constructed white plaster arch on the Bunder pier that was replaced in 1927 by the present Gateway of India, designed by George Wittet, with its cosmopolitan mélange of traditional Hindu, Muslim, and Gujarati styles, notably the minarets and trellis-work *jalis*. India Gate was also the site where on February 28, 1948, the Somerset Light Infantry, to the tune of *Auld Lang Syne*, wrapped up the Union Jack and boarded vessels for England, ending more than two centuries of British rule.

OPPOSITE: The Taj Mahal Hotel's "1900" disco is frequented by Bombay's fashionable in-crowd. ABOVE: Tourist boats moor in front of the Gateway of India, scene of departure ceremonies when Britain left India in 1948, ending more than two centuries of rule.

The **Sassoon Docks**, a 1.5-km (0.9-mile) walk south of the Bunder, named after Bombay's famous Sephardic Jew, David Sassoon, are recommended for the dawn spectacle of fishermen unloading their catch. It's a 10-minute walk from here to the tranquil **Afghan Memorial Church of St John the Evangelist**, built in 1847 to commemorate British soldiers killed in the Sind and Afghan campaigns of 1838 and 1843.

Adjacent to the Apollo Bunder is the bustling **Colaba** area — the main tourist center — crowded with antique shops, cheap lodgings (such as the infamous Stiffles Hotel, which bears a quaint resemblance to a New Orleans

science. There's an array of Harappan artifacts, Assyrian tablets, Tibetan-Buddhist sculptures and scrolls (and gruesome carvings from human bone), antique cloisonné-ware, and oil paintings. Open daily except Monday from 10 am to 6:30 pm, with a Rs 2 entry fee (but free on Tuesdays). Next door is the **Jehangir Art Gallery** (closed on public holidays) and its pleasant Samovar Cafe. Hawkers in this area sell factory seconds — acid-washed denim, cotton dresses, and bright shirts — giant balloons, and garish stuffed animals.

Nariman Point is the place to see small armies of sinewy, white Gandhi-capped *dabba-*

brothel and lists its room rates in Arabic), cafés, and street-stalls selling a medley of bright shirts, plastic flowers, good leather shoes, and electronic watches. Tucked behind the Taj is the **Royal Bombay Yacht Club**, an oasis of musty, nautical charm.

Nearby is the Wittet-designed **Prince of Wales Museum**, set in a circular garden on Mahatma Gandhi Road, which commemorates that monarch's first visit to India. This leafy marble oasis in the midst of Bombay's bustle contains one of India's best collections of art and artifacts. The natural history section contains numerous strange creatures snared and stored in formaldehyde by proud Victorian men of

wallahs delivering cartloads of tiffin boxes to waiting office workers at lunchtime.

The Fort on Foot

The "Fort area" is a rather elastic term for the area that encompassed the original **Fort St George** cantonment, and is now the heart of civic Bombay. This is a fascinating place to stroll around, with its musty antique shops, architectural monuments, and colorful street-hawkers, notably the sandwich-wallahs who serve multi-layered offerings from boxes strapped around their necks. In this area are some of the most daunting official buildings ever constructed on the outposts of the British Empire. These architectural talismans of the High Victorian age were built when Bombay was flushed with commercial success and governed by an ardent imperialist, Sir Bartle Frere (1862—1867), who imported British

ABOVE: Clocktower at Bombay University.
OPPOSITE: Bombay's antique shops attract visitors from all over the world.

architects to execute a massive palisade of public offices in the fashionable Gothic Revival style.

An excursion into the city's history can begin at the **Bandstand** south of the Oval Maiden, where cricket games are held on Sundays. Fronting the sea is a remarkable collection of buildings, beginning with the Venetian-Gothic **Secretariat**, flanked by Sir Gilbert Scott's 1874 French-Gothic **University Campus, University Library**, and the **Rajabai Clock Tower** (excellent for a view over the city). Further along is the **High Court**, completed in 1878. In the noon-day sun, bewigged lawyers flit about in its large courtyard like black crows, and affidavits are painstakingly drafted under flapping palm-mat awnings. The smaller building next to it is the **Public Works Building**, and adjacent is James Trubshawe's **Central Telegraph Office**.

An alternative tour starts from **Hautatama Chowk**, formerly Flora Fountain, where a short walk east brings you to Horniman's Circle and **St Thomas' Cathedral**, whose foundation stone was laid in 1675. The ornate façade was a gift from the East India Company, and the cathedral still exhibits the chairs King George and Queen Mary occupied during their visit in 1911, and a profusion of brass plaques and marble figures.

Beyond the cathedral is a stately sweep of buildings, including the Doric-style **Town Hall**, designed by Col. Thomas Cowper. Opened in 1833, it also functions as the Asiatic Society Library, the oldest and largest library in the city. The basement contains many cloth-covered statues of former colonial rulers, removed after Independence. Beyond this you can glimpse the **Mint**, built in 1829 (permission to visit requires an application to the Mint Master).

But the greatest building of all is the magnificently preposterous **Victoria Terminus** at the north end of the Fort, designed by Frederick William Stevens in 1888. Its façade teems with contorted gargoyles, turreted spires, and a petrified menagerie of rats, peacocks, and snakes. A life-size statue of Queen Victoria once stood in front of the façade, but it has been relocated (with regal hauteur intact) to a corner of the Bombay Zoo. At dusk, the throngs of suburb-bound workers beneath the giant arches give Victoria Terminus the appearance of a metropolitan Hades, watched over sternly by busts of the founding company chairman and his managing director. Lady Dufferin, vicerine when the terminus was completed, thought it "much too magnificent for a bustling crowd of railway passengers."

The Markets
Crawford Market, built by Arthur Crawford in 1867, is the most grandiose market building in

India. Tattered sunlight turns the dust into incense-scented screens as you wander through the chaotic maze of cool passages, each a division of wares. The best time to visit is around seven in the morning, when armies of slender coolies balance silvery basins of fresh fish on their heads, chickens run riot, and immense troughs of fruits and vegetables are unloaded amidst a cacophony of squeals, shouts, and thuds. It has immense character: here you find sly Marwari traders hawking false mustaches and crocheted caps, the frail leaf-like dried bummelo fish, giant sacks of grain, brightly colored spices, caged Assam parrots, labrador

puppies, and fighting cocks. If you crane your neck, it's possible to make out Rudyard's father, Lockwood Kipling's bas reliefs on the market's façade.

Within a two-kilometer (just over a mile) radius of Crawford Market and concentrated between Victoria Terminus and Maulana Shaukatali (Grant) Road are literally dozens of specialist bazaars set amidst a labyrinth of temples, mosques, and narrow, spindly seventeenth-century Gujarati houses. It's easy to spend hours strolling from one bazaar to another. Even Bombayites throw up their hands in mock despair when asked to name them all, but listed here are some of the most interesting. North of Crawford Market, off Abdul Rahman Street, are the **Zaveri** and adjacent silver bazaars, where plump merchants recline on white cushions while prospective wives barter for gold and diamond jewelry — the more ostentatious the better. Around the corner is the sneeze-inducing dry fruits and spices bazaar, called **Mirchi Gully**, where every conceivable kind of chili is sold, along with piles of Afghani almonds and pistachio nuts.

For rows of glittering brass and copper, go to the **Bhuleshwar** area at the top of Kalbadevi Road, where you can also visit the Mumbadevi temple and tank, reconstructed from the original built in 1737 and a shrine of the Koli or fisherfolk, whose sacred goddess gave Bombay its name.

To the north, on Mutton Street, is the best of them all: **Chor** or **Thieves Bazaar**. Stroll past retired car engines to the antique section of the market where grandfather clocks, intricately carved rosewood furniture, chinaware, nautical instruments, and His Master's Voice gramophones are sold by shrewd dealers. The rest of Chor bazaar gets more peculiar — secondhand army surplus, rows of shoelaces, and even a section for stolen airline headphones. The **leather market** in Dhaboo Street is just parallel and worth exploring for wallets, bags, and shoes.

The Marine Promenade

Locals never call Marine Drive by its new name, Netaji Subhash Road; they prefer to call it "Queen's Necklace" for its sparkle of lamps at night. Reclaimed as recently as 1920, it stretches along the seafront from Nariman Point to Malabar Hill and is well-patronized by early morning joggers, king-coconut sellers, and courting couples. Towards the Chowpatty end is the **Taraporewala Aquarium**, which is worth a visit. Opened in 1951, it houses a wide variety of marine and freshwater fish, and even sells fish and chips at its small café! Open 11 am to 8 pm weekdays (except Monday) and 10 am to 8 pm on Sundays, with a Rs 1 entrance fee.

At the north end of Marine Drive is **Chowpatty Beach,** a stretch of sand offering donkey-rides, candy-floss, and piping-hot midnight snacks. This is also the focus for political rallies and where the **Ganesh Chaturthi** festival is staged every year during September's full moon. Bombayites are devoted to this plump, elephant-headed fellow, the deity of material advancement, and honor him with a massive parade along Marine Drive with as many as 6,000 Ganesh images, some towering to nine meters (30 ft) and strung with flashing lights and blaring loudspeakers. The grand finale is the immersion of these effigies in the sea at Chowpatty Beach and the cheers from the crowd as they either buckle and sink or float gaily toward the horizon. In the late nineteenth century, when political meetings were banned by the British, the early Independence movement used the

Ganesh festival as a way of communicating political messages through dance and drama.

From dawn to dusk, Chowpatty Beach is a drifting circus of scrawny beggars, hawkers, aimless sadhus with long tousled hair, and scrums of young men in flared trousers. Families flock here on Sundays, wandering from the donkey stand to impromptu wrestling competitions and the triple row of Bombay's best fast food vendors. Here is the place to sample *channa bhatura, bhel-puri, ragada*, and the queen of Bombay's snacks, *pau bhaji*, a spicy vegetable gravy served with a fried bun.

It's about a 15-minute stroll to August Kranti Gardens, and **Mani Bhavan** — a little brown house at 19 Laburnam Road — is just parallel. This was Mahatma Gandhi's residence during his visits to Bombay between 1917 and 1934. From here, Gandhi launched many of his fa-

mous *satyagraha* (non-violence) campaigns. Today, Mani Bhavan is a museum housing replicas of Gandhi's daily utensils, ascetic bed, spinning wheel, and well-worn sandals. There's a section depicting the Mahatma's life through a collection of dolls, a picture gallery, and an excellent library. Also on exhibit are copies of historic documents signed by Gandhi. Open from 9:30 am to 6 pm, except Sunday. Entrance fee Rs 1.

Malabar Hill

At the top of nearby Malabar Hill are the **Hanging Gardens**, which were landscaped in 1881 and immediately became popular with memsahib watercolorists as a locale for botanical sketches. Despite the Gothic-sounding name, the gardens are very sedate but do have one intriguing attraction — a gardener who trans-

forms his hedges into astonishing abstract art compositions.

Adjacent to the gardens in a private enclave and hidden by dense foliage is the **Tower of Silence**, the round stone construction in which the Parsis place their dead to be devoured by vultures. These structures are designed in much the same way as a lobster-net — to prevent vultures from flying out with body parts in their talons. A series of towers have been built since Aungier leased the Parsi community the one-square kilometer (0.4-sq mile) site in 1673, and today the area is potentially some of the most valuable real estate in Bombay, but is ardently protected by the Parsis. Visitors are strictly forbidden.

Bombay's swish Marine Drive, is known as the "Queen's Necklace" for its sparkle of lights at night.

Just across the road is the **Kamala Nehru Children's Park**, with its colorful playground, floral clock, and spectacular views across Back Bay, Chowpatty Beach, and Marine Drive. Just near the park's entrance is the **Naaz Cafe**, where the top terrace is the best place for a chilled beer at sunset.

At the **Adishwarji Jain Temple**, on B.G. Kher Marg, just down the road from the gardens, you can admire the intricate marble carvings, many of great antiquity, which were placed here after the temple's construction in 1903. Its upper story contains exquisite silver doors, and the ground floor has rows of recesses with statues of Jain

nymphs can be found here alongside the sky-scrapers. On the southern tip, Malabar Point, is **Raj Bhavan**, the Chief Minister's residence, which is closed to the public but can be seen from Marine Drive. Nearby is the **Walkeshwar Temple**, dating back to the eleventh century, where legend has it Rama stopped to make a devotional lingam on his way to rescue his kidnapped wife, Sita, from the clutches of the evil Ceylonese god-king.

Opposite is the **Banganga Tank**, where Rama is supposed to have shot an arrow into the scorched earth when he was thirsty. Today the ancient stone stairs are used to dry clothes and

tirthankaras. One of the most colorful Jain cere-monies to witness here is the Siddh-Chakra, a purification ritual before marriage. (The best time to see it is just before the marriage season begins in December to January). The young men undergoing the ritual wear dhotis and cover their faces with the distinctive Jain gauze mask (to discourage the swallowing of insects), and sit amidst elaborate patterns of blossoms and symbolic *thali*-dishes, humming scriptures with the temple priests as musicians play stirring tunes — all recorded by proud parents on their video cameras.

Malabar Hill and the neighboring suburb of **Breach Candy** are Bombay's most exclusive addresses, where much of the city's famed so-cializing takes place. Majestic eighteenth-cen-tury mansions with ornately carved façades and marble fountains writhing with naked

the tank's mythically pure water has turned to a chocolate-colored swill.

Haji Ali's Tomb and Dhobi Ghats

Little is known about Haji Ali, the turreted mau-soleum built in the late eighteenth century at the end of a rocky causeway reached only at low tide near Mahalaxmi. According to popu-lar belief, the tomb was built in memory of a merchant who renounced his wealth and lived on the barren rocks after a pilgrimage (hajj) to Mecca. His sister, Ma Hajiani, became his com-panion in ascetic suffering and a mausoleum was built for her a little distance away on Worli Bay. This is not the place to leave your shoes unguarded — the tomb is full of quick-eyed beg-gar urchins eager to whisk away your sneakers. Muslim pilgrims have developed a ritual to deal with the row of pitiful, wailing beggars who perform *khel* (beggar's tricks) along the narrow walkway — they exchange rupees for a handful of paise and distribute the equivalent of a few grains of rice to each one. At the entrance are dozens of stalls selling sticky white (and sickly sweet) *prasad*, reflective-glass scripture pictures, *burqa* (the encompassing garment worn by Muslim women), and plug-in Taj Mahal baubles, which shine in the dark. There's also the **Hajiali Juice Center,** which makes the best fresh juice in town. Also try their specialty, *sitafel* (custard-apple), and pomegranate juice.

Two of Bombay's elite social institutions, the ultra-proper Willingdon Club and the **Mahalaxmi Race Course,** are close by. The racecourse is named for the goddess of the nearby Hindu temple, who is the deity of wealth. The annual Derby here in February and March creates a frenzy of social activity. Stroll to the **Mahalaxmi Junction** station over-bridge to see Bombay's dhobi ghats, where hundreds of dhobi-wallahs (washermen) live and work. It's a giant maze of troughs, bubbling with suds and echoing with the noise of stains being tirelessly whacked out of the city's laundry. Like the *dabba*-wallahs, the dhobi-ghats operate almost infallibly on a system of hieroglyphic squiggles on each piece of fabric to identify the owner.

The Museum Round-up Tour

The **Victoria and Albert Museum** is situated in spacious gardens close to the entrance of the Jijamata Udyan in Byculla, which was once the premier European suburb in Bombay. The museum has many Indian paintings, antique coins, and weaponry, but its highlight is "Bombay: a Photorama", which portrays the story of Bombay from 1661 to 1931 through a series of old prints, maps, and 250 old and rare photographs. It is open every day except Wednesday.

The **Victoria Gardens** are Bombay's best and largest, laid out in 1861 with broad paths, ornamental ferneries, and many rare species of tropical plants. A blackboard near the entrance lists "flowering" attractions of the day. The **Bombay Zoo** is here, and children can take elephant, camel, and pony rides. Open Thursday—Tuesday from 8 am to 6 pm.

The **National Maritime Museum** is the only one of its kind in India, with a rich collection of naval and maritime memorabilia dating back to the time of Alexander the Great. It's located on Middle Island, a coastal battery owned by the Western Naval Command, and reached by tourist boats which leave from the nearby Gateway of India. Open between 2 pm and 5:30 pm on Saturdays and 10 am and 5 pm on Sundays and public holidays.

The **F.D. Alpaiwalla Museum,** located at Khareghat Memorial Hall in Khareghat Colony,

houses an extensive collection of antique memorabilia, Gandhara sculptures, 80 albums of picture postcards, fragments of Sir John Marshall's Taxila excavations, Chinese porcelain, and a mummified hand from Egypt.

The **Nehru Planetarium** in Worli has daily star-gazing shows in English at 3 pm and 6 pm (except Mondays), admission Rs 5.

OUT OF BOMBAY

On a small green island just 10 km (six miles) northeast of the Apollo Bunder are four magnificent rock-cut cave temples of Elephanta, dating

from AD 450 to 750 and dedicated to Lord Shiva. It's an hour's journey to **Elephanta Island** and ferries leave every hour between 9 am and 2 pm from the Gateway of India. Tickets are either deluxe Rs 40 or ordinary Rs 16 — the deluxe boats are preferable because they have archaeology graduates as guides.

Long before Bombay came into existence, Elephanta Island was the capital city of the Silahara dynasty (first century AD) and was called Gharapuri, "place of idols". Much later, the Portuguese claimed part of the island and renamed it after discovering a massive elephant sculpture, which now stands in the Victoria Gardens. Portuguese soldiers used the carved temple deities for target practice, and natural decay has added to the damage. From the primitive wooden jetty, the caves are reached by an easy climb (or palanquins for those who don't mind being hoisted up the hill by four semi-naked men). The cave temples contain a combination of Hindu, Jain, and Buddhist iconography, and the sinuous, enraptured figures were considered shockingly Dionysian by the straitlaced Christian visitors. On Sundays and

OPPOSITE: Haji Ali's Muslim tomb of mysterious origin. ABOVE: Boats used for tours of the Elephanta Caves.

public holidays, Elephanta Island is unbearable, with creaking ferry-loads of fellow tourists and a motley crowd of persistent hawkers. Avoid the rabble by taking the earliest boat during the week.

The **Kanheri Caves**, 42 km (26 miles) from Bombay, are far more impressive. This is one of the largest of a series of Buddhist rock-cut monasteries in western India, cut into the hills and valleys of the mountain chain known as the Western Ghats, of which the most famous are at Ajanta and Ellora. The pillars are hewn from the rock in such a way that they appear to support the weight of the mountain above. There are 109 caves in all, dating from about the first to the ninth century AD, and all are excavated from a gigantic circular rock.

The earlier caves belong to the Hinayana phase of Buddhist architecture. Many served as simple monks' quarters and are of little interest, but caves 1, 2, and 3 are notable for their massive pillars, sculptures, and stupas. Most impressive is cave 3, a Buddhist *chaitya* (or chapel), with its monumental pillars and elaborate images of Buddha.

The ruins at **Bassein**, 77 km (48 miles) from Bombay on the mainland, make a perfect picnic spot. This is where the Portuguese built a walled city overlooking the sea after taking possession of the territory from its Muslim rulers in 1534. It grew into a grand settlement, with cathedrals and elegant homes where the fiercely Jesuit Portuguese aristocrats, the Hildalgos, lived in dissolute splendor, using Bassein as a naval base for converting the natives, often under threat of death, and amassing considerable wealth. They were forced to flee suddenly in 1739 during an invasion by the local Mahratta army, and the ruins now serve as a poignant reminder of Portuguese rule. Trains run to Bassein Road station from Victoria Terminus, and the settlement ruins are only four kilometers (2.5 miles) away. It's best to make this a full day's excursion.

GENERAL INFORMATION

The Maharashtra Tourism Development Corporation (MTDC) runs well-organized conducted city bus tours that bulldoze through the main places of interest and cost Rs 40. Daily, except Mondays, at 9 am to 1 pm, and 2 pm to 7 pm. Other guided tours include daily boat trips to the Elephanta Caves at 10 am to 2 pm and 2:30 pm to 6:30 pm for Rs 30, and a full day's excursion that includes the Kanheri Caves, the Lion Safari Park, and Juhu Beach, at 10 am to 7 pm, costing Rs 65.

MTDC Office, CDO Hutments, Madame Cama Road. ©202-6713, 202-7762.

India Tourism Development Corporation (ITDC), ©242-3343.

Government of India Tourist Office, 123 Maharshi Karve Road, opposite Churchgate station. ©293144. Open 9 am to 5 pm, alternate Saturdays 9 am to 12:30 pm, closed Sundays.

Useful Reading

The monthly *Bombay Calling* has an extensive directory for all hotels, restaurants, information centers, travel reservation offices, museums, etc and is available from hotels and newsstands. The Government of India Tourist Office also publishes a fortnightly diary of cultural events in Bombay.

THE WESTERN TRAIL

From Bombay, travelers usually explore western India by one or a combination of three routes through **Goa**, **Maharashtra**, and **Gujarat**. Many make Goa's sandy, palm-lined beaches and colonial Portuguese sights their first priority. But both Maharashtra and Gujarat are equally rewarding destinations, though they are often neglected by tourists.

In Maharashtra, carved from the bare rocks of the Deccan Plateau, are India's finest ancient cave sculptures and frescoes at Ellora and Ajanta.

Gujarat's capital, Ahmedabad, contains many relics of its grand Mughal past and fine art and textile museums. Nearby, the former princely capital, Vadodara (Baroda), is a stately city of Gothic palaces, parks, and museums. But the real pleasures lie in rural Gujarat, from its northern tip at the Rann of Kutch, the home of brightly attired tribal nomads, through the Sasan-Gir wildlife sanctuary and elaborate Jain temples in the south.

GOA

BALMY DAYS AND PORTUGUESE RELICS

Goa is justifiably famous for its dazzling 100-km (62-mile) sweep of palm-lined coastline fringed by the turquoise Arabian Sea. Unspoilt and rustic, Goa's fertile green plains are covered with cashew, mango, and jackfruit groves, and crisscrossed by the Mandovi and Zuari rivers, from which rise forested hills up to the Western Ghats mountain range.

Goa has a seductive Latin atmosphere that feels peculiarly unIndian, and is perfect for relaxing, swimming, sunbathing, and eating seafood.

The Mauryan Empire established settlements along this coastal sweep in the third century BC and the area passed through a succession of rulers in seesaw wars and conflicts between the Muslims from the north and the Hindu-dominated dynasties of the south.

But Goa owes its exotic personality to the Portuguese, who seized it from the Bijapur kings of the Deccan in 1510 under the command of Afonso Albuquerque after failing to secure a base on the Malabar coast further south. Traders from Lisbon used Goa as well as the smaller possessions of Diman and Diu to the north in Gujarat as staging posts for plying the eastern spice routes to Indonesia and Sri Lanka to amass fortunes from ginger, pepper, nutmegs, and saffron.

Zealous missionaries followed, and their terrifying threats of a fiery hell prompted mass conversions of local Hindus, aided by the arrival of an Inquisition party in 1560. At the height of its prosperity, Goa was a magnificent city, full of majestic cathedrals and mansions, some of which can still be seen in old Goa today. But Portuguese power declined rapidly after the seventeenth century, falling prey to occupation by the Dutch in 1603, and later by the British during the Napoleonic wars in Europe. During the full-blown days of the Raj, Goa was regarded as a quaint and harmless vestige, appreciated for its cheap wine. A British guide book of 1898, *Picturesque India*, referred to Goa as "a pathetic wilderness of ruined churches and palaces". The Portuguese held control until 1961, when the remaining colonials were thrown out in a largely bloodless invasion by India.

The colonial heritage is apparent everywhere, in the street tavernas, dilapidated Iberian-style villas, women's preference for frocks over saris, and numerous smatterings of Portuguese in the local Konkan vernacular.

Although India has some 6,000 km (3,700 miles) of coastline, most of it is completely undeveloped. Goa is India's most superior beach resort. This is as much due to its variety of beautiful beaches and hotels as it is to the gregarious Goanese who have a Mediterranean enthusiasm for their hybrid cuisine and locally brewed *feni*, a coconut, palm, or cashew whiskey.

WHEN TO GO

India has few destinations where it is possible to feel comfortable all year round, but Goa is one of them. It's best to visit between October and February, but the monsoon period of June to September is often dramatically beautiful. Sadly, Goa's famous pre-Advent Carnival (held late February to early March), once an exuberant, bacchanalian ritual of floats and costumes, has become drab of late owing to political disputes between its organizers. If you are in Goa for any major Christian festival or for the *Novidades* harvest celebration on August 24, it's likely that bull-fights will be staged, advertised by word of mouth only. During Easter and Christmas, Goa dons full sixteenth century-style regalia for remarkable processions in Old Goa's ghost city of cathedrals and basilicas.

HOW TO GET THERE

By far the most enjoyable way of arriving in Goa is by steamer from Bombay, which operates daily except Tuesday between October and May, but closes down during the June—September monsoon months. The boat leaves from Bombay's Ferry Wharf at around 10 am and drifts into Goa early next morning. Berths can be reserved, but even so, it is best to arrive early to claim your place as operators often double-book. A deluxe cabin on the upper deck costs between Rs 235 and Rs 300 but is recommended over the rigors of traveling in the congested cargo class. However, the lower deck is a mere Rs 48 and for many travelers proves a more interesting experience. Meals and beer are served on board. The return journey from Goa leaves daily except Wednesday; again, berths can be booked in advance.

Goa's Dabolim airport is connected by Indian Airlines flights from Bombay, Delhi,

Bangalore, Cochin, and Trivandrum. Panaji, the capital, is 27 km (16.8 miles) away and the resort beaches are even further, so it's worth utilizing the free reception coaches provided by the major hotels for prospective guests. Otherwise, there's a Rs 20 airport bus into town.

Train journeys to Goa's Vasco da Gama station, some 30 km (18.6 miles) from Panaji, take 22 hours from Bombay and 46 hours from New Delhi. The route from Bombay slices through some spectacular scenery, but the New Delhi journey can be arduous. Luxury buses take 16 hours from Bombay, but most are notorious video-coaches. The best choice is MTDC's air-conditioned "luxury" bus, with no video, departing at 3 pm daily (Rs 105).

GETTING AROUND

Goa looks deceptively tiny on the map, but in reality it is very spread out, and transport is needed to appreciate its varied landscape. Taxis are freely available for day hire and charge around Rs 2 per kilometer (0.62 mile). Hiring a motorbike is far more exhilarating, and rates can vary from Rs 50 to Rs 100 per day. Your hotel should be able to arrange a newish vehicle, but make sure you wear a crash helmet as the local constabulary often extract "simple police fines" from bareheaded tourists.

Goa's four main towns are connected by a regular bus service. **Panaji**, the center, is close to Dona Paula and Miramar beaches; **Mapusa** (13 km, or eight miles) has bus connections along the northern coast; **Margao** (34 km, or 21 miles) is very Portuguese, with fine parks and old mansions, and connects to the southern beaches of Majorda, Colva, Benaulim, Betelbatim, and Betel; and **Vasco da Gama** (30 km, or 18.6 miles) is close to the Oberoi Resort at Bogmalo Beach. The nicest way to explore Old Goa from Panaji is by taking a mid-morning ferry for a languid chug down the Mandovi River. The tourist office runs enjoyable evening river cruises from Panaji's jetty at 6 pm. Full moon nights are spectacular, with dinner and lively Portuguese music and dancing on deck.

SIGHTSEEING

Panaji
Panaji still looks and feels like a sleepy Portuguese town. It is set along the southern bank of the salty Mandovi River, with broad avenues spilling into cobbled squares, grand public buildings, red-tiled houses, narrow lanes, and tavernas.

Start with the **Secretariat** building, originally built by the Sultan of Bijipur who quartered his Arabian horses and elephants in the Moorish courtyard. The Portuguese rebuilt it in 1615 as the official residence for viceroys and generals. Beyond Largo Da Palacio (Palace Square) is Panaji's lively quay where the steamer from Bombay arrives each morning. Nearby is the baroque **Church of the Immaculate Conception**, with its distinctive twin towers. Just beyond the church is the residential Fontainahas area, a languid maze of shuttered, balustraded villas, painted ochre, blue, or mint green, behind which plump matrons slice spinach for the lunchtime Goan favorite, *caldo verde*. This area is full of musty, antiquated shops selling sacks of raw cashews and lumps of Goa's mango-flavored cheese. Shadowed lanes reveal cafés where old men in straw hats gather to sip feni in the siesta hours. For a spectacular view across the town, take a 15-minute walk up to **Altino Hill** and the **Patriarch Palace**, where Pope John Paul II stayed during his 1986 visit.

Old Goa: Conquistadors and Cathedrals
The Portuguese called their prized Indian possession "Goa Dourada", or Golden Goa, but it was not the beautiful beaches they were referring to. Portuguese wealth and power was concentrated in Old Goa, its "Rome of the Orient", where the vast hybrid oriental-baroque cathedrals are layered with African gold.

In the sixteenth century, Goa was famed for its eight square kilometers (three square miles) of majestic churches, monasteries, convents, and stately mansions, boasting a larger population than Lisbon, Paris, or London. Old Goa was abandoned after a series of virulent plagues in 1534, 1635, and 1735 that wiped out nearly 80 percent of the population. The survivors created Panaji, nine kilometers (5.5 miles) away, as the new capital in 1835. Today, Old Goa is still fairly deserted, and its lime-white churches hover above the jungle like a Christian Angkor Wat.

The **Basilica of Bom Jesus**, completed in 1604, contains a remarkable Baroque gilded altar. In an airtight silver and glass casket lie the sacred remains of St Francis Xavier, Goa's patron saint, who spent his life spreading Christianity through the Portuguese colonies. His mottled skull is eerily lit by a naked bulb. Beneath the basilica is a beautifully sculpted mausoleum donated by the Grand Duke of Tuscany. Xavier died in China in 1552, and his mummified corpse criss-crossed the globe before it was brought to Goa in 1613. For a "small donation" you can view his silver-encased feet. Every 10 years, the basilica becomes a mad throng of pilgrims for the "public veneration" of the

OPPOSITE: Goan scenes: TOP: Aguada Beach. BELOW: Restaurant on Baga Beach.

202

Bombay and the West

skeleton. A small gallery displays portraits and various relics attributed to the famous saint. The basilica is open 9 am to 6 pm daily (open 10 am Sundays for service).

Across the road is the majestic **Chapel of St Catherine**, completed in 1619 and dedicated to St Catherine of Alexandria, a pagan girl who became an ardent Christian and was later beheaded on the very same day, November 25, that Afonso Albuquerque gunned his way down the Mandovi to wrest Goa from the Muslims. Many regard the cathedral as Asia's largest and most magnificent Christian church, a grand renaissance structure with an ornate gilded inte-

The **Church of St Cajetan**, near old Goa's ferry wharf, was built by Italian friars to resemble St Peters' basilica in Rome. Look for the **Viceroy's Arch**, the ceremonial entranceway for disembarking Portuguese governors. On Monte Santo (holy hill) is the **St Augustine Tower**, all that remains of what was once Goa's biggest church. Opposite is the buttressed, fortress-style **Convent of St Monica**, India's largest nunnery. A gate leads to the secluded **Church of Our Lady of the Rosary**, one of the earliest built in Goa, which contains the tomb of Dona Caterina, wife of the tenth viceroy and the first Portuguese woman to venture to Goa.

rior. Beautifully detailed panels around the center altarpiece depict St Catherine's life. The font is believed to have been used by St Francis Xavier. The cathedral has five bells, one of which is the "Golden Bell", one of the biggest in the world, which was used to announce the burning of pagans and heretics during the Inquisition.

The nearby **Convent and Church of Francis of Assisi**, built in the rare Manueline style, was originally a small Franciscan chapel. It was completely remodeled in 1661 with gilded, beautifully carved woodwork, exquisite panel frescoes, and fascinating gravestones bearing coats of arms. It houses the Archaeological Museum, which has a gallery of portraits of Portuguese governors and viceroys and a notable collection of ancient Indian sculpture recovered from Goan Hindu shrines sacked by both Muslims and Christians in fits of religious monomania.

Stately Mansions
The tourist department in Panaji can provide a list of 20 private villas and mansions which can be visited by appointment. Some are more than 400 years old and still lived in by the original families, with very beautiful collections of Portuguese colonial and Indian furniture and fittings. The Alvarez mansion in Margao and that of cartoonist Mario Miranda at Lotulim are well worth a visit. Don't turn up on their doorsteps without ringing first, as these are private residences.

Sea and Sand
If you're not heading straight for the main luxury resorts at Aguada and Bogmala beaches, then you face a daunting array of beaches and hotels from which to choose. Generally, the northern coastline is popular for a good range

of hotels, beaches, and restaurants, while the southern coast is more primitive and secluded, though it contains two of Goa's resort hotels.

The Northern Beaches
North of Fort Aguada are the twin beaches of **Calangute** and **Candolim**, a seven-kilometer (4.3-mile) sandy stretch scattered with dozens of hotels and lodging houses and, on the beachfront, makeshift bars and restaurants made from wood and palm leaves. Children cross the sands to tempt reclining tourists with their fruit baskets, and at dawn each morning fishermen unload their catch. During the mid-1960's, when

hippies began colonizing Goa's beaches — to the slightly outraged astonishment of local villagers — Calangute became the center of Flower Power adherents. Stalls in Calangute still do a roaring trade in leather G-strings, hessian trousers, and ethnic sandals.

Two kilometers (just over a mile) further north is **Baga Beach**, backed by a steep hill and probably one of the best of the northern beaches. Its uncluttered sands have an authentic feel, with traditional fishing boats hauled past the high-tide mark, and chaperoning nuns and schoolchildren spending the siesta under the coconut palms. Baga also has a good windsurfing school.

From Baga's northern headland, it's a 10-minute walk to **Anjuna Beach**, a faded paradise for the "love generation" who live in crude matting shacks along the cliff face. The nude

sunbathing attracts squads of Indian men, who are sometimes known to conceal cameras in their pockets. Daily life here centers on exhibitionist yoga, Frisbee games, and the smoking of vast amounts of hashish from elaborate pipes. Worthwhile Anjuna institutions are the Wednesday flea market and the Friday evening Haystack, the brainchild of Goa's most noted musician, August Braganza, whose backyard turns into a canopied showcase for local talent, with folk dances, singing, and music performed and good Goan food served.

The small rocky inlets of **Chapora** and **Vagator** are three kilometers (just under two miles) further north. Chapora is overlooked by the ruins of a Portuguese fort, built in 1717, with fine views from the ramparts. Vagator is more idyllic and secluded, with only one good hotel. A number of local residents here rent out rooms in the village, and it's possible to rent an entire house for Rs 2,400 per month.

The Southern Beaches
Bogmalo is small by Goan standards and largely patronized by guests of the Oberoi's luxury resort which dominates the crescent-shaped bay. For secluded beauty, **Colva**'s 40-km (25-mile) stretch of powdery sand and pristine, warm water is Goa's most paradisical. Away from the main cluster of tourist lodgings and beach cafés, you can virtually have the sands to yourself.

WHERE TO STAY

PANAJI
Hotel Mandovi, Goa's oldest, D.B. Bandodkar Road, ℰ6270-9, still has a certain charm despite suffering from a 1960's decor overhaul. Nothing has changed much since Evelyn Waugh stayed here and observed that the hotel bookshop contained only cheap detective novels, sex psychology, and rationalist education books. Rates: inexpensive.
Hotel Fidalgo, 18th June Road, ℰ6291-99, is more modern but fairly characterless, and inexpensive.

THE NORTHERN BEACHES
The **Fort Aguada Beach Resort**, ℰ7501-9, is Goa's premier resort at Sinquerim, Bardez. Built by the Taj Group within extensive gardens and the ruins of a seventeenth-century fort, the hotel building has tasteful sea-facing rooms, some with terraces.

On the hillside are tiers of self-contained cottages, perfect for a couple. On an even higher level is **The Hermitage**, a series of elite dwellings used for the 1983 Commonwealth heads

---

ABOVE: Church of Immaculate Conception, Panaji, Goa. OPPOSITE: Church of St Cajetan in old Goa.

of government conference, with one cottage named after Britain's Prime Minister Margaret Thatcher. These cost about Rs 2,500. Overlooking the seemingly endless white sands of Calangute Beach, the **Fort Aguada** is perfect for a lazy, luxurious holiday and has an impressive sports complex with good instructors for waterskiing, windsurfing, fishing, scuba diving, and parasailing. The latter, costing Rs 125 for five minutes, always attracts large crowds.

Next door, right on the beach, is the affiliated **Taj Holiday Village**, ℂ7518-7, rates expensive to very expensive with less expensive functional cottages, and access to all Fort

motorbikes, river cruises, waterskiing, fishing, and traditional folk dances.

The **Ronil Beach Resort**, a modern Spanish-style resort around a freshwater swimming pool with an outdoor restaurant is highly recommended and moderately priced. A last Baga Beach option is **Cavala**, which offers simple, rooms without air-conditioning and has a quaint bar and good Goanese restaurant.

Vagator Beach Resort, ℂ41, has the only worthwhile accommodation on the other northern beaches, with charming beachfront cottages and cheaper rooms in the main building. There is an excellent open-air restaurant.

Aguada's facilities.

On Calangute Beach, the best choice is the **Varma Beach Resort**, with large, moderately priced, well-kept, air-conditioned rooms and three small cottages, situated just across the road from the Taj Village. Excellent breakfasts of piping-hot Goanese bread, eggs, fruit, and delicious coffee. Nearby is **Villa Ludovici** (which is exactly the way V.S. Naipaul's "House for Mr Biswas" ought to look) with quaint inexpensive rooms and **O'Sombreiro**, a veranda restaurant serving home-cooked Goan dishes, lobster, and prawns. The secluded **Essa Beach Resort**, ℂ92, has a choice of pleasant sea-facing rooms. Cheap.

On Baga Beach, **Hotel Baia Do Sol**, ℂ84-6, offers the best accommodation. Literally set on the sands, it has casual, well-kept rooms, a great outdoor seafood restaurant, and excellent value riverside cottages. The helpful staff can arrange

THE SOUTHERN BEACHES

The **Oberoi Bogmalo Beach Resort**, ℂ2191, is only 10 minutes from the airport, with pleasant rooms; small balconies face either the sea or a beautiful rear garden. The resort boasts excellent water-sports, a freshwater swimming pool, health club, and a variety of restaurants serving good traditional Goan and seafood dishes. And Colva, Goa's most spectacular beach, is close by. Rooms are expensive but drop to almost half during the low season from May to September.

Colva's **Hotel Silver Sands**, ℂ21645, has good, moderately priced air-conditioned rooms, but it's preferable to stay at **Golden House Cottages**, much cheaper and a pleasant five-minute walk from the beach. Run by a gentle fishing family, you can dine like a king on fresh crab and lobster every night.

Cicade de Goa, Vainguinim Beach, Dona Paula, ©3301, was designed by Indian architect Charles Correa to create the feeling of a Moorish village. The Goan-style rooms and courtyards have views across the Zuari estuary and Mormugao harbor. Excellent facilities, including good poolside and indoor restaurants. Rates: expensive.

Prainha Cottages, Dona Paula, ©4004. These 13 tasteful, white stucco cottages with bougainvillea-fringed balconies are set among palm trees in a secluded, black-sanded bay. Very clean and restful, with the family-run O'Pescador seafood restaurant a two-minute walk away. Rates: expensive.

Accommodation Footnote: The state-run tourism department offers for Rs 20 to Rs 100 a range of unembellished but well-kept tourist hotels and cottages in Goa's main towns and on Bardez, Calangute, Colva, and Bicholim beaches.

GOA A LA CARTE

All over Goa, from city restaurants to the simplest village taverna, it's possible to eat magnificently. Here the unique hybrid cuisine finds a perfect companion in the famous *feni*—a potent local brew made from cashew, coconut palm, or apple. Goans are particularly proud of their robust cuisine, and never turn down an invitation to dine at a family home, where the most authentic food is found.

Indianized Portuguese dishes are usually spicy, but delicious, such as *xacuti*, a high-powered dish of either mutton or chicken with a coconut masala sauce, or *caldinhe*, a delicately seasoned fish dish. These are usually accompanied by *pau*, a small soft bread roll leavened with palm toddy. Pork is a staple meat and is used in *chourisso*, a sausage, and *sorpotal*, pig's liver pickled in a savory sauce.

But the real splendor of Goan cuisine is in the numerous preparations of fresh seafood — king prawns, lobster, kingfish, oysters, mussels, shrimps, and crabs — roasted, grilled, or curried in mouthwatering ways. Goan wines are unexceptional, though much cheaper than other Indian varieties, and all come in screw-top bottles. It is easy to develop a taste for *feni*, which is best taken diluted with soda. The smoother, double-distilled variant flavored with cumin, ginger, or sarsaparilla makes an unusual drink.

Eating Out

Every Goan has a list of favorite eating places, and the only bias tends to be proximity, as Goa is very spread out. Most of the main hotels have good indoor and outdoor restaurants, but the following places are highly recommended.

The outdoor **Beach House** restaurant at the Taj Village has simple wooden benches on the sand under a thatch roof, where you can enjoy exceptional Goan and seafood specialties.

But the best place to head for after sunset is **Casa Portuguesa**, Baga Beach, an exquisitely restored Portuguese villa owned by Francisco Sousa, a wealthy Goan lawyer. This may well be India's most elegant restaurant, with candlelit tables spread through the Iberian-style vaulted rooms, small veranda, and tropical garden. It serves classic Portuguese dishes and standard Goan fare, including such delicacies as Whole Shark *Rachieada*, Mussels in Wine, and Grilled Oysters. Goa's cognoscente flock here as much for the wonderful food as to hear Fran-

cisco perform *fado*, the lugubrious Portuguese love songs. Try either to book or to come early — the Casa Portuguesa serves only dinner and fills up at about 9 pm.

On the Baga beachfront is **St Anthony's Bar**, which has been part of Goan mythology since it opened in 1968. This weathered beach shack, with its peeling formica-top tables, slumbering dogs, and rock-bottom prices, serves everything with a Midas touch, from fruit whips and waffles to grilled mackerel and clams cooked in coconut sauce. **Lilly's** authentic Goan restaurant on Vagator Beach is run by an enterprising Indian woman who was expelled from Mozambique by the Portuguese in the sixties in retaliation for the Indian occupation of Goa.

For good Goan and seafood dishes, also try **O'Coqueriro**, at Porvoim (four kilometers, or 2.5 miles, from the Panaji bridge), the popular **O'Pescador** restaurant at Dona Paula, and **La Paz** and **Zuari Hotel**, both at Vasco. In Panaji, the old Mandovi Hotel's **Rio Rico** has excellent Goan dishes in a period atmosphere, with its antiquated waiters insisting on silver service, its faded chintz, and the view across casuarina

OPPOSITE: One of Goa's upmarket beach resorts. ABOVE: Maharashtra girl hawking handicrafts on the beach.

trees to the Mandovi River, although it is plagued with the sound of an electric organ playing *Swannee River*.

Far more rustic is **Martin's Beach Corner** at Caranzalem, past the Mandovi promenade down a road scattered with dogs, chickens, and pigs. It's an open-air café on the river's edge, with a magnificent view of the Fort Aguada, and is famous for its decadent seafood dishes, such as a fist-size fish roe poached in fish stock and served with powdered rock salt, or more conventional fresh oysters, sautéed squid, and grilled prawns. Gregory Peck and Roger Moore have both dined here.

GENERAL INFORMATION

Government of India Tourist Office, Communidade Building, Church Square, Panaji. ©3412.
Tourist Information and Tour Counter, Tourist Home, Patto Bridge, Panaji. ©5583, 5715, 4757.

HOW TO GET THERE

Overnight Ferry Service: Bombay: New Ferry Wharf, Mallet Bunder. ©864071. Panaji: V.S. Dempo (Travel Division) opposite the Port Jetty, D.B. Bandodkar Marg, Panaji. ©3842.

MUSEUMS AND ART GALLERIES

Archaeological Museum and Portrait Gallery, Old Goa. ©5941. 10 am to 12 pm and 1 pm to 5 pm. Closed Fridays.
Archives Museum of Goa, Arhirwad Building, 1st floor, Santa Inez, Panaji. ©6006. 9:30 am to 1 pm and 2 pm to 5:30 pm. Closed Saturdays, Sundays, and public holidays.

ABOVE: Dusk at Bogmalo Beach, Goa.

MAHARASHTRA

LEGACY OF STONE

Set high on the dry, weathered Deccan Plateau, Maharashtra's craggy heartland stands in stark contrast to the tropical bustle of Bombay, the state capital. A rural patchwork of thatch-huts, fields of giant sunflowers, cotton, and mustard plants, and deep, dried-out ravines, Maharashtra has an eerie, primitive beauty. The state was once the center of the mighty Maratha empire, which ruled much of central India during the seventeenth century, waging fierce battles with Muslim invaders. Much earlier, however, between the second century BC and thirteenth century AD, the area witnessed the creation of the finest of all cave temples and monasteries in India, a technical *tour de force* carved from solid rock with brilliant technical and artistic skill. These are the famous caves at **Ajanta** and **Ellora**, some 60 in total, near the city of Aurangabad. The work of itinerant communities of Buddhist (and later Hindu and Jain) monks who had among their ranks exceptionally skilled sculptors and artists, the caves at Ajanta and Ellora are so exquisite in their execution that they rank with the Taj Mahal, the temples of Khajaraho and Kanchipuram, and the ruined city of Fatehpur Sikri as the country's greatest wonders.

Today's tourists pass through the musty cave recesses to marvel at the skill and beauty of these caves, but for earlier generations of largely illiterate devotees they were an overwhelming visual sermon, enshrining the history of myth, religion, and architecture of ancient India.

After Buddhism declined in India, these cave masterpieces were neglected and fell into obscurity under layers of earth and vegetation until 1819, when a group of British soldiers stumbled upon a cave while tiger hunting on the Deccan Plateau.

AURANGABAD

Although primarily used as a base for the cave temples of Ajanta and Ellora, Aurangabad has several historical attractions and some very interesting Buddhist caves of its own. Originally called Khadke, it was later renamed during the Mughal emperor Aurangzeb's reign from 1650 to 1670. Aurangabad is surrounded by crumbling fortifications and contains several fine Mughal monuments, including Aurangzeb's duplicate Taj Mahal, the Bibi-ka-Maqbara, built as a mausoleum for his wife.

GETTING THERE

From Bombay there is a daily direct flight, leaving at 6:15 am and arriving at 6:55. It's worth bearing in mind that the MTDC tours to both Ellora and Ajanta leave at around 8 am, which makes it difficult if you have to search for a hotel first. You can also fly to Aurangabad direct from Udaipur, Jaipur, and Delhi.

Trains run to Aurangabad from Bombay, but this is a long, awkward journey (eight to nine hours) involving a change at Manmad junction. It's still a popular route, however, and you are required to book four days in advance from Bombay. Jalgaon is the nearest railhead for the Ajanta Caves (56 km, or 35 miles, from Aurangabad), and both Manmad and Jalgaon are linked to Bombay, Delhi, and Calcutta.

Of the overnight buses which ply the winding, mountainous route to Aurangabad, the best choice is the MTDC air-conditioned coach, which leaves Bombay at 8:30 pm (Rs 111). There are frequent buses to both Ellora (29 km, or 18 miles) and Ajanta (106 km, or 66 miles), but you may prefer to take either or both of MTDC's daily, well-conducted full-day Ellora and City Tour and the Ajanta Excursion. The former covers Daulatabad Fort, Grishnewshwar Temple, Ellora Caves, the Aurangabad Caves, tomb at Khuldabad, Bibi-ka-Maqbara, and Panchakki for Rs 15 (ordinary bus), Rs 30 (luxury bus), while the latter covers the Ajanta viewpoint and the Ajanta Caves for Rs 50.

These tours are a very economical way of covering all the main areas of interest in and around the city, and their accompanying guides are all knowledgeable archaeology graduates.

For those who prefer to study India's finest cave temples at leisure, an organized tour can be frustrating. If you are pressed for time, it is possible (but tiring) to see everything in one day. A hired Ambassador taxi (seats four) will cost around Rs 600 for the day, and there are many pleasant picnic spots along the way if you bring a packed lunch.

The best season to visit is October to November, after the monsoon, when the fields brim with sunflower plantations, or December to March, when it is comfortably warm and sunny. As early as April to May, Maharashtra becomes unpleasantly hot, and a supply of mineral water is an absolute necessity.

HOTELS

Aurangabad's best tourist class hotels are the **Welcomgroup Rama International**, ©82340, and the **Ajanta Ambassador Hotel**, ©82211, both centrally located on Airport Road and

moderately priced with pleasant decor and facilities at around Rs 600 a night. Just down the road is the cheaper, recently opened **Hotel Rajdoot**, ©4307, with unremarkable but clean accommodation. In the heart of Aurangabad town is the moderately priced Hotel **Aurangabad Ashok**, ©4520, in Dr Rajendra Prasad Marg. If you are traveling on a budget, eschew the cluster of rather nasty hotels around the railway station and try the MTDC Government Holiday Camp in Station Road, with reliably basic rooms (plus mosquito nets) for Rs 60.

EATING OUT

Both the **Rama International** and the **Ajanta Ambassador** have good Indian/continental restaurants, with almost doting service and evening sitar recitals. The **Mingling Restaurant**, attached to the Hotel Rajdoot, is currently in vogue with Aurangabad's safari suit and pearl set for its excellent Mughlai fare, spotless kitch pastel decor, and crooning *ghazal* singers who perform at both lunch and dinner. By comparison, the adjacent **Shaolin Chinese Restaurant** looks murky and decrepit, but locals swear by its extensive menu of Indianized Chinese food, all laced with chili to please local palates and not a chopstick in sight.

The **Tandoor**, near the railway station on Begumpura Road, is also recent and already very popular for its Punjabi specialties and definitive version of chicken *tikka*. Otherwise try the **Food Walla's Bhoj Restaurant**, on Station Road, for good vegetarian fare.

GETTING AROUND

Aurangabad is a small, rather sleepy, town, with all the useful tourist facilities — railway station, central bus stand, hotels, restaurants, and tourist office — fairly close together. Auto-rickshaws seem to outnumber taxis, and are the best way to negotiate Aurangabad's narrow back-alleys, where the Muslim influence is strongly evident in street-side mosques and *burqa*-clad women. With its better facilities, Aurangabad is perfect as a base for daily excursions to Ajanta and Ellora, and you should plan to spend at least two days here to see everything properly.

SIGHTSEEING

Aurangabad Caves
Few visitors to Aurangabad venture up the stony hillside rock-cleft three kilometers (just under two miles) out of town to see these unfinished, but still magnificent, cave temples. There are 10 of them in all, excavated

by Buddhist monks between the third and the seventh century AD. It's convenient to start with the western group of caves by walking "backwards" from cave 10 to cave 6. Amongst this group, cave 7 is by far the most spectacular, with its central frieze depicting an enormous Siddhartha on the verge of his transformation into Buddha, praying for protection from eight fears — sword, fire, chains, shipwreck, lions, snakes, crazed elephants, and the writhing demons of death. Cave 6 has a curious mixture of Hindu and Buddhist iconography that indicates the gradual absorption of Buddhist thought into Hinduism.

From these caves, it's a rambling 20-minute stroll across to the eastern side of the hill where caves 1 to 5 are located. Cave 4 is the only *chaitya*, or temple, in the series, all the others being *viharas*, or monastery prayer halls.

It is best to travel to the caves by solid Ambassador taxi — the alternative, an auto-rickshaw, is much bumpier. The caves are open from sunrise to 6 pm. A stroll back to Aurangabad is a pleasant finale, and it's easy to find your bearings: just stride across the empty plains towards the white minarets of the Taj-clone, Bibi-ka-Maqbara, and from here you can hire a rickshaw for a Rs 4 ride back into town.

The orthodox Mughal emperor Aurangzeb built the Bibi-ka-Maqbara in 1679 for his wife, known as Rabia Durrani, ordering his architects to construct a masterpiece that would outshine his father Shah Jehan's then recently completed Taj Mahal in Agra. Thrifty even in his grief, Aurangzeb's mausoleum is far less ornamental, costing 300 times less than its immortal rival. Open from sunrise to 10 pm, with a 50 paise entrance fee.

Overlooking Aurangabad's Kaum River in the heart of the city is the **Panchakki**, an impressive pre-Mughal water mill harnessed to operate large grain-grinding stones. It was built in 1624 to commemorate the memory of the Sufi saint Baba Shah Musafir, whose tomb lies nearby. Open from sunrise to 10 pm, with a 50 paise entrance fee.

Aurangabad is famous for its *himroo* shawls, cotton brocade, *bidri* ware, and Aurangabad silk, but the antiquated traditional handloom methods are rapidly disappearing. It's worth paying a visit to one of the few family businesses existing in the city. The most characterful is the Aurangabad Himroo Factory in Shahganj, opposite Gandhi Square, where the owner and arch-weaver, A.H. Qureshi, will explain the technique and mourn the death of the trade,

RIGHT: Carved out of solid rock over a period of some 400 years, the Ellora caves are the most elaborate cave temples in India.

while his spindly fingers blur in the motion of knotting and threading.

Daulatabad Fort

A remarkable medieval fortress towering high on a pyramidal hill above the dusty plains some 13 km (eight miles) from Aurangabad, Daulatabad's eerie beauty is full of references to its former despotic rulers and bloody history. Originally it was the capital of the Yadava dynasty in the thirteenth century, who called it Devagiri, or "hill of the gods". It caught the quixotic imagination of the mad Delhi sultan, Muhammed Tughlaq, who captured the for-

tress, renaming it Daulatabad, or "fortunate city", for his new capital. His unfortunate subjects were forced to walk 1,100 km (680 miles) here from Delhi in 1327; then, only 17 years later, he realized the impracticality of the location and marched the remaining survivors back again.

The medieval equivalent of Fort Knox, Daulatabad is surrounded by six kilometers (3.7 miles) of thick walls, rows of terrifying spikes at its entrance to deter charging elephants, a huge moat that once seethed with hungry crocodiles, and dead-end passages where trapped intruders ended their lives under vat-loads of boiling oil.

With its labyrinth of musty passages, Daulatabad is fascinating to wander through, but bring a torch to avoid stumbling in its dark stairwells. Just inside the entrance gate is the 60-m (197-ft) -high Chand Minar pillar, built in 1435 as a monument of victory. From the dried-out moat, it's a half-hour climb to the top, passing the blue-tiled Chini Mahal Palace where prestigious nobles were kept prisoner. On the hill's crest stands a formidable cannon engraved with Aurangzeb's name, and there's a black, spiralling pit once used to hurl burning coals down on to invaders. Open from sunrise to sunset.

Aurangzeb's Grave

When Aurangzeb died in 1707, he was buried according to his instructions in a bare earth grave open to the sky at Khuldabad ("heavenly abode"), 26 km (16 miles) from Aurangabad on the route to Ellora. Once a fortified village (Aurangzeb built the battlements around it), its most interesting monument is the Karbala, or holy shrine of Deccan Muslims, which contains the remains of many historical figures. In his will, Aurangzeb stated that his funeral costs were to be covered only by the four and a half rupees earned from the sale of caps sewn by the emperor himself. As a final request, the money earned from the sale of his hand-copied Korans was to be divided amongst holy men on the day of his death. It would have displeased Aurangzeb to see the decorative marble screen that surrounds his grave — a donation from the wealthy Nizam of Hyderabad. As contrived as this austerity must have seemed, it came to symbolize Aurangzeb's troubled legacy, for although his descendants were to rule fitfully for another century and a half, Aurangzeb was the last of the Great Mughals. Standing in this tranquil sunlit spot, you may find your musings on this theme interrupted by a meaningful cough by the elderly mosque keeper with a carrot-colored beard, a well-thumbed Koran, and a monetary gleam in his eyes.

Ellora

Some 29 km (18 miles) from Aurangabad are the most elaborate cave temples in India. Although Buddhist monks began excavating in the seventh century, the site grew to include Hindu and Jain temples as the Buddhist faith waned in popularity toward the end of the seventh century. There are 34 caves — 12 Buddhist (AD 600–800), 17 Hindu (around AD 900), and five Jain (AD 800–1000) — and they are numbered in that order as you progress from south to north.

It's convenient to start with the Buddhist caves first, though these are the least interesting. Ten of these can be traced to the Mahayana schism of Buddhism by their contemplative images of Buddha vilified by the more orthodox relic-worshiping Hinayana sect which was responsible for building caves 1 and 7. The wealthy merchants who financed the construction of these caves did so in the belief that their pious contributions helped them to accumulate religious merit. Cave 10 is the only *chaitya* of the group, with its immense Buddha on a lion throne, surrounded by attendants and fronted by a nine-meter (29.5-ft) -high stupa.

If you're on the MTDC tour you'll be whisked speedily past most of the Hindu temples, stopping to admire in detail only the most spectacular. This is cave 16, the Kailasha Temple, named after Shiva's mountain home in the Himalayas. It was built by 7,000 stonecutters, working in squadrons constantly over a period of 150 years during the Rashtrakuta dynasty in the eighth century, an expenditure in manpower and rupees equal to that of conducting a major protracted war.

Carved from a single rock as large as the Parthenon in Athens, the Kailasha Temple is an awesome feat of engineering: begun from the top (much of which is now open to the sky) and chiseled down to the floor, creating arches, passageways, towers, and ornate friezes along the way. A bridge at the entrance leads to an en-

but none are particularly good. The best (and nearest to the caves) is the **Kailash Hotel,** ©43.

Ajanta

It's a long, winding drive from Aurangabad to the Ajanta caves (104 km, or 65 miles), but at journey's end is one of the world's most fascinating collections of wall paintings and frescoes. Unfortunately, the wall paintings are becoming progressively bleached by exposure to the atmosphere and, despite efforts by experts to preserve them with sealing fluids, are slowly fading away. The light wreaks havoc with the delicate colors, so the caves are kept in murky

closed courtyard, where immense flagstaffs and stone elephants surround the main two-storied shrine and Nandi pavilion. The cool, sandalwood-scented interior chambers are filled with ornate Dravidian sculptures depicting stories from the *Ramayana.*

The Jain temples are a short stroll to the north. Although noteworthy for their delicacy and detail, the Jain temples appear rather anemic after the energetic brilliance of the Kailasha Temple. The "Assembly Hall of Indra", cave 32, is the most interesting of this group, with its simple ground floor enlivened by curving lotus reliefs on the ceiling, and the upper story is notable for its decorative friezes and lotus-design columns. The shrine is dedicated to Mahavira, the last of the 24 Tirthankas and founder of the Jain religion.

There are several hotels near Ellora if you want to spend more time looking at the caves,

darkness. Come prepared with a strong flashlight, or pay the "lighting charge" at the entrance. For a small sum, a wizened attendant in a Nehru cap will try to reflect rays of sunlight into the cave using a sheet of corrugated iron. If you're not with a tour, it's advisable to hire a "deluxe" guide from the entrance (the bone fide ones wear accredited badges).

The 30 caves chiseled into Ajanta's crescent-shaped granite gorge represent the highest artistic achievement of the Buddhist monks who arrived here in the second century BC to establish a monastic retreat. Most of the caves were completed by the second century AD; the others date from the fifth to the seventh century, before

ABOVE: Entrance to the Ellora caves.
OPPOSITE: Daulatabad Fort has an eerie beauty and a bloody history.

the site was mysteriously abandoned for nearby Ellora. For hundreds of years, the caves were obscured under thick foliage, and this accounts for the near-perfect state of preservation in which they were found.

The caves are a perfect showcase for understanding the progression of Buddhist art and thought. The early Hinayana school disapproved of earthly pleasures, believing that the best way to attain salvation was through pain. Caves 8, 9, 10, 12, and 13 date from the older Hinayana period, and images of Buddha are notably absent. In the second century BC, the more worldly Mahayana school's liberal ideas

Cave 4 is the largest *vihara* (residence) cave, supported by 28 pillars. Along with caves 17, 19, and 26, it has the best sculptures in the group. The oldest cave is cave 10. The caves are open from 9:30 am to 5:30 pm.

The best local accommodation is five kilometers (three miles) away in Fardapur, with a choice between the **Guest House**, ©4874, and the **Holiday Resort**, ©4713, both of which offer cheap, clean rooms and meals. The tourist hostel directly opposite the caves has extremely surly staff, and it's restaurant should not be trusted with anything more complex than fresh-lime sodas.

shocked Hinayana Buddhists to the core, but created a renaissance in Indian art. Here the frescoes are full of Brueghel-like scenes, far more diverting than the central theme of the Ajanta caves, the life and times of Buddha. This more realistic and sensual art reached its zenith under the Gupta dynasty, AD 320—647.

All the caves at Ajanta are monolithic: scooped out to create a complex granite husk complete with pillars, façades, dormitories, and galleries of sculpted Buddhas, all carved from the same piece of rock. Beneath the frescoes are layers of clay, cow dung, powdered rice husk, and lime plaster. Crushed pebbles, ochre, and ground lapis lazuli were used as colors, and applied with squirrel-hair brushes. Cave 1 is the largest and most impressive of the Ajanta caves, with the best frescoes and relief carvings. Caves 2, 16, 17, and 19 also contain beautiful frescoes.

GENERAL INFORMATION

Government of India Tourist Office, Krishna Vilas, Station Road, ©4017. **Government of Maharashtra Tourist Office**, Holiday Camp, Aurangabad ©4713.

GUJARAT

WOVEN COLORS AND CREEDS

Few travelers venture to Gujarat, yet the state is saturated with historical attractions and, as a

The Ajanta caves boast one of the world's most fascinating collections of wall paintings and frescoes.

relatively untrodden tourist trail, has retained much of its traditional lifestyle. Gujarat is a colorful mixture of modern and old-age cultures. In Gujarat's capital, Ahmedabad—one of India's most highly developed commercial cities — the whole city grinds to a halt during the siesta hours from noon to 4 pm, and camels continue to traipse its main streets as they have done for centuries. Rural Gujarat appears barely touched by the twentieth century — villagers still wear traditional dress and practice skilled crafts, particularly weaving and wood carving.

Gujarat contains many of the ancient sites of Hindu mythology. The story goes that the Som-

With the expansion of the British Empire, mainland Gujarat was governed by the British, while the southern Kathiawar peninsula, now known as Saurashtra, had 282 princely states in an area roughly the size of Ireland.

Mahatma Gandhi, who was born in Gujarat's Porbander state, believed that his penchant for pacifism and social reform was an inherent Gujarati trait and took the motto "non-violence is the supreme religion" from the Jains. More noticeably, Gujaratis are renowned for their shrewd business acumen, and many have emigrated and now thrive in communities around the world.

nath shore temple in the south was built by Soma, the Moon God, to mark the creation of the universe. Legend also places Lord Krishna's kingdom at Dwarka, on Gujarat's west coast. Its first communities appeared with the Indus Valley civilization in about 2500 BC, and the world's earliest Asian and Western literature refers to the value of Gujarat's trade goods. Anti-caste Buddhists and Jains ruled until the end of the eighth century, and the latter are still a dominant force in Gujarat today, being responsible for the state's almost total vegetarianism. During India's Middle Ages, these peaceful cultures were invaded by the feudal Hindu Rajputs, and for several centuries much of the present state fell under first Muslim, then Mughal, rule. Opportunistic Portuguese traders established key ports in Damen and Diu on the southern coast, retaining possession until 1961.

A good mini-tour of Gujarat begins with **Ahmedabad** and covers the main destinations of the Jain pilgrimage centers of **Palitana** and **Junagadh**, the **Sasan-Gir Wildlife Sanctuary** and **Somnath Temple** in the south, and palace-filled **Vadodara** in the southeast. Adventurous travelers can explore the northern **Rann of Kutch**, a salt desert inhabited by the colorful nomadic Malderi tribe. Most of Gujarat's hotels are inexpensive and simple, but are subject to a sliding state imposed luxury tax that can add 30 percent to the bill.

WHEN TO GO

Gujarat has an abundance of fairs and festivals throughout the year, but it's well worth coinciding with the **Makara Sankranti Kite Festival** on January 14, or the **Navrati Festival** which celebrates the goddess Amba, held on the cusp of September to October, with nine days of impromptu street dances and *bhavai* folk theater.

The mild winter months from November to March are the best times for Gujarat, although the monsoon season has its own charm. Bring light clothes for the day and a sweater for winter evenings.

AHMEDABAD: GATEWAY TO GUJARAT

Ahmedabad's congested urban sprawl con-

tains the husk of an original city built by the Muslim ruler Ahmed Shah during the fifteenth century, and much grand Islamic architecture still stands. Toward the end of the sixteenth century, Ahmedabad had a thousand mosques, cenotaphs, and tombs, all surrounded by carefully kept gardens. In 1615, Sir Thomas Roe, the British emissary to Emperor Jehangir in Delhi, described Ahmedabad as being "as large as London, the handsomest city in Hindustan and perhaps the world". It was here that Mahatma Gandhi founded his *ashram* and later launched his famous Salt March to protest British hegemony. Now an industrial center plagued by pollution and noise, Ahmedabad is no longer a beautiful city, but visitors will find it has many pockets of unexpected charm. It has fine museums and boasts a cultivated patronage of the arts that is quite unique in India. Beyond the

remains of the medieval wall and its stone gateways, in the Byzantine confusion of Ahmedabad's old city, are many sixteenth-century *havelis*, so delicately carved they resemble wooden cobwebs, and the *pols*, or living quarters, of the artisan and merchant communities. At almost any hour, weavers, hand-block printers, and wood-workers can be seen in these musty lanes toiling over their work.

Despite Gandhi's legacy, communal enmities run deep in Ahmedabad, which has seen grisly clashes between its Muslim and Hindu communities in the old city.

HOW TO GET THERE

There are daily flights to Ahmedabad's airport (eight kilometers, or five miles, away) from Bombay, Delhi, Calcutta, Jaipur, and Jodphur, and you can also fly there from Vadodara, Bangalore, Madras, Hyderabad, Aurangabad, and Srinagar. From Ahmedabad there are air connections to Gujarat's main cities, notably Vadodara, Keshod, Jamnagar, Rajkot, Porbandar, Bhuj, and Bhavnagar. Daily trains run there from Bombay (the 492-km, or 306-mile, trip takes nine hours by fast mail train and 15 hours by normal service). If you have the stamina, it's fun to experience a lengthy train ride at least once, and the Delhi to Ahmedabad (626 km, or 390 miles, 24 hours) has a drawn-out charm. It stops at Ajmer, Jaipur, and Mount Abu, and passes through dry desert tundra, enlivened by clusters of nomadic camels, brilliant splashes of dandified tribal dress, vendors who wander through the swaying train, and itinerant musicians who jump aboard and sing evocative Rajasthani *ragas*.

There are bus services from Bombay, Mount Abu, and Udaipur, and from Ahmedabad to destinations throughout the state.

WHERE TO STAY

There are only two good hotels, both in the heart of the city overlooking the river and frequently booked out. The **Ritz Hotel**, Lal Darwaja, ©353-6737, is a quaint establishment, originally an eighteenth-century family home, set in a secluded garden with prompt service and characterful, air-conditioned rooms. Inexpensive. **Hotel Cama**, Khanpur Road, ©25281-9, is pleasant and modern, with efficient staff, car rental, a liquor shop, good chemist, and a restaurant that serves delicious lunchtime *thalis*. Rates: moderate. Otherwise, try either the **Riveria**

OPPOSITE and ABOVE LEFT: Pockets of unexpected charm are found in the bustling city of Ahmedabad, such as the Manek Chowk market area where sacred cows wander at will.

Hotel, ©24201-7 or the **Ambassador Hotel**, ©392244, in the cheap to moderate range, both on Khanpur Road. If you're on a low budget, try the **Circuit House**, Shahibagh, ©65033. The **Gandhi Ashram Guest House**, ©867652, six kilometers (3.7 miles) away opposite Gandhi's Ashram, is a pleasant option, with peaceful, balconied rooms set in a small garden for Rs 75 to Rs 100 plus 10 percent tax a night, with a good restaurant attached.

EATING OUT

Ahmedabad's best evening entertainment and authentic Gujarati cuisine is a 15-minute drive south of the city center, at the mock-Gujarati **Vishalla** village, on Sarkhej Road. It's best to arrive no later than 8:30 pm, and then to wander about the decorated mud huts where artisans pot, weave, and make *paan*. The excellent Vechaar Utensils Museum situated here houses a remarkable collection of 2,500 metalware utensils collected from all over Gujarat — including betel nut cutters, hookahs, guns, unique vessels for milking camels, and dowry items — and stays open until 10 pm.

To the accompaniment of folk music or a traditional puppet show, dinner is taken in true cross-legged Gujarati style, served on a brass *thali*. A superb feast of subtly spiced vegetable dishes, fragrant rice, lightly fried *puris*, and chutneys, followed by mugs of sweet buttermilk, and outrageously sweet *jalebis* for dessert. Lunch is equally pleasant, served from 11 am to 1 pm.

Both the **Ritz** and the **Cama** have good restaurants, but Ahmedabad's modest, proletarian-style eating houses are more authentic. The best of these are the popular **Hotel Chetna**, next to the Krishna Talkies on Relief Road, with all-you-can-eat *thalis* for Rs 20, **Hotel Sabar** (opposite the Cama), and **Gopi**, near the Town Hall.

Gujaratis are usually strict vegetarians. Popular dishes include *undhyoo*, a winter dish of aubergines, potato, broad beans, and sweet potato buried under a hot fire, *srikand*, hot *puris* eaten with rich candied yogurt, and *khaman dhokla*, a chick-pea flour cake.

Gujarat makes India's best ice-cream, crammed with fruit and nuts, and with unusual seasonal favorites such as custard apple and cashew. Gujaratis have a fetish for it, and there's a parlor on every block. For the best range, try **Havmor** on Relief Road, or the Vadilal Soda **Fountain**, Bhadra.

SIGHTSEEING

The domes and minarets of the Muslim mosques, pavilions, and monuments built during the

fifteenth century are dotted throughout central Ahmedabad. Built of local honey-colored stone, these structures are a fusion of austere Islamic design and ornately decorative Hindu art, and mark the birth of the Indo-Saracenic style. The most beautiful are within the heart of the city. **Rani Sipri's Mosque and Tomb** (1514) is believed to have been built by a wife of Sultan Mehmood Begada after he executed her son in a fit of anger. Nearby is the **Rani Rupmati's Mosque** (1440), with its exquisite traceries and *jali* screens.

The gracious Friday mosque, **Jumma Masjid** (1424), was built by Ahmed Shah, the city's founder. According to local myth, the large

black stone slab near the main door once formed the base of a Jain idol, which was buried upside down and trampled on to express distaste for other religions. Just outside the mosque's east gate is **Ahmed Shah's Tomb**. Women are refused entry to the central chamber. The tombs of his queens are across the street, but almost impossible to find in the dense bazaars.

Sidi Saiyad's Mosque (1430), close to the river end of Relief Road, was built by one of Ahmed Shah's slaves. Its pierced marble latticework arches are alone worth coming to Ahmedabad to see. Their design and workmanship outshine even the windows of the Taj Mahal in Agra. Unfortunately, the mosque now forms part of a traffic island.

Also a Muslim creation, and unique to Gujarat, are the ornately carved *baolis* (step wells), resembling watery amphitheaters. The most beautiful is the **Adalaj Vav**, built in 1499 by Queen Rudabai of the Waghela dynasty, with its richly carved ornamental friezes and five-story structure, 19 km (12 miles) from the city. Closer at hand is the **Dada Hari** *baoli* in town (closed for siesta 1 to 4 pm), with spiral staircases and decorative friezes.

Just outside the Delhi Gate, to the north of the old city, lies the white marble **Hatheesingh Temple**, a well-patronized Jain citadel erected in 1848 by a wealthy merchant.

For restful strolls, the **Kankaria** artificial lake, almost 1.6 km (a mile) long, is four kilometers (2.5 miles) southeast of the city. Built by the Sultan Qutb-ud-Din in 1451, it has an island palace where Emperor Jehangir and his beautiful empress Nur Jehan came to escape from the dust of Ahmedabad. Today, it's refreshingly peaceful, with lakeside cafés, boating, and a well-stocked zoo. The **Sarkej** monuments, 10 km (six miles) southwest of the city, make a pleasant excursion. This was once an isolated oasis around a stone-stepped *baoli*. The remnants of the palace, pavilions, mosque, and tombs, built by Sultan Mehmud Shah Beghara and his queen Raj Bai in around 1460, are of an elegant, unembellished design.

Gandhi's Ashram

The Sabarmati Ashram (six kilometers, or 3.7 miles, from Ahmedabad) was founded by India's most famous Gujarati, Mahatma Gandhi (1869—1948) in 1915. He moved here two years later with his wife, Kasturba, and remained until 1930. This was where he launched his great civil disobedience movement which led to the freeing of India after two and a half centuries of British rule. It was from here that Gandhi began his famous Dandi march in 1930 to protest the British Salt Law, which effectively barred Indians from the salt business. Of all the memorials throughout India associated with Gandhi, this small collection of whitewashed thatched cottages and personal possessions is the most moving. Open from dawn until the close of the nightly sound and light show (conducted in Hindi, Gujarati, and English on different nights), the Ashram contains a pictorial history of Gandhi's life, a handicrafts center, and a spinning wheel factory. The English sound and light show is held on Wednesdays, Fridays, and Sundays at 8:30 pm.

Pols and Pigeons

Old Ahmedabad is thick with bazaars and tiny shops selling a wonderful array of treasures. **Manek Chowk** is the old city's main marketplace, a bustling mêlée where merchants sell an array of embroidered beadwork, silver jewelry, antique carved wooden doorways, trays

of spices, quaint stuffed toys, regimental silver, and brass teapots. For serious shoppers, this is where the best variety of Gujarat's distinctive fabrics is to be found. Look especially for hand-painted or wood-blocked prints in the traditional black, maroon, red, and ochre patterns, *bandhana* (tie-dyed) silks and cottons, *zari* (gold) work; and the unusual patola silk sari, a traditional design woven with tie-dyed threads much coveted by Gujarati girls and costing anything from Rs 2,000 to Rs 30,000 depending on the quality. If you're uncertain as to whether you are getting a bargain or being thoroughly hoodwinked, try either **Gurjari**

Handicrafts Emporium or **Bangshree**, opposite Vidhyapith, both back in the commercial part of the city on Ashram Road, which offer a good range of traditional products at government prices.

This is Ahmedabad's oldest residential area, divided into confusingly dense pols or culs de sac, which house extended families or clans. Ask directions for the **Doshiwada-ni-pol**, where the most beautiful of the old *havelis* are found. Often only one room wide, they can be as high as five stories and are covered with beautiful carvings. Sadly, these are rapidly being dismantled and sold as antiques or placed in museums.

Ahmedabad is a city of mosques, temples and monuments. OPPOSITE: Jami Masjid, known as the Friday mosque. ABOVE: Hutheesingh Temple.

In this area you'll see bird-feeding squares, called parabdis, where the nature-respecting Jains throw grain to the pigeons. In this most dense part of the old city, it's common to see men wearing the distinctive Gujarati dress — the white, pin-tucked and embroidered tunic worn to almost girlish effect — and *burqa*-clad women.

Museums

Ahmedabad's museums are wonderful, though they tend to be closed during the siesta hours and on state holidays. The best is the **Sarabhais' Calico Museum**, a rare collection of textiles

tribal costumes, decorations, and crafts (open 9 to 11 am, 4 to 7 pm, closed Wednesdays), and the **Tribal Museum** in Gujarat Vidyapith, Ashram Road (open weekdays 4:30 to 5:30 pm), provide a good introduction to Gujarati culture and mythology.

The **N.C. Mehta Museum**, housed in Le Corbusier's Sanskar Kendra Municipal Museum, Paldi, has a fine collection of Indian miniature paintings. Open Tuesday to Sunday, 11 am to noon, 3 to 5 pm. The **Vechaar Utensils Museum** in the Vishalla village (see EATING OUT, page 217) is open Monday to Saturday, 5 to 11 pm, Sunday 5 to 10 pm.

dating to the seventeenth century housed in the gardens of the family mansion in Shahibag, the old elite Civil Lines. There's also an extensive reference library on textiles which can be seen on request. Open April—June, 8:30 to 10:30 am, July to March, 11 am to noon and 3 to 5 pm, open daily, except Wednesdays and public holidays. The Sarabhais are the barons of India's textile industry, a talented Jain family who made their fortune during the cotton boom last century, and live in great style in the leafy compound surrounding the museum. The stately old Sarabhai mansion can be visited, and is now a center for Hindu studies.

The **Shreyas Folk Art Museum**, off Circular Road, which displays a unique array of

ABOVE: Textile factory at Aurangabad.
ABOVE RIGHT: Darwaza Market, Ahmedabad.

OUT OF AHMEDABAD: LOTHAL

The famous archaeological ruins at Lothal, 87 km (54 miles) from Ahmedabad, are well worth a day's excursion. It was once an important Harappan port which traded with Eygpt and Mesopotamia in around 2400 to 1500 BC, and is thus the earliest known civilization in the subcontinent. Other major Harappan sites are in Pakistan at Mohenjo-Daro and Harappa. Discovered in 1954, excavations reveal a systematically planned port city, with a scientific knowledge of the tides applied to its underground drains, planned streets and houses with baths and fireplaces, burial grounds, and dockyards. Terracotta figurines, ivory and shell objects, beads, bangles and semi-precious stones, painted bowls, bronze and copper implements, and seals with Indus Valley script are on display at an excellent on-site museum.

GENERAL INFORMATION

Government conducted tours covering the city's sights leave each day from the Lal Darwaja bus-stand at 8 am and 2:30 pm, costing Rs 12. These are useful if you have very little time and for getting your bearings. Contact the Tourist Office for details on their longer (four or five days) tours around north and south Gujarat and Saurashtra, costing about Rs 450 to Rs 700. **Tourist Corporation of Gujarat**, H.K. House, Ashram Road, ©449683, Open 10:30 am to 1:30 pm, 2 to 5:30 pm.

There are also tourist counters at the airport and railway station.

JAIN FOOTSTEPS

PALITANA

The most revered of the Jains' five temple-covered sacred hills, Palitana's nearby **Shatrunjaya Hill** is a marble jungle of some 863 magnificent Jain temples, some of which date back to the eleventh century. The other sacred hills are at Girnar, near Junagadh, Mount Abu in Rajasthan, Parasnath in Bihar, and Gwalior in Madhya Pradesh.

Jainism became a powerful force in the sixth century BC, largely in reaction to strict, caste-bound Hinduism. It was founded by Prince Mahavira (559–527 BC), the 24th and last Jain Tirthankara, or saint, who became a *jina*, or conqueror of spiritual knowledge, and his disciples, Jains.

The temple complex, known as the "abode of the gods", is a marvel of complex architecture, each temple within a *tuk*, or enclosure, and richly ornamented with carved spires and towers.

The temple chambers are frequently thronged with Jain pilgrims who prostrate themselves before the rows of impassive-looking idols, whose eyes out gleam fiercely in the gloom. Wiry, shaven-headed priests administer to the temple duties and keep a watchful eye out for tourists who neglect to leave their shoes at the door. A stern sign at the entrance to the complex forbids menstruating women to enter, lest they defile the temple's purity. Largest and most ornate temple is the Chaumukh temple, built by a wealthy banker in 1618 in the hope of saving his soul. But most pilgrims make a bee-line for the most sacred temple, dedicated to Sri Adishwara, the first Tirthankara, whose image is studded with gold and enormous diamonds. An unusual addition is the Angar Pir, a Moslem shrine, where childless women make offerings of miniature cradles and pray for children.

The magnificence of these temples is due largely to the Jain belief that reincarnation and salvation can be influenced by, amongst other things, temple building and *ahimsa*, reverence for all life. The truly devout are not only complete vegetarians, excluding even eggs and milk from their diet, but also wear white gauze masks to prevent the accidental swallowing of small insects.

It's best to make Palitana an early morning expedition, before the heat makes climbing the four kilometers (2.5 miles) of steps unbearable. At dawn, the route throngs with white-clad pilgrims, the aged and disabled carried in *dolis*, string sedan chairs, which are also utilized by exhausted tourists. Priests hand a ticket to each leaving visitor who, after an hour's tiring descent, can exchange it for a restorative breakfast of sweetmeats and sugary tea. Open from 7 am to 7 pm, when even the priests withdraw to leave the gods to themselves.

GENERAL INFORMATION

Palitana, 215 km (134 miles) from Ahmedabad, has many resthouses, but these are exclusively for Jain pilgrims. There's a choice of either the state-run **Hotel Sumeru Toran**, ©227, on Station Road, or the new **Hotel Shravak**, ©328, opposite the bus station, both offering a variety of rooms under Rs 100 and cheap *thalis* at mealtimes. If hunger strikes at odd hours, try the popular snack alley next to the Shravak.

It's far preferable to stay in the larger port city of Bhavnagar, 56 km (35 miles) away, at the **Nilambag Palace Hotel**, ©24340. This local maharaja's former palace has charming, inexpensive, period suites.

Bhavnagar, 244 km (152 miles) from Ahmedabad, has the nearest airport, with regular train and bus services for visiting Palitana. From Ahmedabad, there's a train which takes between nine and 11 hours and stops just before Palitana, at Sihor. Express buses take four hours.

JUNAGADH

A picturesque city of much archaeological importance, Junagadh is rather off the beaten track, but of great significance to Jains for the sacred, temple-covered **Girnar Hill** nearby, which is no less impressive than Palitana, and a much gentler climb at only 2,000 steps! Betrothed couples come to worship at the topmost Amba Mata temple to ensure a harmonious marriage. It's a good place to spend a day before continuing on to Sasan-Gir wildlife sanctuary, 58 km (36 miles) away.

Junagadh is thought to date back to around 250 BC, when the Mauryan emperor Ashoka ordered his edicts inscribed on a boulder, which can still be seen on the way to Girnar Hill. On Junagadh's outskirts lies **Uparkot**, a walled city with its own palace, Jami Masjid, and Buddhist caves with spiral staircases, built by the militaristic Chudasamal Rajputs during the ninth century. It was the scene of an epic 12-year siege over the heart of a beautiful potter's daughter who rejected the advances of a neighboring king and married the Rajput ruler of Junagadh instead. In 1094, the Junagadh raja was slain — in a Pyrrhic victory, since the coveted woman committed sati shortly afterwards.

In town, see the **Rang Mahal**, the nineteenth-century palace now used as government offices, in which the dog-loving Nawab of Junagadh staged canine weddings and gave each of his 800 dogs its own room with a telephone and servant. At the time of Partition, the Nawab wished to have his tiny state merged with Pakistan, and having failed to do so, lived in disgraced exile. Within the palace is the **Durbar Hall** museum, with palace relics, weaponry, and a portrait gallery. Open 9:30 to 11:45 am, 3 to 5:30 pm. The tourist office is right next door.

Also see the ornate **Maqbara**, the royal mausoleum, with minarets and spiral staircases; the **Sakkar Bagh** museum and zoo; and the **Rupayatan Institute for Handicrafts** where craftsmen work on traditional embroidery and patchwork.

GENERAL INFORMATION

There are a number of small, cheap hotels in Junagadh, but none is very good. Try **Hotel Vaibhav**, close to the bus station, which has a mirrored dining room with good *thalis* for Rs 10 and excellent mango milkshakes. The nearest airport is Keshod, 47 km (29 miles) away, with flights from Bombay and Ahmedabad. The *Somnath Mail* runs between Ahmedabad and Veraval/Somnath via Junagadh, a 13-hour journey. Buses connect Junagadh with Ahmedabad, Vereval/Somnath, Palitana, and the Sasan-Gir.

SOMNATH

According to Hindu myth, Somnath Temple, which overlooks the Arabian Sea, was built by Soma, the Moon God, at the dawn of creation. Archaeologists date the shore temple to around the first century AD.

Although destroyed and rebuilt more than seven times, the present temple retains much of its legendary beauty. By the sixth century, Somnath was renowned as the richest temple in India, and consequently was sacked by the Mahmud of Ghazni, who required a vast caravanserai of elephants, camels, and mules to carry all the gold and precious ornaments. Over the next 700 years, the temple was repeatedly smashed, then rebuilt by devout priests. The Mughal Aurangzeb, vowing to crush the "heretical" temple, powdered it to dust in 1706. Only in 1950 was it restored to its present state.

Somnath contains one of the 12 *jyotirlingas*, or Shiva shrines, in India and has two major festivals: the vibrant **Kartika Poornima**, a village fair with traditional dance, theater, and chanting of vedic hymns, held in November/December, and the **Mahashivratri**, held in February/March, which attracts hundreds of thousands of Indian pilgrims.

It's best to visit at sunrise or sunset, when the priests perform an elaborate ritual to worship Shiva.

The nearby government-run **Prabhas Patan Museum** is very disorganized, but contains ancient relics of the various versions of Somnath Temple. Open 9 am to noon, 3 to 6 pm daily, except Wednesday.

Somnath has only one decent hotel — the **Hotel Mayuram**, Triveni Road (©Prabhas Patan 362, 268). Somnath's only source of tourist information is the Manager of the Somnath Temple Trust whose office is next to the temple.

SASAN-GIR

One of India's finest wildlife sanctuaries, set in 1,295 sq km (500 sq miles) of lush deciduous forest, the Sasan-Gir is the final refuge of the rare Asiatic lion, once found throughout the Middle East and both north and east India, but hunted as a coveted trophy item during the British Raj era. The famine of 1899 so decimated the Asiatic lion population that Lord Curzon cancelled his shoot at Gir, where he was the guest of the Nawab of Junagadh. Curzon persuaded the Nawab to protect the remaining lions, who now number around 200. The sanctuary is open from mid-October to mid-June, but the cool season between November and February is the best time for sighting the lions, who generally retire to the forest's interior during the summer. The forest also has wild boar, bears, panthers, antelopes, hyenas, leopards, and the unusual Indian *chowsingha* (antelope) whose buck has four horns. The monsoon months of July to September are good for seeing almost 200 varieties of birds.

The Gir Forestry Department organizes "lion shows" by guide-conducted jeeps, and ensures that lions can be viewed at close range by sending trackers on early morning missions to stake out large groups of lions. Shows take place each Sunday between 3 and 6 pm, and can be booked from the Forest Lodge between 4 and 6 pm at Rs 15. If you wish to explore the sanctuary on your own, it's possible to hire a jeep and guide at the rate of Rs 2.25 per kilometer (0.62 mile). Within the Gir Forest are the scenic **Tulishyam Hot Springs**, 90 km (56 miles) from the sanctuary's entrance, where you can bathe in the natural sulfur springs and, if desired, find cheap accommodation at the Holiday Camp Lodge.

GENERAL INFORMATION

There are two lodges, both of which are state-run and inexpensive, with good facilities. The three-star **Lion Safari Lodge**, ©21 has upper-story rooms overlook the reserve. Otherwise try the **Forest Guest House**.

The Gujarat State Tourism Corporation offers a special two-day package tour to Sasan-Gir, which includes reception at Keshod, 90 km (56 miles) away, the nearest airport (an 80-minute flight from Bombay), accommodation at the Forest Lodge, sanctuary tour, and visit to Somnath. The Government Gujarat Tourist Office, Dhanraj Mahal, C. Shivaji Road, Bombay, ©202-6886, will supply further details.

VADODARA (BARODA)

Located 120 km (75 miles) southeast of Ahmedabad, the former capital of the vastly wealthy Gaekwads (whose name means "protector of cows") of Baroda is a city of sprawling parks and lakes, palaces and museums, with a campus atmosphere. Predictably, perhaps, its charms are muted by ugly industrial expansion. It's a good base for excursions to the beautiful ruined fort of **Champaner,** 47 km (29 miles) away.

SIGHTSEEING

On the city's periphery is the **Lakshmi Vilas Palace**, a Gothic-domed, Indo-Saracenic extravaganza with a 150-m (500-ft) facade. It was completed in 1890 for the Maharaja of Sayajirao, who campaigned against purdah and tried to introduce a form of separation for unhappily married women. His legendary wealth included the Baroda collection of jewels, a pearl carpet studded with diamonds, rubies, emeralds, and woven with gold, and thick gold anklets worn by the palace elephants. Unfortunately, the palace and its fabulous collection of armor and sculpture is rarely open to the public.

Back in the city, the **Baroda Museum and Art Gallery** in the **Sayaji Park** (complete with a zoo, miniature train, and large lake) has an excellent collection of Mughal miniatures and European paintings. Open Fridays and Sundays from 9:30 am to 4:45 pm, and Saturdays, 10 am to 5:45 pm. Nearby is the **Maharaja Fateh Singh Museum**, the Gaekwad's lavish art collection, which includes works by Titian, Raphael, Murillo, and displays of Graeco-Roman, Chinese, Japanese, and Indian paintings. Situated within the palace grounds, the museum is open Tuesdays to Sundays from 9 am to noon, 3 to 6 pm from July to March, 4 to 7 pm from April to June.

Old Baroda's faded splendor is best appreciated by visiting several of the Gaekwad's smaller palaces scattered around the city, the most impressive being the **Pratap Vilas Palace**, now used as the Railway Staff College. The **Maharaja Sayajirao University of Vadodara** is a grand palisade of Gothic-inspired architecture leading to Sayaji Park, with a renowned Arts faculty that organizes regular evening performances by India's top artistes. Its Art College is considered one of India's best. Other places to see are the **Kirti Mandir**, the Gaekwad's family vault, and the exquisite **Tambekarwada**, a four-story *haveli* covered with murals. Managed by the Archaeological Survey of India, it is open daily and hard to find, so obtain directions from the Tourist Office opposite the railway station. The **Naulakhi** well, just near the Lakshmi Vilas Palace, is a good example of Gujarati *baoli*, or step-well. The Islamic **Maqbara** has beautiful filigree carvings, and the **Sarsagar Lake** is good for boating.

Some 47 km (29 miles) northeast of Vadodara, the ruins of **Champaner**, Sultan Mahmud Shah Begda's fortified fifteenth-century palace-town, and its grand Jami Masjid mosque lie on the flame-red Pavagadh Hill. It's a sight worth seeing, and it's possible to stay at Champaner's Holiday Home.

General Information

Vadodara connects by air with Delhi and Bombay, and by rail with Ahmedabad, Bombay, and Delhi. The only five-star accommodation is the **Welcomgroup Vadodara**, R.C. Dutt Road, ©323232, with a swimming pool, excellent Mughali restaurant, and a good travel counter. **Hotel Surya Palace**, ©328213, is moderately priced, and comfortable with an excellent restaurant for Gujarati *thalis* (great value for Rs 25).

Calcutta
and
the East

CALCUTTA

Calcutta offers unexpected charms, perhaps all the more striking when contrasted with the image of impoverishment it is more widely associated with. It is easily the country's most fascinating city, a unique and compelling mixture of Raj-era relics, Bengali culture and communist politics. The state capital of West Bengal, it is one of the world's largest cities with a population of more than 11 million people.

Once Calcutta was the second city of the British empire after London, and it remains above all a monument to imperial decline, for it is the most British of all Indian cities. It has a legacy of patrician English Classical buildings, fine museums, the university, the prestigious Royal Asiatic society, the Botanical Gardens and its Pall Mall stretch of exclusive social clubs, not to mention the Edwardian spoonerisms so beloved by the local English press.

Calcutta is the action-packed center of the exuberant Bengali culture, and here literature, politics and the visual and performing arts thrive as the city's ruling passions. The Bengalis are a civilized, gregarious people, given to volatile outbursts but quick to smile and offer their help and hospitality. Calcutta is India's "Left Bank" with its "café society, Bohemian airs, political argument and love of gossip," noted Trevor Fishlock, the author of *India File*.

The city both mocks and fulfills a prophecy, apparently attributed to Lenin, that the "road to world revolution lies through Peking, Shanghai and Calcutta." For over a decade, flags emblazoned with the hammer and sickle have fluttered from the state Secretariat, the former British Writers Building. Its central Maiden has statues of Lenin and the local hero Subhas Chandra Bose who courted both Hitler and the Japanese during World War II in the hope that they would rid India of the British, dying before his plans came to fruition in a wartime plane crash. With deliberate tongue in cheek, Calcuttan authorities renamed the historic Clive Street after Bose, just as they renamed the street in which the American consulate is located after Ho Chi Minh during the Vietnam war.

By Indian standards, Calcutta is comparatively young. It was founded for trade and profit in 1690 by Job Charnock, the local agent of the British East India Company. Desiring a permanent trading post in wealthy Bengal, Charnock selected the site of three villages amid swamp and jungle. One of these was called Kalikata, named by locals after the most fearsome goddess in the Hindu pantheon, Kali, the destroyer. These early settlers lost no time in Anglicizing it to Calcutta and erecting the

first Fort William near the present Dalhousie Square six years later. They faced heavy losses, not only from random bloodshed when defending their patch from regional Muslim officials, but because their immune systems balked at a whole host of hitherto unknown diseases. Calcutta became known as Golgotha or "Place of Skulls" long before it was to earn the sobriquet "City of Palaces" for the Palladian mansions and grand English classical buildings that rose with the city's fortunes. Mortality rates of the European population during the eighteenth century climbed to above 50 percent, and the British penchant for excessive quantities of port, wild boar and puddings may not have helped matters.

Calcutta grew steadily as trade prospered. Opportunistic merchants soon began reaping vast profits in jute, tea, indigo, cotton, silk and minerals, luring scores of young men to make the 18-week journey from England to work as Company hacks or "writers," banking on making their fortunes by dabbling in free trade. The British Residency of Calcutta received a temporary set-back when Fort William was attacked by the Nabob of Murshidabad in 1757, recaptured by Robert Clive, who arrived too late to rescue 123 Europeans who perished in an underground cellar, that later came to be called the "Black Hole of Calcutta."

Soon Calcutta boasted a second, well-fortified fortress town, and in 1772, it was proclaimed the capital of British India by its first Governor, Warren Hastings. The grand imperial architecture is the relic of Calcutta at its zenith, when the British lived and worked behind the iron gates of their splendid homes, offices and social clubs, attended by ever-increasing tiers of servants. James Morris set the scene for the ghosts of the past in Pax Britanica: "In the evenings, the richer British box-wallahs emerged in top hats and frock coats to promenade the Maiden, driving steadily here and there in broughams, hansoms and victorias, exchanging bows and transient assessments." During the nineteenth century, Calcutta was the focus for the early independence movement, motivating the British to shift the vice-regal seat to Delhi in 1911. After Independence it lost its commercial clout with the waning of colonial-based trade, when new industries sprang up in Bombay — and its grand imperial infrastructure fell into neglect and decay.

Calcutta's modern reality is one of impossible overcrowding, pavement slums, congested traffic, inoperable phones, daily electricity blackouts, with water shortages alternating with floods — living conditions that by any standards are intolerable. It was Kipling's "city of dreadful night... the packed and pestilential town." It is true that Calcutta is a virtual synonym for dreadful squalor. It remains off the beaten track for many travelers, and tales of the city's suffering and filth do not add to its attractions. Yet Calcuttans defend their city with a kind of fierce pride, and few would choose to live anywhere else, including its two most famous personalities — Mother Teresa, a Calcuttan by adoption and the famous film-maker Satyajit Ray. Tourists who come to sample its peculiar, yet stimulating attractions will discover that above all, this city radiates the unforgettable triumph of life, laughter and the human spirit against tremendous odds, and few fail to be moved by its unique energy.

WHEN TO GO

"Enough to make a doorknob mushy." So said Mark Twain of Calcutta's intensely humid climate, created that way by its proximity to the sea and low altitude. For comfort, avoid its torrential monsoon from June to September, and visit instead during November to February. Calcutta explodes with revelry during its spectacular three-week **Durga Puja** festival in September/October, when tinseled glitter, colorful pageantry, music, dance and infectious gaiety spill out on the streets. This is the Bengal version of Dussehra, celebrating the goddess Durga, destroyer of evil, portrayed as riding a tiger. On the final day, floats of ornate idols are paraded through the main boulevards, later dunked in the Hooghly at sunset, accompanied by cheering crowds, flashing strobes and Hindi "disco" music.

Calcuttans adore festivals, and are as enthusiastic about the Diwali and the Muslim Id as they are about Christmas, the latter culminating in a grand candlelight mass at St Paul's Cathedral. Since there are about 20 official holidays in the Bengali year, it's rare to arrive without something going on. Bengali New Year in April/May is riotous but hot.

A BIRD'S EYE VIEW

Calcutta is immense. Its greater area sprawls for some 102 sq km (39 sq miles), and just crossing the relatively compact, but very congested city center can easily take an hour by taxi. For the visitor the most relevant part of Calcutta is its central core, which sprawls along the west bank of the Hooghly River from the Zoological Gardens in the south to the Howrah Bridge some five kilometers (three miles) north. Over the bridge is the industrial ship-building and jute industry heartland, and the beautiful Botanical Gardens. The inner city core is the huge green expanse of the Maiden, hugged by the bus-

tling strip popularly known as Chowringhee, now renamed Jawaharlal Nehru Road, where most of the hotels, restaurants, travel and airline offices are found. At the southern end of Chowringhee you'll find the Government of India Tourist Office on and nearby the Birla Planetarium, St Paul's Cathedral and the Victoria Memorial. Slightly north lies BBD Bagh (Dalhousie Square), where the GPO, the international telephone office, the West Bengal Tourist Office, various railway reservation offices, the Writers Building and the American Express office are located.

TRANSPORT

Calcutta can be a dastardly city for getting around in. Visitors are often perplexed by its duplication of street names, since nobody seems to know whether to use the old Raj-era or new post-Independence version. Even maps aren't consistent. The best way to deal with Calcutta's anarchic traffic is treat it as one of the city's most amazing "sights" — an endless heaving tide of garishly painted lorries, double-decker buses, clanging trams, bullock carts, with man-powered rickshaws pulling decorously perched passengers, weaving to and fro. Astonishing things happen on the streets — during one short ten-minute ride for example, I witnessed a naked sadhu casually wander past, a flock of goats milling past the university gates, rows of cycle-rickshaws pulling school-children kept "safe" for their parents in cages and a Calcutta "ambulance," actually an Ambassador taxi with a man waving a red flag leaning out the window making siren noises!

Rush hour literally lasts all day, easing up only in the early hours of the morning and after seven at night. The new subway — India's first — has helped to solve some of Calcutta's transport problems. After years of tunneling, delayed by waterlogging with the annual monsoon, it has opened a four kilometer (two and a half mile) stretch of an astonishingly clean and efficient alternative to the bedlam above. It's still only half completed, running from Tollygunge in the south to Esplanade, but eventually will run all the way out to Dum Dum Airport. Many tourists make use of it to get out to Kalighat, which takes 10 minutes by the underground contrasted with up to an hour's drive.

Taxis and auto-rickshaws provide the most comfortable transport, found at any hour around the Sudder Street area. Both refuse to use their meters, but are prepared to bargain on a fixed fare beforehand. Sudder Street from Howrah Station, for example should be about Rs 20. Buses are a test of Darwinian fitness — watch Calcutta's office-workers hurl themselves like human javelins or cling desperately to dangling hands while attempting to board — then decide whether this mode of transport is for you.

Calcutta is the world's last stronghold of the human-powered cart rickshaw — originally introduced by the Chinese immigrants during the eighteenth century, and now an enduring symbol of the city. Over 30,000 ply the inner city trade, and they have their own union for protection against Calcutta's authorities who have often tried to eradicate them as an embarrassing reminder of human degradation. Tourists often feel guiltily imperialistic perched above a struggling rickshaw wallah — but it's worth remembering that they depend on miserly wages (and generous tips) to fill their stomachs. At night they hook themselves into their contraptions to slumber. For short hops, they can be invaluable for weaving in and out of clogged traffic.

ACCESS

Indian Airlines run direct flights to Calcutta from Delhi, Bombay, Bangalore, Bagdogra (for Darjeeling), Bhubaneswar, Hyderabad, Madras, Varanasi, Patna and Port Blair in the Andaman Islands. Various international carriers connect it with Rome, London, Bangkok, Tokyo, Dubai, New York, Osaka, Moscow, Kathmandu and Dhaka. and domestic flights.

Calcutta's Dum Dum Airport complex combines both international and domestic services and is the most efficient clean and well-organised complex in the country. It's named after a small-arms factory nearby, which in 1898 produced the notoriously effective Dum Dum bullet, which punched fist-sized holes into tribal Afridis and was banned after the Boer War. It's best to get a pre-paid taxi for the 40-minute ride into the city center, costing about Rs 80 either way. There's also a Rs 13 airport bus which stops at Chowringhee, near the Oberoi Grand and Sudder Street, but this service becomes irregular in the evenings.

There are two rail stations, but travelers are most likely to enter the city through the teeming bedlam of Howrah station, just over the Howrah bridge, which has overnight and day rail services out to most major destinations, including Madras (33 hours), Delhi (16 hours), Bombay (36 hours), and Varanasi (12 hours). Give yourself at least an hour to reach Howrah by taxi from the city center. The less congested Sealdah station, 20 minutes north-east of the city, services Darjeeling (24 hours).

HOTELS

Calcutta's **Oberoi Grand**, ©292323, 15 Jawaharlal Nehru Road, is one of India's most styl-

ish and efficient hotels, rated by frequent business travelers as their personal favorite, even compared favorably by some with London's Savoy Hotel. Tucked behind Chowringhee's bustling arcades, it is a haven of luxury, with its sweeping Georgian façade, brass-buttoned bell-hops, immaculate 1930's style marble interior, and staff in period uniforms. Its fortunes are a mini-chronicle of Calcutta: originally built as a fantasy home by one Colonel Grand in the late nineteenth century, then sold to an entrepreneurial Armenian, and during World War II became a glorified doss-house for British troops, known locally as Mrs Monks Guest House. It's

now the Oberoi chain's flagstaff hotel, miraculously managing to function in Calcutta, a city notorious for its frequent power cuts, tainted water and non-operative telephones. It has a beautiful swimming pool and terrace garden, excellent health club facilities including saunas, Turkish baths, gymnasiums and massage-cum beauty parlors. It offers Calcutta's best restaurants, cultural Dances of India performances, a stylish cocktail lounge, an airy 24-hour coffee shop and the city's only discotheque, the Pink Elephant, full of brass palm trees, flashing strobes, and the latest tunes, but open only to guests and club members. Other facilities include a well-equipped business center, shopping arcade, travel desk and in-house astrologer. Stylish comfort extends to all rooms, with their pastel pink, marble and mahogany decor. Rates: very expensive.

The Taj Group opened their new **Taj Bengal**, ©494664, 494986, in late 1989, at 34B Belvedere Road in Alipore in residential south Calcutta. Other than that, the only real luxury alternative to the Oberoi is the **Tollygunge Club**, ©463141, 120 Deshapran Sasmal Road, also in south Calcutta. Set amid a beautiful 81-hectare

ABOVE: A nag-drawn *tonga*, or traditional horse-drawn taxi, outside Howrah Station.

(200-acre) estate, this historic club-house was built in 1788, and for a time became the residence of the desposed sons of Tipu "Tiger" Sultan. During the heyday of the British Raj, it became the most exclusive of all European clubs. It's run by an English couple, Bob and Anne Wright, and facilities include polo and horse-riding fields, squash and tennis courts and a swimming pool. Rates: inexpensive and non-members must advance book.

The **Fairlawn Hotel** ©244460, 241835, 13A Sudder Street, is delightfully eccentric, trussed up like a Brighton boarding house. It is dominated by its formidable Armenian proprietress,

Mrs Smith, whose entourage includes a fleet of lap dogs and a corps of beaming retainers in faded khaki and Nehru caps. Once the entrance gate is closed, Calcutta's tumultuous street-life recedes (although rickshaw boys bed down on the pavement outside) and the guest can unwind in the small leafy courtyard strewn with cane chairs, statues and fairy-lights. Rooms are very pukka — with floral drapes, lace dollies, and old fashioned baths — and you'll have a "bearer" assigned to your room to bring "bed-tea" and Britannica biscuits, collect washing for the *dhobi wallah* and refill water. Mealtimes are sounded with a resounding gong, with as many as four courses ritually served in a dining room crammed with extraordinary monarchist memorabilia. The daily Anglo-Indian menus read like samples from a Victorian handbook for *memsahibs* in the tropics, frequently delicious, particularly the fish course. With its homely, time-warp atmosphere, the Fairlawn often steals nostalgic British guests away from the more luxurious Oberoi, and attracts an interesting array of travelers, who are more or less thrown into each other's company. Videotaped

episodes of *The Good Life, Yes Minister* not to mention the nuptials of Prince Charles and bride Diana, can be viewed in the lounge. Rates are moderate and include three huge meals a day.

After the Fairlawn everything else pales into insignifiance. But of other pleasant centrally located Raj-era options, try the moderately priced three-star **Park Hotel**, ©297941, 17 Park Road, which offers comfortable rooms or the inexpensive **Hotel New Kenilworth**, ©448394-99, 1-2 Little Russell Street, conveniently located close to the tourist office and government emporiums. Just around the corner, the **Astor Hotel**, ©44950, 15 Shakespeare Sarani, is a quaint inexpensive Tudor-style establishment in a peaceful courtyard with evening barbecues. Then there's the **Great Eastern Hotel**, ©232269, 1-2 Old Court Road, whose once-considerable charms are barely perceptible through a haze of grime and tat, although it still charges inflated room rates because Rudyard Kipling stayed there for a few months typing out dispatches for the *Civil and Military Gazette*.

Sudder Street has the greatest concentration of cheap tourist lodges. At 2 Sudder Street is the **Salvation Army Red Shield Guest House**, ©242895, with spartan, but spotless fan-cooled singles rooms with attached bath. Dorm beds cost Rs 13, and guests can use communal bathrooms. Budget travelers rate it highly, although its water supply is not always up to scratch. It's possible to put valuables into "safekeeping" at the front desk. Another popular and cheap tourist lodge is the **Shilton Hotel**, ©243613, a few doors away, at 5A.

Calcutta's YMCA's are quite grand. The most creakily Gothic of all, the **YMCA**, ©292192, on Jawaharial Nehru Road, was originally built in 1902, and has a spooky "Turn of the Screw" feel. It still retains its mystifying plaque "No pets or private servants allowed!" it's unisex, and the room rate — Rs 180 for singles, Rs 230 for doubles — is expensive by YMCA standards, but includes three hearty meals a day, plus tanin-saturated "bed-tea".

RESTAURANTS

It's possible to dine at the Oberoi Grand on Russian caviar, blinis and champagne at Rs 1,000 a shot, if it suits your whim and pocket — it's also possible to join the hungry queue outside the "begger's restaurant" — run by beggers for beggers — just outside Sealdah station, where for Rs 1 you are given a plate, made from melded leaves, heaped with rice, dal and *chapatis*. Given the wide array of excellent restaurants in between, it can be surprisingly difficult to sample Calcutta's exotic Bengali cuisine. That's because most Calcuttan families tend in

---

The Oberoi Grand Hotel, considered by many Calcuttans to be the epitome of elegance and the good life.

eat in — believing, quite rightly, that home cooking is best. This may stem partly from tradition and partly because Bengali dishes rely heavily on subtle herbs, fresh fish and mustard oil — a combination of which does not keep well together for long. Traditionally, meals are served course by course on plantain leaves. When Calcuttans go out, they like to do so in style — opting for swish European, Chinese or north-Indian food, and "cabarets" with Goan bands — both of which are affected by the state's partial prohibition on Thursdays and Saturdays.

The **Suruchi** at 89 Elliot Road, near Sudder Street, gets the highest praise from locals for its typical Bengali dishes. It's best to concentrate on their fresh fish dishes, particularly *doi mach*, an unforgettable curry of river fish, yogurt, ginger, raisins and spices; *dabey chingri* shellfish baked with coconut; *maccher paturi* steamed mustard fish; delicious but bony smoked *hilsa* fish, and prawns sauteed in mustard oil and spiced with coriander and garlic. All are eaten with a variety of rice dishes or with *loochi* a deep-fried bread, and hot, syrupy mango chutney. Benagli sweets are positively devilish for sugar-addicts — usually milk and curd based, like *barfi, rosgulla, rasmalai,* and *sandhesh* — all made to tantalize the taste buds. Another favorite Bengali dessert is *misthi dohi,* a sweet curd with raw *jaggery.*

The Oberoi Grand offers the best Mughali, Szechuen and French food in Calcutta with such sophisticated food and stylish decor that it barely seems possible that the "City of Dreadful Night" hovers outside. The city's elite adore **La Rotisserie** for its classic French cuisine, with such decadent delights as Strasbourg goose liver and truffles, Scottish pheasant, fresh rainbow trout, and New Zealand prime steak — all flown in fresh. Desserts are no less appetizing, and there's an extensive wine list (at extensive prices). A full-blown dinner for two, without imported wine, costs around Rs 1,600, or you can sample their good-value set lunch buffets, and the dinner-time "Dances of India" performance, every night at 6:30 pm (except Tuesdays).

Calcutta's main drag, Park Street, is festooned with faded neon, garish "cabaret" club porticoes and shop façades left over from the thirties and forties, crammed with the city's best-loved restaurants.

The **Sky Room**, ©294362 at number 57 is the most quirkily elegant with its Art Deco decor, fake "sky" ceiling, and old-fashioned waiters clad in spotless white. Order their excellent Bengali and Mughali dishes, all beautifully served on silverware. Here it's possible to buy 1930's style brocade ties (displayed at the front counter) now back in fashion. It's best to

pre-book as city-smart locals flock here in their chiffon-clad and Bengali-dhotied droves, but be forewarned, no alcohol is sold here. Other well-patronized haunts for standard tri-cuisine include **Kwaility**, at number 17, one of the biggest and best of the chain, the **Moulin Rouge** at number 31, fronted by a fake windmill façade, and the **Blue Fox** at N° 55. Just behind Sudder Street, **Amber**, 11 Waterloo Road is the place to sample north-Indian Punjabi food.

Calcutta's Chinese immigrants have endowed the city with numerous authentic regional Chinese restaurants, still mainly catering to the small colony who patronize them for their Peking duck, other homely dishes and continuous green tea. One of the best is **How Hwa**, Mirza Ghalib Road, which offers a staggering 32 different kinds of soups, including the house specialty, Chimney Soup, an mélange of prawn wantons, fish, crab meat and homemade bean curd cooked with a garlic-ginger stock in a Mongolian hot-pot. Special dishes can be ordered in 24 hours in advance, notably luscious roasted Peking duck served with plum sauce, scallions and pancakes, a steal at Rs 100. Other popular "Chinese" include the **Nanking**, 22 Blackburn Lane, and the **Peiping**, 1/1 Park Street, (with its partitioned sections a concession to Muslim patrons), renowned for its steamed garlic and ginger fish and giant king prawns.

Flury's, on Park Street, is a classic Raj-era tearoom with an adjoining pastry shop. it's open early for British breakfasts of baked beans on toast, and is a popular rendezvous place for all-day pastries, club sandwiches and Vienna coffees. **Kathleen's**, 12 Free School Street, at the end of Sudder Street, also has a great restaurant-cum-bakery, always well patronized since Calcuttans adore their cream cakes! Backpackers gravitate to the **Blue Sky Café**, in Sudder Street, which bills itself "The Only Café for You Kind of People!" and serves good fruit *lassis,* Western-style breakfasts, and burgers.

If you're strolling down College Street's "book strip" don't miss one of Calcutta's most lively hang-outs, the **Indian Coffee Worker's Co-operative**, at 15 Bankim Chatterjee Street nearby. It occupies the cavernous Albert Hall, noted as the venue for the First National Congress Conference in 1885. Climb up the "balcony seat" for a delicious iced coffee and observe this hub of political and cultural discussion, echoing to the sounds of urgent Bengali, wafts of high-brow English and emphatic fists on tables. Calcutta's Bengali students may look threadbare, and exist only on coffee and cigarettes, but they sure know their Marxist dialectics. Giant fans dangle like low propellers, waiters flit about dressed in bizarre plumed caps, soiled white uniforms and *cummerbunds*. It's a great place to strike up conversations, and dine well for next to nothing.

"Cabaret-restaurants", provide the glitz for Calcutta's nightlife, and the most famous is "**Trinca's**" at 17B, just outside the Park Hotel. It might be "Exotic Mina and the Twisters", a plump mulatto from Trinaded in a lame dress crooning to the accompaniment of bandsmen in sequinned large lapelled suits one night, or the "Shaheed and the Goanese All-Stars" the next.

SIGHTSEEING

Going "sightseeing" in Calcutta is almost an anachronism. Many travelers stay for weeks, becoming so fascinated by its unbelievably tumultuous street-life that they spend all their time in a half-intoxicated dread-state, combing through the cobbled streets of the decaying imperial center, fossicking in bazaars and simply being a witness to the city's incredible pace of life. At the end of their stay, they've probably worn out their shoe leather, but may not have seen many of Calcutta's historic "sights" at all.

A successful itinerary is planned on the basis of geographical proximity rather than attempting to see things in a particular order. Walking the long distances between one general locality can not only become confusingly complicated if following a less-than accurate Calcutta street map, but gets exhausting too. So hail some form of transport — be it mechanical, animal, or in the case of Calcutta, even human — and move on to wherever else seems the most interesting. The tours devised below are tailor-made for this approach, best spread over several days of sightseeing.

CITY TOUR

If you're staying in the central Chowringhee/Sudder Street area, the most decadent start to any sightseeing is breakfast in the Oberoi Maidens, followed by a short stroll down Chowringhee, now called Jawaharlal Nehru Road. It's lined with decaying Palladian palaces and mansions, formerly inhabited by the wealthy and powerful British and Bengali *bhandralok,* the enterprising Westernized Indian middle class. Today they are used as commercial offices, amid Chowringhee's frenetic melee of garish movie billboards, bazaars, cafés, and hotels.

The Maiden

Across the road is the **Maiden**, Calcutta's three-kilometer (two-mile) -long Hyde Park where everything from massive political rallies to

early morning yoga lessons takes place. Itinerant performers, ash-smeared sadhus and tired tourists alike enjoy the shade of its leafy trees, and it's also famous as the venue for the "Mukta Mela," a sort of informal cultural fair held from time to time, in which poets recite their verses to one another, artists discuss their canvases and free-thinkers bring along their soap-boxes. The Maiden was created in the wake of the massacres of the Indian Mutiny of 1857, when the British decided to replace their original Fort William near Dalhousie Square with a new more massive and impregnable version, whose white-washed fortifications and trenches overlook the Hooghly River further west. The Maiden was originally designed to give the fort's cannons a clear line of fire — today it echoes to the sound of cricket shots. Indian cricket was actually born on the Maiden with a two-day

white flannel match in 1802 between the "Old Etonians" versus a "Calcutta" brigade of East India Company nabobs.

To the south lies the Royal Calcutta Turf Club, which has an active season from November to mid-March, but draws India's horse-mad elite for its climactic annual Queen Elizabeth II Derby in January.

At the southern end of the Maiden rises the dazzling white marble **Victoria Memorial**, one of the most pompous, grandiloquent edifices ever built by the British in India. When the Poet W.H. Auden visited during the fifties, he recorded being vastly amused when a freelance guide told him that it had been designed by the same man who created the Taj Mahal! It has been called an imperial "blamanche" of Classical and Mughal architecture, and it was in fact inspired by the Taj Mahal, with its four rudi-

mentary minarets, gleaming white dome and exterior of solid Macarana marble.

It was commisioned by Lord Curzon, Viceroy of India, and raised entirely with money from voluntary contributions, as the ultimate compliment to Queen Victoria after her death in 1901. Built between 1906 and 1921 at a cost of Rs 7.5 million, it's set amid 26 hectares (64 acres) of lawns, fountains, herbaceous borders and dotted with statues of former British rulers which used to adorn street corners all along Chowringhee and the Maiden. Looking dourly imperious, the Empress of India sits enthroned in bronze at the entrance marble staircase, wearing the regal Order of the Star of India. Above her, a 4.9-m (16-ft) -high bronze winged Angel

Families picnicking in the lush statuary-dotted gardens of the pompously grand Victoria Memorial.

of Victory is poised to fly from atop the central dome.

Inside houses the most remarkable collection of memorabilia of British India ever amassed under one roof — 3,500 exhibits on 25 galleries. The entrance dome is etched with the text of Queen Victoria's proclaimation speech of herself as Empress, while the surrounding-galleries are crammed with pageant-like paintings relating to the major episodes in the monarch's life (coronation, marriage to Albert, baptism of her son and heir Edward VII, going riding with her faithful retainer, John Brown, pompish celebrations of the golden and silver

King Edward VII) making his grand tour of Jaipur in 1876, the works of the Victorian artists, Thomas and William Daniells, and Johann Zoffany's portrait of William Hastings and his family. Rare extant documents, treaties, an armory and a Historic Calcutta exhibition complete the fascinating collection. The Publications Office sells excellent catalogues, books and posters. It's open Tuesdays to Sundays, from 10 am to 4:30 pm from March to October, and until 3:30 pm during November to February, closed on public holidays.

St Paul's Cathedral, barely five minutes walk across the gardens is the first Church of England

jubilees, and many others) as well as several of her personal possessions: the baby-grand piano on which she played as a child, her personal writing desk and embroidered armchair. There are even scrapbooks of her letters in Hindustani, for she was tutored in the language by her favorite India attendant Abdul Karim. Entire wings are lined with portraits and busts of famous British figures, who each in their own way added their contribution to British India, including Robert Clive, General Stringer Lawrence (father of the Indian army), Lord Bentinck who outlawed suttee, William Makepeace Thackeray who was born here, and Florence Nightingale, who only ever took a distant interest in India. Among the many excellent paintings, look especially for Burne-Jones's portrait of Rudyard Kipling, Verestchagin's monumental depiction of the Prince of Wales, (the future

cathedral of British India, built in 1847 with East India Company funds as their Gothic imitation Canterbury Cathedral. Inside see the ornate communion plate presented by Queen Victoria, Burne-Jones's stained glass west window, Francis Chantrey's statue of Bishop Heber and Sir Arthur Blomfield's mosaics around the altar.

Further south-east lies the **Zoological Gardens**, off Belvedere Road, open sunrise to sunset, its main attraction being a captive rare white tiger from Rewa.

Opposite is **Raj Bhawan**, the Government House from which Viceroys ruled India until 1911. It was built in 1803 upon the orders of the Governor General of Bengal, Lord Wellesley who was determined to have a palace equal to his station. He tactfully omited to mention how palatial his palace was, only sending the bill to his superiors in London when it was safely

234

completed, and the East India Company was forced to foot the cost — then two million rupees. However future viceroys found this replica of Kedleston Hall in Derbyshire very much to their tastes. Inside is a grand marble hall dominated by 12 busts of Caesar, staircase sphinxes — and the various contributions left behind by previous occupant's: Warren Hasting's gravel from Bayswater, Lord Ellenborough's Chinese cannon on a brass dragon, Lord Curzon's fretted-iron lift. It's now the part-residence of the Chief Minister and part-Secretariat of West Bengal, not open to the public.

Close by, along Council House Street, you'll find the Greco-colonial **St John's Church**, Calcutta's oldest British cemetry. It was built in 1787, modelled on London's St Martin-in-the-Fields and used as a temporary cathedral by the East India Company's burgeoning populace until St Paul's Cathedral was completed. Its quaint interior is dominated by Zoffany's Raj-version of the "Last Supper", whose saintly diciples actually resemble their less-than angelic sitters, a corps of young clerks, who Zoffany later wryly noted, passed the time taking swigs at brandy bottles. Within the overgrown churchyard, crammed with moss-encrusted masonry, one of the oldest tombstones belongs to Job Charncock, who died in 1692, two years after founding Calcutta. Admiral Watson, who supported Clive in retaking Calcutta from Suraj-ud-daula, is also buried here. Other tombstones illustrate the perils faced by the early British settlers — premature deaths caused by heat, exotic malaises, too much port or ill-fated adventures.

From here, it's a 20 minute stroll down to **Dalhousie Square**, now renamed **BBD Bagh**, in memory of Benoy, Badal and Dinesh, three freedom-fighting Bengali martyrs. For more than 150 years, Dalhousie Square was British India's headquarters, and it is still Calcutta's commercial hub. Bengali bureaucrats, lawyers, stock-brokers and businessmen deftly pick their way past beggers, coolies, shattered pavements and rattling trams. To Western eyes, this imperial muddle of dilapidated Victorian buildings, swept-up Doric colonnades, grand mahogany doors and Romanesque-lettered brass nameplates looks eerily familiar, yet with its overlapping chaotic squalor, almost like a sort of post-Holocaust London. Half-naked men and boys briskly lather themselves in muddy gushes sloshed from burst pipes and clean their teeth with *neem* twigs; thin pavement clerks hunch over battered Remingtons typing out applications for queues of illiterates; tiny urchins chatter over shared *chapatis*. Once this was Job Charncock's Tank Square, where *bheesties* or water carriers serviced the houses of the early

European settlers. The tank still brims today, and its high fence does nothing to discourage early morning swimmers and tribes of dhobi-wallahs, who tirelessly thwack spirals of cloth against the concrete slopes. The square is dominated by the huge 14-storyed **Writer's Building**, built in 1880, with its Early English porticos and burnt–sienna façade crowned by rooftop statues who strike allegorical poses representing imperial ethos: Justice, Virtue, Faith, Charity, and so on. Originally it was just a squat barrack-house where the runtish clerks or "writers", who came out with the East India Company, lived and worked. As Benaglis are apt to ex-

plain, India's notoriously complex bureaucracy dates back to when these early British "writers" scribbled records of business transactions in this very building, now used as the Secretariat of Communist West Bengal. Their modern counterparts, the Bengali *bapus* carry on the tradition of painstakingly-typed letters, receipts and memoranda in triplicate. Tourists who venture inside, usually seeking permission to go the Sunderbans or Darjeeling, find labyrinthine passages, branching off into dusty cavernous rooms where peons shuffle papers, sip tea and wile away time in a trance against pyramids of yellowing files. To the west of Dalhousie

ABOVE: Imposing façade of the Writer's Building in BBD Bagh. OPPOSITE: The Marble Palace is the "Miss Haversham" of grand Calcutta mansions, full of cobwebbed charm.

Square is the imposing Corinthian-pillared **GPO**, which occupies the site of the original Fort William that was demolished by the Nabob Siraj-ud-Daulah in 1756. Calcutta's infamous "black hole", was actually a guard room that stood at the north-east corner of the GPO, but since independence all indications of its presence have been removed, save a tiny brass plaque. It's fascinating to walk along Netaji Subhas Road, Calcutta's main business strip adjoining the square, lined with the old British commercial houses that continue to flourish in Indian hands. Whiffs of tea grow stronger nearer **R.N. Mukherjee Street**, where the city's tea auctions are held, brawny coolies lug stacks of paper for printing industries, and frenzied dealing goes on at the Lyon's Range Stock Exchange, just beyond Clive Street.

A PATCHWORK OF LEGACIES

Howrah Bridge

The colossal cantilevered bridge is the city's most famous landmark. The 27,000-ton plank joining Calcutta with the jute-mill and ship-building settlement of Howrah across the khaki waters of the Hooghly opened in 1943 and is now one of the busiest bridges in the world with some two million people crossing it daily. No other sight captures Calcutta's hectic energy quite so dramatically — from dawn until late into the night it's permanently choked a tide of sardine-can buses, taxis, hideously polluting trucks, buffalo-drawn carts, clanging hordes of bicycles and rickshaws. Sprightly laborers balancing mountainous loads weaving in and out among the larger vehicles. Astonishingly, during high summer, this steel mesh bridge expands some four feet each day in the heat, shrinking back to normal during the night. Beneath it along the river banks, is a constant jamboree of itinerant masseuses, barbers, and flower sellers.

The Marble Palace

Some three kilometers (nearly two miles) north of the city center off Chittaranjan Avenue, lies one of Calcutta's most extraordinary sights. This Palladian mansion and its ornamental garden was built in 1835 by a wealthy Bengali merchant, Raja Rajendra Mullick, who had been orphaned at three and given an English guardian, Sir James Hogg, by the Supreme Court. He started building at the age of 16, amassing an eclectic mix of 126 varieties of marble to line the floors, wall panels and tables. Pelicans and peacocks strut through the colonnaded inner courtyard, and tiny stairwells lead to rooms and apartments crammed with ornate objets d'art and paintings studiously collected from auc-

tions and dispossessed households across the globe — all slowly consumed by Dickensian decay, mildew and dust. Lurking somewhere in this charmed gloom hang oils by Titians, Sir Joshua Reynolds, Murillo and Rubens — amid a jumble of Venetian glass, statues of Greek gods, enormous chandeliers, Parisian furniture, gilt goblets from Bohemia and Teutonic stag heads. An unusually nubile-looking Queen Victoria dominates a red marble room, facing many po-faced plaster busts. Guests are free to wander through between the hours of 10 am to 4 pm, although it's not a museum, but the Mullick family's private home. Respecting the wishes of Mullick senior, their allow beggar children to play in their fairy-tale garden, and provide free meals for queues of destitutes every day at noon. It's closed on Monday and Thursdays.

Nearby, off Rabindra Sarani, is the **Rabindra-Bharati Museum**, the stately ancestral home of the gifted and influential Tagore family. This is where India's famous poet, philosopher and fervent nationalist, Rabindranath Tagore was born and later died. His talents as poet won him the Nobel Prize in 1913, and he also composed the song *Jana Gana Mana Adhinayaka* which was adopted as the National Anthem after Independence. It's a fascinating treasure trove filled with family heirlooms, manuscripts and paintings. It's open from Monday to Friday from 10 am to 7 pm, Saturdays 10 am to 1 pm, and Sundays, 11 am to 2 pm.

It's a 15-minute drive north-east to the **Jain Temple**, built by the fabulously rich Birla family in 1867. It's actually a collection of four pagoda-like shrines set in geometrical gardens and ponds. They have exquisite interiors encrusted with mirror-glass mosaics, Venetian glass, gilt dome ceilings and precious stones, inlaid by a jeweler — all dedicated to Sitalnathji, tenth of the 24 Jain *tirthankars* (prophets).

Returning to the city center, make a short detour to the junction of Rabindra Sarani and Zakaria Street, to see the magnificent **Nakhoda Mosque**, whose giant two 46-m (150-ft) -high minarets and copper-green domes are visible from afar. It's the center of Calcutta's Muslim community, modeled on Akbar's tomb at Sikandra near Agra and able to accommodate up to 10,000 people during major festivals. The most spectacular of these is Muharram, when the surrounding streets come alive with bands, and men dancing like whirling dervishes with long curving swords.

Back in central Calcutta, round off sightseeing with a visit to the historic **South Park Cemetery**, in Park Street, a leafy enclosure congested with classical mausoleums of Calcutta's distinguished Europeans, replacing St John's cemetery in 1767. Among those buried here is William Hickey's wife Charlotte Barry; Colonel Charles Russell Deare, who perished in the fight against Tipu Sultan; Colonel Kyd, the founder of the Botanical Gardens; the early Indologist William Jones, founder of the Royal Asiatic Society, the novelist William Makepeace Thackeray's father, and sons of Charles Dickens and Captain Cook. Among the crumbling tombstones is that of Rose Aylmer, a young beauty who captured Thackeray's heart but died in her late teens after eating infected pineapple. The custodian is full of stories, and it's open all day.

Goddess Kali and the Sisters of Mercy

Take the underground metro to Kalighat to see the temple of Calcutta's patron goddess, Kali, the malevolent destroyer, located about 10 minutes walk from the station. The present temple was built in 1809, but this site of **Kali Khetra** — from which Calcutta derived its name — has long been associated with legend. It is said to be the home of Kali, "the black one," who rose as a incarnation of Devi, Shiva's wife. The story goes that Shiva was so distraught about when Devi died, that the other gods feared he would pound the earth to dust in his grief. So Vishnu surreptitiously removed Devi's offending corpse from Shiva's sight, slicing it into 52 pieces. One of her severed toes fell here, becoming Kali. Devi represented Shiva's feminine energy in its manifold forms. Thus she took on many incarnations, of which Kali and the more saintly Durga, (the focus of Calcutta's annual Durga Puja festival), are the most important. Rather unappetisingly, the temple is notorious for its daily animal sacrifice — usually goats or sheep — when pilgrims are whipped into a frenzy, scrabbling up the marble stairs to make *puja* of sweetmeats, flowers or coconuts. Kali is usually depicted as a gorgon-like creature with beady red eyes, dripping with blood, and triumphantly holding up weapons, snakes, and severed heads in her ten arms. Of all the Hindu deities, her wrath is most feared, and hence revered most slavishly. The temple is open until 10 pm.

Nirmal Hriday, the Place of the Pure Heart, the most famous of Mother Theresa's homes for the dying, stands beside the Kali temple in a former pilgrim's hostel, at 54A Lower Circular Road, (©247115). Visitors are allowed during the early morning and between 4 and 6 pm. It's here that dying men and women with nothing and no one come to be cared for by the Sisters of Mercy in their distinctive white blue-bordered saris, before "going home to God". Mother Theresa started alone in 1948 in a Calcutta slum, and since then the Missionary Sisters have grown to more than a 1,000-strong and a separate Brotherhood has also been formed. Under

her auspices, the Sisters and Brothers now operate over 81 schools, 325 mobile dispensaries serving 1,600,000 people annually, 28 family planning centers, 67 leprosy clinics and 32 homes for dying destitute men and women. It's easy to see why this iron-willed crusader has earned world-wide admiration for her courageous efforts to redress Calcutta's overwhelming human suffering.

Bengali Biblomania

Calcuttans pride themselves on being a literary people. The British began the trend, founding the prestigious Royal Asiatic Society and the National Library here, but the Bengalis were behind Calcutta's nineteenth century literary renaissance that gave zeal to the early independence movement. There are more than 800 newspapers in the state, more than 1,600 poetry magazines, and the bulk of India's creative theater emerges from here. Even the subway system reflects Calcutta's mania for poetical message, one station almost entirely covered in Tagore's poems and artistic doodles. Provocative graffiti crams the city's walls, usually a compelling mixture of the poetic and the political.

Nowhere is the Bengali obsession with words so amply illustrated than the city's Portabello Road of books, **College Street**, near the university, where the air is trapped with dust particles from thousands upon thousands of books — stacked high on the pavement, in tiny stalls, spilling out from large awnings. You'll find almost anything here in almost every language — Victorian lithographs to Russian textbooks — along this kilometer-long strip. Nearby is the **National Library,** the grand former residence of the British Lieutenant Governor, with its eight million books, including rare manuscripts. For brand-new books go to the **Oxford Book Company** on Park Street.

Arrive well primed for Calcutta by reading Geoffrey Moorehouse's classic *1971 Calcutta*, published by Penguin — easily the most fascinating in-depth study around. Dominique Lapierre's *City of Joy* is less critically acclaimed, but makes compulsive reading.

Terra-cotta Pompeii

The unsung heroes of Calcutta's spectacular Durga Puja parade are the idol-makers who fashion clay gods by the thousands. Squatting in cotton *lunghis*, deftly molding wet mud over straw cones, these pavement artisans work in the community known as **Kumar Tulli,** or **"Potter's Lane"**, located near the river in north Calcutta, just off Chitpur Road. Unpainted, yet extraordinarily life-like terra-cotta images of Durga, Kali, Ganesh and Laxmi and many other gods clutter the streets to bake in the sun, looking eerily like a kind of terra-cotta Pompeii. Later they will be painted up in gaudy colors, threaded with tinsel and dressed in glittering costumes as part of the Durga Puja's mammoth float parade.

CULTURE AND CRAFTS ROUND-UP

Of all Indian cities, Calcutta has the most fascinating array of museums, art galleries and cultural "happenings."

Keep an eye out for what's on by consulting the daily *Amrita Bazaar Patrika* and *Sunday Telegraph* newspapers, or consult the tourist office's *Calcutta This Fortnight* leaflet. Opposite the Calcutta Club on Acharaya Bose Road is an excellent information center and box office for the arts. The most active hall is **Rabindra Sadan,** ©449936 on Cathedral Road, Calcutta's cultural hub, where Indian dancers, writers and musicians perform. You're bound to find something happening most nights. Other main halls include the **Academy of Fine Arts, Birla Academy** and the **Sisir Mancha.** It's worth catching a performance of Indian classical dance, particularly the eastern dance styles of Manipuri, Odissa and Chahau, usually recounting stories from the Mahabharata or the Ramayana.

Of Calcutta's 30 or so museums, make time for the country's largest, and most extensive, the **Indian Museum,** located at the junction of Chowringhee and Sudder Street. Founded in 1814 to house the burgeoning collection of the prestigious Asiatic Society, it's a huge Classical-style building with a Corinthian portico and a cavernous proscenium-style arch auditorium. Its vast collection is spread across six departments: archaeology, anthropology, zoology, geology, botany and art. Look especially for its fine coin collection, textiles, *bidri* ware, Indian miniature paintings, and the Sunga and Gandhara sculpture. Intriguing oddities abound, including giant prehistoric coconuts, an eight-legged, four-eared preserved goat, bangles from the belly of a captured crocodile. At the entrance, get a map to help you find your way around its giant corridors, some barely disturbed, with priceless treasures sharing dust-filled rooms with nesting pigeons. It's open daily except Mondays from 10 am to 4:30 pm. Equally impressive is the **Austosh Museum of Modern Art,** housed in Calcutta University on College Street, a fabulous showcase of the rich artistic legacy of eastern India, with sculpture, folk-art, textiles and fine collection of

Kalighat paintings and terra-cottas. It's open from Monday to Friday from 10:30 am to 5 pm with half-days on Saturdays.

Of others to explore, the following are closed on Mondays unless otherwise specified. The **Academy of Fine Arts,** Cathedral Road, open 3 to 8 pm. The **Birla Academy of Art and Culture,** 108-9 Southern Avenue, open 4 to 8 pm. The **Birla Planetarium** at 96 J. Nehru Road, the largest and best organized in India, well patronized by city workers for its air-conditioned environment during the hot summers — most seem to doze off during the soothing drone of its lectures! There are at least two English sessions daily between 2:30 and 6:30 pm.

You can visit the preserved home of **Netaji Subhas Chandra Bose,** the errant Indian nationalist leader who joined forces with the Japanese during World War II, at 38/2 Lala Lajpat Rai Sarani, open Monday to Friday from 6 to 8 pm and on Sundays 9 am to 12 pm. The **Nehru Children's Museum,** 94 J. Nehru Road, open noon to 8 pm. The **Royal Asiatic Society,** 1 Park Street, open for studying only from Monday to Friday noon to 7 pm. The **State Archaeological Museum,** 33 Chittaranjan Avenue, open Monday to Friday 11 am to 5:30 pm, Saturdays from 11 am to 2 pm.

SHOPPING

Calcutta is an oasis of traditional Bengali handicrafts and textiles. Try browsing first at the **Bengal Home Industries Association,** at 57 Jawaharlal Nehru Road and the **West Bengal Government Sales Emporium** on Lindsay Street. Stars to search for include the village terra-cotta figurines, made throughout rural Bengal as icons of occupation; rice-measuring bowls made from wood inlaid with brass, often in a shell design; brass oil lamps crafted to resemble figures or animals; conch-shell bangles, carved ivory, delicate silver jewelry and dolls made from papier mâché or cotton. The queen of Bengali textiles is the Baluchari brocade sari, noted for its highly complicated floral and story-telling motifs, developed by eighteenth century Gujurati migrants. Delicate cotton and lace embroidery is another speciality, best bought at the **All Bengal Women's Home** at 89 Elliot Street. Round off any shopping with a visit to the historic **Hogg's Market,** now known as **New Market,** tucked behind the Oberoi Grand. Its Victorian red-brickwork and awnings were built almost a century ago, and it remains Calcutta's chief bartering place, particularly for its brimming animal and bird mart. Squads of eager porters rush up to prospective buyers, offering to lug your purchases around in panier-like baskets before you've even bought them.

Bystanders wait for some temple action outside the Kali Temple at Kalighat.

AROUND CALCUTTA

THE BANYAN BOULEVARD

Across the Hooghly's banks, south of Howrah, are India's most beautiful **Botanical Gardens** — a perfect bolt-hole from Calcutta proper. It's a 40 minute drive (20 km or 11.4 miles) from the city center. Laid out by one Colonel Kyd in 1786 as a pleasure retreat for the East India Company, it stretches for about a kilometer along the river-front, with palm, orchid and cacti houses, a

herbarium, lakes and altogether some 30,000 varieties of tropical plants and trees. It was at these gardens that the tea now grown in Assam and Darjeeling was first developed. Its world-famous attraction is its 225 year-old banyan tree, the largest on earth. It has a circumference of 417 m (1,367 ft) and some 1,600 aerial roots, resembling a small forest, not a single tree. It's most pleasant to make this a morning exursion, taking a ferry cruise across the Hooghly from Chandpal or Takta Ghats, checking first that the Botanical Gardens Ghat is open.

THE BELUR MATH

Some 10 km (6.2 miles) north, still on the east bank of the Hooghly, is the **Belur Math,** the headquarters of the Ramakrishna Mission. This was established in 1898 by Swami Vivekananda, resuscitating the ideals of the sage Rama Krishna who preached the essential unity of all religions. Illustrating this belief, it looks like a church, Hindu temple or mosque — depending on the way you look at it.

On safari in the Sunderbans. ABOVE: A tawny Royal Bengal tiger. OPPOSITE TOP: Pastoral peace as the sun sets over the marshlands. OPPOSITE BOTTOM: Waiting for a boat to ferry passengers through the mangrove swamps.

General Information

The best Government of India Tourist Office, © 441402, 443521, is at 4 Shakespeare Sarani. It's both friendly and well-stocked with information, particularly helpful for advice about permit requirements for Darjeeling. The West Bengal Tourist Bureau, © 238271 is at 3/2 BBD Bagh. Both the state and national tourist offices have counters at the airport. Both run daily morning and afternoon conducted city tours, good for orientation if you don't have time to sightsee at leisure, and getting out to far-flung sights.

In the Dalhousie Square (BBD Bagh) area, you can make overseas calls at to the Central Telegraph Office at 8 Red Cross Place and collect Poste Restante letters at the large GPO. The Foreigner's Registration Office, © 44301 is at 237 Acharya J C Bose Road. Lastly, you'll save yourself much time and energy by entrusting your travel plans/predicaments to a reliable travel agent. Good ones to try include the Travel Corporation of India, © 445469, or Mercury Travels (© 443555 both at 46C Jawaharlal Nehru Road, or Sita World Travels, © 240935, at 3B Camac Street.

Indian Airlines can be reached at © 260730, 263390, 39 Chittaranhan Avenue. For rail bookings, there are two main offices situated quite close together, both within BBD Square (Dalhousie Square): Eastern Railways, © 222291, at 6 Fairlee Place, BBD Square, and South Eastern Railways, © 235074, Esplanade Mansions, 14A Strand Road. You can waste hours negotiating endless reservations queues, so if possible, let a travel agent handle your bookings. The main bus terminus for city and state transport is off Jawaharlal Nehru Road.

MANGROVES AND TIGERS

The **Sunderbans,** which lies 131 km (81 miles) east of Calcutta where the Ganges spills into the Bay of Bengal sea, is the world's largest mangrove swamp and the home of the magnificent Royal Bengal tiger. Few tourists ever venture to this vast 2,500 sq km (965 sq miles) esturine land of mud flats, mangroves and dense forest, which sprawls across to Bangladesh and is accessible only by riverine waterways. Among those who returned impressed was Alfred Hitchcock, who begged former prime minister Indira Gandhi to let him make a horror film here, writing that it was the most "devilish, foreboding landscape" he had ever seen. She turned Hitchcock down, having already refused him permission to film in the Taj Mahal. However lonely or perilous its landscape, it is certainly crammed with spectacular wildlife. Tribal villagers who eke out a living by honey collecting and fishing here wear brightly painted masks on the backs of their

Calcutta and the East

heads to lessen their chances of becoming tiger fodder. This is the largest natural habitat of tigers in the world, with some 300 roaming free in the central Project Tiger reserve. Among other wildlife, you have a good chance of seeing wild boar, jungle cat, spotted deer, giant crocodiles, king cobras, lizards and monitors including the rare Salvator lizard. Part of the Sunderbans is the **Sajnakhali Bird Sanctuary.**

The main embarkation point for river cruises through the sanctuary is **Canning, 54 km** (33.5 miles) from Calcutta, reached by car, train or bus. It's possible to hire private launches, but safest and easiest to go on the conducted trips

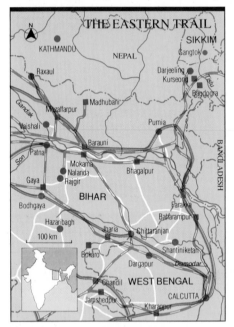

run by the West Bengal Tourist Bureau, who operate a luxury launch, which has sleeping quarters and armed guard for Project Tiger areas, and can anchor in mid-channel to stay overnight. Accomodation can also be had at the **Sundar Cheetal Lodge** at Sajnakhali. It is best visited from mid-September to mid-March. Foreign visitors have to contact the Secretary, Department of Forest and Tourism, Government of West Bengal, Writer's Building, Calcutta.

THE EASTERN TRAIL

From Calcutta you have a diverse array of destinations no more than an hour's flight away. To the west is rural **Bihar,** which has many pilgrimage places sacred to Buddhists. To the north lie the cool, exotic Himalayan destinations of **Darjeeling, Sikkim** and the north-eastern fron-

tier states. To the south is lush, temple-dotted **Orissa,** while off the south-eastern coast lie scattered the beautiful virgin **Andaman** and **Nicobar** archipelago.

If you plan a visit to Darjeeling or the Andaman and Nicobar islands, but particularly to any of the north-eastern states, you'll be required to obtain special visas and permits in advance. In the case of Darjeeling and the Andaman capital, Port Blair, however, permits may be issued upon arrival, provided you make the journey by air. It's advisable to check with the Tourist Office or the travel agencies listed above for any up-to-date stipulations or changes and general information on these more politically delicate areas.

BIHAR: THE BUDDHIST TRAIL

Buddha lived and preached most of his life in the north-eastern state of rural Bihar. Of especial interest to Buddhists, Bihar is off the beaten track for most tourists.

In the sixth century BC Pataliputra, the site of Bihar's modern capital **Patna,** became the capital of the Magadhans, and later the Mauryans and of other successive empires that promoted Buddhist culture and philosophy.

Within the state, **Bodhgaya** is a hallowed place for Buddhists and where Buddha achieved his enlightenment beneath the Bodhi Tree. Close by are **Nalanda,** with the ruins of the world's oldest university and **Rajgir,** capital of the Magadha empire, and the place where Buddha and Mahavira (founder of the Jain faith) lived in retreat and delivered sermons.

DARJEELING

Darjeeling was the unsurpassed "Queen of the Hill Stations" during the British Raj, the goal of jaded Europeans seeking to revive their tempers amid its refreshing cool charm and lovely scenery, far away from muggy Calcutta. It is an exotic patch of Anglo–Himalaya, perched on the Ghoom–Senchal Ridge at an altitude of 2,134 m (7,000 ft), with magnificent views across Mt. Kanchenjunga and Mt. Everest. Its surrounding landscape has range upon range of snowy cloud and mountain peaks, with steeply sloping conifer forests and terraced tea plantations. The lively town is a labyrinth puzzle of interlacing steps, chalet-style huts and colorful bazaars selling handicrafts, the famous Darjeeling tea, and an object of much practical value in Darjeeling — the umbrella. Its cobbled streets bustle with all the races of the Himalayas, often in colorful tribal costume: the martially formidable Gurkhas, the famous mountaineering

Sherpas, Nepali women swaddled in red flannel, their chests hung with huge silver and turquoise necklaces, Mongol-featured urchins, elfin Lepchas and fair-skinned Sikkimese, Tibetan Lamas in saffron robes, Gurung farmers from western Nepal, and serene-faced Bhutanese. Stunted ponies lumber up and down the steps, taking market goods on the way down to town, and giggling apple-cheeked school-children on the way up, bundled in large baskets.

Until the beginning of the eighteenth century, Darjeeling was ruled by the Rajahs of Sikkim, who lost their domain to invading tribes of Gurkhas from Nepal in 1780. Two British

tute. It's also a botanist's paradise, with over 4,000 species of flowers. Nearby destinations include Tiger Hill, which offers incomparable views of the Himalayas, and the **Ghoom Monastery,** dedicated to Maitreya, said by the Tibetans to be the "Buddha Yet to Come."

Darjeeling is of course renowned throughout the world for its tea. However, what is so good for the tea plantations is not always so good for the visitor. The torrential monsoon, which erupts from mid-June to mid-September, can blot out the views, wash out the roads and seriously dampen the pleasure of a visit to Darjeeling. The hill station is most sunily

officers stumbled on this remote Shangri-La in 1828, realizing its potential as a strategic link in the Nepal/Tibet mountain passes, as well as a hill-station sanatorium. At that time, locals called their home "Dorje Ling" or "Place of the Thunderbolt". According to legend, Darjeeling was struck by a mystic thunderbolt of the Lamaist religion, said to be the scepter of Indra, Lord of the Gods, which supposedly fell on the site known as Observatory Hill.

Darjeeling is steeped in British legacies, nattily preserved in Anglican, Scottish and Roman Catholic churches, Tudor-style cottages, village squares, the polo ground — but above all in the tea plantations — begun by the British using seeds smuggled from China.

Darjeeling is a major base for trekking expeditions in the eastern Himalayas, the center of the Himalayan Mountaineering Insti-

idyllic during March to mid-June when rhododendron, magnolia and hollyhocks bloom. Views across to the divine mass of the Himalayas are at their most crisply spectacular during the wintry months of mid-September to December, when Darjeeling is carpeted with snow. Visitors should come prepared with an umbrella, a light raincoat and some warm clothing for the nippy evenings.

PERMITS

Darjeeling is classified as a so-called "sensitive area" by the Indian Government, due in part to the activities of the GNLF (Gurkha National

Impoverished villagers swaddled against steam fumes as they are sped on a ticketless journey through the arid hinterland of Bihar.

Liberation Front). There's a real possibility at the present time of meeting strikes and violence, both of a random and directed kind.

You won't require a permit if flying up to Darjeeling, as your passport will be automatically stamped when you arrive at Bagdogra airport, allowing you to stay for 15 days. It's wise to check with tourist authorities before leaving, as the situation is sometimes prone to changes.

A special permit to visit for seven days must be obtained in advance by those who travel there by train. Arrive early (10:30 am opening time) with your passport and rail tickets, and you may have your case "expedited." Alternatively, you may approach the Political Department, 3rd Floor at the Writer's Building.

Once you're actually in Darjeeling, it's not very easy to extend your stay, but if you want to chance your luck, approach the Darjeeling Foreigner's Registration Department, ©2261, in Laden-La Road.

How to Get There

Indian Airlines operates daily direct flights to Bagdogra airport from Delhi, Calcutta, Patna, Imphal and Guwahati. Bagdogra airport is 90 km (56 miles) away from Darjeeling and reached either by a 3-hour drive by airport bus, taxi or jeep; or by taking the famous miniature two-foot narrow gauge "Toy Train", completed in 1881, from nearby Siliguri/New Jalpaiguri.

The "express" *Darjeeling Mail* (12 hours) leaves Calcutta's Sealdah Station daily at 7:15 pm, bound for New Jalpaiguri. Reservations can be made at the Eastern Railways Booking Office, Fairlee Place, Calcutta. The last leg of the journey takes place on a miniature railway, (about three departures daily) which chugs, puffs and winds through deep jungles, tea gardens and pine forests, culminating in the famous "Agony Loop" just outside Darjeeling. Train addicts have called it India's greatest train journey, but mere mortals often find that the spectacular scenery begins to pall at the crawling pace of 10 kph (6 mph). It frequently takes much longer than its advertised time of seven to eight hours, and some travelers reported arriving in Darjeeling in the small hours after an epic 12 hour run, finding all hotels closed. Check with the tourist office in Calcutta whether the Toy Train is running, as there have occasionally been times when the service has been disrupted. You'll reach Darjeeling much faster (and get the same views) by express bus, although you'll also anticipate a hundred deaths! Quirky roadside warnings, like "Lovers, Don't Leap!" or "Beware of Falling Trucks"

quickly convince you that its not just you being neurotic.

Room with a View

Darjeeling offers a wide-range of hotels, many with breathtaking mountain and valley views. Prices vary a good deal according to season and most hotels include meals in their tariffs. Whatever your accommodation, you'll require heating facilities (Darjeeling gets bone-pinchingly chilly) and a window across the surrounding landscape.

Luxury chateau-style accommodation is best at **Hotel Everest**, (©2616-7, rates: expensive), 29 Gandhi Road. Rooms have superb views, and facilities include a reliably good restaurant, shopping arcade, health club and beauty salon. The **Windamere**, (©2397, rates: mod-

erate), Bhanu Sarani, The Mall, has a delightfully eccentric Raj-era ambience — rather like Calcutta's Fairlawn — with homely log fires in the bedrooms and a "hottie" magically slipped beneath the floral bedspread at night. There's a fusty library, bar, sweet garden, miniature golf course and badminton court. Good quality Indian, Chinese and Continental dishes are guaranteed to restore the body and soul after a long day's traipsing.

Spectacular views from all rooms are just as good at the **Luxury Tourist Lodge**, Bhanu Sarani (✆2611; rates: economy), where rooms have good heaters. Breakfast and dinner are included in the room tariff.

The most sought budget accommodation is the **Youth Hostel**, (✆2290; rates: very cheap), Dr Zakir Hussain Road. It's absurdly good value at Rs 25 for a double room with attached bathroom, with skid row Rs 8 dormitory beds. It's often full, being very popular, since not only is it dirt cheap, clean and equipped with hot showers, but being situated high up on the ridge, it has fantastic views. Its drawback is that its location requires a mandatory 15 minute puffing ascent from the bus or rail stations. The best alternative budget option is the **Shamrock Hotel**, Upper Beachwood Road, family-run and spotlessly clean, with buckets of hot water supplied on request. Room 13 has the best mountain views.

Darjeeling is not renowned for its appetizing cuisine. Addicts of traditional Tibetan *momos*, steamed mincemeat balls flavored with onion

---

Bathed in bright Himalayan sunshine, the ornate Yiga Chhoiling monastery is worthy of a detour in Ghoom.

and ginger, will have a field day — otherwise expect your taste-buds to remain untantalized. The best food is found at the **Oberoi** and the **Windamere,** otherwise go to **Glenary's,** in Laden-La Road, for quaintly cummerbunded waiters but unexceptional mainstream Indian dishes, or to **Chowrasta,** Chowrasta Square, an open-air café serving good-value vegetarian south Indian fare. Another popular rendezvous place is the Himalaya, near the Post Office, with freshly baked Tibetan bread, non-greasy chips, omelets and apple-pancakes. If all else fails — Darjeeling tea and the dry, locally produced Kalimpong cheese help quell hunger pangs.

ORIENTATION

Only the most dedicated sightseer could rise bright and early for energetic expeditions on the first day in Darjeeling. Its high altitude leaves most people feeling slightly enervated for at least a day or so. Bearing this is mind, allow yourself at least three days to see Dajee-ling's main attractions — which can be covered on foot if you've a penchant for healthy, rugged walking. Alternatively, you can inquire at the Tourist Bureau, (©2050) 1 Laden-La Road about hiring private taxis, jeeps, Land-rovers for get-ting about, as well as picking up their useful local map. Ponies might look spindly, but their sturdy knobbled legs are breed for lug-ging heavy loads around — including visiting tourists.

On the first day, develop your Himalayan sea legs by winding your way around Darjeeling town's two main thoroughfares — Laden-La, officially known as Nehru Road leading up to Chowrasta Square, a bustling strip where you'll find most of the hotels, restaurants, shops, banks, cinemas and the Tourist Bureau — and Cart Road at the bottom of the steep ridge, which is crammed with winding bazaars overflowing with odd-shaped vegetables, putrid-smelling Tibetan potions, and colorful Himalayan hand-icrafts — a mixture of Nepali, Tibetan, Sikkimese and Bhutanese folk art, wooden carvings, woven fabric, knits, carpets, local jewelry, and bric-à-brac. Look especially for the interesting, well-organized **Tibetan Self Help Centre,** es-tablished in 1959 to assist Darjeeling's large Ti-betan refugee community (who fled China-oc-cupied Tibet to India along with the 13th Dalai Lama) create their own cottage industry work-shops, and crammed with curios, carpets, leather work, jewelry and wood carvings. Also visit **Hayden Hall,** where Tibetan women in striped tunics sell their brilliantly-hued knitted crea-tions. Darjeeling's main markets pack away their baskets and stalls all day Thursday, while shops are shuttered on Sundays and half-day Saturdays. **Cart Road** is where the rail and bus stations, as well as the taxi stand, are located.

HIGH ON THE HIMALAYAS

Witnessing dawn is Darjeeling's ultimate ex-perience. The curtain is raised and there it is: Mt. Kanchenjunga — and, on a clear morning — Mt. Everest, standing tremendously in the background, surrounded by Markala, Lhotose and several other Eastern Himalayan peaks, their snows flushed rosy-pink with first light, fringed by glittering pyramids of ice, snow and rock.

The best vantage point is **Tiger Hill,** at an altitude of 2,590 m (8,482 ft), situated 11 km (6.9 miles) away. On a clear day, you'll become part of a noisy, exhaust-spluttering convoy along the mountain roads all sharing the same objec-tive. Sightseeing buses and jeeps make the hour-long trip there each morning, arriving at 4 am to await dawn. To avoid the melee, stay over-night for an early rising at the simple, but ade-quate **Tiger Hill Tourist Lodge** (©2813, rates: very cheap), which has a strategic location on a scenic plateau directly facing Mt. Kanchenjunga.

It's worth making the sturdy 40-minute trek from the Tiger Hill viewing platform to **Ghoom Buddhist Monastry,** the largest and most fa-mous religious center of its kind in Darjeeling, with an entrance of fluttering prayer flags. It was established in 1850 by a Mongolian astrol-oger-monk, and contains a giant seated image of Maitreya, the "Buddha to Come", surrounded by bowed-headed Yellow Sect Buddhists, sticks of incense, bells, drums and ornate thangka scrolls. You can ask to view a collection of precious Buddhist manuscripts, and will be asked for a small donation in return. The fun part of this excursion is returning to Darjeeling by another miniature "toy train", which leaves from Ghoom's small station, a half-hour scenic trip.

FLORA AND FAUNA

In town there are plenty of attractions worth a look. Start with the institutions founded by zealously scholarly "mad-dog" British butter-

its inmates — mostly Siberian tiger, Himalayan black bear, deer, panda and black jaguar — up in squalid little cages.

Also worth visiting is the **Himalayan Mountaineering Institute**, famous for its training courses, also has a museum with fascinating photos, equipment and exhibits relating to famous mountaineering expeditions. It's open daily 9 am to 5 pm (summer), 9 am to 4 am (winter). Close by, there's an interesting, well-manicured cemetery of former Raj residents, also containing the tomb of nineteenth century Alexander Kôrôs, a Hungarian orientologist who traveled to Darjeeling set on establishing

fly-catching botanists: **The Bengal Natural History Museum**, set up in 1903, is quite simply a taxidermist's heaven. Expertly presented, it's eccentric enough to warrant a visit purely for the sensation of being "watched" by 4,300 beady stuffed animals and insects, all captured, or stuffed into chloroform bottles, along the Eastern Himalayan belt. It's open from 10 am to 4 pm, closed Thursdays. **Lloyd's Botanical Gardens**, laid out in 1865 with beautiful orchid hothouses containing over 2,000 species and a representative collection of the flora of the Sikkim Himayalas. It's open from 6 am to 5 pm and admission is free. Take directions from the gardens to Victoria Road, then proceed along the pretty half-hour walk to the **Victoria Falls** — one of the most beautiful, secluded strolls in the area, although the waterfall itself is hardly impressive. Darjeeling's **Zoo** is notorious for shutting

that Tibetan and Hungarian peoples shared a common ancestry. He became a national hero to the Tibetan people after publishing his dictionary and grammar of the Tibetan language.

Kalimpong, 51 km (32 miles) from Darjeeling, makes a pleasant day's excursion. This scenic mountain bazaar town, perched at an altitude of 1,250 m (4,100 ft) has spectacular views, picturesque hill-folk and flower nurseries.

TEA PLANTATIONS

Darjeeling is one of the world's most famous tea-growing centers, producing India's most

ABOVE: The brass-studded interior of the Ghoom Monastery famous for its enshrined image of the Maitreya Buddha. OPPOSITE: The magical spectacle of dawn unfolding over the lofty peaks of Mount Kanchenjunga above Darjeeling.

celebrated tea, its refined taste apparently due to its uniquely favorable climate. Altogether, the hill station is dotted with some 78 tea plantations which employ some 48,000 people, many of them Nepalis, and produces some 10.5 million kilos (23 million pounds) of tea annually, all of which is packed in giant tea crates and sent off Calcutta's tea auctions. Pure Darjeeling tea is so expensive — from Rs 60 up to Rs 2,000 for a single kilo — that it's usually blended with leaves from other areas. India is still the largest consumer of its own tea, but the Soviet Union is a major importer of the thoroughbred Darjeeling tea, which they mix with their own leaves

and then sell off as "pure" Russian Tea! The traditional way of judging tea is by to take a pinch in the curl of your hand, then breathe on it to moisten the leaves, and judge the quality from the aroma. Darjeeling's leaves end up at the world's longest tea tasting table at Calcutta's Nilhat House, where highly trained tannin testers fastidiously sip, sniff and swill in the practiced manner of wine-tasters.

You're welcome to visit the **Happy Valley Tea Gardens,** three kilometers (1.9 miles) from the center of town, to see how tea is produced in the so called "orthodox" method, in which the fresh leaves are placed in "withering" troughs,

dried out by high-speed fan, then successively rolled, pressed and painstakingly fermented on a conveyer belt. Finally the tea is sorted out into grades of Golden Flowery Orange Pekoe (unbroken leaves), then Golden Broken Orange Pekoe, Orange Fanning and Dust (broken leaves). It's open from daily, except Mondays, from 8 am to noon, and 1 to 4:30 pm, open only from 1 to 4:30 pm on Sundays.

RECREATION

Just combing this hillside town's vertiginous slopes should be enough to ensure that most visitors sink into their beds at night with their muscles aching all over. If all this pony-riding and strolling don't satisfy athletic urges for the great outdoors, try golfing at the Senchal Golf Club, one of the world's highest; fishing on the Rangeet River at Singla, (8 km or 5 miles) or at the Teesta River at Riyand, (41 km or 25 miles), first obtaining permits from the District Officer. Darjeeling's treks are another popular option, since they are short—two to three days to a week — easily managed and covering spectacular scenery. If you decide to embark on an organized trek, with Sherpa guides, ponies and tents, contact either **Summit** or **Himal Ventures,** both located at Indreni Lodge, ✆ 2710, or **Tenzing Kanchenjunga Tours,** ✆ 3508, 1/D B. Giri Road. These agencies will arrange everything for the equivalent of Rs 200 a day. If you decide to go it alone, trails are well marked with plenty of good lodges for overnight stays along the routes.

The most popular trails go to **Sandakphu, Tonglu** and **Phalut,** all offering marvelous views of the whole Kachenjunga range and Mt. Everest. For detailed information on various trekking possibilities, contact the Tourist Bureau in Darjeeling. You'll also need to notify the Foreigner's Registration Office, and permission is usually granted on production of your permit.

SIKKIM

Button-holed between Bhutan and Nepal, Sikkim was a remote independent Himalayan kingdom until it was annexed by India in 1975. It still has a hermitic flavor, with its Buddhist monasteries, prayer flags fluttering from pagoda-style houses and red-robed lamas chanting mantras to the sound of drums and man-size horns, all against the breathtaking backdrop of the mighty Kanchanjunga range. The Sikkimese are a friendly mix of Lepcha, Bhutanese and Nepalese communities, and their land offers beautiful mountain scenery, good trekking, exotic varieties of fauna and flora. It boasts 600 species of orchid. The best season to visit is during February to May and

ABOVE: Layered tea gardens at the Happy Valley Plantation are typical of the landscape of Darjeeling. OPPOSITE: Tibetan-style façade of Rumtek Monastery, 24 km from Gangtok in Sikkim.

October to December. Get there by flying to Bagdogra, then make the 125 km (77 miles) journey to the capital, **Gangtok,** either by helicopter, taxi or bus. In the capital, comfortable moderately priced accommodation is best at the **Nor-Khill Hotel,** (©2386), the **Hotel Tashi Delek** (©2038), and the **Ashok Mayur** (©2558).

In Gangtok visit the **Tsuklakhang Palace,** the **Institute of Tibetology,** the **Orchid Sanctuary,** the **Cottage Industries Institute,** the **Enchey Monastery and Deer Park.** Make trekking excursions to **Bakkim** and **Dzongri.** Sikkim has remarkable monasteries at **Pemayangtse, Tashiding, Rumtek** and **Phodang,** which have vivid

wall frescoes, exquisite silk brocade thangkas or hangings, rare hand-painted scrolls, magnificent carvings and precious icons of silver and gold. Devotees seek blessings by walking in circles around small Buddhist monuments called *chortens*. Sikkim's religious festivals are celebrated in the monastery courtyards with lively mask dances by ornately costumed lamas.

The Tourist Information Centre (©2064) in Gangtok bazaar can assist with tours, car and guide hire. Good trekking firms in Gangtok are Sikkim Himalayan Adventure, Yak and Yeti Travels and Snow Lion Travels.

THE NORTH-EAST

The north-east is India's last frontier, and regrettably is mostly forbidden to travelers hoping to

explore this vast fertile region of rice paddies, mountains and jungle, wedged between Nepal and China to the north, Bangladesh to the west and Burma to the east. Connected to the rest of Hindu-dominated India by a sliver of territory above Bangladesh, its inhabitants have cultural affinities more toward South East Asia than the subcontinent.

Arunachal Pradesh, Nagaland and Tripura states and the territory of Mizoram are sensitive border zones and off limits. But visitors who do not mind the lack of comforts and can tolerate some restrictions on their movements can, with prior planning, visit the states of As-

sam, Meghalaya and Manipur. Traveling here yields magnificent scenery and exotic wildlife and the experience of one of the least known areas of the globe. The north-east is the home to many tribal peoples, with many different cultures, languages and an infectious love of festivals, music and dance. Part of the Indian government's policy of banning outsiders stems from Jawaharlal Nehru's fear that wholesale exposure to newcomers could spell doom for these unique cultures.

ASSAM

Assam may be synonymous with fine tea, but exotic wildlife reserves are its principal attraction, and home to India's rare one-horned rhinoceros that Marco Polo called the "hideous unicorn". The state capital **Guwahati** lies on the banks of the great Brahmaputra, classified in Hindu cosmology as India's only male river. The city has some grand Hindu temples, but is primarily an airport gateway to the north-east and a jump-off spot for visiting the wildlife reserves. You can either fly there directly from Calcutta, or make the 24-hour journey by train. New Delhi is 40 hours away, even on the express Assam Mail. In Guwahati, the best bet is Hotel Bramaputra Ashok, ©32632, MG Road. Rates: moderate. In town, visit the **Kamakshya Temple,** which honors the Hindu goddess Shakti, the essence of female energy, and the **Assam State Zoo and Museum.** Chug 20 km (12miles) up the Brahmaputra by steamer to visit the silk-weaving community at **Sualkashi,** where the rich Endi, Muga and Pat silks are made. The Tourist Information Centre (©24475) is on Station Road. The best season to visit is January to March and November to December, and the Assamese mark the harvesting season with **bihus,** festivals celebrated by bathing in the Brahmaputra.

WILDLIFE PARKS

Kaziranga Wildlife Sanctuary is located north-east of Guwahati on the banks of the Brahmaputra. Assam's premier nature park has some 430 sq km (158 sq miles) of steamy primeval forest which can be explored by elephant, car and boat. It is home to some 1,000 rhinos, 800 wild elephants and 700 wild buffalo, along with swamp deer, hog deer, tigers and Himalayan bears. The rhinos are watched closely by park guards, but about 30 are believed to be killed illegally each year by poachers, as Chinese value rhino blood, skin and bones for medicinal brews, and pay up to US$200 for an ounce of powdered horn, prized as a reputedly potent aphrodisiac.

Kaziranga can be reached by air from Calcutta to Jorhat, 84 km (52 miles) from the park, or the 235 km (146 mile) trip from Guwahati can be made by bus or taxi through verdant rice paddies and thatched hut villages. Stay in the ITDC **Kaziranga Forest Lodge,** making reservations in advance through the Divisional Forest Officer, Sibasagar Division, PO Box Kaziranga.

Manas Wildlife Sanctuary is nestled in the Himalayan foothills bordering Bhutan, 175 km (108 miles) north-west of Guwahati. It has 270 sq km (104 sq miles) of riverine forest that attracts many varieties of bird and animal life, and was the site where Project Tiger was launched. Stay at the **Forestry Department Bungalow or the Manas Tourist Lodge,** bookable through the Division Forest Officer, Wildlife Division, Sarania, Guwahati.

MEGHLAYA

Only 100 km (62 miles) from Guwahati, Meghlaya's capital of **Shillong** is 1,495 m (4,900 ft) high, a pretty Raj-era hill station with landscape and climate that British colonialist called the "Scotland of the East." It is pleasant most of the year for its quaint cottages, waterfalls, pine groves and flowers, as well as to see dancing by the local Khasi, Jantia and Garo tribes. Avoid the monsoon. **Cherrapunji,** just 60 km (37 miles) away, is reported to be the wettest place on the planet, with an annual average rainfall of nearly

11.5 m or 40 ft! **Shillong** is a regional melting pot, and **Bara** bazaar bustles with colorful costumed Nagas, Mizos and Manipurs from the neighboring states. There are Naga-style woven rugs, silver jewelry, bamboo handicrafts and rare butterflies compressed in glass to buy.

Arrive via Guwahati and stay at the modest **Hotel Pinewood Ashok,** (©23116 rates: inexpensive). In town, play golf at an 18-hole course, and go fishing on Umiam Lake, 16 km (10 miles) away.

MANIPUR

Bordering Nagaland, Mizoram and Burma, **Manipur** is rich in tribal culture, wooded hills and lakes. Visit the capital, **Imphal** for its spectacular Rash Lila festival of Manipuri dance in October/November. Stay at the **Hotel Ranjit,** (©382, rates: cheap), Thangal Bazaar. See the golden **Shri Govindaji** temple museum. Visit the tribal village of **Moraing** (folk culture), 37 km (23 miles) away. Buy woven goods and local handicrafts in the large **Khwairamband** bazaar.

ABOVE: Gangtok's bustling marketplace.
OPPOSITE LEFT and RIGHT: Youthful Buddhist monks in Sikkim.

ENTRY FORMALITIES

Given that some parts of these areas are open to visitors, foreign tourists will need a separate permit for each state. The permit may specify that only part of the state can be visited and many are valid for only seven days. If planning to visit this area, try to obtain all the necessary papers before leaving home from your Indian mission, as some states can require up to four months notice. If booking the trip in India, apply for permits at any Foreigners Registration Office. For the most up-to-date information, contact the Deputy Secretary, Ministry of Home Affairs, Government of New Delhi, (F-10), North Block, New Delhi 110001.

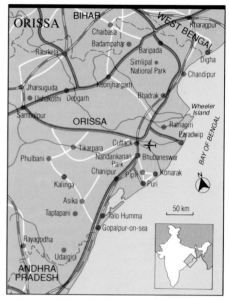

ORISSA

Tucked alongside the north-eastern coastline off the Bay of Bengal, this green, semitropical state is one of India's undiscovered gems — it is said that if one knows Orissa, one knows India. To a visitor's eyes, this quiet, rural state seems barely industrialized at all. Its capital, Bhubaneswar is surrounded by intricate bee-hive-sculpted temples and tiny villages of ocher-red mud huts whose exteriors are traced with pretty rice-flour patterns. Its unspoiled pastoral landscape is a patchwork of palm and cashew plantations, pools covered with mauve water-hyancinths, conspicuously empty of tourists, yet busy with ebony-skinned villagers dressed in loincloths, bullock-carts and plumaged parakeets flickering through the trees.

Orissa has a rich culture, colorful festivals and distinctive folk art. What's more, it even has white-sanded beaches, a tantalizing local cuisine, and a growing network of luxury hotels — in other words, a perfect place just to switch off and relax. For generations, Bengalis have come here to escape the squalor, poverty and rampant social divisions of Calcutta. It's only a matter of time before foreign tourists start flocking to Orissa too.

Above all else, Orissa is famous for its astonishing number of magnificent Hindu and Jain temples. The state is best visited with a view to exploring its compact "temple triangle," beginning with the state capital, Bhubaneswar, a cathedral city of more than 500 temples, built during the heyday of Oriyan Hindu culture between the seventh and fifteenth centuries, some of the most superb religious architecture the world has ever produced. It also has Jain and Buddhist caves, fine museums, and beautiful botanical and zoological gardens. The seaside resort of Puri lies 61 km (38 miles) away,

a vital pilgrimage center where life revolves around the famous temple of Lord Jagannath, culminating in one of India's most extraordinary and spectacular festivals, the Ratha Yatra, held every summer.

Just 31 km (19 miles) along the coastal road from Puri, past paddy fields and villages, is **Konarak,** with its magnificent, densely-carved Sun Temple built in the shape of a huge chariot.

Recorded history documents Orissa's earliest ruler as Kalinga, a powerful warlord who lost his domain to Ashoka, the powerful Mauryan emperor, in 260 BC at a battlefield near modern-day Bhubaneswar. According to lore, Ashoka was so repulsed by the bloody carnage he witnessed here that he pledged to renounce warfare, taking up the Buddhist faith of non-violence and compassion. To commemorate his epoch-making conversion, he left a famous set of rock edicts at Dhauli, 8 km, (5 miles) south of Bhubaneswar.

Buddhism rapidly declined however, and Jainism took root, reaching its zenith during the second century BC under the Chedi king, Khavravela, who encouraged monks to create the excavated cave temples of Udayagiri and Khandagiri, 8 km, (5 miles) west of Bhubaneswar. By the seventh century, Orissa had adopted Hinduism, like much of south India, entered its golden age of temple architecture.

Under successive Hindu Kesari and Ganga kings, the temple for Lord Jagannath was built at Puri; the cult of Shiva, or Shaivism, inspired the creation of many temples in Bhubaneswar, and the worship of Surya, the Sun God, flour-

252

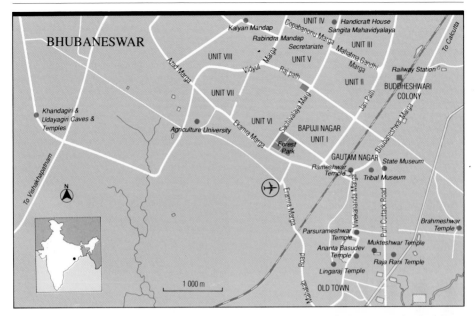

ished, culminating in Konarak's famous Sun Temple, built during the thirteenth century.

Yet Muslim invasions from both the north and the southern kingdom of Golconda resulted in the overthrow of the Hindu rulers, not to mention the decimation of countless temples. Thereafter, Orissa was claimed successively by the Afghans, the Marathas, and the British in 1803.

Orissa is at its most steamy, lush and beautiful just after the monsoon in October, and comfortable to visit until February when the mercury starts to climb. Puri is pleasant and popular as a bolt-hole from Calcutta all the year round. Otherwise, it's well worth braving heat and human waves to witness the Rath Yatra festival held every June to July. Pre-monsoon breakers (May to June) produce the best coasters if you like body-surfing. Puri and Bhubaneswar make the best bases for day-long excursions — there are few hotels of any repute at Konarak.

GETTING THERE

You can fly to Bhubaneswar daily from Calcutta, and there are direct flights from Hyderabad and Varanasi.

It can be more fun to make the journey by overnight train — at least one way. Bhubaneswar is on the main Calcutta to Madras railway line so there are plenty of trains to Bhubaneswar, as well as trains terminating at Puri. From Calcutta, take the "super-fast" overnight Coromandel Express to Bhubaneswar (7 hours) or the slower pilgrim-packed Howrah-Puri Ex-

press (12 hours). Bhubaneswar also has direct rail links with Hyderabad, Delhi and Bombay.

BHUBANESWAR

In ancient times, Bhubaneswar was known as Ekamrakshetra, one of five religious cities in the ancient Kalingan state which now comprises modern-day Orissa. Locals will tell you that Lord Shiva makes his "holidays" here, ranking it second only to Varanasi as his favorite "resort." Here in Bhubaneswar, Shiva is known as Tribuhuvaneswara or "Lord of the Three Worlds," from which the city derives its name. In its heyday, between the seventh to the fifteenth centuries, it was a magnetic and powerful pilgrimage center. More than 7000 sandstone temples once fringed its sacred Bindusagar "Ocean Drop," tank, said to contain water from every holy stream, river and pool in India, and hence a great place for washing away sins. All but 500 or so were destroyed during the Mughal conquest of the sixteenth century. Among these are many perfectly preserved examples of the profusely carved Oriyan style of temple architecture.

Modern Bhubaneswar is delightfully rural for a state capital that administers the affairs of 25 million Oriyans — largely free of pollution, traffic and high-rise buildings. Its hallowed temples are concentrated in the old town, very exotic with its cobbled alleys, palm groves and frangipani trees dotted around the khaki-colored Bindusagar Tank, where local lads go spearfishing for sacred fish.

GETTING AROUND

In town, use taxis, auto-rickshaws or buses. Go temple-hopping by cycle-rickshaw (Rs 30 for a three-hour tour), often wired up with black sun-umbrellas. Bicycles can be hired easily through any hotel, perfect for a day's excursion.

The OTDC Tourist Information Center, ©50099, Jayadev Marg, near Pantha Niwas Tourist Bungalow run useful sightseeing tours. The city tour (8:45 am to 6 pm daily, except Monday) costs Rs 24, and covers Bhubaneswar's major temples, the Udayagiri and Khandagiri caves, Nandankanan Park and Dhauli. There's a regular Puri/Konarak tour (9 am to 6 pm) which costs Rs 34. Both have good guides and leave from the Pantha Niwas Tourist Bungalow. You can also hire trained guides and private cars for sightseeing here. Expect to pay about Rs 400 for a round trip from Bhubaneswar to Puri and Konarak, or Rs 250 one way.

Otherwise, frequent local buses make the 1½ hour journey to Puri, leaving from the main bus station. Buses to Konarak can be irregular, and it's wise to check departures with the tourist office before planning your day. From Puri to Konarak, regular minibuses take passengers on a "fill-her-up" basis for the 35 minute 30 km (18.8 miles). If you take an early-morning bus from Puri and an afternoon bus back (or onto Bhubaneswar), you'll have ample time to see the Sun Temple.

WHERE TO STAY

The **Hotel Oberoi Bhubaneswar,** ©56116, Nayapalli, offers luxury accommodation at remarkably reasonable rates. One of India's most beautiful hotels, its distinctive, temple-inspired design features polished sandstone, Oriyan decor and brass lamps throughout, with a lovely swimming pool and tennis courts set in palm-dotted landscaped gardens. A choice of restaurants offer excellent food, ranging from local specialities to Mughali, Western and Chinese. Facilities include a health club, shopping arcade, travel desk and beauty salon with car-hire for temple-hopping. It's located seven kilometers from the capital. There's a courtesy shuttle service between the airport and the hotel.

Within the city center, choose from three moderately priced hotels, all close to the temples. Best is the **New Kenilworth Hotel,** ©54330-1, at Gautam Nagar, which has comfortably furnished rooms, efficient staff and good restaurants and travel desk. Breakfast at their coffee shop — delicious yogurt, fresh fruit, toast, eggs and coffee — is astoundingly good at only Rs 15. Around the corner, the ITDC-run

Kalinga Ashok, ©53318, is quite stylish, and its useful facilities include a bank, several restaurants, travel agency, swimming pool and doctor. **Hotel Swosti,** ©54178-9 on Janpath is slightly cheaper, with immaculately clean rooms, friendly staff, excellent restaurant, and good facilities including bank, shopping arcade, travel counter and bar.

Hotel Prachi, (©52689, rates: inexpensive), further along Janpath, is functional and clean, with good food, swimming pool and tennis courts. The state-run **Pantha Niwas Tourist Bungalow,** (©54515, rates: inexpensive to cheap) is located close to the temples on Lewis Road,

offers practical comfort: each room comes with fans, mosquito net and shower. It also has Rs 30 dorm rooms. It's right next door to the tourist office and is the departure point for sightseeing tours. Similar quality can be found at the big, well-kept **Bhubaneswar Hotel,** (©51977, rates: cheap) directly behind the railway station.

EATING OUT

Orissa's cuisine is similar to that of Bengal — liberal quantities of fresh seafood (lobster, prawns, crab and fish), traditionally cooked with coconut milk or curd, and given zing with pinches of *fenugreek* and mustard seeds. Order an Oriyan *thali* for starters — fluffy white rice, *bekti* or *rui* fish, vegetable dishes, including the staple green, *kara saag* (spinach), delicate *puris*, rounded off with the local caramel custard, *chena purd patha* (cheese-burnt-sweet) or *khiri*, rice cooked with milk, sugar, cardamoms and cashew nuts.

Other delicious specialties to look out for are *dahi maccha* fish cooked with curd and coriander; *saag bhaja*, fried spinach; and *khajun khata*, an unusual combination of tomato cooked with dates. Local curd is devastatingly rich and creamy — perfect with fresh fruit for breakfast.

A pleasant ride north of town, the **Hotel Oberoi** offers the most stylish dining experience — its **Pushpaneri** restaurant has exceptional Oriyan and Indian fare (both vegetarian and non-vegetarian) for around Rs 80 per head. You'll

able to see style and form developing, expanding and refining before your eyes.

Oriyan temple design was governed by mathematical formulae, even down to the most seemingly innocuous detail. All follow an essential structure consisting of an entrance porch *(jagamohan)* and an inner sanctum for the image of the deity *(deul)*, above which soars a ribbed conical tower *(shikara)* rises. Endless additions could be incorporated — sub-shrines, halls where offerings could be made, and dancing halls for the ritualized dance that later blossomed into the lithe, exotic Odissi style. The exterior was always lavishly carved with geo-

also dine well at slightly cheaper prices at the **Hotel Swosti** and the **Hotel Kalinga Ashok,** both of which offer incredibly good value lunchtime Oriyan thalis, as well as offering a diverse range of Indian, Continental and Chinese food. Few restaurants are worth visiting outside the hotels — most are glorified grubby tea stalls — although the **Angar South Indian Restaurant,** near Station Square, is very popular for its excellent Indian-style breakfasts for Rs 10.

THE TEMPLE TRAIL

Bhubaneswar's famous temples are best covered leisurely on your own, preferably in the quiet cool of early morning. By concentrating on a cluster of impeccably preserved temples, you will be taken on a curator's walk though five centuries of temple architecture,

metrical designs, flowers, animals, mythological figures, humans and gods. In the earlier, squat shrines, these carvings are simple storytelling devices, but in the later extravagant, tapering temples, the stone comes alive with sharp precision, and provocative female figures appear, at their most poutingly playful at the Rajarani and Brahmesvara temples and at the Sun Temple at Konarak, where scrutiny of close-up detail reveals some highly athletic dalliances.

What to See
Bhubaneswar's eleventh century **Lingaraj Temple**, dedicated to Shiva as Lord Lingaraj, or

ABOVE: Post-monsoon ablutions at the Mukteshwar Temple in Bhubaneswar.
OPPOSITE Detail of an exquisitely ornate frieze adorning the Rajarani Temple in Bhubaneswar.

"Lord of the Universe," is considered the pinnacle of Oriyan architecture, but it's so sacred to Hindus that "heathens" aren't allowed inside, and instead are restricted to peering at it from a platform (erected for Lord Curzon) outside the compound wall. Binoculars are useful, otherwise you'll see the temple's ornately carved 46-m (150-ft) -high spire, covered with sculpted lions crushing elephants, said to symbolize the re-emergence of Hinduism over Buddhism. There's little else for foreigners to look at except elderly temple priests napping under a giant Banyan tree. The temple is dedicated to Lord Shiva, and the granite lingam which represents him is dutifully lathered each day with water, milk and bhang (hashish). Amazingly, the entire walled compound contains some 50 small shrines, each of importance to the gift-bearing devotees. Thousands of pilgrims gather here for the major Shivrati festival in February/March, holding candles on the night of the full moon as the Lingaraj deity is ritually bathed in the nearby Bindusagar tank to mark his birth anniversary.

Skirting the eastern side of Bindusagar is a cluster of about 20 smaller temples. Look especially for the small, decorative **Sisneswar Temple** and the double-storied **Vaital Deul Temple**, both dating to the eighth century, the latter thought to be a tantric shrine where humans were once sacrificed for the presiding eight-armed deity, Kapalini, depicted wearing here with garlands of skulls and reclining on a corpse. It's one of the few non-Shiva temples in Bhubaneswar, being dedicated to the Goddess Durga.

At the top of Tankpani Road, you'll find the **Parumeshwar Temple** (seventh century) said to be the home of Ganesh's brother Parumeshwar (Muruga). It's the best preserved of all Bhubaneswar's most ancient temples, and has detailed bas-reliefs of elephant and horse processions. Close by is the **Mukteshwar Temple** (ninth century), with its exquisite carved lotus entrance canopy, each petal bearing an image of a deity. Within its enclosure are many mango and jackfruit trees, plus a pint-sized sacred tank, where childless women bathe on the full moon of March/April to become fertile.

Continuing along Tankpani Road, look out for the **Rajarani Temple**, (twelfth century) set in pretty gardens. It is a "love temple," covered with coyly erotic carvings of women and couples, built by a Rajah for his wife, the Rani — hence the name. Once the Rajah was interred within, the temple became a mausoleum and was no longer used for worship.

Finally, the **Brahmeshwar Temple** (eleventh century) lies on the outskirts of the old city. It's actually a complex of shrines, notable for its elaborate exterior carvings, particularly its dancing girls, and higher up, the Orissan lion, which was hunted to extinction during the British Raj.

If you care to take a look, just across the field from the Brahmeshwar Temple are the part excavated ruins of **Sisupalgarh**, thought to be the remains of the city founded by Ashoka, occupied from the third century BC to the fourth century AD.

In town, also visit the **Orissa State Museum**, opposite the Kalinga Ashok for its rich collection relating to Orissa's history, culture, architecture and many tribal people, open 10 am to 5 pm every day except Monday.

The Tribal Research Bureau is located here, filled with sheaves of yellowing theses on Orissa's 62 distinct tribal groups of aboriginal people whose ancestors existed before the Aryan invasion of India. These "hunter-gatherers" live according to their own customs in the mountain ridges of the central Orissa. Among the better known are the Kondhs, the bugbear of British missionaries for their reluctance to give up their habit of human sacrifice — today slaughter is mostly confined to roosters, goats and bullocks. Then there are the Bondas, famous in India for their licentious attitude to premarital sex, and the fact that their young women choose their husbands on the basis of their sexual skills. Other major tribes are the Juangs, the Santals, the Parajas, the Koyas and the Godabas.

OUT OF TOWN

Either take the OTDC tour or hire a taxi for the afternoon to round-off Bhubaneswar's sights. Some 8 km (5 miles) into the surrounding countryside lie the twin hills of **Udaigiri** and **Khandagiri**, honeycombed with ancient Jain and Buddhist caves. Scattered at various levels, they were hollowed out by monks during the reign of Kharavela, the Kalinga emperor during the second century BC. Udayagiri has 44 caves, many extensively carved. The most historically interesting is the Hathi Gumpha or Elephant Cave, which contains one of India's most important extant Pali scripts — a detailed record of Kharavela's religious, military and civil accomplishments. Khandagiri has 19 caves, and is crowned by a series of Jain temples.

Ashoka's famous **Dhauli Edicts** are about 8 km south of Bhubaneswar, carved on a giant rock overlooking the plain below where the climactic Kalinga battle took place. The 13 inscriptions are still remarkably legible after 2000 years. Above them, the elephant carved out of the rock above symbolizes Buddha, and is the earliest known sculpture in Orissa. The hill is topped by the modern white Shanti Stupa, or Peace Pagoda, built by Japanese Buddhists and visible for miles and notable for its marked resemblance to a UFO, with its five antennae-like "umbrella" representing the Buddhist virtues of faith, hope, compassion, forgiveness and non-violence.

The extensive **Nandankanan Park**, 20 km (12.5 miles) away, is a scenic wildlife and botanical garden, unique as the only place where the rare white tiger has ever been breed in captivity. It's also India's largest Lion Safari Park in India, measuring over 20 hectares (50 acres). It's also home to rhinos, monkeys, gharials, pelicans, pythons, brown bear and India's rare white crocodile. Buses run visitors out on regular "wildlife patrols." There are pleasant facilities to stay at the Tourist Cottages or Forest Rest House. It's open 7 am to 6 pm during April to September, and 7:30 am to 5 pm, September to March. Local buses ply there every hour from Bhubaneswar.

SHOPPING FOR CRAFTS

Orissa was traditionally known as "Utkal," or "Land of Art" for its talented communities of sculptors, painters, potters, weavers and embroiderers whose skills created her exquisite temple complexes and kept her rulers beautifully garbed — today these arts are kept alive in Orissa's timeless villages. By far the most popular tourist purchase is Orissa's famous colorful patchwork applique, fashioned into sun umbrellas, hanging lanterns, canopies and cushions, and her silk and cotton hand loom *ikat* design textiles. Other good buys include the animal motif papier mâché masks originally used for epic play; *patachitra* paintings on muslin cloth; etched palm-leaf manuscripts, silver filigree jewelry, soapstone and wood carvings, brass and bell metal work and shellcraft. At Puri you can buy little carved replicas of Lord Jagannath and his brother and sister.

In Bhubaneswar the best places to shop are the **Utkalika Handicrafts Emporium** and the **Handloom Cooperative Society**, both in the Market Building halfway up Rajpath. These give an overview of contemporary Orissan crafts, with everything sold at fixed prices. They can also arrange visits to see skilled craftsmen at work.

Throughout the state, you'll find lanes, neighborhoods and sometimes, entire villages devoted to one particular craft. Wander into any of these areas, and you'll be welcome to watch the work in progress, meet the family and, if you like, make a purchase. All of this commercial activity comes to a head in **Pipli**, 20 km (12.5 miles) enroute from Bhubaneswar to Puri, where the main street consists entirely of stalls aimed at passing tourists. The speciality here is

colorful applique work, often utilizing decorative motifs of animals, birds and flowers. Much of has become rather mass-produced, although there are still elderly artists who still remember how to make the delicate elaborate work of the last century. Others to visit include the bell-metal village of **Belakati**, 9 km (5½ miles) from Bhubaneswar; the palm-etcher's village of **Ragurajpur**, just outside Puri; and the beautiful fresco-covered houses of **Pathuria Sahi** or "Stone Carver's Lane" in Puri itself.

In the major bazaar areas, such as that around the Jagannath Temple in Puri, bargaining is expected, and whittling down prices is

part of the fun, carried out with bantering good humor. By contrast, the individual artists working from their homes tend to quote fair prices for their work — exceedingly low in relation to the painstaking time, skill and talent which has gone into its making.

PURI

Fringed by sand dunes and casuarina trees, Puri is one of India's four holiest places, a goal for countless pilgrims, from ash-smeared fakirs to Bombay film-stars. It's also India's Brighton, a

---

ABOVE: An white-clad widow clasps her hands and gazes with fretful adoration at a garish painted idol before the commencement of the Rath Yatra or Car festival in Puri.

scented bath and laid out for siesta. Meals are placed before him and later removed — untouched but sanctified. None of these age-old ceremonies may be witnessed by an non-Hindu, for the temple is a forbidden citadel to outsiders.

Puri's religious fervor reaches a spectacular pitch during the **Rath Yatra**, the "Car Festival," held during June and July. To celebrate Krishna's journey from Gokul to Mathura, the images of Lord Jagannath and his siblings are hauled through Puri on vast *raths* (chariots) to the nearby Gundicha Mandir (garden house) for

popular seaside resort with a rambling country-club style hotel, dilapidated Bengali villas and conical-capped lifeguards.

Puri is home to the "Formless One," Lord Jagannath, said to represent the primordial essence of the cosmos. His palatial apartment is the twelfth century **Jagannath Temple**, the focus of this atmospheric, worship-obsessed town. He is an incarnation of Lord Krishna, and one of the reasons for his popularity is that all castes are equal before him.

Millions have dropped to their knees before his image — a white-faced, legless, brightly-painted wooden idol with glaring eyes. Stumpy arms emerge from his forehead, which glitters with a large diamond. He shares the temple with his black-faced brother Balaram, and his yellow-faced sister, Subshadra. He commands more than six thousand "servants" who dedicate their lives to him, either as priests, temple wardens or pilgrim guides, altogether forming a complex hierarchy of 37 orders and 97 classes. Like an infant emperor, Lord Jagannath has his teeth brushed, his face anointed, his fine clothes changed, his body given a fragrant sandalwood-

their annual week's holiday, before being dragged back home.

Puri becomes massed with hundreds of thousands of delirious, swaying humans, riveted by the spectacle of three huge wooden chariots, as large as houses, and surmounted by decorated pavilions where the three gods sit on brocade cushions for their mile-long journey. The largest is Jagannath's, some 14 m (45 ft) high, 11 m (35 ft) square and supported by 16 wheels, each 2.1 m (7 ft) tall — adding the word Juggernaut to the English language. Ritual decrees that each wagon is pulled by 4,200 men, girdled with thick rope, and accompanied by musicians bashing cymbals, drums and horns in wild abandon. People press forward, throwing rice, marigolds, and coconut shards for blessings, and cases of frenzied self-sacrifice beneath the wheels are not unknown. After delivering the gods back home, the chariots are broken up and the discarded timbers are sold as sacred relics.

Four faces of devotion at Puri's Rath Yatra. Clockwise from ABOVE LEFT: Fierce gaze from a shaven-headed woman, one of thousands, has dedicated her locks to Lord Jagganath; A "servant" of Lord Jagganath bears a totemic staff in the image of his master; Ash-smeared sadhu or holy man; A Shaivite or follower of Lord Shiva, his forehead smeared with the phallic symbol of the lingam.

ON THE BEACH

Puri's endless white sand beach is good for long strolls, fresh air, sun-bathing, swims; watching sunrises, sunsets and local fishermen dressed in loincloths and conical hats repairing nets and putting out to sea in their catamarans. Local urchins tag along, selling shells, cloth and semiprecious gems. Pilgrims take a holy dip, staggering and giggling in the surf getting their clothes drenched, believing that its extremely salty waters will, in the words of a local guide, "bring broadness of mind and do away with all meanness."

Tourists preparing to don skimpy swimsuits will soon discover that sun-bathing is considered highly eccentric in Orissa — what goes in Goa does not "go" here. The sight of partially exposed flesh causes local fishermen to stampede across the sands, rapt at having cornered a rare Westerner on their shores. You'll be peppered

with friendly invitations to explore their village, become a star guest at a seafood sizzle-up on the sands or spend a day going fishing with them. It's certainly fascinating to watch their catamarans being constructed on the sands, made from solid tree trunks, split longitudinally and bound together. When they're not being used, they're untied and the planks laid out on the beach to dry out, like giant matchsticks.

Strong currents fringe the shoreline, resulting in Puri's eccentric corps of elderly "life-

guards", actually retired fishermen, easily recognized by their wicker-work hats. They'll lead you down to surf with heroic displays of chivalry, then "guard" your clothes for a few rupees. One Dutch traveler related that he was snatched by a current out to sea, and started shouting for help, only to see the "lifeguard" wave encouragingly from the shore, while his traveling companions had to swim out to rescue him!

Unfortunately, locals seem to use much of their otherwise glorious beach as a public latrine — a good reason for escaping to the more pristine, (hygienic) sands at Gopalpur-on-sea, further south.

WHERE TO STAY

Stay at the **South Eastern Railway Hotel,** (✆2063, rates:moderate), a delightful pre-World War I establishment set in a manicured garden on sand's edge, originally built as the grand residence of one Lady Ashworth. It was taken over the Bengal Nagpur Railway and opened as a hotel in 1925. It's now run by the South Eastern Railway, but still referred to as the "BNR." Rooms are kept spotless, with sand whisked out twice a day, and have quaint four-posters, mosquito nets, porcelain baths, sea-facing shuttered windows, and adjoining verandahs. Some are grander than others and priced accordingly. Convalescent bath-chairs are set for taking "bed tea" and "after tea," delivered by hotel "boys" wearing cummer-

bunds and BNR hats with big brass buttons. Huge quantities of Raj-era food are served downstairs in the dining room, included within the room rates, but open to non-residents. Signs in the hallway request silence during the siesta hours. Facilities include billiards, table tennis, bar and library. The manager is friendly and helpful, particularly for travel arrangements. As you open your shutters in the morning, life-guards wave hopefully from the gate, cooing, "Sahib, Madam, beach is ready and waiting!"

Other accommodation will seem characterless by comparison. Best of Puri's many resorts is **Hotel Prachi Puri**, (©2638, rates: moderate), located at the west end of Puri beach. It offers Puri's best Indian, Continental and Chinese food, and has a pretty outdoor bar. The **Pantha Niwas Tourist Bungalow** (©562; rates: cheap) has clean comfortable rooms, with an attached restaurant for good mealtime thalis.

Small guesthouses provide cheap accommodation for those who like to travel rough, most clustered towards the eastern end of the beach. In current vogue with back-packers are the **Sea Foam Hotel** and the **Z Hotel**, both clean, with fans, mosquito nets and the option of shared or attached bathrooms. Puri's skid row is the big, modern **Youth Hostel**, ©424, where dormitory beds segregate the sexes and cost Rs 8 per night.

THE MAIN DRAG

All sandy tracks in Puri lead to its broad central **Baradand** or **Grand Road** which runs from the Jagannath Temple to the Gundicha Mandir. It's nicest to visit at sunset, when gas lamps and candles form a flickering action-packed strip of jostling pilgrims, prospecting beggars, bullock carts, cycle-rickshaws, and street stalls selling trinkets, vegetarian snacks, and religious paraphernalia.

The magnificent **Jagannath Temple** stands at the center, built during the twelfth century by the Kalingan king Chodaganga. It is Orissa's tallest temple, and its 65 m high (212 ft) spire is a landmark for miles around. Each of its four gates has an animal theme: horse (south), elephant (north), tiger (west) and lion (east). Pilgrims enter by the Lion Gate to pay respects to Lord Jagannath, laden with gifts of coconuts and flowers. Devout women emerge bald-headed, having offered their shining tresses as a symbol of sacrifice. In front of the main entrance is a beautiful pillar, uprooted from the Sun Temple at Konarak.

Non-Hindus aren't allowed inside, but can peer over the walls on a nearby viewing platform on the roof of the Raghunandan Library.

A sign inside warns "Be Aware of Monkeys," and you are given a big stick, just in case. From here you'll get a clear view all the way down to the Gundicha Mandir, Lord Jagannath's summer temple. On the way down, ask to see the library's good collection of antique Pali manuscripts can be available on request —you'll be asked for a donation in any case.

UP THE COAST

If you're looking for a place to get away from it all with clean private beaches, head for

Gopalpur-on-sea, three hours drive south of Puri. Comfortable accommodation is found at the **Oberoi Palm Beach Hotel** (©23, rates: moderate), a charming British country house-style resort just 100 meters from the empty golden sands. Excellent facilities include good restaurants, car rental, badminton and tennis, and arrangements can be made for riding, sailing and fishing. It's 172 km (107 miles) from Bhubaneswar and 16 km (10 miles) from the Berhampur railway station which links with Bhubaneswar and Calcutta. It's a good base for an excursion to Chilka Lake, on the coast between Puri and Gopalpur-on-sea, a beautiful island-dotted bird sanctuary best seen at sunrise by taking a boat out from Balligan or Rambha.

KONARAK

The thirteenth century **Sun Temple** stands on a desolate stretch of blowing sand, an awesome relic of Konarak's ancient legacy as a busy center of Orissan culture and commerce. This

ABOVE: Frenzied devotees hurl themselves on a fragment of a painted wooden *rath* or chariot. OPPOSITE: Seething crowds and enough medieval pageantry to rival a Cecil B. de Mille epic at the Rath Yatra.

unique ruin was conceived as an immense stone chariot which pulls the Sun God, Surya, across the heavens. Steps ascend to the main entrance, flanked by seven gigantic straining horses, representing the seven colors of the prism. Around its base are 24 huge wheels, each signifying the changing cycle of the sun. The entire structure is covered with carvings, sculptures, figures and bas-reliefs. It was designed so that the sun's first rays would strike first the dancing hall, then the hall of audience, and finally the head of the Sun God in the main temple, harnessing its energy and life-force. According to popular lore, it was here that the cult of

complete between 1243–1255. The main temple has fallen into ruins, yet a remaining audience hall is proof of the colossal scale on which the temple was executed. Every aspect of contemporary life was recorded in its painstaking carvings, from courtly procedures like law, administration, civic life and war to erotic imagery of human love as marvelous and detailed as those seen at Khajuraho. Originally the temple had a huge spire, soaring to 70 m (277 ft), and was nicknamed the "Black Pagoda" by early mariners navigating their passage to Calcutta, apparently due to the superstition that the temple's iron filings lured unwary ships to the shore.

sun-worship began some 5,000 years ago. The legend relates that Krishna, irritated by a disrespectful son-in-law, Samba, cursed him with leprosy, and advised him to do penance for the sun-god Surya for 12 years. Once cured of his disease, Samba erected a small temple to Surya — said to be buried beneath the present temple.

The Sun Temple was commissioned by King Narasimha of the Ganga dynasty to commemorate his victorious expansion into Bengal, and as a symbol of Hindu might against the encroaching Muslims. It took 1200 masons and sculptors, and 12,000 laborers 12 years to

Outside the temple grounds, there's a small but interesting **museum** which houses excavated sculptures and fragments, and stocks Debala Mitra's inexpensive guide to Konarak here. It's open 10 am to 5 pm, closed on Fridays.

Konarak's deserted, beautiful beach may tempt some travelers to stay on. The **Tourist Bungalow** (✆21 rates: cheap) is next to the temple, has clean rooms with fans and attached baths.

ANDAMAN AND NICOBAR ISLANDS

This chain of 321 virgin tropical islands stretches across the eastern Bay of Bengal, midway between India and the tip of Sumatra. Only 38 of the islands are inhabited. The

ABOVE : Elderly *dhoti*-clad couple admire friezes worn to a spidery frailty after seven centuries of exposure to the elements at the Sun Temple in Konarak. RIGHT: One of 24 gigantic wheels adorning the base of the Sun Temple.

archipelago possesses a smoldering primitive beauty, with dense forests woven with canopies of vines and deserted white-sand beaches lapped by clear turquoise waters. This exotic, unspoilt landscape hardly feels part of India at all.

Port Blair, the Andamans' capital, is tranquil and rustic, with wooden houses smothered in bougainvillea, scenic views across to nearby islands, and an unpolluted wharf with old ships and cackling seagulls.

There is still something unconquered and mysterious about much of the archipelago, which is home to six aboriginal tribal groups, each with different physiognomies, languages, and beliefs that have changed little since the Paleolithic age. Many of these indigenous tribes are hostile toward intruders, be they government officials carrying presents of plastic buckets, watches, or chocolates, or gaping tourists fumbling for their cameras. Islands inhabited by these tribes are now off limits to casual visitors. Only the xenophobic and handsome Sentinelese, who live on North Sentinel Island, have remained completely isolated from the world, repulsing all intruders with their expertly hurled two-meter (6.5-ft) poisoned arrows. The Greater Andamese from the north, the Jarawas from the Middle Andamans, and the Nicobarese and Shompens from the Nicobar Islands simply prefer to be left alone. Others, like the naked, body-painted Onges from South Andaman, a tribe of hunters and gatherers, have become quite blasé about visits from anthropologists and curious onlookers, and eagerly swap their tasseled G-strings for polyester nighties or T-shirts, and their fresh fish for tins of baked beans.

The powerful Marathas from central India first annexed the Andaman and Nicobar islands in the late seventeenth century as a convenient base for plundering British, Dutch, and Portuguese merchant ships. After several attempts, the British finally ousted the Marathas in the nineteenth century and established a penal colony at Port Blair in the aftermath of the 1857 Indian Mutiny, earning the archipelago the notorious sobriquet *"kala pani"*, or "water of death". During World War II, the Andamans were the only part of India to be occupied by the Japanese, who between 1942 and 1945 massacred large numbers of prisoners and local tribespeople.

Port Blair's main industry is the export of timber, and vast areas of its teak, mahogany, and rosewood forests have been razed. The capital has a mixed community of mainland Indians and Burmese, and makes a perfect base for exploring the nearby coral reefs.

ENTRY FORMALITIES

Foreigners require a permit to visit the Andaman and Nicobar islands, but this is easily obtained from the authorities on arrival at Port Blair, regardless of whether you arrive by air or ship. The permit is valid for 15 days, but it can be extended. It applies only to Port Blair's municipal area and the nearby coral reef islands of Jolly Buoy, Red Skin, Cinque, Neil, and Havelock. Permits are issued from the Tourist Office (©20694) in the Secretariat building on VIP Road, Port Blair. You'll have to make another visit to get a "departure" stamp in your passport before leaving. Those wishing to visit other islands need to approach the Ministry of Home Affairs, Government of India, North Block, New Delhi, but the southern Nicobar Islands are completely off limits to foreign tourists, as are any islands inhabited by tribal groups.

ACCESS

Indian Airlines operates four flights weekly to Port Blair and back from Calcutta and Madras. The flight takes about two hours.

The other alternative is to make the three-day sea crossing to Port Blair from either Calcutta or Madras. Schedules can be irregular, particularly during the monsoon months, and the lurching journey can induce seasickness, but those with a yen for sea travel will find glamour in being adrift in the Bay of Bengal, sighting dolphins and sharks, and being privy to the slightly farcical shipboard atmosphere with its salty seadog captain, aged bearers in soiled caps, and sinewy Dravidian ship-boys. It's certainly much cheaper than flying — one-way fares range from deluxe air-conditioned private cabins with attached bathrooms at Rs 558, Class B at Rs 389, and Class C at Rs 355, all the way down the scale to Rs 69 bunk class, with fold-down planks. Shipboard meals cost extra and tend to be monotonous *thali* affairs, although the Western-style breakfasts are good. To book berths or inquire about the next sailing, contact the Shipping Corporation of India (©239456), 13 Strand Road in Calcutta, or their Madras agents, KPV Sheikh Muhammed Rowther and Co (©510346), 41 Linghi Chetty Street. The SCI also have an office in Bombay at 229–232 Madame Cama Road.

WHEN TO GO

The Andamans are at their most idyllic between mid-November and mid-May, when the weather is generally warm with cooling sea breezes. Port Blair's "off" season coincides with the monsoon period (late May to early October), when it has a steamy, primeval beauty but snorkeling and scuba diving become impossible.

HOTELS

Welcomgroup Bay Island, ©20881, is a spacious, well-designed resort hotel atop Marine Hill, fitted out with local and natural wood furniture. The rooms all have balconies, which provide breathtaking views across Phoenix Bay. Both the bar and restaurant overlook the sea, and hotel fare includes Indian, Burmese, and local seafood dishes. Rates: moderate. Facilities include a seawater pool (there is no attached beach), health club, indoor games, and video screenings of several interesting films on the tribal people of the islands. Mrs Vasan operates the hotel's travel desk, and her efficiency and prodigious knowledge of the islands make this service far superior to that provided by the sleepy tourist office. She'll take rapid care of any ticketing, and can arrange transport facilities (taxi, boat hire, helicopter rides) as well as snorkeling and scuba equipment.

Andaman Beach Resort, ©20599, is modern and functional with a beachfront location at Corbyn's Cove, Port Blair's most swimmable beach. The hotel supplies equipment for windsurfing, water-skiing, sailing, scuba diving, snorkeling, and fishing. Other facilities include a restaurant, bar, travel desk, and tennis courts. Rates: moderate.

Good inexpensive options include the **Shompen Hotel**, ©20360, at Middle Point, which has friendly service, a restaurant, and rooms with attached bathrooms and the popular **Megapode Nest**, ©2207, Haddo, overlooking Phoenix Bay, both bookable through Port Blair's Deputy Director of Tourism (©20694). There are also two quite pleasant government guesthouses, one atop Marine Hill and one in Corbyn's Cove: both offer clean, basic accommodation.

The two resort hotels have the town's only established restaurants — otherwise go to Aberdeen Bazaar to stock up on provisions and delicious local fruits, or sample fish patties and samosas from cheap *chai* cafés. The **Annapurna Cafe**, near the Shompen Hotel, serves good fish and chips and mealtime *thalis*.

SIGHTSEEING

What most people have in mind when they visit the Andamans archipelago is a week or two of idyllic leisure, hopping from one secluded oys-

ter-shell bay to another, basking in clear waters, and exploring the underwater enchantment of colorful coral reefs. But Port Blair has its own charm, and it's worth spending a day or two making a relaxed bicycle tour of its sights.

Start with the **Cellular Jail**, the eerie edifice constructed by the British in 1906 and used to incarcerate many hundreds of "dangerous" Indian political prisoners until 1938. Set on the sea coast of Atlanta Point, it resembles a vast wheel, with the central watchtower joined by seven triple-storied wings, all pocketed with hundreds of tiny crypt-like cells where prisoners were kept in solitary confinement. For the British, it was a highly effective way of paralyzing the Independence movement: elite and literate freedom fighters shared their plight of isolation, hard labor, and brutal torture with common criminals, and many were driven to insanity and suicide.

But by far the worst atrocities took place during the Japanese occupation of Port Blair from 1942 to 1945, when there were mass executions of prisoners as well as villagers suspected of being spies for the Allied forces.

The prison grounds are open from 9 am to noon and 2 to 5 pm every day, and a *son et lumière* show is scheduled to begin in early 1989. There are several informative booklets for sale at the entrance booth.

Winding down the road to Aberdeen Jetty you'll find the **Marine Museum**, a dusty chamber which has over 350 pickled exhibits of different species, charts of tropical fish, shells, coral, and an exotic collection of turtle eggs. Come here before you start scuba diving so you'll recognize what lurks beneath the Andamans' ocean waves. It's open 8:30 am to 12:30 pm and 1:30 to 4 pm, but is closed on Sundays and public holidays.

From here it's a hilly climb through Aberdeen Bazaar up to the **Anthropological Museum**, which has a fascinating collection of photographs and descriptions of the Andaman and Nicobar tribal groups, and displays of ceremonial costumes and objects, such as crab claw pipes, flax tassel G-strings, leaf-palm umbrellas, human mandible necklaces, and nautilus shell cups. But there is frustratingly little solid information, and if you wish to know more about the region's tribal people, try to strike up a conversation with the head researcher in residence, Mr Baha. The museum is open from 9 am to noon and 1 to 4 pm, closed Saturdays and public holidays. From here, ask for directions to the nearby **Cottage Industries Emporium**, which sells delicate shell jewelry, shell-lamps, and a wide range of local handicrafts. It's open 8:15 am to 12:30 pm and 1 to 4:45 pm except during the weekend.

Halfway down the road leading to Chatham Wharf is Port Blair's well-kept **Mini Zoo**, which houses an array of indigenous plumed birds, monitor lizards, wild boars, macaque monkeys, bears, and deer. There's also a crocodile breeding farm, and a captivating Painted Stork, as poised and eccentric as an old count in a multicolored tuxedo. It's open from 7 am to noon, 1 to 5 pm, and is closed on Mondays. The two last stops are eccentric Port Blair tourist attractions: the gigantic Victorian-era Chatham Saw Mill, and the Wimco Match Factory, where most of India's matchsticks are made.

HARBOR CRUISES

The tourist office employs old khaki-clad sailors to run afternoon cruises on quaint, brass-studded Bristol boats, which meander around the harbor stopping at places of interest and return just as sunset casts a molten light over the landscape. First stop is at the Bamboo Jetty Market, where excited islanders in folded-up dhotis and large lapels haggle passionately for fish, jackfruit, and Tupperware. The most interesting stop on this trip is at **Viper Island**. The first prison for chain-gang convicts in British India was built here in 1867; later it was used for female prisoners. Ironically, the view from the gallows — all that remains of the prison — is one of incomparable loveliness. The boat leaves from the end of the Phoenix Bay dockyard at 3 pm, and tickets cost Rs 26.

There's also an early morning Rs 14 cruise from the same jetty across to **Ross Island**, which was once a well-fortified cantonment from which the British could survey their penal settlement in style, well protected from convicts and naked "heathen" tribespeople. Established in 1858, Ross Island had a splendid Georgian-style Residency, a combined officers' mess and club, colonial bungalows, a church and graveyard, numerous administrative offices, and even a printing press and swimming pool. Its residents dressed formally for dinner, as though they were dining in a Pall Mall club. Lady Duff Cooper once spent a night here while fleeing Singapore for England, and thought it very "select". Banyan trees now have the crumbling settlement in a macabre embrace that resembles flesh grafted on to stone. Spotted deer and peacocks run wild and take shelter in the deserted buildings. The island is occupied by the Indian Navy, and is open to visitors only until 12:30 pm. The Tourist Information Centre, ©20380, at the Tourist Home in Haddo, can confirm boat timings.

BEACH PARADISE AND CORAL REEFS

The easiest way to arrange a visit to the outer islands is to contact either Island Travels, Aberdeen Bazaar, ©21358, their branch at the Bay Island Hotel, or the TCI travel desk at the Andaman Beach Resort. They'll give you an update on which islands are open to visitors, and save you the hassle of hiring a boat or organizing helicopter transport to **Havelock** and **Neil** islands (where it's possible to stay overnight at PWD bungalows). They'll also arrange snorkeling and scuba diving equipment. To organize your own trip, contact the Marine Department or the Oceanic Company, on M.G. Road, Middle Point. Boat trips include visits to the paradisical uninhabited islands of **Red Skin**, **Jolly Buoy**, and **Cinque** (actually a handful of small islands connected by sandbars), all fringed by beaches and sheer blue waters with visibility up to six meters (20 ft). The calm lagoons enclosed by coral reefs around these islands are particularly good for snorkeling and diving — just like floating through a huge aquarium with shifting kaleidoscopic hues and technicolor tropical fish. As you cruise between the islands, you'll quite often see gamboling dolphins, flying fish, and large sea crocodiles.

If you plan a diving trip to the Andamans, be sure to avoid the monsoon period between June and September when the sea is turbulent, khaki-colored, and massed with venomous jellyfish. During this period of sudden squalls, boat-owners usually refuse to take tourists to the outer islands.

Two enjoyable excursions from Port Blair are just an hour's drive away. **Chiriya Tapu** is a magnificent beach at the southern tip of the South Andamans, surrounded by lush mangrove swamps. Rare exotic birds can be seen by early risers, and there's plenty of good fishing to be had in the mangrove creeks. You can stay overnight at a guesthouse set atop a hill overlooking the sea. On the west coast lies **Wandoor Beach**, with secluded clear waters and rich coral reefs. It's a convenient base for exploring nearby **Jolly Buoy** and **Red Skin** islands.

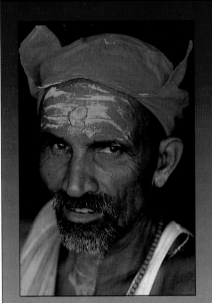

Across
the
Deccan

HYDERABAD

Capital of Andhra Pradesh, Hyderabad is India's sixth largest city. The beautiful architectural relics of its legendary Muslim grandeur are rapidly being swallowed up by an ugly industrial hinterland that sprawls across to Secunderabad, the modern twin capital. Yet locked within Hyderabad's heart are countless layers of its medieval Islamic heritage. Magnificent mosques and peeling nineteenth-century courtly mansions stand cheek to jowl with a shantytown of modern buildings and factory shacks.

With a skyline distinguished by slender minarets, Hyderabad represents a curious Muslim foothold in the south's Hindu heartland. It was founded in 1591 by the Qutub Shahi dynasty, a line of Muslim rulers who had ruled the mainly Hindu subjects of the surrounding southern Deccan since the fourteenth century. Mohammed Quli, the fourth of the Qutub Shahis, built his new capital near the Musi River as an alternative to his cramped, disease-ridden fortress city at Golconda, 11 km (seven miles) away, which today lends its name to locally produced wine.

Hyderabad's first major monument remains its most magnificent emblem: the Charminar arch, which straddles the city's original grid of broad intersecting boulevards. As a thriving trading center, Hyderabad — and the lure of its local diamond industry — proved irresistible to the Mughal emperor Aurangzeb who captured the region in 1650. In the wake of Aurangzeb's death in 1707, Hyderabad was snatched up in 1713 by one of the dead emperor's most trusted generals, Mir Kamruddin Khan, of the Asaf Jahn dynasty. He retained his Mughal title, Nizam-ul-Mulk, and became the independent ruler of Hyderabad.

Successive Nizams amassed legendary fortunes, despite having part of their Deccan domain chipped down to the size of Italy by the French, the Marathas, and the British. When the tenth and last Nizam, Mir Osman Ali Khan, came to power in 1911, he was arguably the richest man in the world. His giant palace teemed with some 11,000 servants — 38 were required to dust the chandeliers, while others did nothing except grind spices — entire wings were used to house mammoth quantities of precious jewels and gold bullion, and he used egg-sized diamonds as paperweights. Yet the Nizam's parsimony was equally fabled: he wore the same oil-streaked fez and soiled jacket for 30 years, was said to knit his own socks, and haggled over the price of local Charminar cigarettes. When India gained its independence in 1947, the Nizam flatly refused to relinquish his control of the state, grimly hanging on for two years before Indian troops massed at his borders forced him to capitulate.

Hyderabad's landscape is fringed by its boulder-strewn Banjara Hills, once the rugged home of a gypsy tribe from distant Rajasthan and now an elite enclave. The Banjara tribespeople still add their colorful presence to the city's bazaars, their women costumed in rustic Rajput finery, with heavy, jingling jewelry and embroidered camel slippers. It's most pleasant to visit the city between October and February, when it is fanned by cool breezes from its numerous reservoirs. But from March onwards, Hyderabad becomes unbearably stifling, with the waves of dry, sauna-hot air reducing even determined sightseers to a dehydrated frazzle.

ACCESS

Indian Airlines operates daily direct flights to Hyderabad from Delhi, Bangalore, Bombay, Madras, and Calcutta, and regular flights from Bhubaneswar.

Alternatively, Vayudoot provide direct links from Goa, Bangalore, and Mysore. Hyderabad is connected by train to all major Indian cities, and popular rail journeys to south Indian destinations include the 19-hour trip to Bangalore and the 15-hour overnight express to Madras. Both these trains can be taken from the central Kachiguda station, saving the drive to the main station in Secunderabad, eight kilometers (five miles) away. As elsewhere in India, the express overnight trains are freqently booked out, so try to reserve your sleeper as soon as possible. Regular buses ply between Hyderabad and Bangalore, Madras, and Bombay.

HOTELS

The new **Krishna Oberoi**, ©222121, Road No. 1, Banjara Hills, is Hyderabad's most elegant luxury hotel with plush pastel decor, indoor fountains, and impeccably efficient staff. It's situated 10 minutes from the airport amid landscaped gardens which overlook the city. (From the the the top floors you can see Golconda Fort, 13 km, or eight miles, away). Comfortable, tastefully furnished double rooms come with all the latest Indian mod-cons — push-button telephones, vast televisions linked to cable TV, and mini-bars. Rates: expensive. Its two stylish restaurants, which offer excellent Hyderabadi and Chinese cuisine, are heavily patronized by the city's elite, and there's also a good bar and 24-hour coffee shop. Facilities include a very modern health club with grounds for squash,

---

OPPOSITE: Care-worn and ash-smeared old man of Hyderabad.

tennis, and golf, a beauty parlor, swimming pool, travel desk, and the adjacent Krishna Plaza, a slick shopping arcade.

Situated close by is **Hotel Banjara**, ©222222, which lacks the Oberoi's polish but has good facilities, including several restaurants, a small swimming pool, shopping arcade, beauty salon, and lakeside boating. The **Ritz Hotel**, ©233571, Hillfort Palace, is more central and has far more character. Built in a Scottish baronial style, this former palace is now a charming — if slightly dilapidated — hotel smothered with white-wash, dusty chandeliers, and bright bougain-villea creepers. The dining room serves Indian, continental, and Chinese food, but has dreary 1950's decor and a befuddled evening band called the "The Minarettes". There are tennis courts and a small pool which is used by locals for swimming lessons. Spacious, air-conditioned ground floor rooms with quaint furniture are best. Rates: inexpensive.

For inexpensive accommodation, try the **Rock Castle Hotel**, ©33541, Road No. 6, Banjara Hills, a colonial-era lodging house now slightly run-down but still quaint, with friendly staff and good food. Within the city center, **Hotel Sarovar**, © 237638, on Secretariat Road has clean, comfortable rooms and an excellent all-day South Indian restaurant with generous Rs 11 *thalis*. The towering annexe under construction next door will offer four-star accommodation at much higher rates. For cheap accommodation try **Hotel Taj Mahal**, ©237988, on King Kothi Road, in Abids, the city's bustling shopping area, which is very popular with budget travelers. There's a pleasant rooftop café, and a colorful array of freelance gurus hovering at the entrance, sometimes catnapping under black umbrellas. One sign reads: "Mr Bakshi, the world's greatest scientific palmist who can solve all life's problems!"

RESTAURANTS

For sophisticated dining and good service: the Oberoi hotel has two plush restaurants, both overlooking cascading fountains: **Firdaus** for faultless Persian-influenced Hyderabadi Mughali dishes — with delicious baronial *raan*, tandoor leg of lamb — and the **Szechuan Garden** for regional Chinese food.

Hotel Banjara's evening **Kebab-e-Bahar** outdoor terrace restaurant is deservedly popular for its Mughali dishes, aromatic kebabs, and handkerchief-thin *roomali rotis*. But no visit to Hyderabad is complete without an authentic experience of the city's Islamic culture in one of the Irani cafés: always cheap, filthy, full of capped Muslims, *burqa*-clad matrons, marble-topped tables, and glittering mosaic walls. The

best (cleanest) to try are the **Hotel Madina**, near the Charminar, and **Rainbow Restaurant** on Abid Road (also known as Mahatma Gandhi Road). Specialties to order include *haleem*, a spiced mutton curry cooked with delicately pounded wheat; *paya*, chicken soup served with flat bread, and *pauna*, sweet spiced tea. Local sweetmeats include *ashrafi*, an edible "coin" stamped with a Mughal seal, and *badam ki jali*, almond-studded halva. Good south Indian food is found at **Hotel Sampurna International** and **Kamath Hotel** near the Indian Airlines office in Saifabad. Well-heeled locals favor a handful of "classy" restaurants, all heavily air-conditioned with fake rococo, mirror-lined decor and a pulsating disco beat, serving good Mughali, Chinese, and continental dishes: **Golden Deer** restaurant and bar, just opposite the Santhosh cinema in Abids; the rooftop **Palace Heights** nearby (just look up, you can't miss its towering neon sign); **Fifth Avenue** and **Blue Fox**, both next to each other on Lakdia-kapol. The **Indian Coffee House**, in the Secretariat grounds, has delicious hot or cold coffee and south Indian snacks — good for a break after visiting the nearby Government Archaeological Museum in the Public Gardens. It's open 9:30 am to 5 pm.

SIGHTSEEING

Hyderabad is very spread out, so it's worth having a definite strategy before setting off for a day's sightseeing. Golconda Fort (see page 273) is best enjoyed in the cool early morning, leaving you free to explore the city's museums, mosques, and markets in the afternoon. Conducted city tours are convenient time-savers, but offer only a fleeting glimpse of Hyderabad's real charm, which is concentrated in its vi-brantly colorful bazaars. Personal guides and transport can be hired at the Tourist Information Bureau and if you're set on cycling the 11 km (seven miles) out to Golconda Fort — a pleasant, relatively straight-foward route if you've got a map on hand — hotels should be able to advise on bicycle hire.

Mosques, Markets, and Museums

At the heart of the old walled city stands Hyderabad's emblematic **Charminar**, a magnificent archway framed by four tapering minarets, each 56 m (184 ft) high. It was built in 1591 by Muhammed Quli Qutub Shahi as a sort of architectural talisman against a plague that was devastating the newly-founded city. You can make the spiraling ascent up to a tiny second-floor mosque for views across the city. The image of the Charminar follows you all across India on the country's No. 1 brand of glorified

Across the Deccan

HYDERABAD

Anandnagar
Railway Station

Raj Bhavan Road

Secretariat Road

Adarshnagar

Collectorate

Ravindra Bharathi

Gaganmahal Road

T T D Information Centre

Chikadpalli Road

Himayatnagar Road

SAIFABAD

Red Hills

Public
Gardens

HIMAYATNAGAR

Lal Bahadur
Stadium

Old MLA Quarters Road

University Rd

NALLAKUNTA

Hyderabad
Railway Station

Public Gardens Road

NAMPALLI

Mahatma Gandhi Road

King Kothi Palace

Narayanguda Road

Vir Savarkar Road

Kacheguda
Railway Station

MEHDI PATNAM

Afsal Sagar

Dabuslam Road

ABIDS

Troop Bazaar

Mukar Ramjahi Road

Sultan Bazaar

Bhagya Reddy Road

KACHIGUDA

Moti Bazaar

National Highway Road

Gosha Mahal Rd

Goshamahal
Stadium

J Nehru Road

Maharani Jhansi Road

Turrebaz Khan

Maulvi Alauddin Road

Begam Bazaar

City Bus
Terminus

Malakpet
Railway Station

MALAKPET

AFZALGANJ

Maharani Jhansi Road

Musi River

500 m

Salar Jung Museum

Rejendranagar Road

Gandhi Bazaar

Sardar Patel Road

Daripura
Railway Station

CHARMINAR

Mecca Masjid

Railway Station

N

beedi cigarettes. It's open from 9 am to 4:30 pm, and expect to find its cavernous interior teeming with swaddled alms-seekers.

Just beyond the Charminar, you'll see the colossal **Mecca Masjid**, the largest mosque in South India. Construction began under Muhammed Quli Qutub Shahi in 1614, but it was finished as an act of Islamic faith by the next conqueror of the Deccan, the Mughal emperor Aurangzeb, in 1687. Modeled on the famous mosque at Mecca, it's built on an awe-inspiring scale with lofty monolithic pillars, vast calligraphy-emblazoned archways, and towering gold-tipped 30-m (100-ft) -high minarets. Pigeons and hornets swoop around it like dark clouds and build nests in its inaccessible upper regions. Against its severe granite walls, the interior glitters in contrast with dangling Belgian chandeliers, and decorative marbled inscriptions from the Koran. This is Hyderabad's principal place of Muslim worship, and during Fridays and Muslim festivals it can accommodate more than 10,000 kneeling devotees. During the Muslim holy month of Ramadan, many thousands more spill

across the streets outside. To the left of the courtyard is a marbled row of the Nizam's decorative tombstones — their womenfolk lie beneath flat tablets. Old men with hennaed beards commiserate with each other in the shadows, and ragged urchins sprawl across the tombstones. The mosque's workers scatter grain across the courtyard for bedraggled flocks of goats, pigeons, chickens, and in the courtyard's far right-hand corner is a solid black marble seat, brought from Iran 200 years ago. Locals say that those who sit on it are destined to return to Hyderabad — you'll have to find that out for yourself!

From here, any number of cobbled lanes will plunge you into the bustling, medieval pantomime of Hyderabad's **Old Bazaar**. Wind your way through crowded alleys strewn with sandalwood screw-curls and dung, side-step loitering buffaloes and knots of conversing merchants, and charge bravely through the riotous traffic.

Crocheted-capped merchants gossip on upturned flower-pots; *burqa*-clad women with heavily kohl-rimmed downcast eyes flit by; and craftsmen stoop over spun silver or run plump

Across the Deccan

271

fingers through rows of pearls. The lanes glitter with glass bangles and open sacks dot the pavement with the color and scent of every imaginable spice. Hyderabad is a major pearl processing center for pearls from the Middle East, Japan, and China, and loose pearls can be purchased at about 20 percent of London prices — and although in many shops you might bargain over the price, you can also pay by credit card. Himroo brocades, delicate silver jewelry, rare Urdu books or decadently gilded Korans, lacquered sandalwood toys, and traditional *bidri* work with its distinctive silver designs against black metal are the best products to buy.

Several old and decaying city palaces lie within walking distance of the bazaar area. They include the **Panch Mahal, Chow Mahala, King Kothi**, and **Baradari** palaces, the latter notable for the battalions of Amazonian female sepoys, used to patrol the palace's zenana, or women's quarters, during the reign of Nizam Ali in the eighteenth century. Court documents as well as local lore record that this Nizam made his Italian mistress the colonel in charge of these female soldiers. But having gained military clout, she lost her original appeal for the Nizam, and he resolved to remove her. Acting on a tip-off, she escaped to Poona (now Pune, in Maharashtra state) accompanied by her loyal female sepoys, where she lived until her death. The next resident of the Baradari was a prime minister renowned for his elegant eccentricities, who trained his soldiers to ride ostriches in

the gardens. By far the most extravagant of these palaces is the **Faluknuma Palace**, five kilometers (three miles) south, a palatial neo-classical mansion fronted by a vast marble stairway and vestibule fountains. It was built in 1897, and was used as the Nizam's guesthouse, accommodating touring viceroys and graced by British royalty. Its grand gilt-edged reception room is left just as it was, cluttered with period furniture, chandeliers, and figurines. To visit, contact the tourist office or apply to Mr Asadullah, the Secretary of the Nizam's Trust Fund, near Lal Bahadur Stadium.

Located on the south bank of the Musi River, the **Salar Jung Museum** is one of Hyderabad's highlights. It houses the extraordinary private collection of the eclectic Nabob Salar Jung III, who served as prime minister to the Nizam of Hyderabad early this century until he resigned in 1914 to devote himself to the serious pursuit of collecting. The Nabob traveled incessantly, immense reserves of gold, and the sight of his sallow, serious face caused ripples of excitement taking with him Europe's leading auction houses. He died in 1949, aged 60 and a bachelor, and his priceless collection of over 35,000 exhibits from all over the world spans 35 galleries, each devoted to a certain theme. There's a vast range of Indian antiques — family heirlooms, sculptures, paintings, manuscripts, textiles, ivory and jade carvings, arms and armour — as well as galleries devoted to Middle Eastern, Far Eastern, and European art, with novelty collections of toys and antique clocks. The top floor contains an India researcher's gold-mine — the Nabob's library of over 60,000 books, many original historical documents and rare state annals. In one corner, an army of plaster busts, a veritable Who's Who of British Empire builders, gathers dust, with their faces turned to the wall like errant children. There's a ground floor cafeteria for tea and snacks. The museum is open daily except Fridays from 10 am to 5 pm, and bags and cameras must be deposited at the entrance.

On the other side of the River Musi lies the former **British Residency**, a fine Greco-colonial building fronted by two crouching sphinxes, built in 1803, and now used as a college. Other nearby architectural relics include the remarkable ocher-red **High Court** and the **Osmania Hospital**, both built in the Indo–Saracenic style in the late nineteenth century.

The **Government Archaeological Museum**, adjacent to the imposing colonial-era Indo–Saracenic Secretariat near the Public Gardens has a fine collection of antique Indian sculpture, prehistoric utensils, coins, manuscripts, old arms, eighteenth-century *bidri*-ware, textiles, and china. Close by is the **Ajanta Pavilion**, which displays full-size copies of the Ajanta frescoes. The gardens are good for a peaceful stroll away from the city's choatic muddle. Rather incongrously, just outside the Secretariat, a row of medicine men seem to have claimed their turf, selling a lurid array of peacock feathers, musty pills, tiger teeth, flayed buffalo skin, and cats' and rats' tails.

If you're going to visit any zoo in India, then make it the **Nehru Zoological Park**, located just outside the old city walls on Bangalore Road, quite near the Charminar. Wandering around its lush, well-landscaped, miniature lake-studded 121-hectare (300-acre) enclosure

the Public Gardens. During the reign of the Qutab Shahis, royal proclamations were announced from here, with drum rolls for effect. Built by the mega-wealthy Birla family and decorated with ornate bas-reliefs depicting scenes from the Hindu epics, the temple is open to all castes and creeds. It's liveliest at sunset, when crowds clamor to offer scented garlands and coconuts — a symbol of a fufilling life — to the temple deity, Lord Venkateshwara. So many coconuts are offered, in fact, that a sign says: "Please Leave Your Coconuts Here" at a locker used to babysit coconuts at the rate of 10 paise an hour! Hawkers sell medicinal bottles of

makes an enjoyable afternoon's excursion. Some 1,600 animals and 240 species of birds live in the near-natural surroundings. The highlight is undoubtedly the **Lion Safari Park**, with its free-roaming herds of lions. It's about a 20-minute walk from the zoo's main entrance, and every 15 minutes between 9:30 am and 12:15 pm and 2 to 4:30 pm, crowded mini-buses leave for a "safari" circuit. There are several cafeterias, and leafy grounds for picnics. During the hot season, avoid visiting in the afternoon, when the animals are slumped in deep siesta. The **National History Museum, Aquarium**, and **Ancient Life Museum** are worth visiting, located just near the entrance. The complex is open between 9 am and 6 pm daily, except Monday.

If you're still in need of stimulation, visit the **Birla Mandir** (Naubat Prahad), the modern white marble temple atop a rocky hill opposite

"Guaranteed Pure Ganga Water", plastic trinkets, and candyfloss at the temple's entrance. On the adjacent hill stands the **Birla Planetarium** (Adarsh Nagar), which offers "Japanese Technology Sky Theater" and English sessions at 11:30 am, 4 and 6 pm daily (Sundays at 11:30 am, 3:45 and 6 pm).

Golconda Fort

The majestic ruins of this rambling fortress capital have an almost biblical quality, looming high above dusty, sepia scrubland, 11 km (seven miles) west of Hyderabad. Golconda was the virtully impregnable medieval citadel of the Qutub Shahi kings, a city fabled for its exotic

OPPOSITE and ABOVE: Everything from silver and pearls to daily fruit and vegetables are on sale at Hyderabad's bustling and colorful bazaars.

bazaars selling diamonds, silver jewelry, and precious gems. Its mines produced the legendary Orloff, Regent, and Kohinoor diamonds.

Eyewitness accounts by Marco Polo and the seventeenth-century French traveler Jean-Baptiste Tavernier spread the legend of Golconda's decadence and wealth. Founded in the thirteenth century by the Hindu Kakatiya kings of Warangal, it was originally just a simple hilltop mud settlement called "Golla" (shepherd) "Konda" (hill). Golconda was ceded to the powerful fourteenth-century Muslim Bahmani rulers, and later passed into the hands of the Persian Qutub Shahi dynasty, who ruled the surrounding region between 1518 and 1687. Under the Qutub Shahis, Golconda emerged as a formidable stronghold; built entirely of solid granite boulders, it seemed almost part of the mountain itself. The city within its walls, had a complex civil and military administration, gem-studded royal palaces, mosques, harem quarters with interior fountains, Turkish baths, assembly halls, pavilioned gardens, and even a mortuary. Water was raised by an ingenious system through laminated clay pipes and Persian water wheels gushed water through the fountains and irrigated the flower-strewn roof gardens at the citadel's heights. One of Golconda's most intriguing features is its acoustical system, which enables a handclap sounded at the gates to be heard clearly right up in the citadel. Golconda was virtually impregnable: it was encircled by some seven kilometers (four and a half miles) of triple-tiered ramparts dotted with eight formidable iron-spiked gates, 87 semicircular watchposts, and a wide moat. It withstood eight months under seige by Aurangzeb's armies, falling only when a turncoat general betrayed the Qutub Shahis and allowed the enemy's forces to stream through the grand entrance gate. Aurangzeb annexed Golconda as part of his empire in 1687, and the fortress citadel soon crumbled into decline.

Golconda's fragmented ruins and winding medieval passages come to life with the help of a knowledgeable guide — but it's also the sort of place that is nice to ramble about in at will, making discoveries of your own. Experienced guides can be hired from the tourist bureau, or you can buy the very informative *Guide of Golconda Fort* which has a its clearly marked map.

Northwest of Golconda lie the **Qutub Shahi Tombs**, a necropolis of more than a dozen magnificent domed tombs built for the Qutub Shahi rulers and their families set amid peaceful gardens. The tombs are reminiscent of the famous

Lodhi tombs of Delhi, and the finest is that of Muhammed Quli Qutub Shahi, the founder of Hyderabad, which rises to a height of 55 m (180 ft).

GENERAL INFORMATION

The Andhra Pradesh Tourist Information Bureau, ©556493, 556523, first and fifth floors, Gargan Vihar, Mukkaram Jahi Road, provide local information, city maps, and tickets for their conducted city tours (8 am to 6 pm every day except Friday). For booking and travel arrangements, both Indian Airlines, ©36902, 72051, and Vayudoot, ©36902, are located at Safiabad, and good travel agents include Trade Wings, ©30545, 3 Public Gardens Road, and Sita World Travel, ©223628, Sita House, Hyderguda.

THE DECCAN TRAIL TO BANGALORE

From Hyderabad, many travelers head straight for Karnataka's capital, Bangalore, picking up the popular route through Mysore to Ooty. Few venture southwest across the Deccan Plateau's arid, boulder-strewn terrain to explore its deserted medieval cities, forts, and temples — the legacy of the powerful Mughal, Chalukya, Telegu, and Hoysala kingdoms who made this region their battleground. Those who make the effort — involving long, hot hours of bus and train travel — will be richly rewarded. The region is full of decaying architectural treasures and rustic towns where life seems barely to have changed for centuries. A good network of state-run hotels offer overnight facilities at all main destinations.

Ideally, you could spend a week or so on the Deccan trail, starting in north Karnataka with **Bidar**, 130 km (81 miles) from Hyderabad, the former capital of the Muslim Bahmanis, with its well-preserved fifteenth-century city fort, palaces, pavilions, and fine tombs; and the fabulous medieval walled city of **Bijapur**, described by historian James Grant Duff as "exceeding anything of its kind in Europe". Bijapur was the sixteenth-century stronghold of the Adil Shahi dynasty, whose legacy of majestic monuments includes the Gol Gumbaz, with a massive dome said to be second in size only to that of St Peter's in Rome, and a "whispering gallery" where the slightest whisper echoes inside the dome 12 times over. To the south lie clustered trio of sculptured caves and stone temple sites — **Badami, Pattadakal**, and **Aihole** — dating back to the sixth century when the early Chalukya kings ruled the region. But the culmination of the Deccan trail is found in the

---

OPPOSITE: The palatial Neo-Dravidian style Vidhana Soudha, which houses Bangalore's Secretariat and Legislature.

splendid isolation of **Hampi**, the fourteenth-century kingdom of the mighty Vijaynagars, whose Hindu empire was the largest in India's history. Its impressive medieval ruins — full of fortified battlements, palaces, temples, pavilions, shrines, baths, and bazaars — spread across 26 sq km (10 sq miles). From Hampi you can link up to Bangalore, 358 km (222 miles) away, either by rail or express bus. For more detailed information on these destinations, and how to reach them, consult with the Government of India Tourist Office in Hyderabad, at its new location in the A.P. Tourist Information Bureau, Gargan Vihar, Mukkaram Jahi Road.

BANGALORE

Karnataka's state capital is an attractive, efficient city with a well-planned grid of treelined boulevards, stately old public buildings, and beautiful gardens. Dubbed India's "Silicon Valley" for its burgeoning computer industry, Bangalore is the country's main center for scientific and technological research, eclipsing the city's traditional industries of coffee-trading, stud farm horse-breeding, and indefatigable movie-making. There's a cosmopolitan, almost campus-like, air to Bangalore, which has a constant stream of foreign business travelers and draws people from all over India for higher education, business opportunities, and research. It's an ideal base for planning trips through South India, with several interesting sights of its own, plenty of good hotels, and a thriving nightlife with an array of restaurants, bars, and thirties-era art deco cinemas.

Legend has it that Kempe Gowda, a feudal chief from the Vijayanagar kingdom, founded Bangalore, which means "city of boiled beans", in 1537 in memory of the spot where he was offered a meal of beans by a kindly hermit when lost in the forest. His medieval mud fort was later enlarged and rebuilt in stone by the Muslim leader Hyder Ali and his son, Tipu Sultan, in the late eighteenth century. After defeating Tipu "Tiger" Sultan at Srirangapatna, the British arrived in 1809 to build a cantonment, and present-day Bangalore is dotted with Raj-era bougainvillea-shrouded bungalows, churches, clubs, pavilioned gardens, quaint shopping malls, as well as racing grounds and breweries. Ironically, it was the Maharaja of Mysore who produced the most extravagant parody of Victorian England in his Bangalore Palace, a vast, ivy-swathed turreted model of Windsor Palace, now eerily silent amidst its large gardens on the outskirts of the old cantonment town.

Set high above the stifling plains, Bangalore is a popular summer bolt-hole, though its climate is pleasant all year round. The city's extensive parks — notably Cubbon Park and Lal Bagh — are at their best during January and August, and it can be fun to participate in the horse-racing mania that grips Bangaloreans between November and March and from mid-April to July.

ACCESS

Bangalore has excellent air connections to the rest of India, with daily direct flights to Bombay, Delhi, Hyderabad, and Madras, as well as regular services to Ahmedabad, Calcutta, Cochin, Coimbature, Goa, Trivandrum, and other centers. India's second-flag airline, Vayudoot, operates between Bangalore and Mysore, Hyderabad, and Tirupati. Daily express trains run to Bangalore from all major Indian cities, and popular journeys include the seven-hour *Brindhavan Express* or *Bangalore Mail* from Madras, the twice-weekly 38-hour *Karnataka Express* from Delhi, and the 27-hour trip from Bombay. Bangalore is also well-serviced by state coaches from all the main Indian cities, with an efficient daily network of buses plying throughout southern and central India. When planning a long bus journey, try to avoid the notorious "video coaches", which feature Hindi movies in "glorious technicolor" as a ploy to lure customers. Insomniacal Indians seem to adore these spoof extravaganzas full of wet saris, paunchy villains, and dance sequences on wildly elaborate sets. Most video coaches carry the sign "If the Video Fails We Are Not Responsible", but alas, it never does.

HOTELS

Welcomgroup's **Windsor Manor**, ©79431, 25 Sankey Road, is very stylish, with meticulous Regency-style decor throughout — from the lobby's balustraded marble staircase to the staff uniforms — prompt service, excellent restaurants, and a poolside barbecue. Rooms are plush, pastel-colored, and fitted with cable TV. Rates: moderate. Facilities include a swimming pool, health club, beauty salon, bookshop, travel counter, and business desk. A classic English bar serves pints of chilled draught beer. **West End Hotel**, ©29281, Race Course Road, run by the Taj Group, is Bangalore's oldest hotel. Set in eight hectares (20 acres) of landscaped gardens, and despite a characterless modern annex, it still radiates Raj-era charm. Ask for a Victorian room in the original whitewashed hotel, where rooms come with balconies, wicker furniture, and huge British bathtubs. Rates: expensive.

There's a good pool, several restaurants, and the lawns are perfect for candlelit cocktails. **Taj Residency**, ©568888, 14 Mahatma Gandhi Road, is a modern, five-star hotel with extensive facilities aimed at business travelers. Its restaurants and bar are considered top-notch by locals. Rates: moderate.

In cheap bracket, try the **Hotel Hoysala**, ©365311, 212 S.C. Road, Seshadri Puram for reliably clean rooms; the **New Victoria Hotel**, ©570336, 47–48 Residency Road, for vintage charm; or **Luciya International**, ©224145-8, 6 O.T.C. Road, which offers comfortable rooms, a restaurant, and a tourist bus service. Accommodation in the very chea range are crammed around the central market area. One of the best is **Sudha Lodge**, ©605420, 6 Cottonpet Main Road, with simple, clean lodgings, hot

and cold water, and friendly owners. If this is full, try the **Tourist Hotel** on Race Course Road, a rabbit warren of clean cubicle-style rooms.

BARS AND RESTAURANTS

Bangalore is the only south Indian city with a thriving nightlife, and most travelers find it a welcome oasis of good restaurants, bars, English-style pubs, and even a discotheque. It's also the only place in India which makes decent draught beer, best sampled at **The Pub**, Church Street. Modeled on an English pub, it comes complete with stained-glass windows, bar stools, and the daily draught on tap is only Rs 7 per glass. It's open from 11:30 am to 10:30 pm. Just next door you'll find **Mac's Fast**

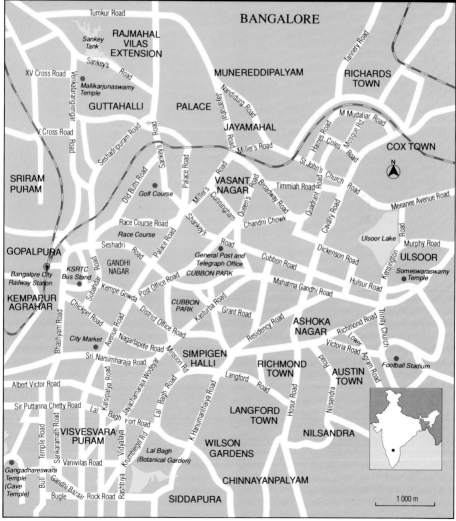

Food, a casual eatery with (buffalo meat) hamburgers, french fries, pizzas, and shakes. Other pubs to try include **Ramda Pub**, off M.G. Road, Indiana, St Patrick's Complex, Residency Road, and **Waikikee**, 11 Brigade Road.

Of the leading hotels, the **Windsor Manor** has several elegant restaurants serving particularly good Indian, North-west Frontier, Chinese, and continental food. Discriminating locals flock to the lobby-level Royal Derby, a classic London tavern which serves excellent Rs 45 pub lunches including a pint of draught beer. In town, try **Princes**, Curzon Complex, Brigade Road, the last word in Bangalore chic, with its

banana leaf platter, can be found at both **Amaravathi**, off M.G. Road, and **RR Plantation Leaf**, opposite The Pub in Church Street. **Woodlands Hotel**, 5 Sampangi Tank Road, offers delicious south-Indian vegetarian food, with as-much-as-you-can-eat Rs 20 mealtime *thalis* and delicious freshly squeezed grape juice. At Bangalore's clean, proletarian Udipi cafés — located mainly around the Gandhi Nagar–Chickpet area near the rail and bus stations — it's possible to dine well on delicious south Indian fare for less than Rs 7! One of the best to try, the **Dai Vihar**, is a few doors down from the Badami House Tourist Office on N.R. Square. It has

plush Regency decor, potted palms, and tailored waiters. A blow-out three-course meal of Waldorf Salad, Prawns Crème Gratin, and Chateaubriand Steak, plus coffee comes to around Rs 150. Right next door is the **Knock-Out Disco**, the city's only discotheque, where overweight sari-clad ladies wobble with their husbands under flashing strobe lights. Entry is free to Princes' restaurant customers — otherwise there's a Rs 40 entrance fee. It's open from Tuesday to Thursday. Other local favorites, with good and reasonably priced Mughali, Chinese, and continental dishes, are the **Blue Fox**, at 80 M.G. Road, with its old-time band and two-step dance-floor; and the **Jewel Box** and **Koshy's Parade Cafe**, both with vintage waiters and excellent food, located within the quaint Raj-era Koshy's Corner, opposite St Mark's Cathedral on Church Road. Excellent Andhra-style food, served on a

Rs 5.50 *thalis*, fresh fruit juices, and great *lassis* mixed in a machine that looks just like a 1920's dentist's drill. There's a quaint **Indian Coffee House** at 78 M.G. Road for early breakfasts with good strong coffee. It's full of amusement value — with its aged waiters in Nehru caps, worn convict-like cotton uniforms, and walls plastered with faded posters of Mahatma Gandhi.

SIGHTSEEING

Bangalore's few places of interest are concentrated around its large sprawling gardens. In the city center, it's worth making a promenade down Vidhana Vidhi (Bangalore's Champs-Elysées) to see an extraordinary Raj-era palisade of Greco-colonial public buildings bordering Cubbon Park. Here you'll see India's most impressive **Post Office**, the sienna-colored

High Court (given a medieval look by straw "tatties" nailed up to keep out the sun), and the ash-red public library. The most magnificent building of all stands on the north side of the park — the palatial **Vidhana Soudha**, which houses the Secretariat and Legislature. Built in 1954, this four-story Neo-Dravidian-style citadel is worth a closer look. Permission to visit after 5:30 pm can be obtained from the Under Secretary (Protocol), Dept. Social and Administrative Reforms, Vidhana Soudha (©79401).

The **Government Museum** is located on Kasturba Road. Established in 1886, it has 18 wings displaying an extensive collection of sculptures, coins, artifacts, inscriptions, and paintings excavated from both the neolithic-period Chandraval site and the great Harappan site at Mohenjodhao in Sind Province, as well as a portrait gallery with rare miniatures and paintings of the bejewelled, sybaritic Tanjore and Mysore rulers. The **Venkatappa Art Gallery** is a spacious modern extension, and houses many paintings by Venkatappa, who was court painter to the Mysore maharaja early this century. Works by India's top contemporary artists are also on display. It's open every day except Wednesday from 9 am to 5 pm. Neither the **Technological Museum** nor the **Aquarium** close by are really worth visiting. This could be a useful time to visit the Tourist Office, almost directly across the road, for information on sightseeing tours. At the entrance to **Cubbon Park**, opposite, it's impossible to miss one of the few imposing statues of Queen Victoria allowed to remain standing in India. Laid out in 1864, the park's wide sweeping green has original wrought-iron benches and is relaxing for sunset strolls.

About four kilometers (2.5 miles) south of the city's bustling market area stands Bangalore's historic **Kempegowda Fort**, Hyder Ali's eighteenth-century stone reconstruction of the orginal mud fort. Inside the fort walls is Tipu Sultan's wooden palace, with just enough elaborate paintwork surviving on the walls, niches, and twirling columns to give an idea of its former glory. Don't miss the tiny museum here; the antique etchings, documents, and family portraits provide a pocket history of the legendary Muslim leader Tipu Sultan (British India's arch rival) and his life and times. It's open from 6 am to 6 pm daily, and is particularly worth seeing if you plan to visit Tipu Sultan's fortress capital, Sriringapatna, 125 km (77.5 miles) away. The finely wrought marble temple almost directly adjacent to Tipu's palace will undoubtedly catch your eye — it's the Venkataramanaswamy Temple, built by the Wodeyars in the seventeenth century.

Bangalore's beautiful **Lalbagh Botanical Gardens**, situated a two kilometer (just over a mile) taxi ride southeast of the city center, were laid out over 100 hectares (240 acres) by Hyder Ali in 1760 with exotic plants supplied by ambassadors from Persia, Kabul, Mauritius, and France. With much zeal, the British added nineteenth-century pavilions, pebble paths lined with elegant lamps, fountains, flowerbeds, and a beautiful cast-iron glasshouse modeled on Crystal Palace. Every afternoon, a band comprised of aged pensioners in epauletted costumes sends warbling, reedy notes from a bygone era wafting across the park. Magnifi-

cent flower shows are held twice a year — on August 15 to mark Independence Day and on January 26, Republic Day. From the gardens, you can make a detour up the nearby Bugle Hill to see the **Bull Temple** with its 6.2-m (20-ft) -high stone monolith Nandi bull, which locals claim grows larger every year. Close by is the **Ganesh Temple**, with a devotional idol of the elephant-headed god carved in 110 kilos (243 lb) of solid butter! Amazingly, it never seems to melt, and when it is ritually cut up every four years and meted out to pilgrims, another replica is created from the proceeds donated by wealthy patrons.

Cultural entertainment in Bangalore is best from March to April, being the peak season for performances of traditional Karnataka dance and music. Performances are always listed alongside the cinema guide in the city's daily *Deccan Herald*. Otherwise inquire at the Chowdiah Memorial Hall, Sankey Road, or Bharatiya Bhavan, on Race Course Road, where the shows are usually held.

ABOVE: Exuberantly-colored powders coaxed into finger-swirled pyramids, terra-cotta pots and dangling necklaces make up some of the *puja* items sold at this stall in Mysore's Devaraja Market. OPPOSITE: The Lalbagh Botanical Gardens in Bangalore.

Across the Deccan

GENERAL INFORMATION

The Karnataka Tourist Office, ©578901, at 10/4 Kasturba Road, Queen's Circle, is the most efficient of a handful of offices dotted around the city. It's worth investigating a number of the well-planned and reasonably priced sight-seeing tours on offer. Aside from useful city tours, there's an excellent 16-hour tour out to Mysore, Srirangapatna, and Brindhaven Gardens, with various overnight tours to the Hoysala temple towns of Belur and Halebid, the Vijayanagar ruins of Hampi, Ootacamund, and the wildlife sanctuaries of Bandipur and Nagarhole.

For air bookings, Indian Airlines, ©79431, is located in the Cauvery Bhavan complex in District Office Road.

MYSORE

Mysore once held sway as Karnataka's princely capital, and an aura of faded grandeur still lingers in this leisurely city of angel-cake palaces, manicured gardens, and treelined avenues. Eclipsed by bustling, industrial Bangalore as the modern capital, Mysore is a quaintly rustic town with thirties-era architecture. This is India's "Sandalwood City", where much of the country's incense is produced, filling the air with dusky whiffs of jasmine, sandalwood, musk, and rose.

Mysore's name stems from Mahishasura, a ruthless demon king who, according to Hindu lore, tyrranized the people of this region until he was slaughtered by the goddess Chamundi. The city has been the seat of a succession of powerful ruling dynasties of the south since ancient times. The first to leave a significant legacy were the Hoysalas, who governed the area from the twelfth to the fourteenth century and were renowned for their patronage of art and architecture. Their magnificent temples and buildings can be seen at nearby Somnathpur, Belur, and Halebid. The Wadiyar maharajas then made Mysore their capital, ruling until 1759 when their kingdom was snatched away by the monarch's own commander-in-chief, the renegade Hyder Ali. In 1799, the British defeated Tipu Sultan, Hyder Ali's powerful son, annexed half his state, and restored an infant Wadiyar heir to the Mysore throne. The British set about expanding their empire in the south, and the Wadiyar maharajas ruled more or less under the protective thumb of the Raj until Independence in 1947. The British referred to prosperous, semi-democratic Mysore as a "model princely state",

and adored attending the domain's lavish royal extravanganzas. The most famous of these was the annual *khedda,* a ritual round-up of wild elephants, with specially constructed spectators' huts complete with electricty and running water, as well as evening entertainment in the form of banquets and a full-piece orchestra — all in the middle of dense jungle.

Today, Mysore boasts India's most spectacular Dassera festival (called Dussehra in northern India). Held during September/October, it celebrates the goddess Chamundi's victory over Mahishasura. This 10-day carnival of dance and musical festivities climaxes with a stunning procession of richly caparisoned elephants, liveried cavalry, and regal silver and gold carriages, accompanied by parading bands, flower-strewn floats, and fireworks.

ACCESS

Vayudoot flies to Mysore from Bangalore and Hyderabad, although Bangalore (140 km, or 87 miles) is the nearest destination for making Indian Airlines connections with most parts of the country. From Bangalore, buses depart throughout the day for the three-hour journey, or there's a regular train service which takes slightly longer.

HOTELS

There are two luxury palace-hotels, both moderately priced quirkily grand and built by the Maharaja of Mysore during the thirties. The most conveniently located is **Lalitha Mahal Palace Hotel**, ©27650, on T. Narasipur Road overlooking the city, an immense former guest

palace painted with a confectioner's palette of white marble, lemon yellow, pale blue, and peppermint green. Its dome was designed after St Paul's Cathedral in London. Suites are crammed with rickety period furniture, and open on to balustraded terraces. Moderately priced. **Rajendra Vilas Palace**, ©22050, is a charming European-style villa set high on Chamundi Hill. Both the rooms and the former royal staff are delightfully archaic. There are stunning views across Mysore from the garden pavilions, especially at night. Transport is essential for getting up and down the hill. Rooms are inexpensive. In the city center, **Hotel Southern Star**, ©27217,

ABOVE: A scalloped archway frames Amber Villas, the fantasy palace built for the Maharaja of Mysore, a passionate Anglophile who also created a replica of Windsor Palace on the outskirts of Bangalore.

13 Vinoba Road, is modern and efficient. Rates: inexpensive. In the same league but slighty out of town is **Hotel Dasaprakash Paradise**, ©26666, 105 Yadavagiri Road, Mysore's top Indian-style hotel. It has a superb south Indian vegetarian restaurant. Heartily recommended for its comfortable colonial charm is **Hotel Metropole**, ©20681, 5 Jhansi Laxshimibai Road, in the city's heart. It has affable khaki-clad staff, rattan-lined verandas, and leafy gardens for sipping cold beers at twilight. Spacious Raj-era rooms have mosquito net-clad bedsteads and old tiled bathrooms. Rates: inexpensive. Excellent Indian, Chinese, and Western dishes are served at

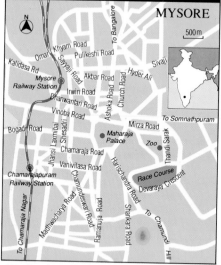

the restaurant. Across the road is the KSTDC-run **Hotel Mayura Hoysala**, ©25349, the best of the mid-range hotels. This quaint old building has clean, very cheap single rooms comfortable air-conditioned suites in the cheap range. A courtyard restaurant serves good travelers' fare, and the Tourist Office is just next door. Another good cheap option is **Hotel Dasaprakash**, ©26666, in Gandhi Square, with a vegetarian restaurant and an ice-cream parlor. Cheaper budget lodges are crammed around the central Gandhi Square area, but you'll find the best value for money at **Hotel Anugraha**, ©30768, in the Thejus Complex, Sayaji Rao Road; **Hotel Durbar**, ©20029, with Rs 50 balcony doubles with attached bathrooms, and a popular rooftop café; and the **Hotel Indra Bhavan**, ©23933, on Dhanvantri Road.

RESTAURANTS

Adventurous eaters will favor Mysore's unexpectedly good streetside south Indian cafés in and around Dhanvantri Road over the predict-

able fare provided by the main hotels. Try **RRR Restaurant** on Gandhi Square, or **RR Plantation Leaf** on Chandraguptha Road, for delicious Andhra Pradesh-style Rs 13 *thalis* served on a banana leaf. **Hotel Dasaprakash**'s cafeteria serves freshly prepared South Indian snacks throughout the day and great Rs 15 mealtime "tiffins" with 15 or so assorted dishes. Freshly squeezed grape juice is their specialty, though it's much nicer if you ask them to leave out the sugar. Opposite the Amber Vilas is the **Gun House**, formerly the royal armory and now a pleasantly restored restaurant with an outside terrace. It's open from mid-morning for drinks and snacks, with excellent Mughali dishes and a Goan band at night. **Hotel Shilpashi**, in CPC Building, Gandhi Square, is the current travelers' favorite for relaxed evening dining. There's a good bar and the pretty rooftop restaurant serves excellent Mughali food, as well as Chinese and Western-style dishes, at around Rs 50 a head. Another popular establishment is the **Punjabi Restaurant and Bombay Juice Centre**, 397 Dhanvantri Road, for good North Indian dishes and fluffy cappuccinos. It's run by an eccentric proprietor who bears an uncanny resemblence to *Coronation Street's* Ena Sharples in drag. **New Bombay Tiffinys**, near the Thesus Complex on Sayyaji Rao Road, is renowned for its overwhelming array of Indian confectionery, with an upstairs café for sampling them with a glass of chilled *lassi*. The vintage **Cold Drinks House** (founded in 1934 as the Brahman Soda Factory), Sardar Patel Road near Gandhi Square, has excellent chilled sweetened milk and fresh fruit juices served in clean glasses with straws. It's run by the spritly Mr Rao, who swears that his good health is due to his grandfather's recipe for delicious Rs 1.25 Sarsparalla Soda.

SIGHTSEEING

Mysore is pleasantly small, so most of its sights can easily be covered on foot or in short hops by taxi or auto-rickshaw. The Tourist Office runs excellent all-day city sightseeing tours that include visits to Brindhavan Gardens and excursions to Somnathpur and Sriringpatna. The city tour starts with **St Philomena's Church**, three kilometers (two miles) north of town. Built in 1931, this neo-Gothic cathedral with its two tapering spires and dazzling medieval-style stained-glass interior appears to have been uprooted from rural France and set down again on the other side of the world. In town is the **Sri Chamarajendra Art Gallery**, housed in the eighteenth-century Jaganmohan Palace near Gandhi Square, with many fine oil portraits of Mysore's royal family, miniature paintings, and all sorts of antique treasures including fine pieces of sculpture, Hoysala carvings, and rare musical instruments. It's open daily from 8 am to 5 pm. There's a brief stop at the **Zoological Gardens**, on Lalitha Palace Road, open daily 8 am to 5 pm, where over 1,500 species of animals and birds reside in leafy captivity.

The city's main attraction is **Amber Vilas,** the late maharaja's palace, a lavish Arabian Nights fantasy of domes, turrets, archways, and fluted colonnades which stands amid garden pavilions in the town center. Designed by the English architect Henry Irwin in the Indo–Saracenic style, it was built over a period of 15 years (1897–1912) to replace the former palace which

the entrance. Avoid the nightmarish crowds during weekends and public holidays, and return on Sunday evenings when Amber Villas, lit up by thousands of flame-colored bulbs, looks like an illuminated mirage. The tour goes to **Chamundi Hill** (13 km, eight miles, by road, or four kilometers, 2.5 miles, by climbing the seventeenth-century pilgrims' steps), a picnic spot 1,065 m (3,500 ft) above the city. It was named for the goddess Chamundi, the family deity of the Mysore rulers. Atop the hill is the 2,000-year-old **Chamundeshwari Temple**, with its sculpted multi-tiered pyramidal tower added only three centuries ago. Nearby is the lurid

had been partially destroyed by fire. Only the public quarters of this rambling fairytale palace are open to view, as this is still a royal residence. It's filled with eccentric enchantments: a vast Durbar Hall dotted with candy-striped gilt pillars, lined with giant murals depicting the life of the maharaja, and topped by a beautiful stained-glass roof. One extravagant room is followed by another, each a confused marvel of styles, with Italianate furniture, Byzantine mosaics, the local Hoysala-style carvings, solid silver doors, art deco statues, sweeping marble staircases, and plumed ostrich-feather chairs with *punkah-wallah* attachments. A fascinating portrait gallery is incorporated within the palace, with another museum of paintings and royal relics in the courtyard near several ornate temples. The palace is open daily from 10:30 am to 5:30 pm. Cameras and shoes must be left at

statue of the ferocious demon Mahishasura — complete with a caddish, cheesy leer — who, according to legend, met his death at the hands of the vengeful goddess Chamundi, thus bringing peace to the local people. Halfway down the hill you'll see the 4.9-m (16-ft) -high **Nandi**, Shiva's holy bull, hewn in 1859 from a single black boulder with wreaths of carved bells and garlands.

The tour ends with a visit to the beautifully terraced **Brindhavan Gardens**, 19 km (12 miles) from Mysore, laid out against the Krishnarasagar Dam on the Cauvery River. Evenings have a gala atmosphere, with the whole park illuminated like a fluorescent fishbowl with

ABOVE: Victorian-era steam-train and an old Austin colorfully adapted into a bogie are two of the exhibits at Mysore's Rail Museum.

sparkling lights and cascading computer controlled fountains synchronized with music! It's possible to stay overnight at the ex-palace **Hotel Krishnajasagar** (©Mysore 20681), rates: inexpensive and views across the gardens, or at the KSTDC Tourist Home, rates: very cheap.

Back in Mysore, one of the city's highlights is the **Devaraja Fruit and Spice Market**, located behind Gandhi Square. It's an intoxicating maze-like strip of heaped flowers, incense stalls, and exotic fruit. Even if you're not shopping for Mysore's famous incense, sandalwood handicrafts, or silks, it's fun to stroll through the city's excellent emporiums. Among the best are **Cauvery Arts and Crafts Emporium** on Sayaji Rao Road, **Karnataka Silk Industries Corporation** on Mananthody Road, and the **Government Sandalwood Oil Factory**, located in the city's southern outskirts, where you can watch the distilling process and see how incense is made and then browse in the shop (open Monday to Saturday 9 to 11 am, 2 to 4 pm).

Train buffs should visit the **Rail Museum**, in KRS Road near the railway station, with its rows of vintage engines, decadent royal coaches, signals, and Raj-era memorabilia. Open daily from 10 am to 1 pm, and from 3 to 5 pm.

It's well worth making an excursion to the island fortress at **Sriringapatna**, 16 km (10 miles) from Mysore, stands between two tributaries of the Cauvery River and was once the stronghold of the powerful eighteenth-century Muslim ruler Hyder Ali and his legendary son, Tipu Sultan. Tipu Sultan was British India's most mercilessly powerful foe. He led two successful battles against East India Company forces before finally dying while defending his fortress capital against Lord Wellesley's army in 1799.

Tipu's larger-than-life persona, virulent hatred of Englishmen, and obsession with surrounding himself with tigers (both live and symbolic) make him one of India's most flamboyant historical figures. One of his most famous artifacts now lies in the Victoria and Albert Museum — the so-called Tiger Man Organ, an ingenious mechanical toy which represents a gleeful tiger swallowing a petrified English sahib.

Only sprawling battle-scarred ruins remain of Tipu Sultan's splendid fortress, although the dungeon where many British soldiers were imprisoned has been preserved. To the right of the entrance, look for a small plaque commemorating the exact spot where the fatally wounded leader died. Also see Tipu's mosque with its twin minarets and the ancient multi-columned **Sri Ranganathawamy Temple**, built in AD 894, with its large reclining image of Vishnu in his *avatar* as sea-serpent and central brass pillar.

Tipu Sultan's magnificent summer palace, **Daria Daulat Bagh**, and the family mausoleum,

the white-domed **Gumbaz** — with its interior lacquered with Tipu's tiger stripe emblem — stand unscathed amid ornamental gardens outside the fort. The Indo-Islamic palace, built in 1784 almost entirely of wood, has an extravagant multicolored interior of gilded walls and ornate arches. Stylized eighteenth-century frescoes depict the lifestyles of the Muslim nabobs and famous battle scenes, each full of symbolic intrigue. Upstairs is a fascinating museum displaying an array of Tipu's tiger-studded possessions, documents, and lithographs, as well as fine ink drawings of him and his family. The palace is open from 9 am to 5 pm daily.

THE HOYSALA TEMPLES

No visit to Karnataka is quite complete without appreciating the artistic grandeur of the Hoysala dynasty in the magnificent temple architecture found at **Somnathpur, Belur**, and **Halebid**. The Hoysala dynasty ruled the surrounding region between about AD 950 to 1310 when they were crushed by the iconoclastic Muslim rulers of Delhi. The finesse and artistry of these Hoysala temples is remarkable, with the fine-grained black stone so finely chiseled that it attains the lace-like delicacy of carved sandalwood or ivory. Hoysala temples typically have origami-pleated walls, ascending friezes, rise from a star-shaped platform, and unlike other south Indian temples have no towering *goporams*.

HASSAN

Hassan, 187 km (116 miles) northwest of Bangalore or 120 km (74 miles) northwest of Mysore, is a convenient base for visiting **Belur** and **Halebid,** and can be reached easily by rail or bus. The **Hassan Ashok Hotel**, ©8330, provides the most comfortable accommodation, or there's a choice of several budget hostels. En route, make a detour to **Sravanabelagola**, 93 km (58 miles) from Mysore, to see its astonishing 1,000 year-old 17-m (56 ft) -high monolithic statue of the naked Jain saint Lord Gomateswara. Every 12 years, there's a near riot here as Jain pilgrims clamber up scaffolding to pour thousands of pots of water, milk, curds, ghee, flowers, vermilion, and saffron across the saint's implacable face in a sacred anointing ritual.

BELUR

Belur, 39 km (14 miles) from Hassan, which flourished as the Hoysala capital 800 years ago, contains the ornately carved **Chennakeshava Temple**, built in 1116. According to local lore, the Muslim conquerors came to Belur intent on razing this temple, but left awed by its magnificence. Every deity in the Hindu pantheon is said to be represented here, and some many times over.

HALEBID

Halebid, 16 km (10 miles) away, offers the equally splendid double-shrined **Hoysalesvara Temple**, built in 1126 and considered one of the most skilled architectural feats in the world. As you walk around the temple, the carved walls begin to seem like a voluminous scroll unfurled before your eyes, laden with an infinite variety of ornamental decoration. Nearby, an open-air museum displays an excellent collection of Hoysala-period sculpture salvaged from other temples. The Tourist Office runs day tours to Belur and Halebid every Wednesday, Friday, and Sunday.

SOMNATHPUR

Somnathpur, built in the thirteenth century, was the last of the Hoysala temples and is the culmination of their artistic achievement.

The triple-shrined temple, dedicated to Keshava, stands on a star-shaped base within a cloistered enclosure and is covered with panels of exquisite sculpted friezes depicting narratives from the great Hindu epics, the *Ramayana*, *Mahabharata*, and *Bhagavad Gita*. It ranks alongside the temples of Khajuraho and Bhubaneswar for the skilled execution and delicacy of its exterior carvings, and is especially noted for the six horizontal bands of decorative friezes ascending with lathe-turn precision from the temple base. The temple is open from 9 am to 5 pm daily. For a more informed account of the temple's history, ask the curator for a Rs 6 copy of P.K. Mishra's *The Hoysalas*.

KARNATAKA'S WILDLIFE SANCTUARIES

From Mysore, two of Karnataka's loveliest wildlife sanctuaries are only a couple of hours' driving distance away. **Bandipur Wildlife Sanctuary** in the Nilgiri foothills, lies 80 km (50 miles) south on the Mysore–Ooty Road. Amidst Bandipur's lush 400 sq km (154 sq miles) of bamboo, teak, and rosewood jungle live many elephants, leopards, Indian bison, spotted deer, macaques, and a great variety of bird-life. It's possible to observe the animals at close range, particularly elephant herds, from the road, from atop an elephant, or from a boat on the Moyer River. The best season is from September to April. Accommodation (which must be pre-booked) as well as all transport within the forest

is arranged through Bandipur's Forest Lodge and Guest House. Write to the Field Director, Project Tiger, Government House Complex, Mysore, or ©20901, 24980.

Nagarhole National Park, 94 km (58 miles) southwest of Mysore, in the beautiful Kodagu district, is famous for its coffee. The park spans 294 sq km (114 sq miles) of tropical forest, undulating streams, and swampland. It's inhabited by tigers, elephants, leopards, sloth bears, wild boar, several species of crocodile, and a rich variety of bird-life. Nagarhole, which translates as "snaking water", is crisscrossed with meandering streams thick with plump mahseer for fishing. Arrangements for hiring jeeps, elephants, and boats, for visiting Heballa elephant training camp, are made either through the hotel or Nagarhole's Forest Department. Delightful accommodation is offered by Tiger Top's riverside Kabini River Lodge, located just outside the park, which includes a converted royal hunting lodge. Excellent food is served, and there's a well-stocked bar. They also run the safari-style Karapur Tented Camp, six kilometers (four miles) into the forest, and both are open to coincide with the park's season from mid-September to mid-June, and bookable through Jungle Lodges and Resorts, 348/9 Brooklands, 13th Main, Rajmahal Villas Extension, Bangalore, or ©362820.

OOTACAMUND (OOTY)

Set 2,285 m (7,500 ft) high in the lush Nilgiri Hills at the apex of Tamil Nadu, Kerala, and Karnataka, "Ooty" was the former summer headquarters of the British Government of Madras. Ooty was their mock-Sussex retreat: a bracing, eucalyptus-scented region of softly undulating hills grazed by plump Jersey cows, rhododendron-lined country roads, Victorian gingerbread cottages, milky streams thrashing with trout, and a cobbled town bazaar called Charing Cross. Today, India's elite spend their summers in a "Snooty Ooty" slightly gone to seed, playing snooker in the Ooty Club (a young subaltern called Neville Chamberlain first invented snooker here in 1875) and attending the annual fox-hunting, garden, and dog galas.

Ooty derives its name from the local Toda word *udhagamandalam*, or "village of huts". The area's original settlers were the Todas, a cattle-worshipping tribe whose women often have as many as four husbands apiece, and still live in small beehive huts on Ooty's outskirts. John Sullivan, the Collector of Coimbature and avid botanist who founded the first European settlement here, stumbled across Ooty's idyllic scenery in 1819 during one of his nomadic searches for rare flowers. By 1869, Ooty was the southern summer capital and an icon of Victorian India with its full social season and pastoral round of "at home" calls, horse-riding, and punting on the lake. Indian royalty soon followed, each vying to build a more extravagant palace than the last.

Raj relics survive everywhere in the pavilioned Botanical Gardens, the Anglican church spires, the nineteenth-century shops, and the dwindling community of British pensioners who preferred to stay on after Independence.

Ooty's main industry is oil extraction, particularly from the eucalyptus trees introduced during the nineteenth century, but also from

Bombay, and Bangalore. Coimbature is also a major rail junction, with an efficient network of trains to all the main cities.

From Mysore, the 159-km (100-mile) bus journey takes about four hours. The route corkscrews up thickly forested slopes dotted with precarious alpine villages, past the sun-drenched glades of Karnataka's Bandipur and Tamil Nadu's Mudumalai wildlife sanctuaries where elephants and monkeys loiter by the roadside. Mysore–Ooty buses (Rs 25) leave the depot throughout the day, but the 6:15 am bus is best for quieter roads.

If you're heading for Coimbature from Ooty,

lemongrass, geranium, clove, and camphor. Tea plantations in the neighboring hills produce distinctive blends of masala, chocolate, and cardamom tea. Ooty's popular "season" lasts from September to October and from April to May, but the place is far more peaceful and less expensive during February and March. In winter and during the nippy (sometimes downright freezing) monsoon months, bring warm woolens and waterproof shoes to guard against sudden flash floods.

ACCESS

Ooty's nearest airport is at **Coimbature,** 88 km (55 miles) away, with direct flights to Madras,

the quickest option is the three-hour bus trip. But be warned: this is a white-knuckle affair, as the bus tends to hurtle down the switchback roads. Between 20 and 30 buses leave Ooty station each day. The best option, though, is India's most enchanting rail journey. Ooty's vintage Swiss miniature train steams slowly down the steep slopes via the Coonoor Hills with their soaring rainforests and waterfalls to the lowland railhead of Mettapalayam. There's a 2:55 pm departure from Ooty which arrives in Mettapalayam in time to connect with the 7:30 pm *Nilgiri Express* (which also stops in Coimbature an hour later en route to Madras).

HOTELS

Savoy Hotel, ©2572, 2463, Club Road, which first opened in 1841, offers deluxe rooms in the

ABOVE: The Raj-era parish church of St Stephen's in Ooty.

original old hotel or in whitewashed cottages, both with comfortable thirties-era furniture and wooden floors, at Rs 650 to Rs 850. On nippy winter nights, aged retainers shuffle in with hot-water bottles and light the wood fires. Good Anglo–Indian cuisine is served in the rosewood-paneled dining room, with afternoon cream teas served on the lawn. Mr Gordon at the front desk can arrange pony-riding, trout-fishing, golf, and visits to nearby tea plantations.

Hotel Fernhill Imperial, ©2055, a vast Swiss Alpine-style former summer palace of the Maharaja of Mysore, offers views across the blue Nilgiri mountains, romantically overgrown gardens, pavilions, and tennis courts. Each room is different. The multi-chambered suites at Rs 250 to Rs 350 a night are filled with Edwardian furniture, old sepia photographs, and dusty objets d'art. The service is theatrically bad. Meals are served in the opulent Gothic-style ballroom. **Hotel Palace**, ©2866, has a similar vintage charm. It is the Nizam of Hyderabad's former retreat, complete with an annex for his summer "wives". Double rooms are Rs 250.

For mid-range accommodation, try **Hotel Mayura Sudarshan**, ©2577, **Hotel Tamil Nadu**, ©2543, or **Hotel Nilgiri Dasaprakah**, ©2434, famed for its south Indian vegetarian restaurant; all offer clean, simple double rooms from Rs 100 to Rs 200. The **YWCA**, ©2218, Anandagri, which takes both men and women, is particularly good value. It has carpeted single rooms with log-fires for Rs 22 to Rs 53, doubles for Rs 140, and a good restaurant. The **Youth Hostel**, ©3665, has cheap dormitory beds for Rs 15. For lakeside vistas — most pleasant during the peaceful off-season — stay at **Hotel Lakeview**, ©2026 located outside town overlooking Ooty Lake.

During the off-season, hotels and lodges reduce their rates substantially.

RESTAURANTS

Ooty's main bazaar area is crammed with eating places catering for the seasonal droves of Indian tourists, but the **Hotel Hills Palace**, at 66 Commercial Road, has particularly good Gujarati Rs 20 mealtime *thalis* and a never-ending menu with something to please everyone from fussy Brahmans to brain-eating Zoroastrians. Your status as a "meat-eater or not, sahib?" is demanded at the door, as a kind of food apartheid is in force: partition walls separate the carnivorous types from the herds of herbivores. Up the road is **Tandoor Mahal**, good for Mughali and tandoor dishes, and the ice-cream parlour next door serves creamy concoctions made with real strawberries, figs, and mango. Both **Chungwah**, on Commercial Road, and **Shinkows**, on Commissioner's Road, are run by

Chinese families whose curry-laced Sino–Indian dishes are quite appetizing. **Tehrani's**, opposite the Youth Hostel, caters for Western tastebuds with delicious Rs 13 pizzas (made with Ooty's Cheddar cheese), baked beans on toast, and apple pie. **King Star**, "The English Confectionery" opposite the Tourist Office, sells moreish filled chocolates and divine fudge by the kilo. Prohibition is in force, but both the Savoy and Fernhill Palace hotel bars serve liquor without demanding permits.

SIGHTSEEING

Ooty's charming landscape provides a soothing break from the scorched lowlands, with plenty of opportunities for long strolls in the Nilgiri Hills, horse-riding, boating on the lake, or simply relaxing in rickety Raj-era splendor. Ooty town is very small, and its sights are easily covered on foot in a day; longer distances can be covered by bus, taxi, or auto-rickshaw.

Start with the terraced **Botanical Gardens**, a sprawling 21-hectare (50-acre) manicured paradise created by the Marquis of Tweedale in 1847 and brimming with some 650 varieties of plants. Visitors can buy seedlings and fresh-cut flowers from the curator's office. Ooty's "season" reaches its peak during May, with the annual Flower Show and Dog Show. A half-hour climb up the main winding path past ornamental floral beds and exotic thickets is the grand Raj-era Government House, still used by the Tamil Nadu Governor as a summer retreat. At the top of the ridge is a Toda community, whose lifestyle has been "modernized" with concrete shacks and Western-style clothing. (To see a Toda settlement where the tribespeople live traditionally in tiny domed huts and wear decorative tattoos, vivid handwoven shawls, and corkscrew curls, go to **Kandal Mund**, a village nine kilometers, or 5.5 miles, from Ooty.) From the Gardens' high cast-iron entrance gates, it's a 20-minute stroll back along Garden Road (turning left at Higgins Road) to **St Stephen's**, a parish church set in an English cemetery. It was built during the early nineteenth century with immense teak beams pillaged from Tipu Sultan's palace at Srirangapatna. Nearby is **Spencer's Store**, an old British emporium with 1940's merchandise and excellent local Cheddar and Wensleydale cheeses, and the red-brick Scottish **Nilgiri Library**, opened in 1868, where old men wearing pince-nez and mufflers study dated copies of Punch magazine and glance disapprovingly at intruders.

Just down the road, near the Savoy Hotel, is the **Ooty Club** (more properly called the Ootacamund Planter's Club), with its faded photographs of stiff-collared British military officers and tea planters, snarling rows of mounted prey, hunting trophies, and a board listing Masters of the Ooty Hunt. The billiard room behind the club is a shrine to the game of snooker, remaining exactly as it was when the game was invented. You'll need to write or ring the Secretary for permission to visit the club.

From here, either jump aboard a bus or take a two-kilometer (one-and-a-quarter-mile) stroll to Ooty's **scenic lake**, the main focus of activity for coy honeymooners and large, raucous family groups. The **Boat House** (open from 8 am to 6 pm) hires out row-, paddle-, and motorboats, and also has facilities for fishing. A handpainted sign proclaims: "Rowers are available for rowing capacity including the rower's rowing cooly charges extra!" Nearby is a children's toy railway which circles the lake, and a small snack bar. At the open-air market by the lakeside, you can hire ponies for about Rs 45 an hour, with or without a hired escort, to trot along Ooty's mountain trails. You can also arrange to have ponies delivered to your hotel for a day excursion.

Ooty's **bazaar**, which stretches from Hospital Road and Commercial Road down to Charing Cross, is good for a leisurely stroll. There are all sorts of musty oddities: Chinese tailors who still use 1930's pattern books, shops specializing only in rosewood pipes and walking sticks, and photographers' shops displaying "Box Brownies" and yellowing photographs of pale-skinned debutantes. For the best collection of antique silver Toda jewelry go to **Suraaj,** about midway down the main bazaar (with a twin shop at the Savoy Hotel), and buy embroidered Toda shawls from a cluster of shops near Charing Cross. The bazaar is crammed with tiny shops selling oils, tea, and delicious Nilgiri honey. The Tourist Office at Charing Cross seems consistently to lack useful Ooty maps and pamphlets; you'll have better luck at Higginbothams bookshop nearby.

OOTY EXCURSIONS

Aside from walking, pony-riding, boating, and a scenic golf course open to paying non-members, anglers will find excellent trout and carp fishing in streams at Avalanche Emerald, and Parson's valleys, as well as in Ooty Lake. A license and tackle are available from the Assistant Director of Fisheries, ©2232, Fishdale, near the bus-stand.

There are plenty of invigorating walks across the hills, particularly to **Wenlock Downs**, eight kilometers (five miles) away, with impressive views across the Nilgiri Hills to **Dodabatta Heights**, 10 km (6.2 miles), which looms behind the Botanical Gardens and is the highest peak in Tamil Nadu at nearly 3,000 m (9,845 ft). Take

a bus there from the main bus-stand, and enjoy spectacular views all the way down to the Coimbature lowlands from the topmost observation point. From there, it's a glorious 45-minute walk back to town, descending past tea gardens, forest thickets, and rolling meadows. (If you start to wilt, there are plenty of buses plying the route back to town.) Nearby picnic spots include **Catherine Falls** and **Elk Hill** (both eight kilometers, or five miles), and **Kodanad View Point** (16 km, or 10 miles) for superb views across the hazel-colored mountains, and the hill station of **Coonoor** (13 km, or eight miles), where you can stay overnight at the delightful Raj-era Hampton Manor, ©244, on Church Road with period suites for Rs 200. Visits to Glen Morgan (24 km, or 15 miles), one of the most beautiful tea estates in the region, can be arranged through Mr Gordon of the Savoy Hotel. Given advance notice, the estate owners will guide visitors around and explain the tea production process; they can also arrange an afternoon tea.

To visit **Mudumalai Wildlife Sanctuary**, 64 km (40 miles) away, take the two-hour express bus to Theppukady, where the sanctuary's reception center is located. Mudumalai covers some 320 sq km (about 125 sq miles), a dense, deciduous hill forest wedged between Bandipur and Wynad sanctuaries. Its remoter regions are exceptionally rich in wildlife, and can be explored by jeep or atop elephants on a four-seater howdah. You're likely to see tigers, panthers, wild bears, spotted deer, gaur (Indian bison), sambar, reptiles (including the scaly anteater), and a great variety of bird life. The park also contains an Elephant Camp, where the harnessed heavyweights are tutored in the logging trade. The best season to visit is February to May, and you can conveniently arrange accommodation and in-park transport whilst in Ooty through the District Forest Officer (North), ©2235. There are lots of options ranging from basic Rs 8 dormitory beds in forest lodges to the most comfortable deluxe rooms for Rs 75 to Rs 180 at **Bamboo Banks Farm House** in Musingudi Village.

GENERAL INFORMATION

The Tourist Office, ©2416, situated in the Super Market building, Charing Cross, runs daily sightseeing tours around Ooty, as well as to Coonor and Mudumalai Wildlife Sanctuary. Talk to S.D. Vincent, Venus Travels, at Hotel Weston, ©3700, about ticketing or transport arrangements.

OPPOSITE: A village woman carries firewood across a rustic meadow in Ooty.

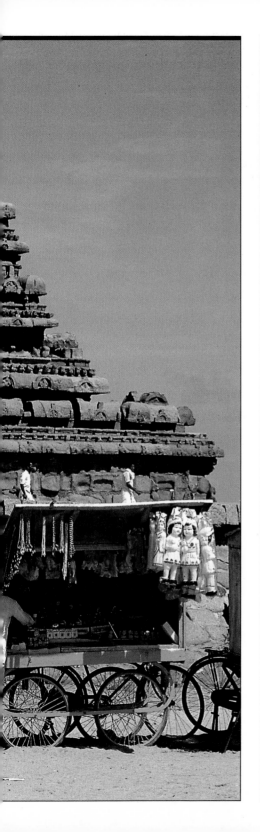

Madras
and the
Temple
Towns

TAMIL NADU

Tamil Nadu, India's most southerly state — dubbed India's Bible Belt — brims with magnificent architecture, exotic pageantry, and age-old traditions — the legacy of the South's ancient Dravidian culture. Following the route from Madras through Kanchipuram, Mahabalipuram, and Madurai — the main trio of temple towns — you'll see some of India's most impressive temple architecture and experience the warmth and color of rustic Tamil Nadu.

TEMPLE ARCHITECTURE OF THE SOUTH

Dravidian architecture and sculpture achieved its zenith with the construction of vast, imposing temple complexes. These were not the single buildings of further north, but sprawling edifices in which the main shrine was lost amidst a warren of passages, sweeping pillared halls, courtyards, bazaars, and sacred bathing pools. Encased by concentric outer walls and dominated by gigantic, multi-tiered *goporum* gateway towers, they are stunning in their rich decorative detail. These places of worship were also public forums, where villagers would come to gossip, listen to devotional readings from ancient palm leaf manuscripts, and debate administrative and court matters.

Dravidian temple architecture follows a basic pattern, regardless of a temple's size, with a rectangular ground plan dominated by the distinctive *goporum*, believed to exert talismanic protection over the temple complex. Often rising to a height of more than 50 m (164 ft), these archways swarm with cavorting deities and mythological creatures — some human and some fantastic hybrids — which act out scenes from the great Hindu epics. Up until Independence, caste Hindus barred harijans, or so-called "untouchables", from entering the temples, so these poor pariahs could only worship the deities on the *goporums*, getting cricked necks in the bargain. Nowadays, temple authorities bow to modern public taste and have them painted up in an outrageous technicolor gloss, disfiguring their great antiquity.

Inside the temple complex stands the pyramid-shaped *vimana*, the wall and tower over the main shrine. This is entered through *mandapas*, cool cloistered passages. In the later Dravidian temple complexes, the designs of these passages became more elaborate, culminating in the so-called "thousand-pillared halls", although rarely do these halls contain this exact number. For instance, Madurai's famous

Madras and the Temple Towns

Meenakshi Temple's Hall of Thousand Pillars actually has only 997. Each temple also has its own sacred tank, several smaller shrines, often a score of ceremonial elephants, and its own ornate *ratha*, or wooden temple chariot. On the annual chariot festival day, the *ratha* is mounted with ornate bronze idols and paraded through the town in a ritual climax of religious fanfare. Most temples you'll encounter in Tamil Nadu's temple towns bar non-Hindus from entering the inner shrine, the sacred *sanctum sanctorum*, but there's still much to admire, with each detail crafted as though that particular panel, door, or fresco was in itself an individual work of art.

SOUTH INDIAN CUISINE

While south Indian dishes are often very hot, they are tempered with plenty of cooling fresh yogurt, grated coconut, and rice, and are generally much lighter on the palate than the rich, ghee-laden cuisine of the north. Fish is always plentiful along the coastal stretches of the south, and you can usually take your pick of pomfret, lobster, mussels, prawns, and crabs, traditionally cooked with spice-laced coconut milk.

The easiest way to order is to request a "tiffin" *thali*, which will either be served the traditional way on a banana leaf or on a large round metal tray. Even in modest cafés — known variously as *udipi vihars*, tiffin houses, and military hotels (the latter denoting non-vegetarian) — you'll be given six or so assorted vegetarian dishes that are constantly refurbished, a dollop of steaming rice, *papads*, puffed wheat *puri*, fresh *dahi* (yogurt), chutneys, and mango pickle. You'll soon catch on to the south Indian way of using fingers as expert all-purpose eating utensils — and marvel how Madras girls manage to make this look almost graceful — but remember to observe the Indian etiquette of using only your right hand, as using the left will earn you horrified glances from neighboring tables. You'll notice how the locals scrub their hands scrupulously clean before settling down to their finger-scrum meal. Don't touch the water which is slapped down as soon as you sit down; stick to bottled drinks, or well-boiled tea and coffee.

Typical south Indian staples include a dozen varieties of *dosa*, a crispy-thin rice pancake filled with spiced vegetables; *idli*, steamed fermented rice cakes; *vadai*, doughnut-shaped, black peppercorn-studded balls of deep-fried lentils and rice; and *utthapam*, a thick rice pan-

OPPOSITE: Weathered stone bulls guard the seventh century Shore Temple at Mahabalipuram.

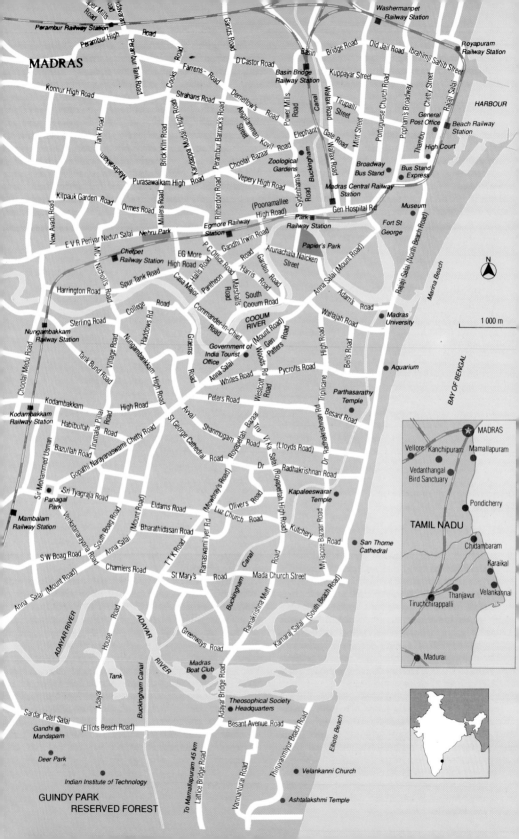

cake which always comes with a topping — akin to a pizza — of tomatoes, onions, and green chilies. All are accompanied by fresh coconut chutney and sambhar, a spicy lentil dish, and make a nourishing protein-packed meal in themselves. Soothe away the chilies with a lassi, freshly squeezed fruit juice, or refreshing fresh coconut milk sipped straight from the husk with a straw. The finale to any meal is always a cup or two of the local filtered coffee, which is hard to beat anywhere in the world. Don't be alarmed at the waiter's antics if he starts sloshing the boiling brew from one beaker to another at rapid speed — he's performing "coffee by the yard", a south Indian courtesy which froths and cools it down to drinking temperature!

MADRAS: THE SOUTHERN GATEWAY

As a gateway to Tamil Nadu, Madras offers relative comfort, good cuisine, and a refined charm to travelers embarking on a tour through the state's temple heartland. Tamil Nadu's tropical seaside capital is full of commercial bustle, yet despite its sprawling skyline, it lacks the brash poverty of India's three larger cities — Bombay, New Delhi, and Calcutta — and has a languid, almost rustic, atmosphere that reflects the essence of south India. This is partly due to its breezy, surf-sprayed locale on the eastern Coromandel Coast, but also to the city's irrepressibly affable, Dravidian-featured, dark-skinned Tamils, whose easy-going ways, lilting language, vivacious culture, and devastatingly hot cuisine give even the seasoned India traveler the odd sensation of encountering another nation altogether.

Four centuries ago, Madras was still Madraspatnam, a small fishing village within a region that was ruled over by the greatest dynasties of the south, the Cholas and the Pallavas. Yet Madras has a long, colorful history of association with seafaring traders and missionaries: St Thomas the Apostle was thought to have been martyred here in AD 72, and Arab, Chinese, and Phoenician merchants first began trading along the Coromandel Coast some 1,500 years ago. A Portuguese cathedral bears witness to a transient occupation by traders from Lisbon during the fourteenth century.

In the early seventeenth century, Madras played a strategic role in the history of the British in India, long before India Britannica was a gleam in Queen Victoria's eye. The city's founder, Sir Francis Day, arrived with the East India Company in 1639, and leased 10 km (six miles) of coastal territory from a descendant of the Raja of Vijayanagar to build Fort St George. The garrison camp within the fort's walls became known as "White Town;" outside sprang up Madraspatam or "Black Town" where the Indian community lived, many of whom were employed as weavers for the cloth trade. This was the husk of modern Madras, which rapidly eclipsed the East India Company's original settlement at Surat on India's northwest coast. In 1688, James II granted Fort St George the first municipal charter in India, and by 1740, Company trade represented over 10 percent of the entire British public revenue. At this time, however, the Company faced a formidable rival in the French who were just as intent as the British on reaping profits from India. They finally came to blows after war broke out in Europe — first the War of the Austrian Succession (1740–1748) then, with reversed alliances, the Seven Years War (1756–1763). The French attacked and took Fort St George in 1746, although in the pause between the two European wars, Madras was restored to the British in exchange for Cape Breton Island in North America. Madras was barely back in British hands before another battle for supremacy in the south followed — but this time the British defeated the French in a dramatic, unexpected assault on nearby Arcot in 1751, taking it against a force twice its size and saved only by timely reinforcements. From this battle emerged one of British India's lasting heroes — the young Robert Clive, who had persuaded his commander to let him seize Arcot and who later became the governor of Madras.

By 1772, Calcutta had become the most important British city, and Madras, despite its busy commerce, grand Victorian buildings, spacious mansions, and glorious coastline, was destined to be the most provincial of British India's quartet of major capitals. Nowadays, Madras combines its old legacy with a sprawling manufacturing belt for its main industries — textiles, tannery, cycles, and automobiles. It's also a major producer of films, and gaudy cinema billboards are the city's trademark.

Madras offers the perfect introduction for a first-time India traveler, as it lacks the intensity, crowds and strain of Bombay, New Delhi, and Calcutta, and is both unusually spacious and easy to negotiate. Madrassis are often ingenuously friendly, forever flashing mirthful grins at passing tourists. Somehow, long after you've left Madras, you'll be charmed by its simplicity — the men perfectly at ease in a knotted, sarong-style *lunghi*, and the women with fragrant blossoms wound into their hair with the same artless grace.

Madras and the Temple Towns

ACCESS

International travelers can fly direct to Madras from Colombo, Kuala Lumpur, Singapore, Shahjah, and Abu Dhabi, and British Airways will soon start operating flights from London. Madras is the most convenient base from which to explore south India, with direct Indian Airlines flights to Ahmedabad, Bangalore, Bombay, Calcutta, Cochin, Delhi, Hyderabad, Madurai, Port Blair, Trivandrum, and several other centers. Both the smart new domestic terminal and the international airport are situated quite close together about 15 km (nine miles) from the city. If arriving by air, there's a PTC bus service (from 5 am to 10 pm) running between both airports and the city, which drops passengers at Egmore railway station and most major hotels on request. Madras port has passenger shipping links with Penang, Singapore, and Port Blair.

Madras has two railway stations: Egmore, which serves most of south India, and Central for the rest of India. Both are located quite close together in the city center near Poomallee High Road. Popular train journeys include the overnight *Madras–Cochin Express* (departs 7:20 pm, arrives 9:40 am), the *Madras–Madurai–Quilon Mail* (departs 7 pm, arrives Madurai 6:40 am, Quilon, 2:45 pm), the *Bangalore Mail* (seven hours), and the *Hyderabad Express* (16 hours). From either station, you can make the short city hop north to Fort St George or eight kilometers (five miles) south to the Guindy National Park. Avoid bottleneck queues for rail tickets and head for the Indrail office on the second floor of the Central station, open from 10 am to 6 pm. Trains are generally slower, but safer, than the battered sardine-tin state buses which make traveling long distances a grueling endurance test. Both the Tamil Nadu State Transport and the privately-run Tiruvalluvar Transport Corporation have their terminals off Esplanade Road. If you intend to do much traveling by bus, buy the Rs 2 monthly *Jaico Time table* from any newsstand, which lists all destinations, revised schedules, and fares in south India.

THE CITY

Despite its ever-expanding boundaries, Madras is refreshingly flat, spacious, and uncrowded. Most of the city's sights are concentrated around three main areas. The historic seafront, **Fort St George**, site of the original East India Company settlement, is bordered by bustling **Georgetown** to the north — you'll find the main bazaars, budget hotels, and Raj-era architecture dotted around its main boulevard, Netaji Subhash Bose Road (known by old Madras-hands as

Parry's Corner). Close by are the two main railway stations, **Central** and **Egmore**, and the two main long-distance bus terminals. To the south, **Anna Salai Road**, also known as Mount Road, is the city's main 16-km (10-mile) -long boulevard, and its commercial nerve center — here you'll find many state tourist offices, emporia, shops, restaurants, consulates, airline offices, and many of the top-range hotels and restaurants. Further south lies the **Guindy/-Adyar** area, bordered by Elliot's Beach, with the nearby attractions of the Guindy reserves and temples. Along the Adyar River, one of the city's major waterways, stands a leafy pocket of grand old mansions, including the Madras Club, the Raja's Chettinad Palace, and the Theosophical Society.

Like most of the southern region, Madras has a balmy, hot climate throughout the year, although it reaches sunstroke levels between March and May when temperatures average 37°C (99°F) — compared by one eighteenth-century English diarist to standing within the "oppressive influence of a steam furnace" — and in the July to September months the area is prey to heavy monsoon rains and coastal squalls, sending huge breakers crashing on to the beach-front sands. The most comfortable time to visit is during its short-sleeved winter from mid-December to February, when the city comes alive with music and dance festivals, with performances of *Bharatanatayam* and classical music every evening. The English daily *The Hindu* offers a useful daily entertainment guide. It's certainly worth timing your visit to coincide with south India's most exuberant festival, *Pongal*, which celebrates the early harvest during four riotous, rice-throwing days during mid-January. You'll watch in amazement as Madras goes cattle-crazy, with people adorning their sacred cows with turmeric, garlands of flowers, sugarcane, coconut, and mango leaves, parading them through the crowded bazaars, and even staging bull rodeos on Marina Beach.

GETTING AROUND

Madras's streets can seem quite intimidating to the first-time visitor, with streets and lanes arranged in haphazard fashion and many of the old British place-names still in currency, despite an official emphasis on new, tongue-twisting, post-Independence names. To save problems, it's often worth asking someone to write in Tamil the names of places you want to visit before setting out. It's most enjoyable to explore Madras by taxi, stopping off at the city's three main sightseeing areas and then simply strolling at whim. You'll find cabs at any of the major hotels and at the main railway station, and can also hail them in the street. Fares are very reasonable at about Rs 1.70 per kilometer (0.62 mile) and you can always bargain for a day rate, giving a list of the places you wish to see. Auto-rickshaws can do the same job for much less, taking you as far as the airport if desired, and cycle-rickshaws are perfect for negotiating the frenetic back-alleys of the city center, but remember to agree on the fare before climbing aboard. Madras has an easy-to-use city bus system — almost orderly compared to India's other main cities — and if you plan to cover much distance this way, buy the useful *Hallo Madras* booklet for a list of all the city bus routes.

Otherwise, the tourist office runs excellent Rs 25 conducted tours, staffed by knowledgeable guides, which whisk you to all the main places of interest in an afternoon. You'll get a good overview of Madras this way, and can always return to Fort St George and the Government Museum — where the tour stops are tantalizingly brief — for a less-harried inspection. The tours leave daily at 2 pm from outside the ITDC office at 154 Anna Salai Road.

Bicycles are perfect for gliding along Madras's flat Italianate Marina Parade for panoramic views across the steel-gray Bay of Bengal and lungsful of salty, incense-scented air, dodging balloon-sellers, donkeys, fakirs, and family scrums. If you follow your nose southward, you'll eventually arrive at Elliots Beach, 11 km (seven miles) away, where the sea starts to look inviting enough for a swim.

HOTELS

The stately **Hotel Connemara**, ©810051, 82166, Binny's Road, has served as both a nabob's palace and a British residency and is an elegant oasis within the city's business district. Its ornately carved wooden lobby is filled with centerpieces from a dismantled antique Dravidian temple, and service is splendidly efficient. Ask to be put in the delightful old wing overlooking the pool, with spacious, luxurious Raj-era rooms. Facilities include possibly the best bookshop in Madras, a choice of bars, a good shopping arcade, travel desk, beauty salon, several excellent restaurants, a coffee shop, and a pastry shop. Rates: moderate.

Two other five-star hotels with similar room rates are located near the city center. There's the **Welcomgroup Chola Sheraton**, ©473347, 10 Cathedral Road, which has executive business facilities, a good swimming pool, a variety of restaurants including the city's best Northwest Frontier cuisine at its replica of the Maurya Sheraton's famous Bukhara restaurant in New Delhi. The best rooms for panoramic city views

are those on the top floor. The **Taj Coromandel**, ©474849, 17 Nungambakkam High Road, provides luxury accommodation despite its drab concrete exterior. As with the Sheraton, the top-floor rooms are the best. Of several restaurants, the Taj's Mysore restaurant is particularly worthwhile for Mughali and regional Indian specialties, with evening Bharatanatayam dance performances and musicians. **Welcomgroup Adayar Park**, ©452525, 132 Mowbray's Road, lies about 15 minutes' drive from the city center and is popular with business travelers for its comfort and efficiency. Facilities include excellent Indian and Chinese restaurants, a health club, and a large swimming pool which at night sets the scene for an evening barbecue. Rates: expensive.

Good centrally located and inexpensive hotels include the **Hotel New Victoria**, ©847738, 3 Kenneth Lane, Egmore; and the **Hotel Imperial**, ©847076, 14 Whannels Road, Egmore, set in gracious gardens and courtyards. Both have good Chinese, Indian and continental restaurants. A little less expensive and good value is **Hotel Maris**, ©470541, right next door to the Chola Sheraton and despite its unexciting, utilitarian decor. In more secluded, downtown Mylapore are two reliably good and clean inexpensive hotels, both on Dr Radhakrishnan Road. At No. 69 is **Hotel Savera**, ©474700, and at No. 72, **New Woodland's Hotel**, ©473111, which has the added attraction of an excellent, cheap south Indian vegetarian restaurant.

But by far the best hotel in the very cheap range is **Broadlands Lodge**, ©845573, 848131, 16 Vallabha Agraham Street, opposite Star Talkies in Triplicane. It's an immaculate old Moorish merchant's house with pastel-blue shutters — a traveler's oasis with simple rooms, a sunroof, a peaceful garden courtyard strewn with deck chairs and swing-seats, room-service meals, and boiled and filtered water. Proprietor Mr Kumar anticipates most essential needs: here you can make international calls, leave valuables and luggage in a safehold, hire bikes, and use the well-stocked, multilingual library. The accommodation choice is single rooms, doubles with attached bathrooms, and the coveted rooftop cottage. The rooftop terrace, popular for sunbathing, overlooks a large modern mosque. Broadlands' staff are a cast of characters, particularly Laxmiah, the rotund comic barber/masseur with his 1920's leather doctor's bag filled with archaic scissors and lotions — but he works wonders with a five-day bristle or an aching back.

If Broadlands' is full, other good economy options worth trying are the **Tourist Home**, ©844079, 21 Gandhi Irwin Road; the **YMCA** in Westcott Road, opposite the Royapetah Hospital, which offers both men and women basic, clean single rooms; or the **YWCA Guest House and Camping Ground**, ©34945, at 1086 Poonamallee High Road.

RESTAURANTS

For stylish dining, try Hotel Connemara's outdoor mock-rustic **Raintree** restaurant, which serves the delicious Tamil Nadu Chettinad cuisine. Specialties include *chettinadu meen kozambu*, an aromatic fish curry, *kozhi varutha*, a subtly spiced chicken curry, and *paayasam*, a moist rice pudding with almonds, raisins, and

cardamoms. Each of the four main hotels has a potpourri of good restaurants and bars, but some are outstanding: the Chola Sheraton's **Peshawri** for superb North-west Frontier food; the Taj Coromandel's **Mysore** for a variety of Indian regional dishes and evening dance performances; and the **Golden Dragon** for Chinese food. Both the Hotel Connemara and the Welcomgroup Adyar Park offer outstanding buffet lunches — with a pick-and-choose mixture of Indian, Chinese, and Western dishes — complete with dessert and coffee for around Rs 70 per head.

For those with a newly-acquired enthusiasm for the almost exclusively vegetarian south Indian cuisine, Madras is a gold mine for good, extraordinarily cheap restaurants and it's fun to experience south Indian cuisine in more authentic surroundings.

Amaravathi, ©476416, 1 Cathedral Road, is nothing less than an eating experience, and won the city's 1987 Best Restaurant Award for its superb Andhra-style food. Try their crab *masala* and *sora puttu*, grilled fish with spices, or opt for their spectacular Rs 11 set meal, served on a banana leaf. This includes a variety of vegetarian dishes, fish, prawns, or chicken, and, if desired, curd and fluffy rice, which the waiter liberally sprinkles with a fine lentil powder and hot ghee, leaving the traditional tamarind paste up to your discretion. Your fingers are supposed to do the rest (you're given finger bowls and hot towels before and after the meal), but if you find the idea off-putting just ask for a fork and spoon.

Other excellent south Indian restaurants to try are **Woodlands Drive-In** restaurant near the top of Cathedral Road, open daily for early morning breakfasts of fresh *idlis, dosas,* and *vadas,* with generous *thali* platters served for lunch and dinner; **Hotel Dasaprakash's** pleasant rooftop restaurant on Poonamallee Road; and **Mathura** restaurant, on the second floor, Tarapore Towers, Anna Salai Road, which specializes in regional vegetarian fare, with a bewildering array of *thali* choices. Here you can dine on the pretty fairy-lit terrace or in air-conditioned comfort.

Along Anna Salai Road, you'll find an overwhelming variety of small eating houses, most open all day serving simple *dipi*, south Indian *thalis*, snacks, and frothed-up *lassis*. One of the best is **Mansara**, at 819 Anna Salai, and highlights here include their immense Rs 7 mealtime *thalis*, fresh grape juice, their "Family Rost", a Rs 15 one-meter (three-foot) -long *dosa* (only served if at least five people solemnly swear they will eat it!), and the urchins in pixie caps who wheel trolleys to and fro like dim-sum ladies in a Hong Kong restaurant. Nearby is one of the city's historic cafés, the **Coronation Durbar Restaurant**, just off Anna Salai at 123 Waljara Road. Head straight for its pleasant rooftop garden restaurant for cheap, reliably good Indian, continental and Chinese dishes. Just opposite the Tourist Office in Spencer's Building — the Harrods of the Raj — is **Fiesta**, extremely popular with tourists and students for its all-day fruity ice-cream, milk shakes, and good Indian and continental food. Outside the hotels, the best Chinese restaurant is **Chinatown**, opposite the Chola Sheraton on Cathedral Road, where the Madras chic converge for excellent Szechuan and Chinese regional dishes amidst an attractive bold red and green decor, dangling Chinese lanterns, and monkey-box screens. The **Chungking**, 67 Anna Salai, is another local old-time favorite for Sino–Indian fare. Set in a quiet leafy cul-de-sac above a musty music shop, it serves good garlic prawns, sweet and sour pomfret, and spring rolls, and you can dine well for under Rs 30 per head. When you feel you can't look at another *thali*, try the **Taco Tavern**'s good vegetarian Mexican tacos and pizzas, located in the Willingdon Estate Building on Commander-in-Chief Road.

SIGHTSEEING

There are two main aspects to sightseeing in Madras—the historic Raj-era architecture within the city's environs and a host of surrounding attractions in the southern Guindy / Adyar area.

cal Survey Office), **Wellesley House**, and the original Officers' Mess (1780–1790), now converted into the **Fort St George Museum**. There's an extraordinarily rich collection of East India Company memorabilia, including original historical documents, a superb portrait gallery, armory, coins, medals, uniforms, antique clocks, and furniture. The museum's highlights include many fine original eighteenth-century lithographs and paintings by the Daniell brothers; a painting attributed to George Chinnery depicting the East India Company's plump adventurer Major Stringer Lawrence companionably walking with the Nabob of Carnatic; and a tiny

If you're taking the conducted tour, you'll first stop at **Fort St George**, established by the East India Company in 1641. The husk of the fort's original "White Town" still stands, much of it rebuilt after the French surrendered the fort in 1749. The ghosts of the Company's East Indiamen still seem to linger in these Georgian gesso-surfaced buildings.

The imposing eleventh-century **Governor's House**, with its grand black Charnockite Corinthian columns, now serves as the city's Legislative Assembly and Council, as well as the offices of the State Secretariat. Its marble-like surface is actually *chunam,* a hard plaster made from ground shells which gleams with high polish. Party men come to chat in the cool of the nearby **Cornwallis Cupola**, above which soars India's tallest flagpole. Other fine historic buildings include **Clive House** (next to the Archaeologi-

wooden cage into which one Captain Phillip Anstruther of the Madras Artillery, a huge, bearded officer, was squashed from September 1839 to February 1840 after he was captured in China while on some forgotten imperial mission. He spent his time sketching on old scraps of bark, the result of which so impressed his captors that they built him a slightly larger cage for more arm movement! Admission is free and the museum is open daily except Fridays from 9 am to 5 pm.

The oldest Anglican church in the East, **St Mary's Church** stands in a leafy, shaded corner of the garrison and still attracts a large

ABOVE: The bulbously-domed Indo-Saracenic High Court is the second largest judicial building in the world. OPPOSITE: Army *jawan* bicycles past a historic building within Fort St George.

congregation of Madras Christians. Designed by William Dixon and built from solid stone between 1678 and 1680 this exquisite chapel is suffused with the spirit of early Empire. Its courtyard is paved with some of the oldest British tombstones in Asia. The church's interior is cluttered with ornate marble sarcophagi decorated with mourning angels. Job Charncock, the founder of Calcutta, who rescued his Indian mistress from her suttee pyre, baptized their three daughters at the church font; Lord Robert Clive married at an altarpiece captured from the French at Pondicherry; and eight former governors lie buried within its environs. Permission can be granted to look at the register of baptisms, marriages, and burials dating from 1680. St Mary's Church is open daily from 8:30 am to 5:30 pm.

Just north of the fort, near Parry's Corner, stands the bulbously domed, ash-red **High Court**, reputed to be India's most remarkable Indo–Saracenic structure and the second-largest judicial building in the world, after London. Designed by Henry Irwin (who designed the Mysore Palace) and J.H. Stephens in 1892, it towers surrealistically over the bustling chaos of modern Madras. If you're on a tour bus, you will probably make a mental note to return for a more lingering inspection. You're free to wander through to its grand central cupola, where impromptu affidavits can be typed out by spectacled, cross-legged peons, and through its vaulted arcades where black-cloaked lawyers, wigs askew, converse in the shade of giant sparrow-infested matted *tatties*. Other spectacularly pompous Victorian buildings clustered nearby to include in your own tour of Madras are the Southern Headquarters of the State Bank of India and the General Post Office further north. Westward from here stands the Indo–Saracenic Central Railway Station with its classic clock-tower, Moore Market, and the Government Museum and National Art Gallery, all of which were designed by Irwin, one of the most prolific architects of the Raj period.

The tour stops next at the **Government Museum** in Pantheon Road, Egmore. First opened in 1857, it is one of the country's best museums, with entire wings devoted to natural history and archaeological relics. Its highlight is India's most extensive collection of Dravidian bronze sculpture, mainly from the Pallava (AD 700–900) Chola (AD 850–1350) and Vijaynagar (1350–1600) periods. Pallava bronzes are easily identified by their elongated grace and distinctive oval faces. The Cholas achieved an artistic peak with their robustly sensuous and ornately-clad bronzes, their archetypal females dressed in bejeweled harem pants, exposing boyish waists, perfect navels, and protruding breasts. Perhaps

the best-known of Chola bronzes is the *Nataraj,* or Shiva, in a cosmic dance pose framed by a decorative ring. Also on display are many rare second-century Buddhist sculptures and the immense Amaravati stupa, said to have been erected over Gautama Buddha's relics. A pebble path leads to the turreted and domed **National Art Gallery**, which has a fine collection of old and modern paintings, including rare Rajput-, Mughal-, and south Indian-style paintings. Both complexes are open from 10 am to 5 pm daily except Friday, and there's a small cafeteria for cool drinks and snacks.

Heading southward, the next stop is **Valluvar Kottam**, in Nungambakkum, a giant concrete memorial to the ancient poet-saint Thiruvalluvar, impressive only for its ornate "temple chariot" shrine, a replica of the famed temple chariot at Tiruvarur. Opened in 1976, its vast

auditorium looks like an aircraft hanger, and contains 1,330 of the poet's verses inscribed on granite tablets.

A further six kilometers (3.7 miles) south lies the **Guindy Snake Park**, the brainchild of American conservationist Romunlus Whitiker. It houses a fascinating, well-documented reptilium, with over 200 species of snakes, lizards, crocodiles, tortoises, and spiders, all living in pits. Look especially for the massive 11-m (33-ft) -long Regal Python and the very poisonous Russells Viper, whose fangs inspired the invention of the hypodermic needle, and the swarming "Snake-Worship Termite-Hill", decked with flowers and lamps every Friday. There's an impressive hourly bout of un-fanged snake handling, and you can witness venom extraction on Saturdays and Sundays between 4 and 5 pm. The fully-fledged research center

here manufactures anti-venom for snake-bite cures. It's open every day from 8:30 am to 5:30 pm.

You can return later to visit the nearby **Raj Bhavan**, a former governor's Banqueting Hall built in the style of a Greek temple, with grand Corinthian and Ionic columns and marble terraces. It was commissioned by Edward Clive, son of Lord Robert Clive, in 1802. Renamed Rajaji Hall, and used for important public functions, it is open from 10 am to 6 pm daily. It lies on the periphery of the **Guindy National Park**, a 121-hectare (300-acre) wildlife reserve only eight kilometers (five miles) from central

ABOVE: Kapaleeswarar Temple in Madras, dominated by a giant multi-tiered pyramid goporum (gateway) that is believed to exert a protective influence over the temple complex.

Madras. It was once part of the governor's gigantic domain, and rare black buck, spotted deer, cheetah, civet cats, jackals, mongoose, and monkeys roam wild. You can return for an enjoyable day's excursion, either taking the urban train or the No. 45 bus from Anna Square.

Crossing the Cooum River into the historic Mylapore district, the tour continues to the **Kapaleeswarar Temple**, off R.K. Mutt Road down an alley lined with hawkers selling flowers, sacred ash, and tulsi-wood beads. It's a magnificent example of Dravidian temple architecture, dominated by a towering *goporum* gateway writhing with colorful, ornately-carved mythological figures.

The present Shiva temple was built by the Vijaynagar kings in the sixteenth century on the site of an earlier temple destroyed during the Portuguese occupation of Mylapore in 1566. Its spacious flagstone-paved courtyard has a bustling, forum-like atmosphere. It is best visited at sunset, when the temple priest conducts the evening *puja*, or worshiping ceremony, to a backdrop of cymbals, flutes, gongs, smoldering incense, and muttered prayers. Pilgrims stream in, clutching blossoms, shredded coconuts, and rice-strands and stopping to have their temples smeared with a blood-red *tikka* mark. The colorful 11-day *Arupathumoovar* festival staged here every March to April is most spectacular on the eighth day, when bronze images of the 63 *nayanmars*, or devotees of Lord Shiva, are paraded around the courtyard. You can also unearth treasures — silks, jewelry, and traditional brass vessels — from the tiny shops surrounding the temples.

Another ancient temple is the **Krishna Parthasarathy Temple** on Triplicane High Road. The tour makes a paddle-stop at **Elliots Beach**, the Long Beach of Madras, which is more peaceful than Marina Beach but not recommended for swimming. You'll notice a small memorial facing the sea, erected in the memory of a sixteenth-century Danish sailor called Schimdt who fell in love with a beautiful Tamil girl. So disconsolate was Schimdt when his mistress drowned at sea that he set sail, vowing to comb the waves in search of her body, and was never seen again. The tour finishes at the **San Thome Cathedral Basilica** on the Main Beach Road, said to contain the mortal remains of St Thomas the Apostle, who was martyred by stone-throwing assailants in AD 72 at the nearby hillock (you'll see it on your way in from the airport) now called **St Thomas Mount**. The present Gothic cathedral, with sepia-colored towers and lovely stained-glass windows, was built in 1896 on a site occupied by several churches since the original fourteenth-century Portuguese church. If you venture to St Thomas Mount, you'll find a little chapel and a cell, said to have been his dwelling, with holes in the ground worn away by his knees in constant prayer.

The Theosophical Society

It's worth making a special visit to the stately nineteenth-century mansion housing the **Theosophical Society**, located amid an oasis of 100 hectares (247 acres) of forested parkland on the southern banks of the Adyar River. The Society, whose advocates essentially explored the spiritual nature of man, was co-founded in 1875 by the Russian Madame Blavatsky and her American financial mentor, Colonel Henry Olcott, who established their world headquarters in Madras two years later. A tireless traveler, Madame Blavatsky survived a disastrous marriage at the age of 14, and despite being described as "fat, unprepossessing and irascible", went on to build an impressive international organization, astounding skeptics by such feats as materializing a shower of roses. In her later years, she taught that evolution would soon dispense with the human sexual organs and that there would be two spinal cords in the body. Among those profoundly influenced by her doctrines were the poet W.B. Yeats, the artists Kandinsky and Mondrian, India-reformer Annie Besant, and Oscar Wilde's wife, Constance. There's an enormous library — open from 9 to 10 am and from 2 to 4 pm — stacked with some 17,000 books and many ancient manuscripts encompassing all religions and philosophies. You can picnic undisturbed in the leafy gardens which are massed with ancient banyan trees, and house a spiritual supermarket of a church, Buddhist and Hindu temples, a Zoroastrian shrine, and a mosque. The Society is open daily from 8 to 11 am and from 2 to 5 pm except Sundays, and the gardens from sunrise to sunset.

Nearby is the **Kalashetra Centre**, where students come from all over India (and overseas) to study Bharatanatayam, possibly India's most ancient classical dance form, traditionally performed by *devadassis*, young girls dedicated to south Indian temples.

Beaches and Bazaars

Marina Beach stands between Madras and the deep-blue Bay of Bengal. This 13-km (eight-mile) -long mustard-yellow sandy strip fringed by palms and casuarina trees is not exactly the French Riviera, but its balmy seafront throbs with activity. By twilight it throngs with milling families, resembling a sort of shantytown Hades of lamp-lit stalls, pavement entertainers, and wandering hawkers. Along its Italianate Raj-era esplanade lie several imposing public buildings facing the ocean — the Nabob's

Palace, the University, Presidency College, and the new lighthouse. Along Marina Beach are parks dotted with statues of famous Tamil writers and sages, flanked at either end by memorials to two former Chief Ministers, the late C.N. Annadurai and M.G. Ramachandran, who was a former matinee idol known for his Superman roles before he turned to politics. Fishing fleets bob into shore on their catamarans (from the Tamil, meaning "tied-logs") just before dusk, providing an interesting spectacle as they pile their seething catch on the sands and haggle with waiting marketers. Walking southward, at the junction of Pycroft Road and South Beach

day, Blacktown had an added oriental swagger in its shifting population of merchants from Portugal, China, Europe, and Arabia, who all added their personality to this historic grid of interlocking streets filled with crumbling façades and decaying godowns. A good walking tour starts at **Armenian Street**, just off Parry's Corner or Netaji Subhash Chandra Bose Road. You can't miss the **Armenian Church**, built in 1724, with its whitewashed interior hung with icons and paintings, and a leafy inner courtyard and cemetery containing the gravestone of a Christian who died in 1630, the earliest in Madras. The church is beautifully maintained,

Corner, you'll reach the **Aquarium** and the historic eighteenth-century **Ice House**, which used to store immense chunks of ice brought by ships from American lakes before the days of refrigerators and air-conditioners. If you're serious about swimming, head out for **Golden Beach**, about 21 km (13 miles) south of Madras, where the sea is clean and calm, or simply head for the beach resorts of Mahabalipuram, 61 km (38 miles) away.

Back in the city, much of Madras's maritime history is crammed into the spice-laden cobbled bazaars of central **Georgetown**, west of the dock area and north of Fort St George. When King George V visited Madras in 1911, he raised his eyebrows at Blacktown, the original East India Company's indelicate sobriquet for the native quarter, and suggested it be renamed. During Madras's late seventeenth-century trading hey-

with a fascinating array of documents relating to the history of Armenians in India, yet has no priest or congregation. Clustered nearby, you'll find the **China Bazaar** and **Portuguese Church Street**. For livelier street-life go to the modern **Burma Bazaar**, located directly opposite the Customs House on First Line Beach Road near Parry's Corner. It's full of cheap electronics smuggled from the Gulf, fake Rolex watches, murky bottles of Johnny Walker, reflective sunglasses by the case-load, and shifty salesmen. Moving southwest toward Anna Salai Road, **Evening Bazaar** is riddled with tiny alleys each specializing in different household items. Its musty antique shops are open until about 9:30 pm.

ABOVE: Windbreaking palm trees along lonely coastal stretch in Tamil Nadu.

ENTERTAINMENT

Enthusiasts of Indian classical dance and music should time their visit to Madras to coincide with the annual cultural bonanza held during December and January, when performances are staged each evening. A dozen cultural halls stage performances throughout the year, notably the **Kalashetra Centre,** the **Music Academy Raja Annamalai Hall**, and the **Fairlands Tourist Exhibition Centre** on Marina Beach. The week's upcoming events are listed in Friday's *The Hindu.* Otherwise, this is your once-in-a-lifetime chance

ayyanars, traditionally made throughout Tamil Nadu as symbolic protection of home and hearth. Purchases can be shipped home, usually with minimum fuss, through either Beanie and Company Shipping Division, ©26894, Armenian Street, and KPV Sheikh Muhammed Rawther and Company, ©510346, 202 Linghi Chetti Street.

The best, and most convenient, items to buy are inexpensive, good quality silks, cottons, and handloom fabrics. **Co-Optrex**, Kuralagam, on N.S.C. Bose Road, has the most extensive range, with a ground floor devoted just to silks and handloom fabrics, sold at fixed prices. **India**

to experience the outrageous fortunes and lachrymose antics of south Indian cinema. The best centrally located air-conditioned cinemas are Sathyam, Devi, and Safire, and if that only whets your appetite, approach the Tourist Office about arranging a visit to one of Madras's film studios.

SHOPPING

Madras is one of India's largest cottage industry centers for textiles, glazed Thanjuver pottery, leather ware, and numerous types of handicrafts. Treasure-hunters will also find Madras full of musty curio shops and excellent well-stocked state emporia, and may find themselves making improbable "impulse" buys of giant brass-studded temple doors, elaborate south Indian temple lamps, or irresistible brightly painted terra-cotta horses known as

Silk House, on 846 Anna Salai Road, also has an excellent range. If you're beginning to feel rather travel-worn, Madras is the perfect place to stock up on fresh cheap cotton garments, many of them "export seconds" in the latest designs. Try **Hanif Bros**, 15-A, Nungambakkam High Road, for quality "Madras plaid" shirts, or simply comb an almost endless line of hawkers' wares along Anna Salai Road. Here you'll also find the state emporia, of which Tamil Nadu's **Poompahur** (at 818), Kerala's **Kairali** (at 138), Karanataka's **Kaveri** in the LIC Building, and the **Victoria Technical Institute** (at 765), are the best.

Poompahur has an especially good range of bronze figures, all reproductions of original tenth- to twelfth-century Chola sculptures. Interesting curio shops to poke through for sculpture, Raj-era relics, brass, and paintings include

N. Balakrishnan and Company, 62 Montieth Lane, the **Heritage**, 135 Anna Salai Road, **Kalimuthi**, Krishnamuthi Mudali Street, next to Triplicane High Road, and **Aparna Art Gallery**, 781 Anna Salai Road. However, bear in mind that faking antiques is a well-developed business throughout India, and that it's illegal to take anything more than a hundred years old out of the country. Reproductions are often excellent, provided they are presented and priced as such and not as the genuine article. Excellent quality leatherware — stylish luggage, wallets, jackets, belts, and shoes — is best at **Sarala Art Centre**, at the Hotel Connemara. The **Reptile**

House, 161 Anna Salai Road, is also worth a try. And its neighbor, **Higginbothams Bookshop**, established in 1844, is the city's largest.

GENERAL INFORMATION

The **Tamil Nadu Government Tourist Office**, ©869685, 143 Anna Salai Road, is friendly, efficient, and well-stocked with city maps and leaflets, as well as information on upcoming dance performances. Here you can book the Madras city tour, as well as the highly rewarding day tour to Kanchipuram, Thirukalikundram, and Mahabalipuram, which leaves at 7:30 am and returns at 6 pm daily, costing Rs 60. There's even a week-long package tour which covers all important destinations in south India, which leaves every Saturday at 6:30 am and costs Rs 1,075. Boarding points are at the express bus-stand and out-

side the Government of India Tourist Office, 154 Anna Salai Road. Otherwise, consult the encyclopedic monthly booklet, *Hallo Madras*, found at every newsagent and most hotels, which has an exhaustive list of all airline offices, information centers, and travel agents likely to be of use.

THE TEMPLE TOWNS

Tamil Nadu's main trio of temple towns — **Kanchipuram, Mahabalipuram**, and **Madurai** — offer the perfect introduction to the cultural fabric of south India, with its Hindu faith, rustic simplicity, and deep respect for tradition.

At least two days are recommended for relaxed enjoyment of both Kanchipuram and Mahabalipuram, with excellent accommodation at the latter. Buses ply from these temple towns to Madurai, but it's more interesting and comfortable to return to Madras first along the scenic coastal road, and then take either the daily flight, eight-hour train trip, or deluxe bus to Madurai.

KANCHIPURAM

Kanchipuram, or "Golden City", 76 km (47 miles) southwest of Madras, is one of the most spectacular of Tamil Nadu's pilgrimage centers. The skyline of this rustic town is massed with towering *goporums*, for within its environs stand no less than a thousand ancient temples, many of them well-preserved masterpieces of Dravidian architecture. Kanchipuram is one of India's Seven Sacred Cities, but differs from the others — Varanasi, Mathura, Ujjian, Hardwar, Dwarka, and Ajodhya — in that it offers worship to both Shiva and Vishnu, rather than one or the other. Few of Tamil Nadu's temple towns are as interesting and beguiling to explore as Kanchipuram, with its almost constant festival pageantry, exquisite temples, swarms of kohl-eyed children, and tiny hut porticoes decorated with rice-powder *kolam*. Outside the entrance to the main temples, wizened hawkers sell assorted piles of blossoms, coconuts, powdered ash, camphor, sugar lumps (a symbol of wealth), incense sticks, conch shells, and sacred threads for Brahmans, the latter with a point-of-sale mantra hummed over it!

Kanchipuram is also renowned for its brightly colored, fine-quality silk, and silver and gold brocaded fabrics. In the surrounding countryside, skeins of brilliant silk and cotton

OPPOSITE and ABOVE: South India is well known for its traditional dance and drama. Special performances are held in Madras in December and January.

hang to dry beneath the trees, and the town itself is a hive of weaving activity: back alleys are matted with silk threads and hum with the click-clacking of looms.

Kanchipuram first flourished as the capital of the Pallava dynasty, great patrons of art who ruled much of the far south between the sixth and eighth centuries. The Pallavas were prolific builders who also turned their talents to establishing the traditions of silk-weaving and the choreography of Bharatanatayam dance, performed within pillared halls by barefoot *devadassis*, half-hidden by silken veils, who lived within the temple enclosures.

Of all the Pallava kings, Mahendravarman I (600–630), a dramatist and poet, encouraged the most inspired developments in Dravidian — the Pallava term for Tamil Nadu — temple architecture. His reign witnessed not only some of the monolithic *rathas*, or "chariot temples", carved out at Mahabalipuram, but also the beginnings of the towering *goporum* gate-towers clustered with writhing deities that became a Dravidian temple trademark. In its heyday, Kanchipuram was not just a major religious pilgrimage center, but also a seat of learning, attracting scholars, sculptors, artists, and musicians. The sixth-century sage Shankaracharya, who has been called the "Brahman Aquinas", set up an episcopal seat here which exists to this day. But by the ninth century, the Pallavas were on the wane, and Kanchipuram fell to a succession of rulers — the Cholas, the Badami Chalukyas, and the Vijaynagar rajas — all of whom stamped their own artistic style on the elaborate temples that can be seen today.

To see Kanchipuram at its exuberant best, try to time your visit to coincide with one of the major temple festivals. The most spectacular is the "car festival" held at the Kamakshiamman Temple on the lunar cusp of February and March, when temple deities are paraded in elaborately decorated wooden chariots against an extravagant backdrop of firecrackers, fairs, street acrobats, and folk theater. Similar festivals are held on a smaller scale by every temple to celebrate the south Indian new year during April, when the equally carnival-like *Brahmothsavam* festival also takes place.

Access and Accommodation

Kanchipuram is easily reached from Madras, either by regular bus services or daily trains from Madras, connecting at Chengalpattu. If you're taking the TTDC tour, which leaves Madras at 6:45 am and returns at 6 pm, you'll make only a brief morning stop at the main temples. It's best to explore at your own leisurely pace, staying overnight at the TTDC-run **Hotel Tamil Nadu**, ℂ2561, Kamatshi Sannathi Street, near

the railway station, which is cheaply priced and serves good south Indian fare. Bicycles are perfect for cruising Kanchipuram's flat, spacious streets, and there are plenty of bike-hire places, the daily rate being about Rs 10. There is no tourist office, but the Archaeological Survey Office opposite the Kailasanatha Temple can usually supply maps.

Sightseeing

Scattered in and around Kanchipuram are some 1,000 temples, about 200 of which are within the city itself. Only a handful are especially outstanding, and these are mainly clustered toward

the northern end of the town, near the bus station.

There are a few basic guidelines to bear in mind before setting off on your temple tour. First, all "living" temples (where pilgrims still come to make *puja* worship) take a siesta break between 1 and 4 pm, so that early mornings and late afternoon are best for sightseeing. Secondly, be prepared for a barrage of dirty beggars and frantic, credential-waving "guides", and remember that one stern-faced "No!" is more effective than a dozen apologetic smiles. But have plenty of spare change at hand anyway in case you get talking with temple priests or custodians,

---

ABOVE: Temple wall buttressed by stone guardians in the pilgrimage town of Kanchipuram. OPPOSITE: Courtyard view of the Ekambareshwara Temple in Kanchipuram.

whose knowledge is genuine and their tales often fascinating. They will sometimes let you clamber to the top of temple *gopora* for stunning views, but they'll expect of token of thanks, something in the realm of Rs 5 to Rs 10.

The **Kailasanthar Temple**, located east of the town center down Nellukkara and Putteri Streets, is one of Kanchipuram's earliest and most exquisite temples. It's a masterpiece of early Dravidian architecture, with a small prototypical *gopora* and *mandapam*, and its sculptures, carved reliefs, and overall design poses a vitality and austere elegance closer in style to the monolithic rock-cut temples at Mahabali-

-high *rajagoporum* and massive fortress-like outer walls built by the Vijaynagar king Krishna Devaraja in 1500. Dedicated to Shiva, this is Kanchipuram's largest, most magnificent "living" temple, spread across nine hectares (22 acres). It was originally built by the Pallavas, and became a fusion of successive Chola and Vijaynagar craftsmanship. Within the dim coolness of its airy sandalwood-scented enclosures, the barefoot pilgrims seem dwarfed. Long pillared hallways lead to a monkey puzzle of ornately-carved enclosures, small shrines, and the inner *sanctum sanctorum*. Within a tiny courtyard stands a gnarled mango tree, said to be

puram. It was built entirely in sandstone by the Pallava king Rayasimha in the late seventh century, with the more elaborate frontispiece added later by his son, Mahendravarman III. Within the temple pavilion stand the three telltale signs of a "living" temple where pilgrims gather to worship Lord Shiva: the Nandi bull (Shiva's trusty stead), the tall *durajasthamba* flagstaff, and the *balipitha*, shaped like an inverted lotus leaf, where offerings are made. The temple's inner courtyard wall contains many miniature shrines, and if you peer closely, some of these have the fragments of beautifully painted stucco-work frescoes, just enough to give an impression of the temple's original splendor.

To the left of the nearby Nellukkara and Putteri Streets junction lies the **Ekambareshwara Temple**, with its soaring 57-m (187-ft)

some 2,500 years old. The temple was built around this tree, and owes its name to a corruption of *Eka Amra Nathar*, Lord of the Mango tree. Novice priests seem to materialize like ghosts from the shadows — some are barely eight years old, already self-assured, with sacred threads twined across their thin chests, heads shaved but for a tuft of hair.

A five-minute stroll further left, you'll find the **Kamakshiamman Temple**, with its large watchtower *goporums*. Built by the Cholas during the fourteenth century, it is one of India's three holy places dedicated to Sakthi (the goddess Parvati when she married Lord Shiva), considered particularly auspicious for marriage-blessings. Close by is the large Vishnu temple, the **Vaikuntha Perumal**, built by the Pallavan emperor, Nadivarman II, in the seventh century. It has beautiful lion-pillared cloisters and sculpted bas-reliefs around the main shrine, portraying the history of the Pallavas and the wars fought by them. Another impressive Vishnu temple is the Vijaynagar **Varasdaraja Temple**, with its 30-m (98-ft) -high *gorporum*, thousand-pillared hall, and many ornate sculptures, among which is a huge chain carved out of a single piece of stone. But these are only the most famous of the town's temples, and you're bound to stumble across countless discoveries of your own, including fascinating weaving workshops. If you're serious about shopping, drop in at the **Weaver's Service Centre**, at 20 Railway Station Road, or **Srinavas Silk House**, at 17A T.K. Nambi Street, for reasonably priced selections of fine silks and brocades. Kanchipuram's delightful **India Coffee House** just down Gandhi Road, serves excellent cold coffee.

TIRUKKALIKUNDRAM

The TTDC tour makes a brief stop at this small pilgrimage town, 50 km (31 miles) from Kanchipuram and 15 km (nine miles) from Mahabalipuram. It's notable for its medieval Shiva temple atop the 160-m (525-ft) -high Vedagiri hill, where two eagles are said to come to be fed by temple priests every day at noon. Legend has it that these two eagles are actually saints who stop to rest at this temple on their daily flight between the holy cities of Varanasi and Rameswaram. But somehow, the birds have either "just been" or are "delayed", when visitors clamber up to witness this daily ritual! The vertiginous climb up the hill's 500 granite-hewn steps is the equivalent of a Jane Fonda work-out and earns you spectacular views. The less-fit get themselves slung into baskets for an alarming swaying ascent at the hands of the *dandi*-wallahs, whose one false step could send their human baggage plummeting all the way down! Another much larger Shiva temple stands within the village center and houses Tamil Nadu's "Lourdes" — a tank believed to have healing powers. Locals swear that every 12 years, a conch mysteriously rises from its waters, a phenomenon which attracts streams of pilgrims. These conchs are displayed in the Shiva temple.

MAHABALIPURAM (MAMMALLAPURAM)

This popular seaside resort lies on the gloriously empty white-sanded Coromandel Coast, 65 km (40 miles) east of Kanchipuram, or 58 km (36 miles) south of Madras, and is easily reached by bus. It began as a seaport almost 2,000 years ago, and was known to Phoenician, Arab, and Greek traders. Between the seventh and tenth

centuries, it thrived as a busy trade center established by Narasimhavarman I, nicknamed *"mamalla"* or "great wrestler", hence the village's original name of Mamallapuram. The Pallavas left an astonishing legacy of unique monolithic rock-cut temples, caves, massive bas-reliefs, and one remaining shore temple — and these are the oriental marvels that visitors flock to see today.

Collectively, these open-air structures are the earliest known examples of Dravidian architecture in existence, built by the Pallava kings during a creative frenzy of temple-building in the seventh century. Mysteriously, the Pallavas

deserted the site, and these ancient architectural treasures lay undiscovered until the late eighteenth century.

You could start your tour close to the village center, with the most famous of the bas-reliefs: the immense **"Arjuna's Penance"**, a huge 27-m (88-ft) -long and nine-meter (30-ft) -high frieze crammed with a Noah's Ark of beasts, birds, and mythological figures — including life-sized elephants — sculpted across a whaleback-shaped rock. Built during the reign of Narasimhavarman Pallava (circa 630–670), archaeologists have long debated whether it portrays the Mahabharata fable in which the mortal Arjuna undergoes penance to Lord Shiva for his guilt in killing his fellow humans alongside Krishna; or the mythical tale of the descent of the holy river Ganges to the earth — depicted by a natural fissure in the rock face. To the right, you'll see Lord Shiva letting the floodwaters flow through his hair, preventing the world from being destroyed by the impact of its descent. Either way, the panel is nothing less than

ABOVE: Gypsy waifs are eerily dwarfed beside Krishna's gravity-defying "Butterball" on the mountain slopes of Mahabalipuram. OPPOSITE: Ancient stone-hewn temples within the group of the Five Rathas at Mabalipuram.

a brilliant piece of artistry, filled with realistic, humorous touches: cavorting mice at the elephants' feet, a deer scratching its face with its hoof, and an emaciated hermit doing penance by standing on one foot, whose ascetic posturing is mocked by a cat striking the same pose.

The nearby hillside is dotted with eight *mandapams*, shallow rock-cut cave temples, each sculpted with fine bas-reliefs depicting scenes from Hindu mythology, although two were left unfinished. The finest and largest of these is the **Krishna Mandapam**, which shows Krishna using Mount Govardhann as a sort of protective umbrella to save his flocks of shepherds and animals from Indra, a vengeful rain-god. Take the path just left of the "Penance" for an easy climb up the hill — site of several scattered temple *mandapams*, and **Krishna's Butterball**, a massive boulder precariously balanced on the hill's slope. For stunning views across Mahabalipuram, climb the tall lighthouse at the rear of the hill, open to visitors until noon. Just below the lighthouse, the **Mahisha-suramardhini Cave**, fronted by a lion-pillared portico, has especially exquisite reliefs, with bas-reliefs of Lord Vishnu sleeping on the coils of the serpent Adisesha and of the Goddess Durga, better known as Kali, seated on a lion about to kill the buffalo-headed demon, Mahishasura.

Back on Beach Road, take the road to your left for a 15-minute walk down to the casuarina tree-sheltered sandy clearing containing the monolithic seventh-century **Five Rathas**. Each of these miniature "temple chariots" is a stupendous work of art, sculpted into architecture from gigantic boulders, and covered with ornate porches, pillars, and statuary. Although these temples have stylistic links to early Buddhist chapels and monasteries, they contain the embryonic forms of later Dravidian architecture — the *goporums, vimanas*, and multi-pillared halls. They are named after the Pancha Pandava, the five hero brothers of the epic *Maharabharata*, and guarded by three stone guardians: a lion, an elephant, and a nandi-bull.

Of Mahabalipuram's ancient "Seven Pagodas", only a single desolate **Shore Temple** stands on the coastline, at the end of the main Beach Road. Built by the Pallava king Rajasimha during the late seventh century, this simple, pagoda-roofed structure is one of south India's oldest temples. Assaulted by the elements, many of the temple's exquisite reliefs have been worn to obscurity, but its original splendor is still visible. This two-spired temple is unique in that it houses shrines to both Shiva and Vishnu, the latter containing a splendid 2.5-m (eight-ft) -long bas-relief of Vishnu reclining on his serpent couch. A rear chamber contains rem-

nants of a 16-sided granite phallic lingam, which originally touched the ceiling, and a bas-relief depicting a sacred cow forever in the throes of sacrificial slaughter. Rows of stone bulls guard the temple courtyard. The temple's modern neighbor is a bulbously ugly nuclear power plant, visible 10 km (six miles) further up the coastline.

Back in town, there's a good open-air museum, dozens of tiny souvenir shops, and a government-funded **School of Sculpture**, where sculptors create excellent replicas of ancient Indian carvings in marble, soapstone, and granite, all sold at reasonable prices. It's diagonally opposite the bus-stop and is open from 9 am to 1 pm, and 2 to 6 pm, closed Tuesdays. Local information is provided by the tourist office, ✆ 32, in East Raja Street, and the useful Guide to Mahabalipuram booklet.

Hotels

For a winning combination of comfortable lodgings, excellent food, and a perfect, quiet stretch of surf for swimming, go to **Silversands Beach Resort** ℂ283-4, about two kilometers (1.2 miles) along the coast. It has sea-facing air-conditioned deluxe rooms or deluxe beach villas, all with tasteful south Indian decor. Good Indian, continental, and Chinese food is served, but fresh seafood dishes here are simply outstanding. Rates: inexpensive. The ITDC-run **Ashok Temple Bay Resort**, ℂ251, is slightly more expensive yet is less stylish, despite secluded cottages, a swimming pool, restaurant, and bar. The TTDC-run **Shore Temple Beach Resort**, ℂ235, 268, is cheap-range resort option, with a complex of double-tiered cottages right on the sands. There's a simple cafeteria-style restaurant, swimming pool, and tennis court. Shoe-

string budget lodges in town include the **Mamalla Bhavan**, ℂ50, and the ITDC-run **Youth Camp**, near the Shore Temple, which has dormitory beds for Rs 10, and spartan mosquito-infested rooms for Rs 30. Some visitors swear by the "authentic" experience of lodging with village families, paying about Rs 50 per week for the local version of "bed and breakfast" — *charpoy* and *chai*. Of a host of friendly, ramshackle budget beach-cafés, try the **Village Restaurant**, the **Sunset**, and the **Rose Garden** for excellent fresh seafood and travelers' fare.

The **Mahabalipuram–Madras Road** is worth several stops. This 58-km (36-mile)-long coastal ribbon of road takes you first to the **Crocodile**

ABOVE: A wandering showman orchestrates a beachfront battle between a mongoose and a cobra near the Shore Temple.

Farm, which lies 16 km (10 miles) from Mahabalipuram. Like Madras' Snake Farm, it was established by Romulus Whitaker to breed rare species of crocodiles in captivity. Visitors peer down into large swampy enclosures housing some 516 reptiles. "Jaws 3", the largest captive crocodile in India, is the star attraction, and crowds form to watch him chew his way through a lunch of bandicoots and beef steaks.

At the sleepy historic fishing village of **Covelong**, 20 km (12 miles) from Mahabalipuram, the remains of an old fort have been converted into the Coromandel Coast's finest luxury resort: the five-star, **Fishermen's Cove**, ©4114-268, run by the Taj Group and comparable to their Fort Aguada resort in Goa. There's a choice of well-furnished, sea-facing rooms outfitted with all modern conveniences, or private beach cottages right on the sands. Facilities include wind-surfing, car rental, a lovely swimming pool, terrace restaurant and bar, shopping arcade, and business services. Rates: inexpensive to moderate.

Just 18 km (11 miles) short of Madras is the **Cholamandalam Artists Village**, a seaside commune started during the sixties where a community of artists, sculptors, and potters live and work. There's a continual exhibition of works for sale, and visitors are often invited in to meet the artists. Those with a creative bent can stay at a clean, simple guesthouse and attend workshops in batik-dyeing, sculpture, painting, or fabric-printing.

MADURAI

Lying 472 km (293 miles) south of Madras, Madurai is one of India's oldest and most illustrious cities, an oasis of traditional Tamil culture dominated by magnificent towering temple complexes. Founded over 2,500 years ago on the lushly fertile banks of the Vaigai River, it retains much of its distinctive heritage, along with a leisurely old-world charm. The most famous of all Tamil Nadu's pilgrimage centers, Madurai's overwhelming attraction for visitors is the giant fortress-like medieval Meenakshi Temple, with its nine soaring stucco-work *goporums*. Acknowledged as the finest, and one of the largest, examples of Dravidian architecture, it embraces much of the city with ever-rippling rings of stone battlements, tanks, and corridors. The elaborate ebb and flow of its temple life has changed little for centuries, and its exotic bazaars hum with a carnival atmosphere and are full of temple-offerings, barefoot devotees, sacred ash-smeared mystics, and wailing music. Tiny shops are full of unexpected treasures — traditional brass temple lamps, jewelry, hand-woven silks, tie-dye fabrics, and stone carvings.

Legend tells how Madurai, "the city of nectar", was formed by a single drop of water shaken from Lord Shiva's locks, in answer to a prayer of the Pandyan king Kulasekera for a new capital during the sixth century BC. The Pandyas ruled much of south India from Madurai until the thirteenth century, initiating a renaissance of Tamil literature, art, and architecture as the seat of the *Sangam*, or Tamil Academy. The city fell to the Cholas during the eleventh and twelfth centuries, and was to change hands several times — first to the Delhi Sultans, then the Vijaynagars, followed by the cultivated Nayak rulers who built Madurai as we see it today, laid out in the pattern of a lotus flower with the immense Meenakshi Temple at its core. The Nayaks ruled from 1599 to 1781, when they were ousted by British troops who destroyed the temple's defenses, filled in its moat fort, and built four broad streets known as the *veli*, or "outer streets", which now mark the limits of the old city. You'll find most of Madurai's sights concentrated here, as well as the budget lodges, restaurants, the main Tourist Office (©22957, West Veli Street), GPO, bus stations, and railway station. Madurai's modern cantonment area lies on the northern banks of the Vaigai River — there's little to see here, but this is where the better hotels are located. Allow yourself at least two days for leisurely sightseeing, either on foot or by handy cycle-rickshaw, nicest in the cool of early evening.

The best time to visit is the cool season from October to March, but it's worth coming a little later for the most spectacular month-long **Chithirai Festival** in April and May, when Madurai explodes with bizarre and wonderful pageantry for the "marriage" of Goddess Meenakshi and Lord Sundareswarar. As many as 10,000 pilgrims stream into the city each day. The **Teppam**, or **"Float" Festival** which is just as interesting, is held during January and February at the Mariamman tank's island temple.

Access

Madurai is easily accessible from Madras, with a choice of a daily flight, an eight-hour train journey, and frequent buses. From either Kanchipuram or Mahabalipuram, buses take about 10 wearisome hours. Madurai is also connected by air to Cochin and Bangalore, and well-connected by rail directly with Bangalore, Quilon, and — for temple-addicts — the other major Tamil temple cities of Rameswaram, Tiruchirapalli (Trichy), Thanjavur (Tanjore), and Tirupati. Buses ply to all major south Indian centers, and from here, Kanya Kumari, the "Land's End" of India, is only 150 km (94 miles), a six-hour bus journey. From Kanya Kumari you can conveniently continue travelling through

Kerala state by taking the early morning express bus to Kovalam beach, a pleasant 3½ hour trip.

Hotels

Of Madurai's two top-class hotels, the best is the Taj Group's three-star **Pandyan Hotel**, ©42471, Race Course Road, set in a pretty garden with pleasant, well-furnished rooms. Rates: inexpensive. It has Madurai's best restaurant, and useful facilities include a car rental, travel agency, bank, beauty parlor, and shopping arcade. Otherwise, try the similarly priced **Hotel Madurai Ashok**, ©42531, Algarkoil Road, which has clean rooms, or the more central, cheaply priced TTDC-run **Hotel Tamil Nadu**, ©31435, West Veli Street, with good air-conditioned doubles, even cheaper "fan-cooled" rooms and classic south Indian meals. You'll see dozens of very cheap hotels and cafés clustered along Town Hall Road within the old town, but **Hotel Apsara**, ©31444, West Masi Street, rates high with travelers. Outside the hotels, good, simple south Indian breakfasts and *thali* meals can be had at **Amutham** and the **Indo–Ceylon Restaurant**, both on Town Hall Road.

Sightseeing

Located in the center of the old town, the magnificent **Meenakshi Temple** is the classic monument to Madurai's Dravidian heritage, and seethes with an astonishing profusion of sculpted figures, ornamental pillars, and cloistered courtyards. Much of this massive complex — which covers six hectares (15 acres) — was built during the seventeenth century by the Nayak kings, although the Vijaynagar rulers renovated it extensively. It comprises two main sanctums, one dedicated to the goddess Meenakshi — a "fish-eyed" Pandyan princess born with three breasts, one of which miraculously disappeared when she met her true love, Shiva, in the form of Lord Sundareswara, up on Mount Kailasha; the other is dedicated to her famous consort, Shiva himself. Of four leviathan tapering *goporums* surrounding the temple complex, the southern gateway eclipses them all with a height of nearly 50 m (164 ft). Within are five smaller *goporums*, enclosing two slender, gilt-smothered *vimanas*, or central shrines. Highlights include its famous **Musical Pillars** — 22 tapering rods, each carved out of a single block of granite, which sound an arpeggio of musical notes when tapped; and the ornate **Hall of a Thousand Pillars**, actually 985, with two small shrines standing in the space reserved for the remaining 15 pillars. Part of the hall has been turned into a museum with a fascinating, though poorly-lit, display of antique art treasures, sculpture, religious icons, and photographs charting the development of Dravidian architecture. There's plenty to see — one enthusiastic visitor said he spent two entire days wandering through its imposing enclosure — and only the inner sanctum is barred to non-Hindus. Evenings can be spent very pleasantly listening to temple music performed outside the Meenakshi Amman shrine between 6 to 7:30 pm and 9 to 10 pm. The main temple complex is open daily from 5 am to 12:30 pm and 4 to 10 pm, and there's a peculiar rule that photos can only be taken between 1 and 4 pm on payment of Rs 5.

A short 10-minute cycle-rickshaw ride brings you to the seventeenth-century **Tirumalai Nayak Palace**, a vast Indo–Saracenic abode notable for its elegant domes, colonnades, and pavilions. As a sort of south Indian Versailles, it so captivated Lord Napier, the Governor of Madras during the 1860's, that he restored it, although today it is only a quarter of its original size. Its imposing Main Hall, as big as a football field, was originally Tirumalai Nayak's boudoir, where he was royally entertained by dancers, musicians, and court fakirs. The courtyard outside was used for religious pageants and gladiatorial fights. Open from 8 am to 4 pm daily, there's a museum and a good sound and light show here daily at 6:45 pm, relating the history of the Nayak dynasty.

There are several other places of interest. The **Mariamman Teppakkulam Tank**, built in 1646, with its picturesque island temple reached by boat, lies five kilometers (three miles) east of the city center. There's a good **Gandhi Museum**, five kilometers (three miles) north of the city center, which houses many of the Mahatma's personal relics, including the bloodstained dhoti he was assassinated in and his glasses. Within the same complex is the **Government Museum** and various south Indian crafts and textile displays, all open daily between 10 am to 1 pm and 2 to 6 pm except Wednesdays.

From the central bus-stand, you can take a No. 5 bus out to the impressive rock-cut temple of **Tirupparankundrum**, eight kilometers (five miles) away. Carved into the side of a mountain, it is one of the six holy shrines of Subrahmanya, the second son of Shiva, and throbs with colorful activity as pilgrims, holy-men, and holidaying Indians come armed with lamp-lit bowls, coconuts, garlands, and incense for Shiva's blessings.

The Deep South Trail

KERALA: COCONUTS AND CATHEDRALS

Kerala instantly disarms travel-weary visitors with its beautiful, shimmering beaches, sun-filtered glades of palms trees, and green lowlands.

Villagers claim their land was created by the war-mongering god Parashurama, who was persuaded to change his bloodthirsty ways and throw away his axe. So noble was his gesture, the legend goes, that when the axe fell from heaven it landed in Southern India and formed the fertile Malabar Coast on the Arabian Sea.

This narrow, verdant strip of land is one of India's wealthiest states, criss-crossed with mossed backwaters and bursting with paddy fields and coconut, rubber, and cashew plantations. Cut off from the rest of India by the towering Sahyadri mountain range to the east, Kerala evolved a distinctive culture of dance, drama, and temple arts under the royal Chera dynasty, and defied even the Mughal's efforts to incorporate it into their empire.

Although isolated by land, Kerala claims an unusually cosmopolitan history. Missionaries were among its earliest visitors: St Thomas the Apostle is believed to have established the earliest Christian colony in Kerala in AD 52, followed by Syrian Christian settlers from Alexandria, whose cathedrals and churches still attract large congregations throughout the state. Kerala's lush Malabar coast lured legions of ancient Phoenician, Chinese, Arab, and Jewish traders in search of ivory, pepper, spices, incense, and myrrh. In the period spanning the fifteenth to the seventeenth century, Kerala became the battleground for numerous colonizing struggles between the Portuguese, the French, the Dutch, and, finally, the British, who gained control in 1795.

Modern Kerala — "land of the Cheras", or "land of kera" (coconuts) — was created in 1956 by the joining together of lands that comprised the ancient kingdoms of Tranvancore, Cochin, and Malabar. A year later, the people of Kerala were the first in the world to voluntarily elect a Communist regime. Today, religious piety and Marxist–Leninism are the reigning passions. Novelist Arthur Koestler described the state as "a kind of tropical Marxist Ruritania, where Cabinet Ministers were known to consult their horoscopes to deduce the Party-line from the stars and Catholic missions, deriving from St Francis Xavier, were still the most important cultural influence."

Kerala does not suffer from the extreme poverty found in the larger northern cities of Bombay, Delhi, and Calcutta. The state boasts a literacy rate of 70 percent and one of the lowest birthrates in India. The balmy climate is softened by strong sea breezes and is most pleasant from December to January, although it's still comfortable to travel between October and March.

TRIVANDRUM

Trivandrum, Kerala's languid seaside capital, sprawls over seven hills covered with colonial-era government buildings and traditional wooden houses hidden among lush parks and gardens.

Trivandrum was originally called Thiru Ananthapuram, or "abode of the snake", after an ancient myth that it was the home of Anantha, the sacred serpent often depicted curling around Lord Vishnu's body. Raja Marthanda Varma of Travancore made this his capital in 1750 and dedicated his entire kingdom to Lord Vishnu, the god of creation. He decreed that he and his successors would be the *dasis,* or servants of Vishnu. The present ex-raja still makes a daily morning pilgrimage from his palace to the Padmanabhaswamy Temple to prostrate himself before the reclining image of the family deity.

Most travelers prefer the sunny indolence of Kovalam's beaches, which are only 13 km (eight miles) away, and visit Trivandrum for a full-day tour of its museums, art galleries, temples, and zoo.

ACCESS

Trivandrum's airport is a useful jumping-off point for Air India, Air Lanka, or Indian Airlines flights to Sri Lanka and the Maldives. Indian Airlines flies direct from Madras, Cochin, Bombay, Goa, Bangalore, and Delhi. Kerala offers some of India's most enjoyable train journeys — gentle swaying rides past spectacular palm-fringed coastal backwaters and vast fields busy with *lunghi*-clad rice-planters. Many travelers make the 18-hour, 920-km (570-mile) journey from Madras by the *Trivandrum Mail,* and then continue up Kerala's coastline to Cochin, 219 km (136 miles) away, by a combination of train, backwater trails, and buses.

From Trivandrum, KSRTC runs frequent buses to all the main cities in Kerala as well as long-distance services to Madras, Madurai, Mysore, and Bangalore; all leave from the bus depot opposite the railway station. If you're planning to take the backwater trip from Quilon (71 km, or 44 miles), buses start at 7:30 am for Ernakulam/Cochin and pass through Quilon about two hours later. There's also a daily bus to the

OPPOSITE: Bustling street scene in the Connemara Market, Trivandrum.

Thekkady Wildlife Sanctuary (272 km, or 170 miles) which takes eight hours.

Locating the right bus at Trivandrum's bus depot can be quite infuriating, as destinations are written in Malayam script and there are no bus bays, so that you have to join the mêlée each time a bus arrives to find out if it is the one you want. It's usually possible to find a seat on these buses but near impossible to book.

HOTELS

The three-star **Luciya Continental**, ⌀73443, near the old East Fort, is Trivandrum's most

which has a cafeteria-style coffee shop that serves reliably good south Indian *thalis* and refreshing fruit *lassis*. Others include **Hotel Arulakam**, ⌀79788, on Station Road, which attracts many Indian tourists, is spartan, but clean. There's a good all-day vegetarian restaurant with plentiful *thalis* at the lobby level. **Hotel Aristo**, ⌀63622, located at Aristo Junction, near the railway station, has a pretty cottage-style exterior and very cheap, pleasant rooms. Find rock-botton accommodation at the **YMCA Guest House**, ⌀77690, in Palatam, and the **Youth Hostel**, ⌀71364, in the Veli area of Trivandrum.

luxurious hotel. It is comfortable and inexpensive, and has novelty suites in Arabic, Chinese, and Keralan styles, and the city's best restaurant for Indian and continental fare. The KTDC-run **Hotel Mascot**, ⌀68990, is a quaint colonial bungalow set in a leafy part of town expanded to accommodate Soviet trade delegations and legions of Russian tourists. The nicest rooms are on the top floor. It's very conveniently located, with the Indian Airlines office just opposite, and the museum, zoo, and tourist office within a 10-minute walk away. Rates: inexpensive. A good cheap-range option is **Hotel Chaithram**, ⌀75777, near the railway station on Thampanoor Road

ABOVE: The multi-storied Padmanabhaswamy Temple in Trivandrum makes an easy landmark in the low-lying capital.

RESTAURANTS

Trivandrum has plenty of small eating houses which serve very good south Indian vegetarian food for next to nothing. One of the best is **Arul Jyothi**, just across the road from the Secretariat, where plentiful *thalis* with fresh red grape juice cost only Rs 6. They serve "rocket roasts", immense paper-thin *dosas* curved up like stetsons and served with *sambhar* and coconut chutney for Rs 5, and have a large selection of delicious *lassis* and sweets. Other good places to try include the excellent vegetarian restaurant at **Hotel Woodlands**, the **Indian Coffee House** (north of Statue Road and between the museum and the Secretariat), and the **Khyber Restaurant**, near Station Road, which also has Chinese and Western food. The railway station's cafeteria must be India's cleanest, with delicious and very cheap *thalis* and south Indian snacks served with a mug of steaming cardamom tea.

SIGHTSEEING

Trivandrum's most famous sight is the **Pad-manabhaswamy Temple**, which has a seven-storyed *goporum*, or pyramid-shaped archway, writhing with carved mythological figures. Raja Marthanda Varma poured much of his personal wealth into glorifying this temple in 1733 as his tribute to Lord Vishnu. Non-Hindus are not allowed inside, and can only admire its ornate exterior — the interior has fine murals and reliefs — and observe male devotees self-consciously disrobing on the temple stairs, partly concealed behind their wives. Clad in their rented Rs 1 dhotis, they disappear into the cool, sandalwood scented interior, from which is heard occasional humming and the clang of a temple bell. Two major temple festivals take place here in March to April and October to November, each lasting 10 days and climaxing in processions of caparisoned elephants, dev-otees carrying golden deities on palanquins, and marching musicians, all led by the dhoti-clad maharaja down to the sea.

It's worth timing your visit around noon to catch the daily procession of temple priests. Then stroll through the back streets branching off Mahatma Gandhi Road for a poke through the government emporium, and the book and antique shops dotted throughout the area. Look out for Kairali, the excellent government handi-crafts emporium, opposite the Secretariat.

From here it's a short rickshaw ride north to Trivandrum's magnificent hilltop **Zoo and Bo-tanical Gardens** (64 acre or 26 hectare), which are open daily and have several museums within the grounds. The **Napier Museum** is a brightly tur-reted pagoda designed in 1880 by an English architect to honor the Governor of Madras, Lord Napier. It houses a superb collection of rare eighth-century, Chola-period sculpture, stone carvings, delicate antique jewelry, intriguing musical instruments, and memorabilia from the royal Travancore household. An excellent guidebook with anecdotes about the various items on display is sold at the front desk. The museum is open from 10 am to 5 pm except Mondays and Wednesdays. Other museums include the **Sri Chitra Art Gallery**, with its fine collection of contemporary Indian paintings, and the **Aquarium**, which has natural history displays of ghoulish stuffed specimens.

The **Connemara Market**, which is easily found by its entrance archway near the Secretariat along M.G. Road, is an interesting place to wander through: a joss-scented strip lined with mer-chants squatting under black umbrellas like wizened monkeys, wiry boys splashing water on heaped blossoms, and chickens running among piles of mangoes, jackfruit and coconuts. This is the city's colorful market forum, where everything from wedding finery to pet parrots can be found.

EXCURSIONS FROM TRIVANDRUM

Trivandrum makes a good base for visiting **Kanya Kumari**, also known as Cape Comorin, 87 km (54 miles) to the southeast in neighboring Tamil Nadu state. This is India's "Land's End", where the waters of the Arabian Sea, Indian Ocean, and the Bay of Bengal merge. Hindu pilgrims throng to its beachfront ghats, or steps, in the belief that bathing in these waters washes away their sins. It's a spectacular, wind-blown location, with nothing but endless sky and sea on the horizon, and its sunsets and sunrises are unique. On full moon nights, sunset and moon-rise occur simultaneously, hovering together like a tangerine and a golf ball. It's worth staying overnight to see at least one sunset and one sunrise.

The two best hotels are the TTDC-run and **Cape Hotel**, ✆22, with Western-style suites, and **Hotel Tamil Nadu**, ✆57, Both have beachfront locations, rooms overlooking the sea, and mealtime *thalis*. Rates: cheap. To get there, you can either take a local bus from Trivandrum (or Kovalam Beach), or go on the Rs 60 day-tour organized by the Kerala Tourist Development Corporation (KTDC), which leaves at 7:30 am and returns at 9 pm and also covers Kovalam Beach and **Padmanbhapuram Palace**, which is 32 km (20 miles) from Kanya Kumari and 55 km (34 miles) from Trivandrum. This is one of Ker-ala's most impressive buildings, built in 1550 for the Travancore rulers of this former capital city. It's a marvel of design and delicate crafts-manship, built of teak wood with Chinese-in-fluenced low gabled roofs with elaborate carved interiors opening out on to private courtyards and some 40 panels of murals throughout. As you wander through, look for the carved open hall where the king held court, and the ornate council chambers, dance hall, temple, women's quarters, and the palace tower, where the top-most room was reserved for the god Vishnu, complete with murals and a bed — the maharaja occupied the room just beneath it. The complex is open daily, except Mondays, from 7 am to 9 pm.

GENERAL INFORMATION

The Tourist Information Centre, ✆61132, on Park View Road, Trivandrum, is very friendly, infor-mative, and conveniently located just opposite the gateway entrance to the zoo, gardens, and museum. You can ask here about Kathakali dance performances run by the Trivandrum Kathakali Club.

The KTDC office, ©75031, Station Road, Thampanoor, runs good sightseeing tours around the city, Padmanabhapuram palace, Kanya Kumari, and to Thekkady Wildlife Sanctuary.

KOVALAM

Kerala's dramatic Malabar coast is a continuous stretch of unspoilt, white-sanded bays,

beach, just to the south, resembles a seaside commune crammed with budget hotels, well-tanned tourists, and cheap restaurants serving delicious fresh seafood and Western-style dishes.

It's not a place for peaceful solitude. Garrulous fisherwomen try to barter their haul of wriggling crabs or sackfuls of pawpaw for your wristwatch, and semi-nude body-surfers attract regular busloads of daytripping Indians. Swimmers should keep close to the shore as Kovalam's waters are renowned for dangerous undertows that frequently carry the unwitting out to sea. After a record 11 deaths in 1986, a

but the only beach resort is at Kovalam, just 13 km (eight miles) from Trivandrum. Here you'll find a series of small, sheltered coves with powder-soft sand, fringed by palm groves and paddy fields. Kovalam is perfect for unwinding after a bout of travel, with its good range of hotels, beach cafés, and plenty of sun and surf.

Compared to Goa's sprawling sands, Kovalam's two main beaches are quite contained and both within easy strolling distance of each other. At one end is Kovalam's five-star Beach Resort, landscaped across a palm-lined hillside with its own secluded bay. The other main

long-term Kovalam resident, clothes-designer Tim Heineman, an American citizen born in Tamil Nadu who has adopted Indian nationality, formed India's first professional team of lifeguards, who rescue an average of two swimmers a day.

ACCESS

Kovalam is only 13 km (8 miles) from Trivandrum and can be reached either by taxi, which costs about Rs 90 one way, or a bus service every half-hour from platform 19 at Trivandrum's city bus depot opposite the Padmanabhaswamy Temple.

Kovalam's optimum season is from September to April, after which the summer's heat and the monsoon send most tourists fleeing to Kashmir and the Himalayas.

Kovalam's lush scenery and palm-fringed beaches are a perfect location for tropical indolence. ABOVE: Poolside vista from the Kovalam Ashok Beach Hotel. OPPOSITE: A seemingly endless stretch of unspoilt coastline.

HOTELS

Kerala's luxury five-star resort, the **Kovalam Ashok Beach Resort**, ℡68010, is stunningly located atop a palm-scattered cliff face. Of a Mediterranean-style design which has won awards from the Royal Institute of British Architects, it sprawls across several tiers that drop down to the beach. but has become quite rundown of late. Facilities include an extensive yoga and massage center, water-sports (including waterskiing, motorboats, and paddleboats), a large pool, and a tennis court. Kovalam's only bank is located within the main lobby. Either stay in the main hotel building, or at the Kovalam Grove, a cluster of self-contained cottages, each with a terrace, along the seafront sands. For quaint vintage splendor, stay at a suite in the 100-year-old Halcyon Castle, the Maharaja of Travancore's former summer palace with beautiful views across the Lakshadweep Sea. Rates moderate to expensive.

The KTDC-run **Hotel Samudra**, ℡62089, overlooking the adjacent secluded bay, is pleasant and inexpensively priced.

Along the main tourist beach, **Rockholm**, ℡306, just above the lighthouse, has a winning combination of spacious, clean rooms (complete with vases of fresh flowers), a friendly management, the beach's most attractive balcony restaurant, and a well-thumbed library. Try to snare one of the coveted rooftop rooms for privacy and a spectacular view. Rates: cheap. Just opposite is **Sharma Cottages** which rents rooms cheaply to long-staying tourists. Nearby, both **Hotel Seaweed**, ℡391, and **Hotel Samudra Tara**, ℡76644, offer comfortable rooms for less than Rs 200. There are also many very cheap lodging houses along the main beach. You might try the **Hotel Moonlight**, ℡584311, near the Kovalam Post Office, with incredibly spotless, spacious rooms run by the solicitous Mr Anand, or **Hotel Neelakanta**, basic but clean. Just outside is Tim Heineman's "Rags Express" shop, which sells clothes especially devised for travelers in India. The hottest-selling item is his "travel pants", with ingenious interior pockets for passports, airline tickets, and travelers' checks.

RESTAURANTS

The ex-fishermen chefs who staff Kovalam's many beach cafés are culinary dynamos, serving up delectable seafood as well as popular Italian, Chinese, English, and French dishes.

Rockholm Hotel's **Balcony Restaurant** has an enchanting view, and serves chilled beer, excellent seafood dishes, and strong, fragrant coffee. Portions are gargantuan by Kovalam standards.

The **Lucky Coral** rooftop restaurant above Hotel Seaweed is almost as pleasant, and plays Talking Heads and David Bowie for its music-conscious patrons. Try Fish Welewska, served with a veloute sauce with shrimps (Rs 25) or Lobster Thermidor (Rs 50).

On the beach, **Hotel Searock's Café** has a talented Goan chef, whose classic Goan dishes are as good as his grilled or baked seafood served with the house lemon-butter garlic sauce. This is also the place for an excellent Rs 25 "executive breakfast", with your toes in the sand and a crumpled copy of yesterday's *Indian Express*.

But for almost unbelievably good value and haphazard charm, both **My Dream**, which serves the best fish and chips in the subcontinent, and the **Black Cat** (for delicious garlic prawns and hot banana pancakes) are heartily recommended.

BEACHES

Apart from these two beaches, there's an almost endless unspoilt coastline to explore. Further south, strung between Kovalam's candy-striped lighthouse and a mini Taj Mahal-style mosque perched on the headland's tip, is a sheltered, slightly more private, beach. In the opposite direction, the almost deserted bay just beyond the Hotel Samudra (past Kovalam's Beach Resort) makes a pleasant afternoon's excursion and is safe for swimming. From here, the beaches get more bewitching the further you stroll.

It's worth rising early one morning to witness Kovalam's fishing community hauling ashore their catamarans and proudly inspecting the morning's catch of tuna, squid, crabs, lobster, sharks and, occasionally, an illicit turtle. From the lighthouse, it's a 10-minute walk across the headland to the fishing village, with a small path leading down to the beach. En route, stop by at the Marine Research Laboratory, which has displays of local marine life and the methods used to catch them. There is also an extensive library, though you must first request permission from the custodian to browse.

THE BACKWATERS

The palm-fringed, balmy backwaters, or *kayals*, stretch along the coastal strip from Quilon to Cochin. Local ferries chug gently through this unexpected version of rural India, providing one of south India's most profound pleasures: a cruise in the heart of a tropical Venice. Go armed with a large floppy hat, a pair of binoculars, a zoom-lens camera, and a bagful of oranges and delicious fresh cashewnuts for optimum enjoyment. Local ferries from **Quilon, Alleppey,** or **Kottayam** — the main backwater towns — cost less than the cashewnuts and offer an *African Queen* fantasy plowing through winding waterways that are peopled by slender riverbank dwellers, and heady with the scent of frangipani and ripe jackfruit trees.

It's also possible to hire a small boat for a watery jaunt for Rs 100 an hour, or if you can muster a large group, there are government barges which seat 15 and cost Rs 235 for four hours. Be sure to agree on the payment details with the boatman before embarking on your journey.

It's worth traveling to Alleppey and Kottayam for the late August/early September 10-day Onam harvest festival, when the backwaters churn with colorful water carnivals and snake boat races. The most spectacular is the Nehru Trophy Boat Race, held in Alleppey on the second Saturday of August, when boats carrying up to 100 paddlers each compete in a colorful regatta.

The backwaters are best visited from December to February, because by early March the heat becomes oppressive and the swarms of mosquitoes can be deflected only by applying continual lathers of repellent.

The picturesque town of Allepey is a favorite setting out point for barge cruises through Kerala's winding coils of backwaters.

QUILON

On the edge of Ashtamudi Lake, 73 km (45 miles) from Trivandrum, Quilon is the most picturesque of the *kayal* towns. It's full of pastel-painted wooden villas and labyrinthine alleys, and policemen wearing quaint Raj-style topees. It's also one of Kerala's most historic ports: the Phoenicians, Persians, Greeks, Romans, and Arabs all used Quilon as a stopover for plying the backwaters. From the seventh to the tenth century, the Chinese established a busy trading base here, leaving a visible legacy of low-slung, pagoda-style architecture and Chinese fishing nets. This strategic, fertile district later became a source of rivalry between the Portuguese, Dutch, and British. It's still possible to see the dilapidated ruins of an old Portuguese fort near Thangasseri Beach, three kilometers (almost two miles) away.

Travelers come to Quilon to embark on the longest and most varied of the backwater routes. It takes eight and a half hours to meander along the 85-km (53-mile) stretch to Alleppey. There are two ferries daily, but you'll see more if you take the earlier one which departs at 10 am and glides into Allepey just after dusk. (This trip can also be made in the opposite direction.)

It's worth staying overnight in Quilon for one of Kerala's best accommodation surprises, the charming lakeside **Tourist Bungalow**, a former British Residency set in leafy gardens on the outskirts of town. Pristine rooms are furnished in local wooden furniture, all with shower, tub, and hot water and very cheap. The stately balcony-level drawing room is full of old Raj-era memorabilia. It's always popular, so book in advance in writing or through a KTDC office.

The more central **Hotel Sudarshan**, ©3755, on Parameswar Nagar, is only 10 minutes' walk from the ferry jetty, and has very cheap, fan-cooled rooms or more expensive air-conditioned ones. You can dine well at either of its two restaurants on a choice of Indian, Chinese, and European specialties, or opt for cheap, delicious vegetarian *thalis* at Hotel Guru Prasad on Main Street.

ALLEPPEY

Alleppey, 83 km (52 miles) from Quilon, is a small, picturesque, oriental Amsterdam, with interlocking canals and bridges, and a center for backwater cruises.

From here you can take the two-and-a-half-hour scenic cruise to Kottayam, which for many is quite long enough to enjoy the *kayals*. Gliding along the canals, which cross the extensive

Vembanad Lake stretching north to Cochin, you'll see flotillas of dug-outs laden with coconuts, and lovely inland lagoons snaking into narrow, waterlily-covered stretches.

Ferries leave for Kottayam throughout the day, starting at 5 am, but the early morning or mid-afternoon departures ensure optimum comfort. There's an alternative, and equally beautiful, four-hour round-trip from Alleppey inland to Changanacherry, with frequent ferries from 6 am to 4:45 pm.

The bus-stand and boat jetty are fairly close together; Alleppey has no rail connection with other destinations in Kerala.

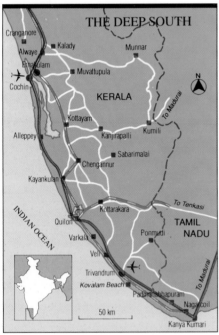

The two-star **Alleppey Prince Hotel**, ℂ3752, on A.S. Road, on the National Highway, provides very comfortable Rs 100 to Rs 150 rooms in a pleasant setting a short distance out of town, and has a good restaurant and swimming pool. Just opposite the boat jetty is **Hotel Komala**, ℂ3631, with a choice of air-conditioned doubles for Rs 120 or non air-conditioned for Rs 50.

St George Lodge, ℂ3373, is popular for its friendly staff and spotless rooms with attached bath for a scant Rs 20, or try the modern **Sheeba Lodge**, near Hotel Komala, for similar prices.

At the **Indian Coffee House**, a five-minute rickshaw ride from the center, waiters clad in ornate turbans and striped cummerbunds serve excellent filter coffee and cheap meals in a simple but relaxing café — perfect for frittering away an hour or so before setting out for the backwaters. For good vegetarian *thalis*, try **Shree Durga Bhavan** restaurant in the Udipi Hotel on Cullen Road.

KOTTAYAM

Less than 30 km (18 miles) from Alleppey, and situated slightly inland from the Malabar coast, Kottayam is a busy commercial city, famous for its rubber, tea, coffee, pepper, and cardamom plantations, and primarily visited by tourists as a stopping-off point on the way to the Periyar Wildlife Sanctuary, 117 km (73 miles) away. A stronghold of the Syrian Christian sect, which has existed in Kerala since AD 190, Kottayam has many beautiful churches, including the Valiapalli Church, five kilometers (three miles) northwest of the railway station, which contains a cross believed to have come from the original church founded by St Thomas the Apostle in Cranganore.

Kottayam is part of the rail network and has two bus stations: a local depot and an interstate stand that is roughly a kilometer (just over half a mile) from the boat jetty.

Stay at **Vembanad Lake Resort**, ℂ62866, Kodimatha, five kilometers (three miles) out of town, with peaceful, pleasant cheap rooms. Regardless of where you choose to stay, take the mid-morning Alleppey–Kottayam ferry and arrive at the Vembanad at lunchtime to order Keralan specialties such as *karimeen*, a local freshwater fish prepared in a fiery sauce of onions, green chilies, and spices, and a variety of vegetarian dishes eaten al fresco by the lakeside at Kottayam's best restaurant.

The brand-new **Hotel Sears**, ℂ3013, on Shastri Road, a five-minute rickshaw ride from the railway station, has good-value, quiet rooms at Rs 35 to Rs 50. In town, stay either at **Anjali Hotel**, ℂ3661, on KK Road with a good coffee shop and clean, comfortable, air-conditioned inexpensive rooms, or at the unusual **Tourist Bungalow**, a former British officers' barracks, with spacious antiquated rooms. Very cheap. It's a 15-minute trek from the boat jetty, and you'll need to ask for directions, as it's a little difficult to find.

PERIYAR (THEKKADY)

The **Periyar Wildlife Sanctuary** is one of the most beautiful forest stretches of the south. Set in the Cardamom Hills near the border with Tamil Nadu, it is a 777 sq km (300 sq mile) jungle refuge for tigers, elephants, bison, antelope, sloth bear, otter, monkeys, and the occasional panther or leopard. Among the sanctuary's creepers, spice vines, and blossoming trees, bird-watchers may spot darters, flycatchers, hornbills, blue-winged parakeets, bulbuls, herons, and egrets.

This is the finest Indian sanctuary for watching and photographing wild elephants, and as a member of Project Tiger, it has 40 of India's 3,000 or so remaining tigers. The enormous Periyar Lake, 24 sq km (9.3 sq miles) in area, was created in 1895 by the British government in Madras for use in irrigation, but it became part of the newly formed sanctuary in 1934. While cruising along the shore in a motorboat, you can watch herds of elephants, bison, deer, and the occasional tiger, grazing at the water's edge.

On the lake's edge, **Aranya Niwas Hotel**, ©23, has comfortable rooms ranging from cheap to inexpensive. In the rather tatty dining room, gravy-stained waiters rush around with such creations as "Lassie", "Mutton Fuyong", "Raw Eggs", and "Two Numbers, Only". Far more enjoyable is the quaint, three-roomed **Government Rest House**, although this is frequently full, or the KTDC-run **Periyar House**, ©26, about a kilometer (just over half a mile) away in the forest, with pleasant airy rooms, hot water, and food that is worth the hike.

At Kumily town, five kilometers (three miles) away, the **Lake Queen Tourist Home**,

ACCESS

There are bus connections to Periyar from all main cities in Kerala, but the most popular scenic route is from Kottayam, 117 km (73 miles) away. The four- to five-hour journey winds up to a 305 m (1000 ft) plateau of leafy cardamom, pepper, and coffee plantations.

HOTELS

The **Lake Palace Hotel**, © Kumily 24, has the most romantic location for overnight stays. This large old bungalow sits on a small island on Thekkady Lake, has a good bar and restaurant, and guests have been known to spot tigers from the windows of their rooms. Rooms have an antiquated Raj-era charm. Rates: inexpensive.

The Deep South Trail

opposite the post office is another pleasant option. It's best to book in advance for hotels in Periyar, which can be done through any KTDC office; otherwise, ask the staff at the tourist office in Kumily to check which hotels have rooms available. They'll also give you useful boat-trip tickets, maps, and walking/trekking permits.

SIGHTSEEING

Tickets for the motorboat cruises on Lake Periyar, which last for 1½ hours, are available from the Wildlife Office, near the boat jetty. You're likely to see more if you take the earliest

ABOVE: Rice-beds create lush headlands all the way along the backwater trail.

boat at 7 am, when the misty waters resemble England's Lake District, and the herds come down for their morning drink.

The Wildlife Office also organizes three-hour group treks through the forest, which are most informative about the sanctuary's flora and fauna, but frustrating as the noise of so many people frightens most animals away. A far more satisfying alternative is to hire a private Wildlife Office guide to take you to the best vantage points and *machans,* or tree houses, so that you see far more wildlife at close range. The Wildlife Office can also arrange elephant rides and private boat rides.

COCHIN

Cochin is Kerala's largest and most beautiful city, with its lush islands, backwaters, faded colonial architecture, and an unusual history. It comprises the Fort Cochin/Mattancherry southern peninsula, the modern business district on Ernakulum mainland, and Willindon, Bolgatty, Gundu, and Vypeen islands. It is one of India's biggest naval bases and busiest ports, exporting vast amounts of coir, rubber, seafood, and spices to foreign countries. Despite its bustling harbour, Cochin is full of languid charm and is perfect for exploring on foot or by boat.

ABOVE: Swaying palms dwarf a canal-side village along the backwaters.

Phoenician, Israelite, Greek, Roman, Arab, and Chinese traders all visited or settled in this tropical port, leaving behind Muslim, Christian, and Jewish communities that still exist today. It was Cochin's Jews who founded the first large community, over 1,000 years ago. These were the "black Jews", who arrived as early as AD 52 from Yemen and Babylon to trade olive oil and dates for peacocks and spices, and intermarried with the local population. Another wave of Jewish refugees came from Spain in the fifteenth century and were given protection by the Raja of Cochin. These "white Jews" were more insular and frowned on mixed marriages; they still exist, though in ever-dwindling numbers, today.

Vasco da Gama took Cochin for Lisbon in 1502, but the Dutch, who coveted its spices, incense, myrrh, and ivory, usurped the Portuguese in 1663. Then in 1795 the city passed to the British. Fort Cochin and Mattancherry Island are littered with the architectural relics — Dutch Palaces, Portuguese churches, and British bungalows — of these conquerors.

ACCESS

Cochin can be reached by daily direct flights from Madras, Trivandrum, Bangalore, Goa, Bombay, and Delhi. There are also direct train routes linking the city with all major cities. Daily trains service nearby destinations from Cochin: an Ernakulam–Kottayam train at 7 am and 5:30 pm, and the Ernakulam–Quilon service at 11:30 am.

Buses depart from the Central Bus Station on Stadium Road in Ernakulam, with regular shuttles several times daily to Trichur, Alleppey, Quilon, Thekkady, and Trivandrum, and links to major cities in neighboring Karnataka and Tamil Nadu states.

WHERE TO STAY

The **Malabar Hotel**, ℗6811, Willingdon Island, is by far the best hotel in Cochin, with air-conditioned rooms tastefully decorated with woven rugs and wicker furniture. Set on the edge of the island with its own lawns and jetty, it has a glorious view across the busy harbor to Mattancherry Island. The hotel has a swimming pool, restaurant, unexceptional coffee shop, and bar and, as part of the Taj-Group, it is being expanded to a total of 100 sea-facing rooms. Located right next to the tourist office, the hotel is convenient to the airport and a short ferry or taxi ride from either Fort Cochin or Ernakulam. Rates: moderate.

Also on Willingdon Island is the inexpensively priced **Casino Hotel**, ℗6821, just up the road. Built in the 1950's, it lacks a harbour view, but is very efficient, with a pleasant old wing. There's a swimming pool and an excellent seafood restaurant that has one drawback — an intrusive live band crooning Western numbers each night. Both hotels have boat services to neighboring islands. Cheaper options on this pleasant island include the **Maruthi Tourist Home**, ©6365, and just next door, **Island Inn**, ©6816.

For travelers in search of faded elegance, the 250-year-old **Bolgatty Palace Hotel**, ©355003, has antique furniture, ceiling fans, mosquito nets draped on four-poster beds and a languid terrace for sipping afternoon beers. Located on the narrow, palm-fringed Bolgatty Island, this was once a Dutch Palace and later the British Residency. Run by the state government, it is deluged with Indian holidaymakers during peak season, and becomes a haven of peace only during off-season. rates: cheap.

In Ernakulam, stay at the three-star, **Sea Lord Hotel**, Shanmugham Road, © 352682, with good air-conditioned rooms. Rates: cheap. Another choice in the cheap bracket with optional air-conditioning is **Hotel International**, ©353911, and cheaper still is **Woodlands Hotel**, ©351372. both on Mahatma Gandhi Road. The latter has an excellent vegetarian restaurant. **Biju's Tourist Home**, ©369881, is the best of the budget hotels with rooms, including baths, very friendly staff, and a convenient location opposite the ferry jetty.

On Fort Cochin, **Hotel Seagull**, ©28128, Calvety Road, overlooks the harbor and the Chinese fishing nets in a sleepy, cul-de-sac of pastel-hued villas, just five minutes' walk from the jetty. It has pleasant very cheap rooms with bath and a popular balcony restaurant. Otherwise, the spartan **PWD Tourist Rest Home**, ©25797, near the beach, offers basic accommodation with a big advantage — mosquito nets.

RESTAURANTS

Kerala cuisine is distinctive for its variety of spicy, coconut-flavored dishes and fresh seafood specialties. The **Riceboat Restaurant** at the Malabar Hotel is decorated to resemble Kerala's cargo boats. The walls are adorned with paddles and coolie hats, and their seafood specialties are very good, especially the prawn shashlik Oriental.

In Ernakulam, the **Sealord Restaurant**, at the Sealord Hotel, serves a special fish Veronique (stuffed with grapes), and offers a range of delicious seafood dishes. **Swagath**, the bustling upstairs eatery at Dwarka Hotel on M.G. Road, is a favorite of Cochin's locals for its air-conditioned annex and generous *thalis*. It offers a choice of the massive mini-*thali* at Rs 8,

or the "executive power lunch" *thalis* at Rs 15, with a staggering array of dishes, as well as good *lassis* and south Indian specialties. **Woodlands**, just down the road, is also recommended for excellent cheap vegetarian *thalis*. Just behind the Dwarka Hotel is Cochin's best Chinese restaurant, the **Chinese Garden**, which serves excellent seafood dishes. The **Indian Coffee House**, opposite the ferry jetty, serves strong, freshly ground coffee, Western-style omelets, and "butter jam" toast as early as 6 am. **Jancy Cafe**, on Shanmugam Road, serves delicious south Indian snacks, with particularly good fluffy *iddlies* and crisp, doughnut-shaped *vadas*.

SIGHTSEEING

If you take a ferry to the historic Fort Cochin/Mattancherry district, you'll alight at the old docks, now a sprawling neighborhood of shuttered merchants' houses and warehouses. Almost directly opposite is the elegant **Mattancherry Palace**, set in a cluster of mango trees. Built by the Portuguese in 1557, it was presented to the Cochin raja, Veera Kerala Varma (1537–1567), in exchange for trading privileges. It was later repaired by the occupying Dutch, gaining the misnomer "Dutch Palace". An annex of the Mattancherry is now a museum. One room contains portraits of former Cochin rajas, a line of imperious mandarin-like faces with fixed, inscrutable gazes; another displays a collection of their elaborate costumes, including ornate robes, brilliant turbans, silk parasols, and an ivory palanquin. The upstairs bedchambers are adorned with seventeenth-century frescoes depicting lively scenes from the Indian epics, the *Ramayana* and the *Mahabharata*, painted with colors created from charcoal, lime, leaves, and flowers. Open from 10 am to 5 pm every day except Friday and public holidays.

Near Mattancherry Palace, up a winding street filled with interesting antique shops and heady with the scent of pepper, cardamom, and cloves, is **Jewtown**. The Jews of Cochin once numbered as many as 4,000, but today only eight families remain, with many families having emigrated to Israel, Australia, and Canada. Almost hidden at the end of a cul-de-sac is the **Jewish Synagogue**. Built in 1568, it is the oldest synagogue in the Commonwealth. It was destroyed by the Portuguese in 1662, and rebuilt by the Dutch in 1664. Its interior glitters with nineteenth-century Belgian chandeliers, hand-painted eighteenth-century Chinese willow-pattern tiles, and in one corner, a brass pulpit and gold raja's crown. Jackie Cohen, the synogogue's custodian, has an expert knowledge of Jewish settlements in Asia, and displays the synagogue's prized possessions on request:

a papyrus whorl that is an ancient copy of the Great Scrolls of the Old Testament and the copperplate grants of privilege made by the Cochin rajas to the Jewish merchant Joseph Rabin. The synagogue is open from 10 am to noon, and from 3 to 5 pm every day except Saturday and Jewish holidays.

By cycle or rickshaw, it's two kilometers (one and a quarter miles) to the northern isthmus of **Fort Cochin**, a neighborhood of pastel-washed villas, sixteenth century bastions, and cobbled streets. Along the way, stop to watch Cochin's fishermen working their Chinese fishing nets, first introduced by visitors from the court of

Kublai Khan, whose influence also remains throughout Kerala in pagoda-style temples, conical fishermen's hats, and Chinese methods of making porcelain and paper. The filmy blue nets, suspended from poles lashed together and cantilevered out over the water, are counterbalanced with a primitive system of rock-weights. To see them in action, return an hour before dusk, when the nets look like giant birds dipping in and out of the water with their silvery cargo.

It's a 10-minute stroll through the winding streets to **St Francis Church**, established by Portuguese Franciscan friars in 1504. This unadorned structure, originally made from wood and later rebuilt in stone, is the oldest European church in India. As invaders conquered Cochin, it passed from the Catholic Portuguese to the Protestant Dutch and the British Anglican, and today functions as a Church of Southern India. The Portuguese explorer Vasco da Gama, who landed in Cochin in 1498 and was known to have terrorized the natives by slicing off the noses, ears, and hands of his captives, was buried here in 1524, although his remains were shipped back to Lisbon 14 years later. The tombstones of da Gama and other settlers, written in Portuguese on one side, and Dutch on the other, can be seen in St Francis Church.

A short stroll south, down Prince Street, is the Roman Catholic **Santa Cruz Church**, built in 1557, with a mock-marble interior painted in lurid colors.

Across the water, on **Gundu Island**, is an old Raj-era coir factory where weavers use the area's abundant supply of coconut husks to fashion practical doormats, ropes, and matting.

The easiest way to become acquainted with Cochin is to take the KTDC's boat tour. It leaves twice a day (9:30 am and 1:30 pm) from Ernakulam's boat jetty opposite the Sealord Hotel, and includes a stop at Bolgatty Palace. The Rs 15 tickets must be purchased as the tourist office, not on board the boat.

If you have a free afternoon, Cochin's scenic backwaters between Ernakulam and Varpaoja make a pleasant trip. The ferry leaves from Ernakulam's main jetty every hour, and takes two hours each way.

In Ernakulam, see the **Cochin Archaeological Museum** in Durbar Hall Road, with its assortment of exhibits plucked from the Cochin royal family's collection. Otherwise buy teas, spices, and fresh cashewnuts in Ernakulam market, and meander along Mahatma Gandhi Road where various emporiums sell *lunghis* the colorful cloth worn tied at the waist, rosewood carvings, jewelry, and Kathakali masks. At the government emporium, look out for a curious collection of Hindu deities with bobbing heads in contemporary garb, with Hanuman, the Monkey god, dressed up like a Japanese *yakuza!*

KATHAKALI

A performance of the traditional Kathakali dance is one of Cochin's highlights. This form of dance theater, dating back 500 years, can be seen nightly, with explanation and narration, all over the city. By tradition, all dancers are male and wear elaborate costumes and mask-like make-up to mime stories from the great Hindu epics, the *Ramayana* and the *Mahabharata*. Arrive early for the performance and peer backstage to see the lean, athletic performers transform themselves into oversized deities attired in bulky tutu-like burlap underskirts, layers of bright garments, heavy jewelry, and head-dress. These make-up is highly symbolic: green denotes the hero king or god, and black and red denote demons. The actor slips a seed from the *cunlappuvu*, or eggplant vine, under his eyelids to make his eyes red.

As much an act of worship as a highly dramatic folk theater, Kathakali is traditionally performed by the flickering light of temple-lamps, accompanied by musicians and a chanting Brahman priest. Artistes use a vast repertoire of acrobatic eye movements, dramatic facial expressions, and perfect muscle control that require years of training. In Ernakulam, there are three equally good daily performances: at the **Cochin Cultural Centre**, ©353732, at the Durbar Hall Ground next to the Cochin Museum, from 6:30 to 8 pm; **Art Kerala**, Menon and Krishna Annexe, from 7 to 8:30 pm and **See India Foundation**, ©369471, Kathathi–Parambil Lane, from 7 to 8:30 pm.

GENERAL INFORMATION

Government of India Tourist Office, ©6045, Willingdon Island (next to the Malabar Hotel).

Open 9 am to 2 pm daily except Sunday. Contact the KTDC Tourist Reception Centre, ©353234, Shanmugham Road, Ernakulam, to make reservations for the conducted boat tours around Cochin.

OUT OF COCHIN: TRICHUR

Trichur, a picturesque pilgrimage town just south of the Nilgiri Hills, set amongst paddy fields and coconut and pineapple plantations, makes an enjoyable overnight excursion from Cochin, 80 km (50 miles) away. If you're visiting Kerala during late April to early May, it's worth planning your itinerary around Trichur's exuberant Pooram procession, the most spectacular of Kerala's temple festivals. Trichur's streets explode into rich pageantry, with a day-long parade of 30 gaily caparisoned "tusker" elephants,

each carrying a Brahman priest seated under silk parasols and giant feathers. After dusk, zthere's a massive fireworks display which lasts until dawn.

Trichur's most remarkable feature is its magnificent Vadakkunath Temple complex in the low-slung, wooden pagoda style unique to Kerala's traditional temple architecture. The main temple shrine contains a curious three-meter (10-ft) mound of hardened cows' ghee, or clarified butter, under which a devotional lingam dedicated to Lord Shiva is completely embedded. The shrine also contains a panel of exquisite murals narrating the epic *Mahabharata*.

A museum and a zoo with a renowned collection of snakes are the other attractions. In Trichur, stay either at the **Ambassador Hotel** or the **Government Guest House**. If you've discovered a fascination for Kathakali dance, it's well worth making the 27-km (17-mile) trip to Cheruthuruthy where the **Kerala Kala Mandalam**, the state's renowned Kathakali dance school, is located. The instructors are usually delighted to let you watch their rigorous early morning training sessions, and there are evening dance performances.

ABOVE LEFT and RIGHT: Two faces of Kathakali dance artistes, displaying the traditional elaborate make-up and stylized dress. OPPOSITE: A vestige of the Portuguese legacy in the old European enclave of the Fort Cochin.

The Deep South Trail

Travelers'
Tips

GETTING THERE

Getting to India is easy. The nation's main gateways of Calcutta, New Delhi, Bombay, and Madras are serviced by most major international airlines. Each airport is linked to the rest of India by its internal air network. It is best to book tickets well in advance, so that you have a firm reservation with the airline of your choice and a date around which to begin planning travel arrangements within India. When booking your international flight, seats on internal Indian Airlines flights can also be booked through your travel agent.

AIR INDIA

Flagship Air India offers flights from Asian capitals, Australia, Europe, the Middle East, Africa, the Soviet Union, and North America.

FROM EUROPE

The London *Independent*'s travel section is good for checking out tours and package deals. Many cut-price flights are offered by Arab or Soviet-bloc airlines, which often make long stopovers and can be delayed in obscure or bizarre locations. It is much better to pay the extra amount and take a direct flight on an established international carrier which at least gives a certain guarantee of arriving on time. Air India, Alitalia, Air France, British Airways, Air Canada, Japan Airlines, Lufthansa, Pan Am, SAS, Swissair, Singapore Airlines, Thai Airways, and Qantus all have good, regular and reliable services to India. Several reliable London travel agencies for low-cost tickets are Trail Finders Travel Centre at 46 Earls Court Road, London W8, GSA Hindustan Travel Service, 30 Poland Street, London WC1, and STA Travel at Old Brompton Court Road London SW7 or 117 Euston Road, London NW1. Typical fares being quoted vary from around £225 one way or £325 or £440 return, but prices depend very much on the carrier.

From the UK and Europe, bargain-hunting can be rewarded by some remarkably cheap deals. ("Bucket shops" advertise in the newspapers and in magazines like *Time Out*, *LAM*, and the *Australasian Express*.)

FROM AUSTRALASIA

Travelers from Australasia often stop off in India for very little extra cost on the grand overland route to Europe. It's possible to get cheap or Apex fares to Singapore, Bangkok or Hong Kong, and then fly on to India from there. Advance-purchase return fares from Australia to London

or other European cities with India as a stopover cost around A$1,500. The price varies according to the season and destination in India, and Sydney and Perth offer the cheapest deals. Travel Specialists, 7 Piccadilly Arcade, 222 Pitt Street, Sydney 2000, has a good reputation.

FROM THE UNITED STATES

American visitors, for whom India is virtually the opposite side of the world, are provided with limited direct air connections and are advised to explore discount fares offered in New York, Los Angeles, and San Francisco, mostly by Asian carriers. Only a few airlines, notably Air India, Pan Am, and TWA, service India directly. New York has the greatest frequency of direct flights to New Delhi, Bombay and Madras, and has at least one weekly flight to Calcutta. Only a few airliners, notably Air India, Pan-Am and TWA service India directly, and the cheapest return fares to India are around US$1,000. Check the Sunday travel sections of papers like the *New York Times*, the *Los Angeles Times* or the *San Francisco Examiner/Chronicle*. Cheaper fares can be found through Apex and the STA "Inter-Asia" discounts offered by several Asian airlines. American travelers may wish to forsake the direct-flight option and and travel to India via London or from an Asian gateway city. From Hong Kong, Bangkok and Singapore you can find one-way flights for around US$230 to US$300.

VISAS

A tourist visa is required for all visitors to India, and it is absolutely imperative to receive clearance from India's local embassy before departing. Immigration officials steadfastly refuse to allow entry to anyone without proper documentation, and most airlines check the passports of all India-bound passengers as in the past they have borne the cost of deporting numerous travelers.

Apply well in advance, as visas usually take about two weeks to clear. Indian officials usually grant a four-month (120-day) stay, and charge the reciprocal equivalent of what your country charges for Indians to enter. If you plan to stay longer than the 120 days' tourist visa limit, you can apply any Superintendent of Police in all district headquarters, the **Foreigner's Regional Registration Offices** in Bombay, Calcutta and Madras. In Delhi the **Foreigner's Registration Office**, ©331-8179, is at 1st Floor, Hans Bhawan, Tilak Bridge, New Delhi 110-002. Special permits for entry into "restricted areas" are requested from the Under Secretary, Foreigner's Division, at the Ministry of Home Affairs, Lok Nayak Bhawan, Khan Market. After the six-month period, officials prefer you to leave, and Indian missions will be reluctant to grant you another entry visa for at least a year.

CUSTOMS

Visitors are allowed to carry in one duty-free bottle of spirits and 200 cigarettes. But customs officials are ever-vigilant about items that may be sold at great profit, and require all foreigners to declare gold, jewelry, and electronic goods, particularly video cameras, which are subject to a 280 percent duty. They will write the serial number of the item on the back page of your passport, and the item must be produced when you leave the country.

India has heavy penalties for smuggling, and unless you really desire a jail term, don't even think about bringing in any illicit goods or smuggling in expensive items. Recent political extremism in India has led to greatly enhanced security, so do not be surprised if after you have been cleared through Customs, your bags are run through an X-ray machine. The four main international airports have red and green channels, and customs officials will be available at the red channel for any foreigners wishing to register dutiable goods. Visitors with more than US$1,000 in cash or travelers' checks are also required to obtain currency declaration forms. There is no restriction on how much money you may bring in, but when you leave you may be asked to show exchange receipts from a state-owned bank to prove that the hard currency was not swapped on the black-market.

CURRENCY

Currency is based on the decimal system, with 100 paise to the rupee, which is available in denominations of 1, 2, 5, 10, 20, 50, and 100. Avoid swapping hard currency on the black-market, as there are serious penalties for offenders and the unofficial exchange rate is usually not more than 10 to 20 percent above what the government banks offer.

The exchange rate at press time was Rs 100 to US$5.92. Exchanging cash and travelers' checks can be a hassle, involving the filling in of endless forms and being referred to at least four different officers before you get the money in your pocket. For this reason, it is often best to change a sizable sum of money at a time so as to minimize the time spent on such procedures. Your passport is essential identification for changing money, and travelers' checks

generally have a better rate of exchange than cash.

It can be difficult to change a Rs 100 note on the street, so it is wise to get some small change at the bank for rickshaws, tips, and fending off persistent street urchins.

There is also a reluctance to accept any bills that are ripped or worn, so be careful that your change does not include notes that will prove difficult to get rid of. Banks and five-star hotels will graciously accept this exhausted currency.

Credit cards have found widespread acceptance at shops and restaurants across India, and you will find the American Express and Visa logos in some of the most distant and obscure locations. While plastic is a convenient way of reserving travel funds, most private shopkeepers will try to charge you the percentage that they are meant to pay the card company. It is rare that wily traders can be persuaded out of this uncharitable state of mind, so be prepared to pay three percent for American Express, and six percent for credit cards such as Visa and Diners Club.

However, plastic is an advantage when paying in five-star hotels, which will add a seven percent "luxury tax" for food and accommodation if you are paying with foreign currency.

Foreigners are generally required to use hard currency to settle accounts at hotels, but can use rupees if they present an encashment certificate proving the source of their local currency was an official bank. This system is chaotic, and you can repeatedly use the same certificate, which may not have any correlation to the rupees you are spending.

WHEN TO GO

It is possible to go to India at any time of the year and avoid extreme heat and monsoons, provided you select the right area. When it is blisteringly hot in the south, it can be crisply pleasant in Delhi and the Himalayas.

In general, the optimum season to travel to northern India — to Delhi, Agra, and Rajasthan — is between September and March, although it can get very cold during the winter months of December and January. It is best to avoid the plains during the hot months between April and June. Southern India is hot all the time, but is best between November and February. To the east, a combination of heat, humidity, and monsoon again makes November to February the most comfortable time to visit. The Himalayas are best appreciated between May and July, so unless you have been bitten by the ski-bug, avoid the winter snows. The extreme pre-monsoon heat, the torrential rain, and the post-monsoon humidity apply everywhere, at varying times, between May and September.

WHAT TO TAKE

Naturally, it is best to travel as lightly as possible if you want to avoid your trip becoming an endurance test, and unless you have a safe base to leave luggage, confine yourself to one main bag. You'll find it near impossible not to accumulate purchases as you travel, so that you'll leave with considerably more than what you did when you arrived. A sound lock, preferably a combination lock is constantly useful to guard against having your luggage pilfered. Always keep all your important documents in your hand luggage: passports, air tickets, credit cards, insurance policies, and immunization certificates etc.

The type of clothing you take is naturally based on your destination. Many travelers, believing that India is a land of perpetual heat and dust, have landed in New Delhi in midwinter with a bag full of breezy Hawaiian shirts. Read the international temperature guide in your local newspaper before deciding your wardrobe. For most of the year, the most practical clothing for India will be loose cotton clothes and sensible walking shoes. Sunglasses provide essential protection against the relentless sun.

There are other items worth taking to India so that you can more easily cope with the unforeseen. Bring spare passport photographs as these are often required for permits to restricted areas. A basic first aid kit should include Lomototil tablets (non-antibiotic pills for diarrhea), sunscreen, water purification pills, multi-vitamins, aspirin, insect repellent and antiseptic cream. As far as toiletries go, bring whatever you feel you couldn't live without for more than a week. Indian chemists usually have a baffling array of pharmaceuticals, but are short on good quality shampoo, cosmetics, suntan lotion, razors, dental floss, contraceptives and tampons.

Photographic film should be purchased outside India, as items sold in India have often been spoiled from being unrefrigerated. A small torch will provide illumination during power cuts and while exploring caves and gloomy ruins. Electrical appliances such as hair dryers, travel irons, and shavers must run on 220 volts. A small pair of binoculars can be useful for spotting wildlife.

India has a great range of bookshops which stock most leading titles, so it is not necessary to bring with you all the reading material you think you might need.

It can be a good idea to carry a a supply of music cassettes, film, cigarettes, alcohol, toiletries, lighters, and pens to be given away as gifts in return for favors or hospitality.

HEALTH

IMMUNIZATIONS

Prevention is always the best cure. A course of immunization vaccinations and a supply of malaria tablets are essential to safeguard you against most of the dreaded maladies India has to offer. These are not essential requirements for entering the country unless you have arrived from Africa, South America, or any area infested with smallpox, yellow-fever, or cholera.

Vaccinations are recommended against cholera, typhoid, tetanus, and hepatitis A. These diseases can easily be contracted and will not only put you in hospital, but may well impair your health permanently. Have your injections at least a fortnight before departing, so that the immunizations have time to take full effect and you can recover from any lingering reaction. Cholera vaccines remain active for six months. The vaccine against hepatitis A, gamma globulin, is effective for two months, so those intending a longer stay should ask for a double dose.

Also make sure that your teeth are in good order, as Indian dentistry can look fearsomly antiquated to Western eyes! If you have capped teeth, you may want to take spare caps and a glue kit. India's swirling dust spells pure hell for travelers who wear contact lenses, so it's more comfortable to wear glasses.

Malaria is a widespread problem, particularly during the monsoon and in tropical areas where mosquitoes are rampant, and there are numerous theories as to the pros and cons of anti-malaria preparations. There is evidence that long-term use can be damaging to the retina and the liver, and many travelers prefer to smother themselves with mosquito repellents and string up nets around their beds at night. Also, pills do not offer complete protection. However, many people who have contracted a severe case of malaria have survived only because they were on a course of pills.

Doctors usually prescribe Chloroquine tablets, which can be taken either daily or weekly. Pregnant women should avoid Chloroquine, and instead take Proguanil, while an anti-malarial syrup is available for children. Other alternatives, known by the brand names Fansidar, Faladar, Antemal, and Methidox, can trigger adverse reactions. It's best to start taking the tablets 10 days before departure, which will give you a chance to change them if they don't agree with you. For full protection, you are supposed to continue taking them for six weeks after you leave the country, as malaria germs are incredibly resilient.

Anti-malarial tablets are overpriced in the United States, where a single course can cost up to US$100 on prescription, compared with US$10 in Europe, Britain, or Australia. In most parts of Asia, anti-malarials are sold without a prescription and cost only US$1.

Rabies vaccinations are now available, but as a general rule, avoid stray dogs and monkeys. Macaque monkeys may look cuddlesome as they gambol across ancient forts and temples, but they can become vicious if they decide to take food from you. If bitten by any animal, clean the wound thoroughly and then admit yourself into the nearest hospital for the 14-day-long series of injections to thwart the potentially fatal disease.

ON THE ROAD

The budget travelers' slogan "Eat Well, Sleep Hard" was probably coined in India, where your health is more important than the bumpy beds you may have to endure. It's quite normal to experience a few minor bodily hiccups in adjusting to the Indian diet and climate, especially during the first few days after arrival when your system is particularly sensitive. There are plenty of tales about India's holiday-ruining ailments, but if you observe some basic rules you should return home in good shape.

Food and drink tend to be the biggest worries for most visitors. Since most diseases in the subcontinent are waterborne, you will need to be particularly careful about your liquid consumption, especially as several liters of fluid a day is necessary to stave off dehydration from India's notoriously hot and dusty summer months.

No matter what old India-hands tell you, avoid any water that has not been boiled for at least 10 minutes and filtered or sterilized with water purification tablets. Always inquire whether water served in hotels and restaurants has been processed, as water that has only been filtered may still harbor a few resilient bugs. Indian Airlines serves unfiltered, un-boiled water on its flights, and it is best to carry on planes, buses, and trains a few bottles of mineral water. When ordering bottled water, make sure that the seal is removed before your eyes, since crafty vendors and waiters have been known to top bottles up with tap water so that they can make a little money on the sly. Also avoid ice cubes, which are, after all, just frozen water. You'll need to take twice as much water on train or bus journeys as you think you will consume, and if your supply runs out, stick to hot tea, soft drinks, or juicy oranges. It's a good idea to bring an all-purpose plastic cup with you, so that you avoid using dirty *chai* glasses which can carry hepatitis. Get into the habit of brushing your teeth with boiled, bottled, or even soda water, and try to remember not to swallow water while you practice arias in the shower!

Adjust to the highly-spiced Indian diet slowly, sticking for the first couple of days to fairly bland dishes like rice, yogurt, breads, and boiled

eggs. In general, it is risky to eat street food prepared by pavement vendors, raw vegetables, un-peeled or unsterilized fruits, and food with a high water content, such as lettuce, tomatoes, and watermelon. India has a fantastic array of vegetarian dishes and many travelers avoid red meats and pork as these can contain nasty parasites. Poultry is usually safe but can contain salmonella, particularly if it is under-cooked, and it is advisable to choose chicken *tikka* over chicken tandoori as the former dish is equally as tasty but cooked more thoroughly, being served off the bone. Seafood is best eaten in the coastal regions and avoided inland, as refrigerated trucks have been known to break down.

However, you must not be overly fastidious or you will miss sampling the remarkable fare that India offers. Food freshly cooked and sold straight from the brazier at roadside *dhabas*, or cafés, is delicious and usually safe. Ice-cream can be a breeding ground for typhoid when thawed and re-frozen, but is also a most delicious treat, particularly in the dairy state of Gujarat. The best rule is to eat at places with a high turnover so that the food served is usually fresh. Ironically, five-star hotels often produce

ABOVE: Platform hawkers sell their spicy wares as a train stands to a halt at a rural station.

tummy troubles as they serve food with sauces and dressings such as mayonnaise that are best left alone. Be sensible, and if something looks or smells borderline, do not eat it. Smaller restaurants often do not provide utensils, in keeping with the Indian custom of eating with one's right hand, and so it is best to wash your hands before chowing down.

If you are smitten by diarrhea or an upset tummy, treat all spiced and oily foods as taboo. Eat sparing amounts of bland boiled rice, yogurt, and bananas, and drink plenty of black tea and water. It is best to try and work the bugs out of your system, but if your travel itinerary demands an immediate calmed stomach, take some Lomotil tablets to halt diarrhea. Avoid taking antibiotics immediately, as these will kill the bugs but also any other bacterial resistance you have accumulated, making you susceptible for a second bout. If problems persist for more than two days, particularly if accompanied by fever, consult a doctor as you may be suffering from dysentery, an illness that will require treatment.

ACCOMMODATION

India has a vast array of accommodation, from opulent palaces to seedy dives, and as tourism becomes a major industry, service standards have generally improved.

In this guide, accommodation has been divided into categories which fall into set price ranges, as follows: Very Expensive: Rs 1,500 plus; Expensive: Rs :900 to Rs 1,500; Moderate: Rs 600 to Rs 900; Inexpensive: Rs 350 to Rs 600; Cheap: Rs 100 to Rs 350; and Very Cheap: Rs 100 and below.

Five-star hotels are the scene of much socializing in the major cities and are usually up to international standards, having an array of restaurants, health clubs, business centers, and all essential services.

Rajasthan has many former palaces converted into hotels, and it is worth staying in one of these for an unforgettable experience of comfort, cuisine, service amid architectural magnificence, and a pleasant change from the modern hotels of the West.

Former lodges of British colonial rulers provide solid and often sumptuous accommodation in the hill stations, and wildlife parks often have comfortable bungalows run by state authorities.

Quite frequently, you will arrive at your hotel and the staff will deny all knowledge of your booking, usually because your room has been given to a guest willing to pay a higher price. In such a situation, have ready all the paperwork necessary to prove your booking, and usually a room will suddenly become vacant.

Cheap accommodation is typically clustered around bus or rail stations, and despite being spartan, is usually available for under Rs 50 a night. If you are traveling through malaria-infested areas and see slogans declaring "get blood test for all fever cases", this is a cue to use a mosquito net. Cotton nets are better than nylon because the natural fabric breathes and allows your sweat to evaporate from the net, cooling you underneath. If you have no net, turn on a ceiling fan — mosquitoes hate direct air currents so this will hopefully ward them off.

Always lock up your luggage when you leave your room if your accommodation is in any way disreputable. The real thieves, sad to say, are usually other foreign tourists who have fallen on hard times or are into hard drugs. French and Italian junkies have the worst reputation for ripping off everything you own, so if you see any one acting suspiciously, change hotels or take protective measures by either carrying your cash and passport with you or leaving it with the hotel manager for safekeeping.

TOURIST INFORMATION

The main **Government of India Tourist Office** is in Delhi, ©332-0005 and 333-0008, at 88 Janpath and is open from 9 am to 6 pm daily except Sundays offers answers to queries about all Indian destinations. **State Tourist Offices** in Delhi are useful for gathering specialized material and are either at Kanishka Shopping Plaza, 19 Ashok Road (Jammu and Kashmir, Kerala, Madhya Pradesh); C-4 Chanderlok Building, 36 Janpath (Rajasthan, Uttar Pradesh, Himachel Pradesh, and Haryana); B-1 Baba Kharak Singh Marg, (Andhhra Pradesh, Assam, Gujarat, Karnataka, Maharashtra, Orissa, Tamil Nadu and West Bengal) or at Hotel Janpath (Sikkim).

Tourist information can also be obtained from the following overseas offices of the Government of India Tourist Office:
Australia
Sydney: 65 Elizabeth Street, Sydney, NSW 2000, ©(02)232-1600.
Canada
Toronto: 60 Bloor Street, West Suite No. 1003, Ontario M4W 3B8, ©416962, 3787/88.
Thailand
Bangkok: Singapore Airlines Building, 3rd Floor, 62/5 Thaniya Road, ©2352585.

United Kingdom

London: 7 Cork Street, London W1X 2AB, ✆01-437-3677/8.

United States of America

Los Angeles: 3550 Wilshire Blvd, Suite 204, California 90010, ✆(213) 380-8855.

Chicago: 230 North Michigan Avenue, Illinois 60601, ✆(312) 236-6899/7869.

New York: 30 Rockeffeller Plaza, Room 15, North Mezzanine, NY 10020, ✆(212)586-4901/-2/3.

GETTING AROUND

India is different for everyone. Some people swear that a rough-and-tumble style of traveling is the only way to get close to its soul. Others enjoy adventurous sightseeing, but not at the expense of comfort.

Perhaps the best strategy is the middle ground of traveling independently with an emphasis on comfort. Try to strike a balance between insulation from India's grand panorama that comes from the cloistered atmosphere of organized tours and five-star hotels, and being snared in by the day-to-day hassles of tight budget traveling.

Most people underestimate India's size, and many travelers' itineraries have been thrown out of kilter by failing to appreciate the considerable time it takes to cover distances. The country has a remarkable transport infrastructure that somehow always gets you where you want to go, and mostly it is a trade-off between time by train and money by plane.

DOMESTIC AIRLINES

Indian Airlines, the main domestic carrier, flies to most major cities in its fleet of Airbuses and Boeing 737s. More obscure regional points are now being serviced by a smaller airline, Vayudoot, named after the Hindu god of speed. Flights on both airlines generally cost about double that of a first-class rail ticket, but the investment is usually worthwhile for covering vast distances that take days by train.

Try to buy tickets well in advance and ensure that seats are confirmed, as flights are typically overbooked. If you purchase your ticket with rupees, you will be asked to produce a bank receipt to prove your foreign currency was changed at a bank. Foreigners pay 50 percent more than residents, but are given a higher priority on flights and greater flexibility in changing tickets.

Political extremism has made tight security a facet of Indian air travel, so ensure that any pocket-knives are stashed inside your checked luggage, and expect batteries to be confiscated as these are designated as capable of powering a bomb.

Indian civil aviation is very overstressed and it is best to give yourself plenty of time between connections as planes are frequently delayed.

Indian Airlines offer several discount travel schemes. The "Youth Fare", restricted to 12- to 30-year-olds, gives a 25 percent discount on the US dollar fare for any internal flight for up to 90 days. The "Discover India" scheme offers 21 days' unlimited travel for a flat US$400. The "Tour India" ticket is similar (US$300 for

14 days spread over six sectors of the country), as is the "Wonderfare" ticket (US$200 for seven days). With all these schemes, you are allowed to visit no airport more than once, except for the purpose of a connecting flight or when in transit.

RIDING THE RAILS

The Indian rail system was established by the British largely as a means of transporting troops and extracting raw materials, and it remains one of the more beneficial colonial legacies, carrying more than three billion passengers each year on its services that ply across the country.

ABOVE: Luckily for these hardy travelers, India is a land of endless horizons and few life-endangering tunnels.

In contrast to the brisk, buckled-up anxiety of a plane journey, Indian train trips are made vivid by one's fellow passengers, and a ticket buys a front-row seat for the greatest drama on earth — the human condition.

The network services the most far-flung areas of the country, and no visit to India would be complete without experiencing a train journey, which remains the most practical and reliable form of travel. There are several scenic routes worth taking during the day, but it is generally best to cover longer distances by overnight sleeper, which will save you money and time.

From first-class air-conditioned sleeper to third-class bench, there will be a mode of rail travel to suit your budget. A quota of berths are reserved for tourists, but these are rapidly allocated so it is best to book well in advance. The system works surprisingly well, and many an astonished traveler has arrived at a remote station to see a clerk open an immense ledger in which their name is listed for a reserved seat. Ticketing is computerized along the main trunk routes, where there are also international travel bureaus that save you the inconvenience of queuing for hours in the main ticket hall.

Not all trains have first-class compartments, and the second-class compartments are usually overcrowded. Even if you have reserved a berth, and it can be difficult to avoid unlikely bed partners. An old man may respectfully request that he be allowed to perch on the edge of your seat, and when you consent, he may be joined by many relatives. In a totally crammed train, it would look very selfish for you to want to take so much room when such people have so little. For this reason, request the top bench that unfolds from the wall. These cannot be shared and usually provide a cozy location for a good night's sleep.

Thieves do prey upon snoozing travelers, so be sure to use your luggage as a pillow. Dining cars are rare on Indian trains, as snacks and refreshments are sold by hawkers at each station. For a more comfortable journey it is best to take along some food and bottles of mineral water.

Indrail Passes are particularly good value for those planning an extended tour of India by train. The pass must be purchased in foreign currency. Prices range from US$160 for air-conditioned first-class travel for seven days and US$600 for 90 days in the same class, to US$80 and US$130 for air-conditioned second class for the same periods. The passes can be purchased only in India, through leading travel agents or the Central Reservations Offices in Delhi, Bombay, Calcutta, Madras, Secunderabad, and Hyderabad. Railway timetables are available from most large stations; the most useful ones are the *All India Railway Timetable* and the concise but comprehensive *Trains at a Glance*.

Well-heeled travelers may want to experience the "Palace on Wheels," a remarkable eight-day rail tour through Rajasthan aboard sumptuous carriages belonging to erstwhile maharajas. Scarlet-turbaned waiters serve Indian and continental cuisine as you chug through the desert state aboard the vintage train, which has private cabins with showers. The tour rolls out from Delhi and stops at Jaipur, Chittaurgarh, Udaipur, Jaisalmer, Jodhpur, and Bharatpur/-Fatehpur Sikri/Agra. The tour runs between October and May. Reservations are through the Rajasthan Tourism Development Corporation, Chandralok Building, 36 Janpath, New Delhi 110001.

BUSES

Buses are less comfortable than trains, but are cheaper and go to more obscure locations not reached by rail. Buses are another quintessential Indian experience, and no one quite forgets the near-collisions above mountain ravines or the constant blaring of horns. The latest addition to the fleets are "video buses", coaches that have mounted behind the driver a television set showing the latest Hindi-language films. While

ABOVE: A second-class carriage scene.

these productions yield remarkable insights into the dynamics of India, the soundtracks ensure insomnia and, unless you have come equipped with earplugs, it is advisable to slip the conductor Rs 20 with the instruction that the video is broken. At the height of summer, it is worth paying extra to travel aboard an air-conditioned vehicle.

URBAN TRANSPORT

Indian towns and cities usually have bus and sometimes rail systems, but most travelers find it best to get around by taxi and auto-rickshaw, for which there are certain ground rules.

Drivers will often insist their meter is not working so that they can charge more; and if you accept this principle, always agree on a price before setting off. It can be helpful to ask a local what a fair price should be. If there is a queue of auto-rickshaws, the lead driver may turn you down if he feels the fare is too low to justify losing his place at the front of the line. If this is the case, just go to the last driver, who will have little to lose by taking you to your destination, even if it is nearby.

Auto-rickshaws are the cheapest and most convenient way of negotiating short distances, but are best avoided for longer trips as it is invariably a rough ride, and the vehicle are prone to break down and have accidents.

Taxis are about double the price, but it is worthwhile paying for the added comfort and speed. The vehicle will either be the ubiquitous Ambassador, a clanking 1957 Morris Oxford still produced in India, or the Padmini, a zippier 1950's-model Fiat.

Drivers usually treat their vehicle reverently, rather like sacred cows, and know weird and wonderful ways to keep them functioning. I once saw a taxi-wallah beat his engine back to life with a rock. Drivers will also wait quite happily if you want to retain them while you go off for an hour of so of sightseeing or shopping, but you must agree to pay a waiting charge of about Rs 15 per hour. Drivers are also entitled to charge on top of the meter a 25 percent "night charge" between 10 pm and 6 am. Different rules apply in different cities, and it is best to check with hotel personnel as to the correct local rate.

COMMUNICATIONS

TIME

Indian Standard Time is 5½ hours ahead of Greenwich Mean Time and 9½ hours ahead of

US EST. However time is a very elastic concept in India. Indeed in Hindi, the same word is used to describe both "yesterday" and "tomorrow."

POSTAL SERVICES

Mail services in India are generally good, although it's best to make sure that staff frank letters to ensure that the stamp is not immediately peeled off and resold — a common practice. Sending a parcel abroad can be a complicated, time-consuming business. Either bear with excess luggage or get government emporiums to ship your shopping home.

TELEPHONES

India has one of the world's oldest telephone systems, an archaic network established by the British during Queen Victoria's reign. The government is updating its mechanical exchanges with digital systems, but in most of the country faulty, idiosyncratic telephones are a way of life. The old maxim: If at first you don't succeed, try, try again, has a special ring to it here. Telephone systems, like water and electricity supplies, tend to run fairly efficiently in upmarket neighborhoods and large hotels. Otherwise, getting through on local or long-distance calls can be a matter of luck. You often have to redial several times, or wait for a gaggle of loquacious squatters to quit double-parking on your line and ring off. Wrong numbers are frequent, and a national habit is to bellow "hello" several times to establish that the line is open.

If you are staying in a five-star hotel in a big city, it is quite easy to make calls internationally or long-distance within India by direct dialing. Otherwise, calls must be made through an operator, either from crowded booths at the local post office or from your hotel. It can take anything from five minutes to an entire day to get the line, and the process is much faster if you request a Demand Call, which costs more but gives you a higher priority in an overburdened system. A Lightning Call goes through immediately, but can cost up to eight times the regular amount.

Hotels usually whack a stiff service charge on telephone calls, so it is worth checking their terms before you begin a calling binge.

TELEX, TELEGRAMS, AND FACSIMILE

Domestic and international telex and telegram services in India are fairly reliable and reasonably priced. Again, you have a choice of either queuing up at the GPO or using the facilities of a large hotel. The advantage of the telex is that it gives you a record of having reconfirmed hotel or flight bookings, and can be a highly useful piece of paper if knowledge of your booking is denied.

Facsimile facilities have yet to make an impact in India. Most five-star hotels have business centers with fax services, but rates tend to be pricey at Rs 230 per page, plus an additional 10 percent service charge for an international destination.

Filing information by a computer modem through a telephone line can be erratic, as one line hit will disrupt the data flow, but after two or three attempts the message is usually received at the other end.

MEDIA

India has a large number of English-language dailies and hundreds of vernacular newspapers, for one of its beauties is an unshackled press. The dailies, written in a dense Edwardian prose packed with remarkable colloquialisms, become an addictive beginning to the day if you wish to understand the complexities of Indian politics. The *Times of India* is the largest in circulation and, along with the *Statesman of Calcutta*, plots a centrist path. The *Indian Express* is anti-government and prone to printing glaring exposés on its front page. The *Hindu of Madras* has a strong science section and solid coverage of southern India, while the *Hindustan Times* is pro-government and good for getting the views of the status quo. The *Telegraph* and the newly-created *India Post* are more upbeat, with solid features and good photographs. Newspapers also advertise ongoing cultural events, but the coverage is haphazard, with events often being advertised after they have occurred. Major cities usually have a weekly journal dedicated to local events, such as the capital's *Delhi Diary, Bombay Calling* and *Hallo Madras*, brimming with practical information and directory listings.

Sunday newspapers contain matrimonial columns that amply illustrate how Indian marriages are frequently transactions based on pragmatic assessment. For women, a "wheatish complexion" is an asset, and both sexes are rated by their caste, profession, income, and prospects.

More in-depth coverage is found in news magazines, such as The *Illustrated Weekly* or *Sunday*. But the best read is *India Today*, a fortnightly publication crammed with well-written and well-researched articles covering all aspects of Indian life.

The government controls the electronic media, and All India Radio and the two-channel Doordarshan television network are notoriously dull, essentially reporting on news of process (politicians planting trees) or cricket matches. Television does have its high points, notably the screening of soap operas based on the Hindu epics. The programs enjoy a massive following, with entire villages turning out to watch a television set that has been garlanded and blessed for the weekly showing.

India has the world's largest film industry, annually churning out more than 1,000 films compared with Hollywood's paltry 400. The industry is centered in Bombay, and the finished products usually resemble to the Western eye 1940's-style pantomimes of heroes, villains, and damsels in distress bursting into song between gun battles.

Cinema has been seriously undermined throughout the country by the rise of the video. Cassettes of new Western films are pirated and appear in India within weeks of their release in the United States or Europe.

INDIA'S NIGHTLIFE

Nightlife is virtually non-existent in small towns and villages, but New Delhi, Bombay, and Calcutta have discos and an array of cultural events that will keep you out until the wee hours.

Wealthy, well-educated, and socially elite Indians tend to lead incredibly hectic social lives, and simply adore formal dress functions, which is what the winter wedding season is all about. Visitors drawn into well-connected party circles find themselves taken behind India's "Brocade Curtain" into a high-powered series of social engagements in private homes, five-star hotels, and exclusive clubs. Here, dress, manners, and informed conversation count for everything. Time-honored tradition ensures that while guests are plied with drinks, food often doesn't arrive until past midnight. By the time it does, your surroundings may have become an amiable blur of perfume, silk brocade saris, handlebar mustaches, and tinkling laughs. Most guests tend to eat very quickly, then melt away into the night. Whiskey on an empty stomach followed by rich, spicy food taxes the body, and the best counter-measure is to have a snack before going out and then to drink and eat lightly.

Discos are found in most five-star hotels in the big cities, but cover charges and bar prices tend to be outrageously high. Hotel guests are charged only a nominal amount, but high membership fees deter all but the wealthy sons and daughters of the shakers and movers.

BENEATH THE WHIRLING FAN

Every visitor to India encounters its bureaucracy, the leviathan that runs the affairs of the nation's multitudes.

Many formalities in India require bouts of form-filling, but anything slightly more complex — like getting a refund on a railway ticket or permission to go to a restricted area — can escalate into a Kafkaesque adventure. India's bureaucratic warrens usually house rows of bespectacled shrunken clerks, cowering peons in faded khaki shuffling about delivering sahib's

tea, whirring fans, and great sheaves of yellowing files held down by paperweights or quite literally bound by "red tape". The expression was born in India during the early days of the British Civil Service, when red ribbons were first used to hold together official documents. To the untutored eye, these office dens may appear totally haphazard — bustling with people and transactions, while replies to your queries may appear confusing, or even cryptic. You may find yourself wondering what originally launched you on your bureaucratic odyssey in the first place.

But take heart. Be assured that behind every formality lies a reason. By following some general ground rules, keeping reasonably patient, and always maintaining a sense of humor, you'll find things can get done. As a foreigner, it is sometimes difficult to understand all the labyrinthine ins-and-outs of the system. Since transactions can often be frustrating and time-consuming, use an age-old management technique: delegate responsibility. Most hotels can produce a number of willing young men who for a small tip will wait in long queues to purchase tickets at airline offices, rail or bus stations. In local parlance, they will "do the needful" while you follow your own schedule. Always check that the person you are about to trust with your money has been vetted by hotel staff. Travel agencies in India tend to charge only nominal rates for their services, and often secure bookings magically through their own quotas, even on services you've been assured are completely "full up".

More important procedures, such as extending one's visa or seeking a permit to visit a restricted area, require making a personal appearance. Often all that is required is a stamp and an indecipherable scrawl in the right place on the right piece of paper by the right official, but without this your holiday may be ruined. Officials tend to take a very dim view of foreigners who arrive in India without a visa, over-stay, or wind up in areas deemed strategically "sensitive".

The trials and eventual triumphs of dealing with officialdom in India are just part of adjusting to the pace of life on the subcontinent. Never underestimate the power of the person wielding the needed rubber stamp, and always conduct your business in a very polite, but reasonably firm manner.

Officials usually sit in a cramped room and deal with hundreds of people daily, all of whom think their case is more important than yours, so it is easy to see why any display of rudeness or arrogance can go against the grain. Heat and inexplicable delays can drive even paragons of patience to tantrums, but try to remember that India is run according to different rules.

Jovial small talk and a zestful handshake with the appropriate official will go a long way toward getting your case cleared. Some travelers swear that a tip oils the cogs, and this may work in distant regions. But most Indian officials staunchly oppose the suggestion of a bribe, and unless a demand is clearly made, do not risk being arrested for trying to corrupt an officer of the government of India.

BAKSHEESH, BEGGING AND BARGAINING

One of the first words a traveler learns in India is **"baksheesh"**. Loosely translated, it is some-

ABOVE: An Indian policeman wearing a *kepi* in Pondicherry, Tamil Nadu, once a French enclave.

thing you pay to get things done — a little gift or a bribe, a payment for services rendered or even to get rid of a pest. It is usually a small amount, generally less than Rs 5. Beggars moan "baksheesh, sahib", on street corners. Taxi drivers keep their palms out and demand "baksheesh" after you've just given them the correct fare. The judicious use of baksheesh can save you many tedious hours of queue-waiting, while a boy waits for you for a few rupees. Begging is a part of Indian life, despite being officially illegal. India in many ways forces a traveler to make choices, and the baksheesh decision is one for which there can be no guid-

ance. Coping with beggars is all part of traveling in India.

The most deserving of your sympathy are the lepers, multiple amputees, and other misfortunates whose permanent, life-crippling diseases prohibit them from doing much else. Elderly women begging on the streets are invariably widows, who have a lowly place in society once their husband has died. Half-naked children with large eyes can be very endearing, but are often employed by local rackets who make begging a profession. Mothers with screaming babies whom they deliberately pinch should come much lower on the compassion scale.

Bargaining is one of India's great institutions. Once you have experienced the satisfaction of whittling down the price of a carpet, silver necklace or carved statue, no shopping expedition in India will ever be the same again. Traders expect their customers to haggle, and are inwardly astonished if items are purchased without even a hint of dissent.

Bargaining requires a little acting ability — traders do their showmanship routine, offering syrupy tea, and pulling out stock so that their shop takes on the appearance of a sty-pen —

ABOVE: Ritual beggars at Dasaswanadh Ghat in Varanasi.

and you should do your part by appearing disinterested in the items you most covet, by picking out little defects, and disdainfully scorning the prices being quoted. The last stage of bargaining involves getting up, shaking your head and commenting on how the price is just too high. Usually you won't get far before having your shirt sleeves tugged back inside, with prices dropping with each shrug of your shoulders. Bear in mind that no merchant worth his salt is going to sell at anything less than his cost price — and they'll often try to sell goods at up to 70 percent higher than that.

The main thing to remember is that bargaining is only the means to an end. When you see something that you really want, or that you know will make a perfect gift for someone, don't feel that if you can't whittle the price down then it's not worth having. In India as anywhere, quality and fine workmanship will always come with a price-tag attached.

TRAVELERS' HINDI

Hullo/Goodbye *Namaste*
Goodbye/See you again *Phir milenge*
How are you *Aap kaise hain*
Very Good *Bahut Acha*
Bad *Kharab*
Please *Kripaya*
Thank you *Dhanyavad, Shukriya*
Yes *Han, Anchi*
No *Nahi*
Excuse me *Maaf Karna*
What is your name *Aap ka naam kya hai*
My name is John *Meera naam John hai*
What is the time *Kya bara hai*
Where is the ... *Kahan hai ...*
How much is this *Kitne ka hai*
Too much *Bahut zyada hai*
Lower your price *Kum karo*
Left *Bai*
Right *Dai*
Stop *Roko/ Bas*
Go Straight *Seedha jaaiye*
Hurry up *Jaldi kare*
Slow Down *Aahista*
Go away *Chale jao or Chelo*
Big *Bada*
Small *Chhota*
Beautiful *Sundar*
Toilet *Bakhana*
Train *Gadi*
Prayer *Puja, pratha*
Sleep *Sana*
Friend *Dosta*
Smile *Muskarana*
Bill please *Bill lao*
Water *Panni*

Quick Reference A–Z Guide
to Places and Topics of Interest with Listed Accommodation, Restaurants and Useful Telephone Numbers